Handbook of
Exposure Therapies

Handbook of
Exposure Therapies

Dr. David C. S. Richard

Rollins College
Department of Psychology

Dr. Dean Lauterbach

Eastern Michigan University
Department of Psychology

ELSEVIER

AMSTERDAM • BOSTON • HEIDELBERG • LONDON
NEW YORK • OXFORD • PARIS • SAN DIEGO
SAN FRANCISCO • SINGAPORE • SYDNEY • TOKYO

An imprint of Elsevier

Academic Press is an imprint of Elsevier
30 Corporate Drive, Suite 400, Burlington, MA 01803, USA
525 B Street, Suite 1900, San Diego, California 92101-4495, USA
84 Theobald's Road, London WC1X 8RR, UK

This book is printed on acid-free paper. ∞

Library of Congress Cataloging-in-Publication Data
Application submitted

British Library Cataloguing-in-Publication Data
A catalogue record for this book is available from the British Library.

ISBN 13: 978-0-12-587421-2
ISBN 10: 0-12-587421-9

For information on all Academic Press publications
visit our Web site at www.books.elsevier.com

Printed in the United States of America
06 07 08 09 10 9 8 7 6 5 4 3 2 1

Contents

Contributing Authors

Jonathan S. Abramowitz, Ph.D., A.B.P.P.   Dr. Abramowitz earned his Ph.D. in clinical psychology from the University of Memphis in 1998. He is currently Associate Professor of Psychology and Director of the OCD/Anxiety Disorders Program in the Department of Psychiatry and Psychology at the Mayo Clinic. In addition to his clinical and supervisory work, he conducts research on OCD and other anxiety disorders and has authored over 50 research articles and book chapters. Dr. Abramowitz sits on the Editorial Board of several scientific journals, is a member of the Obsessive Compulsive Foundation's Scientific Advisory Board, the Anxiety Disorders Association of America's Clinical Advisory Board. He also served on the DSM-IV-TR Anxiety Disorders Work Group.

Dean T. Acheson, B.A.   Dean T. Acheson is a graduate student in clinical psychology at the University at Albany, SUNY. He earned his B.A. in psychology from Purdue University. His research focuses on investigating the role of learning mechanisms in the etiology and maintenance of fear and anxiety.

Velma Barrios, B.A.   Velma Barrios is a graduate student in clinical psychology at the University at Albany, SUNY. She earned her B.A. in Psychology from the University of California, Los Angeles. Her research focuses on the influence of contextual factors on the acquisition and amelioration of anxiety disorders, including acceptance and mindfulness-based interventions targeting emotion regulation processes in anxiety pathology.

Stéphane Bouchard   Dr. Bouchard is Professor at the Université du Québec en Outa-ouais (UQO) and he holds the Canada Research Chair in Clinical Cyberpsychology. He graduated in Psychology in 1995 from the Université Laval in Québec at the same time as he was completing a one year postdoctoral position. His research initially focused on treatment efficacy and treatment mechanisms of anxiety disorders. In 1999, he started work on delivering cognitive-behavior therapy through videoconferencing to people in rural areas. Since then, his research interests have included the use of virtual reality to treat anxiety disorders and understanding the concept of presence. He has received numerous infrastructure and operating research grants and is co-director of the Cyberpsychology Lab at UQO. He has published more than 50 articles and book chapters and hundreds of scientific communications. As a clinical psychologist and university professor, he has supervised more than 45 students. His research continues to investigate the application of cyberpsychology to the treatment of clinical disorders.

Shawn Cahill   Dr. Cahill is Assistant Professor of Psychology in Psychiatry at the University of Pennsylvania's Center for the Treatment and Study of Anxiety, where he is involved in treatment and research into the nature of anxiety disorders, with a particular interest in PTSD.

Frank Castro   Frank Castro is a doctoral student in Clinical Psychology at Temple University. His research focuses on the role of trauma and oppression in identity development and plasticity. Other interests include examining how client and therapist expectancies during the therapy process mediate treatment outcome.

Heather Cochran   Heather M. Cochran is completing her Ph.D. in Clinical Psychology from Central Michigan University. Her primary research interests are related to sexual assault of college women, treatment of anxiety disorders, and issues related to child abuse and neglect. Her clinical interests are treatment of anxiety disorders, behavioral medicine, and parent training.

Sophie Côté, Ph.D.   Dr. Côté recently completed her doctoral thesis addressing the cognitive mechanisms underlying the efficacy of virtual reality exposure for arachnophobia. She specializes in anxiety disorders, in health psychology, and in virtual reality. Her extensive clinical experience in virtual reality exposure makes her one of the experts in Canada in this field, both in fundamental and clinical research. Previously part of the Cyberpsychology Lab of UQO and a lab in Montreal studying obsessive-compulsive disorder, depersonalization, and specific phobias in children, she currently is working on implementing virtual reality interventions in hospital settings to help patients cope with cancer and painful medical procedures.

Michael Davis, Ph.D.   Dr. Davis was appointed the Robert W. Woodruff Professor of Psychiatry and Behavioral Sciences in the Department of Psychiatry at Emory University, September 1, 1998. Prior to this, Dr. Davis was on the faculty at Yale University for 29 years in the Departments of Psychiatry and Psychology. His faculty appointment began immediately after he received his Ph.D. in Experimental Psychology at Yale in 1969, where he worked with Allan Wagner, following undergraduate training at Northwestern University. Dr. Davis is world renowned for his work on the neural basis of fear, the role of the amygdala in conditioned fear and memory, and the acoustic startle reflex. He is a member of seven editorial boards and an elected Fellow in several professional organizations. He held an NIMH Career Development and Research Scientist Award for 25 years, and has had generous support from the National Science Foundation and National Institute of Mental Health (NIMH), including two consecutive 10-year NIMH MERIT Awards. Currently, he has about 250 publications and is exploring intracellular processes in the amygdala in connection with the formation and storage of long-term fear memories as well as studying brain systems involved in the reduction of fear and anxiety.

Brett Deacon, Ph.D.   Dr. Deacon is Assistant Professor of Psychology at the University of Wyoming. He received his Ph.D. from Northern Illinois University and completed a two-year postdoctoral fellowship specializing in anxiety disorders at the Mayo Clinic in Rochester, Minnesota. Dr. Deacon's clinical interests involve using exposure therapy, often in a brief, intensive fashion, to treat individuals with anxiety disorders. Dr. Deacon has published numerous research articles on the nature and treatment of anxiety disorders and regularly presents scientific papers and clinical workshops on exposure therapy at regional and national conferences.

Carlos G. Finlay, Ph.D.   Dr. Finlay is currently a postdoctoral associate at the Research Institute on Addictions in Buffalo, New York. He received his degree from the University at Albany, State University of New York and completed his clinical internship at the University of Mississippi Medical Center/G.V. ("Sonny") Montgomery VAMC Consortium. His research interests include the etiology, maintenance, treatment, and threat of relapse of anxiety disorders, primarily panic disorder and post-traumatic stress disorder (PTSD).

John P. Forsyth, Ph.D.   Dr. Forsyth earned his Ph.D. in Clinical Psychology from West Virginia University in 1997 after serving as Chief Resident in the Department of Psychiatry and Human Behavior at the University of Mississippi Medical Center. He is Associate Professor and Director of the Anxiety Disorders Research Program in the Department of Psychology at the University at Albany, SUNY. His basic and applied research focuses on variables and processes that contribute to the etiology, maintenance, and treatment of anxiety-related disorders. He has written widely on acceptance and experiential avoidance, and on the role of emotion regulatory processes in the etiology and treatment of anxiety disorders. Dr. Forsyth was the recipient of the 2000 B. F. Skinner New Research Award by Division 25 of the American Psychological Association and the 1999 Outstanding Dissertation Award by the Society for a Science of Clinical Psychology. He has authored over 50 scientific journal articles, numerous book chapters, and several teaching supplements for courses in abnormal psychology. He is a licensed clinical psychologist in New York State, serves on the editorial boards of several leading clinical psychology journals, and is associate editor of the Journal of Behavior Therapy and Experimental Psychiatry. He also is an author of two forthcoming books – *Acceptance and Commitment Therapy for Anxiety Disorders: A Practitioner's Treatment Guide to Using Mindfulness, Acceptance, and Value-Based Behavior Change Strategies* and *ACT on Life, Not on Anger* – describing the application of Acceptance and Commitment Therapy (ACT) for persons struggling with anxiety disorders and problem anger. He routinely gives talks and workshops on ACT and Cognitive-Behavior Therapy for anxiety and related disorders.

Mary Gillis, B.A.   Mary Gillis is a graduate student in the clinical-behavioral master's program at Eastern Michigan University. After earning a bachelor's degree in Literature from Wayne State University, she worked for 15 years as a copy-editor and contributor to reference books before returning to school. In addition to teaching and research duties associated with her fellowship award, Mary presented on blood-injury-injection phobia at the Behavior Analysis Association of Michigan conference in 2004. Her current research concerns social supports for caregivers of bone marrow and stem cell transplant patients.

Andrew Gloster, Ph.D.   Dr. Gloster completed his undergraduate work at Boston University before traveling to Europe to study the trumpet. After developing an interest in music performance anxiety, Andrew was admitted to the Ph.D. program in clinical psychology at Eastern Michigan University. His master's thesis was a unique application of ecological momentary assessment (EMA) methodology to study anxiety in musicians who were required to give a live performance before a panel of judges. In May of this year, Andrew successfully defended his dissertation, an EMA study of individuals with obsessive-compulsive disorder, and then finished his clinical internship at the University of Texas—Houston Medical School. He recently accepted a position in Germany as Assistant Professor at the Technical University of Dresden, where he will be Head of Anxiety Research. Dr. Gloster's research interests focus on the development and maintenance of anxiety, cognitive and behavioral treatments for anxiety and worry, issues surrounding comorbidity, patient accuracy in estimating functional relations of variables related to anxiety, treatment dissemination, and cross-cultural anxiety research.

Elizabeth Hembree, Ph.D.   Dr. Hembree is Assistant Professor of Psychology in Psychiatry at the University of Pennsylvania, and serves as the Director of Clinical Training in the Center for the Treatment and Study of Anxiety. Her primary research interest and area of specialization is the study and dissemination of cognitive behavioral treatments for post-traumatic stress disorder (PTSD).

Joe Himle, Ph.D.   Dr. Himle is an Assistant Professor at the University of Michigan School of Social Work. His research interests focus on both adult and youth obsessive-compulsive disorder, telemedicine, and cognitive-behavioral interventions for adults with depression and diabetes. He is also interested in the relationship between social anxiety and welfare and the interplay between psychosocial interventions and neurobiological variables. Dr. Himle has a joint appointment with the University of Michigan Department of Psychiatry.

Michiyo Hirai, Ph.D.   Dr. Hirai is Assistant Professor at Washington State University. She received a Ph.D. in Clinical Psychology from Virginia Polytechnic Institute and State University in 2002. Her research areas include etiology, assessment and cognitive-behavioral treatment of anxiety disorders, the application of web-based assessment and interventions, and the role of emotions in developing and maintaining anxiety symptoms.

Jody Hoffman, Ph.D.   Dr. Hoffman received her Ph.D. in Clinical Psychology and Industrial-Organizational Psychology from Bowling Green State University in 2003. She is currently a psychologist with Ann Arbor Consultation Services. Her research interests include evaluation of the effect of affirmative action programs, the use of ecological momentary assessment, health and the workplace, and the role of organizational value statements in recruitment.

Flora Hoodin, Ph.D.   Flora Hoodin is Associate Professor of Psychology at Eastern Michigan University, Ypsilanti, Michigan. She completed a postdoctoral fellowship in Health Psychology and Rehabilitation Psychology at the Rehabilitation Institute of Michigan after earning her doctorate in Clinical Psychology from Wayne State University, Detroit, Michigan. For several years thereafter, she provided clinical services to patients with chronic intractable head pain in an inpatient interdisciplinary setting. Now in academia, her research focus shadowing her clinical interests, she has published in the areas of chronic headache management and psychosocial aspects of bone marrow transplant survivorship. Recently, her research team has widened its purview to investigate how certain spinal deformities and orthopedic treatments affect and are affected by behavioral variables.

Ellen Koch, Ph.D.   Dr. Koch earned her Ph.D. in Clinical Psychology from Western Michigan University in 2001. She is currently Assistant Professor in the Department of Psychology at Eastern Michigan University. In addition to her teaching and supervisory work, she conducts research on behavioral and cognitive-behavioral treatments for anxiety disorders.

Karin E. Larsen, Ph.D.   Dr. Larsen is a Medical Psychology Fellow in the Department of Psychiatry and Psychology, Mayo Clinic and an Instructor at Mayo Clinic College of Medicine. She earned her Ph.D. in Clinical Psychology from the University of Iowa. Her research and clinical work has centered on women's health with a focus on psychological factors affecting perinatal health and sexual functioning. Currently, she is researching the relationship between women's moods and cardiovascular health.

Dean Lauterbach, Ph.D.   Dr. Lauterbach earned his baccalaureate degree from the University of Wisconsin and his advanced degrees from Purdue University. Following completion of his clinical internship, he accepted a faculty position at Northwestern State University (NSU). He remained at NSU from 1995 to 2001, and during this time his research focused primarily on risk and resilience factors among college-age trauma victims. In 2001, Dr. Lauterbach accepted a position as Associate Professor of Clinical Psychology at Eastern Michigan University. He has continued his work on risk and resilience factors but has also expanded his interests to include victims of natural disasters and child abuse/neglect.

Teresa Leyro, B.A.   Teresa Leyro received her B.A. in Psychology from Colby College, and is now a research assistant at Boston University. Her research experience includes helping implement novel online survey procedures to assess addictive disorders in college-aged students. Her current work on translational research investigates rates of fear learning and extinction among individuals from different diagnostic groups.

Judith Lyons, Ph.D.   Dr. Lyons studied in Montreal (B.A., 1979, McGill University; M.A., 1982 and Ph.D., 1985, Concordia University) then completed her clinical internship in Jackson, Mississippi (1984-85). After serving as the founding clinical director of the Traumatic Stress Disorder Center at the Boston VA (1985-87), she returned to Jackson, MS to establish the Trauma Recovery Program at the G.V. ("Sonny") Montgomery VA Medical Center. She assesses and treats traumatic stress through her work with the VA, consults on personal injury and criminal cases, and participates in disaster response work with the American Red Cross. She is Associate Professor of Psychiatry and Human Behavior at the University of Mississippi Medical Center and conducts research with the support of the VA's South Central Mental Illness Research, Education and Clinical Center (MIRECC).

Brian Marx, Ph.D.   Dr. Marx received his undergraduate degree from Boston University in 1987 and his Ph.D. in Clinical Psychology from the University of Mississippi in 1996. Following a clinical internship at the University of Mississippi Medical Center, his first academic position was at Oklahoma State University. In 1999, he joined the faculty at Temple University. Dr. Marx has published widely on a variety of topics related to posttraumatic stress and sexual abuse. His research has been funded by the Centers for Disease Control and Prevention, the Alcoholic Beverage Medical Research Foundation, and the Pennsylvania Department of Health. Dr. Marx has also served as a grant reviewer for the National Institutes of Health and has served as a reviewer for several scientific journals.

Sandra Mendlowitz, Ph.D.   Dr. Mendlowitz received her doctorate from the University of Toronto in 1996. She is currently an assistant professor in the Department of Child Psychiatry at the University of Toronto, a full-time psychologist on the Anxiety Disorders Team, and is affiliated with the Hospital for Sick Children. Her research has primarily focused on the development and evaluation of effective treatment interventions for children and adolescents. She is also interested in how a person's readiness to change mediates treatment outcome. Several years ago, she published with Dr. Stéphane Bouchard a paper reporting the use of exposure and response prevention for bingeing with anorexic and bulimic females.

Michael W. Otto, Ph.D.   Dr. Otto received his doctorate from the University of New Mexico, completed an internship at Brown University, and subsequently served as the Director of the Cognitive Behavior Therapy Program at Massachusetts General Hospital and Harvard Medical School. Dr. Otto is currently Professor of Psychology at Boston University. Dr. Otto's research activities are closely tied to his clinical interests and target investigations of the etiology and treatment of anxiety, mood, and substance-use disorders. Of particular interest to Dr. Otto is the development and testing of new treatments, including the combination of pharmacologic and cognitive-behavioral strategies for treatment- refractory and substance abusing patients, and the modification of treatment packages for novel populations (e.g., Cambodian refugees). He has published over 190 articles, book chapters, and books spanning these research interests. Dr. Otto is President-Elect for the Association for Behavioral and Cognitive Therapies, a fellow of the American Psychological Association, and a member of the Scientific Advisory Board for the Anxiety Disorders Association of America. He also serves as a section editor for *Cognitive and Behavioral Practice,* and on the editorial boards of *Anxiety, Behavior Research and Therapy, Clinical Psychology: Science and Practice, Journal of Anxiety Disorders, Journal Watch in Psychiatry,* and *Psychotherapy and Psychosomatics.*

Janet L. Pietrowski, M.S.   Janet L. Pietrowski is a doctoral candidate in clinical psychology in the Department of Psychology at Eastern Michigan University. She earned her Master of Science degree in Clinical Behavioral Psychology at Eastern Michigan University. She has been convention manager of the Behavior Analysis Association of Michigan. Her research includes establishing schedule-induced behavior as an animal model of obsessive-compulsive disorder in humans. She has also studied resilience in unwed teenage mothers with a focus on how receipt of social support influences success.

Mark B. Powers, Ph.D.   Mark Powers received his bachelor's degree in 1996 from the University of California at Santa Barbara, and a master's degree from Pepperdine University in 1997 while working under Dr. Joseph Wolpe as the managing editor for the *Journal of Behavior Therapy and Experimental Psychiatry.* He devoted two years to the management of clinical trials in schizophrenia, depression, chronic pain, generalized anxiety disorder, PTSD, panic disorder, social phobia, and pain disorder while working as a research coordinator at the University of

California at Los Angeles before entering a doctoral program at the University of Texas, and subsequently a predoctoral research position at Boston University. Dr. Powers completed his psychology internship at the University of Washington. His research has focused on the conditions that influence extinction learning, and he has published 27 journal articles and chapters. Dr. Powers has also served on the Committee on Science and Practice in Division 12 of the American Psychological Association (formerly the Task Force on Psychological Interventions or Empirically Supported Treatments). He is currently an assistant professor on the faculty of Social and Behavioral Sciences at the University of Amsterdam.

Sarah Reiland, B.S.   Sarah Reiland earned her Bachelor of Science degree in Psychology from Seattle Pacific University in 2004 and is currently enrolled in the doctoral program in Clinical Psychology at Eastern Michigan University. Her research primarily involves risk and resilience factors in trauma survivors.

Kerry James Ressler, M.D., Ph.D.   Dr. Ressler is Assistant Professor of Psychiatry and Behavioral Sciences at Emory University School of Medicine and an affiliate scientist at Yerkes National Primate Research Center. Dr. Ressler was trained as a molecular biologist at Harvard Medical School and as a behavioral scientist at Emory with Michael Davis, Ph.D. His current work focuses on translational research that bridges molecular neurobiology with clinical research on fear and anxiety disorders. Dr. Ressler has received several prestigious national research awards for his basic research, including the 2003 Anxiety Disorders Association of America Junior Faculty Award, two NARSAD Young Investigator awards, a Rockefeller Brothers Fund Young Investigator Scholarship, and a K01 award from NIMH.

David C. S. Richard, Ph.D.   Dr. Richard is Director of the Psychology and Organizational Behavior programs in the Hamilton Holt School at Rollins College in Winter Park, Florida. He received his undergraduate degree in political science from the University of California at San Diego, a master's degree in Counseling and Consulting Psychology from Harvard University, and his Ph.D. in Clinical Psychology from the University of Hawaii. After completing his clinical internship at the University of Mississippi Medical Center, he held positions at Southwest Missouri State University (now Missouri State University) and Eastern Michigan University. He has published in the areas of psychological and behavioral assessment, the integration of computer technology in psychotherapy and behavior therapy, and interrater variability in the scoring of intelligence test protocols. His research interests focus on psychological and behavioral assessment, post-traumatic stress disorder and exposure therapy, ecological momentary assessment, the application of signal detection theory to diagnostic formulations of mental health disorders, and biased recall of psychological symptoms. In his spare time, he tends to a fledgling garden and refines his mai tai–making skills.

Barbara Olasov Rothbaum, Ph.D.   Dr. Rothbaum is Associate Professor of Psychiatry at the Emory School of Medicine in the Department of Psychiatry and Behavioral Sciences and director of the Trauma and Anxiety Recovery Program at Emory. Dr. Rothbaum specializes in research on the treatment of individuals with affective disorders, particularly focusing on anxiety and post-traumatic stress disorder (PTSD). She has won both state and national awards for her research, is an invited speaker internationally, authors scientific papers and chapters, has published two books on the treatment of PTSD, and received the

Diplomate in Behavioral Psychology from the American Board of Professional Psychology. She is currently president of the International Society of Traumatic Stress Studies (ISTSS). Dr. Rothbaum is also a pioneer in the application of virtual reality to the treatment of psychological disorders.

Jasper A. J. Smits, Ph.D.   Jasper Smits received his Ph.D. from the University of Texas at Austin. As part of his research and clinical training, he completed a fellowship at Harvard Medical School/Massachusetts General Hospital. Currently, Dr. Smits is Assistant Professor in the Department of Psychology at Southern Methodist University, where he directs the Anxiety Research & Treatment Program. With the intent to increase the efficacy of existing interventions for the anxiety disorders, and specifically for social anxiety disorder and panic disorder, Dr. Smits' research program focuses on (a) enhancing the understanding of factors that drive or maintain pathological anxiety; and (b) the development of techniques that facilitate anxiety reduction and decrease the risk of relapse. He has authored several empirical papers elucidating mediators and moderators of exposure treatment efficacy, as well as a number of review articles that help hone clinicians' attention on factors that may attenuate the effectiveness of exposure-based treatments for anxiety disorders.

James Todd, Ph.D.   Dr. Todd is Professor of Psychology at Eastern Michigan University. He holds a Ph.D. in Developmental and Child Psychology from the University of Kansas. He is co-editor, with Edward K. Morris, of *Modern Perspectives on John B. Watson and Classical Behaviorism* and *Modern Perspectives on B.F. Skinner and Contemporary Behaviorism*. He is past-President and current Secretary-Treasurer of the Behavior Analysis Association of Michigan. He has written on the history of Division 25 (Experimental Analysis) of the American Psychological Association, evolution of psychology textbooks, and misconceptions about behavior analysis. His current research includes establishing schedule-induced behavior as a model of obsessive-compulsive disorder and determining the basic behavioral processes underlying activity anorexia.

Laura Vernon, Ph.D.   Dr. Laura Vernon is Assistant Professor at Auburn University. She received her Ph.D. in clinical psychology from the University of Illinois at Urbana-Champaign in 2000. Her research focuses on the role of emotion, cognitive processes, and coping in the anxiety disorders.

Stacey A. Waller, Ph.D.   Dr. Waller earned her doctoral degree in Clinical Psychology from Western Michigan University in 2004. She is currently a staff psychologist in the Department of Behavioral Medicine and Psychiatry at West Virginia University School of Medicine. Her primary area of interest is cognitive-behavioral treatment of anxiety disorders.

Preface

C. S. Lewis once wrote that courage is the highest virtue because all other virtues depend upon it. For individuals with long-standing fears, a healthy dose of courage may be needed before taking the plunge into exposure therapy. Although exposure remains one of behavior therapy's most efficacious treatments, it is not for the faint of heart. Exposure treatments require that clients tolerate the very fear and anxiety they have so deliberately avoided. Over time, the effects of exposure therapy may be seen not only in the reduction of anxiety, but in the emergence of new and more adaptive behavioral repertoires that promote greater client self-efficacy for managing previously feared situations.

This book arose from an observation a couple of years ago that the proliferation of research surrounding exposure therapy over the last four decades had not produced a volume that conveniently brought together an accounting of its application across the anxiety disorders. Individual chapters describing exposure, meta-analyses comparing exposure to other psychotherapeutic interventions, and treatment manuals detailing the proper application of exposure therapy, are relatively common. However, a single volume that brought together an array of voices who considered exposure therapy from a multiplicity of perspectives was needed.

With the help of our publisher, Academic Press, we set about convening leading clinicians and researchers in exposure therapy and behavior analysis to produce a volume that was at once accessible both to novices and experienced clinicians. The book starts with an introduction to exposure therapy that presents essential features of exposure techniques, mechanisms of action, and issues pertaining to assessment. Jim Todd and Janet Pietrowski then detail the contribution animal models have made in our understanding of how exposure therapy works. John Forsyth, Velma Barrios, and Dean Acheson follow with a consideration of exposure therapy in light of the evolution of behavior therapy and highlight the role of verbal processes in mediating and sustaining fear reactions. In the fourth chapter, Mark Powers, Jasper Smits, Teresa Leyro, and Michael Otto discuss the limitations of understanding the effects of exposure therapy solely in terms of extinction and discuss the clinical implications of context effects, particularly with regard to relapse.

With the first four chapters serving as a foundation, the book then moves into consideration of specific anxiety disorders. Dean Lauterbach and Sarah Reiland discuss exposure therapy in the context of post-traumatic stress disorder. Frank Castro and Brian Marx follow with a chapter on adult survivors of childhood sexual abuse. Rounding out the chapters considering trauma-related themes, Carlos Finlay and Judith Lyons discuss issues surrounding the use of exposure therapy with war veterans.

The next two chapters focus on the use of exposure therapy with individuals diagnosed with obsessive-compulsive disorder. Jonathan Abramowitz and Karin Larsen provide a review of the research literature and a case study report in Chapter 8, and Sandra Mendlowitz describes the use of exposure therapy with a child in Chapter 9.

Panic and phobia are considered in the next two chapters. Ellen Koch, Andrew Gloster, and Stacey Waller review the use of exposure therapy in the treatment of panic disorder in Chapter 10 and supplement the review with a case study of a man who developed panic symptoms after the deaths of two close relatives. Michiyo Hirai, Heather Cochran, and Laura Vernon then review the use of exposure therapy in the treatment of phobia in Chapter 11.

The next four chapters focus on the use of exposure therapy in behavioral medicine and recent developments in psychopharmacology. In Chapter 12, Flora Hoodin and Mary Gillis review the use of exposure in individuals complaining of pain anxiety or experiencing a blood injection phobia. In the next chapter, Joe Himle and Jody Hoffman discuss novel application of exposure therapy in the treatment of a case of hypochondriasis. Chapters 14 and 15 highlight psychopharmacology as Brett Deacon comprehensively reviews outcome studies examining combined pharmacotherapy and exposure therapy treatment regimens. Kerry Ressler, Michael Davis, and Barbara Rothbaum then describe exciting recent advances in the understanding of the biological bases of extinction and how the pharmacological blockade of N-methyl-D-aspartate (NMDA) receptors speeds extinction learning.

The last three chapters in the book offer an exploration of contemporary developments and trends in the field. Stéphane Bouchard, Sophie Côté, and David Richard review the outcome literature for virtual reality applications of exposure therapy in Chapter 16. Elizabeth Hembree and Shawn Cahill then discuss obstacles to successful implementation of exposure therapy and myths surrounding the use of exposure. The book closes with a chapter by David Richard and Andrew Gloster in which they review litigation pertaining to exposure therapy (or, more appropriately, the lack of evidence of litigation) and discuss the results of an empirical study examining attitudes that clinicians, clients, and others hold toward various forms of exposure therapy.

The book is a healthy mix of literature review, theory, case studies, and empirical research. The overall format of the book was purposefully eclectic and designed to share with the reader the rich history and varied application of exposure therapy. We hope that it will serve as a useful reference for years to come. We would like to thank all the chapter contributors, our diligent undergraduate and graduate student assistants (especially Shawn Mason, Jennifer Mainka, and Laszlo Erdodi), and the helpful staff at Academic Press for their efforts. Your willingness to be a part of this project is greatly appreciated. We would also like to extend a special thanks to our families for their support and encouragement.

David C. S. Richard
Dean Lauterbach
July 25, 2006

CHAPTER 1

Description, Mechanisms of Action, and Assessment

David C. S. Richard
Rollins College

Dean Lauterbach
Eastern Michigan University

Andrew T. Gloster
Technical University of Dresden, Germany

There can be no doubt that exposure therapy in its many variations represents one of the most efficacious treatment approaches available to clinical psychologists. Even today, however, exposure therapy is frequently overlooked as a preferred treatment for anxiety in favor of other treatments that have garnered less empirical support. To complicate matters, popular accounts of the causes and treatment of anxiety symptoms frequently omit mention of learning mechanisms or exposure therapy. For example, in a recent article in *Scientific American Mind*, Siegel (2006) claims that "once a person has learned to feel apprehensive about something, he or she may always feel dread associated with that experience (p. 47)," even though there is ample evidence that behavioral treatments for anxiety can reduce apprehension and in many cases, eliminate it. To complicate matters, he then contends that the best way to defeat fear is to practice the "five Rs": regular sleep, regular meals, regular entertainment, regular exercise, and regular work schedule. Although the five Rs are probably helpful, they represent recommendations that could apply to anyone, not just individuals with an anxiety disorder.

Omitting mention of the success exposure therapy has had in treating a variety of anxiety-related problems is commonplace in the popular media and leads one to a curious yet disheartening conclusion. Despite years of empirical work that points overwhelmingly to the efficacy of exposure therapy across a number of anxiety disorders, as well as significant efforts to disseminate these results, both the public-at-large and mental health workers seem to know little about exposure therapy and/or the reasons why it works. For example, in the aforementioned article, the author fails to mention exposure therapy, let alone distinguish it from other treatments that are less empirically supported. Instead, he generically describes therapy as "time-consuming" and asks rhetorically, "is such verbal support enough?" (p. 46). Of course, for decades, behavior therapists have resoundingly responded to this question in the negative.

Unfortunately, one article in the popular press may have a greater effect on public awareness than the most rigorously designed empirical study. It is not so much that exposure therapy is *dismissed* as it is *ignored*. We speculate that the roots of neglect are complex, are applicable to behavioral approaches more generally, and probably stem from the fact that many clinical psychologists either are not well versed in learning theory, routinely assume behavioral approaches are superficial in their treatment of complex human suffering, or reject principles of conditioning as being irrelevant to the therapeutic enterprise.

This chapter has multiple goals. First, we define the key characteristics of exposure therapy. As we will see, exposure techniques come in many forms, but all share certain features in common. In addition, some techniques that have not tradition-ally been considered a form of exposure therapy clearly include certain exposure elements. It is our position that exposure is a critical component of any successful therapy for anxiety and that exposure is an active treatment mechanism in therapies that were not originally construed as a form of exposure (e.g., written disclosure, eye movement desensitization and reprocessing (EMDR), systematic desensitiza-tion, anger management).

Second, we present different perspectives as to why exposure therapy works. Our coverage is introductory with an emphasis on contemporary models. More comprehensive reviews of mechanisms of action in exposure therapy have been published elsewhere (e.g., Tryon, 2005). Finally, we address the assessment of fear reduction as it relates to exposure therapy. Because clinicians most often use expo-sure therapy with individual clients, we discuss the different methods for assess-ing treatment-related fear reduction and the complexities of reliable, repeated assessment of individuals.

WHAT IS EXPOSURE THERAPY?

Characteristics of the Feared Stimulus

Exposure therapy has been shown to be effective in the treatment of anxiety problems. The term *exposure* broadly means exposure to a feared stimulus of some sort. Anxiety-evoking stimuli can be animate (e.g., spiders, dogs), inanimate (e.g., thunderstorms, earthquakes, germs), represent feared situations (e.g., fear of public speaking, test anxiety), or be intrusive thoughts or memories of past events (e.g., a repeated recollection of a prior sexual abuse). Reactions to these various stimuli can range from mild anxiety to full-blown panic symptoms. Further, anxiety may be exacerbated in the absence of a physical stimulus through exaggerated expectations of impending doom. Thus, although the stimulus itself may be easily identified in treatment, anxiety to the feared stimulus is usually compounded by catastrophic self-statements that magnify the perceived threat an individual may experience.

By its very nature, exposure therapy implies that new learning occurs as a person is exposed to a feared stimulus, or representation of the feared stimulus, in the absence of an actual threat. Although there is some debate as to what exactly occurs in the brain during exposure, new behavioral repertoires are developed and reinforced each time an individual successfully manages a previously feared situation. How exposure is conducted in treatment is often a function of the nature of the fear. For example, although it may be possible to develop an approach task for a spider phobic that utilizes a real spider, an example of exposure in vivo, the same option is not available for a female adult survivor of child molestation. Instead, imaginal exposure would be preferred, for both practical and ethical reasons. In either case, successful exposure to the actual stimulus (a spider) or to the memory of an event (child molestation) implies a reduction in one's physiological response to the feared stimulus, as well as the probability that subsequent avoidance and escape responses will occur.

Characteristics of the Anxiety Response

In the brain, responses to feared stimuli are first mediated by the visual thalamus, visual cortex, and amygdala. The brain then activates the sympathetic nervous system, which is responsible for initiating a fight–flight response. The fight–flight response is the body's way of preparing for and reacting to a threat. Although all individuals have experienced the fight–flight response at some point in their lives, exposure therapy is justified when conditional stimuli, or cues, associated with the feared stimulus frequently occur in the person's natural environment and have the effect of evoking a response. Typically, individuals then develop avoidance and escape strategies to minimize exposure to cues that may have a significant effect on the quality of one's life. For example, we know of one individual who survived a horrific automobile accident and subsequently refused to drive or ride in an automobile. As a result, he commuted to work using the city bus, even though the trip took two hours in each direction.

Pervasiveness

Although the terms *frequency, intensity,* and *duration* may be obvious to the reader, generalized responding (or pervasiveness) is a hallmark of pathological anxiety. Anxiety is pervasive when a stimulus evokes fear or avoidance behavior irrespective of context. For example, a fear of spiders is pervasive if it occurs regardless of how a spider is encountered (e.g., in the backyard, at the zoo, in the bedroom, in one's imagination). A person with obsessive-compulsive disease (OCD) may have a strong fear of germs that does not depend on the way he or she contacts the germ.

Persistence

Another hallmark feature of fears typically treated using exposure therapy is the persistence of the problem. Most clients do not seek exposure therapy as their first treatment option. Instead, they often agree to exposure therapy after other treatment efforts have failed. Sometimes, this might be after many years of suffering. The fact that anxiety responses do not seem to alleviate appreciably over a long period implies that new learning has not taken place. Ironically, those individuals who have not experienced success using other treatment modalities are often the most proficient at using elaborate avoidance and escape responses that preempt new learning from occurring.

Core Elements of Exposure Therapy

Although there are many variations of exposure therapy, all share some common elements. Our purpose here is to describe the similarities in different forms of exposure therapy without recourse to proposed underlying mechanisms of action.

Systematic Exposure to a Stimulus

Exposure therapy, as its name implies, involves deliberate and planned exposure to a feared stimulus, or representation of the stimulus, until the intensity of a person's distress recedes to a level that is (1) lower than pretreatment levels and (2) acceptable to the client. A feared stimulus is one that reliably evokes changes in multiple modes of behavior characteristic of an anxiety response (e.g., physiological responses, subjective experience of fear, catastrophic cognitions) and may be detected across multiple methods of assessment (e.g., self-report, behavioral observation, psychophysiological measures), although perfect congruence of data across assessment measures is not necessarily expected. Although reduction of *all* anxiety is not the goal of treatment, reduced anxiety in the presence of the previously feared stimulus has been commonly interpreted as evidence of habituation and therefore, therapeutic gain (Foa & Kozak, 1986). Systematic exposure to a feared stimulus or representation of the stimulus constitutes the core element of any exposure therapy.

For some individuals, the stimulus does not evoke anxieties but rather cravings that are physiologically mediated and difficult to resist, as in the case with cigarettes, alcohol, opiates, and other recreational and illicit drugs. Similarly, some environments set in motion a chain of behaviors that occur at high rates and are maladaptive, as in the case of persons with gambling problems. Cue exposure therapy is an extinction-based treatment paradigm that has attempted to moderate cue reactivity associated with drugs or gambling through repeated exposure to conditional stimuli while preventing the stereotyped response from occurring. The efficacy of cue exposure therapy remains contested, with a recent meta-analysis concluding there is no demonstrated efficacy for its use (Conklin & Tiffany, 2002), although some researchers questioned the wisdom of conducting the analysis across heterogeneous addiction populations (Drummond, 2002). Although cues encountered by individuals with a substance use or gambling problem can certainly evoke responses characterized by anxiety and distress, individuals with addiction problems typically do not *fear* the cues. Instead, the distress a person feels results from efforts to inhibit select behaviors that, in the short term, gratify the urge evoked by the cues. Thus, an individual does not fear a hypodermic needle, cigarette, or slot machine; anxiety results when an individual attempts to resist engaging in behaviors previously associated with these conditional stimuli and reinforced by the past effects of their use (e.g., a "rush" when shooting heroin, a nicotine high when smoking a cigarette, or the thrill of winning money on the slots).

A critical difference between cue exposure approaches and the use of exposure therapy for anxiety disorders, therefore, is that the problem behavior in the former almost always is characterized by a maladaptive *approach* response. The response, or chain of behaviors, is ultimately reinforced by the potent pharmacological properties of the drug and the physiological consequences of not taking the drug (e.g., withdrawal symptoms). Anxiety disorders, on the other hand, are characterized by maladaptive avoidance and/or escape responses that are reinforced by their *supposed* effects. For example, the focal problem for an individual with OCD may be anxiety that develops in response to an object that possesses germs or toxins. Avoidance and escape behaviors (e.g., washing money with an antibacterial soap, cleaning one's hands with alcohol) function to reduce anxiety in the short term by placating the individual's exaggerated fear of potential harm to self. Exposure and response prevention techniques provide the individual with corrective information that has the effect of recalibrating the person's estimates of potential harm so as to more realistically align with actual probabilities. When an individual learns that harm is no more likely to occur as the result of not engaging in the avoidance or response behavior, the supposed value of the behavior in warding off a threat is weakened.

Although cue exposure therapy is similar in its rationale to the various forms of exposure described in this volume, the focus here is on reducing avoidance and escape behaviors as they apply to stimuli that are *feared*. Exposure therapists aim to expose individuals to previously feared stimuli in the absence of an actual threat to create a corrective learning experience that subsequently moderates the client's estimated probability of the presence of a real threat. Exposure therapy also has the effect of reinforcing an alternative behavioral repertoire that supplants the maladaptive avoidance and escape responses. Thus the focus of this volume is not on responses associated with addiction but on the application of exposure therapy to anxiety-disordered populations.

Representation

Exposure therapy also implies presentation or representation of the feared stimulus for therapeutic purposes. The stimulus may be presented in reality (in vivo), imaginally, virtually (in virtuo), or as part of a writing exercise. Systematically exposing the client to the stimulus, or parts of it, distinguishes exposure therapy from other treatments that may have an incidental exposure component. Simply referencing a feared stimulus, or reinterpreting its meaning, may include an element of exposure (and may have a therapeutic effect) but does not constitute formal exposure therapy. Talking about the meaning of a traumatic event is one step removed from actually processing horrific images encountered during an event and the memories associated with them. Although a client may imagine the feared stimulus or situation as the result of a cognitive intervention (e.g., the mere mention of the word *Vietnam* may conjure up memories from a firefight), exposure in this instance is secondary to the larger goal of having the client reinterpret the meaning of the event or reevaluate the validity of beliefs and cognitions associated with the event. In exposure therapy, the exposure itself is conceived as a necessary precondition for change, with all subsequent modifications in cognitions, and interpretations of meaningfulness, occurring as a result of fear reduction. Thus, although it is not the express purpose of exposure therapy to facilitate reinterpretation of a feared situation, this often is a by-product of the intervention.

Repeated and/or Prolonged Exposure

Although there have been reports of significant clinical change after a prolonged single session of exposure therapy (Heading, Kirkby, Martin, Daniels, Gilroy, & Menzies, 2001; Thom, Sartory, & Jöhren, 2000; Veltman, Tuinebreijer, Windelman, Lammertsma, Witter, Dolan, et al., 2004; Breitholtz & Öst, 1997, Öst, 1989), a central feature of exposure therapy is that intervention is repeated across sessions and/or prolonged within-session. Guidelines for prolonged exposure have been developed by Hembree, Rauch, and Foa (2003). Repeated and prolonged exposure has been justified in terms of habituation—a decrement in a fear response owing to repeated processing or reliving of the event. Others have argued that repeated exposure in quick succession may lead to superior extinction effects in humans, as it does in mice (Quirk, 2004).

Additional Elements of an Exposure Therapy Treatment Package

Response Prevention

Most forms of exposure therapy also include a response prevention component. Because avoidance and escape responses, by definition, function to reduce the individual's exposure to an aversive stimulus, a consequential effect is that individuals fail to acquire new learning regarding the feared stimulus. Thus, avoidance and escape responses have powerful short-term effects because they preempt or alleviate anxiety. However, they also inhibit new learning and prevent introduction of corrective information that would ultimately reduce the intensity of an individual's emotional response.

Although response prevention can take any of a number of forms, a common misconception is that response prevention is coercive, in that the therapist is responsible for preventing an escape response in a client. Unfortunately, the term itself errantly implies a heavy-handedness on the part of the therapist. In truth, prevention occurs only with the willing and informed participation of the client. The therapist usually serves to prompt or remind the individual not to engage in the behavior when it occurs and encourages the client to engage in alternative behaviors that function as an alternative response repertoire. As a result, response prevention serves both to prevent the occurrence of maladaptive behaviors and to reinforce more adaptive or appropriate behavior.

Fear Hierarchy

Therapists rarely expose patients to their greatest fear without some level of preparation. Clients often progress through a graded hierarchy of fears that are arranged from least to most fear evoking. For example, a hierarchy might be composed of several progressively challenging scenarios involving a feared object. Alternatively, clients may recount a sequence of events from a traumatic memory, starting with those events that evoke the least anxiety and progressing to the most distressing images and recollections.

Reduction of Distractions

Research on the effectiveness of exposure therapy has shown that removing distractions during the exposure sessions is associated with better treatment outcome. Distractions can take several forms and may include the perception of available safety. This finding is not surprising, as distractions enable the patient to avoid thinking about a feared stimulus and therefore inhibit new learning.

Experiencing the Present

Regardless of the way exposure therapy is conducted, clients are encouraged to confront their fears in the present tense. For example, a client recounting a traumatic event in exposure therapy is encouraged to describe the event as if it were being relived. Treatment focuses on processing the emotions as though they were recurring. As a result, clients are gently prompted during recall to avoid using past tense verbiage, as it implies temporal distance from the events and reduces the degree to which the client may be immersed in the processing. Thus, a client who says "I felt horrified" would be prompted by the therapist to say "I feel horrified." In vivo and in virtuo treatments also stress the importance of processing emotion in the present by exposing the client to a feared stimulus (in vivo) or simulated imagery of the feared stimulus (in virtuo).

Use of Adjunctive Treatments

Therapists rarely use exposure in the absence of other treatments. In fact, exposure therapy is often used in conjunction with other treatments and in many cases, only after other treatments have had little or no effect on reducing client symptoms. When using exposure therapy, clinicians must determine whether concurrent treatments will inhibit or potentiate the effects of exposure therapy. In this regard, there are many considerations. For example, anxiolytic medications may inhibit the client's ability to experience anxiety during an exposure session. Other medications may enhance the effects of exposure therapy and speed extinction.[1]

Interactive effects are not limited to pharmacological treatments, however. Psychosocial interventions may encourage the development of coping skills that functionally distract the patient from confronting a feared stimulus during exposure. Alternatively, a client who is also participating in group therapy may converse with other patients who may be skeptical of the treatment if they do not understand its rationale. In any case, there is a general consensus among exposure therapy practitioners that selection of adjunctive treatments should carefully consider the treatment's potential interaction with exposure therapy.

MECHANISMS OF ACTION

Complexities in Isolating Mechanisms of Action

As Foa and Kozak (1986) note, exposure may represent a common mechanism that explains therapeutic change in treatment across theoretically disparate approaches. Most forms of therapy involve exposure to aversive stimuli in some way, whether the exposure involves talking about a distressing event, promoting mastery, or framing the exposure in the context of resolving long-standing intrapsychic issues. Further, any treatment technique that reduces the probability of escape and avoidance behavior in response to an aversive stimulus should have the effect of facilitating corrective learning experiences and reinforcing a repertoire of alternative adaptive behaviors.

To the degree that elements of exposure, whether incidental or systematic, occur in theoretically dissimilar treatments that supposedly work as a result of mechanisms that are actually inert, the power of inferential statistical methods to detect statistically significant differences between exposure therapy and other treatments

---

[1]See the chapter discussing N-methyl-D-aspartate (NMDA) receptor antagonists by Ressler, Davis, and Rothbaum in this volume.

is reduced. This issue has been at the center of the debate surrounding EMDR, since a number of dismantling studies concluded that eye movements have no effect therapeutically beyond what appeared to be a core exposure element to treatment (see McNally, 1999, for a review). In this case, the supposed equivalence of treatment effects reflected nothing more than a comparison of topographically dissimilar, yet functionally equivalent, treatment methods. Viewed in this way, EMDR is not so much a new treatment as a repackaged version of exposure elements with additional components that have yet to show incremental treatment validity above and beyond the effects of exposure alone. Because EMDR without finger waving bears a strong likeness to imaginal exposure, McNally concluded that, "what is effective in EMDR (imaginal exposure) is not new, and what is new (eye movements) is not effective" (p. 1). The idea that EMDR shares similar mechanisms of action with exposure therapy has been echoed by others as well (e.g., Spates & Koch, 2003; Spates, Waller, & Koch, 2000).

A problem in designing sophisticated comparative outcome studies involves isolating treatment mechanisms that are orthogonally represented across conditions. Unfortunately, there are inherent limits to treatment dismantling. Because most treatment packages represent a constellation of techniques that may or may not be directly relevant to the underlying theory, dismantling designs often sacrifice ecological validity by creating an artificial treatment context that is unrepresentative of actual practice. For example, removing the exposure elements inherent in EMDR yields an unrepresentative facsimile of EMDR. Alternatively, researchers may design dismantling studies that assess the incremental treatment validity of a supplemental procedure (e.g., finger oscillation) for exposure therapy. Because exposure therapy is known to be efficacious, however, there is a ceiling as to the effect supplemental procedures can have beyond the treatment effect of exposure therapy alone. If the ceiling of maximum possible improvement under any therapeutic condition is close to the current ceiling for exposure therapy, then the unique effect attributable to any supplemental procedure will necessarily be small. Detection of a statistically significant and clinically meaningful treatment effect for such a small effect would require a level of statistical power greater than current studies possess.

Similarly, Pennebaker and Beall's (1986) written emotional disclosure paradigm appears to contain significant exposure elements, despite the fact that Pennebaker and colleagues have claimed that no one theory can account for the therapeutic effects of written disclosure. Written emotional disclosure, however, clearly possesses a strong exposure element. In a cleverly crafted study, Sloan, Marx, and Epstein (2005) assigned 79 college students to one of three groups: written disclosure about a specific traumatic event, written exposure about any traumatic event (different events could be disclosed across sessions), and a control condition in which participants wrote about trivial life events. They found that only individuals in the group writing about a specific event showed statistically significant and clinically meaningful changes in post-traumatic stress disorder (PTSD) symptoms, depressive symptomatology, and subsequent physical health complaints. In contrast, the disclosure group that wrote about more than one event did not show any greater improvement than the control condition by the end of the study. Their results supported the hypothesis that the mechanism of action for written disclosure involves repeated exposure to, or writing about, a single traumatic event. Other studies, however, have found therapeutic gains when participants are not instructed to write about a single event, suggesting that it may not be exposure per se but disclosure of emotionally charged information that accounts for change (Sloan & Marx, 2004).

Mowrer's Two-Factor Theory of Fear Acquisition and Maintenance

Although not a theory of how exposure therapy works, Mowrer's (1960) two-factor learning theory of fear acquisition and maintenance continues to influence the way many behavior therapists conceptualize treatment action in exposure therapy. Mowrer proposed that fears are initially learned through associative learning and respondent conditioning. Conditional stimuli present at the time of the initial learning become discriminative stimuli (commonly referred to as cues) for eliciting a conditional emotional response (CER). Because CERs are subjectively and physiologically distressing to an individual, avoidance and escape behaviors that remove an individual from contact with relevant cues are strengthened through negative reinforcement. Thus, any behavior that functions to assist a person in either avoiding or escaping conditions likely to evoke a CER will be strengthened over time.

With regard to exposure therapy, Mowrer's two-factor theory suggests that exposure therapy is effective for at least three reasons. First, fear should lessen, or extinguish, after repeated trials in which discriminative stimuli are presented in the absence of a paired aversive stimulus (i.e., an unconditional stimulus). For example, a child who fears dogs subsequent to a dog bite should experience reduced fear after exposure to several friendly dogs. An alternative explanation for the fear reduction is that repeated trials change the subjective probability estimates made by individuals as to the likelihood that an aversive experience will occur when put in contact with previously feared stimuli.

Second, prevention of avoidance and escape responses encourages the development of alternative behavioral repertoires that function to keep an individual in a previously feared situation. By remaining in the situation, the individual now has the opportunity to learn new information about the feared stimulus. For example, a child may learn that dogs are more likely to bite when surprised or approached from the rear. Conversely, permitting a dog to sniff one's hand first reduces the likelihood that the animal will bite. Neither the new information nor behavior would have been acquired if the child had continued to use avoidance and escape strategies.

Finally, people usually do not remain anxious indefinitely in the absence of a real threat. Presentation of a feared stimulus may initially lead to feelings of anxiety, but these feelings often subside either within or between sessions.

Criticisms of Mowrer's Two-Factor Theory

Critics of Mowrer's two-factor theory have pointed out that individuals may report aversive experiences and acquire consequent fear responses yet do not engage in avoidance or escape behaviors, even though their fear does not remit. Alternatively, other people may engage in avoidance and escape behaviors despite reporting no longer subjectively experiencing distress at the time they engage in the behavior. Another criticism has been that many people do not recall having had a learning experience related to their particular fear even though the fear may develop late enough in life that the person should have a memory of a precipitating event.

Some recent research has also shown that fear pathogenesis and maintenance involves more than the combined effects of a respondent and operant conditioning sequence. Specifically, the therapeutic benefit of exposure therapy may be related to changes in an individual's fear of experiencing future anxiety. Smits, Powers, Cho, and Telch (2004) found that self-reported fear of having a panic attack mediated the effect cognitive-behavioral therapy (CBT) had on global disability in functioning, and to a lesser extent, panic frequency, anxiety, and agoraphobic avoidance, in a sample of 130 participants completing a 12-week CBT program that included two exposure components. The results were consistent with the hypothesis that CBT exerts its effects by reducing an individual's "fear of fear," which, in turn, improves functioning and reduces symptom expression.

Finally, although the two-factor theory may account for phobic fears, it is less satisfactory in accounting for the complexities of other fears that are diffuse or involve relational themes. For example, the sequelae of repeated sexual assault in childhood by a family member may go well beyond the effects explained by the two-factor model and include subsequent disturbances in identity formation, dissociative responses to stress, and impaired interpersonal relations. It is difficult to see how such effects can be explained as conditioned emotional responses.

Lang's Bioinformational Theory

Dissatisfaction with a purely learning approach to fear acquisition and maintenance led many researchers to posit stronger cognitive and physiological aspects to fear and its treatment. Lang's bioinformational theory (e.g., 1977; 1985; 1995; Lang, Bradley, & Cuthbert, 1990) describes anxiety as an emotional memory stored within a semantic network in the brain. The structure of emotional memories is hypothesized to contain three categories of information: (1) information about the stimulus or situation that evokes the emotional memory structure; (2) information regarding an individual's responses (i.e., verbal-cognitive, overt motor, and covert-physiological); and (3) semantic elaboration that defines the meaning of the stimulus and response. Most emotional networks are understood to be products of one's individual conditioning history, especially experiences necessary for survival (Lang, 1995). Nevertheless, neurological hardwiring provides the parameters within which the emotional networks develop (Lang, 1985). In this context, emotions are defined as stored action dispositions, released when specific stimulus contexts activate the semantic network. Expression of emotions occurs when an individual's context sufficiently matches input information and information stored in the semantic network.

According to Lang (1985), the concordance of response systems (i.e., cognitive, motor, and physiological) depends on arousal level, valence of the stimuli, and degree of control. One would expect concordance between the systems only in extreme situations (i.e., circumstances in which high arousal, negative valence, and no control are present). Otherwise, discordance between the verbal-cognitive (e.g., subjective thoughts, images, and reports), overt motor (e.g., behavioral actions), and covert physiological (e.g., autonomic arousal) responses is expected.

When an emotional network contains erroneous information leading to subjective distress, therapeutic intervention may be necessary. The therapeutic relevance of Lang's theory results from the multifaceted description of semantic networks. That is, variations exist in the type of information and response possibilities stored in these networks. By way of extension, individuals must activate relevant aspects of the emotional network to process pathological anxiety. For example, eliciting verbal-linguistic representations of anxiety will lead to changes only in those variables mediated by verbal-linguistic expression. If one asks a client about his or her panic attacks, only those dimensions of the panic attack accessible via the verbal-linguistic channel may be altered. Although physiological sensations are presumably an intricate aspect of the memory structure, they may not be altered using a verbally mediated intervention. Partial activation of the network, inferred by discordance in response systems, leads to partial processing. As a result, a more comprehensive evocation of the structure is needed and suggests a multimethod and multimodal approach to treatment.

Lang's concept of complex emotional networks is consistent with modern behavior therapies built on a theory of human language (Hayes, Barnes-Holmes, & Roche, 2001; Hayes, Strosahl, & Wilson, 1999) and predates more complex neural network models described later. Hayes and colleagues have demonstrated the multitude of complications resulting from human verbal-linguistic processes. One's thoughts and memories about an anxious experience often become anxiety provoking in their own right. Thus, asking a social phobic to think about a feared social interaction elicits an anxious response even in the absence of feared stimuli. In turn, the thoughts themselves are avoided in an effort to control and limit anxious feelings. In the context of Lang's theory, these thoughts are derived or learned associations tied into the broader semantic memory. The implication is that a therapist cannot concentrate simply on the content of the thoughts but must also attend to the process by which the associative learning is fostered (Hayes et al., 1999). This is consistent with Wilson and Murrell's (2004) observation that successful exposure results in increased breadth and flexibility of one's behavioral repertoire, including verbal behaviors, and not simply a reduction in arousal and avoidance. Again, this observation is conceptually consistent with Lang's semantic network, while acknowledging that exposure therapy also serves to differentially reinforce other more adaptive behavioral repertoires.

Lang (1985) also hypothesized that anxiety disorders exist on a continuum of affective memory organization. Placing anxiety disorders in a hierarchy of network coherence resulted in the following list: "focal phobia, obsessions and compulsions, social anxiety, agoraphobia, panic, and generalized anxiety states" (p. 167). An implication of the hierarchy is that the efficacy of a therapeutic intervention is a function of the degree to which the treatment addresses activated components of the network. Lang's own words summarize this best: "It may prove that the most effective therapy will not be similarly unimodal, but will depend on careful consideration of all three affective parameters [i.e., valence, arousal, and control]" (p. 169).

Rachman's Emotional Processing Theory

Building on Lang's work, Rachman (1980) proposed the concept of emotional processing, which he defined as "a process whereby emotional disturbances are absorbed and decline to the extent that other experiences and behavior can proceed without disruption" (p. 51). Refining this concept, Rachman stipulated that emotional processing has occurred when an emotional disturbance declines in intensity and a person returns to a normal, routine behavioral pattern. The emphasis on a return to normal functioning emphasizes that not every emotion requires emotional processing, only those that represent a problematic deviation in functioning.

Rachman stated that the degree of emotional processing can be observed and tested via "probes," including "the person's ability to talk about, see, listen to or be reminded of the emotional events without experiencing distress or disruptions" (p. 52). For example, an individual can be presented with a feared stimulus several months after exposure therapy to determine the progress of emotional processing. Although Rachman considered test probes a primary method of measuring change, he proposed the use of several other techniques and indices that functioned to indirectly assess signs of distress. Foa and Kozak (1986) subsequently called into question the adequacy of probes for eliciting fear responses because the response could be attenuated for any of a number of reasons that had little to do with successful emotional processing.

Although Rachman's theory does not elaborate extensively on the specific mechanism of action for emotional processing, he does cite Lang's work on vividness of imagery and physiological elicitation (Lang, 1977) as an important factor. In this sense, Rachman's concept of emotional processing is nearly identical to Lang's ideas of processing emotions within an emotional memory network.

In an attempt to account for the fact that most emotional events are processed by individuals without giving rise to emotional difficulties, Rachman predicted that four factors mediated effective emotional processing: (1) state factors, (2) personality factors, (3) stimulus factors, and (4) associated activity factors. For example, a general state of relaxation should inhibit anxiety and emotional expression, and a general state of fatigue and sleeplessness should exacerbate symptoms. Similarly, personality factors such as broad competence and stability are believed to exert a protective effect, whereas neuroticism and introversion may have the opposite effect. As a result, emotional processing is contingent on a wide array of factors extrinsic to the approach itself, factors that should be assessed carefully by clinicians before treatment.

Rachman (1980) also proposed several within-treatment factors that could influence the effectiveness of emotional processing. According to Rachman, factors that facilitate emotional processing included strong engagement during exposure, calm rehearsals, habituation training, extinction, vivid and prolonged presentations of feared stimuli, repeated practice, and relaxation. Factors hypothesized to impede emotional processing included avoidance behavior, agitated rehearsals, silence, distractions during treatment, poorly implemented treatment procedures, excessively brief presentations to feared stimuli, fatigue, and lack of an autonomic response to feared stimuli.

Foa and Kozak's Emotional Processing Model

Foa and Kozak (1986) extended the work of Lang and Rachman by hypothesizing that fear reduction could occur only through the modification of a latent fear structure that encompassed all knowledge, information, and behaviors relevant to a feared stimulus. Of special relevance to exposure therapy, Foa and Kozak's theory of emotional processing suggests that fear reduction occurs not only because of a weakening of associations, but also because it reflects changes in meaning in the composition of the underlying fear structure.

A fear structure is differentiated from other information structures in terms of the emotional valence of the structure and the number of cues that can activate the structure. Foa and Kozak describe a fear structure as a "program to escape danger," and pathological fear structures are characterized both by excessive response elements (e.g., heightened physiological reactivity in response to a feared stimulus, avoidance behaviors) and resistance to change. Activation of the fear structure in treatment is inferred by a patient's increased physiological reactivity when exposed to a feared stimulus (regardless of the medium of exposure), changes in subjective self-reports, and behavioral observations of increased anxiety.

From this perspective, exposure therapy is responsible for three important changes in emotional processing. First, exposure to the feared stimulus activates its associated fear structure, a necessary prerequisite for any subsequent habituation. Second, repeated and prolonged exposure to the feared stimulus introduces corrective information that has the effect of modifying the fear structure and reducing the person's fear. Fear reduction is indicated initially through within-session habituation, which then sets the stage for between-session habituation. Between-session habituation is considered better evidence of sustained fear reduction and is more reliably associated with long-term therapeutic change than within-session habituation. Foa and Kozak contend that within-session habituation does not necessarily involve modification of higher cortical processes and must occur in order for between-session habituation to take place. Within-session habituation is suggested when measures of anxiety (i.e., physiological measures, self-report, and behavioral observations) show a steady return to a pre-arousal or baseline state even though the person continues to be exposed to a feared stimulus. In contrast, between-session habituation is signaled by lowered physiological arousal to previously feared stimuli at the beginning of subsequent exposure sessions and is thought to reflect higher order changes in the person's interpretation of the meaning of the feared stimulus. Specifically, changes in meaning include reductions in the exaggerated probability of harm or catastrophe occurring when exposed to a feared object or situation, modification of the belief that anxiety will persist until escape is realized, and reconsideration of the negative emotional valence associated with the feared stimulus.

Should exposure therapy be ineffective with a client, any of a number of causes are implied by the theory. All share a common theme, however: failure to activate and modify the fear structure. Such failure may occur because a large discrepancy exists between the individual's fear structure and the information that is communicated during exposure therapy (e.g., stimuli used during exposure may not reliably match important stimulus parameters represented in memory). Alternatively, inattention, concentrating on nonfearful elements in a situation, and subtle cognitive avoidance strategies may cause a client to fail to encode information and activate the fear structure. Beyond in-session variables that mediate the effectiveness of exposure therapy, Foa and Kozak also propose that certain patient characteristics may impede or lead to poor treatment outcome, including high tonic arousal (i.e., high resting heart rate, skin conductance) and mood disorders such as depression.

A Revised Theory

Foa and McNally (1996) revised the emotional processing approach 10 years later to emphasize that exposure therapy serves not just to weaken old associations but to reinforce new associations. The revised view contends that successful exposure therapy reflects more than modification of existing fear structures, but instead the creation of new structures that override the former's effects (Bouton, 1988). The new, nonpathological structures are susceptible to encroachment by the preexisting fear structures to the extent that contexts, settings, and internal states (e.g., dysphoric mood) successfully activate the fear structure (i.e., reinstatement of fear). As a result, it may be that fear structures are not so much modified as inhibited by the development of new structures that represent the effects of corrective learning. To this end, Foa and McNally (1996) recommend that treatment should address generalization of inhibitory responding (i.e., strengthening the new structures) in contexts that would have previously evoked a fear response.

Perceived Control and Self-Efficacy

The work of Foa and colleagues was followed by a chapter by Mineka and Thomas (1999) that questioned some of the central tenets of the emotional processing theory while proposing an alternative explanation for therapeutic change. Mineka and Thomas pointed out that emotional processing models cannot account for a number of findings in the exposure literature that appear to be at odds with emotional processing approaches. From their perspective, any model that relies on an information-processing approach has difficulty explaining why the *way* in which information is presented may have an effect on fear reduction. For example, they cite studies by Kazdin (1975, 1976) that showed observation of a group of models engaging in a safety behavior led to greater fear reduction in anxious individuals than observation of individual models engaging in the same safety behavior. Further, Mineka and Thomas note Barlow's (1988) observation that Foa and Kozak's model may not be able to account for those individuals who reported subjective decreases in anxiety as a result of exposure therapy in the absence of physiological changes that typically occur during extinction.

In response to these shortcomings, Mineka and Thomas proposed an alternative explanatory theory that blended Bandura's self-efficacy theory with Foa and Kozak's emotional processing approach. Their approach emphasizes the role of perceived control and self-efficacy in managing situations where a feared stimulus is present. In short, they contend that other theories have generally overlooked the importance that restoring control in a person's life can have on anxiety reduction. It is not so much that theories that rely on extinction and habituation are incorrect as it is that they are incomplete.

Because successful anxiety reduction during exposure therapy leads to an increased sense of control, a corresponding increase in self-efficacy results. Increases in self-efficacy correspondingly lead to an increased sense of self-competence and greater ability to tolerate previously intolerable situations. Thus, Mineka and Thomas emphasize the importance of an individual's perceived control of aversive stimuli and argue that the *expectation* that one's actions are effective in changing the environment is at least as important as the *knowledge* about the effects of those actions.

Mineka and Thomas point out that the effects of exposure therapy appear to generalize across contexts and situations. Generalization of treatment effects appears to be inconsistent with more specific and localized effects commonly attributed to extinction procedures. In extinction, lack of generalization is thought to occur because context cues serve as discriminative stimuli for extinction. To the degree that new contexts are absent of discriminative stimuli, extinction effects will not occur. However, increased perceived control may better explain generalization effects because responses that suggest an increase in an individual's sense of perceived control (e.g., covert self-statements) are context-independent and act as safety signals in a wide variety of situations. An effective coping response therefore "will provide more generalizable safety information than is provided by context alone following simple Pavlovian fear extinction" (Mineka & Thomas, 1999, p. 754).

Neural Networking Models

Tryon (2005) comprehensively reviewed proposed mechanisms of action for desensitization and exposure therapy and concluded that a parallel, distributed processing connectionist neural network model provided the most satisfactory explanation for the exposure therapy's effects. Tryon's approach shares with other approaches a general networking model but is much more specific about the way the network is activated and maintained. Briefly, learning presumes retention and is interdependent with a memory network in the brain. The *learning-memory principle* acknowledges that learning and memory are intertwined at the synaptic level, with new learning trials functioning to change synaptic connections by changing the connection weight of their respective neurons. Thus, the *learning-memory mechanism* may be a common factor that could explain the effects of a variety of behavioral phenomena (e.g., extinction, habituation, reinforcement). Learning is modeled, in part, by changing the connection weights for two neurons to reflect the effect new information has on their association. The network architecture is characterized as a layered system in which each layer consists of nodes, and the nodes are connected via synapses both within and across layers. Although nodes can communicate via synapses within-layer, connections can only be made with adjacent layers. Thus, nodes in stimulus input layers only communicate indirectly with a distal behavioral response layer, as communications are mediated by an intervening layer representing concepts stored in the neural network. Nodal connections can be either excitatory or inhibitory, with network activation cascading to different nodes contingent on the a priori synaptic strength of nodal connections. The strength of the behavioral response to neural activation depends on the dynamically changing connection weights of activated neurons. Learning, as mentioned previously, entails modification of the connection weights and subsequent changes in the cascading pattern of neural activation. Thus, as Tryon notes, "learning-driven connection weight changes" (p. 81) form the basis for changes in the emphasis that the network puts on stimulus characteristics, thereby changing the meaning attributed to any sensory input and fostering therapeutic gains.

Explanatory models that incorporate networking features have been proposed elsewhere (see also Creamer, Burgess, & Patterson, 1992; Chemtob, Roitblat, Hamada, Carlson, & Twentyman, 1988) and represent sophisticated approaches to understanding behavioral phenomena that were previously understood without recourse to cognitive mechanisms.

ASSESSMENT

Although exposure therapy has historically been considered a behavioral intervention, and much of the underlying notions of the way in which exposure therapy functions are rooted in learning theory, the preceding discussion should make it clear that any satisfactory explanation of mechanisms of action will probably go beyond extinction and habituation to include a learning component that interacts with complex, interdependent memory systems. Further, an adequate accounting of mechanisms of change must account not only for the weakening of associations related to pathological responding but for the strengthening of alternative cognitive and behavioral repertoires (i.e., new learning) that function to supplant or override maladaptive beliefs and avoidance behaviors. To the extent that adequate assessment is a prerequisite for understanding the magnitude of treatment change and the mechanisms responsible for change, the issue is complicated by the fact that certain kinds of measurement methods and change indices inherently limit the strength of inferences that may be drawn from them. In short, the assessment of idiosyncratic therapeutic change is more complex than initially thought.

Unfortunately, assessment of change is not treated with the care it deserves when conducting treatment outcome research. As noted by DeVellis (1991), "poor measurement imposes an absolute limit on the validity of the conclusions one can reach" (p. 13). Moreover, an important issue that is frequently overlooked is that measurement error can significantly affect the power of both between- and within-group indices of change.

This section has several goals. We first outline the purposes of assessment before, during, and after treatment and provide exemplars of specific techniques that have been used. The focus is on *techniques* and not specific instruments, as this is far beyond the scope of a single chapter. The chapter concludes with a discussion of broad assessment-related issues and their applicability to different research contexts.

Assessment Goals

Pretreatment Assessment

In treatment outcome research, the primary goals of pretreatment assessment are to identify potential subjects, evaluate stability and severity of presenting symptoms, assess for the presence of contraindicated conditions, make decisions regarding treatment eligibility, and provide a baseline against which to compare treatment effects. Decisions regarding treatment eligibility can be based on the presence of a disorder and/or predetermined event (Foa, Hembree, Cahill, Rauch, Riggs, Feeny, et al., 2005) or a score on a standardized measure of the focal disorder. For example, in a study of public speaking phobia, a group of undergraduate students were pre-screened regarding their level of confidence as a public speaker (Harris, Kemmer-ling, & North, 2002). Persons with scores exceeding a predetermined cutoff score were contacted and assigned to either a wait-list control group or an exposure treatment group.

Exclusionary criteria can vary greatly in scope and co-vary with perceived client vulnerability, intensity of treatment, and the overall purpose or hypotheses of the study. For example, a large-scale randomized trial of prolonged exposure therapy for female sexual and nonsexual assault victims (Foa, et al., 2005) included the following exclusionary criteria: (1) being in an abusive relationship, (2) current diagnosis of organic mental disorder, schizophrenia (or other psychotic disorder) that is not medicated, (3) symptomatic bipolar disorder, (4) substance dependence, (5) illiteracy in English, (6) high risk for suicidality, and (7) recent history of self-injurious behavior.

A second goal of pretreatment assessment is to assess the stability of symptoms. The importance of assessing symptom stability may seem self-evident, but few research-ers or clinicians reporting case studies include multiple pretreatment assessments to gauge variability of symptom expression. A notable exception, however, is a series of studies conducted by Botella and colleagues, who have used virtual reality expo-sure techniques to treat individuals diagnosed either with claustrophobia or panic disorder with agoraphobia (Botella, Baños, Villa, Perpiñá, & García-Palacios, 2000; Botella, Villa, Baños, Perpiñá, & García-Palacios, 1999).

Assessment During Treatment

Assessment that takes place during treatment can serve both as a manipulation check and an integral part of treatment. As noted earlier in the chapter, Foa and Kozak (1986) argued that exposure therapy works by virtue of activating a fear structure that is subsequently modified through the introduction of corrective information. In a graded exposure paradigm, one would expect that distress scores should vary as a function of exposure content (i.e., the kind of emotional processing being con-ducted), with subjective anxiety peaks corresponding to the most traumatic ele-ments of a memory. The theory also predicts that one would expect to observe within- and between-session habituation of the fear response. It follows that absence of distress, or variability in distress, implies either that the fear is not as great as expected or that the fear structure has not been adequately activated. If the latter, the theory also predicts that exposure therapy may not be effective since modification of the fear structure requires its activation. Conversely, excessive anxiety or distress may produce sensitization effects or lead to premature termination. These reactions have been termed underengagement and overengagement, respectively (Hembree, et al.,

2003). Either of these kinds of responses to treatment could then be addressed with the client-provided assessment was sensitive to their detection.

Post-Treatment Assessment

Assessment of change during treatment requires a post-treatment assessment that contrasts scores on dependent measures against data collected earlier. Of most relevance are changes in diagnostic status, symptom severity, engagement in previously avoided behaviors or activities, secondary gains not initially anticipated, and other variables that do not involve specific avoidance or escape features (e.g., changes in overall functioning, interpersonal relationships, everyday functioning, and so forth). Post-treatment assessment is typically conducted to assist the investigator in making inferential statements regarding the efficacy of treatment and the durability and generalizability of treatment effects. Although there are no guidelines for the timeframe for follow-up assessments, the upper limit is about 2 years. Limited sample sizes for most treatment outcome studies, coupled with participant attrition, conspire to limit the feasibility of long follow-up intervals.

Assessment Techniques

Structured and Semi-Structured Interviews

Structured and semi-structured interviews are typically used to arrive at diagnoses and make decisions regarding treatment eligibility. Commonly used interviews include the Structured Clinical Interview for DSM-IV Axis I disorders (First, Spitzer, Gibbon, & Williams, 1995), the Clinician Administered PTSD Scale (Blake, Weathers, Nagy, Kaloupek, Gusman, Charney, et al., 1995), and the Yale-Brown Obsessive-Compulsive Scale (Goodman, Price, Rasmussen, Mazure, Delgado, Heninger, & Charney, 1989a, 1989b). In some cases, structured or semi-structured interviews are strongly preferred to self-report measures. For example, a study comparing clinician and self-report measures of childhood OCD found that the clinician-rated method more accurately reflected symptom presentation than self-report (Stewart, Ceranoglu, O'Hanley, & Geller, 2005).

It should be noted, however, that the superiority of one assessment method over another should not automatically be assumed. Reliability, validity, and utility of diagnostic and screening instruments may vary across populations (e.g., men, women, children, adolescents, adults, inpatients, outpatients, general population), diagnostic groups, and the intended purpose of the assessment. For example, Herman and Koran (1998) found that clinicians routinely overestimated by as much as a standard deviation the frequency and intensity of OCD clients' symptoms when clinician ratings on the Yale-Brown Obsessive Compulsive Scale (Y-BOCS) were compared to client self-monitoring data collected via a handheld computer.

Subjective Units of Distress (SUD)

Self-reported level of distress and severity of symptoms related to the focal disorder are commonly assessed in exposure-based treatments. The most frequently used technique for assessing general distress is the Subjective Units of Distress (SUD) scale (Wolpe, 1969). Clients are asked to rate their level of distress on a scale from 0 to 100. Participants often provide SUD ratings several times during an exposure session in order for the therapist to monitor a client's arousal and gain a better understanding of behavioral variability during the session. A reduction in scores is thought to reflect changes in subjective anxiety and may suggest within-session habituation. As noted earlier, SUD scores can also be compared across sessions. A reduction in scores across sessions is thought to reflect between-session habituation and is commonly used as one index of treatment effectiveness.

Focal Assessments

Self-report measures of symptoms more closely related to the focal disorder are also frequently administered. There are self-report measures for a host of disorders, including PTSD (Foa, Riggs, Dancu, & Rothbaum, 1993; Lauterbach & Vrana, 1996), depression (Beck, Steer, & Brown, 1996; Radloff, 1977), fear of flying (Howard, Murphy, & Clarke, 1983), and fear of heights (Cohen, 1977), to name a few. When using these instruments to gauge the trajectory of client progress, researchers should carefully examine the timeframe assessed to ensure sensitivity to symptomatic changes.

Behavioral Avoidance Tests

Given that self-reported distress and physiological arousal may not co-vary with behavioral change (Lang, 1979), a frequently used technique to assess behavioral change in the Behavioral Avoidance Test (BAT). In a typical BAT, an individual engages in a task designed to evoke a fear response. For example, a person with a spider phobia may be asked to approach a spider in a glass terrarium. The score on the test would reflect the final proximity of the individual to the spider before discontinuing the task. Also, the person's subjective distress and idiosyncratic behaviors during the task can be recorded and evaluated as further indices of change in treatment. BATs can either be standardized (e.g., Turner, Beidel, & Larkin, 1986) or tailored to the client's specific fears (e.g., Heimberg, Hope, Dodge, & Becker, 1990). Although both standardized and individualized BATs can serve as dependent measures for assessing treatment effects, Becker and Heimberg (1988) concluded that individually tailored BATs maximize client immersion and are more likely to be externally valid. Empirical studies of the validity of BATs support their continued use (Bellack, 1983).

Physiological Measures

Fear and anxiety responses are multimodal in that they occur across a variety of behavioral response systems. Although self-reports may help a clinician understand the magnitude and variability of a client's subjective response, these data are often not sensitive to physiological changes. A number of indices of physiological change have been used across studies as a means of assessing treatment response, including changes in skin conductance, facial electromyography, heart rate, blood pressure, salivary cortisol, and circulating levels of norepinephrine. With regard to heart rate, several studies have found that greater heart rate habituation during exposure therapy is associated with better treatment outcome (Boudewyns & Hyer, 1990; Mueser, Yarnold, & Foy, 1991; Shalev, Orr, & Pitman, 1993).

Broader Assessment Issues to Consider

Change Scores

One strategy for examining the impact of an intervention is to compute individual change scores that reflect the difference between scores before and after treatment. In 1970, Lee J. Cronbach and Lita Furby published a classic article discouraging the use of change scores. They concluded that change scores are unreliable and that researchers should partial out pretest scores instead. Although others have disagreed (e.g., Nesselroade & Ghisletta, 2003), the unreliability of change scores became reified in methods training. In summarizing the current state of the literature, King and King (2004) concluded that unreliability of change scores is likely less problematic than earlier thought. Under most conditions, change scores are reliable, and classical test theory-based conceptualizations of reliability may not be appropriate for assessing the utility of change scores. Consistent with work by Collins (1996) and Collins and Sayer (2001), it may be that a new psychometric theory is needed to elucidate differences in the meaning of interindividual and intraindividual change.

Sensitivity of Global Measures of Change

Many treatment outcome studies use mixed designs and involve repeated assessment of symptom severity using clinician rating instruments. An obvious issue surrounds the relationship between the behavioral anchors on the rating instrument and actual symptom dimensions. If the anchors of the rating instrument are too broad or impressionistic, they may not be able to detect or accurately quantify clinically meaningful changes in specific behaviors. Although measures of changes in global scores may serve as a rough index of changes in overall improvement, they necessarily obscure the specific effects treatment may have on behavior or response modes.

Assessing Clinical Significance

Effect Sizes and Cohen's d

One of the more straightforward strategies for assessing clinical significance is to compute a treatment effect size. Cohen's d, for example, is computed by dividing the difference between pretreatment and post-treatment scores on a dependent measure by *either* the pretreatment standard deviation, the post-treatment standard deviation, or the pooled standard deviation. Labels that qualitatively describe the size of an effect for Cohen's d and other effect size indices (R^2, η^2, etc.) were provided by Cohen (1988). For example, when Cohen's d meets or exceeds .80, the effect size is considered large because the mean for the treatment group is eight-tenths of a standard deviation above the mean for the comparison group. A Cohen's d of .50 is considered a medium effect and a Cohen's d of .20 is considered a small effect. Effect sizes like Cohen's d are useful, as they quantify treatment effects independent of the original measurement metric and may be compared across measures and studies (Cohen, 1988).

Reliability Change Index

Another strategy for assessing clinical significance of change is to compute a reliability change (RC) Index (Jacobson, Follette, & Revenstorf, 1984; Jacobson & Truax, 1991). The RC Index is computed by dividing each participant's pretreatment to post-treatment change score by the standard error of measurement. If the resultant RC Index value exceeds $\pm$ 1.96, change is not likely due to chance. Although conceptually appealing in its simplicity, the fact that scores represent observations drawn from the same individual violates parametric assumptions regarding independence of observations. Further, Speer (1992) suggested that the RC Index neglects possible confounding of improvement rate estimates with regression to the mean. Speer proposed an alternative method that incorporates an adjustment that minimizes this confound when statistical regression is present. A subsequent refinement of the RC Index (called the RC_{ID}) was designed to improve the pre-post difference score by taking into account regression to the mean as a result of measurement unreliability (Hageman & Arrindell, 1993).

Alternative Approaches for Measuring Clinical Significance

Beyond statistical analysis of change scores, interpretation of the meaning of change scores requires that assessors have substantial experience with both the measurement tool and the focal disorder. An alternative strategy for assessing treatment effects in exposure-based therapies is to combine empirical information on performance of nonclinical subjects with that of the focal treatment group. For example, several studies (Garcia-Palacios, Hoffman, Carlin, Furness, & Botella, 2002; Öst,

Stridh, & Wolf, 1998) have operationalized clinically significant change to mean statistically significant changes in scores from pretreatment to post-treatment, provided that mean post-test scores in the treatment group fall within a prespecified range of scores drawn from a nonimpaired sample (e.g., within 2 standard deviations of mean scores from a nonclinical sample). Thus, the procedure prescribes the amount of change required to consider the change clinically significant and implies a cut score based on the functioning of a nonimpaired sample (see Garcia-Palacios et al., 2002, for an example.)

Recommendations for Assessment of Change

When taken together, what are the recommendations for assessment in exposure-based treatments? The answer lies, in part, on the intended goals. If the goal is primarily to provide high-quality treatment, clinicians would be advised to develop an assessment protocol that included the following elements: (1) multiple pre-test scores; (2) multiple measures to assess within- and between-session changes; (3) multimodal assessment of behavioral, cognitive, and physiological indices; (4) assessment before, during, and immediately after exposure; and (5) multiple post-treatment observations. In addition, the assessment results are most meaningful when the assessment not only measures treatment outcome but informs treatment. For example, identification of overengagement or underengagement during a treatment session permits a clinician to titrate the dose of exposure during a given session. Similarly, examination of score variability on all measures may shed light on variables that influence client responses. For example, should a client's scores on a self-efficacy measure unexpectedly rise midway through a 10-session treatment protocol, the clinician could highlight this change for the client. Given the feedback, it would not be surprising if the client's motivation to take full advantage of succeeding sessions increased. Although many of the same recommendations apply to clinical research, the dynamic use of the assessment process has implications for treatment standardization across participants and may result in considerable variation in the nature of the treatment protocol.

SUMMARY

This chapter is the first of four chapters that provide a foundation for the rest of the book. By identifying commonalities in exposure techniques and reviewing proposed mechanisms of action, we hope to provide the reader with a broad rationale for exposure therapy and an appreciation of the sustained work that has occurred in the field over the last 40 or more years. Our discussion of assessment issues was designed to assist the reader in interpreting empirical findings and case study results presented later in the book and to guide thoughtful consideration of the complexities involved whenever one attempts to evaluate cause-effect explanations of individual change. Exposure therapy, continues to be one of the crowning achievements of behavior therapy, and future work will, in all likelihood, address and perhaps even resolve many of the issues reviewed here.

REFERENCES

Barlow, D.H. (1988). *Anxiety and its disorders: The nature and treatment of anxiety and panic*. New York: Guilford Press.

Beck, A.T., Steer, R.A., & Brown, G.K. (1996). *Manual for the Beck Depression Inventory-II*. San Antonio, TX: Psychological Corporation.

Becker, R.E., & Heimberg, R.G. (1988). Assessment of social skills. In A.S. Bellack & M. Hersen (Eds.), *Behavioral assessment: A practical handbook: Pergamon general psychology series* (3rd ed., Vol. 65). Elmsford, NY, US: Pergamon Press, Inc.

Bellack, A.S. (1983). Recurrent problems in the behavioral assessment of social skill. *Behaviour Research & Therapy, 21,* 29–41.

Blake, D.D., Weathers, F.W., Nagy, L.M., Kaloupek, D.G., Gusman, F.D., Charney, D.S., et al. (1995). The development of a Clinician-Administered PTSD Scale. *Journal of Traumatic Stress, 8,* 75–90.

Botella, C., Baños, R. M., Villa, H., Perpiñá, C., & García-Palacios, A. (2000). Virtual reality in the treatment of claustrophobic fear: A controlled, multiple-baseline design. *Behavior Therapy, 31,* 583–595.

Botella, C., Villa, H., Baños, R., Perpiñá, C., & García-Palacios, A. (1999). The treatment of claustrophobia with virtual reality: Changes in other phobic behaviors not specifically treated. *CyberPsychology & Behavior, 2,* 135–141.

Boudewyns, P.A., & Hyer, L.A. (1990). Physiological response to combat memories and preliminary treatment outcome in Vietnam veteran PTSD patients treated with direct therapeutic exposure. *Behavior Therapy, 21,* 63–87.

Bouton, M.E. (1988). Context and ambiguity in the extinction of emotional learning: Implications for exposure therapy. *Behaviour Research and Therapy, 26,* 137–149.

Breitholtz, E., & Öst, L.-G. (1997). Therapist behavior during one-session exposure treatment for spider phobia: Individual vs. group setting. *Scandinavian Journal of Behaviour Therapy, 26,* 171–180.

Chemtob, C., Roitblat, H.L., Hamada, R.S., Carlson, J.G., & Twentyman, C.T. (1988). A cognitive action theory of post-traumatic stress disorder. *Journal of Anxiety Disorders, 2,* 253–275.

Cohen, D.C. (1977). Comparison of self-report and overt-behavioral procedures for assessing acrophobia. *Behavior Therapy, 8,* 17–23.

Cohen, J. (1988). *Statistical power for the behavioral sciences* (2nd ed.). Hillsdale, NJ: Lawrence Erlbaum Associates.

Collins, L.M. (1996). Is reliability obsolete? A commentary on "Are simple gain scores absolute?" *Applied Psychological Measurement, 20,* 289–292.

Collins, L.M., & Sayer, A.G. (Eds.). (2001). *New methods for the analysis of change*. Washington, DC, US: American Psychological Association.

Conklin, C.A., & Tiffany, S.T. (2002). Applying extinction research and theory to cue-exposure addiction treatments. *Addiction, 97,* 155–167.

Creamer, M., Burgess, P., & Pattison, P. (1992). Reaction to trauma: A cognitive processing model. *Journal of Abnormal Psychology, 101,* 452–459.

Cronbach, L.J., & Furby, L. (1970). How we should measure "change": Or should we? *Psychological Bulletin, 74,* 68–80.

DeVellis, R.F. (1991). *Scale development: Theory and applications* (Vol. 26). Thousand Oaks, CA, US: Sage Publications, Inc.

Drummond, D.C. (2002). Is cue exposure cure exposure? *Addiction, 97,* 357–359.

First, M.B., Spitzer, R.L., Gibbon, M., & Williams, J.B. (1995). *Structured clinical interview for DSM-IV Axis I disorders-Patient Edition (SCID-I/P, Version 2)*. New York: State Psychiatric Institute, Biometrics Research Department.

Foa, E.B., & Kozak, M.J. (1986). Emotional processing of fear: Exposure to corrective information. *Psychological Bulletin, 99,* 20–35.

Foa, E.B., & McNally, R.J. (1996). Mechanisms of change in exposure therapy. In R. Rapee (Ed.), *Current controversies in the anxiety disorders* (pp. 329–343). New York: Guilford Press.

Foa, E.B., Hembree, E.A., Cahill, S.P., Rauch, S.A.M., Riggs, D.S., Feeny, N.C., et al. (2005). Randomized trial of prolonged exposure for posttraumatic stress disorder with and without cognitive restructuring: Outcome at academic and community clinics. *Journal of Consulting and Clinical Psychology, 73,* 953–964.

Foa, E.B., Riggs, D.S., Dancu, C.V., & Rothbaum, B.O. (1993). Reliability and validity of a brief instrument for assessing post-traumatic stress disorder. *Journal of Traumatic Stress, 6,* 459–473.

Garcia-Palacios, A., Hoffman, H., Carlin, A., Furness, T.A., III, & Botella, C. (2002). Virtual reality in the treatment of spider phobia: A controlled study. *Behaviour Research & Therapy, 40,* 983–993.

Goodman, W.K., Price, L.H., Rasmussen, S.A., Mazure, C., Delgado, P., Heninger, G.R., & Charney, D.S. (1989a). The Yale-Brown Obsessive Compulsive Scale, I: Development, use, and reliability. *Archives of General Psychiatry, 46,* 1006–1011.

Goodman, W. K., Price, L. H., Rasmussen, S.A., Mazure, C., Delgado, P., Heninger, G.R., & Charney, D.S. (1989b). The Yale-Brown Obsessive Compulsive Scale, II: Validity. *Archives of General Psychiatry, 46,* 1012–1016.

Hageman, W.J., & Arrindell, W.A. (1993). A further refinement of the Reliable Change (RC) Index by improving the pre-post difference score: Introducing $RC_{(ID)}$. *Behaviour Research & Therapy, 31,* 693–700.

Harris, S.R., Kemmerling, R.L., & North, M.M. (2002). Brief virtual reality therapy for public speaking anxiety. *CyberPsychology & Behavior, 5,* 543–550.

Hayes, S.C., Barnes-Holmes, D., & Roche, B. (2001). Relational frame theory: A précis. In S.C. Haynes, D. Barnes-Holmes, and B. Roche (Eds.), *Relational frame theory: A post-Skinnerian account of human language and cognition*. New York: Kluwer Academic/Plenum.

Hayes, S.C., Strosahl, K.D., & Wilson, K.G. (1999). *Acceptance and commitment therapy: An experiential approach to behavior therapy*. New York: Guilford Press.

Heading, K., Kirkby, K.C., Martin, F., Daniels, B.A., Gilroy, L.J., & Menzies, R.G. (2001). Controlled comparison of single-session treatments for spider phobia: Live graded exposure alone versus computer-aided vicarious exposure. *Behaviour Change, 18,* 103–113.

Heimberg, R.G., Hope, D.A., Dodge, C.S., & Becker, R.E. (1990). DSM-III–R subtypes of social phobia: Comparison of generalized social phobics and public speaking phobics. *Journal of Nervous & Mental Disease, 178,* 172–179.

Hembree, E.A., Rauch, S.A.M., & Foa, E.B. (2003). Beyond the manual: The insider's guide to prolonged exposure therapy for PTSD. *Cognitive and Behavioral Practice, 10,* 22–30.

Herman, S., & Koran, L.M. (1998). In vivo measurement of obsessive-compulsive disorder symptoms using palmtop computers. *Computers in Human Behavior, 14,* 449–462.

Howard, W.A., Murphy, S.M., & Clarke, J.C. (1983). The nature and treatment of fear of flying: A controlled investigation. *Behavior Therapy, 14,* 557–567.

Jacobson, N.S., & Truax, P. (1991). Clinical significance: A statistical approach to defining meaningful change in psychotherapy research. *Journal of Consulting & Clinical Psychology, 59,* 12–19.

Jacobson, N.S., Follette, W.C., & Revenstorf, D. (1984). Psychotherapy outcome research: Methods for reporting variability and evaluating clinical significance. *Behavior Therapy, 15,* 336–352.

Kazdin, A.E. (1975). Covert modeling, imagery assessment, and assertive behavior. *Journal of Consulting and Clinical Psychology, 43,* 716–724.

Kazdin, A.E. (1976). Effects of covert modeling, multiple models, and model reinforcement on assertive behavior. *Behavior Therapy, 7,* 211–222.

King, D., & King, L. (2004, November). New longitudinal methods for trauma research. Paper presented at the Conference on Innovations in Trauma Research Methods, New Orleans, LA.

Lang, P.J. (1977). Imagery in therapy: An information processing analysis. *Behavior Therapy, 8,* 862–886.

Lang, P.J. (1979). A bio-informational theory of emotional imagery. *Psychophysiology, 16,* 495–512.

Lang, P.J. (1985). The cognitive psychophysiology of emotion: Fear and anxiety. In A.H. Tuma & J.D. Maser (Eds.), *Anxiety and the anxiety disorders* (pp. 131–170). Hillsdale, NJ: Erlbaum.

Lang, P.J. (1995). The emotion probe: Studies of motivation and attention. *American Psychologist, 50,* 372–385.

Lang, P.J., Bradley, M.M., & Cuthbert, B.N. (1990). Emotion, attention, and the startle reflex. *Psychological Review, 97,* 377–395.

Lang, P.J., Cuthbert, B.N., & Bradley, M.M. (1998). Measuring emotion in therapy: Imagery, activation, and feeling. *Behavior Therapy, 29,* 655–674.

Lauterbach, D., & Vrana, S.R. (1996). Three studies on the reliability and validity of a self-report measure of posttraumatic stress disorder. *Assessment, 3,* 17–25.

McNally, R.J. (1999). Research on eye movement desensitization and reprocessing (EMDR) as a treatment for PTSD. *PTSD Research Quarterly, 10,* 1–7.

Mineka, S., & Thomas, C. (1999). Mechanisms of change in exposure therapy for anxiety disorders. In T. Dagleish and M. Power (Eds.), *Handbook of cognition and emotion* (pp. 747–764). New York: John Wiley and Sons.

Mowrer, O.H. (1960). Two-factor learning theory: Versions one and two. In O.H. Mowrer (Ed.), *Learning theory and behavior* (pp. 63–91). Hoboken, NJ: John Wiley and Sons.

Mueser, K.T., Yarnold, P.R., & Foy, D.W. (1991). Statistical analysis for single-case designs: evaluating outcome of imaginal exposure treatment of chronic PTSD. *Behavior Modification, 15,* 134–155.

Nesselroade, J.R., & Ghisletta, P. Structuring and measuring change over the life span. In U.M. Staudinger & U. Lindenberger (Eds.), *Understanding human development: Dialogues with lifespan psychology* (pp. 317–337). Dordrecht, Netherlands: Kluwer Academic Publishers.

Öst, L.-G. (1989). One-session treatment for specific phobias. *Behaviour Research and Therapies, 27,* 1–7.

Öst, L.-G., Stridh, B.-M., & Wolf, M. (1998). A clinical study of spider phobia: Prediction of outcome after self-help and therapist-directed treatments. *Behaviour Research & Therapy, 36,* 17–35.

Pennebaker, J.W., & Beall, S.K. (1986). Confronting a traumatic event: Toward an understanding of inhibition and disease. *Journal of Abnormal Psychology, 95,* 274–281.

Quirk, G.J. (2004). Learning not to fear, faster. *Learning and Memory, 11,* 125–126.

Rachman, S. (1980). Emotional processing. *Behavior Research and Therapy, 18,* 51–60.

Radloff, L. (1977). The CES-D scale: A self-report depressions scale for research in the general population. *Journal of Applied Psychological Measurement, 1,* 385–402.

Shalev, A.Y., Orr, S.P., & Pitman, R.K. (1993). Psychophysiologic assessment of traumatic imagery in Israeli civilian patients with posttraumatic stress disorder. *American Journal of Psychiatry, 150,* 620–624.

Siegel, M. (2006). Can we cure fear. *Scientific American Mind, 16,* 44–49.

Sloan, D.M., & Marx, B.P. (2004). A closer examination of the structured written disclosure procedure. *Journal of Consulting and Clinical Psychology, 72,* 165–175.

Sloan, D.M., Marx, B.P., & Epstein, E.M. (2005). Further examination of the exposure model underlying the efficacy of written emotional disclosure. *Journal of Consulting and Clinical Psychology, 73,* 549–554.

Smits, J.A.J., Powers, M.B., Cho, Y., & Telch, M.J. (2004). Mechanism of change in cognitive-behavioral treatment of panic disorder: Evidence for the fear of fear mediational hypothesis. *Journal of Consulting and Clinical Psychology, 72,* 646–652.

Spates, R.C., & Koch, E.I. (2003). From eye movement desensitization and reprocessing to exposure therapy: A review of the evidence for shared mechanisms. *Japanese Journal of Behavior Analysis, 18,* 62–76.

Spates, C.R., Waller, S., & Koch, E.I. (2000). A critique of Lohr, et al.'s (1998) review of EMDR and Lipke's commentary: Of messages and messengers. *The Behavior Therapist, 23,* 148–154.

Speer, D.C. (1992). Clinically significant change: Jacobson and Truax (1991) revisited. *Journal of Consulting and Clinical Psychology, 60,* 402–408.

Stewart, E.S., Ceranoglu, T., O'Hanley, T., & Geller, D.A. (2005). Performance of clinician versus self-report measures to identify obsessive-compulsive disorder in children and adolescents. *Journal of Child and Adolescent Psychopharmacology, 15,* 956–963.

Thom, A., Sartory, G., & Jöhren, P. (2000). Comparison between one-session psychological treatment and benzodiazepine in dental phobia. *Journal of Consulting and Clinical Psychology, 68,* 378–387.

Tryon, W.W. (2005). Possible mechanisms for why desensitization and exposure work. *Clinical Psychology Review, 25,* 67–95.

Turner, S.M., Beidel, D.C., & Larkin, K.T. (1986). Situational determinants of social anxiety in clinic and nonclinic samples: Physiological and cognitive correlates. *Journal of Consulting & Clinical Psychology, 54,* 523–527.

Veltman, D.J., Tuinebreijer, W.E., Winkelman, D., Lammertsma, A.A., Witter, M.P., Dolan, R.J., & Emmelkamp, P.M.G. (2004). Neurophysiological correlates of habituation during exposure therapy in spider phobia. *Psychiatry Research: Neuroimaging, 132,* 149–158.

Wilson, K.G., & Murrell, A.R. (2004). Values work in Acceptance and Commitment Therapy: Setting a course for behavioral treatment. In S.C. Hayes, V.M. Follette, & M.M. Linehan (Eds.), *Mindfulness and acceptance: Expanding the cognitive-behavioral tradition* (pp. 66–95). New York: Guilford.

Wolpe, J. (1969). *The practice of behavior therapy.* Oxford, England: Pergamon.

CHAPTER 2

Animal Models of Exposure Therapy: A Selective Review

James T. Todd and
Janet L. Pietrowski
Eastern Michigan University

The term *exposure therapy* refers to a family of highly effective clinical psychological interventions designed to resolve anxiety disorders through the extended contact of the client with the events or stimuli that are presumed to cause the anxiety. The exposure of the client to the anxiety-producing events, usually while the client is prevented from escaping, avoiding, or engaging in other coping responses, reduces the events' anxiety-eliciting functions. By reducing the anxiety directly, the probability and severity of secondary dysfunctional escape or coping responses are reduced. Numerous variations of the basic procedures can be found in the clinical literature and go by names such as exposure and response prevention, graduated exposure, flooding, implosion, and systematic desensitization (Barlow, 1988; Emmelkamp, 1982). Along with contingency management techniques based on operant conditioning (Skinner, 1938, 1953), exposure therapies are among the most effective clinical interventions yet developed. It is estimated that exposure therapies are about 70% effective for alleviating simple phobias, obsessive-compulsive disorder, post-traumatic stress disorder (PTSD), agoraphobia, panic disorder, and related conditions (Barlow, 1988; Emmelkamp & Kuipers, 1979; Meyer & Crisp, 1966).

Like operant techniques, exposure therapies have a long history but have become dominant modes of clinical interventions for anxiety disorders only during the last 25 to 30 years. Operant techniques, which are now most often applied to behavior problems associated with developmental disabilities and head injury, began to be used broadly in the 1960s (Kazdin, 1978), but they have their origins in operant research with animals in the tradition of B.F. Skinner, starting in the

Handbook of Exposure Therapies

1930s (Skinner, 1938, 1953). Exposure therapy also has strong ties to basic research in classical conditioning with animals, going all the way back to Pavlov's work (1927) as depicted in simplified form in John B. Watson's popularizations (Watson, 1916, 1919, 1930; Watson & Morgan, 1917; Samelson, 1994). But the connection between research and therapy is not as direct on the respondent side as it is on the operant side. Exposure therapists can accurately point to Wolpe's (1952) research on reciprocal inhibition in cats as the functional beginning of their enterprise. Unlike the operant program, which has seen a continuous conceptual and programmatic expansion into the applied realm since shortly after its inception (Fuller, 1949; Skinner 1948), behavior therapy's ties to animal research were not as systematic or direct (Breger & McGaugh, 1965). There was a lengthy gap between Wolpe's work, for example, and the earlier attempts to apply Pavlov's principles to understand the etiology and treatment of phobias by Watson and Rayner (1920) in "Conditioned Emotional Reactions" and Mary Cover Jones's 1924, "The Case of Peter" (Jones, 1924, 1974). Some intervening attempts to apply conditioning principles to behavior problems (e.g., Salter, 1948; Dollard & Miller, 1950) were conceptually ambiguous detours that attempted to react against Freudian dynamic mechanisms while also attempting to translate them into conditioning language.

Some cognitive psychologists complain of the conceptual insufficiency of basic conditioning principles for fully understanding anxiety disorders (e.g., Bouton & Moody, 2004; Tryon, 2005). Behavior, it is said, is only an indirect measure of learning. Although cognitive psychology has added a large variety of intervening variables and hypothetical constructs to the analysis of anxiety-related behavior (e.g., Bouton & Moody, 2004; Dickinson, 1989; Pickens & Holland, 2004; Stanton, 2000; Tryon, 2005), therapeutic procedures incorporating these concepts seem hardly much different than those that do not. Standard respondent and operant conditioning procedures remain central and crucial to understanding the etiology and treatment of anxiety disorders (Mineka, 1979; Mineka & Cook, 1988, 1989).

This chapter explores some elements of animal models of exposure therapies. To provide a basis for evaluating the validity and usefulness of the animal models as they have evolved over time, we will explore some of the historical antecedents of modern exposure therapies. Our primary concern, however, is animal models of exposure therapy as it is being currently practiced. In particular, we attend to animal-based attempts to replicate the specific anxiety-reducing elements of exposure therapy. Because the fundamental aspects of animal models of exposure therapy per se have not changed much since Thyer, Baum, and Reid's (1988) thorough review, however, we are going beyond a concentration of animal models of treatment to explore some animal models of the etiology, symptomatology, and prevention of anxiety disorders. The subject of animal models of exposure therapy and relevant related areas comprises a large and varied literature, probably requiring a book-length treatment for proper coverage. Thus, we offer a selective view of animal models to provide a starting point for those who might wish to sample what is available in this area and dig deeper. We begin with a brief look at the major modes of operation of exposure therapy as practiced in the clinic to serve as a foundation for our coverage of animal models.

BASIC TYPES OF EXPOSURE THERAPY

Exposure therapy is not a single procedure. It represents a family of interventions that expand on a common functional element (Emmelkamp, Bouman, & Sholing, 1992; Marks, 1997). The client is exposed to anxiety-producing events in a controlled manner such that the client's behavior will come in contact with the lack of functional consequences of the anxiety. In an operational sense, clients are made to "face their fears" rather than avoid them and discover that "they have nothing to fear but fear itself." Even when the therapy is conducted at an entirely verbal or imaginal level, it remains fundamentally an extinction procedure. Causing the anxiety to occur without a consequence is analogous to Pavlov repeatedly ringing the bell (the conditioned stimulus) without giving the dog the food (the unconditioned response). The conditioned response (the anxiety) is analogous to the salivation and will eventually decrease to undetectable levels. The phobic, compulsive, or other avoidant responses that functioned to alleviate the anxiety no longer occur because anxiety is gone. Most readers will recognize the conceptual basis of this as Mowrer's "two-factor" theory of avoidance learning (Mowrer, 1939a, 1939b, 1940).

Systematic desensitization, considered by many to be the first clinically applied version of exposure therapy, ensures continuous exposure and response prevention by adding a relaxation element (McNeil & Zvolensky, 2000). The client is taught deep muscle relaxation on cue, usually using the Jacobson procedure (Jacobson, 1934). Graduated exposure comes from a hierarchy of subjective units of discomfort that ranges, in a series of even steps, from a mildly fearful situation to a very highly fearful situation. The client is made to relax while exposed systematically to each of the steps of the hierarchy. Only when the client can remain relaxed at a lower step is a higher one attempted. Eventually, the client can remain relaxed even under circumstances that would have previously been unbearable (Wolpe, 1961). Although systematic desensitization differs procedurally from other exposure treatments, and the concept of reciprocal inhibition has been invoked to explain why systematic sensitization is effective, it is probably the case that the efficacy of desensitization procedures is a function of the same mechanism that contributes to the success of other exposure therapy modalities, namely extinction.

Ideally, the stimuli used in therapy are actually those that caused the anxiety and are presented in relevant settings. Training in the natural environment should be more effective, as generalization of treatment effects from the therapeutic setting should be maximized. It is often difficult, however, to arrange treatment in the actual phobic settings. If the procedure is imaginal, the therapist must try to ensure that the client is capable of vivid, accurate, and sustained visualization of the phobic events. Homework might be assigned in which the client attempts to confront fear-producing events between therapy sessions. To bridge the gap between purely imaginal therapy and the ideal of conducting the work in actual problem situations, some therapists are beginning to use virtual reality techniques (e.g., Emmelkamp, Bruynzeel, Drost, van der Mast, 2001; Gershon, Anderson, Graap, Zimand, Hodges, & Rothbaum, 2002; North, North, & Coble, 2002).

As noted earlier, the operational mechanism initially proposed for systematic desensitization was reciprocal inhibition. Two physically incompatible responses cannot be simultaneously elicited in the same organism (Wolpe, 1958). By presenting the anxiety-producing stimuli when they cannot elicit anxiety, the associational bond is broken and the anxiety is alleviated. Since Wolpe's original conceptualization, numerous other mechanisms have been proposed to account for the effectiveness of systematic desensitization (see McGlynn, 2005; Taylor, 2002). Counter-conditioning is similar to reciprocal inhibition but does not require a physiologically antagonistic response. In counter-conditioning, the anxiety response is reduced because it is gradually replaced by a different response, generally relaxation. Because it is difficult to distinguish between reciprocal inhibition and counter-conditioning, they are frequently mentioned together (Dickinson, Mellgren, Fountain, & Dyck, 1977; Marshall, 1975). Others have argued that the relaxation response does not function in either an inhibitory, reciprocal mode or as incompatible replacement response. It simply serves to keep the client engaged with the stimulus long enough to allow extinction or habituation of the anxiety-eliciting stimulus function to occur (see McGlynn, 2005). This is the basis of the view that desensitization is actually a form of graduated exposure and response prevention.

But is the separate relaxation component necessary at all? In a classic article, Meyer (1966) demonstrated the reduction in compulsive responding associated with obsessive-compulsive disorder (OCD) by exposing clients to the anxiety-eliciting events and preventing the compulsive responses from occurring. No programmed relaxation component was included. Before the 1970s, OCD was considered a rare and highly intractable disorder (Foa, 1996). Thus this new, simpler approach garnered considerable attention and led to the widespread adoption of exposure and response prevention techniques for anxiety disorders generally. The advantage of exposure therapy over systematic desensitization is that it is as effective as systematic desensitization but can achieve its effects in fewer sessions because the time-consuming relaxation training component is not included (Rosqvist, 2005). Although exposure therapy is expected to produce higher levels of anxiety during sessions as compared to systematic desensitization, it is not clear that this results in significantly higher numbers of clients failing to complete treatment (although this is a concern frequently expressed by clinicians, see Richard and Gloster's chapter in this volume). Note that while exposure therapy appears to be a fairly straightforward Pavlovian extinction procedure, it was not generally done as an attempt to directly apply animal laboratory principles directly to human behavior problems as has been done in operant-based therapy (see, e.g., Allyon & Azrin, 1968; McDowell, 1988; Wolf, Risley, & Mees, 1964).

Exposure therapy is practiced in two general forms depending on whether the anxiety-producing stimuli are presented gradually or all at once. In graduated exposure, the client is exposed to successively greater levels of the anxiety-producing stimuli while being prevented from making escape or coping responses. In flooding and implosion, the client is confronted with the full version of the anxiety-producing event (or a verbal equivalent) all at once (Boudewyns & Shipley, 1983; Emmelkamp & Wessels, 1975; Marks, 1973; Stampfl & Levis, 1968). The popularity of graduated exposure is probably due to the historical origins of exposure therapy in systematic desensitization. The graduated version exposure therapy is also justified, relative to flooding, on ethical and procedural grounds as a means of preventing the client from experiencing unneeded trauma that might cause the client to self-terminate therapy (Rosqvist, 2005). Many variations have been developed: relatively fewer but longer sessions (massed presentations) versus shorter, more numerous sessions; within-sessions variations of the rate, duration, and intensity of stimulus presentations; and presentation of stimuli in the natural environment, entirely imaginally, or somewhere in between (Foa, Steketee, & Grayson, 1985). Virtual reality techniques are also becoming more common. Therapeutic adjuncts sometimes used can include drugs, modeling of appropriate reactions, cognitive exercises, reinforcement of alternative behavior, instructions, and homework. Anxiety sufferers can avail themselves of a wide range of therapist support: from none at all (if they attempt to implement the therapy on their own from instructions in a book or a website), to relatively nondirective and minimally supportive, to minutely detailed and highly directive. Almost all of these variations have been the subject of animal analogue research.

ANIMAL MODELS

In an ideal animal model of human behavior, all of the stimulus and response functions known to be critical to the animal behavior should correspond directly to stimulus-and-response functions in the human instance. The behavioral topographies of the target responses should be similar, although realities of scale often compel the use of simpler, functionally equivalent surrogates of the human responses (few would expect a researcher to build a tiny elevator for rats to model an elevator phobia). The behavior of interest should also have been acquired in the same way in the human and animals. Once established, the behavior should be similarly sensitive to the same events across corresponding parametric ranges. In other words, the behaviors should be functionally identical but occur in different organisms. One rule of thumb that might be applied is that if we did not know the organisms were of different species, would we conclude that the animal and human versions are the same behavior? For methodological purposes, we might operationally require that the animal and human versions correspond to the greatest degree possible in symptomatology, etiology, prevention, and therapy (see McKinney, 1974; Mineka, 1985, 1987; Seligman, 1974, 1975).

Given the acknowledged effectiveness of exposure therapy with humans, why even use animal models? Scientific curiosity about the basic processes of nature is probably a sufficient reason, but other reasons are valid as well (see Sidman, 1960). At a conceptual level, animal models of exposure therapy are used because the conditioning and learning tradition from which they arise has always incorporated a strong continuity assumption (see Watson, 1913; Skinner, 1938; Tolman, 1932). Thus animal models are just a way to explore the details of exposure therapy (see Skinner, 1953). Animal models are used to test the limits and extent of the behavioral continuity in specific cases (see Mineka, 1985). Ethical and practical considerations sometimes dictate the use of animals (usually rats and monkeys in exposure therapy models) and standard preparations for animal research. The presumption of continuity often gives animal analogue experiments prima facie credibility as a source of useful information about the human instance. But questions can be raised about the degree to which the behavior of a jumpy rat in a box or a drooling dog in a harness is representative of, say, a person who is obsessively counting the number of tiles in the ceiling or afraid to leave the house. Thus, some animal models are designed to test the adequacy of animal models themselves (e.g., Mineka, 1987; Stampfl, 1987). Of course, most models are not designed to explain everything but just to replicate specific functional aspects of the target behavior using familiar and economical animal preparations (Baum, 1971; Martasian, Smith, Neill, & Reig, 1992; Mineka & Cook, 1986). Thus, most animal models would properly be regarded as *partial models*. Mineka (1987, p. 82) has used the term *minimodel* to designate such partial models.

Basic Methodological Features of Animal Models

Animal-based research on exposure therapies has been directed at all aspects of the exposure therapy situation as outlined previously: symptomatology, etiology, prevention, and therapy (see Baum, 1986; McKinney, 1974; Mineka, 1985, Thyer, et al., 1988). A great deal of this research is aimed at the basic processes by which exposure therapy might work: Is it extinction or counterconditioning (Marshall, 1975)? Are massed or distributed sessions more effective (Martasian, et al., 1992)? How do different modes of stimulus presentation affect the short- and long-term effectiveness of exposure (Bouton, 1988)? Some research is designed to test the adequacy of the models themselves (see e.g., Stampfl, 1987). Often these studies are aimed at demonstrating that some aspect of the animal behavior really is or really is not an analogue of the human counterpart (see e.g., Cook & Mineka, 1991). In most cases, however, the research preparations and basic research designs are variations on those that have long been used in investigations of signaled escape and avoidance based on Mowrer's two-factor theory (Mowrer, 1939a, 1939b, 1950a). For example, a large number of studies have been conducted using the ledge box. A rat is placed into a space where an aversive stimulus, usually electric shock, can be presented, usually preceded by a tone as a warning stimulus. Safety from the aversive stimulus is achieved by jumping onto a ledge protruding from the side of the chamber. The ledge can be retracted, dropping the rat back into the chamber, and then reinserted to initiate another trial. The latency to jump is a typical dependent measure in this device (Baum, 1965; Baum, Andrus, & Jacobs, 1990).

Shuttle boxes are also used (Overmier & Seligman, 1967; Solomon & Wynn, 1953). Aversive stimuli are presented in one area, and the animal can escape or avoid the stimuli by moving to an adjacent space. The most important difference between the ledge box and shuttle box is that the shock and safe sides of the shuttle box can be made as similar or different as needed. The functional aspects of the two sides can be reversed to potentially automate the experiment, study reacquisition, and eliminate potential confounds based on ecological dissimilarity of the safe and shock areas. In these boxes, latency is also the primary dependent measure.

Some research, usually using rats, has used variations on the conditioned suppression paradigm of Estes and Skinner (1941). A stable operant response is established in an experimental chamber using a schedule of reinforcement that engenders a moderate, steady rate of responding, such as a variable interval schedule. In a separate setting, a conditioned aversive stimulus is established, usually by pairing a light or tone with shock. This conditioned aversive stimulus is then presented in the original operant training situation, and the suppression of the rate of the operant response relative to the overall rate of responding (a suppression index) is the usually the dependent measure.

Researchers using monkeys (e.g., Mineka, 1987; Cook & Mineka, 1991) use the techniques described previously, plus a variety of species-specific devices and preparations that take advantage of monkeys' excellent vision and sensitivity to observational learning. The Wisconsin General Test Apparatus (Harlow, 1949) requires that the monkey reach across a space into which an anxiety-producing stimulus can be placed. Latency to reach for an item is a common measure. The "Sackett Self-Selection Circus" (Sackett, 1970; Sackett, Porter, & Holmes, 1965) contains a space divided into a central area and multiple surrounding or radiating compartments. The back wall of each compartment is transparent. Various objects are placed on the other side of each wall. The proportion of the total time spent in each compartment is typically measured. Compartments with the lowest occupancy are presumed to correspond to the most highly feared stimuli. Used in combination, the Wisconsin and Sackett preparations can illuminate important distinctions between subjective anxiety, overt avoidance, and physiological elements of fear responses (Mineka, Davidson, Cook, & Keir, 1984). A monkey might spend virtually no time near a feared object in the Sackett apparatus, yet readily reach for a reinforcer near it in the Wisconsin preparation. This is critically important because the relative preference for activities in one situation might not be a useful predictor of the probability of approach or avoidance in other situations. Indeed, in humans, stimuli that seem to evoke strong anxiety responses do not always lead to actual physical avoidance (Hodgson & Rachman, 1974; Rachman & Hodgson, 1974). Finally, because monkeys will watch and respond to video displays as they do to corresponding real-life displays (Capitanio, Boccia, & Colaiannia, 1985; Mineka & Cook, 1986, 1989; Plimpton, Swartz, & Rosenblum, 1981), observational learning in the generation and elimination for anxiety responses can be studied using edited video presentations. The advantage of video is that editing can be used to achieve a wide variety of effects not obtainable if real models were used.

Treatment

Many studies that involve animal models of exposure therapy have been designed to answer questions about the basic parameters of exposure therapy as they relate to clinical outcome. These parameters include duration of exposure, the use of drugs, the nature of response prevention, the rate of presentation of anxiety-producing stimuli (graduated versus flooding), therapist modeling of nonfearful responses, the use of distraction, reinforcement of alternative responses, and the mere presence of nonanxiety-producing stimuli. In general, these animal studies demonstrate a good correspondence with human experience.

Duration and Distribution of Exposure

Although there is little doubt that longer overall durations of exposure and response prevention are superior to shorter exposures (Öst, Alm, Brandberg, & Breitholtz, 2001; Öst, Brandberg, & Alm, 1997; Öst, Hellström, & Kåver, 1992; Thyer, et al., 1988), research with humans has been equivocal in regard to the relative effectiveness of massed exposure of the client to the anxiety-producing stimuli relative to distributed presentations (see Baum, et al., 1990). This is likely due to significant procedural differences between studies and outcome measures used. Some research suggests that massed exposures are more effective for reducing anxiety (see, e.g., Chaplin & Levine, 1981; Marshall, 1985; Stern & Marks, 1973; Foa, Jameson, Turner, & Payne, 1980). Other researchers have reported the superiority of shorter, more numerous sessions (see, e.g., Ramsay, Barends, Breuker, & Kruseman, 1966). Distributed exposure is said to reduce the possibility of future recovery and reacquisition of the anxiety response because multiple sessions more fully extinguish the stimulus function of early-session cues, which are contacted less frequently in multiple sessions. Others see little difference (Lanyon, Manosevitz, & Imber, 1968). More recent studies lend some support to the conclusion that both distributed and massed exposure can produce comparable reductions in anxiety in the short term but that long-term maintenance of anxiety reduction may be enhanced by distributed exposures (Rowe & Craske, 1998; Tsao & Craske, 2000).

In animals, the answers have been similarly equivocal. Several classic studies have seemingly demonstrated the relative superiority of longer, continuous sessions for extinguishing a classically conditioned response (see, e.g., Birch, 1965; Mackintosh, 1970, 1974; Pavlov, 1927; Polin, 1959; Teichner, 1952). Some more recent research, mostly done with rats, seems to demonstrate the superiority of shorter, more numerous sessions (see, e.g., Baum, et al., 1990; Baum & Myran, 1971; Berman & Katzev, 1972, 1974; Franchina, Agee, & Hauser, 1974;). Still others report little or no difference (see, e.g., Shearman, 1970; Martasian & Smith, 1993; Martasian, et al., 1992), although some evidence shows the total time of exposure to be the most important variable (Schiff, Smith, & Prochaska, 1972). As in humans, the answer to the question of massed versus distributed sessions in animals depends greatly on the type and severity of the anxiety, the anxiety-reduction procedures used, and whether long- or short-term measures are taken.

Modeling, Instructions, and Observational Learning

Viewing a model that responds appropriately to anxiety-producing stimuli can sometimes have therapeutic benefits on its own. It reportedly can enhance both the short- and long-term effectiveness of exposure therapy of all kinds (Bandura, Grusec, & Menlove, 1967; Ellissa, Alai-Rosales, Glenn, Rosales-Ruiz, & Greenspoon, 2005; Geer & Turteltaub, 1967; Kornhaber & Schroeder, 1975). In fact, most practitioners of exposure therapy are careful to provide their clients with accurate information about the real dangers posed by the things that produce excessive anxiety in the clients (Ammerman & Hersen, 1993). Even if modeling is not explicitly incorporated into the therapy, modeling of appropriate, nonfearful responses is automatically included in the therapy because the therapist will be interacting closely and nonfearfully with the anxiety-producing stimuli. A lucky therapist (and client) might find providing information alone sufficient to alleviate the problem (Agras, Leitenberg, Barlow, & Thompson, 1969; Foa & Kozak, 1986; Wolpe, 1982), and feedback about internal states such as heart rate can be beneficial (Nunes & Marks, 1975, 1976). Appropriate response modeling and instructions, even from an authority figure such as a psychologist, however, are clearly insufficient to help most individuals with phobias, OCD, PTSD, panic attacks, agoraphobia, and other anxiety disorders.

The difficulties associated with testing the effectiveness of instructions and modeling with animals are obvious but not insurmountable. Monkeys are the subjects of choice for analogues of observational learning, and numerous studies on the acquisition of fear responses employing them have been done by Mineka's group (see, e.g., Mineka, 1985, 1987; Mineka & Cook, 1989). Some work, however, has been done with rats. Baum (1969) has shown that fear-conditioned rats would emit fewer escape responses during extinction when they were in the presence of nonfearful rats than when they were alone. Uno, Greer, and Goates (1973) reported that rats that apparently observed other rats in a response-prevention situation had fewer responses to extinction than rats that had not observed other rats. Whether this effect was obtained through social facilitation or modeling is unclear.

Contingent Reinforcement

Contingent reinforcement and distraction can be added to exposure therapy, usually with beneficial effects (Agras, Leitenberg, & Barlow, 1968; Boer & Sipprelle, 1970; Ellis, et al., in press; Grayson, Foa, & Steketee, 1982, 1986; Leitenberg & Callahan, 1973; Leitenberg Agras, Thompson, & Wright, 1968; Leitenberg, Agras, Edwards, Thompson, & Wincze, 1970; Leitenberg, Agras, Allen, Betz, & Edwards, 1975; Leitenberg, Rawson, & Mulick, 1975). Reinforcement is usually presented to the subject for maintaining contact with the fear-producing stimulus. In one study, for example, performance of math problems by a child with an insect phobia was assessed during verbal descriptions of crickets and in the presence of crickets in an exposure-therapy procedure (Jones & Friman, 1999). Contingent reinforcement was given for completing the math problems. The authors reported no effect of the exposure component alone but a large reduction in fear when exposure was combined with contingent reinforcement.

As for contingent reinforcement in animals, the original counter-conditioning procedure of Wolpe (1952) and Masserman (1943) used food reinforcement to induce nonfearful behavior. Of course, adding contingent reinforcement of an incompatible behavior to extinction is a standard and highly effective procedure for reducing problem behavior in applied behavior analysis (see, e.g., Martin & Pear, 2005; Miltenberger, 2001). Even noncontingent reinforcement seems beneficial (Leitenberg, Rawson, & Mulick, 1975; Rawson, & Leitenberg, 1973). A number of studies have presented noncontingent intracranial reinforcement to rats during extinction from avoidance conditioning and found greater reductions in fear relative to no reinforcement (Baum, LeClerc, & St. Laurent, 1973; Becker, Magnuson, & Reid, 1977; Buss & Reid, 1973; Gordon & Baum, 1971; Hunsicker, Nelson, Reid, 1973; LeClerc, Laurent, & Baum, 1973). As Skinner's classic superstition experiment showed, noncontingent reinforcement is not empty of behavioral value (Skinner, 1948). It might not reinforce a particular response incompatible with escape and avoidance during extinction, but it will generally contact any number of indeterminate responses that happen to be incompatible with the problem behavior. In applied-behavior analysis, periodic noncontingent reinforcement presentations are frequently used to reduce problem behavior because the noncontingent reinforcer is likely to contact more non-target responses than target responses, thereby reducing the rate of the target responses relative to everything else (see, e.g., Coleman & Holmes, 1998; Lindberg, Iwata, Roscoe, Worsdell, & Hanley, 2003).

Distraction

As with contingent reinforcement, adding a distracting stimulus seems to enhance the effectiveness of exposure therapy, although differences between studies make a definite conclusion difficult (Rodriguez & Craske, 1993). Theoretical interpretations are not well developed, but it is believed that reactions to the distracting stimuli are incompatible with avoidance and other coping strategies that a client might use during exposure therapy to avoid contacting the fear-producing stimuli (Kamphuis & Telch, 2000). For example, the distracting tasks usually chosen for humans, such as cognitive problem solving exercises (Telch, Valentiner, Ilai, Young, Powers, Smits, et al., 2004) or playing a video game (e.g., Grayson, et al., 1982, 1986) appear to be incompatible with sustained avoidance responding. Distraction seems also to work to enhance the effects of extinction procedures in animals. Presenting a loud noise to avoidance-trained rats during procedures analogous to exposure and response increases the effectiveness of the procedure in reducing fear (Baum, 1987; Baum & Gordon, 1970; Baum, Pereira, & LeClerc, 1985).

Return of Fear

Return of fear is a critical issue in clinical treatments and has been the subject of numerous reviews and studies (see e.g., Rachman, 1979; Rachman & Lopatka, 1988). A wide variety of causes have been proposed for return of fear, including insufficient initial exposure (Rachman, Robinson, & Lopatka, 1987), distraction during treatment (Kamphuis & Telch, 2000), failure to extinguish fear in relevant contexts (Bouton, 2000; Mineka, Mystkowski, Hladek & Rodriguez, 1999), reacquisition by exposure to the fear-producing stimulus (Rachman & Whittal, 1989), reactivation by exposure to the original fear-producing stimulus (Rescorla & Heth, 1975), and even symptom substitution (Weitzman, 1967).

Many of the factors presumed to cause relapse in humans are well established in animal literature. Spontaneous recovery, which would be expected if an insufficient amount of exposure were used, was well known to Pavlov (1927) and continues to receive attention by animal researchers as a likely cause of some treatment failures (Bouton, 1994, 2000; Robbins, 1990). Re-exposure to the original fear-producing stimuli in rats can reinstate a previously extinguished fear response in rats (Rescorla and Heth, 1975). This effect can also be seen in rats after counter-conditioning (Brooks, Hale, Nelson, & Bouton, 1995) and thus, has relevance for systematic desensitization. Generalization effects may be the most thoroughly studied factor in relapse in recent years (Bouton, 1998). Mood during exposure, distractions during therapy, the physical features of the therapeutic context, the type of anxiety-producing stimuli used during therapy, drug state, and even time of day are all likely to be different outside the therapeutic context when the client encounters troublesome events than during therapy sessions. Merely changing the room in which therapy is conducted and anxiety is later tested can lead to increased fear responses in humans (Mineka, et al., 1999; Rodriguez, Craske, Mineka, & Hladek, 1999; Vansteenwegen, Hermans, Vervliet, Francken, Beckers, Baeyens, et al., 2005; Vervliet, Vansteenwegen, Baeyens, Hermans, & Paul, 2005).

Bouton and his colleagues have done many studies with animals on the relevance of context or generalization in the return of fear (Bouton, 1998). Bouton's contention is that extinction does not weaken or eliminate the association between the conditioned aversive stimulus and anxiety responses but teaches a new response based on the new contextual information (Bouton, 1991, 1994; Bouton & King, 1983; Bouton & Peck, 1989; Bouton & Swartzentruber, 1991). A taste aversion extinguished in a different context than it was trained under will recur when rats are returned to the training context (Rosas & Bouton, 1997). Stimuli presented during extinction of conditioned magazine entry responses will attenuate recovery of the behavior when presented during a recovery test (Brooks & Bouton, 1994). Similar effects were reported in an early study involving a conditioned suppression, paradigm-shocks presented during suppression reinstated the suppressed response only when they were administered in the testing context (Bouton & Bolles, 1979).

The context-dependent effect can also be seen if the aversion training and extinction occur in the same context, but later testing occurs in a different one, the so-called AAB paradigm (Bouton & Ricker, 1994), or when the three phases are conducted in different contexts (ABC). Although Bouton's interpretations of these phenomena carry with them copious references to inferred cognitive processes (see, e.g., Bouton, 1994), his theory does not predict significantly different results than are predicted by classic accounts of the relative irreversibility of behavioral relations arising from nonmediational animal learning viewpoints (see Sidman, 1960). That is, Bouton's theory suggests that extinction trials do not weaken associative connections but teach a different association than was acquired in the training trials. This is not incompatible with a purely behavioral view (Dinsmoor, 1995a, 1995b). Using extinction of one or two of the stimulus-response relationships in an experimental setting inevitably leaves many associations untouched (Sidman, 1960). The point to draw from this research, regardless of how the effects might be interpreted, is the importance of explicitly programming for generalization and maintenance of treatment effects rather than adopting a "train and hope" strategy (Stokes & Baer, 1977).

Drugs

There is little doubt that a variety of medications can reduce troublesome anxiety-induced avoidance and coping responses. Benzodiazepines, selective serotonin reuptake inhibitors, beta-blockers, and other medications have all shown some effectiveness in this regard (Lydiard & Falsetti, 1995; Meyer & Quenzer, 2005). In contrast, there seems to be little evidence that many of these drugs significantly enhance the effectiveness of exposure therapy. Neither benzodiazepines, a class of drugs that includes Valium, Librium, Ativan, and Xanax, nor barbiturates appear to improve the outcome of exposure therapy in humans (Birk, 2004; Leonard, 1997;

Munjack, 1975; Whitehead, Blackwell, & Robinson, 1978; Whitehead, Robinson, Blackwell, & Stutz, 1978). In animals, similar effects are seen. Taub, Taylor, Smith, Kelley, Becker, and Reid, (1977), in an extensive study of the effects of a wide variety of drugs on resistance to extinction after response prevention in more than 400 rats, found that only atropine appeared to enhance the effects of a response-prevention procedure. Benzodiazepines and barbiturates had no effect or actually reduced resistance to extinction. A number of other experiments with animals showed similar results (Baum, 1973; Baum, Roy, & LeClerc, 1985; Cooper, Coon, Mejta, & Reid, 1974; Gorman, Dyak, & Reid, 1979; Kamano, 1972; Weissman, 1959). Alcohol does no better. Thyer, Parrish, Himle, Cameron, Curtis, and Nesse (1986) describe survey data showing alcohol self-administration among phobics is a common coping mechanism. Laboratory research on humans, however, shows that alcohol administered during exposure therapy does not improve outcome (e.g., Cameron, Liepman, Curtis, & Thyer, 1987; Rimm, Briddell, Zimmerman, & Caddy, 1981; Thyer & Curtis, 1984). Administration to animals during extinction sessions in analogue studies retards the progress of extinction procedures (Baum, 1969, 1970, 1971; Skurdal, Eckardt, & Brown, 1975; Taub, et al., 1977), perhaps because organisms that have consumed alcohol simply cannot attend effectively to the relevant events during therapy.

Although most conventional pharmacological agents seem to have limited usefulness as adjuncts to exposure therapy, D-cycloserine (DCS), an antibiotic drug long used to treat tuberculosis, has been shown to enhance the effects of exposure therapy (Koch, 2002; Richardson, Ledgerwood, & Cranney, 2004). A study conducted by Ressler compared the effects of DCS and placebo combined with exposure therapy for fear of heights. Subjects who received DCS and exposure therapy showed greater reductions in a variety of fear measures after 1 week and 3 months (Ressler, Rothbaum, Tannenbaum, Anderson, Graap, Zimand, et al., 2004). DCS alone also seemed to have beneficial effects for PTSD (Heresco-Levy, Kremer, Javitt, Goichman, Resheff, Blanaru, et al., 2002). These results correspond closely to findings in animals. Giving DCS to rats undergoing extinction after fear conditioning involving foot shock enhanced the effects of extinction relative to rats that did not receive DCS (Walker, Ressler, Lu, & Davis, 2002). DCS appears to have multiple anti-anxiety effects. In rats, DCS enhanced the extinction of a fear-producing conditional stimulus (CS) while also reducing fear of a nonextinguished fear-producing CS (Ledgerwood, Richardson, & Cranney, 2005). Thus, DCS can be used alone (Ho, Hsu, Wang, Hsu, Lai, Hsu, et al., Tsai, 2005) or, more effectively, in conjunction with exposure therapy.

Symptomatology

The symptoms of anxiety disorders are fairly well described in the literature, the details of which are more than adequately explored in other chapters in this volume. For the purposes of animal modeling, however, the analogue situation is typically highly simplified relative to what happens to people. Humans are usually free-living, and their daily behavior might be focally or broadly disrupted by various avoidant, compulsive, or fearful responses occurring at the private and public levels. In contrast, in most animal studies, the animals are given a single or small set of anxiety-induced responses that are manifested only in the experimental context. Otherwise the animals' lives are generally normal (for a laboratory animal), and they are burdened by their anxieties only at a prescribed time of the day. This raises some questions of generality. Even so, the close topographical correspondence of the human and animal instances seems to satisfy most in the exposure therapy field that the animal models are valid, even if they are sometimes limited in scope.

Generalized Anxiety

Early studies of experimental neurosis by Pavlov (1957, 1960), Masserman (1943), Liddell (1947), and Wolpe (1952) produced animals that engaged in a wide variety of bizarre, fearful behaviors. After exposure to contexts in which they could not emit functional behaviors to solve difficult stimulus discrimination problems or avoid aversive events, animals would exhibit general avoidance, fear of handling, stereotyped movements, catatonia, health effects associated with stress, phobic reactions, and general helplessness (Masserman, 1943; Liddell, 1947; Wolpe, 1952). These behaviors correspond closely to those seen in people with PTSD, panic disorder, and social phobia. The relative ease of producing these dysfunctional behaviors in otherwise healthy organisms, including rats, cats, dogs, goats, and monkeys, was surprising. Equally surprising was the robustness of the behavior. These elements of animal experimental neurosis also seemed to correspond to the human experience, in which a brief exposure to stressful conditions could establish lifelong problem behaviors. For clinicians, the ease with which an individual can acquire a fear implies greater importance should be given to thoroughly eliminating fear during treatment and training clients in skills that foster adaptive responses to future stressful situations.

Phobic Anxiety

In modern studies, anxiety-resembling phobia is the most common behavior simulated in animal models of exposure therapy (see Thyer, Baum, & Reid, 1988). As we have noted before, the animal is conditioned to be afraid of a stimulus. Then its overt reactions are studied. The reactions are usually unidimensional-escaping when a shock-associated tone is played or when reaching across a feared object to obtain a reinforcer. It is widely recognized, however, that anxiety is not a simple, unitary response. As noted by Lang (1968, 1971, 1985) and others (Hodgson & Rachman, 1974; Mineka, 1979, 1985, 1987; Rachman & Hodgson, 1974), anxiety responses can have a private phenomenological component, a physiological component, and a public component. These components do not necessarily co-vary.

In exposure therapy, it is common for a person with a phobia to be taught to approach feared objects before subjective discomfort subsides (Hodgson & Rachman, 1974). The failure to fully extinguish all components of the anxiety reaction is sometimes blamed for the return of fear (Rachman, 1979; Rachman & Lopatka, 1988; Rachman, Robinson, & Lopatka, 1987). People with OCD will have overt compulsions, private obsessive thoughts, and anxiety reactions. Although the multiple dimensions of OCD do not lend themselves to investigation with animals, some attempts have been made to incorporate Lang's view of phobic anxiety into animal models of anxiety disorders in the hope that doing so will increase the validity of the models and account better for some of the observations about the relative effectiveness of exposure therapy under certain conditions.

Using monkeys, Mineka and her colleagues have attempted to separate some of the three elements of anxiety responses described by Lang (1968, 1971, 1985). In addition to measuring the latency to reach across a feared object (usually a snake) in a Wisconsin apparatus and measuring avoidance of chambers near feared objects in a Sackett Circus, they also measure a set of behaviors known to accompany subjective anxiety in monkeys such as piloerection, grimacing, threat postures, and gaze aversion. In one set of experiments, Mineka used an exposure-like procedure to get fearful monkeys to reach for food near a snake in a Wisconsin apparatus (Mineka & Keir, 1983; Mineka, Keir, & Price, 1980). She also reported, however, that although all the monkeys would reliably reach for the food, taking 18 or fewer exposure sessions to learn to do so, all showed signs of significant subjective anxiety. These monkeys also showed significant relapse during the experiments, and in treatment terms, the overall procedure could be considered a failure. A 6-month follow-up study showed complete relapse. This model corresponds closely to the human experience in exposure therapy and points to the need to measure and eliminate all elements of the anxiety reaction.

The Neurotic Paradox

The so-called neurotic paradox is an important element in understanding the symptomatology of anxiety disorders, especially phobias, and has been addressed by many researchers and theorists from Freud onward (Eglash, 1952; Freud, 1926; Hull, 1929; Mowrer, 1948, 1950b). Its character is well summarized by Mowrer's 1950 observation that phobic reactions are "self-defeating and yet self-perpetuating, instead of self-eliminating" (1950b, p. 351). Essentially, the issue involves the relative ease by which phobias can be established (sometimes by a single aversive pairing or one instance of observation) and then their relative intractability in the face of numerous environmental contingencies that should eliminate the phobia. Without going into this literature deeply, which would require a volume at least, we will present one interesting recent attempt to encompass it within an animal model.

Thomas Stampfl, who is generally credited with the invention of implosion therapy, has attempted to create an animal model to answer concerns raised by

Mineka (1985) about the questionable correspondences between animal avoidance behavior and human phobic responses. First, in the human instance, a presumed conditioned aversive stimulus is being avoided rather than the unconditioned stimulus (e.g., shock) as in animal studies. Sometimes the conditioned stimulus avoided by people is only distantly connected to the actual fear-producing situation. For example, a human with an elevator phobia might become anxious during a conversation about elevators. Second, as previously noted, phobias are sometimes remarkably easily established, requiring only a single aversive exposure or observation of a model. Laboratory avoidance often takes many trials to establish (Mineka, 1985).

Stampfl contends that these concerns are answered by studies already in the literature (e.g., Boyd & Levis, 1976; Kostanek, & Sawrey, 1965; Levis & Boyd, 1979), and the literature of classical conditioning contains numerous examples of strong avoidance responses established in one trial (Garcia & Koelling, 1966; Logue, 1979). Even so, Stampfl has created a new preparation to demonstrate both one-trial acquisition and avoidance of the CS in rats. In Stampfl's experiment, rats were carried on a conveyor belt down an alley. At the end of the alley was a dark compartment where shocks could be delivered. Immediately before the dark compartment the alley walls were painted black. If the rat remained on the belt, it would be carried down the track, past the black walled section, then into to the dark shock compartment. If it ran to the opposite end of the belt, it would break a photobeam and the belt would stop for 3 minutes. Initially, the rat only had to break the photobeam one time to stop the belt, but the requirement was raised to 10 crossings. After a single shock resulting from riding the belt to the end, and subsequent rides to a segment of the alley with the black walls, rats reliably learned to run through the photobeam again as soon as the belt started and avoided the shock compartment on 1000 consecutive trials. Thus, with one presentation of shock, the rats learned to avoid the shock compartment and also, like humans, would make avoidance responses early in the chain of events.

Animal Models of the Etiology and Prevention of Anxiety Disorders

Despite sometimes being criticized as being oversimplified and insufficient to capture the complexities of the situation (Bouton, 1994; Rescorla & Wagner, 1972; Tryon, 2005), the basic mechanisms of aversive classical conditioning worked out in detail by (Pavlov, 1927) and of avoidance learning explained by Mowrer's (1950a) two-factor theory of avoidance remain fundamental components of animal models of anxiety disorders and their treatment. Few animal studies of exposure therapy do not start with signaled avoidance training, in which a tone or other stimulus (the conditioned aversive stimulus) precedes the presentation of a shock or other aversive event (the unconditioned stimulus). The conditioned aversive stimulus is then presented so that the organism can do something to escape from it, as is done in most experimental work on the two-factor theory. Work reported by Pavlov (1927), Masserman (1943), and Wolpe (1952), on the generation of experimental neuroses by presenting conflicting discriminative cues and unpredictable aversive events, also remain central to understanding anxiety and PTSD-like responses in humans. These procedures are not as prevalent as avoidance conditioning for creating anxiety problems in recent animal models of exposure therapy. Cognitive theorists offer a variety of alternative models (see e.g., Tryon, 2005), but these tend to be cognitive reformulations of associative mechanisms (Bouton, 1991; Bouton, Mineka, Barlow, 2001) or attempts to incorporate the mental representations or private verbal responses events into the conditioning process (Mahoney, 1995). These latter processes are difficult to model in animals. But even in humans, the mediational process models are equally inferential. Modeling and instructional control are sometimes labeled "cognitive" (Carroll & Bandura, 1990), but are easily understood in terms of the principles of discriminative stimulus control (Baer & Sherman, 1964; Catania, 2003; Skinner, 1953, 1957).

Like human responses to phobic stimuli, the reactions of monkeys can be complex and multidimensional. A monkey might avoid proximity to the snake in a Sackett Circus, but reach near one to obtain food in a Wisconsin Test Apparatus. Clearly models can be important in the understanding of the etiology of fear responses, and the monkey model has the advantage of eliminating verbal mediating processes. In fact, the correspondences between monkey and human behavior in this respect suggest that verbal processes might be epiphenomenal in many instances of anxiety disorders. Both Freud and Skinner emphasized that there is little reason to expect an individual to be able to accurately recount the conditions under which their own behavior developed. Social psychologists would further caution us that what humans might say about their fears could arise largely from the implicit requirements of the verbal community for one to justify and explain behavior in a logically consistent manner (Kelley, 1967; Festinger & Carlsmith, 1959; Skinner, 1957).

Observational Learning

Observational learning is likely to play a significant role in the acquisition of some anxiety disorders, perhaps a primary one. These observational mechanisms have been extensively studied and validated for a wide variety of behaviors in humans (e.g., Bandura, 1969; Bandura, Ross, & Ross, 1963). They represent a plausible basis for the many instances of anxiety disorders that do not seem to have a basis in associative conditioning or traumatic stress (Green & Osborne, 1985; Marks, 1969). The possibilities for studying the observational acquisition of behavior in animals such as rats is relatively limited, especially given the possibility that social facilitation can resemble imitation. Monkeys, however, are clearly capable of observational learning. According to Mineka (1987, Cook & Mineka, 1991), monkeys are near ideal organisms for the modeling of human fear acquisition because of their close behavioral and genetic resemblance to humans (relative to rats, at least).

In Mineka's standard preparation for observational acquisition of a phobia, a fearful reaction to snakes is established in monkeys, not by signaled avoidance learning but by having nonfearful monkeys observe other monkeys reacting fearfully and nonfearfully to snakes. Cook, Mineka, Wolkenstein, and Laitsch (1985) and Mineka, et al. (1984), for example, demonstrated that monkeys watching models react fearfully to snakes would acquire a fear of snakes without standard avoidance conditioning. The snake phobia was quickly learned and long lived. In another series of experiments, observer monkeys that watched a video recording of wild-reared monkeys reacting fearfully to a snake in the Wisconsin apparatus subsequently reacted fearfully to snakes in the same test (Cook, et al., 1985; Mineka, et al., 1984; Mineka, et al., 1980). This seemed to explain the prevalence of snake fear in wild monkeys, even though few would have actually been harmed by snakes. Such studies indicate that it is likely to be unprofitable to assume that phobic reactions result from an actual encounter between the client and the event that now causes anxiety. There is little reason to believe that anxiety acquired by non-conditioning mechanisms is qualitatively or parametrically different from anxiety acquired through conditioning and little reason to believe it would respond differently to exposure therapy. The concern of the exposure therapist would thus be for the possibility of reacquisition of fear via observational learning.

Selective Associations

Empirical and theoretical attention to selective associations in the acquisition of avoidance responses in animals became prominent in the 1960s and 1970s, with studies in areas such as conditioned taste aversion (Garcia & Koelling, 1966) and species-specific defense reactions (e.g., Bolles, 1970). In humans, the issue of selective associations in fears and phobias followed the publication of work by Seligman (1971; de Silva, Rachman, & Seligman, 1977). It is easier in standard laboratory contexts to establish a conditioned taste aversion in rats to a flavor rather than visual and auditory stimuli associated with food (Garcia & Koelling, 1966). It is reportedly easier to train a pigeon to press a treadle than to peck a key to avoid a shock (Bolles, 1970). The shuttle box and ledge box are used in studying avoidance learning in rats because rats are said to be easier to train to jump to avoid shock than to press a lever (although the abundant literature on avoidance in rats using lever pressing suggests that avoidance by lever pressing is not particularly hard to teach (see e.g., Sidman, 1962). In the analysis of exposure therapy, the most illustrative studies of the relative contributions of specific innate fear reactions and preparedness have been done by Mineka and her colleagues with monkeys (Cook & Mineka, 1991). Studies using edited video suggest that whereas snake phobias are learned, they are also "prepared." Apparently comparable fearful reactions by televised monkeys to flowers and snakes does not produce a fear of flowers but readily produces a fear of snakes, and even toy snakes, in monkeys viewing the models. This effect is highly repeatable and robust, and Mineka has concluded that there is sufficient evidence from this series of studies to conclude that specific phobias are not innate, but the susceptibility to acquiring them is (Cook & Mineka, 1991).

Immunization and Prevention of Fears

Efforts in remediation typically also include attention to prevention—or should if they do not. In the case of anxiety disorders, however, the therapist typically finds the client already in possession of a serious problem. Thus, the therapist is mostly guarding against the reacquisition of the phobia. Prevention must be possible however, because the children of phobics do not acquire their parents' phobias at anywhere near the rate that might be predicted from seeing how easily fears can be established through observational processes (Emmelkamp, 1982; Marks, 1987). It is likely that this effect in humans is due to the relative frequency of nonproblematic contact with the parent's fear-eliciting situation before and concurrent with the observations of fearful responding. Such an effect would typically be attributed to the CS pre-exposure effect or latent inhibition, which has been the subject of many studies in laboratory animals (see e.g., Lubow & Moore, 1959). In such studies, a stimulus is repeatedly presented to an animal before the stimulus is used in standard conditioning trials. This procedure can substantially increase the number of trials required to establish the stimulus as an effective eliciting agent relative to the number that would be required had it not been repeatedly presented (Mackintosh, 1974). This procedure might be conceived of as conducting exposure therapy on the stimulus before it is a fear-producing stimulus. Indeed, it suggests that relapse would be reduced in people who can maintain frequent nonaversive contact with the previously anxiety-producing events.

Monkeys serve as a good model for testing the pre-exposure hypothesis in a human-like observational conditioning situation. Mineka and Cook (1986), for instance, showed eight monkeys a model monkey reaching food near a snake in a Wisconsin Test Apparatus. Six of these eight monkeys subsequently showed significantly less fear of snakes than control animals when they were shown another model repeatedly exhibiting fearful responses to a snake in the Wisconsin apparatus. As previously stated, such exposure is sufficient under ordinary conditions to establish a strong fearful reaction to snakes by monkeys. This study also controlled for the effects of CS pre-exposure by conducting the same number of exposures to the CS shown without a model as with a model.

Feedback Insufficiency

A more recent animal model of OCD is based on the hypothesis that the compulsive responses fail to extinguish because of insufficient feedback during extinction (Daphna & Avisar, 2001). Exposure therapies, although not based on this theory, provide the needed feedback to cause full extinction of the coping responses. In a standard operant conditioning preparation, rats are taught to lever press in the presence of stimulus that signals food deliveries. The relationship between the stimulus and food is then selectively extinguished (feedback attenuation), and excessive lever pressing during extinction occurs (Daphna & Avisar, 2001). Compulsive lever pressing produced in this way seems to be affected by drugs in a manner similar to human OCD (Daphna & Doljansky, 2003). This research does not point to specific changes in the process of exposure therapy, but it is somewhat unusual in suggesting that at least some compulsive behavior might have originated as positively reinforced responses rather than as responses negatively reinforced by the reduction in subjective anxiety.

Nonassociative Processes

Recent laboratory work on schedule-induced polydipsia (SIP) in rats has pointed to some correspondences between it and obsessive-compulsive behavior in humans (Pietrowski, 2005; Woods, Smith, Szewczak, Dunn, Cornfelt, & Corbett, 1993). SIP appears to be the result of the sensitization of the normal eat-drink pattern in rats by the repeated presentation of food (Todd, Cunningham, Janes, Mendelson, & Morris, 1997; Todd & Pietrowski, 2005; Wetherington, 1981). To generate SIP, a rat is fed a small food pellet periodically on a fixed-time schedule of food delivery. After a few sessions, the rat will develop a pattern of robust post-food drinking, drinking after most or all pellet deliveries, and consuming 0.1 to 1.0 ml per drinking bout (see Falk, 1961, 1971; Todd, et al., 1997). These bouts do not resemble the normal eat-drink pattern seen in rats, have a highly stereotyped topography, and are excessive relative to the amount of food consumed and normal drinking patterns. Once established, the unusual post-food drinking topography becomes a lifelong component of a rat's behavioral repertoire and requires no contingent reinforcement for maintenance over the lifetime of the rat (Todd, 1990). SIP appears truly compulsive, and the rat will even adjust other aspects of its behavior to avoid modifying its stereotyped post-food drinking ritual. In a study in which food and water were placed varying distances apart on a runway (15 to 91 cm), the rats adjusted their running rate to maintain a constant eat-drink latency as the distance was varied. That is, as the distance became greater, the rats ran faster. Correspondences exist at the pharmacological level as well. If a selective serotonin reuptake inhibitor is given to a polydipsic rat pressing a lever for food pellets, the operant lever pressing will remain largely unaffected, but the obsessive post-food drinking will be interrupted (Woods, et al., 1993). Preliminary research also suggests that SIP is conditionable through associative process. Odors paired with food deliveries will later elicit drinking when presented alone (Anson & Todd, 2005; Todd & Taylor, 1995). Thus, a stimulus different than the one that originally engendered the compulsive drinking can set the occasion for drinking. Sensitization as a generator process for OCD would explain some elements of its resistance to extinction under ordinary circumstances.

CONCLUSION

As shown in earlier reviews of animal models of exposure therapy (Thyer, et al., 1988) and related areas (Cook & Mineka, 1991; Mineka, 1985, 1987), there remains a high degree of correspondence between observations and research findings on the use of various forms of exposure therapy in humans with the results of animal analogue experiments. The effects of all of the major parameters of exposure therapy procedures, including duration of treatment, the use of distraction and contingent reinforcement, and the action of a range of drugs, are highly similar in animals and humans. Close correspondences have been found for the effects of drugs in combination with exposure therapy. The etiology of anxiety disorders, as they relate to the use of exposure therapy, seems to be accounted for effectively by relatively simple models of avoidance conditioning and observational learning. Anxiety in animals created by both conditioning and observational mechanisms are similar to each other. Anxiety in animals seems to respond to exposure-like treatments, as does anxiety in humans. Reducing the symptoms unique to PTSD, OCD, and social phobias has received less attention by animal modelers, but the developing animal models in these areas seem to contact many of the relevant variables.

One important implication of the close correspondence between animal and human behavior in anxiety and exposure treatment situation has to do with conceptual and pragmatic status of some of the newer modes of theorizing. Great success has been obtained with animal models that remain closely tied to descriptive principles of behavior, such as those offered by Pavlov, Mowrer, and Skinner. Modern cognitive psychologists have offered elaborations and reinterpretations, but it is yet to be established that these are truly superior to more parsimonious models in the description, prediction, and control of anxiety disorders (see e.g., Tryon, 2005; Bouton, 1988, 1991, 1994; Bouton & Moody, 2004; Rescorla & Wagner, 1972).

Continued research is necessary, of course, and will probably concentrate more deeply on mechanisms of the acquisition of anxiety disorders and the effectiveness of new drugs, such as D-cycloserine (DCS), as replacements for, or adjuncts to, behavior therapy. The effectiveness of virtual reality therapies can probably be tested in animals such as monkeys. Additional work on cognitive factors will continue as well, but the role of animal models will be limited relative to conditioning and observational models owing to the metaphorical nature of the constructs involved. In the end, animal modeling will continue to prove an effective means of validating and refining therapeutic interventions for anxiety disorders.

REFERENCES

Agras, W.S., Leitenberg, H., & Barlow, D.H. (1968). Social reinforcement in the modification of agoraphobia. *Archives of General Psychiatry, 19,* 423–427.
Agras, W.S., Leitenberg, H., Barlow, D.H., & Thompson, L.E. (1969). Instructions and reinforcement in the modification of neurotic behavior. *American Journal of Psychiatry, 125,* 1435–1439.

Ammerman, R.T., & Hersen, M. (Eds.). (1993). *Handbook of behavior therapy with children and adults: A developmental and longitudinal perspective.* Needam Heights, MA: Allyn & Bacon.

Anson, H.M., & Todd, J.T. (2005, May). Use of Odor as a Conditioned Stimulus for Schedule Induced Polydipsia in Rats. Poster session presented at the annual meeting of the Association for Behavior Analysis, Chicago, IL.

Ayllon, T., & Azrin, N. (1968). *The token economy: A motivation system for therapy and rehabilitation.* Englewood Cliff, NJ: Appleton-Century-Crofts.

Baer, D.M., & Sherman, J.A. (1964). Reinforcement control of generalized imitation in young children. *Journal of Experimental Child Psychology, 1,* 37–49.

Bandura, A. (1969). *Principles of behavior modification.* Oxford: Holt, Rinehart, & Winston.

Bandura, A., Grusec, J.E., & Menlove, F.L. (1967). Vicarious extinction of avoidance behavior. *Journal of Personality and Social Psychology, 5,* 16–23.

Bandura, A., Ross, D., & Ross, S.A. (1963). Vicarious reinforcement and imitative learning. *Journal of Abnormal & Social Psychology, 67,* 601–607.

Barlow, D.H. (1988). *Anxiety and its disorders: The nature and treatment of anxiety and panic.* New York: Guilford Press.

Baum, M. (1965). An automated apparatus for the avoidance training of rats. *Psychological Reports, 16,* 1205–1211.

Baum, M. (1969). Paradoxical effect of alcohol on the resistance to extinction of an avoidance response in rats. *Journal of Comparative and Physiological Psychology, 69,* 238–240.

Baum, M. (1970). Effect of alcohol on the acquisition and resistance to extinction of avoidance responses in rats. *Psychological Reports, 26,* 759–765.

Baum, M. (1971). Effect of alcohol on the resistance to extinction of an avoidance response: Replication in mice. *Physiology and Behavior, 6,* 307–309.

Baum, M. (1973). Extinction of avoidance in rats: The effects of chlorpromazine and methylphenidate administered in conjunction with flooding (response prevention). *Behaviour Research and Therapy, 11,* 165–169.

Baum, M. (1986). An animal model for agoraphobia using a safety signal analysis. *Behaviour Research and Therapy, 24,* 87–89.

Baum, M. (1987). Distraction during flooding (exposure): Concordance between results in animals and man. *Behaviour Research and Therapy, 25,* 227–228.

Baum, M., Andrus, T., & Jacobs, W.J. (1990). Extinction of a conditioned emotional response. Massed and distributed exposures. *Behaviour Research and Therapy, 28,* 63–68.

Baum, M., & Gordon, A. (1970). Effect of a loud buzzer applied during response prevention (flooding) in rats. *Behaviour Research and Therapy, 8,* 287–292.

Baum, M., LeClerc, R., & St. Laurent, J. (1973). Rewarding vs aversive intracranial stimulation administered during flooding (response prevention) in rats. *Psychological Reports, 32,* 551–558.

Baum, M., & Myran, D.D. (1971). Response prevention (flooding) in rats: The effects of restricting exploration during flooding and of massed vs. distributed flooding. *Canadian Journal of Psychology, 25,* 138–146.

Baum, M., Pereira, J., & LeClerc, R. (1985). Extinction of avoidance responding in rats: The noise intensity parameter in noise facilitation of flooding. *Canadian Journal of Psychology, 39,* 529–535.

Baum, M., Roy, S., & LeClerc, R. (1985). Failure of a peripheral muscle relaxant (suxomethonium bromide) to increase the efficacy of flooding (response prevention) in rats. *Behaviour Research and Therapy, 23,* 361–364.

Becker, B.M., Magnuson, D.J., & Reid, L.D. (1977). Methods of deconditioning persisting avoidance: Intracranial stimulation as a counterconditioner. *Physiological Psychology, 5,* 73–75.

Berman, J.S., & Katzev, R.D. (1972). Factors involved in the rapid elimination of avoidance behavior. *Behaviour Research and Therapy, 10,* 247–256.

Berman, J.S., & Katzev, R.D. (1974). Effect of exposure to conditioned stimulus and control of its termination in the extinction of avoidance behavior. *Journal of Comparative and Physiological Psychology, 87,* 347–353.

Birch, D. (1965). Extended training extinction effect under massed and space extinction trials. *Journal of Experimental Psychology, 70,* 315–322.

Birk, L. (2004). Pharmacotherapy for performance anxiety disorders: Occasionally useful but typically contraindicated. *Journal of Clinical Psychology, 60,* 867–879.

Boer, A.P., & Sipprelle, C.N. (1970). Elimination of avoidance behavior in the clinic and its transfer to the normal environment. *Journal of Behavior Therapy and Experimental Psychiatry, 1,* 169–174.

Bolles, R.C. (1970). Species-specific defense reactions and avoidance learning. *Psychological Review, 77,* 32–48.

Boudewyns, P.A., & Shipley, R.H. (1983). *Flooding and implosive therapy: Direct exposure in clinical practice.* New York: Plenum Press.

Bouton, M.E. (1988). Context and ambiguity in the extinction of emotional learning: Implications for exposure therapy. *Behaviour Research and Therapy, 26,* 137–149.

Bouton, M.E. (1991). A contextual analysis of fear extinction. In P.R. Martin (Ed.), *Handbook of behavior therapy and psychological science: An integrative approach.* (pp. 435–453). Elmsford, NY, Pergamon.

Bouton, M.E. (1994). Conditioning, remembering, and forgetting. *Journal of Experimental Psychology Animal Behavior Processes, 20,* 219–231.

Bouton, M.E. (1998). The role of context in classical conditioning: Some implications for cognitive behavior therapy. In W.T. O'Donahue (Ed.), *Learning and behavior therapy.* (pp. 59–84). Boston, MA: Allyn & Bacon.

Bouton, M.E. (2000). A learning theory perspective on lapse, relapse and the maintenance of behavior change. *Health Psychology, 19,* 57–63.

Bouton, M.E., & Bolles, R.C. (1979). Role of conditioned contextual stimuli in reinstatement of extinguished fear. *Journal of Experimental Psychology: Animal Behavior Processes, 5,* 368–378.

Bouton, M.E., & King, D.A. (1983). Contextual control of the extinction of conditioned fear tests for the associative value of the context. *Journal of Experimental Psychology Animal Behavior Processes, 9,* 248–265.

Bouton, M.E., Mineka, S., & Barlow, D.H. (2001). A modern learning theory perspective on the etiology of panic disorder. *Psychological Review, 108,* 4–32.

Bouton, M.E., & Moody, E.W. (2004). Memory processes in classical conditioning. *Neuroscience and Biobehavioral Reviews, 28,* 663–674.

Bouton, M.E., & Peck, C.A. (1989) Context effects on conditioning, extinction, and reinstatement in an appetitive conditioning preparation, *Animal Learning and Behavior, 17,* 188–198.

Bouton, M.E., & Ricker, S.T. (1994). Renewal of extinguished responding in a second context. *Animal Learning & Behavior, 22,* 317–324.

Bouton, M.E., & Swartzentruber, D. (1991). Sources of relapse after extinction in Pavlovian and instrumental learning. *Clinical Psychology Review, 11,* 123–140.

Boyd, T.L., & Levis, D.J. (1976). The effects of single-component extinction of a three-component serial CS on resistance to extinction of the conditioned avoidance response. *Learning and Motivation, 7,* 517–531.

Breger, L., & McGaugh, J.L. (1965). Critique and reformulation of "learning-theory" approaches to psychotherapy and neurosis. *Psychological Bulletin, 63,* 338–358.

Brooks, D.C., & Bouton, M.E. (1994). A retrieval cue for extinction attenuates response recovery (renewal) caused by a return to the conditioning context, *Journal of Experimental Psychology Animal Behavior Processes, 20,* 366–379.

Brooks, D.C., Hale, B., Nelson, J.B., & Bouton, M.E. (1995). Reinstatement after counterconditioning. *Animal Learning & Behavior, 23,* 383–390.

Buss, R.S., & Reid, L.D. (1973). Deconditioning persisting avoidance: Spacing counterconditioning periods during response prevention. *Bulletin of the Psychonomic Society, 2,* 418–420.

Cameron, O.G., Liepman, M.R., Curtis, G., & Thyer, B.A. (1987). Ethanol retards desensitisation of simple phobias in non-alcoholics. *British Journal of Psychiatry, 150,* 845–849.

Capitanio, J.P., Boccia, M.L., & Colaiannia, D.J. (1985). The influence of rank on affect perception by pigtailed macaques (*Macaca nestrina*). *American Journal of Primatology, 8,* 53–59.

Carroll, W.R., & Bandura. A. (1990). Representational guidance of action production in observational learning: A causal analysis. *Journal of Motor Behavior, 22,* 85–97.

Catania, A.C. (2003). Verbal governance, verbal shaping, and attention to verbal stimuli. In K.A. Lattal & P.N. Chase (Eds.), *Behavior theory and philosophy.* (pp. 301–321). New York: Plenum.

Chaplin, E.W., & Levine, D.A. (1981). The effects of total exposure duration and interrupted versus continuous exposure in flooding therapy. *Behavior Therapy, 12,* 360–368.

Coleman, C.L., & Holmes, P.A. (1998). The use of noncontingent escape to reduce disruptive behavior in children with speech delays. *Journal of Applied Behavior Analysis, 31,* 687–690.

Cook, M., & Mineka, S. (1991). Selective associations in the origins of phobic fears and their implications for behavior therapy. In P.R. Martin (Ed.), *Handbook of behavior therapy and psychological science: An integrative approach* (pp. 413–434). Elmsford, NY: Pergamon.

Cook, M., Mineka, S., Wolkenstein, B., & Laitsch, K. (1985). Observational conditioning of snake fear in unrelated rhesus monkeys. *Journal of Abnormal Psychology, 94,* 591–610.

Cooper, S., Coon, K., Mejta, C., & Reid, L. (1974). Methods of deconditioning persisting avoidance: Amphetamine, chlorpromazine, and chlordiazepoxide as adjuncts to response prevention. *Physiological Psychology, 2,* 519–522.

Daphna, J., & Avisar, A. (2001). Excessive lever pressing following post-training signal attenuation in rats: A possible animal model of obsessive-compulsive disorder? *Behavioural Brain Research, 23,* 77–87.

Daphna, J., & Doljansky, J. (2003). Selective alleviation of compulsive lever-pressing in rats by D-sub-1 but not D-sub-2, blockade: Possible implications for the involvement of D-sub-1 receptors on obsessive-compulsive disorder. *Neuropsychopharmacology, 28,* 77–85.

de Silva, P., Rachman, S., & Seligman, M. (1977). Prepared phobias and obsessions: Therapeutic outcome. *Behaviour Research and Therapy, 15,* 65–77.

Dickinson, A. (1989). Expectancy theory in animal conditioning. In S.B. Klein & R.R. Mowrer (Eds.), *Contemporary learning theories: Pavlovian conditioning and the status of traditional learning theory.* (pp. 279–308). Englewood Cliffs, NJ: Prentice Hall.

Dickinson, A.L., Mellgren, R.L., Fountain, A., & Dyck, D. (1977). Wolpe's reciprocal inhibition procedure: An animal analogue. *Psychological Reports, 40,* 395–401.

Dinsmoor, J. (1995a). Stimulus control: I. *Behavior Analyst, 18*(1), 51–68.

Dinsmoor, J. (1995b). Stimulus control: II. *Behavior Analyst, 18*(2), 253–269.

Dollard, J., & Miller, N.E. (1950). *Personality and psychotherapy: An analysis in terms of learning, thinking, and culture.* New York: McGraw Hill.

Eglash, A. (1952). The dilemma of fear as a motivating force. *Psychological Review, 59,* 376–379.

Ellis, E.M., Ala'i-Rosales, S.S., Glenn, S.G., Rosales-Ruiz, J., & Greenspoon, J. (in press). The effects of graduated exposure, modeling, and contingent social attention on tolerance to skin care products with two children with autism. *Research in Developmental Disabilities.*

Emmelkamp, P.M.G. (1982). *Phobic and obsessive-compulsive disorders: Theory, research, and practice.* New York: Plenum.

Emmelkamp, P.M.G., Bouman, T.K., & Sholing, A. (1992). *Anxiety disorders: A practitioner's guide.* New York: Wiley.

Emmelkamp, P.M.G., Bruynzeel, M., Drost, L., & van der Mast, C.A.P.G. (2001). Virtual reality treatment in acrophobia: A comparison with exposure in vivo. *Psychology and Behavior, 4,* 335–339.

Emmelkamp, P.M.G., & Kuipers, A.C. (1979). Agoraphobia: A follow-up study four years after treatment. *British Journal of Psychiatry, 134,* 352–355.

Emmelkamp, P.M.G., & Wessels, H. (1975). Flooding in imagination versus flooding in vivo. A comparison with agoraphobics. *Behaviour Research and Therapy, 13,* 7–16.

Estes, W.K., & Skinner, B.F. (1941). Some quantitative properties of anxiety. *Journal of Experimental Psychology, 29,* 390–400.

Falk, J.L. (1961). Production of polydipsia in normal rats by an intermittent food schedule. *Science, 133,* 195-196.

Falk, J.L. (1971). The nature and determinants of adjunctive behavior. *Physiology and Behavior, 6,* 577–588.

Festinger, L., & Carlsmith, J.M. (1959). Cognitive consequences of forced compliance. *Journal of Abnormal and Social Psychology, 58,* 203–210.

Foa, E.B. (1996). The efficacy of behavioral therapy with obsessive compulsives. *The Clinical Psychologist, 49,* 19–22.

Foa, E.B., Jameson, J.S., Turner, R.M., & Payne, L.L. (1980). Massed versus spaced exposure sessions in the treatment of agoraphobia. *Behavior Research and Therapy, 18,* 333–338.

Foa, E.B., & Kozak, M.J. (1986). Emotional processing of fear: Exposure to corrective information. *Psychological Bulletin, 99,* 20–35.

Foa, E.B., Steketee, G., & Grayson, J.B. (1985). Imaginal and in vivo exposure: A comparison with obsessive-compulsive checkers. *Behavior Therapy, 16,* 292–302.

Franchina, J.J., Agee, C.M., & Hauser, P.J. (1974). Response prevention and extinction of escape behavior: Duration, frequency, similarity, and retraining variables in rats. *Journal of Comparative and Physiological Psychology, 87,* 354–363.

Freud, S. (1926). *The ego and the id.* Honolulu, HI: Hogarth Press.

Fuller, P.R. (1949). Operant conditioning of a human vegetative organism. *American Journal of Psychology, 62,* 587–590.

Garcia, J., & Koelling, R.A. (1966). Relation of cue to consequence in avoidance learning. *Psychonomic Science, 4,* 123–124.

Geer, J.H., & Turtletaub, A. (1967). Fear reduction following observation of a model. *Journal of Personality and Social Psychology, 6,* 327–331.

Gershon, J., Anderson, P., Graap, K., Zimand, E., Hodges, L., & Rothbaum, B.O. (2002). Virtual reality exposure therapy in the treatment of anxiety disorders. *Scientific Review of Mental Health Practice, 1,* 78–83.

Gordon, A., & Baum, M. (1971). Increased efficacy of flooding (response prevention) in rats through positive intracranial stimulation. *Journal of Comparative and Physiological Psychology, 75,* 68–72.

Gorman, J.E., Dyak, J.D., & Reid, L.D. (1979). Methods of deconditioning persisting avoidance: Diazepam as an adjunct to response prevention. *Bulletin of the Psychonomic Society, 14,* 46–48.

Grayson, J.B., Foa, E.B., & Steketee, G. (1982). Habituation during exposure treatment: Distraction versus attention-focusing. *Behaviour Research and Therapy, 20,* 323–328.

Grayson, J.B., Foa, E.B., & Steketee, G. (1986). Exposure in vivo of obsessive-compulsives under distracting and attention-focusing conditions: Replication and extension. *Behaviour Research and Therapy, 24,* 475–479.

Green, G., & Osborne, J.G. (1985). Does vicarious instigation provide support for observational learning theories? A critical review. *Psychological Bulletin, 97,* 3–17.

Harlow, H.F. (1949). The formation of learning sets. *Psychological Review, 56,* 51–65.

Heresco-Levy, U., Kremer, I., Javitt, D.C., Goichman, R., Reshef, A., Blanaru, M., & Cohen, T. (2002). Pilot-controlled trial of D-cycloserine for the treatment of post-traumatic stress disorder. *International Journal of Neuropsychopharmacology, 5,* 301–307.

Ho, Y., Hsu, L., Wang, C., Hsu, W., Lai, T., Hsu, C., & Tsai, H. (2005). Behavioral effects of D-cycloserine in rats: The role of anxiety level. *Brain Research, 1043,* 179–185.

Hodgson, R., & Rachman, S. (1974). Desynchrony in measures of fear. *Behaviour Research and Therapy, 12,* 319–326.

Hull, C.L. (1929). A functional interpretation of the conditioned reflex. *Psychological Review, 6,* 498–511.

Hunsicker, J.P., Nelson, T.C., & Reid, L.D. (1973). Two kinds of intracranial stimulation as counterconditioners of persisting avoidance in rats. *Physiological Psychology, 13,* 227–230.

Jacobson, E. (1934). *You must relax.* Oxford: Whittlesey House.

Jones, K.M., & Friman, P.C. (1999). A case study of behavioral assessment and treatment of insect phobia. *Journal of Applied Behavior Analysis, 32,* 95–98.

Jones, M.C. (1924). A laboratory study of fear: The case of Peter. *Pedagogical Seminary, 31,* 308–315.

Jones, M.C. (1974). Albert, Peter, and John B. Watson. *American Psychologist, 29,* 581–583.

Kamano, D.K. (1972). Using drugs to modify the effect of response prevention on avoidance extinction. *Behaviour Research and Therapy, 10,* 367–370.

Kamphuis, J.H., & Telch, M.J. (2000). Effects of distraction and guided threat reappraisal on fear reduction during exposure-based treatments for specific fears. *Behaviour Research and Therapy, 38,* 1163–1181.

Kazdin, A.E. (1978). *History of behavior modification: Experimental foundations of contemporary research.* Baltimore, MD: University Park Press.

Kelley, H.H. (1967). Attribution theory in social psychology. In. D. Levine (Ed.), *Nebraska Symposium on Motivation* (pp. 192–238). Lincoln: University of Nebraska Press.

Koch, M. (2002). Pharmakologische Unterstützung der Expositionstherapie bei Angststörungen: Tierexperimentelle Untersuchungen. *Nervenarzt, 73,* 481–483

Kornhaber, R.C., & Schroeder, H.E. (1975). Importance of model similarity on extinction of avoidance behavior in children. *Journal of Counseling and Clinical Psychology, 43,* 601–607.

Kostanek, D.J., & Sawrey, J.M. (1965). Acquisition and extinction of shuttlebox avoidance with complex stimuli. *Psychonomic Science, 3,* 369–-370.

Lang, P. (1968). Fear reduction and fear behavior: Problems in treating a construct. In J. Shlein (Ed.), *Research in psychotherapy* (pp. 90–102). Washington, DC: American Psychological Association.

Lang, P. (1971). The application of psychophysiological methods to the study of psychotherapy and behavior modification. In A. Bergin & S. Garfield (Eds.), *Handbook of psychotherapy and behavior change: An empirical analysis.* (pp. 75–125). New York: Wiley.

Lang, P.J. (1985). The cognitive psychophysiology of emotion: Fear and anxiety. In A. Tuma & J. Maser (Eds.), *Anxiety and anxiety disorders* (pp. 131–170). Hillsdale, NJ: Erlbaum.

Lanyon, R.I., Manosevitz, M., & Imber, R.R. (1968). Systematic desensitization: Distribution of practice and symptom substitution. *Behaviour Research and Therapy, 6,* 323–329.

LeClerc, R., St. Laurent, J., & Baum, M. (1973). Rewarding vs aversive intracranial stimulation administered during flooding (response prevention) in rats. *Psychological Reports, 32,* 551–558.

Ledgerwood, L., Richardson, R., & Cranney, J. (2005). D-cycloserine facilitates extinction of learned fear: Effects on reacquisition and generalized extinction. *Biological Psychiatry, 57,* 841–847.

Leitenberg, H., Agras, W.S., Allen, R., Butz, R., & Edwards, J. (1975). Feedback and therapist praise during treatment of phobia. *Journal of Consulting and Clinical Psychology, 43,* 396–404.

Leitenberg, H., Agras, W.S., Edwards, J.A., Thompson, L.E., & Wincze, J.P. (1970). Practice as a psychotherapeutic variable: An experimental analysis within single cases. *Journal of Psychiatric Research, 7,* 215–225.

Leitenberg, H., Agras, W.S., Thompson, L.E., & Wright, D.E. (1968). Feedback in behavior modification: An experimental analysis in two phobic cases. *Journal of Applied Behavior Analysis, 1,* 131–137.

Leitenberg, H., & Callahan, E.J. (1973). Reinforced practice and reduction of different kinds of fears in adult and children. *Behaviour Research and Therapy, 11,* 19–30.

Leitenberg, H., Rawson, R.A., & Mulick, J.A. (1975). Extinction and reinforcement of alternative behavior. *Journal of Comparative and Physiological Psychology, 88,* 640–652.

Leonard, H.L. (1997). New developments in the treatment of obsessive-compulsive disorder. *Journal of Clinical Psychiatry, 58,* 39–45.

Levis, D.J., & Boyd, T.L. (1979). Symptom maintenance: An infrahuman analysis and extension of the conservation of anxiety principle. *Journal of Abnormal Psychology, 88,* 107–120.

Liddell, H.S. (1947). The experimental neurosis. *Annual Review of Physiology, 9,* 569–580.

Lindberg, J.S., Iwata, B.A., Roscoe, E.M., Worsdell, A.S., & Hanley, G.P. (2003). Treatment efficacy of noncontingent reinforcement during brief and extended application. *Journal of Applied Behavior Analysis, 36,* 1–19.

Logue, A.W. (1979). Taste aversion and the generality of the laws of learning. *Psychological Bulletin, 86,* 276–296.

Lubow, R.E., & Moore, A.U. (1959). Latent inhibition: The effect of nonreinforced pre-exposure to the conditional stimulus. *Journal of Comparative and Physiological Psychology, 52,* 415–419.

Lydiard, R.B., & Falsetti, S.A. (1995). Treatment options for social phobia. *Psychiatric Annals, 25,* 570–576.

Mackintosh, N.J. (1970). Distribution of trials and the partial reinforcement effect in rats. *Journal of Comparative and Physiological Psychology, 73,* 341–348.

Mackintosh, N.J. (1974). *The psychology of animal learning.* New York: Academic Press.

Mahoney, M.J. (1995). Theoretical developments in the cognitive psychotherapies. In: M.J. Mahoney (Ed.), *Cognitive and constructive psychotherapies: Theory, research, and practice* (pp. 3–19). New York: Springer.

Marks, I.M. (1969). *Fears and phobia.* Oxford: Academic Press.

Marks, I.M. (1973). New approaches to the treatment of obsessive-compulsive disorders. *Journal of Nervous and Mental Disease, 156,* 420–426.

Marks, I.M. (1987). *Fears, phobias, and rituals.* New York: Wiley.

Marks, I.M. (1997). Behaviour therapy for obsessive-compulsive disorder: A decade of progress. *Canadian Journal of Psychiatry, 42,* 1021–1027.

Marshall, W.L. (1975). An examination of reciprocal inhibition and counterconditioning explanations of desensitization therapy. *European Journal of Behavioural Analysis and Modification, 12,* 74–86.

Marshall, W.L. (1985). The effects of variable exposure in flooding therapy. *Behavior Therapy, 16,* 117–135.

Martasian, P.J., & Smith, N.F. (1993). A preliminary resolution of the retention of distributed vs massed response prevention in rats. *Psychological Reports, 72,* 1367–1377.

Martasian, P.J., Smith, N.F., Neill, S.A., & Rieg, T.S. (1992). Retention of massed vs distributed response-prevention treatments in rats and a revised training procedure. *Psychological Reports, 70,* 339–355.

Martin, G.L., & Pear, J. (2005). *Behavior modification: What it is and how to do it* (7th ed.). Upper Saddle River, NJ: Prentice-Hall.

Masserman, J.H. (1943). *Behavior and neurosis.* Chicago: University of Chicago Press.

McDowell, J.J. (1988). Matching theory in natural human environments. *Behavior Analyst, 11,* 95–109.

McGlynn, F.D. (2005). Systematic desensitization. In M. Hersen & J. Rosqvist (Eds.), *Encyclopedia of behavior modification and cognitive behavior therapy.* Volume 1: *Adult clinical applications.* (pp. 574–582). Thousand Oaks, CA; Sage.

McKinney, W. (1974). Animal models in psychiatry. *Perspectives and Biology and Medicine, 17,* 529–541.

McNeil, D.W., & Zvolensky, M.J. (2000). Systematic desensitization. In A.E. Kazdin (Ed.), *Encyclopedia of Psychology,* Vol. 7. (pp. 533–535). London: Oxford University Press.

Meyer, J.S., & Quenzer, L.F. (2005). *Psychopharmacology: Drugs, the brain, and behavior.* Sunderland, MA: Sinauer.

Meyer, V. (1966). Modification of expectations in cases with obsessional rituals. *Behaviour Research and Therapy, 4,* 273–280.

Meyer, V., & Crisp, A.H. (1966). Some problems in behavior therapy. *British Journal of Psychiatry, 112,* 367–381.

Miltenberger, R.G. (2001). *Behavior modification: Principles and procedures.* Belmont, CA: Wadsworth.

Mineka, S. (1979). The role of fear in theories of avoidance, flooding, and extinction. *Psychological Bulletin, 86,* 985–1010.

Mineka, S. (1985). Animal models of anxiety disorders: Their usefulness and limitations. In A.H. Tuma & J.D. Maser (Eds.), *Anxiety and anxiety disorders* (199–244). Hillsdale, NJ: Lawrence Erlbaum Associates.

Mineka, S. (1987). A primate model of phobic fears. In H. Eysenck & I. Martin (Eds.), *Theoretical foundations of behavior therapy* (pp. 81–111). New York: Plenum.

Mineka, S., & Cook, M. (1986). Immunization against the observational conditioning of snake fear in rhesus monkeys. *Journal of Abnormal Psychology, 95,* 307–318.

Mineka, S., & Cook, M. (1988). Social learning and the acquisition of snake fear in monkeys. In T. Zentall & B. Galef (Eds.), *Social learning: Psychological and biological perspectives* (pp. 51–73). Hillsdale, NJ: Lawrence Erlbaum.

Mineka, S., & Cook, M. (1989). Mechanisms involved in the observational conditioning of fear. *Journal of Experimental Psychology: General, 122,* 23–38.

Mineka, S., Davidson, M., Cook, M., & Keir, R. (1984). Observational conditioning of snake fear in rhesus monkeys. *Journal of Abnormal Psychology, 93,* 355–372.

Mineka, S., & Keir, R. (1983). The effects of flooding on reducing snake fear in rhesus monkeys: 6-month follow up and further flooding. *Behaviour Research and Therapy, 21,* 527–535.

Mineka, S., Keir, R., & Price, V. (1980). Fear of snakes in wild- and lab-reared rhesus monkeys. *Animal Learning and Behavior, 8,* 653–663.

Mineka, S., Mystkowski, J.L., Hladek, D., & Rodruguez, B.I. (1999). The effects of changing contexts on return of fear following exposure therapy for spider fear. *Journal of Consulting and Clinical Psychology, 67,* 599–604.

Mowrer, O.H. (1939a). Anxiety and learning. *Psychological Bulletin, 36,* 517–518.

Mowrer, O.H. (1939b). A stimulus-response analysis of anxiety and its role as a reinforcing agent. *Psychological Review, 46,* 553–566.

Mowrer, O.H. (1940). An experimental analogue of "regression" with incidental observations on "reaction formation." *Journal of Abnormal and Social Psychology, 35,* 56–87.

Mowrer, O.H. (1948). Learning theory and the neurotic paradox. *American Journal of Orthopsychiatry, 18,* 571–610.

Mowrer, O.H. (1950a). *Implications of a two-factor theory.* Psychological Service Center.

Mowrer, O.H. (1950b). *Learning theory and personality dynamics.* Oxford: Ronald Press.

Munjack, D.J. (1975). Overcoming obstacles to desensitization using in vivo stimuli and Brevital. *Behavior Therapy, 6,* 543–546.

North, M.N., North, S.M., & Coble, J.R. (2002). Virtual reality therapy: An effective treatment for phobias. In: K.M. Stanney, Kay (Ed.), *Handbook of virtual environments: Design, implementation, and applications* (pp. 1065–1078). Mahwah, NJ: Erlbaum.

Nunes, J.S., & Marks, I.M. (1975). Feedback of true heart rate during exposure in vivo. *Archives of General Psychiatry, 32,* 933–936.

Nunes, J.S., & Marks, I.M. (1976). Feedback of true heart rate during exposure in vivo: Partial replication with methodological improvement. *Archives of General Psychiatry, 33,* 1346–1350.

Öst, L.G., Alm, T., Brandberg, M., & Breitholtz, E. (2001). One vs five sessions of exposure and five sessions of cognitive therapy in the treatment of claustrophobia. *Behaviour Research and Therapy, 39,* 167–183.

Öst, L.G., Brandberg, M., & Alm, T. (1997). One versus five sessions of exposure in the treatment of flying phobia. *Behaviour Research and Therapy, 35,* 987–996.

Öst, L.G., Hellström, K., & Kåver, A. (1992). One versus five sessions of exposure treatment of injection phobia. *Behavior Therapy, 23,* 262–282.

Overmier, J.B., & Seligman, M.E.P. (1967). Effects of inescapable shock upon subsequent escape and avoidance responding. *Journal of Comparative and Physiological Psychology, 63,* 28–33.

Pavlov, I.P. (1927). *Conditioned reflexes: An investigation of the physiological activity of the cerebral cortex.* Dover: New York.

Pavlov, I.P. (1957). *Experimental psychology and other essays.* New York: Philosophical Library.

Pavlov, I.P. (1960). *Psychopathology and psychiatry.* New Brunswick, NJ: Transaction Publishers.

Pickens, C.L., & Holland, P.C. (2004). Conditioning and cognition. *Neuroscience and Biobehavioral Reviews, 28,* 651–661.

Pietrowski, J.L. (2005). *Schedule-induced polydipsia: A potential model for obsessive-compulsive behavior in humans.* Unpublished masters thesis, Eastern Michigan University, Ypsilanti, MI.

Plimpton, E.H., Swartz, K.B., & Rosenblum, L.A. (1981). Responses of juvenile bonnet macaques to social stimulation presented through color videotapes. *Developmental Psychobiology, 14,* 109–115.

Polin, A.T. (1959). The effects of flooding and physical suppression as extinction techniques on an anxiety motivated avoidance locomotor response. *Journal of Psychology, 47,* 235–245.

Rachman, S. (1979). The return of fear. *Behaviour Research and Therapy, 17,* 164–166.

Rachman, S., & Hodgson, R. (1974). Synchrony and desynchrony in fear and avoidance. *Behaviour Research and Therapy, 12,* 311–318.

Rachman, S., & Lopatka, C. (1988). Return of fear: Underlearning and overlearning. *Behaviour Research and Therapy, 26,* 99–104.

Rachman, S., Robinson, S., & Lopatka, C. (1987). Is incomplete fear-reduction followed by a return of fear? *Behaviour Research and Therapy, 25,* 67–69.

Rachman, S., & Whittal, M. (1989). The effect of an aversive event on the return of fear. *Behaviour Research and Therapy, 27,* 513–520.

Ramsay, R.W., Barends, J., Breuker, J., & Kruseman, A. (1966). Massed versus spaced desensitization of fear. *Behaviour Research and Therapy, 4,* 205–207.

Rawson, R.A., & Leitenberg, H. (1973). Reinforced alternative behavior during punishment and extinction with rats. *Journal of Comparative and Physiological Psychology, 85,* 593–600.

Rescorla, R.A., & Heth, C.D. (1975). Reinstatement of fear to an extinguished conditioned stimulus. *Journal of Experimental Psychology: Animal Behavior Processes, 1,* 88–96.

Rescorla, R.A., & Wagner, A.R. (1972). A theory of Pavlovian conditioning: Variations in the effectiveness of reinforcement and nonreinforcement. In A.H. Black & W.F. Prokasy (Eds.), *Clinical conditioning II: Current research and theory* (pp. 64–69). New York: Appleton-Century-Crofts.

Ressler, K.J., Rothbaum, B.O., Tannenbaum, L., Anderson, P., Graap, K., Zimand, E., Hodges, L., & Davis, M. (2004). Cognitive enhancers as adjuncts to psychotherapy: Use of D-cycloserine in phobic individuals to facilitate extinction of fear. *Archives of General Psychiatry, 61,* 1136–1144.

Richardson, R., Ledgerwood, L., & Cranney, J. (2004). Facilitation of fear extinction by D-cycloserine: Theoretical and clinical implications. *Learning and Memory, 11*(5), 510–516.

Rimm, D., Briddell, D., Zimmerman, M., & Caddy, G. (1981). The effects of alcohol and the expectancy of alcohol on snake fear. *Addictive Behaviors, 6,* 47–51.

Robbins, S.J. (1990). Mechanisms underlying spontaneous recovery in autoshaping. *Journal of Experimental Psychology: Animal Behavior Processes, 16,* 235–249.

Rodriguez, B.I., & Craske, M.G. (1993). The effects of distraction during exposure to phobic stimuli. *Behaviour Research and Therapy, 31,* 549–558.

Rodriquez, B.I., Craske, M.G., Mineka, S., & Hladek, D. (1999). Context-specificity of relapse: Effects of therapist and environmental context on return of fear. *Behaviour Research and Therapy, 37,* 845–862.

Rosas, J.M., & Bouton, M.E. (1997). Renewal of a conditioned taste aversion upon return to the conditioning context after extinction in another one. *Learning & Motivation, 28,* 216–229.

Rosqvist, J. (2005). Exposure. In M. Hersen & J. Rosqvist (Eds.), *Encyclopedia of behavior modification and cognitive behavior therapy.* Volume 1: *Adult clinical applications.* (pp. 288–292). Thousand Oaks, CA; Sage.

Rowe, M.K., & Craske, M.G, (1998). Effects of an expanding-spaced vs. Massed exposure schedule on fear reduction and return of fear. *Behaviour Research and Therapy, 36,* 701–717.

Sackett, G.P. (1970). Unlearned responses, differential rearing experiences and the development of social attachments by rhesus monkeys. In L. Rosenblum (Ed.), *Primate behavior: Developments in field and laboratory research.* Vol. 1 (pp. 112–140). New York: Academic Press.

Sackett, G.P., Porter, M., & Holmes, H. (1965). Choice behavior in rhesus monkeys: Effect of stimulation during the first month of life. *Science, 140,* 304–306.

Salter, A. (1948). *Conditioned reflex therapy: The direct approach to the reconstruction of personality.* New York: Capricorn.

Samelson, F. (1994). John B. Watson in 1913: Rhetoric and practice. In J.T. Todd & E.K. Morris (Eds.), *Modern perspectives on John B. Watson and classical behaviorism.* (pp. 3–18). Westport, CT: Greenwood Press.

Schiff, R., Smith, N., & Prochaska, J. (1972). Extinction of avoidance in rats as a function of duration and number of blocked trials. *Journal of Comparative and Physiological Psychology, 81,* 356–359.

Seligman, M. (1971). Phobias and preparedness. *Behavior Therapy, 2,* 307–320.

Seligman, M.E.P. (1974). Depression and learned helplessness. In R.J. Friedman & M.M. Katz (Eds.), *The psychology of depression: Contemporary theory and research* (pp. 83–113). San Francisco: Freeman.

Seligman, M.E.P. (1975). *Helplessness: On depression, death, and development.* San Francisco: Freeman.

Shearman, R.W. (1970). Response-contingent CS termination in the extinction of avoidance learning. *Behaviour Research and Therapy, 8,* 227–239.

Sidman, M. (1960). *Tactics of scientific research.* Boston: Authors' Cooperative.

Sidman, M. (1962). Classical avoidance without a warning stimulus. *Journal of the Experimental Analysis of Behavior, 5,* 97–104.

Skinner, B.F. (1938). *The behavior of organisms: An experimental analysis.* New York: Appleton-Century-Crofts.

Skinner, B.F. (1948). "Superstition in the Pigeon." *Journal of Experimental Psychology, 38,* 168–172.

Skinner, B.F. (1953). *Science and human behavior.* New York: McMillan.

Skinner, B.F. (1957). *Verbal behavior.* New York: Appleton-Century-Crofts.

Skurdal, A.J. Eckardt, M.J., & Brown, J.S. (1975). The effects of alcohol on escape learning and on regular and punished extinction in a self-punitive situation with rats. *Physiological Psychology, 3,* 29–34.

Solomon, R.L., & Wynn, L.C. (1953). Traumatic avoidance learning: Acquisition in normal dogs. *Psychological Monographs, 67,* (Whole No. 354).

Stampfl, T.G. (1987). Theoretical implications of the neurotic paradox as a problem in behavior theory: An experimental resolution. *Behavior Analyst, 10,* 161–173.

Stampfl, T.G., & Levis, D.J. (1968). Implosive therapy: A behavioral therapy? *Behaviour Research and Therapy, 6,* 31–36.

Stanton, M.E. (2000). Multiple memory systems, development and conditioning. *Behavioral and Brain Research, 110,* 25–37.

Stern, R.S., & Marks, I.M. (1973). Brief and prolonged flooding: A comparison in agoraphobic patients. *Archives of General Psychiatry, 28,* 270–276.

Stokes, T.F., & Baer, D.M. (1977). An implicit technology of generalization. *Journal of Applied Behavior Analysis, 10*(2), 349–367.

Taub, J., Taylor, P., Smith, M., Kelley, K., Becker, B., & Reid, L. (1977). Methods of deconditioning persisting avoidance: Drugs as adjuncts to response prevention. *Physiological Psychology, 5,* 67–72.

Taylor, S. (2002). Systematic desensitization. In M. Hersen, & W, Sledge (Eds.), *Encyclopedia of Psychotherapy,* Vol. 2 (pp. 755–759). New York: Elsevier.

Teichner, W.H. (1952). Experimental extinction as a function of the intertrial intervals during conditioning and extinction. *Journal of Experimental Psychology, 44,* 170–178.

Telch, M.J., Valentiner, D.P., Ilai, D., Young, P.R., Powers, M.B., & Smits J.A.J. (2004). Fear activation and distraction during the emotional processing of claustrophobic fear. *Journal of Behavior Therapy and Experimental Psychiatry, 35,* 219–232.

Thyer, B.A., Baum, M., & Reid, L.D. (1988). Exposure techniques in the reduction of fear: A comparative review of the procedure in animals and humans. *Advances in Behaviour Research and Therapy, 10,* 105–127.

Thyer, B.A., & Curtis, G.C. (1984). The effects of ethanol intoxication on phobic anxiety. *Behaviour Research and Therapy, 22,* 599–610.

Thyer, B.A., Parrish, R.T., Himle, J., Cameron, O.G., Curtis, G.C., & Nesse, R.M. (1986). Alcohol abuse among clinically anxious patients *Behaviour Research and Therapy, 24,* 357–359.

Todd, J.T. (1990). An experimental analysis of some basic characteristics of schedule-induced polydipsia in rats. Doctoral dissertation, University of Kansas, 1990. Dissertation Abstracts International, 51, no. 11B.

Todd, J.T., Cunningham, L.A., Janes, A.A., Mendelson, J., & Morris, E.K. (1997). The generation and maintenance of schedule-induced polydipsia in normal male rats without weight reduction. *Physiology and Behavior, 62,* 1385–1390.

Todd, J.T., & Pietrowski, J.L. (2005). Schedule-induced behavior. In M. Hersen & J. Rosquist (Eds.), *Encyclopedia of behavior modification and cognitive behavior Therapy,* Vol. 1: *Adult clinical applications.* (pp. 499–501). Thousand Oak, CA: Sage.

Todd, J.T., & Taylor, P.J. (1995, May). *Schedule induced polydipsia: An attempt to elicit drinking with odors paired with reinforcer presentation.* Poster session presented at the convention of the Association for Behavior Analysis, Washington, DC.

Tolman, E.C. (1932). *Purposive behavior in animals and men.* New York: Appleton-Century-Crofts.

Tryon, W.W. (2005). Possible mechanisms for why desensitization and exposure therapy work. *Clinical Psychology Review, 25,* 67–95.

Tsao, J.C.I., & Craske, M.G. (2000). Timing of treatment and return of fear: Effects of massed, uniform-, and expanding-spaced exposure schedules. *Behavior Therapy, 31,* 479–497.

Uno, T., Greer, S.E., & Goates, L. (1973). Observational facilitation of response prevention. *Behaviour Research and Therapy, 11,* 207–212.

Vansteenwegen, D., Hermans, D., Vervliet, B., Francken, G., Beckers, T., Baeyens, F., & Eelen, P. (2005). Return of fear in a human differential conditioning paradigm caused by a return to the original acquisition context. *Behaviour Research & Therapy, 43,* 323–336.

Vervliet, B., Vansteenwegen, D., Baeyens, F., Hermans, D., & Paul, H. (2005). Return of fear in a human differential conditioning paradigm caused by a stimulus change after extinction. *Behaviour Research and Therapy, 43,* 357–371

Walker, D.L., Ressler, K.J., Lu, Kwok-Tung, & Davis, M. (2002). Facilitation of conditioned fear extinction by systemic administration or intra-amygdala infusions of D-cycloserine as assessed with fear-potentiated startle in rats. *Journal of Neuroscience, 22,* 2343–2351.

Watson, J.B. (1913). Psychology as the behaviorist views it. *Psychological Review, 20,* 158–177.

Watson, J.B. (1916). The place of the conditioned reflex in psychology. *Psychological Review, 23,* 89–116.

Watson, J.B. (1919) *Psychology from the standpoint of a behaviorist.* Philadelphia, Lippincott.

Watson, J.B. (1930). *Behaviorism* (rev. ed.). Chicago: University of Chicago Press.

Watson, J.B., & Morgan, J.J.B. (1917). Emotional reactions and psychological experimentation. *American Journal of Psychology, 28,* 163–174.

Watson, J.B., & Rayner, R. (1920). Conditioned emotional reactions. *Journal of Experimental Psychology, 3,* 1–14

Weissman, A. (1959). Differential drug effects upon a three-ply multiple schedule of reinforcement. *Journal of the Experimental Analysis of Behavior, 2,* 271–287.

Weitzman, B. (1967). Behavior therapy and psychotherapy. *Psychological Review, 74,* 300–317

Wetherington, C.L. (1981). Is adjunctive behavior a third class of behavior? *Neuroscience and Biobehavioral Reviews, 6,* 329–350.

Whitehead, W.E., Blackwell, B., & Robinson, A. (1978). Effects of diazepam on phobic avoidance behavior and phobic anxiety. *Biological Psychiatry, 13,* 59–64.

Whitehead, W.E., Robinson, A., Blackwell, B., & Stutz, R.M. (1978). Flooding treatment of phobias: Does chronic diazepam increase effectiveness? *Journal of Behavior Therapy and Experimental Psychiatry, 9,* 219–225.

Wolf, M.M., Risley, T. R., & Mees, H. (1964). Application of operant conditioning procedures to the behavior problems of an autistic child. *Behaviour Research and Therapy, 1,* 305–312.

Wolpe, J. (1952). Experimental neurosis as a learned behavior. *British Journal of Psychology, 43,* 243–268.

Wolpe, J. (1958). *Psychotherapy by reciprocal inhibition.* Stanford, CA: Stanford University Press.

Wolpe, J. (1961). The systematic desensitization treatment of neuroses. *Journal of Nervous and Mental Disease, 132,* 189–203.

Wolpe, J. (1982). The dichotomy between classical conditioned and cognitively learned anxiety. *Journal of Behavior Therapy and Experimental Psychiatry, 12,* 35–42.

Woods, A., Smith, C., Szewczak, M., Dunn, R.W., Cornfeldt, M., & Corbett, R. (1993). Selective serotonin reuptake inhibitors decrease schedule-induced polydipsia in rats: An potential model for obsessive-compulsive disorder. *Psychopharmacology, 112,* 195–198.

CHAPTER 3

Exposure Therapy and Cognitive Interventions for the Anxiety Disorders: Overview and Newer Third-Generation Perspectives

John P. Forsyth, Velma Barrios,
and Dean T. Acheson

University at Albany, State University of New York

The overarching goal of this chapter is to compare behavioral and more explicitly cognitive approaches for the treatment of all anxiety disorders. In so doing, we take a broad brush stroke in describing theoretical rationales, methods of treatment, mechanisms and processes underlying therapeutic change, and work supporting treatment efficacy. The remainder of the chapter outlines psychological and experiential variables and processes that are now considered crucial in explaining the genesis, maintenance, and alleviation of anxiety *disorders* rather than anxiety per se (Barlow, Allen, & Choate, 2004; Craske, 2003). In so doing, we draw attention to broad-band emotion regulatory processes for three reasons.

First, the emerging consensus is that emotional regulation processes, namely the tendency to avoid, suppress, or escape from aversive emotional states and the contexts or cues that may evoke them, characterize virtually all anxiety disorders (Barlow, 2002; Barlow, et al., 2004; Rosen & Schulkin, 1998). Second, findings from the field of emotion regulation suggest that the tendency to regulate emotion is heavily dependent on verbal-cognitive processes, may be harmful when applied to aversive emotional states, and function to transform normal anxiety and fear into disordered anxiety and fear. Third, it is becoming increasingly clear that the application of self and emotion regulation strategies in situations and contexts where it is unnecessary is largely responsible for the wide-ranging functional impairment typical of many persons with anxiety disorders.

Indeed, rigid and inflexible forms of emotion regulation, when juxtaposed with fear-learning experiences and powerful competing approach contingencies that

Handbook of Exposure Therapies

cannot be avoided without significant costs, likely function as an important predisposition for the development and maintenance of *disordered* fear (see Forsyth, Eifert, & Barrios, 2006, for a detailed account). Collectively, this work has led to a rethinking of the mastery and control agenda that has come to characterize many mainstream behavior therapies for the anxiety disorders (Barlow, et al., 2004). It also reaffirms that newer third-generation behavior therapies (e.g., acceptance and commitment therapy, Hayes, Strosahl, & Wilson, 1999; functional analytic psychotherapy, Kohlenberg & Tsai, 1991), including unified treatment protocols based on them for persons suffering from anxiety disorders (see Eifert & Forsyth, 2005), may be on the right track in making emotion regulatory processes explicit targets in therapy.

Our intent here is to provide a broad overview of this work with an eye on how it may help advance our understanding of anxiety disorders and lead to improved clinical interventions, including modifications to the most effective aspects of cognitive-behavioral treatments. To set a context for the discussion, we begin with a brief overview of first (i.e., behavioral) and second (i.e., cognitive) accounts of the anxiety disorders, followed by a critical evaluation of behavioral and cognitive-behavioral accounts of anxiety and fear learning within an emotion regulation context. The remaining sections describe findings from emotion regulation research that are germane to understanding the maintenance of anxiety-related problems and the basic and applied implications that follow from this account. Using acceptance and commitment therapy (ACT; see Eifert & Forsyth, 2005; Hayes, et al., 1999) as an example, we show how acceptance, mindfulness, and value-guided behavior change strategies can be used to alter the function of problematic thoughts and feelings (not their form) in the context of exposure-based interventions. The chapter concludes with a discussion of conceptual and methodological issues and directions for future research.

RATIONALES OF FIRST- AND SECOND-GENERATION BEHAVIOR THERAPY

In this section we briefly review the traditional behavioral and cognitive-behavioral accounts of anxiety. We then describe the core features of a model, described in more detail elsewhere (see Forsyth, et al., 2005), that outlines a new functional behavioral approach. In this model, emotion regulation strategies and language processes are at the core of the transformation from normal experiences of fear and anxiety to disordered experiences of fear and anxiety. We do not address biological theories here because psychological and biological theories of anxiety have largely pursued their own agenda. Rachman (2004) also points out that, with few exceptions, biological theories seek to explain particular disorders. They do not provide broad theories of anxiety that have been the hallmark of behavioral models.

Behavioral Views

Behavior therapy is an intensely empirical, pragmatic, direct, time-limited, and minimally inferential approach. It emerged as a major player on the psychotherapy scene in the 1950s because of these characteristics and for reasons having to do with its close affinity with learning theory, learning principles (both classical and instrumental), and experimental psychology. Learning principles and learning theories provided the chief inspiration for intervention technologies that could be used to achieve concrete clinical outcomes. Behavior therapists focused on direct symptom relief and behavior change, not hypothesized desires, unconscious wishes, beliefs, or clinical concepts and methods that were too subtle, complex, imprecise, or broad in scope (Hayes, 2004a). These first-order change targets became a defining characteristic of behavior therapy, with the anxiety disorders serving as the initial proving ground (Wolpe, 1958). The outcome was a range of learning-based models and intervention technologies that worked not just with anxiety disorders but also a range of other behavioral problems.

Early behavior therapy owes much of its success to the conditioning account of the etiology and maintenance of anxiety disorders: Anxiety disorders are learned or acquired via a process of classical conditioning (Eysenck, 1987; Marks, 1969, 1981; Wolpe, 1958; Wolpe & Rachman, 1960) and maintained via negative reinforcement through operant escape and avoidance behaviors (Mowrer, 1939, 1960). Consistent with this view, phobias and anxiety disorders were conceptualized in fear conditioning terms. Thus, when an otherwise benign stimulus occurs in close contingency with an anxiety-inducing event, it becomes highly likely that the stimulus will later elicit anxiety and fear without further trauma. Such learning can also occur via vicarious observation (Mineka & Cook, 1993; Mineka & Ben Hamida, 1998) and informational transmission (Rachman, 1990).

Regardless of the pathway, it is now becoming increasingly clear that a relation between otherwise neutral stimuli and a false alarm (i.e., a panic attack) may be enough to set this learning in motion (Barlow, 1988; Bouton, Mineka, & Barlow, 2001; Chambless & Gracely, 1989; Forsyth, Daleiden, & Chorpita, 2000; Forsyth, Eifert, & Thompson, 1996; Forsyth & Eifert, 1996a, 1998a, 1998b; Wolpe & Rowan, 1988). This view also is at the core of contemporary thinking about the critical processes involved in fear learning, wherein experiencing panic attacks or panic-like responses function as both critical conditioning events in the genesis of panic and other anxiety disorders (Bouton, et al., 2001) and central targets in exposure-based therapy.

Cognitive and Cognitive-Behavioral Views

One logical consequence of the conditioning account was that successful treatment needs to involve helping clients to confront feared stimuli and contexts in a safe therapeutic environment so as to (1) counter the powerful action tendency to avoid or escape fear-evoking stimuli and situations and thereby (2) allow for new corrective emotional learning via extinction of excessive fear and anxiety (Wolpe, 1958). This view, based largely on exposure as a treatment technology and extinction as a process, survived more or less intact until the 1970s, when criticisms mounted suggesting that fear conditioning does not adequately explain the etiology and maintenance of anxiety disorders (Rachman, 1977, 1991). Learning principles and learning theories had failed to provide an adequate account of human language and cognition. There was limited behavioral research addressing the relation between language and emotional meaning, and very little of this work had any clear practical utility. The need to address thoughts and feelings in a more central way was unmet and set the stage for cognitive theories and constructs.

The cognitive view emerged to provide a more forceful and direct account of how feeling, affect, and cognitive processes contribute to human suffering. Cognitive theorists and therapists initially drew on clinical observation for their theoretical and practical inspirations, and many later turned to information processing models to fill in the gaps with a technical account. This cognitive information-processing perspective (and there are several) draws heavily on mediational constructs (e.g., networks, nodes, expectancies, appraisals, and schemata) borrowed from information and computer science (e.g., Williams, Mathews, & MacLeod, 1996; Williams, Watts, MacLeod, & Mathews, 1988). This approach emphasizes the role of memory, attention, catastrophic thinking patterns, irrational beliefs, unrealistic self-statements and appraisals, and the like in the etiology, maintenance, and treatment of anxiety disorders. Accordingly, pathological anxiety is thought to result from selective processing of information perceived as signifying threat or danger. Distorted information processing, in turn, contributes to physiological, affective, and behavioral symptoms of anxiety disorders.

The traditional cognitive theory posits such beliefs, and interpretations of events based on them become problematic and inflexible and thus, yield emotional distress (Beck, 1979). This view differs from the traditional behavioral account, in that it is the individual's interpretation of events, rather than the events themselves, that leads to distress (Clark, 1986). That is, an individual's belief system may cause them to interpret events in a rigid and maladaptive fashion, thus leading to pathological behavior. For example, individuals with social anxiety disorder tend to hold negative beliefs regarding their own social behavior, rating it more harshly than the behavior of others (Stopa & Clark, 1993). Clients with panic disorder, on the other hand, hold beliefs that their normal bodily sensations are signs of danger (Clark, 1986).

Indeed, most cognitive accounts stipulate that individuals with anxiety disorders experience overactive cognitive patterns that continually structure external and internal experiences as signs of danger (Beck, Emery, & Greenberg, 1985). Despite some nuances, all emphasize how verbal-symbolic processes convey emotional meaning and how emotions and resulting behavior depend on such processes.

The fundamental idea is that emotions are experienced as a result of the way in which events are interpreted or appraised. It is the meaning of events that triggers emotions rather than the events themselves. The particular appraisal made will depend on the context in which an event occurs, the mood the person is in at the time it occurs, and the person's past experiences. Effectively this means that the same event can evoke a different emotion in different people, or even different emotions in the same person on different occasions (Salkovskis, 1996, p. 48).

These notions have had great appeal and were quickly integrated within behavior therapy and became known as cognitive and cognitive-behavior therapy (CBT) (Beck, et al., 1985).

Methods of Treatment

Advances in behavioral and cognitive research and theory over the last 2 decades have led to an improved understanding of variables and processes involved in the etiology and maintenance of anxiety disorders. All have also yielded a range of time-limited intervention technologies that have helped clarify potential therapeutic parameters needed for developing and improving interventions. The collective practical impact of this work is startling: CBTs for each of the anxiety disorders have been empirically supported since their emergence (Chambless, Baker, Baucom, Beutler, Calhoun, Crits-Christoph, et al., 1998) and are now considered the treatments of choice for these disorders (Barlow, 2002). This section describes methods of treatment that follow from behavioral and cognitive-behavioral conceptualizations of anxiety disorders. As will be seen, both behavioral and cognitive interventions are fundamentally about first-order change methods. That is, intervention procedures that are about targeting problematic psychological and emotional content directly.

Exposure-Based Behavioral Approaches

All exposure-based treatments involve clients confronting previously avoided objects or situations, including unwanted thoughts and feelings, while resisting the tendency to avoid or escape from them. In short, exposure-based interventions arrange for structured approach behavior and thus, allow extinction processes to work. Although one cannot infer etiologic process from treatment response, the notion that exposure depends on extinction has a long history and follows from the view that people learn to be afraid; they are not born with an anxiety disorder. Therapy, therefore, presents an opportunity for new corrective emotional learning.

Although there are variants (e.g., flooding), most exposure therapies are conducted in a gradual and systematic fashion under the guidance of a trained therapist. The targets of exposure may be interoceptive (e.g., thoughts, physical sensations, worry, painful memories) and/or exteroceptive (e.g., environmental cues and situations that evoke fear) using either imaginal or in vivo procedures. The process of exposure therapy often begins with the therapist and client developing a hierarchy or rank-ordered list of the least-to-most feared stimuli. Thereafter, clients are encouraged to approach each element of the hierarchy, beginning with the least anxiety-inducing one, and for each step to remain in its presence until anxiety attenuates to manageable levels. By preventing escape or avoidance during such exposure-based procedures, anxiety-related distress, and the probability of the reemergence of fear to specific feared stimuli are eventually minimized (Öst, 1997).

The modality of exposure therapy (i.e., imaginal, in vivo, or virtual reality) and the stimuli targeted during treatment typically depend on a client's unique presenting problems. For example, the target stimulus could consist of a bodily sensation for panic disorder, a social encounter for social phobia, a specific object or situation for specific phobias, contamination for obsessive–compulsive disorder (OCD), a catastrophic image for generalized anxiety disorder, or a traumatic image for post-traumatic stress disorder (PTSD). It should be noted that exposure-based interventions are typically used in conjunction with other therapeutic components, such as cognitive restructuring and relaxation exercises (i.e., breathing retraining, systematic muscle relaxation). This is interesting given that it is widely known that exposure therapy (in vivo, imaginal, and interoceptive) is sufficient for good clinical outcomes when used alone in the treatment of anxiety disorders (Ladouceur, 1983; Marks & Horder, 1987; Emmelkamp, 1994; de Beurs, van Balkom, Lange, Koele, & van Dyck, 1995). This observation highlights the fact that exposure therapy is not a clickety-clack "get rid of anxiety" process, but rather can broadly impact how people think about their anxiety, fear, themselves, and their world.

Cognitive and Cognitive-Behavioral Approaches

Problematic psychological content is thought to play a significant role in the etiology, exacerbation, and maintenance of anxiety disorders. Thus, cognitive approaches involve numerous strategies that target distorted, unrealistic, or inappropriate patterns of thinking directly, namely variants of cognitive restructuring (Newman, 2003). This intervention strategy, in turn, typically begins with helping clients to monitor their cognitive style and understand the role it has in their anxiety problems and associated symptom complaints. Clients are then taught cognitive skills that will allow them to be more flexible and to modify their problematic ways of thinking. The final step is to create new behavioral repertoires that run counter to previous patterns of thinking.

Various homework assignments are often included to facilitate cognitive restructuring. For instance, clients may be asked to keep a daily record of dysfunctional thoughts (Clark, 1986) and to learn to apply methods to challenge such thoughts with more realistic thoughts and appraisals. Yet the ultimate purpose of such interventions is to modify maladaptive cognitive schemas that underlie problematic thinking and patterns of behavior. Viewed through Beck and Clark's (1997) information processing model, cognitive restructuring aims to develop more adaptive and realistic appraisals of threat as a mechanism toward psychological health.

Behavioral experiments are also routinely used to facilitate cognitive restructuring (Clark, 1986). In this procedure, clients test cognitive distortions by engaging in an anxiety-provoking behavior and carefully evaluating the consequences. These exercises aim to identify the faulty nature of the client's cognitions (Dobson & Hamilton, 2003) and can be conducted in-session using exposure or role playing or with in vivo homework assignments (Newman, 2003). For example, an individual with social phobia may believe that she will be laughed at or otherwise ostracized if she attends a party. The therapist would encourage her to attend a party despite her fears and then evaluate the accuracy of her predictions. If the client's predictions were inaccurate, then the therapist would point out and discuss this discrepancy with the goal of modifying the client's threat schema. If the client's prediction for some reason were accurate, the therapist would explore possible reasons for this and work to modify the client's problematic behavior. Thus, most cognitive strategies involve what many would call exposure-based exercises. Indeed, the very act of contacting the problematic thought could be thought of as exposure. For these and other reasons, it is quite difficult to disentangle purely cognitive from more behaviorally based exposure interventions.

MECHANISMS AND PROCESSES UNDERLYING THERAPEUTIC CHANGE

Although the efficacy of exposure and cognitive therapy for the anxiety disorders has been well established (Chambless, et al., 1998), overwhelming evidence suggests that the effectiveness of both is relatively short-lived. Indeed, a significant number of individuals experience the reemergence of symptoms after the end of successful treatment (Rachman, 1989), and many other anxious individuals experience little or no benefit at all from these gold-standard therapies (Craske, 1999). As a result, the past 2 decades has seen increased attention to therapeutic mechanisms of change. This section considers the critical variables that are theorized to account for the therapeutic effects of exposure therapy and cognitive interventions.

Behavioral Interventions

All exposure-based interventions for anxiety disorders involve a complex interaction between classical and instrumental learning processes. Exposure, by definition, involves the simultaneous approach of a feared event and willingness to remain fully in contact with that feared event. To derive maximal benefit from exposure therapy requires that anxious clients fully engage the feared situation without resistance, avoidance, and/or escape, while also allowing themselves to experience anxiety and fear that are likely to occur (Foa & Kozak, 1986). The approach behavior, itself an instrumental or operant response, is designed to counteract the powerful action tendency to avoid or escape from aversive events. Thus, with approach also comes the possibility of new learning and the benefits of collateral extinction processes that may accompany approach behavior. More specifically, exposure therapy attenuates the severity of fear through extinction processes by repeatedly presenting fear-evoking stimuli (i.e., spider) in the absence of traumatic consequences (i.e., spider bite).

The process of extinction has provided a framework that has helped conceptualize important principles within exposure therapy. Since the early days of behavior therapy, in fact, learning theory has guided the development of therapeutic procedures by contributing theoretically and experimentally derived principles with a measure of practical utility. Still, we know much less about why exposure therapy works than the fact that it does work. This is due, in part, to the research agenda in this area that has tended to focus on showing good outcomes, not in elucidating relevant processes responsible for those outcomes.

This state of affairs has resulted in a great deal of confusion about the processes involved in exposure-based interventions. For instance, it is common to hear exposure therapy discussed as unlearning or counter-conditioning or worse, as being noncognitive. None of these are accurate. Indeed, recent theoretical and conceptual developments in learning theory (Bouton, 1993), for instance, showed that extinction is an active learning process whereby conditioned association is not destroyed or unlearned. Bouton and colleagues (1993), for instance, have shown that extinction is an active learning process whereby the conditioned association is not destroyed or unlearned. Instead, this process reflects the development of new relational learning. This learning, in turn, tends to be highly context dependent and thus, does not generalize well outside the extinction context (see Bouton, 2002, for a review). In fact, when a fearful response is extinguished in one context (such as the laboratory or therapist's office), there is a high probability that the fearful response will reemerge when a laboratory animal or human is in a new context that was different from the extinction context (Bouton, 1988, 1994). A handful of studies with clinically anxious individuals have shown as much (Mineka, Mystkowski, Hladek, & Rodriguez, 1999; Mystkowski, Craske, & Echiverri, 2002; Rodriguez, Craske, Mineka, & Hladek, 1999). Thus, when clients are faced with a previously extinguished fear-evoking stimulus in a new context, they are likely to show a return of fearful responding to that stimulus.

Collectively, this work shows that extinction does not depend on unlearning of the emotive properties of a feared stimulus, but rather learning something new about that stimulus in and within a context. When the context changes, so may the functions of the previously feared event. This work, in turn, has numerous implications for relapse after exposure-based interventions for anxiety disorders and can address previous criticisms of the traditional conditioning account where the focus has been on conditioning in relative isolation from contextual factors (Forsyth, et al., 2006; Mineka & Zinbarg, 1996).

Cognitive Interventions

Most cognitive theories of anxiety pathology suggest that effective therapy depends on modifying maladaptive beliefs and ultimately the underlying schemas responsible for these beliefs (Beck, 1979). That is, if pathological anxiety is a result of maladaptive threat schemas, then changing the structure of these schemas should result in symptom alleviation. Unfortunately, because of the unobservable nature of cognitive constructs, it is extremely difficult to establish causality when studying the mechanisms involved in cognitive therapy. The extent to which a schema or belief has been modified must be inferred through self-report measures such as Fear of Negative Evaluation or Irrational Beliefs Test (Mattick & Peters, 1988; Mattick, Peters, & Clarke, 1989). Responses to such measures may, in turn, be confounded with anxiety itself (Feske & Chambless, 1995). Although cognitive therapy sets out to change the structure and content of the clients' thoughts, there are no direct measures of the purported mechanisms and processes underlying cognitive therapy.

Nonetheless, there is a large body of evidence suggesting that changes in self-reported cognitive style may mediate treatment outcome. In the treatment of social phobia, for instance, Foa, Franklin, Perry, and Herbert (1996) showed that estimated social cost and degree of overestimation of negative social consequences was highly associated with symptom levels at post-treatment. Further, Hofmann (2004) compared social phobics receiving either cognitive-behavior group therapy, exposure group therapy, or wait-list control. The results showed changes in estimated social cost-mediated treatment effects in both treatment groups. Yet, only the CBT group continued to improve 6 months post-treatment. This work suggests that cognitive interventions lead to better maintenance of treatment gains, possibly mediated through changes in perceived social cost.

Several studies have also suggested that cognitive mediation plays a role in the treatment of panic disorder and specific phobias. There is ample evidence that changes in catastrophic thinking about panic predict treatment outcome (Chambless & Gracely, 1989; Clark, Salkovskis, Hackmann, Middleton, Anastasiades, & Geldeer, 1994; Margraf, Barlow, Clark, & Telch, 1993; Michelson, Marchione, Greenwald, Giantz, Marchione, & Telsa, 1990). Changes in negative cognitions have also been found to be correlated with phobic fear reduction (Shafran, Booth, & Rachman, 1993; Rachman & Whittal, 1989). Once again, however, the correlational nature of these findings limits the conclusions that can be drawn from this research. Because these correlations run across treatment modalities, it is difficult to identify which elements of treatment are responsible for the changes. It is also equally possible that fear reduction leads to cognitive change. Given this possibility, the role of cognitive change, including the mechanisms underlying such change, in the treatment of anxiety disorders remains unclear.

TREATMENT EFFICACY

In this section, we briefly review the literature on treatment outcome for behavioral and cognitive-behavioral interventions. We again take a broad approach to emphasize the take-home point—namely, that there is little evidence for superiority of behavioral over exclusively cognitive and cognitive-behavioral interventions. Virtually all efficacious intervention for anxiety disorders includes both cognitive and exposure-based procedures, with each of these procedures involving both cognitive and exposure-like elements.

Outcome of Exposure Therapy Across the Anxiety Disorders

Numerous studies have shown that exposure therapy is efficacious in the treatment of all anxiety disorders. For instance, in vivo exposure to internal feared cues (i.e., bodily sensations) and agoraphobic fears is highly effective in reducing symptoms of panic disorder and agoraphobia. A meta-analysis of 55 studies showed that pretreatment versus post-treatment effect sizes for panic disorder ranged from 0.79 to 1.09, whereas effect sizes for agoraphobic avoidance ranged from 1.38 to 1.48 (see Bakker, van Balkom, Spinhoven, Blaauw, & van Dyck, 1998, for a review; Westling & Öst, 1999; van Balkom, Bakker, Spinhoven, Blaauw, Smeenk, & Ruesnik, 1997). Moreover, imaginal exposure to intrusive thoughts or images is particularly effective in the treatment of OCD (Abramowitz, 1996; Foa, Steketee, Turner, & Fischer, 1980).

A meta-analytic review of 45 studies yielded a large pretreatment versus post-treatment effect size for exposure therapy for OCD (1.47; van Balkom, van Oppen, Vermeulen, van Dyck, Nauta, & Vorst, 1994). Similar large-effect sizes were found in a recent meta-analytic review of 13 studies for PTSD, with imaginal and/or in vivo exposure yielding to a pretreatment versus post-treatment effect size of 1.57 (Bradley, Greene, Russ, Dutra, & Westen, 2005). In vivo exposure therapy to circumscribed feared objects or situations has been found to be an effective form of treatment for specific phobias (Biran, Augusto, & Wilson, 1981; Biran & Wilson, 1981; Emmelkamp & Wessels, 1975) and social phobia (see Heimberg, 2002, for a review). Finally, virtual reality exposure therapy for some of the specific phobias (i.e., acrophobia, fear of flying, heights) has recently been shown to be as effective as in vivo exposure (Emmelkamp, Krijn, Hulsbosch, de Vries, Schuemie, & van der Mast, 2002; Rothbaum, Hodges, Anderson, Price, & Smith, 2002). Despite considerable reports attesting to the effectiveness of exposure therapy for anxiety disorders, approximately 10% to 30% of individuals do not benefit from it (Craske, 1999), and some experience a reemergence of fear and anxiety some time after having gone through successful treatment.

Outcome of Cognitive Interventions Across the Anxiety Disorders

Several researchers have compared cognitive therapy with applied relaxation in the treatment of generalized anxiety disorder (Arntz, 2003; Barlow, Rapee & Brown, 1992; Borkovec & Costello, 1993; Öst & Breitholtz, 2000). All studies tended to show immediate equivalence between the two treatments, with one study demonstrating superior outcome for cognitive therapy at 12-month follow-up. Also, Butler, Fennell, Robson, and Gelder (1991) evaluated cognitive therapy for generalized anxiety disorder (Beck et al., 1985) with a version of anxiety management minus any cognitive interventions. They found cognitive therapy to be superior both immediately post-treatment and at 6-month follow-up.

Other studies focused on comparing purely cognitive procedures to exposure-based treatments. For instance, Marks, Lovell, Noshirvani, Livanou, & Thrasher (1998) compared relaxation training, cognitive, behavioral, and cognitive-behavioral treatments for PTSD. Findings suggested that there were no major differences between cognitive, behavioral, and combined treatments at post-treatment and 6-month follow-up. Mattick, et al. (1989) evaluated exposure treatment, cognitive restructuring, and a combination of the two as treatments for social anxiety disorder. Results showed that all three conditions resulted in roughly equal gain, with the cognitive restructuring condition showing better improvements on tests of irrational beliefs and negative self-evaluation. In a similar manner, Taylor, Woody, Koch, McLean, Paterson, & Anderson (1997), in comparing cognitive and exposure-based treatments for social anxiety, found that, in the initial sessions of a treatment, cognitive restructuring produced superior gains compared to a generic filler treatment. In a related study, van Oppen, de Haan, van Balkom, Spinhoven, Hoogduin, & van Dyck (1995) compared exposure and response prevention (ERP) to a purely cognitive intervention for the treatment of OCD. Clients received six sessions of each, followed by 10 sessions of combined treatment. Results suggested that both interventions led to initial symptom reduction, with reduction continuing throughout the combined treatment portion of the study.

Findings appear to suggest equivalence between cognitive and exposure-based treatments, indicating that adding cognitive components to exposure treatments provides little incremental utility. Available outcome literature for cognitive therapy may be difficult to interpret, however, as many studies investigating interventions derived from cognitive therapy have failed to explicitly disentangle these interventions from traditional behavioral interventions (i.e., exposure therapy). A rather stark example is the use of behavioral tests of negative cognitions, which require clients to expose themselves to their feared situations, including distressing thoughts, memories, and the like (e.g., Clark, et al., 1999). Also, the simple process of examining maladaptive cognitions in session may function as imaginal exposure. It is important to note here that cognitive theory views exposure to fearful events as having the fundamental purpose of allowing individuals an opportunity to identify and dispute their cognitive distortions. Although exposure interventions allow for new corrective emotional learning via extinction of excessive fear and anxiety, the therapeutic process of change from a cognitive theory standpoint occurs via changes in cognition that come about through cognitive restructuring. Yet, at a conceptual level, it is exceedingly difficult to evaluate procedures specific to cognitive theory in such investigations, as all could be conceptualized as involving exposure elements. The same is true of exposure-based procedures, wherein extinction and approach behavior likely involves thinking in verbally able organisms. Still, a handful of studies have carefully tested the contribution of purely cognitive interventions, and none have shown that these interventions are superior to exposure-based behavioral interventions (e.g., Emmelkamp & Mersch, 1982; Emmelkamp, van der Helm, van Zanten, & Plochg, 1980).

Efficacy of Combined Cognitive-Behavioral Treatments

CBT refers to the integration of both behavioral and cognitive intervention strategies in manualized treatment protocols. Such integrated treatment packages exist for each of the DSM-defined anxiety disorders. Although cognitive and behavioral intervention components involve direct attempts to reduce maladaptive thoughts, emotions, and behavior that characterize anxiety-related disorders, each differ in theory, therapeutic strategies of change, and targeted processes.

With regard to targeted processes, behavioral interventions focus on alleviating excessive fear and anxiety, including associated avoidance and escape behavior, by targeting them directly via exposure-based strategies. The added cognitive components target problematic thre at appraisals, beliefs, and thinking patterns that are thought to exacerbate and maintain anxiety problems (Brewin, 1996). Collectively, integrated CBT packages teach anxious individuals behavioral and cognitive competencies needed to function more adaptively in their lives. More specifically, the most common therapeutic techniques used in such interventions involve exposure to the feared stimuli to reverse patterns of escape and avoidance, and cognitive restructuring to alter irrational thoughts and beliefs (Heimberg, 2002).

Currently, CBT is the gold standard for the treatment of anxiety disorders. Indeed, CBT has been judged to meet empirical standards of demonstrated efficacy for panic disorder, agoraphobia, social phobia, generalized anxiety disorder, OCD, and specific phobia (Chambless & Ollendick, 2001). Some widely used CBT packages for anxiety disorders include *Master of Your Anxiety and Panic* (MAP-3; Barlow & Craske, 2000), *Cognitive-Behavioral Group Treatment for Social Phobia* (CBGT; Heimberg, Dodge, Hope, Kennedy, Zollo, & Becker, 1990), and *Mastery of Your Anxiety and Worry* (MAW) for generalized anxiety disorder (Craske, Barlow, & O'Leary, 1992). These treatment packages typically contain a combination of exposure-based and more explicitly cognitive strategies.

Across the anxiety disorders, CBT tends to yield relatively large pretreatment versus post-treatment effect sizes. For instance, CBT for panic disorder (i.e., involving interoceptive and situational exposure, cognitive restructuring, and/or relaxation) has yielded a mean effect size (ES) of 0.68 in a meta-analysis of 19 studies (Gould, Otto, & Pollack, 1995). A meta-analytic review of 16 studies comparing the efficacy of cognitive-behavioral treatment (i.e., exposure plus cognitive restructuring) with exposure and cognitive restructuring alone for social phobia suggested that exposure therapy either alone (ES = 0.89) or in combination with cognitive restructuring (*ES* = 0.80) is somewhat more effective than cognitive restructuring alone (*ES* = 0.60; Gould, Buckminster, Pollack, Otto, & Yap, 1997). With respect to generalized anxiety disorder, cognitive-behavioral treatment has been found to be more effective than behavioral or cognitive interventions with effect sizes in 11 studies ranging from 0.91 to 1.01 (Borkovec & Whisman, 1996; Butler, et al., 1991; Gould, Otto, Pollack, & Yap, 1997). Similarly, CBT and exposure and response prevention (ERP) have demonstrated efficacy in the treatment for OCD, with a recent meta analysis showing mean effect sizes ranging from 1.39 for CBT (*n* = 4) to 1.53 for ERP (*n* = 16; see Abramowitz, Foa, & Franklin, 2002; Eddy, Dutra, Bradley, & Westen, 2004). Finally, combined behavioral and cognitive treatment procedures (i.e., CBT: exposure, cognitive restructuring, management skills) for post-traumatic stress disorder has been shown to be effective (*ES* = 1.27; van Etten & Taylor, 1998). The overwhelming weight of evidence here suggests that CBT works for a range of anxiety disorders.

Summary and Evaluation: Toward a New Perspective

During the last 40 years, behavior therapy has led the development of empirically derived and time-limited psychological interventions to assist those suffering from anxiety and fear-related problems. Of these interventions, several randomized, controlled clinical trials have established the efficacy of CBTs and have shown that CBTs are effective regardless of the anxiety disorder. Most of these interventions now exist in the form of manuals and have been remarkably successful. Yet, all is not well.

Although behavioral and CBTs are the treatments of choice for anxiety disorders (Barlow, 2002), there is a growing consensus that more can be done and needs to be done to push the efficacy ceiling. Despite some impressive short-term gains, we are still far from producing overwhelming success rates in terms of long-term recovery and relapse prevention. CBTs are still far from curative. A significant number of anxiety sufferers fail to respond to CBTs, and more people than we would like to admit never even start treatment once they hear what it involves

(Becker & Zayfert, 2001). Many others will drop out before completing treatment. Of those who complete treatment, many will ultimately experience relapse and require additional treatment. It is simply not the case that we have reached the efficacy ceiling with regard to CBTs for anxiety disorders (Barlow, et al., 2004; Foa & Emmelkamp, 1983; Foa & Kozak, 1997a). Far from it. We can and should do better. In fact, we must do better.

Meeting this challenge will require rethinking some of the basic assumptions guiding our views of anxiety-related problems and their treatment. This is precisely what is happening now with newer third-generation behavior therapies that focus on common processes that transform normal fear and anxiety into the life-shattering problems that characterize the anxiety disorders. The remainder of this chapter provides some background for this work and a new perspective.

Critical Evaluation and Evolution

For better or for worse, CBTs have become the treatments of choice for anxiety disorders. Such treatments focus heavily on symptom alleviation as a therapeutic goal, are matched to specific DSM-defined anxiety disorders, and are set within a mastery and control framework. Such treatments imply several things.

First, they suggest that the "symptoms" are the problem. This perspective, by the way, is similar to how clients tend to view their problems (at least early on in therapy). In this sense, CBT therapists and clients appear to be in agreement that symptoms of anxiety cause impairment and suffering. If this were the whole story, then an obvious treatment strategy would be to target the symptoms. Yet there is usually a more important life to be lived behind the symptoms. It is this "living" that is of deep concern to clients, as it is to most human beings. In the past, traditional CBT has not paid sufficient attention to this living and, as a consequence, may have missed important aspects of a person's life situation. It is for this reason that acceptance-based approaches put living front and center of the therapeutic stage.

Second, we must provide a more process-oriented answer to this question: What are the so-called symptoms of anxiety a sign of? If we refer to the problem responses that our clients seek treatment for as symptoms of anxiety, then we must explain what the disorder is. Calling the disorder *anxiety* sounds reasonable, but it is not a viable solution. A problem response (symptom) cannot define a disorder and be a symptom of the disorder at the same time (Williams, 2004). The alternative we suggest in this chapter is to go after the processes that turn normal anxiety into the often life-shattering problems we refer to as anxiety disorders and then target those processes during treatment.

Third, the strategy of matching treatments to different anxiety disorders suggests that the anxiety disorders are truly distinct and thus, warrant different approaches for each. Such differences are obvious at the phenomenological level, particularly if one focuses on events that elicit fear and anxiety across the anxiety disorders. This issue alone is interesting itself and certainly deserves more comment than space would allow for here. Most therapists, however, are quick to point out the high degree of functional and symptom overlap across the presumably different anxiety disorders. For instance, although panic attacks occur most frequently in persons with panic disorder (PD), they also can and do occur in persons with all other anxiety disorders (Barlow, 2002). That similar treatment technologies work for different anxiety disorders (e.g., exposure, cognitive restructuring, relaxation) is a further indication that the disorders are more similar than they have been made out to be. Most important, the tendency to avoid and escape from fear and anxiety is characteristic of just about every individual diagnosed with an anxiety-related disorder (see Salters-Pedneault, Tull, & Roemer, 2004, for a review). The specific types of escape and avoidance behavior may differ at a phenomenological level, but the basic function of those behaviors is the same: they serve to reduce fear and anxiety and get the person out of the situation where he or she experiences fear and anxiety.

There is also considerable overlap between anxiety disorders and major mood disorders (see Mineka, Watson, & Clark, 1998, for a review). For instance, Barlow and colleagues (2004) report that 55% of patients with a principal anxiety or mood disorder had at least 1 other additional anxiety or depressive disorder at the time of assessment. In the majority of cases of coexisting anxiety and depression, anxiety disorders preceded rather than followed the onset of mood disorders. The observable overlapping features of the various anxiety disorders, as well as the large co-occurrence of anxiety and mood disorders, point to a more basic fundamental and functional overlap at the process level that is at the heart of all anxiety disorders: rigid and excessive attempts to avoid experiencing anxiety and unpleasant private content. It is interesting that this perspective has actually been gaining ground in CBT, too. For instance, Barlow has recently proposed a unified treatment protocol and modular approach directed at the core features of all anxiety and related emotional disorders, with the goal of condensing the existing various versions of CBT to one strategic approach that targets those core features (Barlow, et al., 2004). In subsequent sections, we present empirical support for the powerful and self-defeating impact of avoiding negative affect as the core pathological process that fuels all anxiety disorders.

Finally, virtually all cognitive-behavioral treatments are cast within a mastery and symptom control framework. The chief therapeutic goal of such interventions is to teach clients more effective ways to gain control over their anxiety, fear, and related symptoms. Again, this is precisely what clients have come to expect from therapy and a posture that most clients are all too familiar with by the time they enter therapy. That is, clients have tried this or that to master and control their anxiety and fear, often without much success. Now, they expect therapists to provide them with new, "better," gold-plated strategies to do essentially more of the same, hoping that such strategies will be more workable than those they have tried in the past. As we will suggest, this mastery and control agenda is unnecessary and may even be counterproductive. Thoughts and emotions need not be managed to live a valued and meaningful life. Human experience tells us as much. Management and control of our internal private world is not a necessary prerequisite for living a meaningful life.

Our intent is to suggest ways that we can improve on existing CBT interventions while retaining those components of CBT that have clearly proven effective, such as exposure exercises and strategies to counteract avoidance behavior. Helping clients to improve their life situation, however, may require that we rethink the mastery and control change agenda within standard CBTs for anxiety disorders.

Toward a New Behavioral Perspective

The roots of exposure-based interventions are firmly planted in fear-learning research and therapy. Yet, numerous criticisms have been raised about the clinical relevance of fear conditioning research as a model of anxiety disorders. Most of these have followed from an oversimplified view of conditioning preparations and processes. Our intent here is not to redress all of these criticisms (e.g., Marks, 1981; Menzies & Clarke, 1995; Rachman, 1977, 1991), as none of them hold up in light of contemporary learning theory (Bouton, et al., 2001; Forsyth & Eifert, 1996a, 1996b, 1998a, 1998b; Mineka & Zinbarg, 1996). That is, all but one.

As we see it, the chief challenge facing Pavlovian conditioning research is in explaining how an entirely functional and ubiquitous learning process (i.e., conditioning), coupled with equally functional and ubiquitous emotional responses (i.e., fear and anxiety) would send some individuals down the path to an anxiety disorder and not others (cf. Forsyth, et al., 2005). This issue is a bit different than asking whether individual differences moderate fear learning (Eysenck, 1967; 1976; Mineka & Zinbarg, 1996), including events occurring before, during, and after conditioning (e.g., latent inhibition, context). Rather, the question here is about how conditioning itself, when placed in the context of fear, would yield an anxiety disorder and not simply conditioned fear, anxiety, or avoidance that most humans have experienced at some point in their lives. Put simply, what makes fear conditioning helpful in some contexts and problematic in others?

When fear is evoked, for instance, the typical acute consequence is disruption and narrowing of ongoing behavior. Such disruptions function to ready organisms to take immediate action to prepare for, and subsequently to escape from or avoid, potential sources of threat. It makes sense to learn to fear stimuli that have been associated with aversive consequences, and particularly aversive emotional states, even when people are exposed to contingencies between arbitrary stimuli and aversive unconditioned stimuli (UCSs). In fact, evolutionarily it would be exceedingly costly for organisms to fail to show conditioned fear and hence, fail to learn from aversive experiences. These actions function to mobilize all mammals to take appropriate action in response to threat or danger and thus contribute in some sense to survival. After aversive experiences, most mammals will actively avoid exposing themselves to stimuli that predict aversive responses, in part, because it makes adaptive sense to do so. Our challenge then is to explain the parameters and processes that transform such behavior from being adaptive in some contexts to maladaptive or dysfunctional in others.

When Fear Learning Becomes Problematic

Classical fear conditioning emerged as a model of anxiety disorders largely because of Watson and Rayner's (1920) dramatic demonstration of fear acquisition in Little Albert. The correspondence between the behavior of Albert and the phobias and other anxiety problems was striking and led to the recognition of a process by which fear could be acquired. Yet, the recognition of a process should not be confused with saying that fear learning itself is problematic or that fear learning is an adequate analogue of phobias or anxiety disorders. Under the circumstances, Albert behaved in accord with the history he was provided. There were no costs associated with his conditioned fear or his avoidant behavior. By contrast, fear learning and avoidance across the anxiety disorders are typically associated with costs, in large part, because such behavior is set within a context of powerful competing approach contingencies (see Hayes, 1976). Such competing contingencies are typically reflected in the reasons anxious clients seek treatment (e.g., "My fear of driving is driving my husband crazy," or "I just don't like feeling anxious," or "I can't drive to work because I might have a panic attack").

This dual-component view suggests that fear learning becomes problematic only when it (1) removes access to reinforcing events, and/or (2) puts the individual in contact with aversive events. The resulting avoidance, in turn, becomes disruptive when competing contingencies supporting (1) and/or (2) are present. Thus, a pedestrian who hears the blare of a horn of an oncoming car and jumps out of the way would likely experience fear, some conditioning, and clearly demonstrates avoidance. Yet, this person would not be considered phobic, in part because there are few or no approach contingencies in this situation (Costello, 1970; Hayes, 1976). In fact, approach in this context (running into the street) would be extremely punishing. This situation is analogous to animal avoidance learning paradigms wherein a signal is followed by the emission of an avoidance response or else the onset of an aversive stimulus. Such behaviors, as Hayes (1976) points out, are not phobic because there is no competing approach element in the situation. Although etiologically all phobic behavior is avoidance behavior, it is not true that all avoidance behavior is phobic behavior (see Hayes, 1976), nor is it true that all fear learning is phobic learning (cf. Forsyth, et al., 2005).

From a more functional process-oriented perspective, classical fear conditioning is recognized as an enormously powerful means of altering the functions of a range of events and directing behavior as a consequence. Yet, such learning cannot account for the development of an anxiety disorder except under the most extreme and unusual circumstances. If there are no strong approach contingencies in the situation (i.e., approach-avoidance conflict), then fear learning is just fear learning and avoidance is simply avoidance, not a phobia or an anxiety disorder. The implications of this account have yet to be fully tested in human fear conditioning analogues but have been demonstrated reliably in animal research (e.g., see Hayes, Lattal, & Myerson, 1979). Such tests in humans present a challenge, in part, because humans can expand the range and scope of approach-avoidance contingencies, including classical conditioning processes, via language and verbal behavior.

Verbal Processes and Disordered Fear

Humans can respond to approach-avoidance contingencies verbally and symbolically without being confronted with the actual contingencies directly. Thus, a person who learns that fear is bad and must be managed before being able to do important tasks (e.g., go to work, attend a child's play—all approach contingencies) may, in turn, struggle to manage the emotional response first to engage in effective actions second. This type of learning can take approach-avoidance conflict to a new level of complexity and requires consideration of what humans do to manage the experience and expression of emotions. As we will indicate, this is a key difference between nonhuman animals and humans and one that is accounted for, in large part, by social contingencies and the capacity for humans to engage in complex verbally mediated relations, including rule-governed verbal behavior. Such capacities make it possible for humans to engage in self and emotion regulatory actions that are not possible to the same degree in nonverbal organisms, including primates.

Despite ample evidence (e.g., Cook & Mineka, 1991; Suomi, 1999) that primates experience and express pain and chronic states of anxious arousal, there is no indication that they *regulate the experience of having pain and anxiety*. For instance, rhesus monkeys exposed to uncontrollable and unpredictable aversive stimulation experience alarm responses followed by long-term anxious arousal. Primates will also learn to avoid the source and context of aversive stimulation, but as best we can tell, they do not act deliberately and purposefully to regulate their emotional experience. Humans, by contrast, can and do suffer about their own emotional pain and histories by responding to conditioned responses with evaluative verbal behavior and thinking (e.g., "God, this is awful," "I'm going to pass out") and by engaging in efforts to suppress, avoid, or escape from their emotional pain and related thoughts. Thus, humans can become fearful of fear, depressed about anxiety, worried about the future, agonize about the past, and struggle to avoid and escape from unpleasant thoughts, images, sensations, feelings, behavioral tendencies, and the circumstances that have evoked them or those that *may* evoke them in the future. The capacity of language, coupled with powerful social contingencies regarding the experience and expression of emotion, make this possible.

The experience and expression of emotion, as well as the implications of regulating emotional experience for success and personal happiness (Gross, 1998; Hayes, et al., 1999), are largely shaped by social and cultural conventions and contact with other human beings. Much of this learning is heavily dependent on complex forms of relational learning that is entailed in language and verbal-symbolic behavior (Forsyth, 2000; Forsyth, et al., 2005; Forsyth & Eifert, 1996b; Friman, Hayes, & Wilson, 1998). Language serves important symbolic functions by providing humans with emotional experiences without exposure to the actual physical stimuli or events that ordinarily elicit those responses (Staats & Eifert, 1990). For instance, suppose a person has learned to associate fear with "danger," "unpredictability," and "sudden, quick movements" and actions such as "running away." Suppose also that this person has no previous negative history with snakes but hears someone say that snakes make sudden, quick movements. Although this person has not been told to be fearful of snakes, they may now quickly derive that snakes are something to be afraid of, without explicit reinforcement for doing so. They may also derive that snakes are unpredictable and dangerous, too. Although such relations may seem intuitively obvious, the learning that gives rise to such relational capacities is not.

Such verbal-relational tendencies are socialized and emerge by about the age of two and are fundamentally built into human language and cognition (for a more detailed account of relational learning processes, see Hayes, Barnes-Holmes, & Roche, 2001). Such learning begins with an extensive history of reinforcement for relating many stimuli in many different ways based largely on their formal stimulus properties (e.g., beach ball is a ball, a basketball is a ball), and thereafter through more indirect relations (e.g., spoken word "ball" is the same as written word "ball" and other physical examples of balls and not balls). Such a history, in turn, makes it possible for humans to relate other, novel stimuli in numerous ways without being taught to do so (see Blackledge, 2003). Thus, the person described in the example earlier may respond with fear, run away, and may avoid going back into the woods in the future after hearing someone say, "I saw a snake in the woods once." The woods also may become dangerous, unpredictable, and a place that evokes fear. Such learning, in this example, was established indirectly and almost entirely via arbitrary verbal relations. Arbitrary here simply means that the new relations are not dependent on the stimulus properties of the relata (e.g., the woods are not more or less snaky) but rather, established by social convention.

Language Entangles Humans in a Struggle with Emotions

The language-based capacity for humans to evaluate and respond relationally to their own evaluations, thoughts, and feelings with more evaluations also makes it possible for humans to get entangled in a struggle with their own emotions while acting not to have them (Forsyth, et al., 2005). With the preceding example, one can quite literally try to run away from the experience of fear and a host of events with which it might be arbitrarily related without being taught to do so. That is, the experience of fear can now be established via derived relations with many other events, including those that entail strong approach contingencies. Indeed, several studies have shown transfer of fear and avoidance functions, including many other stimulus functions (e.g., discriminative, approach), after a history of learning relations between arbitrary stimuli (e.g., A = B = C; see Augustson & Dougher, 1997; Dougher, Augustson, Markham, Greenway, & Wulfert, 1994). What is interesting about this work is that it shows how language can establish relations between events that are not taught directly. Thus, if painful shock is associated with C, it is likely that A and B will also evoke conditioned emotional responses. This has been demonstrated not only with fear, but also avoidance, numerous other functions (e.g., sexual arousal), and with classes involving more than three members (see Hayes, et al., 2001, for a detailed account).

Collectively, this work points to the kinds of histories that may transform the experience of a sudden, quick movement of the heart into "this is dangerous" and "I might be dying" without direct contact with the aversive contingency (i.e., death). It also points to how language may function to fuse verbal processes with the formal properties of private and public events. When such fusion occurs, a thought is no longer just a thought, and a word is no longer just a sound; rather, actual events can become fused with the words used to describe them, and thus, humans can respond to words about some event as if we were responding to the actual event. Consequently, humans can establish contingencies almost entirely through verbal processes (e.g., "don't touch the hot stove or you'll get burned") and can respond to those verbal constructions even when faced with powerful contradictory natural contingencies (e.g., "I might get 'burned' if I trust that person," meaning hurt).

Although there is evidence that nonverbal organisms can learn relational responses based on the formal properties of relata (e.g., pick a larger object when presented with multiple different objects of varying size and shape), they cannot make more complex relational responses (e.g., pick the *scariest* object when presented with a picture of the moon, a tree, and a small wasp). A nonverbal animal would not be able to respond above chance, whereas a verbally sophisticated human would likely choose the wasp. Here, "scary" is not a formal stimulus property involving any of the five senses but rather, a stimulus property that has been given arbitrary significance by the social verbal community (cf. Blackledge, 2003; Hayes, et al., 2001). One outcome of this process is the tendency to regulate aversive emotional experience so as to suppress, control, avoid, or escape from it. Another is that language processes can greatly expand the scope of limited fear-learning experiences (see earlier example). Both point to the powerful role of socially mediated contingencies in shaping the experience and expression of emotion. When such contingencies are juxtaposed with classical conditioning contingencies, otherwise adaptive fear learning processes can lead some individuals down the path of developing an anxiety disorder (Forsyth, et al., 2005). It is to a discussion of this view that we now turn.

EMOTION REGULATION AND THE ANXIETY DISORDERS

There are several accounts to explain the shift from normal to clinically disordered fear. Most accounts share two notions. First, fear and anxiety are somehow dysregulated, such that either emotional response occurs too frequently, too intensely, or for too long. Second, anxiety and fear are evoked by cues that do not demand such responses. That is, fear and anxiety are evoked in the absence of real threat. Thus, the combination of dysregulated emotion occurring in contexts that do not call for an anxious response may result in wide-ranging functional impairment that CBTs for anxiety disorders target via some combination of cognitive restructuring and exposure-based strategies (Barlow, 2002; Barlow, et al., 2004).

The Nature of Emotion Regulation

Emotion regulation simply refers to a heterogeneous set of actions that are designed to influence "which emotions we have, when we have them, and how we experience and express them" (Gross, 2002, p. 282; see also Gross, 1998). Such actions include, but are not limited to, phenomena captured by terms such as reappraisal, distraction, avoidance, escape, suppression, emotion and problem-focused coping, and use of substances to enhance or blunt emotional experience. Each of these domains subsumes numerous actions that can be applied to both positive and negative emotional states (Parrott, 1993). In the context of aversive emotional states, emotion regulatory processes share a common functional goal, namely to avoid or minimize the frequency, intensity, duration, or situational occurrence of internal feeling states, associated thoughts, and physiological processes (e.g., fear and anxiety). Some regulatory processes may be relatively autonomic or habitual, occurring in or outside of awareness (e.g., selective attention), whereas others may be more purposeful or deliberate (e.g., blame, rumination, suppression, avoidance). Most processes, however, can be characterized by actions (i.e., automatic or controlled) that aim to alter the form or frequency of events that may precede an emotional response, or the consequences of emotional responding, including the very experience of the emotional response itself. The former has been described as antecedent-focused emotion regulation, whereas the later refers to response-focused emotion regulation.

The emerging field of emotion regulation research and theory aims to bring together numerous processes that are involved in the experience, expression, and modulation of emotion, including the positive and negative consequences of emotion regulation itself (e.g., achievement of goals, restriction in life functioning). That is, emotion regulation is best thought of as a broad term that characterizes a range of well-established psychological phenomena that have been shown to influence the experience and expression of emotion. Although emotion regulation is itself not a dysfunctional process, it can become dysfunctional when the emotions concerned cannot and need not be regulated and when the very act of emotion regulation gets in the way of meaningful life activities (i.e., regulation that competes with powerful approach contingencies; see Hayes, 1976). It is for these and other reasons that the very topic of emotion regulation is gaining currency in psychopathology research (Barlow, et al., 2004; Eifert & Forsyth, 2005) and mental health care more generally (Blackledge & Hayes, 2001; Gross & Muñoz, 1995).

Our consensual model of emotion regulation in a fear-learning context (see Forsyth, et al., 2006, for details) suggests that humans may regulate the antecedents and consequences of emotions. Antecedents, in the case of anxiety disorders, may include situations where anxiety and fear are likely to occur, bodily and environmental cues that tend to evoke such reactions, whether emotionally relevant information is attended to, and how such information is evaluated or appraised (e.g., "this isn't so bad," or "I can't get through this"). In Pavlovian conditioning terms, the relevant antecedents would be conditional stimuli (CSs), and quite possibly unconditional stimuli (UCSs), and the contexts where both may occur. Strategies used to regulate emotions on the front end are important precisely because how one responds to emotional inputs, and particularly the verbal evaluation of those inputs (i.e., this is dangerous, awful, harmful), affects the emotional consequences that may follow. Thus, escalation of the emotional sequence can be attenuated or avoided altogether depending on how one manages the antecedents that may evoke or occasion emotional experience.

Once the emotion occurs, regulation efforts tend to focus on the intensity, duration, and general quality of the emotional response and its consequences. Such response-focused regulation strategies may involve taking a break, relaxation, deep breathing, distraction, affiliating with others, or doing something pleasant. There is nothing disordered about such strategies when applied in a context-sensitive and flexible manner. Problems may arise when persons make rigid efforts to down-regulate the cognitive, physiological, or behavioral components of negative emotions when such efforts are unnecessary to engage competing approach contingencies. Such down-regulation strategies are often subtle and idiosyncratic in persons suffering from anxiety disorders and usually take the form of suppression, control, avoidance, or escape (Barlow, 2002; Barlow, et al., 2004).

Healthy and Unhealthy Varieties of Emotion Regulation

Historically, the field of emotion regulation research and theory has been agnostic with regard to the positive and negative consequences of emotion regulation strategies for psychological health and wellness. Increasingly, however, we are learning that certain forms of emotion regulation may be healthier than others and that some may produce human suffering. We briefly summarize findings from this literature that are relevant to a better understanding of how emotion regulation may make fear and fear learning problematic.

Antecedent-Focused Regulation

Antecedent forms of emotion regulation characterize actions occurring before emotional response tendencies are fully engaged. The most studied strategy, reappraisal, refers to verbal-linguistic actions that change the meaning of an emotion-eliciting situation for better or worse (Lazarus & Alfert, 1964). Research suggests that positive reappraisal is a flexible and effective means of minimizing the negative impact of an aversive event (Gross, 1998, 2002). This strategy subsumes numerous actions (e.g., sense making, acceptance) with the goal of reframing an emotion-eliciting situation in less emotional terms. Less functional antecedent strategies include avoidance, distraction, suppression, and escape.

Studies suggest that positive reappraisal strategies are less likely to be used by depressed and anxious persons relative to healthy controls and that infrequent use of such strategies in healthy adolescents is associated with more depressive and anxious symptoms (Garnefski & Spinhoven, 2001). Others have shown that reappraisal is less emotionally and cognitively costly relative to suppression and avoidance and that chronic use of suppression impairs memory for emotional information even after controlling for neuroticism and social desirability (e.g., see Richards & Gross, 1999, 2000). Ochsner and colleagues (2002, 2004) showed that reappraisal, like other emotion regulatory strategies, draws heavily on verbal linguistic processes and that these processes may up- or down-regulate amygdala activity. This circuitry, in turn, is strongly implicated in fear learning (e.g., LeDoux, 2000).

Response and Consequence-Focused Regulation

Studies have demonstrated that suppression of aversive emotions does not provide relief from the psychological experience of that emotion. In fact, just the opposite tends to occur; the emotion becomes stronger and more salient, resulting in increased sympathetic nervous system activity (e.g., cardiovascular and electrodermal response; Gross & Levenson, 1997) and a range of undesired psychological content in the suppressor, as well as those interacting with him or her (see Butler & Gross, 2004, for a review).

Other research suggests that attempts to suppress and control unwanted thoughts and feelings can result in *more* unwanted thoughts and emotions (Wegner, 1994; see also Purdon, 1999, for a review). Moreover, emotion suppression has been shown to contribute to suffering and pain (Hayes, et al., 1999), distress and restriction in life functioning (Marx & Sloan, 2002), diminished contact with meaningful and valued life activities, and poorer overall quality of life (Hayes, 2004a; Hayes, Wilson, Gifford, Follette, & Strosahl, 1996; Hayes, Follette, & Linehan, 2004). Individuals who chronically engage in suppression also tend to report more negative experiences and fewer positive ones (Gross & John, 2003). Such relations appear to be completely mediated by inauthenticity

(John & Gross, 2004), a construct similar to lack of self-acceptance (Hayes, et al., 1999).

The emerging consensus here is that response-focused emotion regulation requires considerable effort, only works to a point, and is counterproductive when the emotions are intense and highly aversive. Thus, reacting to our own reactions can actually amplify those reactions in a vicious self-perpetuating cycle, resulting in an increase of the very emotion that is undesired, particularly in contexts or situations where the regulation of emotion would be most desired (Craske, Miller, Rotunda, & Barlow, 1990).

The Importance of Flexibility

Functional accounts of emotion regulation and other behavioral processes demand attention to contextual factors. In this view, the utility of emotion regulation depends on whether or not it works to achieve desired outcomes and whether it can be flexibly applied depending on the context. That is, because emotion regulation characterizes socially acquired behaviors (not immutable traits), it ought to be sensitive to contextual determinants. For instance, positive reappraisal seems like a useful strategy to defuse or minimize the impact of an aversive emotion compared to avoidance, suppression, and control. Yet, this does not mean that positive reappraisal should be uniformly applied where it does not work. For example, it would not seem advantageous for a person to remain in a highly aversive situation using positive reappraisal when other behavioral options are clearly more viable. Flexibility, or the ability to discriminate between a range of stimuli in and outside a context, seems crucial in any account of the functional utility of emotion regulation strategies in a fear-learning context. In fact, the failure of discrimination—or the tendency to regulate emotions indiscriminately or chronically in a traitlike fashion—is emerging as a core theme that appears to distinguish problematic from more functional forms of emotion regulation and poorer long-term adjustment (Bonanno, Papa, LaLande, Westphal, & Coifman, 2004; John & Gross, 2004).

Language processes can facilitate or interfere with discrimination and contingency-shaped responding (see Hayes, 2004b, for a detailed account). For instance, rules can make learning contingencies more rapid, or they can interfere with learning contingency relations (e.g., Hayes, Brownstein, Zettle, Rosenfarb, & Korn, 1986). The behavioral account of human inflexibility has focused on how language processes diminish contact with approach contingencies by establishing patterns of self and emotion regulation as prerequisites for effective action (Zettle & Hayes, 1982). Experiential avoidance, a recent term used to describe this tendency, refers to behaviors to alter the frequency, duration, or form of unwanted private events (i.e., thoughts, feelings, and physical sensations) and the cues and situations that occasion them (Hayes, et al., 1999). This is a technical definition as much as it is a functional definition. Experiential avoidance characterizes a set of actions that tend to be more rule-governed than contingency shaped. Thus, it yields behaviors that appear more rigid than circumstances warrant.

Because experiential avoidance entails the very same set of processes that can make emotion and thought regulation problematic, it is thought to contribute to numerous problems associated with unwanted psychological and emotional content (Hayes, et al., 1996). In fact, persons so predisposed will likely experience approach-avoidance conflicts across numerous situations for the simple reason that experiential avoidance is rigidly and inflexibly applied and is thus pitted against numerous life contingencies (verbally and nonverbally derived) that demand approach (e.g., going to work, running errands, taking a vacation, being with people).

For instance, persons who use chronic suppression tend to report feeling a sense of incongruence between the private and outer behavior, fear being accepted by others, and thus, use suppression in relationships they care about and are afraid to lose (see John & Gross, 2004, for a review). This example illustrates how emotion regulation interfaces with several verbally derived approach-avoidance conflicts. It also suggests how this tendency may be a potentially self-destructive process that is associated with significant costs and a range of negative outcomes, including functional impairment in interpersonal, social, and occupational domains, overall poorer quality of life (Gross, 1998; Hayes, et al., 1996; Pennebaker & Beall, 1986; Quilty, Van Ameringen, Mancini, Oakman, & Farvolden, 2003), and even illness and greater mortality risk (Denollet, Sys, Stoobant, Rombouts, Gillebert, & Brutsaert, 1996).

The question, then, is why do we avoid thoughts and feelings? From an emotion-regulation perspective, social learning creates a context where forms of experiential avoidance and nonacceptance can thrive (Hayes, et al., 1999). Emotion regulation is used as evidence of maturity, emotional stability, health and wellness, success, fulfillment, and happiness. We typically do not question what life might be like if unpleasant emotions and thoughts were treated simply as events to be experienced as part of being fully human and not as events that must be managed and controlled (cf. Blackledge & Hayes, 2001). We do not question the cultural mandate that equates failures of emotional regulation with suffering and misery and connects "positive" thoughts and feelings with an ability to engage life to its fullest. In this cultural context, anxious thoughts and feelings become obstacles to living and the achievement of valued goals. They are reasonable justifications for inaction and quite often fused with a sense of self worth (e.g., "I'm not good enough," "I am broken"). It follows that unwanted feelings and thoughts must be managed and controlled (e.g., "I need to be fixed before I can do what matters to me"), even at significant cost to the individual.

Paradoxically, the first step toward healthy emotional regulation may involve fostering greater discrimination and less rule-governed behavior, particularly as applied to regulating unwanted emotional experiences. Evidence suggests that this stance puts humans (and most nonverbal organisms) in a much better position to exert control where they have it, namely in responding to natural contingencies. We expand on this next, by showing how experiential avoidance may function to maintain disordered experiences of anxiety and fear and serve as an experiential risk factor for the development and maintenance of anxiety disorders.

Experiential Avoidance: A Learned and Potentially Toxic Form of Emotion Regulation

Experiential avoidance is thought to function as a core psychological diathesis—a way of relating with oneself and the world—underlying the development and maintenance of anxiety disorders and several other forms of psychopathology (Blackledge & Hayes, 2001; Hayes, et al., 1996; Hayes & Wilson, 1993, 1994). It is a process related to how we go about influencing the emotions we have, when we have them, and how we experience and express them. As such, experiential avoidance is best described as an overarching emotion regulation strategy (see Gross, 1998) that differs from largely inherited biological individual differences that may make persons more vulnerable to developing an anxiety disorder (e.g., an overly active behavioral inhibition system [Gray, 1990]; temperament [Kagan, 1989]; neuroticism [Eysenck, 1967]; Eysenck & Rachman [1965]).

Although Gray (1990) and Kagan and Snidman (1999) readily acknowledge the importance of environmental variation in activating and modulating the influence of behavioral inhibition and temperament, they also emphasize the strong heritable components and identified a number of associated brain structures and neurophysiological correlates. Neuroticism is likewise thought of as an important individual difference predisposition—a proxy for biological dysregulation—that co-varies with the tendency to be more or less emotionally reactive (Eysenck, 1967; Flint, 2004; Gross, Sutton, & Ketelaar, 1998; Larsen & Ketelaar, 1998; Tellegen, 1985). Such tendencies describe emotionality, whereas emotion regulation describes how and why emotions direct or disrupt a range of psychological, physiological, and sociobehavioral processes (cf. Blair, Denham, Kochanoff, & Whipple, 2004).

Temperament and other biological individual differences are clearly important in conferring risk for anxiety pathology. Yet, it is important to recognize that the tendency to be more or less emotional is not necessarily problematic unless one is willing to claim that emotions are somehow problematic. Indeed, the tendency to regulate emotions is only modestly related with baseline individual difference domains such as neuroticism (e.g., $r = .03$; see Gross & John, 2003) and extraversion (John & Srivastava, 1999). Such weak relations suggest that the tendency to suppress, and to engage in experiential avoidance more generally, does not occur simply because persons experience more negative affect or negative emotions that need to be regulated. Estimates of the additive and nonadditive heritability of neuroticism are low and comparable to other complex human traits (27% to 31% and 14% to 17%, respectively; see Flint, 2004, for a review). Nonetheless, it remains to be seen whether temperamental factors (e.g., neuroticism, behavioral inhibition) interface with (1) contingencies that help establish less functional forms of emotion regulation, such as a rigid use of avoidance-oriented coping strategies when faced with aversive life events (see Leen-Feldner, Zvolensky, Feldner, & Lejuez, 2004), and (2) concomitant strong approach contingencies that may make emotion and its regulation problematic.

Evidence Supporting Experiential Avoidance as a Toxic Diathesis

To show that emotional avoidance functions as a behavioral diathesis and risk factor for anxiety-related pathology, it is important to demonstrate that this predisposition functions to exacerbate aversive emotional responding in individuals with no known history of psychopathology. Consistent with this view, we have shown that greater predispositions toward emotional avoidance (as assessed using the Acceptance and Action Questionnaire; Hayes, et al., 2004), including the deliberate application of instructed emotion regulation strategies (i.e., emotion suppression), results in more acute emotional distress but not greater autonomic reactivity (Feldner, Zvolensky, Eifert, & Spira, 2003). This study is important, for it is the first to show that emotional avoidance and emotion regulation strategies potentiate experimentally induced acute episodes of emotional distress using panicogenic inhalations of 20% CO_2-enriched air. Most notably, such effects were shown in healthy individuals with no known psychopathology.

We have since replicated these findings and found that emotional avoidance, but not other psychological risk factors for panic (e.g., anxiety sensitivity), tends to covary with more severe panic response, even in healthy individuals (Karekla, Forsyth, & Kelly, 2004; see also Spira, Zvolensky, Eifert, & Feldner, 2004). After several trials of inhaling CO_2-enriched air, individuals high in experiential avoidance endorsed more panic symptoms, more severe cognitive symptoms, and more fear, panic, and uncontrollability than their less avoidant counterparts. Of interest, as in all previous studies we conducted in our laboratories, the magnitude of autonomic responses did not discriminate between groups.

Only one study that we know of has shown a relation between experiential avoidance and physiological reactivity to pleasant, unpleasant, and neutral film clips. In that study, persons with a greater predisposition toward experiential avoidance tended to experience their positive and negative emotions more intensely, but also showed greater heart rate suppression to unpleasant stimuli relative to their less avoidant counterparts (Sloan, 2004). These studies provide further strong evidence that experiential avoidance exacerbates aversive emotional responses and may constitute a risk factor for strong emotional learning and thus, play a role in the development and maintenance of anxiety disorders. Collectively, the work discussed previously and other related studies (Hayes, et al., 1996) suggest that a rigid repertoire of emotional avoidance may constitute an important psychological diathesis and risk factor for the development, maintenance, and potential exacerbation of anxiety-related problems (see Feldner, Zvolensky, & Leen-Feldner, 2004, for a review). For this reason, emotion regulation has increasingly become a primary treatment target in newer behavior therapies.

Experiential Acceptance: An Example of a Broad-Band Nonregulatory Strategy

There have been increasing efforts to test alternative strategies designed to undo excessive emotion regulation and thus, foster greater discrimination and willingness to stay in contact with aversive private experiences without acting on them or because of them. In our own research laboratory, for instance, we compared the effects of creating an acceptance versus an emotion regulation context on avoidance behavior and reported fear in women scoring high in anxiety sensitivity (Eifert & Heffner, 2003). All women were asked to breathe 5.5% CO_2-enriched air for two 10-minute periods. This challenge procedure reliably produces involuntary and largely uncontrollable physiological sensations that are similar to those experienced by people during panic attacks (see Forsyth & Eifert, 1998a). Before the inhalation trials, half the participants were taught how not to fight their reactions but to accept and make space for them, whereas the remaining participants were taught a special breathing skill and were encouraged to use it to regulate and control their reactions. Nearly half the participants instructed to regulate their fear worried that they would lose control. Of interest, quite a few of them (20%) actually did lose control; they dropped out of the study altogether. In contrast, participants taught to accept their reactions reported less intense fear and fewer catastrophic thoughts and were less avoidant behaviorally (0% dropout rate).

Our results were replicated in a study examining the effects of accepting versus suppressing the effects of a panicogenic CO_2 challenge in persons suffering from panic disorder (Levitt, Brown, Orsillo, & Barlow, 2004). Participants in that study were simply instructed to either accept or suppress their responses to the CO_2 challenge. The acceptance group was significantly less anxious and less avoidant than the suppression or no-instruction control groups. Yet, the groups did not differ in terms of self-reported panic symptoms or physiological responses. It is important to reiterate that people in these studies, just like people with panic attacks in natural life, had no choice about having or not having the physical sensations. People cannot choose not to have emotions such as fear and anxiety and quite often fear conditioning episodes. They can, however, choose to regulate fear and anxiety when it shows up.

There are also a number of clinical studies suggesting that client attempts to control anxiety may have negative paradoxical effects (Ascher, 1989). For example, Wegner (1994) found that attempts to control anxiety in the face of ongoing stress exacerbate physiological arousal. Additional work, although based largely on retrospective self-report, confirms that the tendency to suppress thoughts is strongly related to extent of anxiety, OCD complaints, and depression in healthy persons and OCD sufferers (McLaren & Crowe, 2003). Indeed, healthy individuals who tend to suppress personally relevant intrusive thoughts experience more depression, obsessionality, and anxiety compared with their counterparts who tend to accept such thoughts (Marcks & Woods, 2005). Also, Heide and Borkovec (1983) found that many of their participants who went through a relaxation exercise experienced increases rather than the targeted decreases in anxiety. A study by Craske, Rowe, Lewin, and Noriega-Dimitri (1997) also showed that adding slow diaphragmatic breathing did not increase the effectiveness of interoceptive exposure treatment for panic disorder. In fact, breathing retraining, itself a form of emotion regulation, can lead to poorer outcomes compared to treatment without such training (Schmidt, Woolaway-Bickel, Trakowski, Santiago, Storey, Koselka, et al., 2000).

In a more general way, active coping efforts that attempt to minimize the experience of anxiety may (paradoxically and unintentionally) maintain pathological anxiety and increase the anxiogenic effects of interoceptive stimulation (Craske, Street, & Barlow, 1989). For instance, Spira and colleagues (2004) found that avoidant coping strategies (e.g., denial, mental disengagement, substance abuse) predicted more frequent and intense CO_2-induced physical and cognitive panic symptoms than acceptance-based coping strategies. These findings are consistent with earlier studies showing that attempts to avoid aversive private events are largely ineffective and may be counterproductive (Cioffi & Holloway, 1993; McLaren & Crowe, 2003; Pennebaker & Beall, 1986). Together these findings suggest that hiding, actively suppressing, escaping from, or avoiding negative thoughts and emotions is not helpful in the long term. In fact, purposefully trying to control feeling anxious may increase the very anxiety one wants to control (Gross & Levenson, 1997), while also increasing the probability that unwanted emotional responses will recur (often in more severe form) in the future (Cox, Swinson, Norton, & Kuch, 1991; Hayes, 2004a; Hayes, et al., 1996, 1999). Worse yet, anxiety suppression and control efforts can act to decrease positive emotional experiences (Gross, 2002). The result is more anxiety, not less, which will likely be followed by more effort to control the anxiety, in a self-perpetuating cycle.

Fear Learning in an Emotion-Regulation Context

Fear learning provides an important experiential foundation for stimuli and situations to acquire aversive functions and likewise, to alter those functions via exposure-based interventions. Verbal processes, in turn, can expand the range of events that may evoke fear, including avoidance, after aversive learning. Thus, any point in the emotion-generative process could, in principle, be a target of emotion regulation within and outside a fear-learning context (see Forsyth, et al., 2005). For instance, persons may act to avoid or escape from antecedents that may evoke or occasion fearful responding (i.e., CSs, occasion setters, discriminative stimulus [SDs]; aversive stimuli that may evoke fear and anxiety (i.e., UCSs, punishers); contexts or situations that may reliably predict a relation between antecedents and emotional consequences. Persons may also act to avoid or escape from the very experience of fear itself and any accompanying thoughts, sensations, behavioral tendencies, or consequences. Such processes not only interfere with functioning but also work against approach behavior and thus, also act against extinction processes from taking hold.

Although fear learning may temporarily disrupt ongoing behavior (e.g., avoidance or escape), emotion regulation strategies may take this basic form of learning to a whole new level. Specifically, we have proposed (cf. Forsyth, et al., 2005) that fear and fear learning may shift from being a normative process to a disordered process when persons: (1) do not accept the reality that they experience certain emotions, thoughts, memories, or physical sensations they do not like; (2) are unwilling to be in contact with them as they are; (3) take deliberate steps to alter their form and frequency or the circumstances that occasion those experiences; and (4) do so rigidly and inflexibly even at significant personal and interpersonal cost (cf. Forsyth, 2000; Forsyth & Eifert, 1996b, 1998b; Friman, et al., 1998; Hayes, et al., 1996). These four behavioral predispositions, and the verbal-cognitive processes that guide their regulation, are at the core of understanding the development and maintenance of anxiety disorders and figure prominently in several contemporary behavioral approaches to treatment such as *Acceptance and Commitment Therapy* (ACT; Hayes, et al., 1999), *Dialectical Behavior Therapy* (Linehan, 1993), *Functional Analytic Psychotherapy* (Kohlenberg & Tsai, 1991), *Integrative Behavioral Couples Therapy* (Jacobson, Christensen, Prince, Cordova, & Eldridge, 2000), and *Mindfulness-Based Cognitive Therapy* (Segal, Williams, & Teasdale, 2002).

An important element of this model is the very idea that rigid emotion regulation (i.e., control, suppression, avoidance, distraction, escape) may emerge as a consequence of fear learning. Another is that the involvement of language may transform fear learning into anxiety pathology. The very processes that establish and shape emotion regulation may, in turn, function as an important predisposition for fear and fear learning to become problematic (Forsyth, et al., 2005). There are at least two ways this could happen. First, language processes can expand the range of stimuli relevant to previous (adaptive) learning, including logically related events (e.g., "I was afraid in the mall," "I felt trapped," "I could be trapped in an elevator or an open field or a marriage," etc.), imagined futures, or fear itself. Second, language can create self-amplifying loops (e.g., rules about how not to think of fearful things, which when followed evoke thinking about fearful things). Language also provides plenty of strong approach contingencies. Thus, persons can drive themselves with the same relational repertoire that simultaneously is expanding out fear learning into every corner and self-amplifying it through the unworkable combination of rule-governed and contingency-based behavioral regulatory processes. Experiential avoidance is a life-constricting behavior precisely because humans cannot avoid their psychological experience of the world while at the same time engaging powerful approach contingencies in that world.

If this account is, at least in part, correct, then it points to several key processes that may turn emotional and psychological pain, whether conditioned or not, into suffering. One such process is the tendency to self-regulate unpleasant emotions, including associated thoughts, feelings, and behavioral tendencies. The second process points to the role of language in maintaining such regulation tendencies. Verbal relational learning is typically additive not subtractive (Hayes, et al., 2001) and thus, can function to expand the range of events (1) that evoke fear based on limited learning and (2) the range of events for which emotion regulation is applied. These processes can turn emotional pain into suffering precisely because successful emotion regulation—itself a form of avoidance—becomes a prerequisite for effective action. Often such relations take the form of rules such as "I can't fly in a plane because I will have a panic attack," "I don't want to go out because I'm depressed," or "I get too anxious when I'm around people." These examples, and many others like them, hint at the kinds of approach-avoidance relations described early on.

Contrast these with "I can fly and may have a panic attack," "I will go out along with my depression," and "I can be anxious or have an upsetting thought and be around people." These examples include only approach-approach contingencies. They also highlight how excessive emotion regulation may act to facilitate or impair functioning and turn fear learning and fear into disordered fear and fear learning. Emotion regulation and the verbal actions that guide it represent processes that can be targeted directly in prevention and intervention efforts, whereas fear, fear learning, and approach contingencies are facts of life that need not be changed. The posture of acceptance (i.e., nonavoidance) may be a key preventive mechanism that protects persons from developing anxiety disorders.

BASIC AND APPLIED IMPLICATIONS

Up to this point, we have provided a broad outline of our recent arguments for conceptualizing fear learning in an emotion regulation context (see Forsyth, et al., 2006). This perspective does not diminish the relevant work regarding the nature of fear learning itself. Rather, this view suggests that it is critical to evaluate what people do about fear-learning processes when attempting to develop more effective cognitive behavioral interventions for anxiety disorders. Next we briefly highlight some of the basic and applied implications of an emotion regulation account for fear conditioning research and for developing more unified treatments for anxiety disorders.

Implications for Fear-Learning Research

First, it seems clear that certain forms of emotion regulation can exacerbate fearful and anxious responding. Thus, a person who walks into a fear-learning experience with a greater tendency toward experiential avoidance ought to (1) be more likely to respond to that experience negatively, (2) show greater efforts to escape from experiential and psychological aspects of that experience, and (3) show greater disruptions in ongoing behavior, and consequently (4) act to avoid similar kinds of experiences to a greater degree than individuals who are not so predisposed. This process may, in turn, increase the likelihood of strong negative emotional learning and promote resistance to extinction. Indirect support of this can be found in studies that have shown that anxious persons, particularly those with PTSD, tend to show more robust fear learning compared with nonanxious control subjects (e.g., Orr, Metzger, Lasko, Macklin, Peri, & Pitman, 2000; Pitman & Orr, 1986). Although this research is suggestive, it is important to note studies that have not explicitly assessed for, or otherwise attempted to manipulate directly, emotion-regulation strategies in a fear-learning context.

Second, the study of emotion regulation within a fear-learning context has been somewhat limited. Yet, basic conditioning arrangements could be juxtaposed with emotion-regulation processes that are selected for (i.e., individual difference) or manipulated directly (e.g., training to suppress, express, accept the antecedents and consequences of fear learning). Regardless of the strategy used, it will be important to develop experimental preparations that more closely resemble the kinds of contingencies that humans might confront in their natural environments. In the natural environment, for instance, it is often the case that the CS and UCS occur simultaneously and are difficult to distinguish (e.g., a snake bite: the snake and the bite are not perceived as two phenomenologically separate events). Indeed, in the real world it would be unusual for a CS to appear first, then disappear, with this disappearance being followed by a UCS. Yet, this is precisely the kind of contingency used in trace and some forms of delay conditioning. Although such contingencies tend to yield more reliable conditioning in the laboratory, in the natural environment it is more likely that the CS and UCS occur closely together, at times simultaneously, because the CS delivers the UCS. This is particularly true of interoceptive conditioning where the responses to the CS and UCS are bodily changes or sensations.

Third, we know that conditioning in language-able humans is far from being noncognitive. Verbal-symbolic processes are often tightly embedded with human experience and allow for complex forms of relational responding that cannot be readily explained by invoking stimulus generalization, higher-order conditioning, or mediated generalization. Networks of verbal relations are expansive and so too are the functions that may transfer via such relations. As such networks expand, the functions that transfer do not degrade in the same way responding may degrade across a stimulus generalization gradient or via second- or third-order conditioned relations (see Hayes, et al., 2001, for a detailed review). This means that there is probably no such thing as a purely nonverbal conditioning event in verbally able humans, in part, because the experience of human emotion is psychological and relational and verbal. It also means that Pavlovian conditioning preparations may not only involve Pavlovian processes, particularly in humans where both classical and operant learning contingencies typically interact in complex ways to shape and guide behavior. Emotion regulation is one such operant. There are many others.

Fourth, ethical constraints and practical considerations have made it notoriously difficult to model fearful emotional responding in laboratory human conditioning research. For instance, fearful responding in the natural environment—a response that most closely resembles panic—is rarely approximated in the laboratory, the exception being studies using panicogenic challenge agents as UCSs (e.g., CO_2-enriched air; Forsyth & Eifert, 1998a). This needs to change if we are to develop more ecologically valid models of human fear learning. In addition, the tendency to allow participants to set the intensity of aversive UCSs in human conditioning research, however justified for ethical reasons, is far removed from the kinds of conditions that likely operate when fear learning occurs in the natural environment. In fact, it would be difficult to imagine persons being able to set the strength of an aversive event (a form of antecedent regulation), or even their possible reactions to it, before experiencing an aversive learning episode in the real world.

Fifth, and perhaps most important, laboratory fear-learning preparations with humans tend to occur in relative isolation from competing environmental demands. Participants in laboratory fear conditioning studies typically sit idly and are presented with the aversive contingencies. There are no costs associated with such learning, at least from the perspective of the participant. Participants sit, experimenters deliver the contingencies, and participants take it. Yet, in the natural environment, such learning typically occurs in the context of competing approach contingencies and fluid ongoing actions in and within a context. For instance, a rat will cease bar pressing for food in the presence of a CS that has been reliably paired with shock. Most humans will likewise show some disruption and narrowing of ongoing behavior when afraid, regardless of the source, in the natural environment. Eventually, however, the rat will return to bar pressing at CS offset. Most human beings will also return to doing what was important to them.

The tendency toward experiential avoidance, by contrast, can result in less flexible behavior and hence, keep people off track and miserable long after conditioned or unconditioned sources of threat have passed. In this context, experiencing anxiety is not merely a bump in the road but rather costly in psychological terms. Persons with a tendency toward experiential avoidance often build their lives around not having fear and anxiety. These actions are disruptive precisely because they are unnecessary, contextually insensitive, and tend to get in the way of meaningful life activities. That is, approach-avoidance contingencies best characterize problematic experiences of fear and fear learning in the natural environment.

Virtually all human fear-learning research, by contrast, models only aversive contingencies. To the extent possible, fear-learning research needs to attend to competing approach-avoidance contingencies in the laboratory. This work may include study of how emotion regulation potentiates or depotentiates fear learning and how the consequences of fear learning and its regulation disrupt *meaningful* goal-directed actions and hence, result in real costs for the individual. Arguably, modeling such contingencies in the laboratory will be a challenge with humans, but we believe it can and must be done. The same is true of research that aims to evaluate how experiential avoidance functions as a predisposition for, and perhaps even how it may emerge as a consequence of, fear learning and other forms of learning. Numerous emotion regulatory processes could be studied here, either alone or in combination with other regulatory processes. Knowing that such regulatory tendencies account for a good deal of human suffering and are typically salient targets for treatment are two good reasons that such work ought to make its way into fear-conditioning analogue research. This view is now making its way into mainstream cognitive-behavioral therapies for anxiety disorders, resulting in a rethinking of the symptom-focused mastery and control agenda (Barlow, et al., 2004).

General Treatment Implications

The literature on emotion regulation and experiential avoidance suggests a number of related clinical strategies that target the agenda of emotion regulation itself and the verbal processes supporting it (e.g., Eifert & Forsyth, 2005; Hayes, et al., 1999). For instance, experiential exercises based on metaphor and paradox may be used to teach clients how to experience their anxious thoughts and feelings from a mindful, detached, observer perspective, while learning to make space for anxious thoughts and feelings and other unwanted facets of their private world (e.g., physical sensations, images, memories). The goal here would be to foster greater experiential openness and psychological flexibility and less rule-governed behavior. By weakening powerful verbally regulated avoidance contingencies that might set up approach-avoidance conflicts in the natural environment, an acceptance posture also may help free up clients to use their hands and feet to regulate how they live their lives and, thus transform problematic fear and anxiety into just fear and anxiety. This is potentially important, for it suggests that interventions that defuse regulation may result in more approach-approach relations in a client's natural environment and a broader range of functioning. It also suggests that therapists ought to attend to approach-avoidance contingencies in the therapeutic setting and thus, frame exposure in a way so that it models such contingencies and not simply avoidance contingencies (for a detailed treatment guide, see Eifert & Forsyth, 2005).

Also, the verbal-relational properties entailed in language and emotion regulation are additive and expansive and heavily dependent on context (Hayes, et al., 2001). The basic animal and human literature also suggests that extinction is not unlearning but new learning. In fact, it is becoming increasingly clear that contextual factors are important in fear renewal and relapse (Craske, 2003). Language processes also serve as an important context that may function to occasion fear relapse and fear renewal. For instance, suppose a person has learned a relation between panic attacks, elevators, and avoidance. These relations, in turn, are reliably evoked in the context of going to work (approach contingency) and other important activities where closed spaces may be involved. Interoceptive and exteroceptive exposure may be quite successful in altering such relations, including altering the functions of other events that might be part of this network. Yet, a broad transformation across the network may be incomplete. When this happens, other unchecked elements of the network may function to reactivate and solidify previously altered relations, including the very agenda of emotion regulation itself. For instance, suppose this person later finds herself in a relationship and feels "trapped." This feeling, in turn, may evoke panic and avoidance, and because both were related to closed spaces before, she may subsequently experience renewal of fear to elevators and other closed spaces without further panic attacks in those contexts. Unfortunately, we know surprising little about how verbal processes function in exposure therapy and fear renewal. Yet, basic research on verbal processes suggests that such outcomes are likely and may be difficult to prevent entirely (see Hayes, et al., 2001, for a review). This again highlights why disrupting the emotion regulation agenda may be critical, in part, because it helps hold together and make toxic aversive emotional states in the context of competing environmental demands.

Specific Implications for Cognitive-Behavioral Therapies

Mainstream CBTs for anxiety disorders tend to conceptualize unwanted anxiety-related private events as problems that warrant clinical attention (e.g., Beck, et al., 1985). Accordingly, the therapeutic solution is to alleviate symptoms by getting clients to confront feared objects or aversive bodily events in a safe therapeutic context to facilitate corrective emotional learning and fear reduction (e.g., Barlow, 2002). Techniques used include exteroceptive or interoceptive in vivo exposure, imaginal exposure, thought stopping, response prevention, flooding, systematic desensitization, worry control and decatastrophizing, cognitive restructuring, systematic desensitization, guided imagery, breathing retraining, and progressive muscle relaxation. Comprehensive treatment manuals incorporating such techniques are available for all major anxiety disorders: panic disorder (e.g., *Mastery of Your Anxiety and Panic*, Barlow & Craske, 2000), specific phobias (e.g., *Mastery of Your Specific Phobia*; Antony, Craske, & Barlow, 1995), OCD (*Mastery of Obsessive-Compulsive Disorder*; Foa & Kozak, 1997b), and generalized anxiety disorder (*Mastery of Your Anxiety and Worry*; Zinbarg, Craske & Barlow, 1993).

The word *mastery* in the titles of such manuals is not accidental and reflects the underlying philosophy and approach of such treatments. These treatments suggest, either explicitly or implicitly, that having catastrophic or other "maladaptive" thoughts are part of the problem and a cause of human suffering that may interfere with living a successful life. Otherwise, it would make no sense to target them for change in therapy. The goal is to assist clients in becoming better at controlling (i.e., mastering) their thoughts and emotional experiences by teaching them more effective regulation strategies. This is indeed what many anxious clients expect from psychotherapy: They want to learn more effective ways of reducing unwanted private events.

A key problem of traditional CBT is that it tends to play into this system by suggesting to clients that pursuing a control and mastery approach may indeed be a long-term workable solution by attempting to teach clients more effective management strategies than they may have used in the past. The literature on the effects of experiential avoidance, however, suggests that this approach itself may be flawed and points to a different strategy. This strategy involves addressing the agenda of emotion regulation itself so as to help clients give up the struggle to control and avoid unwanted thoughts and feelings. Thus far, people have often desperately tried to relax *away* fear and anxiety by pushing their unwanted thoughts and feelings away. Instead, an acceptance-based behavior therapy approach aims to help people relax *with* their anxiety, whether or not conditioned, by being and moving with it. Anxious thoughts and feelings are not considered "symptomatic" of anything but, rather normal facets of human experience. The task for clients then is no longer to down-regulate anxiety and fear because anxiety and fear per se are not the problem.

Targeting unwanted private experiences in therapy has been shown to be quite efficacious and can produce symptom reduction and relief. This strategy, however, also keeps clients entangled in their struggle with their experience, suggesting that their experience per se is problematic and the cause of life problems. Thus, when anxious thoughts and feelings recur again, clients will be inclined to engage in efforts to change or reduce their intensity fearing that other problems may be potentiated. Yet, what differentiates psychological health and normal pain from disordered suffering is not the absence of negative private events. The difference is whether people are willing to experience whatever it is that they experience and still do what matters most to them. We could aim to teach people how to experience a wide range of emotional experience, willingly and without defense, and behave effectively despite what they may think or feel. *Willing* here is not about brute force of will. It means being open and having what is. It is about finding a way to live a meaningful and productive life *and* taking personal pains and joys along for the ride instead of living to avoid or manage psychological pain. This view is now making its way into mainstream CBT, resulting in a rethinking of the symptom-focused mastery and control agenda (Barlow, et al., 2004).

Acceptance and Commitment Therapy for Anxiety Disorders

New-wave generation behavior therapies (Hayes, 2004a, 2004b) tend to focus on domains of human experience that go well beyond symptom alleviation and control as therapeutic goals. Instead, they emphasize topics traditionally reserved for less empirical wings of psychology such as acceptance, mindfulness, values, spirituality, meaning and purpose, relationships, and quality of life (Hayes, et al., 2004). These approaches challenge the symptom- and syndrome-focused change agenda that has come to characterize much of mainstream CBT. They offer a unique and expanded view of human suffering and what it means to foster psychological health and wellness. To illustrate, we outline briefly the basic elements of an acceptance and commitment therapy (ACT) approach to the treatment of anxiety disorders (for a more detailed session-by-session treatment guide, see Eifert & Forsyth, 2005).

First, within a coherent theoretical and philosophical framework, ACT illuminates the ways that language entangles clients into futile attempts to wage war against their own inner lives. This war is fundamentally about the application of emotion regulation efforts in contexts where such regulation efforts are unnecessary or unworkable. Addressing the struggle head on is what an ACT approach to treatment is about because nonacceptance and struggle with anxiety is the toxic process that makes anxiety disordered. ACT tries to undermine and loosen the hold that excessive, rigid, and inflexible emotion regulation has on the lives of anxiety sufferers. With anxiety disorders, this form of regulation usually centers on anxious thoughts and feelings that are unwanted or undesired, including the situations that might occasion them. They spend their lives focused on not experiencing anxiety and fear rather than doing what is most important to them. Through experiential exercises based on metaphor and paradox, clients learn how to experience their anxious thoughts and feelings from a mindful observer perspective, as they are rather than as how they evaluate them, learning to make space for anxious thoughts and feelings and other unwanted facets of their private world (e.g., physical sensations, images, memories) to foster greater experiential openness and psychological flexibility. This acceptance posture frees up clients to use their hands and feet to regulate how they live their lives consistent with their values and goals.

Second, cognitive-behavioral interventions typically focus on narrow-band clinical outcomes in the form of symptom reduction and relief. To get there, however, clients typically must go through quite a bit of pain by confronting anxiety and fear-evoking cues and situations during in vivo or imaginal exposure exercises. Of interest, this is the point at which more than a few anxious clients drop out of therapy (Becker & Zayfert, 2001). Two recent studies from our laboratories showed the positive effects of an acceptance context for preventing dropout. The first study (Karekla & Forsyth, 2004) showed significant differences in the pattern of attrition rates between CBT and ACT-enhanced CBT for persons suffering from panic disorder. Before introducing the rationales for interoceptive and exteroceptive exposure, none of the CBT clients and only three ACT clients dropped out of therapy prematurely. However, after the introduction of the exposure rationales, five persons discontinued therapy in the PCT group (the only dropouts!) and only one person in the ACT group.

The main difference between the exposure rationales was in how they were framed (i.e., mastery and control of panic vs. mastery of experiencing panic) and for what purpose (i.e., controlling panic symptoms vs. living more fully and consistently with what one values). The results of this study suggest that exposure conducted in the service of feeling better is somewhat limiting and not very inspiring. All the pain of therapy and for what? The hope of feeling less anxious? At some level, anxious persons recognize that feeling less anxious does not mean that they will be anxiety free or that somehow their lives will be better, richer, or more meaningful. In the second related study with highly anxious females (Eifert & Heffner, 2003) who experienced panic-like responses in an acceptance or a control context, we found that 20% of control participants dropped out of the study, whereas none of the acceptance participants did. Here too, by giving up their efforts to gain control, people had actually gained control and strength.

Although ACT allows room for symptom alleviation, it is not a main target or *the* therapeutic goal. Rather, the focus is on what we call broad-band outcomes. Such outcomes are about helping the client move in life directions that they truly care about. For instance, a client may value having deep and meaningful relationships with her children but is letting her anxiety regulation efforts get in the way of that. Within ACT, the focus would be about removing barriers to having that kind of relationship with her children (e.g., unnecessary emotion regulation strategies). Anxiety reduction may occur as a consequence, but it is not an explicit target. Rather, the explicit targets are in areas that most readers will associate with a life lived well, namely living in a manner consistent with meaningful values and goals. Making and keeping value-guided commitments are an important part of an ACT approach to anxiety disorders (Eifert & Forsyth, 2005). Valued living dignifies the treatment and makes the hard work of therapy worthwhile.

Traditional CBT exposure interventions for anxiety have a different feel when used within an ACT approach. Virtually all of them are recast within an Acceptance and Mastery of Experiencing framework. Exposure, for instance, is no longer cast as an eliminative technique within a Mastery and Control of Anxiety framework because it sends a message to the client that anxiety is the problem and must be reduced or managed before a client can live better. Rather, exposure within ACT is framed as one of several experiential exercises, with the goal being to *feel* better (i.e., become better at feeling), not to feel *better* (i.e., feeling less anxiety). This mastery of experience framework for ACT exposure exercises is about helping clients develop willingness to experience thoughts and feelings for what they are. Thus, exposure exercises within ACT are framed in the service of fostering greater psychological flexibility, experiential willingness, and openness. They are about growth and are always done in the service of client values and goals. This approach, which we describe in detail elsewhere (Eifert & Forsyth, 2005), is very much about altering how clients with anxiety respond to their emotional and psychological experiences, not the structure or content of those experiences. We are trying to help clients make room for those experiences, while freeing up psychological and behavioral space for clients to get on with the task of living their lives consistent with, and in the direction of, their chosen values.

Summary

When viewed historically, behavior therapy has been an enormously successful experiment. Its success, in turn, is based in large part on the simple principle of conducting clinical science with at least one eye on practical utility. The utility of fear conditioning research as a clinical analog of anxiety-related suffering is a good news–bad news story. The good news is that Pavlovian fear conditioning research and theory, despite numerous criticisms regarding its scope and clinical relevance, remains at the core of contemporary behavioral accounts of the origins, maintenance, and amelioration of anxiety disorders. The bad news is that first- and second-generation behavior therapies represented classical conditioning and cognitive content as a sufficient model to account for the development of anxiety disorders. This led to the notion that anxiety-related suffering is about excessive physiological responding or other psychological content, including avoidance.

This chapter introduced the notion that fear and its conditioned basis are not disordered processes per se but rather, become so when humans act on them and because of them so as to alter their form, frequency, or occurrence. The regulation of anxiety and fear using any number of strategies may result in temporary relief (e.g., anxiety reduction via negative reinforcement). Yet, the cumulative effect over time of such actions is life constriction and long-term suffering. Such actions, when rigidly and inflexibly applied, can take over a person's life and turn the experience of fear and fear learning into an emotional experience that is a problem, not simply a painful experience that can be had. This work suggests that exposure-based interventions may need to attend to the emotion regulation agenda itself, while reframing exposure in terms of valued life goals (e.g., family, relationships, spirituality, health), not control or attenuation of anxiety and fear as goals. Otherwise, exposure and cognitive change procedures may be used as yet another set of emotion regulation strategies that may, in the end, set clients up for fear renewal and relapse.

The emerging consensus is that such regulation tends to make aversive emotions more intense and more likely to occur: if you don't want it, you've got it. This outcome, when coupled with powerful approach contingencies, may function as a predisposing and maintaining factor for anxiety pathology. As clients learn to give up the struggle and control agenda and focus on life–goal-related activities, they are no longer owned by their unwanted experiences. After developing greater clarity about personal values and committing to needed behavior change, we encourage clients to embark on the journey and put those commitments into action. They are free to live.

REFERENCES

Abramowitz, J.S. (1996). Variants of exposure and response prevention in the treatment of obsessive-compulsive disorder: A meta-analysis. *Behavior Therapy, 27,* 583–600.

Abramowitz, J.S., Foa, E.B., & Franklin, M.E. (2002). Empirical status of cognitive-behavior therapy for obsessive-compulsive disorder: A meta-analysis. *Romanian Journal of Cognitive and Behavioral Therapy, 2*, 89–104.

Antony, M.M., Craske, M.G., & Barlow, D.H. (Eds.). (1995). *Mastery of your specific phobias.* San Antonio, TX: Harcourt Brace.

Arntz, A. (2003). Cognitive therapy versus applied relaxation as treatment of generalized anxiety disorder. *Behavior Research and Therapy, 41*, 633–646.

Ascher, L.M. (1989). Paradoxical intention and recursive anxiety. In L.M. Ascher (Ed.), *Therapeutic paradox* (pp. 93–136). New York: Guilford.

Augustson, E.M., & Dougher, M.J. (1997). The transfer of avoidance evoking functions through stimulus equivalence classes. *Journal of Behavior Therapy and Experimental Psychiatry, 28*, 181–191.

Bakker, A., van Balkom, A.J.L.M., Spinhoven, P., Blaauw, B.M.J.W., & van Dyck, R. (1998). Follow-up on the treatment of panic disorder with or without agoraphobia. *Journal of Nervous and Mental Disease, 186*, 414–419.

Barlow, D.H. (1988). *Anxiety and its disorders: The nature and treatment of anxiety and panic.* New York: Guilford.

Barlow, D.H. (2002). *Anxiety and its disorders: The nature and treatment of anxiety and panic* (2nd ed.). New York: Guilford Press.

Barlow, D.H., & Craske, M.G. (2000). *Mastery of your anxiety and panic: Client for anxiety and panic (MAP-3).* San Antonio, TX: Graywind/Psychological Corporation.

Barlow, D.H., Allen, L.B., & Choate, M.L. (2004). Toward a unified treatment for emotional disorders. *Behavior Therapy, 35*, 205–230.

Barlow, D.H., Rapee, R.M., & Brown, T.A. (1992). Behavioral treatment of generalized anxiety disorder. *Behavior Therapy, 23*, 551–570.

Beck, A.T. (1979). *Cognitive therapy for the emotional disorders.* New York: International Universities Press.

Beck, A.T., & Clark, D.A. (1997). An information processing model of anxiety: Automatic and strategic processes. *Behavior Research and Therapy, 35*(1), 49–58.

Beck, A.T., Emery, G., & Greenberg, R.L. (1985). *Anxiety disorders and phobias: A cognitive perspective.* New York: Basic Books.

Becker, C.B., & Zayfert, C. (2001). Integrating DBT-based techniques and concepts to facilitate treatment for PTSD. *Cognitive and Behavioral Practice, 8*, 107–122.

Biran, M., & Wilson, G.T. (1981). Treatment of phobic disorders using cognitive and exposure methods: A self-efficacy analysis. *Journal of Consulting Clinical Psychology, 49*, 886–899.

Biran, M., Augusto, F., & Wilson, G.T. (1981). In vivo exposure vs. cognitive restructuring in the treatment of scriptophobia. *Behavior Research and Therapy, 19*, 525–532.

Blackledge, J.T. (2003). An introduction to relational frame theory: Basics and applications. *The Behavior Analyst Today, 3*, 421–433.

Blackledge, J.T., & Hayes, S.C. (2001). Emotion regulation in Acceptance and Commitment Therapy. *JCLP/In session: Psychotherapy in Practice, 57*, 243–255.

Blair, K.A., Denham, S.A., Kochanoff, A., & Whipple, B. (2004). Playing it cool: Temperament, emotion regulation, and social behavior in preschoolers. *Journal of School Psychology, 42*, 419–443.

Bonanno, G.A., Papa, A., LaLande, K., Westphal, M., & Coifman, K. (2004). The importance of being flexible: The ability to both enhance and suppress emotional expression predicts long-term adjustment. *Psychological Science, 15*, 482–487.

Borkovec, T.D., & Costello, E. (1993). Efficacy of applied relaxation and cognitive-behavioral therapy in the treatment of generalized anxiety disorder. *Journal of Consulting and Clinical Psychology, 61*, 611–619.

Borkovec, T.D., & Whisman, M.A. (1996). Psychosocial treatment for generalized anxiety disorder. In M. Mavissakalian & R. Prien (Eds.), *Long-term treatment of anxiety disorders.* Washington, D.C.: American Psychiatric Association.

Bouton, M.E. (1988). Context and ambiguity in the extinction of emotional learning: Implications for exposure therapy. *Behaviour Research and Therapy, 26*, 137–149.

Bouton, M.E. (1993). Context, time, and memory retrieval in the interference paradigms of Pavlovian learning. *Psychological Bulletin, 114,* 80–99.

Bouton, M.E. (1994). Conditioning, remembering, and forgetting. *Journal of Experimental Psychology: Animal Behavior Processes, 20,* 219–231.

Bouton, M.E. (2000). A learning theory perspective on lapse, relapse, and the maintenance of behavior change. *Health Psychology, 19* (1) Suppl., 57–63.

Bouton, M.E. (2002). Context, ambiguity, and unlearning: Sources of relapse after behavioral extinction. *Biological Psychiatry, 52,* 976–986.

Bouton, M.E., Mineka, S., & Barlow, D.H. (2001). A modern learning theory perspective on the etiology of panic disorder. *Psychological Review, 108,* 4–32.

Bradley, R., Greene, J., Russ, E., Dutra, L., & Westen, D. (2005). A multidimensional meta-analysis of psychotherapy for PTSD. *American Journal of Psychiatry, 162,* 214–227.

Brewin, C.R. (1996). Theoretical foundations of cognitive-behavior therapy for anxiety and depression. *Annual Review of Psychology, 47,* 33–57.

Butler, E.A., & Gross, J.J. (2004). Hiding feelings in social contexts: Out of sight is not out of mind. In P. Philippot & R.S. Feldman, (Eds.), *The regulation of emotion* (pp. 101–126). Mahwah, NJ: Erlbaum.

Butler, G., Fennell, M., Robson, P., & Gelder, M. (1991). Comparison of behaviour therapy and cognitive behaviour therapy in the treatment of generalized anxiety disorder. *Journal of Consulting and Clinical Psychology, 59,* 167–175.

Chambless, D.L., & Gracely, E.J. (1989). Fear of fear and the anxiety disorders. *Cognitive Therapy and Research, 13,* 9–20.

Chambless, D.L., & Ollendick, T.H. (2001). Empirically supported interventions: Controversies and evidence. *Annual Review of Psychology, 52,* 685–716.

Chambless, D., Baker, M.J., Baucom, D.H., Beutler, L.E., Calhoun, K.S., Crits-Christoph, P., et al. (1998). Update on empirically validated therapies, II. *Clinical Psychologist, 51,* 3–15.

Cioffi, D., & Holloway, J. (1993). Delayed costs of suppressed pain. *Journal of Personality and Social Psychology, 64,* 274–282.

Clark, D.M. (1986). Cognitive therapy for anxiety. *Behavioral Psychotherapy, 14,* 283–294.

Clark, D.M. (1999). Anxiety disorders: Why the persist and how to treat them. *Behavior Research and Therapy, 37,* S5–S27.

Clark, D.M., Salkovskis, P.M., Hackmann, A., Middleton, H., Anastasiades, P., & Geldeer, M.G. (1994). A comparison of cognitive therapy, applied relaxation and imipramine in the treatment of panic disorder. *British Journal of Psychiatry, 164,* 759–769.

Clark, D.M., Salkovskis, P.M., Hackman, A., Wells, A., Ludgate, J., & Gelder, M. (1999). Brief cognitive therapy for panic disorder: A randomized controlled trial. *Journal of Consulting and Clinical Psychology, 67,* 583–589.

Cook, M., & Mineka, S. (1991). Selective associations in the origins of phobic fears and their implications for behavior therapy. In P.R. Martin (Ed.), *Handbook of behavior therapy and psychological science* (pp. 413–434). New York: Pergamon.

Costello, C.G. (1970). Dissimilarities between conditioned avoidance responses and phobias. *Psychological Review, 77,* 250–254.

Cox, B.J., Swinson, R.P., Norton, G.R., & Kuch, K. (1991). Anticipatory anxiety and avoidance in panic disorder with agoraphobia. *Behaviour Research and Therapy, 29,* 363–365.

Craske, M.G. (1999). *Anxiety disorders: Psychological approaches to theory and treatment.* Boulder, CO: Westview Press.

Craske, M.G. (2003). *Origins of phobias and anxiety disorders: Why more women than men?* Oxford, UK: Elsevier.

Craske, M.G., Barlow, D.H., & O'Leary, T.A. (1992). *Mastery of your anxiety and worry.* San Antonio, TX: Psychological Corporation.

Craske, M.G., Street, L., & Barlow, D.H. (1989). Instructions to focus upon or distract from internal cues during exposure treatment of agoraphobic avoidance. *Behaviour Research and Therapy, 27,* 663–672.

Craske, M.G., Miller, P.P., Rotunda, R., & Barlow, D.H. (1990). A descriptive report of features of initial unexpected panic attacks in minimal and extensive avoiders. *Behaviour Research and Therapy, 28,* 395–400.

Craske, M.G., Rowe, M., Lewin, M., & Noriega-Dimitri, R. (1997). Interoceptive exposure versus breathing retraining within cognitive-behavioural therapy for panic disorder with agoraphobia. *British Journal of Clinical Psychology, 36,* 85–99.

de Beurs, E., van Balkom, A.J.L.M., Lange, A., Koele, P., & van Dyck, R. (1995). Treatment of panic disorder with agoraphobia: Comparison of fluvoxamine, placebo, and psychological panic management combined with exposure and of exposure in vivo alone. *American Journal of Psychiatry, 152,* 683–691.

Denollet, J., Sys, S.U., Stoobant, N., Rombouts, H., Gillebert, T.C., & Brutsaert, D.L. (1996). Personality as an independent predictor of long-term mortality in patients with coronary heart disease. *The Lancet, 347,* 417–421.

Dobson, K.S., & Hamilton, K.E. (2003). Cognitive restructuring: Behavioral tests of negative cognitions. In W. O'Donohue, J.E. Fisher, & S.C. Hayes (Eds.), *Cognitive behavior therapy: Applying empirically supported treatments in your practice.* Mahwah, NJ: John Wiley and Sons, Inc.

Dougher, M.J., Augustson, E., Markham, M.R., Greenway, D.E., & Wulfert, E. (1994). The transfer of respondent eliciting and extinction functions through stimulus equivalence. *Journal of the Experimental Analysis of Behavior, 62,* 331–351.

Eddy, K.T., Dutra, L., Bradley, R., & Westen, D. (2004). A multidimensional meta-analysis of psychotherapy and pharmacotherapy for obsessive-compulsive disorder. *Clinical Psychology Review, 24,* 1011–1030.

Eifert, G.H., & Forsyth, J.P. (2005). *Acceptance and commitment therapy for anxiety disorders: A practitioner's treatment guide to using mindfulness, acceptance, and value-based behavior change strategies.* Oakland, CA: New Harbinger.

Eifert, G.H., & Heffner, M. (2003). The effects of acceptance versus control contexts on avoidance of panic-related symptoms. *Journal of Behavior Therapy and Experimental Psychiatry, 34,* 293–312.

Emmelkamp, P.M.G. (1994). Behavior therapy in adults. In A.E. Bergin, & S.L. Garfield (Eds.), *Handbook of psychotherapy and behavior change*(4 th ed.). New York: Wiley.

Emmelkamp, P.M.G., & Mersch, P.P. (1982). Cognition and exposure in vivo in the treatment of agoraphobia: Short-term and delayed effects. *Cognitive Therapy and Research, 6*(1), 77–88.

Emmelkamp, P.M.G., & Wessels, H. (1975). Flooding in imagination vs. flooding in vivo: A comparison with agoraphobia. *Behaviour Research and Therapy, 13,* 7–15.

Emmelkamp, P.M.G., van der Helm, M., van Zanten, B.L., & Plochg, I. (1980). Treatment of obsessive-compulsive patients: The contribution of self-instructional training to the effectiveness of exposure. *Behaviour Research and Therapy, 18,* 61–66.

Emmelkamp, P.M.G., Krijn, M., Hulsbosch, A.M., de Vries, S., Schuemie, M.J., & van der Mast, C.A.P.G. (2002). Virtual reality treatment versus exposure in vivo: A comparative evaluation in acrophobia. *Behaviour Research and Therapy, 40,* 509–516.

Eysenck, H.J. (1967). *The biological basis of personality.* Springhill: C.C. Thomas.

Eysenck, H.H. (1976). The learning theory model of neurosis: a new approach. *Behaviour Research and Therapy, 14,* 251–267.

Eysenck, H.J. (1987). Behavior therapy. In H.J. Eysenck & I. Martin (Eds.), *Theoretical foundations of behavior therapy* (pp. 3–34). New York: Plenum.

Eysenck, H.J., & Rachman, S. (1965). *Causes and cure of neurosis.* London: Routledge and Kagan Paul.

Feldner, M.T., Zvolensky, M.J., & Leen-Feldner, E.W. (2004). A critical review of the empirical literature on coping and panic disorder. *Clinical Psychology Review, 24,* 123–148.

Feldner, M.T., Zvolensky, M.J., Eifert, G.H., & Spira, A.P. (2003). Emotional avoidance: An experimental test of individual differences and response suppression during biological challenge. *Behaviour Research and Therapy, 41,* 403–411.

Feske, U., & Chambless, D.L. (1995). Cognitive-behavioral versus exposure only treatment for social phobia: A meta-analysis. *Behavior Therapy, 26,* 695–720.

Flint, J. (2004). The genetic basis of neuroticism. *Neuroscience and Biobehavioral Reviews, 28,* 307–316.

Foa, E.B., Franklin, M.E., Perry, K.J., & Herbert, J.D. (1996). Cognitive biases in generalized social phobia. *Journal of Abnormal Psychology, 105,* 433–439.

Foa, E.B., & Emmelkamp, P.M.G. (1983). *Failures in behavior therapy.* New York: Wiley.

Foa, E.B., & Kozak, M.J. (1986). Emotional processing of fear: Exposure to corrective information. *Psychological Bulletin, 99,* 20–35.

Foa, E.B., & Kozak, M.J. (1997a). Beyond the efficacy ceiling? Cognitive behavior therapy in search of a theory. *Behavior Therapy, 28,* 601–611.

Foa, E.B., & Kozak, M.J. (1997b). *Mastery of obsessive-compulsive disorder (OCD): A cognitive-behavioral approach.* Boulder, CO: Graywind.

Foa, E.B., Steketee, G., Turner, R.M., & Fischer, S.C. (1980). Effects of imaginal exposure to feared disasters in obsessive-compulsive checkers. *Behaviour Research & Therapy, 18,* 449–455.

Forsyth, J.P. (2000). A process-oriented behavioral approach to the etiology, maintenance, and treatment of anxiety-related disorders. In M.J. Dougher (Ed.), *Clinical behavior analysis* (pp. 153–180). Reno, NV: Context Press.

Forsyth, J.P., & Eifert, G.H. (1996a). Systemic alarms in fear conditioning I: A reappraisal of what is being conditioned. *Behavior Therapy, 27,* 441–462.

Forsyth, J.P., & Eifert, G.H. (1996b). The language of feeling and the feeling of anxiety: Contributions of the behaviorisms toward understanding the function-altering effects of language. *The Psychological Record, 46,* 607–649.

Forsyth, J.P., & Eifert, G.H. (1998a). Response intensity in content-specific fear conditioning comparing 20% versus 13% CO_2-enriched air as unconditioned stimuli. *Journal of Abnormal Psychology, 107,* 291–304.

Forsyth, J.P., & Eifert, G.H. (1998b). Phobic anxiety and panic: An integrative behavioral account of their origin and treatment. In J.J. Plaud & G.H. Eifert (Eds.), *From behavior theory to behavior therapy* (pp. 38–67). Needham, MA: Allyn & Bacon.

Forsyth, J.P., Daleiden, E., & Chorpita, B.F. (2000). Response primacy in fear conditioning: Disentangling the contributions of the UCS vs. The UCR. *The Psychological Record, 50,* 17–33.

Forsyth, J.P., Eifert, G.H., & Barrios, V. (2006). Fear conditioning in an emotion regulation context: A fresh perspective on the origins of anxiety disorders. In M.G. Craske, D. Hermans, & D. Vansteenwegen (Eds.), *Fear and Learning: From Basic Processes to Clinical Implications* (pp. 133–153). Washington, DC: American Psychological Association.

Forsyth, J.P., Eifert, G.H., & Thompson, R.N. (1996). Systemic alarms in fear conditioning II: An experimental methodology using 20% carbon dioxide inhalations as an unconditioned stimulus. *Behavior Therapy, 27,* 391–415.

Friman, P.C., Hayes, S.C., & Wilson, K.G. (1998). Why behavior analysts should study emotion: The example of anxiety. *Journal of Applied Behavior Analysis, 31,* 137–156.

Garnefski, N., & Spinhoven, K.P. (2001). Negative life events, cognitive emotion regulation and emotional problems. *Personality and Individual Differences, 30,* 1311–1327.

Gould, R.A., Otto, M.W., & Pollack, M.H. (1995). A meta-analysis of treatment outcome for panic disorder. *Clinical Psychology Review, 15,* 819–844.

Gould, R.A., Otto, M.W., Pollack, M.H., & Yap, L. (1997). Cognitive-behavioral and pharmacological treatment for generalized anxiety disorder: A meta-analysis. *Clinical Psychology: Science and Practice, 4,* 291–306.

Gould, R.A., Buckminster, S., Pollack, M.H., Otto, M.W., & Yap, L. (1997). Cognitive-behavioral and pharmacological treatment for social phobia: A meta-analysis. *Behavior Therapy, 28,* 285–305.

Gray, J.A. (1990). Brain systems that mediate both emotion and cognition. *Cognition and Emotion, 4,* 269–288.

Gross, J.J. (1998). Antecedent - and response-focused emotion regulation: Divergent consequences for experience, expression, and physiology. *Journal of Personality and Social Psychology, 74,* 224–237.

Gross, J.J. (2002). Emotion regulation: Affective, cognitive, and social consequences. *Psychophysiology, 39,* 281–291.

Gross, J.J., & John, O.P. (2003). Individual differences in two emotion regulation processes: Implications for affect, relationships, and well-being. *Journal of Personality and Social Psychology, 85*, 348–362.

Gross, J.J., & Levenson, R.W. (1997). Hiding feelings: The acute effects of inhibiting negative and positive emotion. *Journal of Abnormal Psychology, 106*, 95–103.

Gross, J.J., & Muñoz, R.F. (1995). Emotion regulation and mental health. *Clinical Psychology: Science and Practice, 2*, 151–164.

Gross, J.J., Sutton, S.K., & Ketelaar, T. (1998). Relations between affect and personality: Support for the affect-level and affect-reactivity views. *Personality and Social Psychology Bulletin, 24*, 279–288.

Hayes, S.C. (1976). The role of approach contingencies in phobic behavior. *Behavior Therapy, 7*, 28–36.

Hayes, S.C. (2004a). Acceptance and Commitment Therapy, Relational Frame Theory, and the third wave of behavioral and cognitive therapies. *Behavior Therapy, 35*, 639–666.

Hayes, S.C. (Ed.) (2004b). *Rule-governed behavior: cognition, contingencies, and instructional control.* Reno, NV: Context Press.

Hayes, S.C., & Wilson, K.G. (1993). Some applied implications of a contemporary behavior-analytic account of verbal events. *The Behavior Analyst, 16*, 283–301.

Hayes, S.C., & Wilson, K.G. (1994). Acceptance and commitment therapy: Altering the verbal support for experiential avoidance. *The Behavior Analyst, 17*, 289–303.

Hayes, S.C., Barnes-Holmes, D., & Roche, B. (2001). *Relational frame theory: A post-Skinnerian account of human language and cognition.* New York: Kluwer.

Hayes, S.C., Follette, V.M., & Linehan, M.M. (2004). *Mindfulness and acceptance: Expanding the cognitive-behavioral tradition.* New York: Guilford.

Hayes, S.C., Lattal, K.A., & Myerson, W.A. (1979). Strength of experimentally induced phobic behavior in rats: Avoidance versus dual-component formulations. *Psychological Reports, 44*, 891–894.

Hayes, S.C., Strosahl, K.D., & Wilson. K.G. (1999). Acceptance and Commitment Therapy: An experiential approach to behavior change. New York: Guilford.

Hayes, S.C., Brownstein, A.J., Zettle, R.D., Rosenfarb, I., & Korn, Z. (1986). Rule-governed behavior and sensitivity to changing consequences of responding. *Journal of the Experimental Analysis of Behavior, 45*, 237–256.

Hayes, S.C., Wilson, K.G., Gifford, E.V., Follette, V.M., & Strosahl, K. (1996). Experiential avoidance and behavioral disorders: A functional dimensional approach to diagnosis and treatment. *Journal of Consulting and Clinical Psychology, 64*, 1152–1168.

Hayes, S.C., Strosahl, K.D., Wilson, K.G., Bissett, R.T., Pistorello, J., Toarmino, D., et al. (2004). Measuring experiential avoidance: A preliminary test of a working model. *The Psychological Record, 54*, 553–578.

Heide, F.J., & Borkovec, T.D. (1983). Relaxation-induced anxiety: Paradoxical anxiety enhancement due to relaxation training. *Journal of Consulting and Clinical Psychology, 51*, 171–182.

Heimberg, R.G. (2002). Cognitive-behavioral therapy for social anxiety disorder: Current status and future directions. *Biological Psychiatry, 51*, 101–108.

Heimberg, R.G., Dodge, C.S., Hope, D.A., Kennedy, C.R., Zollo, L.J., & Becker, R.E. (1990). Cognitive-behavioral group treatment for social phobia: Comparison with a credible placebo control. *Cognitive Therapy and Research, 14*, 1–23.

Hofmann, S.G. (2004). Cognitive mediation of treatment change in social phobia. *Journal of Consulting and Clinical Psychology, 72*, 392–399.

Jacobson, N.S., Christensen, A., Prince, S.E., Cordova, J., & Eldridge, K. (2000). Integrative behavioral couple therapy: An acceptance-based, promising new treatment for couple discord. *Journal of Consulting and Clinical Psychology, 68*, 351–355.

John, O.P., & Gross, J.J. (2004). Healthy and unhealthy emotion regulation: Personality processes, individual differences, and life span development. *Journal of Personality, 72*, 1301–1333.

John, O.P., & Srivastava, S. (1999). The Big Five trait taxonomy: History, measurement, and theoretical perspectives. In L.A. Pervin & O.P. John (Eds.), *Handbook of personality: Theory and research*, 2nd ed. (pp. 102–138). New York: Guilford.

Kagan, J. (1989). Temperamental contributions to social behavior. *American Psychologist, 44,* 668–674.

Kagan, J., & Snidman, N. (1999). Early childhood predictors of adult anxiety disorders. *Biological Psychiatry, 46,* 1536–1541.

Karekla, M., & Forsyth, J.P. (2004, November). A comparison between acceptance enhanced cognitive behavioral and Panic Control Treatment for panic disorder. In S.M. Orsillo (Chair), Acceptance-based behavioral therapies: New directions in the treatment development across the diagnostic spectrum. Paper presented at the 38th annual meeting of the Association for Advancement of Behavior Therapy, New Orleans, LA.

Karekla, M., Forsyth, J.P., & Kelly, M.M. (2004). Emotional avoidance and panicogenic responding to a biological challenge procedure. *Behavior Therapy, 35,* 725–746.

Kohlenberg, R.J., & Tsai, M. (1991). *Functional analytic psychotherapy: Creating intense and curative relationships.* New York: Plenum.

Ladouceur, R. (1983). Participant modeling with or without cognitive treatment for phobias. *Journal of Consulting Clinical Psychology, 51,* 942–944.

Larsen, R.J., & Ketelaar, T. (1989). Extraversion, neuroticism, and susceptibility to positive and negative mood induction procedures. *Personality and Individual Differences, 10,* 1221–1228.

Lazarus, R.S., & Alfert, E. (1964). Short-circuiting of threat by experimentally altering cognitive appraisal. *Journal of Abnormal and Social Psychology, 69,* 195–205.

LeDoux, J.E. (2000). Emotion circuits in the brain. *Annual Review of Neuroscience, 23,* 155–184.

Leen-Feldner, E.W., Zvolensky, M.J., Feldner, M.T., & Lejuez, C.W. (2004). Behavioral inhibition: Relation to negative emotion regulation and reactivity. *Personality and Individual Differences, 36,* 1235–1247.

Levitt, J.T., Brown, T.A., Orsillo, S.M., & Barlow, D.H. (2004). The effects of acceptance versus suppression of emotion on subjective and psychophysiological response to carbon dioxide challenge in patients with panic disorder. *Behavior Therapy, 35,* 747–766.

Linehan, M.M. (1993). *Skills training manual for treating borderline personality disorder.* New York: Guilford.

Margraf J., Barlow D.H., Clark D.M., & Telch M.J. (1993). Psychological treatment of panic: Work in progress on outcome, active ingredients, and follow-up. *Behaviour Research and Therapy, 31,* 1–8.

Marcks, B.A., & Woods, D.W. (2005). A comparison of thought suppression to an acceptance-based technique in the management of personal intrusive thoughts: A controlled evaluation. *Behaviour Research and Therapy, 43,* 433–445.

Marks, I.M. (1969). *Fears and phobias.* New York: Academic Press.

Marks, I. (1981). *Cure and care of neurosis.* New York: Wiley.

Marks, I., & Horder, J. (1987). Phobias and their management. *British Medical Journal, 295,* 589–591.

Marks, I., Lovell, K., Noshirvani, H., Livanou, M., & Thrasher, S. (1998). Treatment of post-traumatic stress disorder by exposure and/or cognitive restructuring: A controlled study. *Archives of General Psychiatry, 55,* 317–325.

Marx, B.P., & Sloan, D.M. (2002). The role of emotion in the psychological functioning of adult survivors of childhood sexual abuse. *Behavior Therapy, 33,* 562–577.

Mattick, R.P., & Peters, L. (1988). Treatment of severe social phobia: Effects of guided exposure with and without cognitive restructuring. *Journal of Consulting and Clinical Psychology, 56,* 251–260.

Mattick, R.P., Peters, L., & Clarke, J.C. (1989). Exposure and cognitive restructuring for social phobia: A controlled study. *Behavior Therapy, 20,* 3–23.

McLaren, S., & Crowe, S.F. (2003). The contribution of perceived control of stressful life events and thought suppression to the symptoms of obsessive-compulsive disorder in both non-clinical and clinical samples. *Journal of Anxiety Disorders, 17,* 389–403.

Menzies, R.G., & Clarke, J.C. (1995). The etiology of phobias: A non-associative account. *Clinical Psychology Review, 15,* 23–48.

Michelson, L.K., Marchione, K., Greenwald, M., Giantz, L., Marchione, N. & Testa, S. (1990). Panic disorder: Cognitive-behavioral treatment. *Behaviour Research and Therapy, 28,* 141–151.

Mineka, S., & Cook, M. (1993). Mechanisms involved in the observational conditioning of fear. *Journal of Experimental Psychology: General, 122,* 23–38.

Mineka, S., & Ben Hamida, S. (1998). Observational and nonconscious learning. In W.T. O'Donohue (Ed.), *Learning and behavior therapy* (pp.421–439). Needham Heights, MA: Allyn and Bacon.

Mineka, S., & Zinbarg, R. (1996). Conditioning and ethological models of anxiety disorders: Stress-in-dynamic context anxiety models. In D.A. Hope (Ed.), *Perspectives on anxiety, panic, and fear: Volume 43 of the Nebraska symposium on motivation* (pp. 135–210). Lincoln: Nebraska University Press.

Mineka, S., Watson, D., & Clark, L.A. (1998). Comorbidity of anxiety and unipolar mood disorders. *Annual Review of Psychology, 49,* 377–412.

Mineka, S., Mystkowski, J., Hladek, D., & Rodriguez, B. (1999). The effects of changing contexts on return of fear following exposure treatment for spider fear. *Journal of Consulting and Clinical Psychology, 67,* 599–604.

Mowrer, O.H. (1939). A stimulus-response analysis of anxiety and its role as a reinforcing agent. *Psychological Review, 46,* 553–565.

Mowrer, O.H. (1960). *Learning theory and behavior.* New York: Wiley.

Mystkowski, J.L., Craske, M.G., & Echiverri, A.M. (2002). Treatment context and return of fear in spider phobia. *Behaviour Therapy, 33,* 399–416.

Newman, C.F. (2003). Cognitive restructuring: Identifying and modifying maladaptive schemas. In W. O'Donohue, J.E. Fisher, & S.C. Hayes (Eds.), *Cognitive behavior therapy: Applying empirically supported treatments in your practice.* Mahwah, NJ: John Wiley and Sons, Inc.

Ochsner, K.N., Bunge, S.A., Gross, J.J., & Gabrieli, J.D.E. (2002). Rethinking feelings: An fMRI study of the cognitive regulation of emotion. *Journal of Cognitive Neuroscience, 14*(8), 1215–1229.

Ochsner, K.N., & Gross, J.J. (2004). Thinking makes it so: A social cognitive neuroscience approach to emotion regulation. In R.F. Baumeister & K.D. Vohs (Eds.), *Handbook of Self-Regulation: Research, Theory, and Applications* (pp. 229–255). New York: Guilford Press.

Orr, S.P., Metzger, L.J., Lasko, N.B., Macklin, M.L., Peri, T., & Pitman, R.K. (2000). De novo conditioning in trauma-exposed individuals with and without posttraumatic stress disorder. *Journal of Abnormal Psychology, 109,* 290–298.

Öst, L.G. (1997). Rapid treatment of specific phobias. In G. Davey (Ed.), *Phobias: A handbook of theory, research, and treatment* (pp. 227–246). Chichester: John Wiley.

Öst, L.G., & Breitholtz, E. (2000). Applied relaxation vs. cognitive therapy in the treatment of generalized anxiety disorder. *Behavior Research and Therapy, 38,* 777–790.

Parrott, W.G. (1993). Beyond hedonism: Motives for inhibiting good moods and for maximizing bad moods. In D.M. Wegner & J.W. Pennebaker (Eds.), *Handbook of mental control* (pp. 278–308). Englewood Cliffs, NJ: Prentice-Hall.

Pennebaker, J.W., & Beall, S.K. (1986). Confronting a traumatic event: Toward an understanding of inhibition and disease. *Journal of Abnormal Psychology, 95,* 274–281.

Pitman, R.K., & Orr, S.P. (1986). Test of the conditioning model of neurosis: Differential aversive conditioning of angry and neutral facial expressions in anxiety disorder patients. *Journal of Abnormal Psychology, 95,* 208–213.

Purdon, C. (1999). Thought suppression and psychopathology. *Behaviour Research and Therapy, 37,* 1029–1054.

Quilty, L.C., Van Ameringen, M., Mancini, C., Oakman, J., & Farvolden, P. (2003). Quality of life and the anxiety disorders. *Journal of Anxiety Disorders, 17,* 405–426.

Rachman, S.J. (1977). The conditioning theory of fear acquisition: A critical examination. *Behaviour Research and Therapy, 15,* 375–387.

Rachman, S. (1989). The return of fear: review and prospect. *Clinical Psychology Review, 9,* 147–168.

Rachman, S. (1990). *Fear and courage,* 2nd ed. New York: W.H. Freeman Co.

Rachman, S. (1991). Neo-conditioning and the classical theory of fear acquisition. *Clinical Psychology Review, 11,* 155–173.

Rachman, S. (2004). *Anxiety,* 2nd ed. New York: Psychology Press.

Rachman, S., & Whittal, M. (1989). Fast, slow and sudden reductions in fear. *Behaviour Research and Therapy, 27,* 613–620.

Richards, J.M., & Gross, J.J. (1999). Composure at any cost?: The cognitive consequences of emotion suppression. *Personality and Social Psychology Bulletin, 25,* 1033–1044.

Richards, J.M., & Gross, J.J. (2000). Emotion regulation and memory: The cognitive costs of keeping one's cool. *Journal of Personality and Social Psychology, 79,* 410–424.

Rodriguez, B.I., Craske, M.G., Mineka, S., & Hladek, D. (1999). Context-specificity of relapse: Effects of therapist and environmental context on return of fear. *Behaviour Research and Therapy, 37,* 845–862.

Rosen, J.B., & Schulkin, J. (1998). From normal fear to pathological anxiety. *Psychological Review, 105,* 325–250.

Rothbaum, B.O., Hodges, L.F., Anderson, P.L., Price, L., & Smith, S. (2002). Twelve-month follow-up of virtual reality and standard exposure therapies for the fear of flying. *Journal of Consulting & Clinical Psychology, 70,* 428–432.

Salkovskis, P.M. (1996). The cognitive approach to anxiety: Threat beliefs, safety seeking behavior, and the special case of health anxiety and obsessions. In P.M. Salkovskis (Ed.), *Frontiers of Cognitive Therapy* (pp. 49–74). New York: Guilford.

Salters-Pedneault, K., Tull, M.T., & Roemer, L. (2004). The role of avoidance of emotional material in the anxiety disorders. *Applied and Preventive Psychology, 11,* 95–114.

Schmidt, N.B., Woolaway-Bickel, K., Trakowski, J., Santiago, H., Storey, J., Koselka, M., et al. (2000). Dismantling cognitive-behavioral treatment for panic disorder: Questioning the utility of breathing retraining. *Journal of Consulting and Clinical Psychology, 68,* 417–424.

Segal, Z.V., Williams, J.M.G., & Teasdale, J.D. (2002). *Mindfulness-based cognitive therapy for depression: A new approach to preventing relapse.* New York: Guilford.

Shafran, R., Booth, R., & Rachman, S. (1993). The reduction of claustrophobia: II. Cognitive analyses. *Behaviour Research and Therapy, 31,* 75–85.

Sloan, D.M. (2004). Emotion regulation in action: Emotional reactivity in experiential avoidance. *Behaviour Research and Therapy, 42,* 1257–1270.

Spira, A.P., Zvolensky, M.J., Eifert, G.H., & Feldner, M.T. (2004). Avoidance-oriented coping as a predictor of anxiety-based physical stress: A test using biological challenge. *Journal of Anxiety Disorders, 18,* 309–323.

Staats, A.W., & Eifert, G.H. (1990). The paradigmatic behaviorism theory of emotions. *Clinical Psychology Review, 10,* 539–566.

Stopa, L., & Clark, D.M. (1993). Cognitive processes in social phobia. *Behavior Research and Therapy, 31,* 255–267.

Suomi, S.J. (1999). Attachment in rhesus monkeys. In J. Cassidy & P.R. Shaver (Eds.), *Handbook of attachment: Theory, research, and clinical application* (pp. 181–197). New York: Guilford Press.

Taylor, S., Woody, S., Koch, W., McLean, P., Paterson, R., & Anderson, K.W. (1997). Cognitive restructuring in the treatment of social phobia: Efficacy and mode of action. *Behavior Modification, 21,* 487–511.

Tellegen, A. (1985). Structures of mood and personality and their relevance to assessing anxiety, with an emphasis on self-report. In A.H. Tuma & J. Maser (Eds.), *Anxiety and the anxiety disorders* (pp. 681–706). Hillsdale, NJ: Lawrence Erlbaum.

van Balkom, A.J.L.M., Bakker, A., Spinhoven, P., Blaauw, B.M.J.W., Smeenk, S., & Ruesink, B. (1997). A meta-analysis of the treatment of panic disorder with or without agoraphobia: A comparison of psychopharmacological, cognitive-behavioral, and combination treatments. *Journal of Nervous and Mental Disease, 185,* 510–516.

van Balkom, A.J.L.M., van Oppen, P., Vermeulen, A.W.A., van Dyck, R., Nauta, M.C.E., & Vorst, H.C.M. (1994). A meta-analysis of the treatment of obsessive-compulsive disorder: A comparison of antidepressants, behavioral, and cognitive therapy. *Clinical Psychological Review, 14,* 359–381.

van Etten, M., & Taylor, S. (1998). Comparative efficacy of treatments for posttraumatic stress disorder: A meta-analysis. *Clinical Psychology and Psychotherapy, 5,* 126–145.

van Oppen, P., de Haan, E., van Balkom, A.J.L.M., Spinhoven, P., Hoogduin, K., & van Dyck, R. (1995). Cognitive therapy and exposure in vivo in the treatment of obsessive compulsive disorder. *Behavior Research and Therapy, 33,* 379–390.

Watson, J.B., & Rayner, R. (1920). Conditioned emotional reactions. *Journal of Experimental Psychology, 3,* 1–14.

Wegner, D.M. (1994). Ironic processes of mental control. *Psychological Review, 101,* 34–52.

Westling, B.E., & Öst, L.-G. (1999). Brief cognitive behaviour therapy of panic disorder. *Scandinavian Journal of Behaviour Therapy, 28,* 49–57.

Williams, J.M.G., Mathews, A., & MacLeod, C. (1996). The emotional stroop task and psychopathology. *Psychological Bulletin, 120,* 3–24.

Williams, J.M.G., Watts, F.N., MacLeod, C., & Mathews, A. (1988). *Cognitive psychology and emotional disorders.* Chichester: Wiley.

Williams, S.L. (2004). Anxiety. In J.E. Maddux & B.A. Winstead (Eds.), Psychopathology: Contemporary issues, theory, and research (pp. 127–154). Hillsdale: Erlbaum.

Wolpe, J. (1958). Psychotherapy by reciprocal inhibition. Stanford, CA: Stanford University Press.

Wolpe, J., & Rachman, S. (1960). Psychoanalytic "evidence": A criticism based on Freud's case of Little Hans. *Journal of Nervous and Mental Disease, 131,* 135–148.

Wolpe, J., & Rowan, V.C. (1988). Panic disorder: A product of classical conditioning. *Behaviour Research and Therapy, 26,* 441–450.

Zettle, R.D., & Hayes, S.C. (1982). Rule governed behavior: A potential theoretical framework for cognitive-behavior therapy. In P.C. Kendall (Ed.), *Advances in cognitive-behavioral research and therapy,* Vol. 1 (pp. 73–118). New York: Academic.

Zinbarg, R.E., Craske, M.G., & Barlow D.H. (1993). *Mastery of your anxiety and worry.* Boulder, CO: Graywind Publications.

CHAPTER 4

Translational Research Perspectives on Maximizing the Effectiveness of Exposure Therapy

Mark B. Powers
Boston University

Jasper A. J. Smits
Southern Methodist University

Teresa M. Leyro and Michael W. Otto
Boston University

This chapter is designed to provide an accounting of the successes, and more important, the failures (nonresponse and relapse) of exposure-based treatment for the anxiety disorders, relative to current conceptualizations of the nature and limits of extinction learning. As compared to early conceptualizations of extinction as the systematic *unlearning* of a learned association, modern learning theory now conceptualizes extinction as the acquisition of *new learning* (e.g., Bouton 2002, 2004; Rescorla, 2001). In terms of fear conditioning, extinction is the relearning of safety to a cue (e.g., a tone) that has been previously associated (e.g., through tone-shock pairings) with fear. This learning occurs as a result of repeated presentations of the tone in the absence of the shock.

As we detail next, the distinction between extinction as an active learning of safety, rather than a passive weakening of fear learning, is especially important for designing strategies to maximize the acquisition and retention of extinction. Indeed, inherent within the "new learning" perspective is the idea that this new learning has to compete with previous learning, and that this competition may be resolved in terms of either the old learning (fear) or the new learning (relative safety). Which learning experiences dominate any current situation appears to depend on the context of the learning and recall cues (Bouton, 2004). For example, in a fear-learning paradigm where a tone is paired with a shock (fear acquisition), fear behaviors decrease when the tone is presented alone, with no shock present (fear extinction); however, learning of extinction appears to be sensitive to the context of learning (Bouton, 2004). Examples of contexts that have been manipulated in the literature include rooms, placement, environment, and other external background stimuli (Bouton, 1993; Smith, 1988; Spear, 1978). If fear conditioning is completed in one context (Context A), but then extinguished in a different context (Context B), the degree to which the conditioned stimulus (tone) elicits fear behaviors is dependent on whether the tone is re-presented in Context A or B (or a novel context C). The reemergence of fear when the cue is presented in the context of original fear learning (Context A) or novel context (Context C) is termed *renewal* (Bouton, 2002).

Related extinction effects that also demonstrate the retention of the original fear learning despite extinction include (1) *reinstatement* (e.g., Bouton, 1984; Delamater, 1997; Pavlov, 1927; Rescorla & Heth, 1975), the reemergence of fear from re-presentation of the unconditioned stimulus (e.g., the shock) in the same context where the CS is later presented, (2) *spontaneous recovery* (e.g., Brooks & Bowker, 2001; Brooks, Karamanlian, & Foster, 2001; Brooks & Bouton, 1993), the reemergence of the original fear learning as the extinction context becomes temporally remote, and (3) *rapid reacquisition* (e.g., Napier, Macrae, & Kehoe, 1992; Bouton, 1986; Bouton, 1993), relearning of the association between the conditioned stimulus (CS) and the unconditioned stimulus (US) is more efficient after extinction than if never learned, although this effect has been demonstrated for associations other than fear extinction. Each of these phenomena provide evidence for the retention of fear learning despite extinction and elucidate the conditions under which the competition between fear and safety learning is likely to be resolved in favor of the fear learning. The bad news, for the goal of eliminating fear, is that fear acquisition appears to be more resilient to changes in context than fear extinction. This phenomenon is nicely illustrated by the renewal effect when three contexts are used: a fear acquisition context (A), an extinction context (B), and a third, novel context (C). After fear acquisition and extinction, fear behavior tends to be renewed in context A while extinction tends to be maintained in context B. But the renewal of fear also occurs in the third, novel context (C), providing evidence for greater context dependence of the extinction as compared to the acquisition learning.

A natural compensatory strategy to help maximize safety learning and reduce the risk of relapse resulting from context dependency is to conduct exposures in varying contexts (Chelonis, Calton, Hart, & Schachtman, 1999; Gunther, Denniston, & Miller, 1998; Vansteenwegen, Dirikx, Hermans, Vervliet, & Eelen, 2006). To investigate the effectiveness of using multiple contexts in extinguishing fears, Gunther, et al. (1998) examined how well animals were able to unlearn an excitatory reaction to a CS that had previously been paired with an aversive consequence in a single context. They found that rats that underwent extinction in three different exposure contexts responded less to the CS when placed in a fifth test context than were those rats that underwent extinction in only one novel context. The authors also found, however, that when rats learned and unlearned the association of the CS and aversive consequence in three contexts, they were no longer more equipped to display dampened reactions to the CS in a test condition than were rats that were learned and unlearned fear associations in one context (Guntherr, et al., 1998). These data suggest that if fear learning occurs in more than one context, it is even more critical to conduct exposures in multiple contexts; however, some researchers have been unable to replicate these findings (Bouton, García-Gutiérrez, Zilski, and Moody, in press).

It is also important to note that contexts include interoceptive stimuli as well as exteroceptive stimuli. Examples of interoceptive contexts that have been manipulated in studies include drug state (Bouton, Kenney, & Rosengard, 1990), hormonal state (Ahlers & Richardson, 1985), mood state (Bower, 1981), deprivation state (Davidson, 1993), recent events (Bouton, Rosengard, Achenbach, Peck, & Brooks, 1993; Rosas & Bouton, 1998), expectation of events (Bouton, et al., 1993), and time (Bouton, 1993). For example, Bouton, et al. (1990) conducted extinction trials with rats that were under the influence of a benzodiazepine or a placebo. Fear was renewed when these rats were later tested in a drug-incongruent state (e.g., extinction in drug state; test in nondrug state or the reverse).

CONTEXT EFFECTS IN CLINICAL STUDIES

Context effects have also been observed in studies with humans with anxiety disorders (Mineka, Mystkowski, Hladek, & Rodriguez, 1999; Mystkowski, Mineka, Vernon, & Zinbarg, 2003) and substance use disorders (Collins & Brandon, 2002). For example, Mineka, et al. (1999) treated 36 spider-fearful participants in a single session of exposure therapy. They were then tested in either the same or different context 1 week later. Context was defined in this study by (1) gender and clothing of the experimenter, (2) room size, (3) visual cues in the room, (4) room location, and (5) size and color of exposure tools such as gloves or the spider container. Consistent with prediction, participants in the different context at the follow-up assessment displayed greater return of fear.

Even stronger evidence for context effects was provided for shifts in internal contexts. Specifically, Mystkowski, et al. (2003) investigated the effects of internal context by having participants ingest either caffeine or placebo during a single session of exposure-based treatment for spider phobia. Both groups improved significantly at the post-treatment assessment on the same day. Context was manipulated at the 1-week follow-up assessment so that participants were reconfronted with the spider under an incongruent condition (i.e., treated while taking caffeine, but tested while taking placebo, or the reverse) or a congruent condition (i.e., treated and tested while taking caffeine or treated and tested while taking placebo). Significantly greater return of fear was found for participants who were retested in the incongruent condition, providing support for a renewal effect linked to internal context.

Elsewhere we have discussed the potential role of internal context effects in the combination treatment literature (Otto, Smits, & Reese, 2005). Specifically, research on context effects suggests that what is learned during exposure while on medication may not transfer well to the nonmedicated state because of a shift in internal context. This effect is nicely exemplified by studies that examined exposure-based cognitive-behavioral therapy (CBT) alone compared with CBT combined with medication. In this design, patients undergoing exposure would be expected to acquire safety in both conditions, but in the combination-treatment group, this "learned safety" is occurring in the context of (the feel of) medication. When medication discontinuation brings a context shift, attenuation of learned safety would be expected. This expectation fits the available data well. Two, large multicenter trials document that some of the benefits of CBT provided during medication treatment are lost when medication is discontinued, so that the long-term effects of combined treatment appear to be inferior to CBT alone (Barlow, Gorman, Shear, & Woods, 2000; Marks, et al., 1993). There is suggestive evidence for a similar effect for the combined treatment of social phobia, with evidence that combined treatment does not have an advantage over CBT alone over longer term intervals (Cottraux, Mollard, Bouvard, & Marks, 1993; Haug, et al., 2003).

CLINICAL IMPLICATIONS OF CONTEXT EFFECTS

The distinction between extinction as an active learning of safety, rather than a passive weakening of fear learning, is especially important for conceptualizing exposure interventions. From a passive learning perspective, the therapist simply needs to arrange for exposure to relevant fear cues (CSs) in the absence of aversive outcomes (USs). From an active-learning perspective, therapists need to marshal resources for the most active discrimination of safety during exposure and the strongest retention of this learning over time. Several corollaries to this general principle deserve attention.

First, exposure needs to target the correct core fears, with attention to the settings and conditions that modulate these fears. Clinicians who treat panic disorder, for example, are well aware of the degree to which contexts influence core fears of anxiety and panic sensations. Sensations of anxiety may be viewed as relatively safe when they occur in the clinician's office but terrifying when occurring outside the office. In addition to being outside the office, these sensations may be further amplified by other external (in a car, driving fast) or internal (feeling sleep deprived) contextual factors that help define the "dangerousness" of the situation. For exposure to accurately target a fear, the complex constellation of fear cues and contexts needs to be understood.

Second, clinicians need to attend to what is *being learned from exposure*, with evaluation of the degree to which conditional safety, as compared to a broader sense of safety, is being acquired. Research on context and renewal effects underscores the limitations in exposure learning (risk for relapse) that comes from exposure in only select contexts. Presumably, for exposure to be broadly effective, experiences with phobic cues need to occur under a wide variety of circumstances so that learned safety is not judged to be specific to these special circumstances (e.g., "I am OK as long as I have my cell phone," "I am OK as long as I am rested," "I am OK as long as I take my pills").

Third, clinicians need to attend to the retention of learned safety. Context is certainly one cue for recall, and hence, the inclusion of multiple practices and multiple cues for recall in exposure sessions is one strategy to aid the recall of safety learning over competing memories of fear learning. The importance of recall is underscored by the brevity of treatment in the lives of patients. For example, a weekly 50-minute session accounts for less than 1% of an average patient's waking life (Otto, 2000). Brief CBT attempts to bring about dramatic changes, using this 1% of time, in as little as a dozen weeks for chronic conditions such as panic disorder (e.g., with a mean duration of disorder of 10 years before treatment; Otto, Pollack, Sachs, O'Neil, & Rosenbaum, 1992). Otto (2000) described the clinical use of stories and metaphors during treatment to enhance the salience of session material to try to bridge the gap between the 1% of clinic time and the 99% of out-of-clinic time. When discussing the salience of memories for exposure or other therapy interventions, it is important to differentiate animal from human learning, given the human ability to use verbal symbolic processing in learning tasks (Blackledge & Hayes, 2001). This verbal learning provides for the efficiencies of instructional learning (i.e., humans learn outside of direct experiences) as well as the liabilities from this learning (i.e., learning independently of experience means that sometimes corrective experiences will be ignored in favor of long-held cognitions). To maximize learned safety, clinicians presumably will want to get their patients' cognitive rehearsals in line with the exposure experiences. In other words, adaptive memories for what is learned from exposure presumably can be enhanced by post-event (post-exposure) processing and verbal rehearsals. Moreover, verbal instruction can be used to help patients discriminate between past fear learning and current safety learning; that is, patients can rehearse, "things are different now, I have learned how to react differently to anxiety so that I shut down my panic cycles."

Figure 4.1 provides a summary of principles drawn from extinction research. Simply, therapists target the relevant fears for extinction learning and work to make this new learning salient, including providing multiple cues for recall. Use of multiple cues and contexts for safety learning helps ensure that learning is independent of contexts that will not be present in future situations (e.g., the therapist, the clinic, medication). Armed with these straightforward principles, we now consider research on the efficacy of exposure and relapse effects. In particular, from the perspective of context effects on extinction, we examine the role of increasing engagement and attention to learned safety, providing multiple cross context cues, enhancing the salience of session material, using multiple contexts under realistic conditions, and ensuring learning is independent of contexts that will not be present in the future (e.g., the therapist) when phobic stimuli are encountered.

Current animal research, with initial confirmatory findings in humans, indicates:

- **Safety learning is an active process of new learning**

- **New learning has to compete with old learning**

- **New learning is particularly context dependent**

- **Contexts can aid or impair recall of extinction depending on their meaning (association with fear or safety)**

Accordingly, exposure-based treatments can be potentially enhanced by:

- **Increasing engagement and attention to exposure-based learning**

- **Providing multiple cues (cross context) for recall of safety (extinction) learning**

- **Increasing the salience and memory of safety learning using exposure parameters,verbal rehearsals, cues, etc.**

- **Using multiple contexts for safety learning, with attention to completing exposure under realistic conditions (variable internal and external contexts)**

- **Ensuring that learning is independent of contexts that will not be present in the future (test) situations (e.g., the therapist, the clinic, pills).**

FIGURE 4.1 Principles drawn from extinction research.

EXPOSURE PARAMETERS FROM A CONTEXT PERSPECTIVE

Focus of Attention

Studies investigating the effects of distraction have often been contradictory (Arntz, Dreessen, & Merckelbach, 1991; Craske, Street, & Barlow, 1989; Craske, Street, Jayaraman, & Barlow, 1991; Kamphuis & Telch, 2000; Grayson, Foa, & Steketee, 1982, 1986; Johnstone, & Page, 2004; Oliver & Page, 2003; Rodriguez & Craske, 1995; van den Bergh, Eelen, & Baeyens, 1989). In some studies, there is a clear advantage when focusing on the core threat (Kamphuis & Telch, 2000), whereas other studies suggest there may be an advantage using distracted exposure through threat irrelevant conversation (Johnstone, & Page, 2004). On closer examination, these data suggest that the *type of distraction may be critical* in determining outcome and may hinge on the useful distinction made by Borkovec and Grayson (1980) between objective presentation of phobic stimuli and attention to and processing of the stimuli: "Objective presentation of the stimuli does not guarantee functional exposure to those stimuli" (p. 118). Accordingly, if participants are able to maintain a "functional" exposure to the stimuli while being distracted, they may fare better, whereas distraction that compromises functional exposure will likely interfere with fear reduction. For example, manipulation of cognitive factors such as attentional focus and feedback during exposure have provided encouraging data suggesting that greater fear reduction is achieved when phobic patients are encouraged to focus on their specific core threat during treatment (Kamphuis & Telch, 2000; Sloan, & Telch, 2002; Telch, Valentiner, Ilai, Young, Powers, & Smits, 2004), and that fear reduction is impeded when patients' attentional resources to focus on the threat are compromised via cognitive load manipulations (Kamphuis & Telch, 2000; Rodriguez & Craske, 1993; Telch et al., 2004). On the other hand, Johnstone and Page (2004) found that distraction that does not interfere with functional exposure may actually enhance fear reduction. They stressed the importance of maintaining visual attention to the phobic stimulus (spider) while engaging in either threat relevant or threat irrelevant conversation. The threat irrelevant group showed a clear advantage both within and between sessions. Taken together, these data suggest the benefit of maintaining focus on the stimulus during exposure but that there may be benefits in "acting" in such a way that is inconsistent with fear (i.e., having a normal conversation). The management of patient responses during exposure has also received particular attention in the study of "safety behaviors."

Safety Behaviors

What we have learned from contextual learning may help explain the deleterious effects of safety behavior use during exposures. Safety behaviors are ubiquitous among the anxiety disorders and include the many subtle avoidance, distraction, and escape strategies that may occur as a strategy to manage fear while a person is engaged in formal exposure (Wells, Clark, Salkovskis, Ludgate, Hackmann, & Gelder, 1995). For example, a socially phobic patient may grip objects tightly to prevent trembling, while a panic disorder patient may check his or her pulse to manage the fear of a heart attack. Safety behaviors often result in symptom reduction, but evidence from laboratory studies suggests that these actions impede the new learning that can be achieved with exposure-based treatment. More specifically, Sloan and Telch (2002) found that safety behavior availability during claustrophobia exposure, such as opening a window or unlocking the door, interfered with fear reduction, compared to exposure without safety behavior availability and focusing on their perceived core threat. However, the investigators found that only some of the participants engaged in the safety behaviors that were made available. It remained unclear whether the interfering effects were due to engaging in safety behavior utilization, the assurance of their availability if necessary, or both. Powers, Smits, and Telch (2004) found that the use or mere availability of the aids equally interfered with fear reduction. This is consistent with persistent fear in patients who carry "rescue medications" such as benzodiazepines in their pockets during in vivo exposures. Even though they don't take the pill, they are still learning conditional safety, "If I have my pill I won't panic." Recommendations based on these data are that the availability of safety behaviors should be identified and faded as part of exposure-based treatment.

Clinical evidence suggests that safety behavior fading indeed facilitates exposure efficacy. Wells and colleagues (1995) treated eight socially phobic patients in a counterbalanced within-subjects design. Exposure combined with the fading of safety behaviors resulted in significantly more fear reduction than exposure alone. Salkovskis, Clark, Hackman, Wells, and Gelder, (1999) also found significantly greater improvement in patients with panic disorder and agoraphobia who were encouraged to fade safety behaviors during exposure compared to those who continued to use them. This principle appears to apply well to the issue of medication discontinuation. As compared to the attenuation of CBT effects in individuals who later go on to discontinue medication, there is evidence of maintenance of expansion of treatment gains when the CBT spans the shift in context caused by medication discontinuation (i.e., exposure occurs during and after medication taper and discontinuation) (see Otto, et al., 2005).

Why are safety behaviors maladaptive? One account is that safety behaviors engender a context where safety learning is particularly conditional—where the specific conditions of the exposure do not adequately represent the patient's core fears ("I knew I could make it if I used my 'tricks,' but who knows what would have happened if I did not use them") and/or place the patient at risk for relapse should the safety behaviors not be fully available in the future. A more cognitive accounting of safety behaviors also underscores the idea of conditional safety and context; Salkovskis (1991) argued that safety behaviors result in misattribution of safety. More specifically, patients may incorrectly attribute "surviving" the exposure exercise to the availability of safety behaviors rather than learning that the situation is indeed innocuous. A similar accounting from a learning perspective emphasizes the role of safety behaviors as conditioned inhibitors that protect the conditioned stimulus from extinction (Bouton, Mineka, & Barlow, 2001). From this perspective, fear reduction occurs as a result of a type of "error correction" between predicted occurrence of the US and actual occurrence of the US in the presence of the CS. With use of a safety behavior, the original CS is changed (it becomes CS + safety cue), and hence, its meaning (its ability to predict the US) is changed. In other words, when a safety behavior (inhibitor) is paired with the CS (excitor) during extinction, it cancels the prediction that the US will occur. Because there is less violation of expectation, there is less learning in relation to the CS. Accordingly, the CS in the absence of the safety behavior retains its strength of prediction and its ability to generate fear.

Coping Versus Acceptance? Safe Only as Long as I Can Relax

A number of cognitive-behavior therapies have incorporated a coping focus into treatment with such strategies as progressive muscle relaxation and breathing retraining (Craske, 1999; Öst, 1988). New directions in the exposure-based methods, however, include a general focus on acceptance (Barlow, Allen, & Choate, 2004; Otto, Safren, & Pollack, 2004; Hayes, Strosahl, & Wilson, 1999). Many therapists struggle with the contradiction of telling a patient that there is nothing harmful about having a panic attack while stressing the importance of coping with or preventing them using relaxation strategies. If coping strategies like these are used as safety behaviors then fear reduction may actually be compromised (Schmidt, Woolaway-Bickel, Trakowski, Santiago, Storey, Koselka, et al., 2000). In fact, attempts to relax may have paradoxical effects (Wegner, et al., 1997). Therefore, a contemporary strategy for exposure is to help patients to do nothing to manage their anxiety when undergoing exposure.

Antiphobic Strategies

Sloan and Telch (2002) proposed that the mere act of engaging in safety behaviors may directly activate the alarm system, much like there are direct neural pathways for sensorimotor information to travel to the limbic system (Ledoux, 1998). Hence, they hypothesized that actions that are not consistent with threat transmission may facilitate fear reduction achieved with exposure-based practice. Such inclusion of antiphobic strategies involves more than eliminating safety behaviors; this is the active programming of behaviors that challenge the notion that one must be "careful" in a phobic situation. Preliminary evidence suggests that the inclusion of antiphobic strategies in exposure-based treatment protocols may indeed enhance outcome. For example, Wolitzky and Telch (2004) reported that participants with height phobia who used antiphobic actions such as jogging toward the railing, and making oneself dizzy near the railing, showed greater fear reduction compared to participants who completed exposure exercises as usual. Again, from a learning perspective, antiphobic strategies may function as "excitors" that increase the over-prediction of the US, thus resulting in a magnified discrepancy between the expectation of negative outcomes and the actual ("relatively safe") outcome achieved in exposure (Bouton, et al., 2001). Therefore, it is likely that the error correction and learning should also be magnified.

Postprocessing and Enhancing Disconfirming Evidence

As discussed earlier, the primary goal in conducting exposures is to help provide the patient with new corrective information that is not consistent with their core fears. In animal models, we simply conduct exposures to the CS without the US. Unfortunately, unlike animal extinction models, humans may not pay attention to what is learned during exposure. This represents the irony that comes with the gift of verbal learning. By guiding a patient's attention during exposures and conducting a post-event review of what was learned from the exposure, clinicians can improve the likelihood that patients are using their cognitive abilities in line with their exposure experiences. Most cognitive errors that anxiety patients make can be divided into an exaggerated estimate of the probability or perceived consequences of the feared event (Butler, & Mathews, 1983). Therefore, it is critical that when the feared outcome does not occur during exposures that we make sure the patient fully processes this fact. For example, outcome significantly improves when participants are guided to reevaluate their feared outcome during and after exposures (Kamphuis, & Telch, 2000; Telch, Valentiner, Ilai, Petruzzi, & Hehmsoth, 2000). It is hypothesized that this strategy works because the discrepancy between the stimuli and threat are made more salient.

Gradation of Exposure

Context research can also inform our choice of basic parameters of exposure-based treatments. Some of these parameters include the gradation of exposures, trial durations, session length, and spacing of sessions. In the case of deciding to use a fear hierarchy over flooding, context effects would predict that the gradation of exposure should not affect outcome unless patients discontinue treatment before reaching the highest item on their list. Only conducting exposures to easier items is in itself a context. This may leave patients thinking that they are safe only when the threat is minor. On the other hand, if the therapist suggests a very high fear item early in treatment and patients quit therapy, then they are in the same predicament. Research suggests that having patients confront easier items on their fear hierarchy versus starting at more advanced items does not often affect outcome (Gelder, Bancroft, Gath, Johnson, Mathews, & Shaw, 1973). Feigenbaum (1988), however, found a clear advantage for intense massed exposure (76% in total remission) compared to graded, spaced exposure (35% symptom free) as evaluated at a 5-year follow-up assessment. Many patients may reject this type of flooding, with evidence that dropouts may be common (Emmelkamp & Ultee, 1974; Emmelkamp & Wessels, 1975). Therefore, treatment manuals often suggest starting at an item with a moderate level of fear (Foa & Wilson, 2001) unless the patient is willing to try a more advanced item. This method affords a compromise in choosing a significantly threatening item while also protecting against potential patient attrition.

Length of Trials and Sessions

The general rule for exposure is to conduct the exposure long enough to ensure that fear decreases during the exposure session, with suggestions to continue a trial of exposure until the patient reports at least a 50% reduction in his or her subjective fear rating (Foa & Wilson, 2001). Research suggests that the more exposure a fearful person has to stimuli, the greater the fear reduction tends to be (Marks, 1975). For example, Chaplin and Levine (1981) compared 25- and 50-minute exposures among speech-anxious participants. There was significantly greater fear reduction in the 50-minute trial group. In fact, examination of the process data in this group showed that fear tended to rise for the first 25 minutes of exposure and then decline rapidly. This study highlights the importance of conducting exposure until fear declines to reap maximum benefit. Similarly, Marshall (1985) found that continuing exposure trials until subjective distress was very low (i.e., a subjective units of distress (SUD) rating of less than 10) outperformed a brief exposure condition (terminating exposure after only a slight reduction in fear or until 75% of maximum distress). Marshall (1985) also found that prolonged exposure (conducting exposures one-third longer than the duration required to reach a minimal distress level, i.e., SUD < 10) showed additional benefits at the 4-week follow-up evaluation.

Distribution of Sessions

Spacing of treatment sessions has also been investigated. Data support massed exposure at the outset of therapy combined with spacing sessions further apart as therapy progresses. More specifically, studies suggest advantages in short-term outcome with massed exposure (Foa, Jameson, Turner, & Payne, 1980; Stern & Marks, 1973) and other benefits (e.g., relapse prevention) in long-term outcome with spaced sessions (Dua, 1972; Rowe & Craske, 1998; Tsao & Craske, 2000). For example, Abramowitz, Foa, and Franklin (2003) found a trend for greater post-treatment improvement in an intensive treatment group (daily) but higher relapse at follow-up compared to twice-weekly therapy (see also Hafner, 1976; Jansson & Öst, 1982 for data on flooding). From the perspective of context learning, an intensive schedule may provide strong learning of safety, but that safety may be context dependent on acute experiences with therapy. With increasing time between treatment termination and subsequent encounters with phobic cues, the original fear learning may come to dominate. Accordingly, long-term outcome may be enhanced with spaced sessions because a time delay from the last exposure becomes part of the context signaling safety rather than fear (i.e., this is the context explanation of spontaneous recovery) (Bouton, 2002).

For purposes of strong acute outcome plus relapse prevention, an expanding schedule of sessions is recommended to accomplish both goals (Bjork & Bjork, 1992; Rowe & Craske, 1998). For example, Bjork and Bjork (1992) attend strongly to the potential competition between fear and safety learning and hypothesize that the new safety learning should be maximized by intensive exposure, but should fade over time, allowing old fear learning to once again dominate. These principles predict that massed exposure should predict superior outcome at post-treatment but that an expanding spaced schedule of exposure should result in greater fear reduction at follow-up evaluation. Indeed, Rowe and Craske (1998) found exactly this. Massed exposure with spider-fearful participants resulted in greater fear reduction at post-assessment, but an expanding spaced schedule of exposure was superior at follow-up assessment. An expanding spaced schedule may offer intense learning experiences early in treatment and then opportunities to further learn safety in the latter stage of treatment when the declining schedule of sessions (e.g., transitioning from weekly to monthly) ensures that passage of time is part of the context cues for successful reentry into phobic situations. Although the effects of massing extinction intertrial intervals are supported by the literature, the beneficial effects of spacing intertrial intervals on relapse are less consistent (Bouton, Woods, Moody, Sunsay, & García-Gutiérrez, in press).

Out-of-Clinic Practice: Adherence

To ensure that learned safety occurs in a context away from the therapist, home exposure assignments are essential. In most cases, these are the exposure assignments that share the most cues with their core fears (i.e., occur in their actual setting) and hence, stand out as being particularly important for the generalization of therapy gains to the nontherapy environment (De Araujo, Ito, & Marks, 1996). Although it stands to reason that more out-of-clinic exposure should be related to better outcome, this relationship has been only inconsistently demonstrated in the empirical literature. For example, research on homework adherence in an agoraphobic population has suggested a positive relationship between homework compliance and long-term follow-up evaluation (Michelson, Mavissakalian, Marchione, Dancu, & Greenwald, 1986. Additional studies of exposure-based treatment for agoraphobia have found mixed outcomes (Edelman & Chambless, 1993) and even no support of a positive relationship between adherence and treatment outcomes (Barlow, O'Brien, & Last, 1984). For the treatment of social phobia, there is limited evidence suggesting a link between homework adherence and lower symptoms during treatment, and an initial finding suggesting that homework adherence is especially crucial during the first and final periods of CBT. Leung and Heimberg (1996) found that patients who complied with home-exposure assignments during these periods experienced lower levels of anxiety after treatment, but surprisingly those who complied during middle phases of treatment were found to have the opposite outcome.

Strategies to increase adherence (Malouff and Schutte, 2004) include the following: (1) psychoeducational efforts to help establish interest and motivation in the homework, with discussions of the elements, importance, and potential benefits of these procedures; (2) careful selection of a starting point for exposure, to allow initial experiences to be attainable and successful (perhaps with in-session rehearsal of relevant tasks); (3) both oral and written assignment of practice; and (4) discussion of where the assignment will be done and how, to aid recall, cues for, and confidence for the homework assignment. Motivational interviewing interventions (Burke, Arkowitz, & Menchola, 2003) and problem-solving methods (Malouff &

Schutte, 2004) are also useful strategies for helping patients solve motivational and practical blocks to adequate practice of therapy principles outside the session.

Pharmacological Strategies for Enhancing Safety Learning

Throughout this chapter we have emphasized the potential competition between fear and safety learning, and have recommended a variety of strategies to enhance the salience of exposure procedures, with the purpose of helping ensure that the exposure experience is salient enough that it will dominate in future recall situations (when confronted by a phobic cue). Management of the content and context of the exposure session, and use of relevant rehearsals and post-exposure processing strategies, are all aimed at helping safety learning emerge as the active memory when confronting the phobic stimulus in the future. Exciting new developments in the animal literature have introduced another strategy for increasing the salience of exposure memories—pharmacological enhancement of safety learning in humans.

This work grew out of the careful documentation of the neural circuits involved in fear and safety learning, with identification of the N-methyl-D-aspartate (NMDA) glutamatergic receptor as especially important in both conditioning and extinction (Davis & Myers, 2002). Administration of an NMDA antagonist blocks fear learning and extinction (Falls, Miserendino, & Davis, 1992; Davis & Myers, 2002), and administration of an NMDA agonist enhances fear extinction (Walker, Ressler, Lu, & Davis, 2002; Ledgerwood, Richardson, & Cranney, 2003). One such NMDA partial agonist is D-cycloserine (DCS), an antibiotic previously used to treat tuberculosis. Based on the animal findings with DCS, Ressler, Rothbaum, Tannenbaum, Anderson, Graap, Zimand, et al. (2004) randomized patients with acrophobia (fear of heights) to exposure plus DCS or exposure plus placebo. Consistent with prediction, patients who underwent exposure with the cognitive enhancer were significantly more improved when later tested without the drug. These exciting findings await replication and extension to other exposure-based treatments but are supportive of the role of DCS, applied in single doses before exposure, as having no in-session effects but promoting the retention of safety learning over time. Given the potential of these results, further investigations of the application of DCS to exposure protocols for the anxiety disorders are currently ongoing in multiple labs across the country, with the goal of showing that DCS speeds the acquisition of learned safety (allowing a strong response with fewer sessions of exposure) and may be helpful for patients who have failed to respond to previous treatment.

CONCLUDING COMMENTS

In this chapter, we emphasized the importance of conceptualizing exposure-based treatment as an active process of new safety learning. This is in opposition to the notion that extinction represents a destruction or replacement of fear learning. As discussed, both fear and safety responses are maintained even after extinction, leaving them in competition whenever the conditioned stimulus (CS) is encountered again. Because studies suggest the importance of context in determining whether safety or fear responses are retrieved on subsequent exposure to the CS, much of the purpose of this chapter was to discuss strategies that tip the scales in favor of the safety learning.

We organized this discussion around several simple principles, underscoring the proposition that contexts can aid or impair recall of extinction depending on their meaning (association with fear or safety) and arguing that clinicians need to actively evaluate the context and nature of learning in exposure assignments. Using this accounting of context effects as a heuristic, a wide variety of findings on exposure parameters—attention, safety behaviors, antiphobic behaviors, post-exposure processing, and the length and spacing of trials—were discussed from a unified perspective. By way of conclusion, we encourage clinicians to address two crucial questions in the construction of exposure assignments: (1) What is the nature of the new memory I need to help this patient form in order to have lasting relief from their anxiety disorder, and (2) What can I do to make this memory especially salient, so that it will be recalled readily in the future? In short, clinicians should construct exposure experiences that make use of as many contexts as possible to aid in the unconditional learning of safety.

REFERENCES

Abramowitz, J.S., Foa, E.B., & Franklin, M.E. (2003). Exposure and ritual prevention for obsessive-compulsive disorder: Effects of intensive versus twice-weekly sessions. *Journal of Consulting and Clinical Psychology, 71,* 394–398.

Ahlers, S.T., & Richardson, R. (1985). Administration of dexamethasone prior to training blocks ACTH-induced recovers of an extinguished avoidance response. *Behavioral Neuroscience, 99,* 760–764.

Arntz, A., Dreessen, L., & Merckelbach, H. (1991). Attention, not anxiety, influences pain. *Behaviour Research and Therapy, 29,* 41–50.

Barlow, D H., Allen, L.B., & Choate, M.L. (2004). Toward a unified treatment for emotional disorders. *Behavior Therapy, 35,* 205–230.

Barlow, D.H., Gorman, J.M., Shear, M.K., & Woods, S.W. (2000). Cognitive-behavior therapy, imipramine, or their combination for panic disorder: A randomized controlled trial. *Journal of the American Medical Association, 283,* 2529–2536.

Barlow, D.H., O'Brien, G.T., & Last, C.G. (1984). Couple treatment of agoraphobia. *Behavior Therapy, 15,* 41–58.

Bjork, R.A., & Bjork, E.L. (1992). A new theory of disuse and an old theory of stimulus fluctuation. In A.F. Healy & S.M. Kosslyn (Eds.), *Essays in honor of William K. Estes:* Vol. 2. *From Learning processes to cognitive processes.* (pp. 35–67). Hillsdale, NJ: Erlbaum.

Blackledge, J.T. & Hayes, S.C. (2001). Emotion regulation in acceptance and commitment therapy. *Journal of Clinical Psychology, 57,* 243–255.

Borkovec, T.D., & Grayson, J.B. (1980). Consequence of increasing the functional impact of internal emotional stimuli. In K. Blanskein, P. Pliner, & J. Policy (Eds.), *Advances in the study of communication and affect: Assessment and modification of emotional behaviour,* Vol. 6. (pp. 117–137). New York: Plenum Press.

Bouton, M.E. (1984). Differential control by context in the inflation and reinstatement paradigms. *Journal of Experimental Psychology: Animal Behavior Processes, 10,* 56–74.

Bouton, M.E. (1986). Slow reacquisition following the extinction of conditioned suppression. *Learning & Motivation, 17,* 1–15.

Bouton, M.E. (1993). Context time and memory retrieval in the interference paradigms of Pavlovian learning. *Psychological Bulletin, 114,* 80–99.

Bouton, M.E. (2002). Context, ambiguity, and unlearning: Sources of relapse after behavioral extinction. *Biological Psychiatry, 52,* 976–986.

Bouton, M.E. (2004). Context and behavioral processes in extinction. *Learning & Memory, 11,* 485–494.

Bouton, M.E., García-Gutiérrez, A., Zilski, J., & Moody, E.W. (in press). Extinction in multiple contexts does not necessarily make extinction less vulnerable to relapse. *Behaviour Research and Therapy.*

Bouton, M. E., Kenney, F. A., & Rosengard, C. (1990). State-dependent fear extinction with two benzodiazepine tranquilizers. *Behavioral Neuroscience, 104,* 44–55.

Bouton, M.E., Mineka, S., & Barlow, D.H. (2001). A modern learning theory perspective on the etiology of panic disorder. *Psychological Review, 108,* 4–32.

Bouton, M.E., Rosengard, C., Achenbach, G.G., Peck, C.A., & Brooks, D.C. (1993). Effects of contextual conditioning and unconditional stimulus presentation on performance in appetitive conditioning. *Quarterly Journal of Experimental Psychology, 46B,* 63–95.

Bouton, M.E., Woods, A.M., Moody, E.W., Sunsay, C., & García-Gutiérrez, A. (in press). Counteracting the context-dependence of extinction: Relapse and some tests of possible methods of relapse prevention. In M.G. Craske, D. Hermans, & D.Vansteenwegen (Eds.), *Fear and learning: Basic science to clinical application.* Washington, DC: American Psychological Association.

Bower, G.H. (1981). Mood and memory. *American Psychologist, 36,* 129–148.

Brooks, D.C. & Bouton, M.E. (1993). A retrieval cue for extinction attenuates spontaneous recovery. *Journal of Experimental Psychology: Animal Behavioral Processes, 19,* 77–89.

Brooks, D. C. & Bowker, J. L. (2001). Further evidence that conditioned inhibition is not the mechanism of an extinction cue's effect: A reinforced cue prevents spontaneous recovery. *Animal Learning and Behavior, 29,* 381–388.

Brooks, D.C., Karamanlian, B.R., & Foster, V.L. (2001). Extinction and spontaneous recovery of ataxic tolerance to ethanol in rats. *Psychopharmacology, 153,* 491–496.

Burke, B.L., Arkowitz, H., & Menchola, M. (2003). The efficacy of motivational interviewing: A meta-analysis of controlled clinical trials. *Journal of Consulting and Clinical Psychology, 71,* 843–861.

Butler, G., & Mathews, A. (1983). Cognitive processes in anxiety. *Advances in Behaviour Research and Therapy, 5,* 51–62.

Chaplin, E.W., & Levine, B.A. (1981). The effects of total exposure duration and interrupted versus continued exposure in flooding therapy. *Behavior Therapy, 12,* 360–368.

Chelonis, J.J., Calton, J.L., Hart, J.A., & Schachtman, T.R. (1999). Attenuation of the renewal effect by extinction in multiple contexts. *Learning and Motivation, 30,* 1–14.

Collins, B.N. & Brandon, T.H. (2002). Effects of extinction context and retrieval cues on alcohol cue reactivity among nonalcoholic drinkers. *Journal of Consulting and Clinical Psychology, 70,* 390–397.

Cottraux, J., Mollard, E., Bouvard, M., & Marks, I. (1993). Exposure therapy, fluvoxamine, or combination treatment in obsessive-compulsive disorder: One-year followup. *Psychiatry Research, 49*(1), 63–75.

Craske, M. (1999). *Anxiety Disorders.* Boulder, CO: Westview Press.

Craske, M.G., Street, L., & Barlow, D.H. (1989). Instructions to focus upon or distract from internal cues during exposure treatment of agoraphobic avoidance. *Behaviour Research and Therapy, 27,* 663–672.

Craske, M.G., Street, L.L., Jayaraman, J., & Barlow, D.H. (1991). Attention versus distraction during in vivo exposure: Snake and spider phobias. *Journal of Anxiety Disorders, 5,* 199–211.

Davidson, T.L. (1993). The nature and function of interoceptive signals to feed: Toward integration of physiological and learning perspectives. *Psychology Review, 100,* 640–657.

Davis, M., & Myers, K.M. (2002). The role of glutamate and gamma-aminobutyric acid in fear extinction: Clinical implications for exposure therapy. *Biological Psychiatry, 52,* 998–1007.

De Araujo, L.A. , Ito, L.M., & Marks, I. (1996). Early compliance and other factors predicting outcome of exposure for obsessive-compulsive disorder. *British Journal of Psychiatry, 169(6),* 747–752.

Delameter, A.R. (1997). Selective reinstatement of stimulus-outcome associations. *Animal Learning and Behavior, 25*(4), 400–412.

Dua, P.S. (1972). Group desensitization of phobia with three massing procedures. *Journal of Counseling Psychology, 19,* 125–129.

Edelman, R.E., & Chambless, D.L. (1993). Compliance during sessions and homework in exposure-based treatment of agoraphobia. *Behaviour Research and Therapy, 31,* 767–773.

Emmelkamp, P.M.G., & Ultee, K.A. (1974). A comparison of "successive approximation" and "self observation" in the treatment of agoraphobia. *Behavior Therapy, 5,* 606–613.

Emmelkamp, P.M.G., & Wessels, H. (1975). Flooding in imagination vs. flooding in vivo: A comparison with agoraphobics. *Behaviour Research and Therapy, 13,* 7–15.

Falls, W.A., Miserendino, M.J., & Davis, M. (1992). Extinction of fear-potentiated startle: Blockade by infusion of an NMDA antagonist into the amygdala. *Journal of Neuroscience, 12,* 854–863.

Feigenbaum, W. (1988). Long-term efficacy of ungraded versus graded massed exposure in agoraphobics. In I. Hand & H. Wittchen (Eds.), *Panic and phobias: Treatments and variables affecting course and outcome.* (pp. 149–158). Berlin: Springer–Verlag.

Foa, E.B., Jameson, J.S., Turner, R.M., & Paynes, L.L. (1980). Massed versus spaced exposure sessions in the treatment if agoraphobia. *Behaviour Research and Therapy, 18,* 333–338.

Foa, E.B., & Wilson, R. (2001). *Stop obsessing!* New York: Bantam Books.

Gelder, M.G., Bancroft, J.J., Gath, D.H., Johnson, D.W., Mathews, A.M., & Shaw, P.M. (1973). Specific and non-specific factors in behavior therapy. *British Journal of Psychiatry, 123,* 445–462.

Grayson, J.B., Foa, E.B., & Steketee, G. (1982). Habituation during exposure treatment: Distraction vs. Attention-focusing. *Behaviour Research and Therapy, 20,* 323–328.

Grayson, J.B., Foa, E.B., & Steketee, G. (1986). Exposure in vivo of obsessive-compulsives under distracting and attention-focusing conditions: Replication and extension. *Behaviour Research and Therapy, 24,* 475–479.

Gunther, L.M., Denniston, J.C., & Miller, R.R. (1998). Conducting exposure treatment in multiple contexts can prevent relapse. *Behaviour Research and Therapy, 36,* 75–91.

Hafner, R.J. (1976). Fresh symptom emergence after intensive behavior therapy. *British Journal of Psychiatry, 129,* 378–383.

Haug, T.T., Blomhoff, S., Hellstrom, K., Holme, I., Humble, M., Madsbu, H.P., & Wold, J.E. (2003). Exposure therapy and sertraline in social phobia: 1-year follow-up of a randomized controlled trial. *Birtish Journal of Psychiatry, 182*(4), 312–318.

Hayes, S.C., Strosahl, K.D., & Wilson, K.G. (1999). *Acceptance and commitment therapy: An experiential approach to behavior change.* New York: Guilford Press.

Jansson, L & Öst, L.G. (1982). Behavioral treatments for agoraphobia : An evaluative review. *Clinical Psychology Review, 2,* 311–336.

Johnstone, K.A., & Page, A.C. (2004). Attention to phobic stimuli during exposure: The effect of distraction on anxiety reduction, self-efficacy and perceived control. *Behaviour Research and Therapy, 42,* 249–275.

Kamphuis, J.H., & Telch, M.J. (2000). Effect of distraction and guided threat reappraisal on fear reduction during exposure-based treatments for specific fears. *Behaviour Research and Therapy, 38*(12), 1163–1181.

Ledgerwood, L., Richardson, R., & Cranney, J. (2003). Effects of D-cycloserine on extinction of conditioned freezing. *Behavioral Neuroscience, 117,* 341–349.

Ledoux, J. (1998). Fear and the brain. Where have we been and where are we going? *Biological Psychiatry, 44,* 1229–1238.

Leung, A.W., & Heimberg, R.G. (1996). Homework compliance, perceptions of control, and out-come of cognitive-behavioral treatment of social phobia. *Behaviour Research and Therapy, 34*(5–6), 423–432.

Malouff, J. & Schutte, N. S. (2004). Strategies for increasing client completion of treatment assignments. *Behavior Therapist, 27,* 118–121.

Marks, I. (1975). Behavioural treatments of phobic and obsessive-compulsive disorders: A critical appraisal. In M. Hersen, R.M. Eisler, & P. M. Miller (Eds.), *Progress in behavior modification,* Vol. 2. New York: Academic Press.

Marks, L.B., Swinson, R.P., Basoglu, M., Kuch, K., Noshirvani, H., O'Sullivan, G., et al. (1993). Alpra-zolam and exposure alone and combined in panic disorder with agoraphobia. A controlled study in London and Toronto. *British Journal of Psychiatry, 162,* 776–787.

Marshall, W.L. (1985). The effects of variable exposure in flooding therapy. *Behavior Therapy, 16,* 117–135.

Michelson, L., Mavissakalian, M., Marchione, K., Dancu, C., & Greenwald, M. (1986). The role of self-directed in vivo exposure in cognitive, behavioral, and psychophysiological treatments of agorapho-bia. *Behavior Therapy, 17,* 91–108.

Mineka, S., Mystkowski, J.L., Hladek, D. & Rodriguez, B.I. (1999). The effects of changing contexts on return of fear following exposure therapy for spider fear. *Journal of Consulting and Clinical Psychology, 67,* 599–604.

Mystkowski, J.L., Mineka, S., Vernon, L.L., & Zinbarg, R.E. (2003). Changes in caffeine states enhance return of fear in spider phobia. *Journal of Consulting and Clinical Psychology, 71,* 243–250.

Napier, R.M., Macrae, M., Kehoe, E. J. (1992). Rapid reacquisition in conditioning of the rabbit's nictitating membrane response. *Journal of Experimental Psychology: Animal Behavioral Processes, 18,* 182–192.

Oliver, N.S., & Page, A.C. (2003). Fear reduction during in vivo exposure to blood-injection stimuli: distraction vs. Attentional focus. *British Journal of Clinical Psychology, 42,* 13–25.

Öst, L.-G. (1988). Applied relaxation vs. progressive relaxation in the treatment of panic disorder. *Behav-iour Research and Therapy, 26,* 12–22.

Otto, M.W. (2000). Stories and metaphors in cognitive-behavior therapy. *Cognitive and Behavioral Practice, 7,* 166–172.

Otto, M.W., Pollack M.H., Sachs, G.S., O'Neil, C. A., & Rosenbaum, J. F. (1992). Alcohol dependence in panic disorder patients. *Journal of Psychiatric Research, 26,* 29–38.

Otto, M.W., Safren, S.A., & Pollack, M.H. (2004). Internal cue exposure and the treatment of substance use disorders: Lessons from the treatment of panic disorder. *Journal of Anxiety Disorders, 18,* 69–87.

Otto, M.W., Smits, J.A.J., & Reese, H.E. (2005). Combined psychotherapy and pharmacotherapy for mood and anxiety disorders in adults: Review and analysis. *Clinical Psychology: Science and Practice, 12,* 72–86.

Pavlov, I.P. (1927). *Conditioned Reflexes.* Oxford, UK: Oxford University Press.

Powers, M.B., Smits, J.A., & Telch, M.J. (2004). Disentangling the effects of safety-behavior utilization and safety-behavior availability during exposure-based treatment: a placebo-controlled trial. *Journal of Consulting and Clinical Psychology, 72*(3), 448–454.

Rescorla, R.A. (2001). Experimental extinction. In R.R. Mowrer & S.B. Klein (Eds.), *Handbook of contemporary learning theories* (pp. 119–154). Mahwah, NJ: Erlbaum.

Rescorla, R.A., & Heth, C.D. (1975). Reinstatement of fear to an extinguished conditioned stimulus. *Journal of Experimental Psychology: Animal Behavioral Processes, 1,* 88–96.

Ressler, K.J., Rothbaum, B.O., Tannenbaum, L., Anderson, P., Graap, K., Zimand, E., Hodges, L., & Davis, M. (2004). Cognitive enhancers as adjuncts to psychotherapy. *Archives of General Psychiatry, 61,* 1136–1144.

Rodriguez, B.I., & Craske, M.G. (1993). The effects of distraction during exposure to phobic stimuli. *Behaviour Research and Therapy, 31,* 549–58.

Rodriguez, B.I., & Craske, M.G. (1995). Does distraction interfere with fear reduction during exposure? A test among animal-fearful subjects. *Behavior Therapy, 26,* 337–349.

Rosas, J.M. & Bouton, M.E. (1998). Context change and retention interval can have additive, rather than interactive effects after taste aversion extinction. *Psychonomic Bulletin & Review, 5*, 79–83.

Rowe, M.K., & Craske, M.G. (1998). Effects of an expanding-spaced vs. Massed exposure schedule on fear reduction and return of fear. *Behaviour Research and Therapy, 36*, 701–717.

Salkovskis, P.M. (1991). The importance of behaviour in the maintenance of anxiety and panic: A cognitive account. *Behavioural. Psychotherapy, 19*, 6–19.

Salkovskis, P.M., Clark, D.M., Hackman, A., Wells, A., & Gelder, M.G. (1999). An experimental investigation of the role of safety-seeking behaviors in the maintenance of panic disorder with agoraphobia. *Behaviour Research and Therapy, 37*, 559–574.

Schmidt, N.B., Woolaway-Bickel, K., Trakowski, J., Santiago, H., Storey, J., Koselka, M., & Cook, J. (2000). Dismantling cognitive-behavioral treatment for panic disorder: Questioning the utility of breathing retraining. *Journal of Consulting and Clinical Psychology, 68*, 417–424.

Sloan, T., & Telch, M.J. (2002). The effects of safety-seeking behavior and guided threat reappraisal on fear reduction during exposure: an experimental investigation. *Behaviour Research and Therapy, 40*, 235–251.

Smith, S.M. (1988). Environmental context-dependent memory. In G.M. Davies & D.M. Thomson (Eds.), *Memory in context: Context in memory* (pp 13–34). New York: John Wiley and Sons.

Spear, N.E. (1978). *The processing of memories: Forgetting and retention.* Hillsdale, NJ: Erlbaum.

Stern, R.S., & Marks, I.M. (1973). Brief and prolonged flooding: A comparison of agoraphobic patients. *Archives of General Psychiatry, 28*, 270–276.

Telch, Valentiner, D.P., Ilai, D., Petruzzi, D., & Hehmsoth, M. (2000). The facilitative effects of heart-rate feedback in the emotional processing of claustrophobic fear. *Behaviour Research and Therapy, 38*, 373–387.

Telch, M.J., Valentiner, D.P., Ilai, D., Young, P.R., Powers, M.B., & Smits, J.A.J. (2004). Fear activation and distraction during the emotional processing of claustrophobic fear. *Journal of Behavior Therapy and Experimental Psychiatry, 35*, 219–232.

Tsao, J.C.I. & Craske, M.G. (2000). Timing of treatment and return of fear: Effects of massed, uniform-, and expanding-spaced exposure schedules. *Behavior Therapy, 31*, 479–497.

van den Bergh, O., Eelen, P., & Baeyens, F. (1989). Brief exposure to fear stimuli: Imagery ability as a condition of fear enhancement and fear decrease. *Behavior Therapy, 20*, 563–572.

Vansteenwegen, Dirikx, Hermans, Vervliet, & Eelen (2006). Multiple contexts during extinction of spider phobia may protect against relapse. In M. G. Craske, E. Hermans, & D. Vansteenwegen (Eds.), *Fear and learning: Basic science to clinical application.* Washington, DC: American Psychological Association.

Walker, D.L., Ressler, K.J., Lu, K.T., & Davis, M. (2002). Facilitation of conditioned fear extinction by systemic administration or intra-amygdala infusions of D-cycloserine as assessed with fear-potentiated startle in rats. *Journal of Neuroscience, 22*, 2343–2351.

Wegner, D.M., & Smart, L. (1997). Deep cognitive activation: A new approach to the unconscious. *Journal of Consulting and Clinical Psychology 65*(6), 984–995.

Wells, A., Clark, D.M., Salkovskis, P., Ludgate, J., Hackmann, A. & Gelder, M. (1995). Social phobia: The role of in-situation safety behaviors in maintaining anxiety and negative beliefs. *Behavior Therapy, 26*, 153–161.

Wolitzky, K.B. & Telch, M.J. (November 2004). Placebo Controlled Trial Investigating the Efficacy of Encouraging *Anti-Phobic Actions* during In Vivo Exposure Therapy: Work in Progress. Paper presented at the annual convention for the Association for the Advancement of Behavior Therapy, New Orleans, LA.

CHAPTER 5

Exposure Therapy and Post-Traumatic Stress Disorder

**Dean Lauterbach and
Sarah Reiland**
Eastern Michigan University

It has long been recognized that exposure to traumatic events can produce a wide range of symptoms (Trimble, 1985). A specific disorder devoted to the sequelae of trauma, however, did not become a part of the diagnostic nomenclature until 1980, with the publication of the third edition of the *Diagnostic and Statistical Manual* (DSM) (American Psychiatric Association, 1980). Its inclusion was driven, in large part, by veterans of the Vietnam conflict, and the initial notion was to label the disorder post-Vietnam syndrome (Helzer, Robins, & McEvoy, 1987). It rapidly became apparent, however, that similar symptoms emerged in victims of other types of trauma including disasters, physical assaults, sexual assaults, and accidents.

Trauma exposure and post-traumatic stress disorder (PTSD) are extremely common. Findings from the national comorbidity survey (Kessler, Sonnega, Bromet, Hughes, & Nelson, 1995) indicate that 60.7% of men and 51.2% of women have experienced an event of sufficient intensity to potentially elicit symptoms of PTSD. Among those exposed to trauma, 8.2% of men and 20.4% of women develop PTSD. PTSD is among the most prevalent disorders, and it has powerful consequences for those affected. For this reason, it is particularly important to identify effective treatments.

This chapter addresses a number of issues. First, the diagnostic characteristics of PTSD are briefly outlined. Next, several theories are presented that frame symptom emergence, persistence, and the mechanisms of change. Some of these theories have received considerable attention and were reviewed earlier in this volume (e.g., Foa & Kozak, 1986), whereas others are relatively new but have the potential to advance

Handbook of Exposure Therapies

thinking in the area. The review of theories is limited to those with a strong behavioral element. Exposure-based treatments have consistently proven effective for adults (Bradley, Greene, Russ, Dutra, & Westen, 2005; Rothbaum & Foa, 1999) and children (Cohen, Deblinger, Mannarino, & Steer, 2004; Feeny, Foa, Treadwell, & March, 2004), but they have not been widely accepted into regular clinical practice. A number of reasons have been proposed for this slow acceptance, and these issues are briefly addressed. Much of the chapter addresses methods of implementation and variations in the basic procedures that hold the promise of expanding the scope of persons who can be treated. In this vein, the chapter concludes with an extended discussion of the "state of the art" and areas in need of investigation.

DEFINITION OF PTSD

PTSD is composed of five diagnostic criteria. First, the individual must have experienced, witnessed, or confronted one or more traumatic events. Second, the response to the trauma must have involved intense fear, helplessness, or horror. Third, the event must be persistently reexperienced through distressing memories, dreams, or flashbacks, and exposure to reminders of the trauma produces distress and physiologically arousal. Fourth, there are efforts made to avoid trauma-related thoughts, feelings, sensations, places, or people. Avoidance strategies may be either direct (active) or indirect. Indirect avoidance symptoms include emotional detachment from others, blunted affect, or a sense of a foreshortened future. Although symptoms of active avoidance and numbing are included in the same diagnostic cluster, a number of studies have found these symptoms to form separate symptom constellations (King & King, 1994; Lauterbach, Vrana, King, & King, 1997).[*] Fifth, after the trauma, there is a persistent increase in physiological arousal. Examples of hyperarousal include difficulty falling/staying asleep, irritability, difficulty concentrating, hypervigilance, or an exaggerated startle reflex. Symptoms must be present for more than 1 month.

Although the DSM eschews theories of etiology for most disorders, the first criterion is clearly related to cause. Research has consistently identified a number of distal variables that may moderate the relationship between trauma exposure and emergence of PTSD symptoms such as preexisting personality, family history, or lack of support (e.g., Kulka, Schlenger, Fairbank, Hough, Jordan, Marmar, et al., 1990; Lauterbach & Vrana, 2001; Ozer, Best, Lipsey, & Weiss, 2003; Schnurr, Friedman, & Rosenberg, 1993), although the most proximal cause is severity of trauma exposure. The severity and chronicity of PTSD symptoms are related to the severity of the trauma as measured objectively (e.g., duration, severity of injuries, number of loved ones lost, amount of property damage) and subjec-

---

[*]McWilliams, Cox, and Asmundson (2005) also obtained a four-factor solution. Close examination of the factors, however, indicates little correspondence between the factor structure obtained and either the existing DSM categories or previous factor analytic findings.

tively (e.g., perception of trauma severity at the time of the event, perception of trauma severity in retrospect, perception of life threat, perception of helplessness/hopelessness). Most of the widely accepted models of development and maintenance of PTSD have borrowed heavily from extant learning theory.

THEORIES OF PTSD

Mowrer's Two-Stage Learning Model

A number of researchers have used Mower's (1947, 1960) two-stage learning model as a framework for understanding symptom emergence, persistence, and the mechanisms of change (Keane, Fairbank, Caddell, Zimering, & Bender, 1985). According to the model, fears are *acquired* via classical conditioning and *maintained* via operant conditioning. In applying this model to PTSD, Keane, et al. (1985) argued that persons who are exposed to a life-threatening situation become conditioned to a wide variety of stimuli present at the time of the trauma. These stimuli could include sights, sounds, smells, or internal emotional/cognitive states. These previously neutral stimuli become classically conditioned with the presence of the trauma. Symptoms are maintained through operant conditioning. Persons with PTSD become adept at avoiding reminders of the trauma. This avoidance is successful in temporarily reducing distress and thus is negatively reinforced. Mechanisms of higher order conditioning and stimulus generalization help explain the expanding web of avoidance symptoms that emerge. The model predicts that symptoms should diminish or disappear with repeated exposure. In naturally occurring situations, however, habituation does not occur because people avoid aversive trauma-related memories.

This model provides a general framework for understanding symptom emergence, maintenance, and a possible mechanism of change. However, it does not address why specific symptoms emerge, such as nightmares, psychogenic amnesia, flashbacks, restricted range of affect, or sense of foreshortened future. Perhaps most important, it does not address the cognitive mediators that appear to influence therapeutic change.

Emotional Processing Theory

Emotional processing theory (Foa & Kozak, 1986) has been the most influential model in the PTSD treatment literature. Emotional processing theory developed in the tradition of Lang's bioinformational model of pathological fear (Lang, 1977, 1979b). Lang argues that fear memory networks are composed of 3 types of information: (1) information about the feared stimulus; (2) information about verbal, physical, and behavioral responses; and (3) information about the meaning of the stimulus and response. This model was initially applied to the fear structure of phobias, and

Foa and Kozak extend the model to PTSD. It is argued that the PTSD fear structure differs from the phobia fear structure in three important ways: (1) intensity of responses, (2) size of the structure, and (3) accessibility of the structure. When PTSD fear structures are activated, they result in more intense responses than those characteristic of phobias. In addition, PTSD fear structures are larger and more accessible than phobia fear structures. To alter the fear structure, the fear memory must be activated and new information must be provided that is incompatible with the existing structure. Fear memories are activated when an individual is presented with information that matches information in the structure. The information can be about the situation, the person's responses, or the meaning of the responses. Thus, there is a direct correspondence between the hypothesized content of the fear structure and the type of stimuli that can activate the structure. A critical number of informational units must be present for the fear memory to be activated. Because the fear structure characteristic of PTSD is large, it is easily matched and activated. For example, in the case of a combat veteran with PTSD, a wide variety of stimuli could activate the fear structure. Fear, anger, horror, sadness, and paranoia are emotional states that may activate the structure. Similarly, a broad array of sights, sounds, smells, and environmental conditions/cues may activate the fear network. Although such a large structure may be easy to activate, it may be difficult to activate in its entirety. For example, a veteran of the first Gulf War might experience a moderate level of network activation when on a hot sandy beach and a high level of activation when nighttime falls. The fear, anger, and paranoia elements of the network might be activated at night as the conditions more closely approximate the conditions under which missile attacks were likely to occur in Iraq. In addition, large structures may be less cohesive than smaller ones, and consequently, associations among elements may be weaker. The strong response elements in PTSD may also promote avoidance, which results in an incomplete activation of the fear structure. According to the model, therapeutic change occurs when there is within-session habituation (through repeated exposure) and exposure to the feared situation results in changes in its threat meaning. Between-session changes are predicted as well. One consequence of successful treatment is that patients will develop a more cohesive trauma narrative (Foa, Molnar, & Cashman, 1995). In other words, patients will become better able to describe the behavioral, cognitive, emotional, and sensory elements of the trauma.

The initial theory has since been elaborated by a number of authors (Foa & Riggs, 1993; Foa & Rothbaum, 1998). One elaboration of the model was to address the relationship between knowledge available before, during, and after the trauma and emergence of PTSD. They argue that persons with rigid views about the self and the world before the trauma are particularly vulnerable to developing PTSD. For example, a woman who had taken numerous self-defense courses and felt extremely confident that she was capable of protecting herself from an attacker would be more likely to develop PTSD after a rape than someone less confident in her self-defense skills. In many ways, this modification is similar to Janoff-Bulman's notion that trauma is most likely to have a profound effect if it violates individual's strongly held notions of their personal competence (Janoff-Bulman, 1992). This revised model also incorporates increased attention to negative appraisals of responses. Negative appraisals crystallize a victim's self-perception of incompetence and influence lifestyle, behavioral choices, and responses to others.

The emotional processing model has been particularly influential because it makes specific predictions about mechanisms of change, and it is closely tied to a specific treatment approach, prolonged exposure. In addition, it provides a framework for understanding why core symptoms of PTSD (i.e., reexperiencing, avoidance, and hyperarousal) emerge and are maintained. Several elements of the model, however, have received equivocal support. A central tenant of the model is that change occurs when the fear structure has been activated and new information is incorporated. Some have found that fear activation is associated with symptom reduction (Foa, Riggs, Massie, & Yarczower, 1995; Pitman, Orr, Altman, Longpre, Poir, Macklin, et al., 1996), but others have found that fear activation is only predictive of treatment success when it is followed by habituation (Jaycox, Foa, & Morral, 1998). Moreover, although within-session habituation is postulated as a central change mechanism, it appears that between-session reductions in fear may be a better predictor of treatment outcome (Jaycox, et al., 1998; Van Minnen & Hagenaars, 2002). This suggests a primary role for integration of new information and a secondary role of habituation.

Finally, it is unclear if trauma severity is associated with more or less cohesive trauma narratives (Amir, Stafford, Freshman, & Foa, 1998; Gray & Lombardo, 2001; Zoellner, Alvarez-Conrad, & Foa, 2002). Although it appears that trauma narratives of persons in treatment become longer and include more feeling statements as therapy progresses (Foa, Molnar, et al., 1995), several studies have found no relationship between *fragmentation* of the narratives and treatment outcome (Foa, Molnar, et al., 1995; Van Minnen, Wessel, Dijkstra, & Roelofs, 2002). In addition, when a change in fragmentation does occur, it is not consistently associated with all dimensions of therapeutic change, suggesting that it is not the principal change mechanism (Foa, Molnar, et al., 1995).

Cognitive Action Theory

Much like the emotional processing theory just described, the cognitive action theory (Chemtob, Roitblat, Hamada, Carlson, & Twentyman, 1988) takes it starting point from Lang's (1979a) bioinformational model of fear. Emotional stimuli are represented by individuals in hierarchically arranged propositional networks. This is similar to fear structures described by Foa and Kozak (1986), but Chemtob, et al. (1988) provide much more detail regarding the structure of the fear network. These structures contain information about the properties of stimuli, including imaginal properties, valences, and behaviors to perform in the presence of the stimuli. The model holds that emotion, action, cognition, and memory all flow from the processing of information contained in mental networks. Information processing occurs by transmitting simple signals through complex structures containing relatively simple units. These structures process information in parallel, thus allowing for information processing by more than one part of the network at a given time.

The schematic information-processing network underlying this model consists of hierarchically arranged lattices of interconnected nodal elements. In the schematic representation of a fear network (Figure 5.1), the threat arousal node is typically always partially potentiated. The detection of threat evidence will increase threat arousal, which in turn potentiates threat expectancy. The net effect of this arousal is that attention becomes focused, and a bias develops to discover (and confirm) evidence for threat.

Levels in the hierarchy roughly correspond to levels of abstraction. Notice that lower elements of the schematic model are behavioral or physiological responses. Higher level nodes interact by transmitting, potentiating, or inhibiting messages. Nodal activation (e.g., activation of threat expectancy) is controlled by the nonlinear combination of the potentiation or inhibition the node receives from other elements in the network and stimuli it receives from the environment. In addition to potentiating or inhibiting lower level nodes, activation of a node can inhibit alternative nodes representing incompatible behaviors or thoughts. Learning can occur in all levels of the network through two mechanisms: (1) formation of new nodes and (2) altering the strength of connections between existing nodes. *Extinction* might weaken the con-

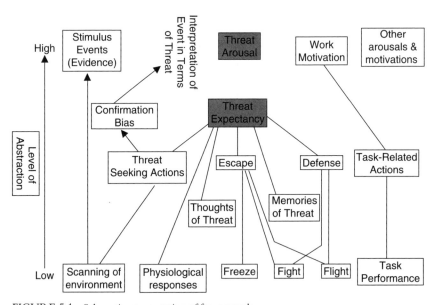

FIGURE 5.1   Schematic representation of fear network.

nection between existing nodes. *Counter-conditioning* results in the formation of new nodes and connections that inhibit previously existing nodes through lateral inhibition of incompatible nodes. The formation of new nodes is consistent with contemporary learning notions that conditioned emotional responses are not forgotten but inhibited by the creation of new learning experiences (Bouton & Swartzentruber, 1991; Jacobs & Nadel, 1985; LeDoux, 1998). Although this information-processing account provides an interesting schematic overview of fear acquisition and maintenance, as well as mechanisms of change, it has received scant attention in the empirical literature.

Control Theory

There is little doubt about the effectiveness of exposure therapy in the treatment of PTSD (Bradley, et al., 2005; Chambless & Ollendick, 2001), but considerable debate remains regarding the mechanisms of change. As mentioned earlier, there is increasing evidence that between-session cognitive changes may account for therapeutic change well beyond what may be accounted for by within-session habituation. Several new models have been proposed that suggest the primary mechanism of change is alternation in one specific cognitive set—perception of control (Holeva, Tarrier, & Wells, 2001; Mineka & Thomas, 1999). There is considerable literature suggesting that perceived control modulates anxiety level and depression. As will become apparent in the section describing exposure-based therapy for PTSD, virtually no treatments involve "just" exposure. One element that has been added to the standard exposure protocol is designed to enhance perceived control (Zayfert, Becker, & Gillock, 2002). Perhaps enhanced perceptions of control become incorporated in the fear network during the time between sessions. Foa and Rothbaum (1998) have proposed that persons with PTSD develop two dysfunctional cognitions: *the world is completely dangerous* (unpredictable), and *I am unable to handle stress*. Consistent with this notion, Foa and Rauch (2004) found that treatment gains were associated with improvements in these cognitions. Similarly, Ehlers, Clark, Dunmore, Jaycox, Meadows, and Foa (1998) hypothesized that persons who experienced *mental defeat* during the trauma were more likely to experience difficulty coping and less likely to respond favorably to exposure therapy. Mental defeat is similar to the construct of hopelessness. It was also hypothesized that persons who felt alienated or felt they had been permanently changed by the event were less likely to respond well to exposure treatment. Treatment outcome was related to both cognitive features.

EXPOSURE THERAPY

Early Reservations Regarding Use of Exposure-Based Treatment

Exposure therapy is an empirically validated approach to the treatment of PTSD (Bradley, et al., 2005; Chambless & Ollendick, 2001), but it has not been widely used in private practice settings and in Veterans Administration (VA) medical centers. A study of practice patterns in VA medical centers (Rosen, Chow, Finney, Greenbaum, Moos, Sheikh, et al., 2004) found that fewer than 20% of PTSD specialists conducted exposure-based treatment, and fewer than 10% did so regularly. This percentage did not rise after the International Society for Traumatic Stress Studies (ISTSS) published its practice guidelines, which supported the use of exposure therapies (Rosen, et al., 2004). The use of exposure therapy to treat anxiety disorders raises a number of issues that at times are at odds with the data. For example, clinicians have not shied away from using exposure therapy to treat specific or social phobias. Although a sizable percentage (one-third to two-thirds) of phobic patients do not recall a relevant aversive conditioning experience, clinicians appear comfortable using a behaviorally focused treatment approach that presupposes such an event. In contrast, many clinicians are reluctant to use exposure therapy with PTSD patients despite the fact that, by definition, 100% of the patients have experienced a traumatic event. There are several reasons why clinicians may be reluctant to use exposure therapy to treat patients with PTSD. Clinicians may fear "retraumatizing" patients and may be concerned that the stress of exposure therapy may cause patients to decompensate or terminate treatment prematurely (Kilpatrick & Best, 1984; Pitman, Altman, Greenwald, Longpre, Macklin, Poir, et al., 1991, Pitman, et al., 1996; Tarrier, Pilgrim, Sommerfield, Faragher, Reynolds, Graham, et al., 1999). Reluctance to use exposure-based therapy based on fear of premature termination, however, appears unwarranted. Hembree, Foa, Dorfan, Street, Kowalski, and Tu (2003) compared termination rates in the following groups: exposure alone, stress inoculation or cognitive therapy alone, combined therapy (exposure plus cognitive therapy or stress inoculation training), eye movement desensitization and reprocessing (EMDR), and control subjects. The average dropout rate was 20.5% from exposure treatments, 22.1% from cognitive therapy (CT) or stress inoculation therapy (SIT), 26.9% from combinations of exposure therapy and other cognitive behavior therapy (CB) techniques, 18.9% from EMDR, and 11.4% from the control group. There were no differences in dropout rates for the four active treatment groups. Hembree, et al. (2003) suggest that the dropout rate of 20.5% compares favorably with dropout rates for treatment of other disorders using exposure therapy, cognitive therapy, or medications.

The issue of symptom exacerbation is important, and arguably, a clinician's first duty is to do no harm. There is evidence that exposure therapy leads to a temporary worsening of symptoms. Nishith, Resick, and Griffin (2002) found that therapeutic exposure is associated with mild symptom exacerbation. This exacerbation was found for both prolonged exposure and exposure embedded in the context of cognitive processing therapy for both treatment completers and intent to completers. Similarly, Foa and colleagues (Foa, Zoellner, Feeney, Hembree, & Alvarez-Conrad, 2002) examined whether onset of imaginal exposure was associated with exacerbation of PTSD, depression, or anxiety symptoms. Most important, they examined whether those with "reliable" exacerbations in symptoms were more likely to drop out of therapy or to be treatment resistant. They found that the majority of patients experiencing prolonged exposure (either alone or in the context of exposure + cognitive restructuring) did not experience symptom exacerbation. Among the patients who did experience an exacerbation of symptoms, the majority were in the prolonged exposure condition. The patients who did experience an exacerbation of symptoms did not benefit less from exposure therapy (comparable end state functioning) and were not more likely to terminate prematurely.

A final concern is that clients might be unwilling to choose a treatment that would involve reexposing themselves to trauma reminders; however, the available data suggest otherwise. For example, Zoellner, Feeny, Cochran, and Pruitt (2003) assessed treatment preference in a sample of 273 women with varying degrees of trauma history and PTSD symptoms. Participants read a scenario describing a traumatic event, imagined that it had happened to them, and were asked to choose from among three treatment options: sertraline (SER), prolonged exposure (PE), or no treatment. Women were more likely to choose PE than SER for the treatment of chronic PTSD. Not surprisingly, the perceived credibility of the treatment coincided with women's choices; however, preference for treatment may not translate into treatment compliance. Scott and Strandling (1997) found low rates of client compliance with exposure exercises in two small treatment outcome studies ($N = 14$ and 37).

The Practice of Exposure Therapy with PTSD Patients

Several caveats should be considered before a clinician engages in exposure therapy. First, there is considerable variation in the precise way in which exposure therapy is conducted. Exposure modalities can be imaginal, in vivo, in virtuo, or narrative, and they can vary in duration. Second, exposure is not the only active treatment element present. Additional elements typically include psychoeducation, cognitive restructuring, and coping skills training. In many cases, however, the exposure is viewed as the essential active treatment ingredient. What follows is a description of the most common ways in which exposure therapy is practiced. It is intended to offer more detail than is typically provided in treatment outcome articles while stopping short of the comprehensive descriptions provided elsewhere (e.g., Foa & Rothbaum, 1998).

This description takes as its starting place the PE protocol described by Foa, Dancu, and Hembree. This protocol is extremely well articulated and is the most comprehensively studied exposure treatment. It is not the only protocol, and where appropriate, recommendations from other programs are included. A comment frequently made by clinicians considering the prospect of conducting exposure therapy is that it seems (on paper) to be a cold, distant set of techniques. It is important to recognize that the *preconditions* necessary for any therapy to be effective, [e.g., client's *positive expectations* (based on effectiveness of technique and therapist skill) and a *facilitative therapeutic relationship* (Grencavage & Norcross, 1990)] must also be met in exposure therapy. From the outset, it is critical to convey the message that the technique is effective and that the therapist is skillful in its implementation. Throughout treatment, it is important to acknowledge the client's courage in confronting the event and convey respect for that decision. Therapists should communicate their attempts to understand the client's symptoms and when possible, incorporate the client's examples of her or his symptoms during exposure sessions. In addition, clinicians should validate the client's experience in an empathic and nonjudgmental manner. This may be the first time the client has related the trauma narrative and the therapist's reaction is important. Although critics have claimed that exposure therapy leads to large power differentials between the therapist and the client, when properly practiced, exposure therapy is an inherently collaborative process. It is essential to incorporate the client's judgment about pace and targets of therapy.

Table 5.1 lists the treatment components in a 10-session PE treatment protocol. Sessions are approximately 90 minutes, and from the outset, the focus of treatment is on the traumatic event. Imaginal exposure and in vivo exposure are two core treatment elements. Imaginal exposure begins in the third session and

TABLE 5.1   Overview of the Prolonged Exposure (PE) Protocol

Session 1
1. Provide a program overview (25–30 minutes).
2. Discuss the treatment procedures.
3. Explain that the focus of the program is on post-traumatic stress disorder (PTSD) symptoms.
4. Collect trauma-relevant information (45 minutes).
5. Assess physiological responsiveness on exposure to internal/external cues or reminders.
6. Assign homework (note: both of the following exercises are assigned after all sessions and will not be repeated).
a. Practice breathing retraining for 10 minutes, 3 times per day.
b. Listen to audiotape of session once.

Session 2
1. Review homework (5–10 minutes) is part of every session and will not be repeated.
2. Discuss common reactions to trauma (25 minutes).
3. Show and then discuss the Dateline videotape. (Get information on how to purchase video and add as footnote).
4. Discuss the rationale for in vivo exposure (10 minutes).
5. Introduce Subjective Units of Distress scales (SUDs) (5 minutes).
6. Construct in vivo hierarchy (20 minutes).
7. Select in vivo assignments for homework (5 minutes).
8. Assign homework (10 minutes).
a. Read handout on common reactions to trauma several times and share with others if helpful.
b. Complete list of avoided situations.
c. Begin in vivo exposure assignment.

(Continued)

TABLE 5.1 *(Continued)*

Session 3
1. Present rationale for imaginal exposure (10 minutes).
2. Conduct imaginal exposure (60 minutes).
3. Process imaginal exposure.
4. Assign homework.
a. Continue in vivo exposure exercises daily working up the hierarchy.

Sessions 4 to 5
1. Conduct imaginal exposure (30–45minutes).
2. Process imaginal exposure with client (15–20 minutes).
3. Discuss/implement in vivo exposure (10–20 minutes).
4. Assign homework.
a. Continue in vivo exposure exercises.

Sessions 6 to 9
1. Conduct imaginal exposure focusing on "hot spots" progressively as therapy advances (30–45 minutes).
2. Process imaginal exposure with client (15–20 minutes).
3. Discuss/implement in vivo exposure (10–20 minutes).
4. Assign homework.
a. Continue in vivo exposure exercises.

Session 10 (Final session)
1. Conduct imaginal exposure focusing on entire trauma (20–30 minutes).
2. Process imaginal exposure and discuss how perception of the trauma has changed.
3. Obtain current SUDs for in vivo hierarchy and discuss how they differ from the original SUDs.
4. Assign "homework."
a. Continue to apply everything learned in therapy.

continues through the remaining sessions. During imaginal exposure, participants are asked to describe and visualize, as vividly as possible, the trauma in the present tense. Visualization focuses on the entire trauma and includes those events that occurred immediately before and after the trauma. Participants are encouraged to keep their eyes closed and provide as much detail as possible to enhance visual imagery and potentiate emotional engagement. Homework sessions also include listening to an audiotape of the therapy session once per day. Clearly, this is a demanding and intensive therapeutic experience, and it is essential that clients have a clear understanding of the rationale for imaginal exposure. As a general rule, it is helpful to frame the rationale for exposure as an opportunity to process (digest) the trauma, organize memories, make sense of the experience, or appropriately compartmentalize the experience. Clients can also be helped to understand that exposure results in habituation, so that the trauma can be remembered without intense disruptive anxiety. This will help them become better at distinguishing between thinking about the trauma and actually "reexperiencing" it. The ultimate goal of the exposure is to provide behavioral evidence that engaging the trauma memory does not result in going crazy or losing control; instead patients experience an enhanced sense of self-control and personal competence.

An important issue in imaginal exposure concerns engagement, or the degree to which the patient becomes immersed in the exposure session. Underengagement refers to difficulty a client may have accessing the total trauma experience. Engagement can be enhanced by revising the rationale for exposure or prompting for thoughts, sensations, and feelings. Overengagement in the exposure session can result in a patient not feeling safe or "grounded" in reality. In severe cases, patients may experience dissociative sensations. Overengagement can be moderated by having clients open their eyes during imagery or altering the instructions to have them describe the event in the past tense (see Hembree, Rauch, & Foa, 2003, for additional procedural modifications for addressing overengagement/underengagement).

Starting with the fourth session, clients begin in vivo exposure. During this element of treatment, clients expose themselves to feared persons or situations that are "realistically" safe. This can be an intimidating experience for clients, and it is important to provide a clear *rationale for in vivo exposure*. For example, clients can be reminded that trauma-related fears are sometimes unrealistic or excessive. Repeated exposure in vivo provides concrete information that the avoided situation is safe and that their fear can and will diminish through habituation. They can also be reminded that in vivo exposure will provide evidence that they are in control and competent. Further, friends, relatives, or a therapist may verbalize similar confidence in their abilities, but these people are easy to discount.

After presenting the rationale for in vivo exposure and discussing its importance, the therapist provides daily life examples of in vivo exposure and habituation. Next, the client and therapist work collaboratively to develop a list of situations that the client has been avoiding, and the therapist introduces the Subjective Units of Distress scales (SUDs) rating system. The therapist asks the client to rate the intensity of anxiety (SUDs) s/he imagines would result from confronting each situation. The client and therapist then arrange the situations in a hierarchy. If the client is unable to identify avoided circumstances, the therapist can suggest typically avoided situations. The therapist also assesses the actual safety of the situations.

Although there is currently only one primary form of PTSD, there is clearly heterogeneity in etiology, symptom presentation, and sex and age of the victim. The sections that follow briefly outline the treatment variations that are driven by the event type, victim characteristics, or a desire to enhance the intensity of the exposure experience.

Virtual Reality Exposure and PTSD

Although Bouchard and colleagues discuss virtual reality (VR) approaches to exposure therapy later in this book, we will touch briefly on the approach with regard to PTSD. As noted earlier, a central notion in exposure therapy is the proposition that the fear structure must be activated for therapy to be effective (Foa & Kozak, 1986). The more thoroughly the fear structure is activated, the more likely it is that therapy will be effective. Historically, this has been accomplished primarily through guided imagery or imaginal exposure; however, there are considerable individual differences in the ability to form and maintain vivid images. A number of researchers, most notably Rothbaum and colleagues, have used VR technology to expose persons to simulated aversive stimuli and situations.

In virtual reality, persons are fitted with a head-mounted device that projects a separate visual display to each eye. All visual contact with the "real" world is eliminated, and the person is completely immersed in the virtual world. Head-mounted sensors react to the participant's movements by reorienting the graphical interface, thus creating the impression of synchronized movement in the virtual environment. In addition, the therapist can observe the participant's movement through the virtual environment on a separate monitor and provide feedback and support via headphones (for an extended discussion of VR, see Rothbaum & Hodges, 1999; Zimand, Anderson, Gershon, Graap, Hodges, & Rothbaum, 2002). In a small open trial using VR exposure to treat 16 male Vietnam combat veterans (Rothbaum, Hodges, Ready, Graap, & Alarcon, 2001), participants were exposed to two virtual environments. One was a virtual Huey helicopter that flew over terrain similar to that seen in Vietnam. The second was a virtual clearing surrounded by jungle (see Hodges, Rothbaum, Alarcon, Ready, Shahar, Graap, et al., 1999 for extended discussion of the virtual environment). Therapy consisted of exposure to the virtual environment, at which time participants were asked to describe in detail memories triggered by the environment. Later sessions involved a combination of virtual exposure coupled with imaginal exposure to the most traumatic memory. Rothbaum, et al. (2001) found significant reductions in PTSD scores measured by self-report and clinical interviews. Clinician-rated gains were maintained at 6-month follow-up period. In addition, modest treatment gains were reported in a case study of a Vietnam combat veteran (Rothbaum, Hodges, Alarcon, Ready, Shahar, Graap, et al., 1999).

Virtual reality exposure has also been used to treat PTSD related to the destruction of the World Trade Center (WTC) (Difede & Hoffman, 2002). The patient was a 26-year-old woman who had unsuccessfully attempted traditional exposure therapy for PTSD symptoms. To enhance emotional engagement, a virtual environment was created that included images of jets crashing into the WTC, animated explosions, sound effects, images of people jumping to their deaths, burning buildings, and ultimately the collapse of the towers and the dust clouds. A graded version of VR exposure was used in this study. There were substantial reductions in depression (83%) and PTSD (90%) symptoms post-treatment.

Narrative Exposure Therapy for Multiply Traumatized Clients

Inherent in the traditional prolonged exposure paradigm is the notion that the survivor has been exposed to a limited number of discrete events; however, many trauma survivors have been exposed to multiple events. For example, refugees from war-torn regions of the world often experience a series of traumatizing events that include physical attacks, sexual assaults, and military actions (De Jong, Komproe, Van Ommeren, El Masri, Araya, Khaled, et al., 2001). In cases of multiple trauma, therapists may have difficulty, or find it impossible, to identify a single traumatic event that accounts for the patient's symptoms. In these cases, a more flexible adaptation of the exposure paradigm may be required (Neuner, Schauer, Roth, & Elbert, 2002).

Narrative exposure therapy (NET) is similar to prolonged exposure in a number of ways. It is a brief (4 sessions), trauma-focused therapy that involves recounting (orally) traumatic experiences in as much detail as possible. It is based on basic principles of cognitive-behavioral therapy with an exposure element that has been adapted to meet the needs of multiply traumatized survivors of war and torture. The duration of exposure is from 60 to 120 minutes or until distress diminishes.

The first session begins with a psychoeducational component that includes a description of the nature and prevalence of PTSD. This is followed by a detailed assessment and a description of the rationale for the treatment. In the exposure sessions, the client narrates (orally) an autobiography that includes, but is not limited to, a detailed description of traumatic events. *Thus, an important point of departure from traditional PE is that NET involves forming a coherent life narrative, not simply a trauma narrative.* During exposure sessions, the therapist probes for sensory, emotional, and cognitive elements. In addition, the therapist identifies areas of ambiguity or inconsistency in the narrative. These inconsistencies are gently pointed out to the client. Much like standard PE, an explicit goal of therapy is development of a less fragmented narrative. There are no explicit instructions to close eyes during the exposure, and in this way, treatment is similar to PE for persons who are overengaged. During the session, the therapist transcribes the client's narrative. In subsequent sessions, the narrative is read to the client and she or he is encouraged to make corrections and add details, particularly regarding emotional and cognitive aspects of the trauma. Given that NET is most frequently used in unstable regions where multiple languages or dialects are spoken, a translator may be needed to transcribe the narrative and/or read it to the client. In the last session, a complete narrative is read to the client. The client, therapist, and possibly the translator sign the autobiography. One copy is given to the client and a second copy is kept by the therapist. In addition, if the client agrees, an additional copy can be sent to human rights organizations to document experiences and to facilitate advocacy. Preliminary findings from a case study of a severely traumatized Kosovar refugee (Neuner, et al., 2002) suggest that NET is effective in reducing symptoms of PTSD and dissociation. A randomized controlled trial comparing NET to a supportive counseling and psychoeducational treatment support its effectiveness (Neuner, Schauer, Klaschik, Karunakara, & Elbert, 2004). One year post-treatment, only 29% of the NET participants met the diagnostic criteria for PTSD. By contrast, 79% and 80% of the supportive counseling and psychoeducation groups, respectively, still met diagnostic criteria for PTSD.

Narrative exposure therapy is a promising treatment for persons exposed to multiple traumas. Thus, it may prove helpful for victims of ongoing physical or sexual abuse or for persons in occupations that involve frequent exposure to trauma, such as police officers, firefighters, or emergency technicians. It is not uncommon for trauma victims to define themselves in terms of the trauma, and NET may be particularly effective in helping place a trauma within the larger context of one's life.

Exposure Therapy for Children Exposed to Trauma

PTSD is often diagnosed in children who have experienced traumatic events such as natural disasters, violent crimes, sexual abuse, serious medical illness, and war (Smith, Perrin, & Yule, 1999). There is increasing evidence that children experience symptoms similar to those found in adults such as reexperiencing, avoidance, and arousal (Smith, et al., 1999); however, children often exhibit additional symptoms and difficulties. Symptoms common in very young children include separation anxiety and regression to behaviors characteristic of earlier childhood such as enuresis, excessive clinginess, and temper tantrums (Rudenberg, Jansen, & Fridjhon, 1998). Adolescents may express a sense of foreshortened future (Buckley & Walsh, 1998) and are at increased risk for depression, drug abuse, and promiscuity (Dawes, 1990). Symptoms can be moderated by age (Dawes, 1990), sex (Cooley-Quille, Boyd, Frantz, & Walsh, 2001), intelligence (Punamäki, Qouta, & El-Sarraj, 2001), social support (Garbarino & Kostelny, 1996), family environment (Miller, Wasserman, Neugebauer, Gorman-Smith, & Kamboukos, 1999), and coping styles (Dempsey, Overstreet, & Moely, 2000). Because PTSD may cause significant impairment in multiple areas of functioning (Giaconia, Reinherz, Silverman, Pakiz, Frost, & Cohen, 1995), and may increase children's risk of developing other disorders (Smith, et al., 1999), it is important to develop effective treatments for children with PTSD.

In conceptualizing PTSD in children, Saigh (1992) drew heavily on Mowrer's two-factor learning theory. Consistent with this theory, prolonged therapeutic exposure to traumatic memories in the absence of the original unconditioned stimulus (i.e., the trauma) will lead to an extinction of the anxiety response (Smith, et al., 1999). Because of the promising results of exposure therapy in reducing post-traumatic stress symptoms in adults, studies examining the use of exposure therapy in children are gaining increased attention.

The procedure for exposure therapy with children is similar to the procedure used with adults (Faust, 2000; Smith, et al., 1999). Therefore, our discussion of treatment with children highlights treatment elements *unique* to the population. Exposure work is often preceded by coping skills training, including deep muscle and breathing relaxation techniques and positive imagery training, in which the child is encouraged to visualize a "safe place" that can enhance the ability to relax. Imagery can be used to help children learn to relax and tense their muscles (e.g., "pretend you are squeezing the juice of an orange with your right hand"; Faust, 2000). Therapists should note the safe place the child chooses to visualize during relaxation. Children may not understand the nature of the activity and may select a location associated with the traumatic event, such as a bedroom where abuse took place (Faust, 2000).

The second step typically involves explaining how to use the SUDs to rate anxiety (Smith, et al., 1999). By this point, it is also important to ensure that children understand the rationale for exposure therapy. Recounting details of the trauma and imagining traumatic scenes can cause distress, and children may not understand why they are being asked to reexperience the trauma (Cocco & Sharpe, 1993). To prevent children from feeling revictimized by the treatment, it is important to explain that some aspects of the treatment will evoke distress but that eventually the distress will dissipate.

The third step involves developing a script of the event or particular scenes that were the most traumatic for the child (Saigh, 1987c; Smith, et al., 1999). Children are prompted to recount the experience in a first-person, present-tense format. Unlike the adult version of PE described earlier, there are no specific prompts to close eyes during imagery. The therapist prompts the child for details of what was seen, heard, felt, and thought during the event. Throughout the child's account of the event, the therapist asks for SUDs ratings. Components of the event that evoke high SUDs ratings are identified as targets for flooding sessions. Children may have difficulty remembering or recounting the trauma, so prompting may be necessary to complete the narrative. Smith, et al. (1999) suggest that drawing and play may facilitate children's recall of events.

The fourth component involves imaginal exposure sessions. These sessions typically begin with 5 to 10 minutes of relaxation and positive imagery (Saigh, 1987c). Then the child recounts the identified traumatic scene or imagines it while the therapist helps the child visualize it. SUDs ratings are obtained throughout the exposure session, and the therapist will ask the child to continue processing the image until SUDs scores decrease. The time devoted to each scene needs to be long enough to allow sufficient time for the distress to decrease as the child continues to hold the scene in mind. At the end of sessions, therapists typically guide clients through 5 to 10 minutes of relaxation to reduce distress (Smith, et al., 1999).

A distinctive element of imaginal exposure therapy for children is the direct assessment of imagery skill (Saigh, Yule, & Inamdar, 1996). One method is to ask the child to close his or her eyes and concentrate on various aspects of the scene. After approximately 3 minutes, the therapist asks the client to rate the image clarity on a 10-point Likert scale (1 = not at all and 10 = very much) (Saigh, 1992). Lower ratings (1 through 4) should be discussed to assess whether additional practice is necessary or whether the selected image should be modified or replaced.

If the child has difficulty imagining a trauma scene (i.e., underengagement), there are several techniques that may be used that are distinctive from exposure with adults. Children can be asked to bring in items that are physically representative of the trauma, such as photographs, videotapes, or articles of clothing (Faust, 2000). Physical representations that more closely approximate an in vivo experience can enhance imagery. Saigh (1987c) used tape-recorded sounds of progressively closer shell and rocket explosions to help a child imagine the components of his traumatic experience.

Children's threshold for fatigue is an important additional consideration in the planning of flooding sessions (Saigh, et al., 1996). The length of exposure should be tailored to the child's developmental stage and capacity for sustained attention. Although sessions need to be long enough to evoke distress and allow distress to dissipate, children should not be expected to maintain an image as long as adults can. Saigh (1986) encourages therapists to note signs of fatigue in children and shorten subsequent flooding sessions to a tolerable length. The frequency of flooding sessions depends on the number of traumatic scenes identified and the amount of time needed to decrease SUDs ratings. Saigh found that two sessions per week for 4 weeks were sufficient to reduce PTSD symptoms in several children who had been exposed to war-related traumatic events (Saigh, 1987b, 1987c).

Much like the adult PE treatment protocol, if the child's symptoms include avoidance of places or other reminders of the trauma, exposure therapy may include in vivo techniques (Abrahams & Udwin, 2000; Smith, et al., 1999). This procedure is typically undertaken only after SUD scores during imaginal exposure have significantly decreased. Thus, although PE with adults may include simultaneous imaginal and in vivo exposure, these approaches are typically staggered with children. Feared situations are identified and ordered from least to most distressing. Starting with the least distressing situation, children are encouraged to engage in the situation until distress decreases. Relaxation is practiced before and after each task. To facilitate task completion and ensure the child's safety, the child's parents are often recruited. As with adults, only avoidance of safe situations should be targeted for change. The therapist needs to carefully weigh the possible benefits against the possible harm involved in the use of extra-therapy tasks with children.

The published literature on the use of exposure therapy with children has yielded promising results. Saigh has published a number of studies using imaginal flooding with children exposed to political violence. The children ranged in age from 6 to 14 years and included boys and girls (Saigh, 1986, 1987a, 1987b, 1987c, 1989). In all of these case studies, exposure therapy resulted in reduced anxiety and depression, improved concentration and memory, fewer intrusive recollections, and improved ability to revisit places and tolerate cues associated with the trauma.

When children are exposed to chronic traumatic events, adjunctive treatments may increase therapeutic effectiveness. Although exposure-based therapies are designed to address symptoms of reexperiencing, avoidance, and arousal, there are frequently other problems that warrant independent attention such as sleep disturbances, separation anxiety, anger and conduct problems, and prolonged grief reactions (Smith, et al., 1999). If a child is experiencing sleep disturbances in conjunction with PTSD, implementing relaxation routines before bed or dream restructuring techniques may be helpful. The use of drawings and play can help children grieve losses they have experienced, and behavioral and cognitive techniques may be used to address conduct and anger problems, as well as separation anxiety. Faust (2000) also suggests using cognitive-behavioral therapy to enhance coping abilities by helping the child replace dysfunctional thoughts and feelings with more adaptive ones.

Many children who have experienced a trauma will also benefit from interventions directed toward the caregivers and other family members (Faust, 2000; Smith, et al., 1999). Family therapy may be particularly important in abuse-related PTSD in which the perpetrator was known to the child. Even when trauma occurred outside of the family, the child's family will still be affected by the experience and may be in a better position to help aid the child's recovery if they are educated about the process of therapy. A specific component of caregivers' psychoeducation may include discussing their attributions about the event and ensuring that caregivers' attributions that are conveyed to the child are congruent with the messages that the therapist is giving. Parents may also be encouraged to develop a safety plan with the child to facilitate a sense of control over the environment and assure the child that the caregivers are concerned with his or her safety.

There is still a need for further research on the treatment of PTSD in children. There is a paucity of research on the use of exposure-based therapies, and most of the current studies have involved children who have been exposed to war-related violence. Research on the effectiveness of exposure therapy with children who have experienced other types of trauma is a necessary component of demonstrating the generalizability of the use of exposure therapies. Studies published thus far, however, suggest that exposure-based therapies may be an effective component of treatment for childhood PTSD.

THOUGHTS FOR THE FUTURE

Elegant Theories and Inelegant Assessment: Lack of Correspondence Between Theory and Assessment

As mentioned previously, Lang's bioinformational model of pathological fear (Lang, 1977, 1979b) forms the theoretical backdrop for emotional processing theory (Foa & Kozak, 1986). Lang argues that fear memory networks are composed of specific types of information, and once one element of the network has been activated, there is a cascade effect with successive elements activating (and inhibiting) compatible (and incompatible) elements in the fear structure. This description suggests a dynamic reactive process akin to waves emanating outward from the point of activation. Although this is an elegant description of a process, it does not correspond to the traditional way in which activation of the fear network is assessed. Typically, network access is assumed based on elevations in scale scores on some standardized measure on exposure to trauma-related cues. In other words, all changes in network activation level are directly linked to presentation of the trauma-related cue and not to a cascade effect.

Similar challenges exist in assessing the validity of cognitive action theory (Chemtob, et al., 1988). Emotional stimuli are represented by individuals in hierarchically arranged lattices of interconnected nodal elements. Levels in the hierarchy roughly correspond to levels of abstraction. Lower elements of the schematic model are behavioral or physiological responses. Higher-level nodes interact by transmitting potentiating *or* inhibiting messages. Nodal activation is controlled by the nonlinear combination of the potentiation or inhibition the node receives from other elements in the network and stimuli it receives from the environment. In addition to potentiating or inhibiting lower level nodes, activation of a node can inhibit alternative nodes representing incompatible behaviors or thoughts. In typical studies examining network activation, little attention is devoted to elements of the network that are inhibited during cued exposure; however, this is not an insurmountable issue.

Ecological momentary assessment (EMA), however, is well suited to studying some of these phenomena. In a typical EMA study, participants carry a personal digital assistant (PDA) throughout the course of the day. Periodically, the PDA signals the participant to complete a series of questions that assess current symptoms, behaviors, or surroundings. More complex EMA designs involve technologies that can assess concurrent physiological or ambulatory processes. Because EMA methodology provides an opportunity to examine how behaviors are functionally related, it may be possible to make a priori predictions of the conditions under which nodal inhibition would occur. For example, surroundings could be coded using the following scheme: (1) trauma symptom agonist, (2) neutral, and (3) trauma symptom antagonist. Nodal inhibition (e.g., PTSD symptoms below baseline) would be hypothesized in trauma symptom antagonist environments.

It should be noted that a number of investigators (Beckham, Feldman, Barefoot, Fairbank, Helms, Haney, et al., 2000; Beckman, Taft, Vrana, Feldman, Barefoot, Moore, et al., 2003; Beckham, Gehrman, McClernon, Collie, & Feldman, 2004; Carlson, 2005) have begun using this methodology but have yet to use it to address the specific questions posed here.

Time for a Paradigm Shift in Training?

The most recent conference of the International Society for Traumatic Stress Studies was devoted to dissemination of information on trauma and its treatment. Although it is possible to train master's level therapists in prolonged exposure therapy (Hembree, Foa, Cahill, Chrestman, Rehm, & Gaulin, 2005), it is rarely the case that clinicians use state-of-of-the-art treatment approaches. There are a variety of barriers to implementing treatment, including lack of adequate training and supervision, therapists' dislike for manualized therapy, and misperceptions concerning the safety and efficacy of exposure techniques (Foa, 2005).

On the other hand, there has been a slow, but steady move toward training therapists in graduate programs to implement empirically supported treatments (ESTs). Although the emphasis of training new therapists in the implementation of ESTs is a relatively new movement, it is hoped that there will soon be a critical mass of therapists who are skilled in the use of efficacious therapeutic interventions. The less optimistic view is that many aspiring clinicians view graduate training as a "necessary evil" that must be endured so that they can eventually practice psychotherapy in whatever way they see fit. This is both a dangerous and unacceptable scenario that may result in clinicians using watered-down hybrid versions of effective treatments that are ineffective, at best, or even harmful. Ultimately, insurance companies may be left responsible for quality control of the profession.

Assuming for the moment that the behaviors of freshly minted clinicians will be guided by best-practices guidelines, the behavior of existing clinicians remains at issue. Although most states require continuing education, few provide specific guidelines as to the nature of the educational experiences. Moreover, there are no guidelines regarding whether clinicians alter their current practice based on best-practice guidelines. This is a rather remarkable set of circumstances. Imagine for a moment that the electrical code in your community changed, and you hire a licensed electrician to complete work in your home. If the electrician knew about the code change but chose to disregard it, the inspector charged with reviewing the electrician's work would provide him a failing mark. In other words, mere knowledge of best practices in the skilled trades is inadequate. Practice guidelines, or codes, must be correctly implemented. Perhaps similar continuing education standards should be applied to providers of mental health services.

What Does the Future Hold?

Although exposure-based therapies are reasonably effective in treating persons with PTSD, a substantial percentage (30% to 40%) would be classified as treatment failures, by virtue of either premature termination or nonresponsiveness. One strategy for dealing with treatment failure has been to increase the level of exposure by use of techniques that increase immersion (e.g., virtual reality therapy). A second strategy is to administer a medication that increases the subjective experience of the exposure (Davis, Myers, Ressler, & Rothbaum, 2005). The advent of these new variations raises important questions in need of serious empirical work. Large scale, multisite studies will be needed to examine: (1) incremental impact of these variants, (2) demographic variables that may influence treatment effectiveness, (3) potentially harmful effects, and (4) empirically validated contraindicants of these procedures. These techniques are relatively new, and their long-term applicability is in need of investigation. The profession has been challenged thus far to integrate exposure-based therapies into clinical practice, and it would appear that the outlook for incorporating more technically complex variations may prove even more problematic. That said, we believe there is considerable promise that future generations of therapists will implement therapies of known efficaciousness.

REFERENCES

Abrahams, S., & Udwin, O. (2000). Treatment of post-traumatic stress disorder in an eleven-year-old boy using imaginal and in vivo exposure. *Clinical Child Psychology and Psychiatry, 5*(3), 387–401.

American Psychiatric Association. (1980). *Diagnostic and statistical manual of mental disorders.* Washington, DC: American Psychiatric Association.

Amir, N., Stafford, J.A., Freshman, M.S., & Foa, E.B. (1998). Relationship between trauma narratives and trauma pathology. *Journal of Traumatic Stress, 11*(2), 385–391.

Beckham, J.C., Feldman, M.E., Barefoot, J.C., Fairbank, J.A., Helms, M.J., Haney, T.L., et al. (2000). Ambulatory cardiovascular activity in Vietnam combat veterans with and without posttraumatic stress disorder. *Journal of Consulting and Clinical Psychology, 68*(2), 269–276.

Beckham, J.C., Gehrman, P.R., McClernon, F.J., Collie, C.F., & Feldman, M.E. (2004). Cigarette smoking, ambulatory cardiovascular monitoring, and mood in Vietnam veterans with and without chronic posttraumatic stress disorder. *Addictive Behaviors, 29*(8), 1579–1593.

Beckham, J.C., Taft, C.T., Vrana, S.R., Feldman, M.E., Barefoot, J.C., Moore, S.D., et al. (2003). Ambulatory monitoring and physical health report in Vietnam veterans with and without chronic posttraumatic stress disorder. *Journal of Traumatic Stress, 16*(4), 329–335.

Bouton, M.E., & Swartzentruber, D. (1991). Sources of relapse after extinction in Pavlovian and instrumental learning. *Clinical Psychology Review Applied Learning Theory: Research Issues for the 1990s, 11*(2), 123–140.

Bradley, R.G., Greene, J., Russ, E., Dutra, L., & Westen, D. (2005). A multidimensional meta-analysis of psychotherapy for PTSD. *American Journal of Psychiatry, 162*(2), 214–227.

Buckley, M.A., & Walsh, M.E. (1998). Children's understanding of violence: A developmental analysis. *Applied Developmental Science, 2*(4), 182–193.

Carlson, E. (2005, November). Use of ecological proximal assessment to study trauma survivors. Paper presented at the Conference on Innovations in Trauma Research Methods, Toronto, CA.

Chambless, D.L., & Ollendick, T.H. (2001). Empirically supported psychological interventions: Controversies and evidence. *Annual Review of Psychology, 52,* 685–716.

Chemtob, C.M., Roitblat, H.L., Hamada, R.S., Carlson, J.G., & Twentyman, C.T. (1988). A cognitive action theory of post-traumatic stress disorder. *Journal of Anxiety Disorders, 2,* 253–275.

Cocco, N., & Sharpe, L. (1993). An auditory variant of eye movement desensitization in a case of childhood post-traumatic stress disorder. *Journal of Behavior Therapy and Experimental Psychiatry, 24*(4), 373–377.

Cohen, J.A., Deblinger, E., Mannarino, A.P., & Steer, R.A. (2004). A multisite, randomized controlled trial for children with sexual abuse-related PTSD symptoms. *Journal of the American Academy of Child and Adolescent Psychiatry, 43*(4), 393–402.

Cooley-Quille, M., Boyd, R.C., Frantz, E., & Walsh, J. (2001). Emotional and behavioral impact of exposure to community violence in inner-city adolescents. *Journal of Clinical Child Psychology, 30*(2), 199–206.

Davis, M., Myers, K.M., Ressler, K.J., & Rothbaum, B.O. (2005). Facilitation of extinction of conditioned fear by cycloserine: Implications for psychotherapy. *Current Directions in Psychological Science 14*(4), 214–219.

Dawes, A. (1990). The effects of political violence on children: A consideration of South African and related studies. *International Journal of Psychology, 25*(1), 13–31.

De Jong, J.T.V.M., Komproe, I.H., Van Ommeren, M., El Masri, M., Araya, M., Khaled, N., et al. (2001). Lifetime events and posttraumatic stress disorder in 4 postconflict settings. *Journal of the American Medical Association, 286*(5), 555–562.

Dempsey, M., Overstreet, S., & Moely, B. (2000). "Approach" and "avoidance" coping and PTSD symptoms in inner-city youth. *Current Psychology: Developmental, Learning, Personality, Social, 19*(1), 28–45.

Difede, J., & Hoffman, H.G. (2002). Virtual reality exposure therapy for World Trade Center post-traumatic stress disorder: A case report. *CyberPsychology and Behavior, 5*(6), 529–535.

Ehlers, A., Clark, D.M., Dunmore, E., Jaycox, L.H., Meadows, E.A., & Foa, E.B. (1998). Predicting response to exposure treatment in PTSD: The role of mental defeat and alienation. *Journal of Traumatic Stress, 11*(3), 457–471.

Faust, J. (2000). Integration of family and cognitive behavioral therapy for treating sexually abused children. *Cognitive and Behavioral Practice, 7*(3), 361–368.

Feeny, N.C., Foa, E.B., Treadwell, K.R.H., & March, J.S. (2004). Posttraumatic stress disorder in youth: A critical review of the cognitive and behavioral treatment outcome literature. *Professional Psychology: Research and Practice, 35*(5), 466–476.

Foa, E.B. (2005, November). Dissemination of effective treatments for PTSD: Successes and challenges. Paper presented at the International Society for Traumatic Stress Studies, Toronto, CA.

Foa, E.B., & Kozak, M.J. (1986). Emotional processing of fear: Exposure to corrective information. *Psychological Bulletin, 99*(1), 20–35.

Foa, E.B., Molnar, C., & Cashman, L. (1995). Change in rape narratives during exposure therapy for posttraumatic stress disorder. *Journal of Traumatic Stress, 8*(4), 675–690.

Foa, E.B., & Rauch, S.A.M. (2004). Cognitive changes during prolonged exposure versus prolonged exposure plus cognitive restructuring in female assault survivors with posttraumatic stress disorder. *Journal of Consulting and Clinical Psychology, 72*(5), 879–884.

Foa, E.B., & Riggs, D.S. (1993). Posttraumatic stress disorder and rape. In J.M.R. Oldham, Michelle B; Tasman, A. (Ed.), *American Psychiatric Press review of psychiatry,* Vol. 12 (pp. 273–303). Washington: American Psychiatric Press.

Foa, E.B., Riggs, D.S., Massie, E.D., & Yarczower, M. (1995). The impact of fear activation and anger on the efficacy of exposure treatment for posttraumatic stress disorder. *Behavior Therapy, 26*(3), 487–499.

Foa, E.B., & Rothbaum, B.O. (1998). *Treating the trauma of rape: Cognitive-behavioral therapy for PTSD.* New York: Guilford Press.

Foa, E.B., Zoellner, L.A., Feeney, N.C., Hembree, E.A., & Alvarez-Conrad, J. (2002). Does imaginal exposure exacerbate PTSD symptoms? *Journal of Consulting and Clinical Psychology, 70*(4), 1022–1028.

Garbarino, J., & Kostelny, K. (1996). The effects of political violence on Palestinian children's behavior problems: A risk accumulation model. *Child Development, 67*(1), 33–45.

Giaconia, R.M., Reinherz, H.Z., Silverman, A.B., Pakiz, B., Frost, A.K., & Cohen, E. (1995). Traumas and posttraumatic stress disorder in a community population of older adolescents. *Journal of the American Academy of Child & Adolescent Psychiatry, 34*(10), 1369–1380.

Gray, M.J., & Lombardo, T.W. (2001). Complexity of trauma narratives as an index of fragmented memory in PTSD: A critical analysis. *Applied Cognitive Psychology, 15*(7), S171–S186.

Grencavage, L.M., & Norcross, J.C. (1990). Where are the commonalities among the therapeutic common factors? *Professional Psychology: Research and Practice, 21*, 372–378.

Helzer, J.E., Robins, L.N., & McEvoy, L. (1987). Post-traumatic stress disorder in the general population: findings of the epidemiologic catchment area survey. *New England Journal of Medicine, 317*(26), 1630–1634.

Hembree, E.A., Foa, E.B., Cahill, S.P., Chrestman, K., Rehm, K., & Gaulin, A. (2005, November). Dissemination of prolonged exposure for PTSD to community clinics: A decade later. Paper presented at the International Society for Traumatic Stress Studies, Toronto, CA.

Hembree, E.A., Foa, E.B., Dorfan, N.M., Street, G.P., Kowalski, J., & Tu, X. (2003). Do patients drop out prematurely from exposure therapy for PTSD? *Journal of Traumatic Stress, 16*(6), 555–562.

Hembree, E.A., Rauch, S.A.M., & Foa, E.B. (2003). Beyond the manual: The insider's guide to prolonged exposure therapy for PTSD. *Cognitive & Behavioral Practice, 10*(1), 22–30.

Hodges, L.F., Rothbaum, B.O., Alarcon, R.D., Ready, D.J., Shahar, F., Graap, K., et al. (1999). A virtual environment for the treatment of chronic combat-related post-traumatic stress disorder. *CyberPsychology and Behavior, 2*(1), 7–14.

Holeva, V., Tarrier, N., & Wells, A. (2001). Prevalence and predictors of acute stress disorder and PTSD following road traffic accidents: Thought control strategies and social support. *Behavior Therapy, 32*(1), 65–83.

Jacobs, W.J., & Nadel, L. (1985). Stress-induced recovery of fears and phobias. *Psychological Review, 92*(4), 512–531.

Janoff-Bulman, R. (1992). *Shattered assumptions: Towards a new psychology of trauma.* New York: Free Press.

Jaycox, L.H., Foa, E.B., & Morral, A.R. (1998). Influence of emotional engagement and habituation on exposure therapy for PTSD. *Journal of Consulting and Clinical Psychology, 66*(1), 185–192.

Keane, T.M., Fairbank, J.A., Caddell, J.M., Zimering, R.T., & Bender, M.E. (1985). A behavioral approach to assessing and treating post-traumatic stress disorder in Vietnam veterans. In C.R. Figley (Ed.), *Trauma and its wake. Vol. I: The study and treatment of post-traumatic stress disorder* (pp. 257–294). New York: Brunner/Mazel.

Kessler, R.C., Sonnega, A., Bromet, E.J., Hughes, M., & Nelson, C.B. (1995). Posttraumatic stress disorder in the National Comorbidity Survey. *Archives of General Psychiatry, 52*(12), 1048–1060.

Kilpatrick, D.G., & Best, C.L. (1984). Some cautionary remarks on treating sexual assault victims with implosion. *Behavior Therapy, 15*(4), 421–423.

King, L.A., & King, D.W. (1994). Latent structure of the Mississippi Scale for Combat-Related Post-Traumatic Stress Disorder: Exploratory and higher-order confirmatory factor analyses. *Assessment, 1*(3), 275–291.

Kulka, R.A., Schlenger, W.E., Fairbank, J.A., Hough, R.L., Jordan, B.K., Marmar, C.R., et al. (1990). Why is it that some developed PTSD and others did not?. In *Trauma and the Vietnam War generation: Report of findings from the National Vietnam Veterans Readjustment Study* (pp. 73–85). New York: Brunner/Mazel.

Lang, P.J. (1977). Imagery in therapy: An information processing analysis of fear. *Behavior Therapy, 8*, 862–886.

Lang, P.J. (1979a). A bio-informational theory of emotional imagery. *Psychophysiology, 16*, 495–510.

Lang, P.J. (1979b). A bio-informational theory of emotional imagery. *Psychophysiology, 16*, 495–512.

Lauterbach, D., & Vrana, S.R. (2001). The relationship among personality variables, exposure to traumatic events, and severity of posttraumatic stress symptoms. *Journal of Traumatic Stress, 14*(1), 29–45.

Lauterbach, D., Vrana, S.R., King, D.W., & King, L.A. (1997). Psychometric properties of the civilian version of the Mississippi PTSD Scale. *Journal of Traumatic Stress, 10*(3), 499–513.

LeDoux, J. (1998). Fear and the brain: Where have we been, and where are we going? *Biological Psychiatry, 44*(12), 1229–1238.

McWilliams, L.A., Cox, B.J., & Asmundson, G.J.G. (2005). Symptom structure of posttraumatic stress disorder in a nationally representative sample. *Journal of Anxiety Disorders, 19*(6), 626–641.

Miller, L.S., Wasserman, G.A., Neugebauer, R., Gorman-Smith, D., & Kamboukos, D. (1999). Witnessed community violence and antisocial behavior in high-risk, urban boys. *Journal of Clinical Child Psychology, 28*(1), 2–11.

Mineka, S., & Thomas, C. (1999). Mechanisms of change in exposure therapy for anxiety disorders. In T. Dalgleish & M.J. Power (Eds.), *Handbook of cognition and emotion* (pp. 747–764). New York: USs Ltd.

Mowrer, O.H. (1947). On the dual nature of learning–a re-interpretation of "conditioning" and "problem-solving." *Harvard Educational Review, 17,* 102–148.

Mowrer, O.H. (1960). *Learning theory and behavior.* New York: Wiley.

Neuner, F., Schauer, M., Klaschik, C., Karunakara, U.K., & Elbert, T. (2004). A comparison of narrative exposure therapy, supportive counseling, and psychoeducation for treating posttraumatic stress disorder in an African refugee settlement. *Journal of Consulting and Clinical Psychology, 72*(4), 579–587.

Neuner, F., Schauer, M., Roth, W.T., & Elbert, T. (2002). A narrative exposure treatment as intervention in a refugee camp: a case report. *Behavioural and Cognitive Psychotherapy, 30* (2), 205–209.

Nishith, P., Resick, P.A., & Griffin, M.G. (2002). Pattern of change in prolonged exposure and cognitive-processing therapy for female rape victims with posttraumatic stress disorder. *Journal of Consulting and Clinical Psychology, 70*(4), 880–886.

Ozer, E.J., Best, S.R., Lipsey, T.L., & Weiss, D.S. (2003). Predictors of posttraumatic stress disorder and symptoms in adults: A meta-analysis. *Psychological Bulletin, 129*(1), 52–73.

Pitman, R.K., Altman, B., Greenwald, E., Longpre, R.E., Macklin, M.L., Poir,, R.E., et al. (1991). Psychiatric complications during flooding therapy for posttraumatic stress disorder. *Journal of Clinical Psychiatry, 52*(1), 17–20.

Pitman, R.K., Orr, S.P., Altman, B., Longpre, R.E., Poir,, R.E., Macklin, M.L., et al. (1996). Emotional processing and outcome of imaginal flooding therapy in Vietnam veterans with chronic posttraumatic stress disorder. *Comprehensive Psychiatry, 37*(6), 409–418.

Punamäki, R.-L., Qouta, S., & El-Sarraj, E. (2001). Resiliency factors predicting psychological adjustment after political violence among Palestinian children. *International Journal of Behavioral Development, 25*(3), 256–267.

Rosen, C.S., Chow, H.C., Finney, J.F., Greenbaum, M.A., Moos, R.H., Sheikh, J.I., et al. (2004). VA practice patterns and practice guidelines for treating posttraumatic stress disorder. *Journal of Traumatic Stress, 17*(3), 213–222.

Rothbaum, B.O., & Foa, E.B. (1999). Exposure therapy for PTSD. *PTSD Research Quarterly, 10*(2), 1–6.

Rothbaum, B.O., & Hodges, L.F. (1999). The use of virtual reality exposure in the treatment of anxiety disorders. *Behavior Modification, 23*(4), 507–525.

Rothbaum, B.O., Hodges, L.F., Alarcon, R.D., Ready, D.J., Shahar, F., Graap, K., et al. (1999). Virtual reality exposure therapy for PTSD Vietnam veterans: a case study. *Journal of Traumatic Stress, 12*(2), 263–271.

Rothbaum, B.O., Hodges, L.F., Ready, D.J., Graap, K., & Alarcon, R.D. (2001). Virtual reality exposure therapy for Vietnam veterans with posttraumatic stress disorder. *Journal of Clinical Psychiatry, 62*(8), 617–622.

Rudenberg, S.L., Jansen, P., & Fridjhon, P. (1998). The effect of exposure during an ongoing climate of violence on children's self-perceptions, as reflected in drawings. *South African Journal of Psychology, 28*(2), 107–115.

Saigh, P.A. (1986). In vitro flooding in the treatment of a 6-yr-old boy's posttraumatic stress disorder. *Behaviour Research and Therapy, 24*(6), 685–688.

Saigh, P.A. (1987a). In vitro flooding of a childhood posttraumatic stress disorder. *School Psychology Review, 16*(2), 203–211.

Saigh, P.A. (1987b). In vitro flooding of an adolescent's posttraumatic stress disorder. *Journal of Clinical Child Psychology, 16*(2), 147–150.

Saigh, P.A. (1987c). In vitro flooding of childhood posttraumatic stress disorders: A systematic replication. *Professional School Psychology, 2*(2), 135–146.

Saigh, P.A. (1989). The use of an in vitro flooding package in the treatment of traumatized adolescents. *Journal of Developmental and Behavioral Pediatrics, 10*(1), 17–21.

Saigh, P.A. (1992). The behavioral treatment of child and adolescent posttraumatic stress disorder. *Advances in Behaviour Research and Therapy, 14*(4), 247–275.

Saigh, P.A., Yule, W., & Inamdar, S.C. (1996). Imaginal flooding of traumatized children and adolescents. *Journal of School Psychology, 34*(2), 163–183.

Schnurr, P.P., Friedman, M.J., & Rosenberg, S.D. (1993). Premilitary MMPI scores as predictors of combat-related PTSD symptoms. *American Journal of Psychiatry, 150*(3), 479–483.

Scott, M.J., & Stradling, S.G. (1997). Client compliance with exposure treatments for posttraumatic stress disorder. *Journal of Traumatic Stress, 10*(3), 523–526.

Smith, P.A., Perrin, S.G., & Yule, W. (1999). Cognitive behaviour therapy for post traumatic stress disorder. *Child Psychology and Psychiatry Review, 4*(4), 177–182.

Tarrier, N., Pilgrim, H., Sommerfield, C., Faragher, B., Reynolds, M., Graham, E., et al. (1999). A randomized trial of cognitive therapy and imaginal exposure in the treatment of chronic posttraumatic stress disorder. *Journal of Consulting and Clinical Psychology, 67*(1), 13–18.

Trimble, M.R. (1985). Post-traumatic stress disorder: History of a concept. In C.R. Figley (Ed.), *Trauma and its wake*. Vol. I. *The study and treatment of post-traumatic stress disorder* (pp. 5–14). New York: Brunner/Mazel.

Van Minnen, A., & Hagenaars, M. (2002). Fear activation and habituation patterns as early process predictors of response to prolonged exposure treatment in PTSD. *Journal of Traumatic Stress, 15*(5), 359–367.

Van Minnen, A., Wessel, I., Dijkstra, T., & Roelofs, K. (2002). Changes in PTSD patients' narratives during prolonged exposure therapy: A replication and extension. *Journal of Traumatic Stress, 15*(3), 255–258.

Zayfert, C., Becker, C.B., & Gillock, K.L. (2002). Managing obstacles to the utilization of exposure therapy with PTSD patients. In L. VandeCreek & T.L. Jackson (Eds.), *Innovations in clinical practice: A source book*, Vol. 20 (pp. 201–222). Sarasota, FL: Professional Resource Press.

Zimand, E., Anderson, P.L., Gershon, J., Graap, K., Hodges, L.F., & Rothbaum, B.O. (2002). Virtual reality therapy: Innovative treatment for anxiety disorders. *Primary Psychiatry, 9*(7), 51–54.

Zoellner, L.A., Alvarez-Conrad, J., & Foa, E.B. (2002). Peritraumatic dissociative experiences, trauma narratives, and trauma pathology. *Journal of Traumatic Stress, 15*(1), 49–57.

Zoellner, L.A., Feeny, N.C., Cochran, B., & Pruitt, L. (2003). Treatment choice for PTSD. *Behaviour Research and Therapy, 41*(8), 879–886.

CHAPTER 6

Exposure Therapy with Adult Survivors of Childhood Sexual Abuse

**Frank Castro and
Brian P. Marx**
Temple University

Childhood sexual abuse (CSA) is often regarded as one of the most traumatic events a child may experience. Although definitions of CSA vary across studies, it is typically defined as an instance in which a child is either forced or coerced to watch or engage in sexual acts (kissing, fondling, masturbation, oral, anal, vaginal penetration, etc.). Studies vary in the age cutoff used to denote childhood (e.g., under the age of 18, under the age of 14). Some studies of CSA incorporate more stringent criteria (e.g., the perpetrator must be 5 years older; contact abuse only) or focus specifically on one gender. Given these measurement differences across studies, as well as participant self-report biases and distortions, CSA prevalence rates vary widely, with rates ranging from 15% to 44% in women and 5% to 39% in men, with the higher percentages reported in clinical samples for both genders (Beitchman, Zucker, Hood, DaCosta, Akman, & Cassavia, 1992; Briere, 1992; Browne & Finkelhor, 1986; Polusny & Follette, 1995).

Long-term effects of CSA on psychological health have been reported in several studies over the last 2 decades. These studies have demonstrated that CSA is associated with both short- and long-term negative outcomes (Beitchman, et al., 1992; Briere, 1992; Browne & Finkelhor, 1986; Polusny & Follette, 1995), including depression, anxiety, post-traumatic stress disorder (PTSD), sexual revictimization, borderline personality disorder, somatization disorder, dissociative disorders, self-mutilation, suicidal ideation and parasuicidal behavior, eating disorders, and substance use disorders (for a comprehensive review of sequelae, see Browne and Finkelhor, 1986, or Polusny and Follette, 1995). In treatment, adult CSA survivors often present with comorbid symptoms that make treatment planning more complex and may require the concurrent or sequential use of more than one treatment modality (e.g., substance use treatment followed by exposure therapy).

In the following sections of this chapter, a theoretical explanation of the traumatic response to CSA is described in detail. Then, exposure therapy, as it is applied in the treatment of the sequelae to CSA, is explored. Specifically, we provide a detailed review of the outcome research to date on exposure therapy in the treatment of the sequelae to CSA, as well as the specific concerns of CSA survivors as they relate to the implementation of exposure therapy. Finally, a critical analysis of the outcome research will examine methodological limitations, as well as important unanswered questions.

THEORETICAL EXPLANATIONS
OF THE RESPONSE TO CSA

CSA experiences may be viewed as a complex set of unconditioned stimuli that elicit an unconditioned response (UCR), namely fear and its associated arousal (Cloitre, 1998; van der Kolk, 1989). Consistent with principles of classical conditioning, stimuli that are paired over a number of trials with CSA experiences may eventually come to elicit the same response as CSA. In addition, stimuli paired only once with intensely aversive situations may result in fear conditioning (Sartory, 1993). Stimuli such as footsteps in a hallway, a darkened room, a bed, or a particular brand of cologne may eventually serve as conditioned stimuli and trigger an intense conditioned fear response. The conditioned response (CR) may also transfer to other stimuli through processes of secondary conditioning, higher-order conditioning, and stimulus generalization. Given that CSA often occurs within the context of close, interpersonal relationships, it is entirely possible that this associated complex set of stimuli, which under normal circumstances elicits a wide range of emotions, may come to consistently elicit a conditioned fear response. Given the pervasiveness of such stimuli (emotional intimacy, interpersonal relationships, etc.), some CSA survivors may then experience conditioned emotional responses in the company of others who unknowingly are associated with the conditioned stimuli. To complicate matters, the UCR can become a conditioned stimulus (CS) for an even more aversive CR. For example, in the case of CSA, the initial fear response (UCR) may subsequently lead to feelings of hopelessness, loss of control, or a sense of guilt. In this way, fear might become a discriminative stimulus for a chain of subsequent emotions and cognitions.

According to Mowrer (1960), conditioned fear is expected to have motivational and reinforcing properties. Specifically, given that fear is an aversive state that serves to increase the strength of behaviors that reduce it, attempts are usually made to either avoid the CS altogether or respond with escape behaviors that function to reduce the conditioned fear response when conditioned stimuli are presented. Responses are strengthened when they result in successful termination or avoidance of stimuli that elicit the conditioned fear. In other words, the conditioned fear response sets the stage for other behaviors that function to avoid situations or stimuli that produce the conditioned fear response.

Because the CR can be extinguished only by presenting the CS without the UCS, (thereby "teaching" the individual that the CS does not reliably produce the CR), individuals will continue to engage in avoidance behavior that prevents extinction of the UCS/CS link. Avoidance behavior also prevents individuals from habituating to the aversive CR, thereby maintaining the anxiety level originally experienced during the presentation of the UCS.

Recent theorists have expanded on this model, incorporating more cognitive aspects. For example, Lang (1979) proposed a bioinformational theory of fear in which fear networks consist of three interconnected nodes: information about the stimuli related to the event, information about the individual's emotional and physiological response to the event, and meaning related to the degree of threat. In this model, pathological fear results from erroneous information contained within these nodes. Similarly, Rachman (1980) suggested that psychopathology is a result of improper encoding and emotional processing of an event.

Foa and Kozak (1986) synthesized these modern views with Mowrer's two-factor conditioning model by proposing that pathological fear results from erroneous information that is encoded when the UCS is paired with the UCR, leading to pathological fear that generalizes to nonthreatening stimuli and avoidance behavior that prevents fear extinction. In summary, many sequelae to CSA may be considered conditioned fear responses, the function of which is to avoid stimuli that may evoke anxiety. Behaviorally, the avoidance and escape responses may take any of a number of forms (e.g., substance abuse, dissociation, promiscuous sex, parasuicidal behavior) and may occur across a variety of diagnostic categories that are relevant to CSA (e.g., PTSD, borderline personality disorder, dissociative identity disorder).

Survivors of CSA may present with other symptoms that cannot easily be explained by traditional and/or contemporary behavioral models of pathological fear. These symptoms include depression, guilt, feelings of helplessness, low self-esteem, feelings of anger and hostility, negative cognitions about self, and poor interpersonal relationships. Foa and Cahill (2001) and Foa and Rauch (2004) have contended that survivors of trauma often encode negative attributions about the world and themselves during the course of a traumatic event. Many trauma survivors deny recalling experiencing these cognitions. In the case of survivors with pathological fear, however, these cognitions are maintained much the same way the conditioned fear response is maintained (i.e., through avoidance and escape repertoires). More specifically, these cognitions are never disconfirmed because the survivor actively avoids or escapes situations that would lead to their extinction.

EXPOSURE THERAPY WITH CSA SURVIVORS

According to Foa and Kozak's (1986) model of exposure, pathological fear can be extinguished only through a process in which the fear structure is first activated and then modified through the provision of corrective information. In the case of CSA survivors, this is accomplished through repeated, imaginal reliving of the traumatic experience.

In imaginal exposure, the client recounts the memory of his or her traumatic experience aloud in the present tense and in great detail. To intensify the experience, clients are asked to close their eyes and visualize the event as they recount it, focusing on their thoughts and feelings. Clients are instructed not to describe the event in the past tense but in the present. To ensure both a heightened level of negative affect and a subsequent decrease of negative affect, clients usually recount the traumatic experience several times within a single session and engage in the procedure across multiple sessions.

In addition, clients may be asked to complete therapist-assisted in vivo exposures where the client confronts situations, settings, or contexts that elicit fear and avoidance responses (e.g., a specific room of a house, basements). A hierarchy of such situations or stimuli is usually developed, and exposure begins with situations that elicit an anxiety response of moderate severity. As with imaginal exposure, repeated exposures are usually needed to reduce or eliminate the CR. Once this occurs, the next item on the fear hierarchy can be confronted; however, generalization often occurs during exposure, and it may not be necessary to proceed through the entire hierarchy.

Some exposure techniques include active imagining and mastery exercises (Smucker, Dancu, Foa, & Niederee, 1995) or counter-conditioning procedures (Paunovic, 2002, 2003). In active imagining and mastery exercises, rather than trying to correct erroneous information, clients relive the experience and change its recounting such that the narrative emphasizes client mastery over the experience. In counter-conditioning, positive memories are paired with neutral stimuli that are eventually used to counter-condition the client's pathological response (for a full review see Paunovic, 2002, 2003). There has been some success using active imaining with CSA survivors (Smucker, et al., 1995a; Smucker & Niederee, 1995b) and counter-conditioning with a case study of a PTSD survivor of rape (Paunovic, 2003). Studies with larger samples, however, must be performed to understand the mechanisms of symptom change and generalization of treatment effects.

In general, exposure therapy with CSA survivors usually includes both imaginal exposure, in vivo exposure, and other treatment components. For example, Foa and colleagues (Foa & Rothbaum, 1998) include psychoeducation and breathing re-training in their version of exposure therapy, prolonged exposure (PE). PE treatment is brief, often lasting only 9 to 12 sessions (Foa & Rothbaum, 1998). Clients who fail to achieve a 70% reduction in symptom severity by the eighth session are offered three additional sessions.

Over the course of exposure therapy, clients learn that heightened negative affect does not persist indefinitely in the presence of feared situations or stimuli (within-session habituation) and that, over time, general anxiety related to the experience of the trauma decreases without avoidance and/or escape (between-session habituation). Correspondingly, there is reduced motivation for engaging in behaviors that are negatively reinforced through fear reduction. Imaginal and in vivo exposure in a supportive setting also has the effect of incorporating safety information into the trauma memory and helps the individual recognize that recalling a trauma is not inherently dangerous. In other words, clients learn that remembering a trauma and processing associated emotions is not the same as the trauma itself and that objectively safe contexts that were associated with the trauma are not inherently dangerous. This process is thought to result in the reduction of hyperarousal symptoms, as clients correspondingly adjust their perceptions of what constitutes safety.

OUTCOME RESEARCH

Numerous treatment outcome studies have provided support for the efficacy of exposure therapy as a treatment for PTSD. The majority of these studies used exposure therapy for PTSD in specific populations such as combat veterans, sexual assault victims, and childhood abuse victims, although recent studies have examined more complex cases (e.g., multiple and heterogeneous trauma; see Foa, Keane, & Friedman, 2000). To date, only a few studies have examined the use of exposure therapy with adult CSA survivors. Considering that CSA prevalence rates are conservatively estimated to range from 15% to 33% in the general population and up to 44% in female clients seeking psychological treatment (Briere, 1992), the fact that only a small number of exposure-based treatment studies have been conducted appears to be a major oversight in the exposure therapy literature.

In the first study to examine the efficacy of exposure in victims of childhood abuse (CA), Cloitre, Koenen, Cohen, and Han (2002) compared a two-phase cognitive-behavioral treatment to wait-list control in 58 women with PTSD related to CA. Consistent with previous research that found affect dysregulation and disturbances in interpersonal skills in adult survivors of CA, Cloitre, et al. (2002) developed a two-phase program (Skills Training in Affect and Interpersonal Regulation-modified Prolonged Exposure (PE); STAIR-modified PE) to address these specific difficulties before the initiation of exposure. Phase 1 of the treatment included eight weekly sessions of skills training in affect and interpersonal regulation. This phase was derived from techniques used in various cognitive-behavioral treatments, as well as dialectical behavior therapy (DBT; Linehan, 1993), which were tailored to address the specific needs of the CA population. Phase 2 consisted of eight weekly sessions of modified prolonged exposure, at which time clients completed imaginal exposure exercises based on Foa and Rothbaum's (1998) treatment program (no in vivo component was included). Three additional components followed each imaginal exposure: a stabilization check where participants were guided in coping with increased affect, an emotion-focused processing intervention aimed at aiding participants in identifying negative feelings, and an additional exercise that helped participants identify negative interpersonal schemas within the exposure narrative. Strengths of the study included multimethod assessment of PTSD by trained clinicians blind to condition assignment, multiple assessment points up to 9-month follow-up period, random monitoring of treatment adherence, and use of a representative sample of CA survivors (i.e., participants with comorbid diagnoses were not excluded).

Relative to participants assigned to the wait-list condition, participants in the active treatment condition showed a decrease in PTSD symptoms and greater improvement in affect regulation and interpersonal skills. Further, these gains were maintained at 3- and 9-month follow-up evaluation. Although results provided preliminary support for the efficacy of exposure with CA survivors, numerous questions remain. First, it is unclear which aspect (and/or phase) of treatment was responsible for changes in PTSD symptoms. Further, the exposure treatment phase included postexposure components not offered in standard prolonged exposure—components that bear great similarity to cognitive restructuring techniques—thereby making it even more difficult to identify mechanism(s) of action. Future research could use dismantling techniques to identify active treatment components and identify how symptoms change (i.e., frequency, intensity) as a function of each technique. In addition, the sample was composed of individuals reporting either sexual or physical abuse in childhood, and it is unclear whether the intervention was equally efficacious for the two groups. These and other methodological issues are reviewed by Cahill, Zoellner, Feeny, and Riggs (2004) and Cloitre, Stovall-McClough, Miranda, and Chemtob (2004b).

In a follow-up investigation, Cloitre, Stovall-McClough, and Levitt (2004a) recruited 49 female CA survivors from two clinical trials of their STAIR/modified PE treatment. Participants met the same criteria for inclusion as the 2002 study, and many had several coexisting diagnoses. Almost 70% of the women completed treatment, with no differences in abuse history or clinical characteristics between completers and noncompleters. Dropouts were significantly younger than noncompleters and most often dropped out, on average, at the end of the STAIR phase of treatment. Results showed that a positive therapeutic alliance at the beginning of treatment reliably predicted PTSD symptom reduction at the end of treatment; however, this relationship was mediated by a woman's ability to successfully regulate her negative emotions. The authors interpreted these findings to suggest that the quality of the therapeutic relationship was an active ingredient in the treatment of CA-related PTSD (e.g., Foa & Kozak, 1986). Similar to the previous study, the generalizability of findings was reduced by the small sample size, the lack of appropriate control groups, and exclusion of male survivors.

In 2002, Resick, Nishith, Weaver, Astin, and Feuer conducted a randomized, controlled trial comparing prolonged exposure, cognitive processing therapy

(CPT), and minimal attention (MA) conditions with 171 sexual assault survivors with chronic PTSD. Individuals in both active treatments experienced a reduction in PTSD and related symptoms, relative to individuals in the no treatment control group. The success of CPT indicated that it might be as effective as prolonged exposure for sexual assault victims. In a secondary analysis of the findings from this study, Resick, Nishith, and Griffin (2003) examined whether or not there were differences between CSA and non-CSA survivors in the reduction of PTSD and other stress symptoms (i.e., alterations in regulating affective arousal, attention and consciousness, systems of meaning, somatization, and chronic characterological changes). After accounting for group differences on pretreatment scores, CSA and non-CSA groups did not differ on their post-treatment scores, irrespective of treatment condition. Further, improvements in both groups were maintained for at least 9 months. The authors concluded that both CPT and PE were effective for treating PTSD and depression, as well as more complex symptoms that have been observed among CSA survivors. In contrast to the findings of Cloitre and colleagues, similar attrition rates and intervention success across treatment conditions suggested that it may not be necessary to include treatment components that specifically target affect and interpersonal regulation skills.

Finally, McDonagh, Friedman, McHugo, Ford, Sengupta, Mueser, et al. (2005) compared individual cognitive-behavioral therapy (CBT), including imaginal and in vivo exposure, with present-focused problem-solving therapy (PST) and a wait-list control condition in 74 women with CSA-related PTSD. All participants were randomly assigned to conditions, and both the CBT and PST interventions were manualized and lasted for 14 weeks. Based on the work of Foa, Dancu, Hembree, Jaycox, Meadows, and Street (1999), the CBT intervention consisted of prolonged imaginal and in vivo exposure, as well as cognitive restructuring. Given that the sample was primarily composed of multiply traumatized individuals, the most distressing CSA memory took precedence for the prolonged exposure portion. Only after habituation of negative affect associated with the memory occurred did the participant and therapist move to the next most distressing memory in the fear hierarchy, which may or may not have been another CSA memory. The other active therapeutic intervention consisted of a systematic approach to coping and problem solving. This intervention was carefully developed so that it did not contain any of the active ingredients of the CBT condition. Participants assigned to CBT and PST conditions were reassessed immediately after treatment, as well as 3- and 6-months post-treatment.

Relative to the other conditions, the CBT condition had a greater dropout rate. The results also showed, however, that individuals assigned to the CBT condition were significantly less likely than PST individuals to meet criteria for PTSD at the follow-up assessments. Further, participants assigned to either the CBT or PST conditions reported less severe PTSD symptoms, trauma-related cognitive distortions, and anxiety compared with wait-list individuals. The findings suggested that, although Foa, et al.'s PE treatment package may result in greater success in achieving remission from PTSD, both treatment packages may be successfully used to improve the psychological functioning of CSA survivors who meet criteria for PTSD. The attrition rate for the CBT group (> 41%) was higher than attrition rates from other similar studies (e.g., Foa, Rothbaum, Riggs, & Murdock, 1991; Foa, et al., 1999; Resick, Nishith, Weaver, Astin, & Feuer, 2002). Most of the CBT attritions occurred during early imaginal exposure sessions (between sessions 4 and 7), suggesting that imaginal exposure may be especially challenging for many CSA survivors (e.g., those with more complex symptom presentations).

SPECIAL CONSIDERATIONS FOR CSA SURVIVORS

As was shown in the study by McDonagh, et al., not all CSA survivors can tolerate exposure-based CBT well, and those with complex symptom presentations may be less tolerant than those with a more simple PTSD presentation. More specifically, CSA survivors who present with intense hyperarousal, emotional numbing and dissociation, intense intrusive thoughts, anger/suicide/therapy interfering behaviors, and substance use problems may not be well suited for exposure-based CBT. In addition, CSA survivors who present with issues related to retraumatization or sexual revictimization and incomplete or suspect narratives may also be poor candidates for exposure-based CBT. Other important concerns, such as the gender of the therapist and sexuality issues, may have implications for whether or not exposure-based therapies are used with CSA survivors.

Hyperarousal

The goal of exposure therapy is to provide corrective information so that it may be incorporated into the fear structure. When experiencing extreme arousal, individuals are often unable to focus on corrective information. As a result, exposure therapy may only serve to exacerbate symptoms. Thus, CSA survivors who evidence excessively high levels of arousal or are especially reactive to the exposure paradigm are poor candidates for exposure therapy.

Numbing/Dissociation

Any behavior that effectively precludes activation of an individual's fear network should decrease the likelihood that exposure techniques will be efficacious. Thus, individuals who do not become sufficiently emotionally aroused, or who are prone to dissociate, will not experience the therapeutic effects of habituation. In cases where a client's depressive symptomatology is interfering with the ability to experience sufficient arousal, interventions such as cognitive therapy (Beck, Rush, Shaw, & Emery, 1979) might be needed to first alleviate depressive symptoms to a level where exposure can then be effective. Alternative treatment considerations may include inpatient care or pharmacological interventions (Foa & Rothbaum 1998).

Intrusive Thoughts

Because the fear network is a distributed system that provides linkages to a host of fear-relevant memories and affective responses, activation of the fear network sometimes results in recollections of other traumatic experiences. Intrusive recollections of peripheral traumas can startle the client and distract him or her from processing a selected event. It is best to preemptively warn the client that this is possible, as well as reserve time during the session to discuss any intrusive or new memories. Making time for discussion of unexpected memories may preempt client rumination about the experience and help the client refocus on the exposure task. Encouraging the client to accept the spontaneous recovery of forgotten memories as a normal byproduct of the exposure therapy experience usually reduces client anxiety over their sudden reemergence.

Affect Regulation and Resistance

Needless to say, clients must be highly motivated to engage in exposure therapy. Resistance to exposure therapy may be expressed in any of a variety of externalizing or acting-out behaviors characterized by poor affect regulation (e.g., high levels of anger or cynicism, parasuicidal behavior). Similarly, clients may not fully engage in exposure, miss sessions, actively disrupt the session, or be noncompliant with homework. In the case of clients with a comorbid Axis II diagnosis (e.g., Borderline Personality Disorder), therapists should confront these issues directly using techniques borrowed from Dialectical Behavior Therapy (DBT; Linehan, 1993). In general, life-threatening issues (e.g., abusive relationships, suicidal or parasuicidal behaviors) take priority over exposure therapy and contraindicate its use until the issues are resolved.

Concurrent Substance Abuse

Substance abuse is a significant problem for exposure therapy, in that individuals may use substances as a means of avoiding unwanted negative affect, thoughts, and memories. Foa and Rothbaum (1998) suggest that sobriety should be an explicit condition of continued treatment, and those individuals who have a history of substance abuse should be clean and sober for at least 90 days before treatment. The client should be referred to an appropriate substance abuse treatment program before participating in any exposure treatment.

Sexual Revictimization or Multiple Assaults

Female CSA survivors are more likely to experience an adult assault than those who do not have a CSA history, a phenomenon known as sexual revictimization (Marx, Calhoun, Wilson, & Meyerson, 2001; Marx, Heidt, & Gold, 2005). It is also common for CSA survivors to experience multiple CSA episodes with one or multiple perpetrators. For the purposes of conducting exposure therapy, it is best for the therapist and client to choose the most traumatic experience to work with, as it will be the event with the highest probability of activating the fear network. In some cases (e.g., when hyperarousal is an issue), it may be advisable to begin working with a less threatening event before processing traumatic experiences that are more difficult to confront. However, the therapist should take care not to reinforce avoidance behavior by confirming the client's suspicions that some memories are too traumatic to deal with.

Therapist Gender

As a result of their experiences, many CSA survivors are uncomfortable with a therapist who is the same gender as their assailant. Accordingly, gender may be a conditioned aversive stimulus that elicits strong negative reactions from the client. Therapist gender issues should be dealt with immediately, and both the therapist and client should jointly explore whether a referral is necessary. During the discussion, it may be worthwhile to discuss how the therapist's gender may actually be an advantage, as it may enhance activation of the client's fear network.

Incomplete or Suspect Narrative

It is often the case that a long interval of time has passed from the trauma to the initial treatment efforts with adult survivors of childhood sexual abuse. Because of this lengthy passage of time, the reconstructive nature of memory, and the relatively underdeveloped cognitive capacities of survivors at the time of the abuse, survivors of CSA may present in therapy with incomplete or inaccurate trauma memories. In these circumstances, the therapist and client might try to obtain additional information about the abuse from other family members, the police, or from medical records. Also, the client might make use of relevant stimuli (e.g., pictures with other family members) to facilitate abuse recollection. Therapists should be creative, within reason, in helping the client remember specific events.

Some clients might present with claims of abuse that are suspect. Claims that are suspect are those in which the individual has no memory of abuse but, for one reason or another, believes abuse occurred. To avoid facilitating the production of a false memory of abuse, some clinicians use an age limit, usually around 5 years of age, where it is plausible for the client to remember the event to distinguish between valid and invalid claims of abuse (Courtois, 2001). A better course of action, however, is to find a reliable means of corroborating the event. This can be accomplished through court, police, or medical records, talking with a parent or older sibling, or other documentation. An important question the therapist should ask in this case is, "Does this person stand to gain anything from having a CSA history and associated diagnoses?" especially if litigation is a possibility. If a therapist remains unsure about the veracity of the client's report, therapy should focus on helping the client cope and develop adaptive skills rather than exposure therapy.

Cognitive Disability and Communication Difficulties

Exposure therapy requires the client to recount his or her story in the first person, present tense. Clients with diminished cognitive ability and/or poor communication skills may not be able to adequately recount their subjective experiences.

Gender and Sexuality Issues

CSA survivors often present with issues specific to sexual and gender identity, and these issues might be related to their original sexual victimization. For example, studies have shown that survivors of CSA are more likely to engage in promiscuous behavior. In a study of male and female practitioners of sadomasochism, Nordling, Sandnabba, and Santtila (2000) found higher incidences of CSA than in nonpractitioners. In a study of internalized homophobia (IH) among gay, bisexual, and transgender adults, Gold, Marx, and Heidt (2003) showed that IH significantly predicted psychological symptomatology among gay male survivors of sexual victimization. Not surprisingly, same-sex victimization may lead survivors to significant questions concerning their own gender identification and sexuality.

Interpersonal Difficulties

Various authors (e.g., Foa & Meadows, 1997; Tarrier, Pilgrim, Sommerfield, Faragher, Reynolds, Graham, et al., 1999) have argued that CSA survivors constitute a qualitatively different class of trauma victims because CSA is likely to interfere with normal developmental processes (see Polusny & Follette, 1995). Despite this recognition, few authors have provided guidance as to how to address these issues in exposure therapy. Foa and Meadows (1997) suggested that adjunctive techniques to PE therapy can educate the individuals regarding "normal" interpersonal interactions, although they do not provide information as to the specific techniques or their timing. Cloitre, et al. (2002) provided the only known examination of an exposure-based therapy for CSA survivors that included skills training in affect and interpersonal regulation.

Beyond Exposure

Provided therapy is successful, CSA survivors often consider disclosing their abuse to their family or significant others. Some even report wishing to confront the perpetrator. Should the client wish to disclose, the therapist should not be dismissive of the client's wish. The choice to disclose or confront is the client's alone. A useful role for the therapist, however, is to help the client fully explore the different ways in which disclosure or confrontation can occur, its timing, and the potential familial or systemic ramifications.

Deciding whether exposure therapy is appropriate for a client may be difficult, especially if the symptom picture is complex. It is strongly suggested that a detailed client history and functional assessment of the client's psychological problems be obtained. A detailed history improves therapist inferences regarding the causes of a client's problems and therefore helps foster a relevant treatment plan. It can also help clinicians identify which traumatic events should be the focus of the exposure sessions and what kind of exposure techniques should be used.

Although it is still unclear how much of the variance in treatment outcome may be attributed to the therapeutic alliance (e.g., Cloitre, et al., 2004a), it is imperative that a strong alliance is formed at the beginning of therapy. By definition, exposure therapy is invasive and may initially evoke high levels of distress. A strong therapeutic alliance can foster the support necessary for the client to tolerate treatment. Several therapist behaviors may contribute to establishing a strong therapeutic alliance, including praise, empathic listening, and adopting a nonjudgmental stance. Another way to forge a strong therapeutic relationship is to involve the client in treatment decision making at all levels. Decisions regarding pace, selection of target behaviors, and even which memories to focus on during imaginal exposure should be made jointly (Hembree, Rauch, & Foa, 2003).

Therapists are also obligated to protect the welfare of their clients. Part of protecting client welfare means ensuring that the therapist is both intellectually and emotionally ready to provide adequate and appropriate treatment for each client. Exposure therapy is not only difficult for the client, it is challenging and strenuous for the therapist. In fact, it is not uncommon for the strong emotional responses of the client during exposure therapy to evoke secondary distress in the therapist. Given these circumstances, it is important for the therapist to accept the treatment rationale, allow the treatment model to guide decisions, and remind oneself as often as possible that the work being done is beneficial (Hembree, et al., 2003).

Given that work to date on the efficacy of exposure therapy with adult CSA survivors has been completed solely using female participants, it remains unclear whether exposure treatments are as effective for male survivors of CSA. Research into the efficacy of exposure for combat-related PTSD has provided mixed findings (Foa & Meadows, 1997). Although the reasons for this are still unclear, it may be that exposure to memories of self-committed brutality (frequently seen among combat veterans with PTSD) may exacerbate PTSD symptoms, as corrective information may not adequately address feelings of guilt (Pitman, Altman, Greenwald, Longpre, Macklin, Poire, et al., 1991). In a similar fashion, adult male CSA survivors may be more likely than female CSA survivors to experience guilt as a result of increased social stigmatization, myths, and stereotypes associated with same-sex CSA. Such guilt may be difficult to treat solely using exposure techniques. For these individuals, additional therapy modalities may be needed to address such concerns. For example, Kubany and colleagues have developed a cognitive therapy package for trauma-related guilt (CT-TRG; Kubany, 1997; Kubany & Manke, 1995); however, CT-TRG has been used with combat veterans and its applicability to CSA survivors is unclear. Other treatment packages, such as cognitive processing therapy (Resick, et al., 2002), that are specifically designed to address guilt and other cognitive distortions occurring in the wake of sexual victimization have proved useful in these circumstances.

SUMMARY AND CONCLUSIONS

CSA is a traumatic experience that affects millions of individuals. Firmly grounded in cognitive-behavioral theory, exposure therapy has displayed great promise as a treatment for those suffering from the sequelae to traumatic experiences, including CSA.

Although the work by Cloitre, et al., Resick, et al. and McDonagh, et al. on the efficacy of exposure with adult CSA survivors is encouraging, given the relative dearth of research on exposure therapy with adult survivors of CSA, more work is needed to determine the relative efficacy of this treatment. In the future, researchers should conduct dismantling studies to identify the most active treatment components of the exposure approach with CSA survivors. Although not every client is well suited for exposure therapy, and many questions remain unanswered, it should be considered a primary treatment option for individuals with psychological difficulties resulting from CSA.

This chapter was supported by funding from the Alcoholic Beverage Medical Research Foundation awarded to Brian P. Marx.

REFERENCES

Beck, A.T., Rush, A.J., Shaw, B.F., & Emery, G. (1979). *Cognitive therapy of depression*. New York: Wiley.

Beitchman, J.H., Zucker, K.J., Hood, J.E., DaCosta, G.A., Akman, D., & Cassavia, E. (1992). A review of the long-term effects of child sexual abuse. *Child Abuse and Neglect, 16,* 101–118.

Briere, J.N. (1992). *Child abuse trauma: Theory and treatment of the lasting effects*. Newbury Park, CA: Sage.

Browne, A., & Finkelhor, D. (1986). Impact of child sexual abuse: A review of the research. *Psychological Bulletin, 99,* 66–77.

Cahill, S.P., Zoellner, L.A., Feeny, N.C, & Riggs, D.S. (2004). Sequential treatment for child abuse-related posttraumatic stress disorder: Methodological comment on Cloitre, Koenen, Cohen, and Han (2002). *Journal of Consulting and Clinical Psychology, 72,* 543–548.

Cloitre, M. (1998). Sexual revictimization: Risk factors and prevention. In V.M. Follette, J.I. Ruzek, & F.R. Abueg (Eds.), *Cognitive-behavioral therapies for trauma* (pp. 278–304). New York: Guilford Press.

Cloitre, M., Koenen, K.C., Cohen, L.C., & Han, H. (2002). Skills training in affective and interpersonal regulation followed by exposure: A phase based treatment for PTSD related to childhood abuse. *Journal of Consulting and Clinical Psychology, 70,* 1067–1074.

Cloitre, M., Stovall-McClough, K.C., & Levitt, J.T. (2004a). Treating life-impairing problems beyond PTSD: Reply to Cahill, Zoellner, Feeny, and Riggs (2004). *Journal of Consulting and Clinical Psychology, 72,* 549–551.

Cloitre, M., Stovall-McClough, K.C., Miranda, R., & Chemtob, C.M. (2004b) Therapeutic alliance, negative mood regulation, and treatment outcome in child abuse-related posttraumatic stress disorder. *Journal of Consulting and Clinical Psychology, 72,* 411–416.

Courtois, C.A. (2001). Implications of the memory controversy for clinical practice: An overview of treatment recommendations and guidelines. *Journal of Child Sexual Abuse, 9,* 183–210.

Foa, E.B., & Cahill, S.P. (2001). Psychological therapies: Emotional processing. In N.J. Smelser & P.B. Bates (Eds.), *International encyclopedia of the social and behavioral sciences* (pp. 12363–12369). Oxford, England: Elsevier.

Foa, E.B., & Kozak, M.J. (1986). Emotional processing of fear: Exposure to corrective information. *Psychological Bulletin, 99,* 20–35.

Foa, E.B., & Meadows, E.A. (1997). Psychological treatments for PTSD: A critical review. *Annual Review of Psychology, 48,* 449–480.

Foa, E.B., & Rauch, S.A.M. (2004). Cognitive changes during prolonged exposure versus prolonged exposure plus cognitive restructuring in female assault survivors with posttraumatic stress disorder. *Journal of Consulting and Clinical Psychology, 72,* 879–884.

Foa, E.B., & Rothbaum, B.O. (1998). *Treating the trauma of rape*. New York: Guilford Press.

Foa, E.B., Dancu, C.V., Hembree, E.A., Jaycox, L.H., Meadows, E.A. & Street, G.P. (1999). Comparison of exposure therapy, stress inoculation training and their combination in reducing post traumatic stress disorder in female assault victims. *Journal of Consulting and Clinical Psychology, 63,* 948–955.

Foa, E.B., Keane, T.M, & Friedman, M.J. (2000). *Effective treatments for PTSD*. New York: Guilford Press.

Gold, S.D., Marx, B.P., & Heidt, J.M. (November, 2003). Lesbian, gay, and bisexual sexual assault victims: The relationship between internalized homophobia and psychological sequelae. Poster presented at the annual meeting of the Association for the Advancement of Behavior Therapy, Boston, MA.

Hembree, E.A., Rauch, S.A.M., & Foa, E.B. (2003). Beyond the manual: The insider's guide to prolonged exposure for PTSD. *Cognitive and Behavioral Practice, 10,* 22–30.

Kubany, E.S. (1997). Application of Cognitive Therapy for Trauma-Related Guilt (CT-TRG) with a Vietnam veteran troubled by multiple sources of guilt. *Cognitive and Behavioral Practice, 4,* 213–244.

Kubany, E.S. & Manke, F.P. (1995). Cognitive therapy for trauma-related guilt: Conceptual bases and treatment outlines. *Cognitive and Behavioral Practice, 2,* 23–61.

Lang, P.J. (1979). A bio-informational theory of emotional imagery. *Psychophysiology, 6,* 495–511.

Linehan, M.M. (1993). *Cognitive-behavioral treatment for borderline personality disorder*. New York: Guilford Press.

Marx, B.P., Calhoun, K.S., Wilson, A.E., & Meyerson, L.A. (2001). Sexual revictimization prevention: An outcome evaluation. *Journal of Consulting and Clinical Psychology, 69,* 25–32.

Marx, B.P., Heidt, J., & Gold, S.D. (2005). Perceived uncontrollability and unpredictability, self-regulation, and sexual revictimization. *Review of General Psychology, 9,* 67–90.

McDonagh, A., Friedman, M.J., McHugo, G., Ford, J. Sengupta, A., Mueser, K., et al. (2005). Randomized trial of cognitive-behavioral therapy for chronic posttraumatic stress disorder in adult survivors of childhood sexual abuse. *Journal of Consulting and Clinical Psychology, 73,* 515–524.

Mowrer, O.H. (1960). *Learning theory and behavior.* New York: Wiley.

Nordling, N., Sandnabba, N. K., & Santtila, P. (2000). The prevalence and effects of self reported childhood sexual abuse among sadomasochistically oriented males and females. *Journal of Child Sexual Abuse, 9,* 53–63.

Paunovic, N. (2002). Prolonged exposure counterconditioning (PEC) as a treatment for chronic posttraumatic stress disorder and major depression in an adult survivor of repeated child sexual and physical abuse. *Clinical Case Studies, 1,* 148–170.

Paunovic, N. (2003). Prolonged exposure counterconditioning as a treatment for chronic posttraumatic stress disorder. *Anxiety Disorders, 17,* 479–499.

Pitman, R.K., Altman, B., Greenwald, E., Longpre, R.E., Macklin, M.L., Poire, R.E., et al. (1991). Psychiatric complications during flooding therapy for posttraumatic stress disorder. *Journal of Clinical Psychiatry, 52,* 17–20.

Polusny, M.A., & Follette, V.M. (1995). Long term correlates of child sexual abuse: Theory and review of the empirical literature. *Applied and Preventive Psychology, 4,* 143–166.

Rachman, S. (1980). Emotional processing. *Behaviour Research and Therapy, 18,* 51–60.

Resick, P.A., Nishith, P., & Griffin, M.G. (2003) How well does cognitive-behavioral therapy treat symptoms of complex PTSD? An examination of child sexual abuse survivors within a clinical trial. *CNS Spectrums, 8,* 340–355.

Resick, P.A., Nishith, P., Weaver, T.L., Astin, M.C., & Feuer, C.A. (2002). A comparison of cognitive-processing therapy with prolonged exposure and a waiting condition for the treatment of chronic posttraumatic stress disorder in female rape victims. *Journal of Consulting and Clinical Psychology, 70,* 867–879.

Sartory, G. (1993). The associative network of fear: How does it come about? In N. Birbaumer & A. Ohman (Eds.), *The Structure of Emotion* (pp. 193–204). Seattle: Hogrefe & Huber Publishers.

Smucker, M.R., & Niederee, J. (1995). Treating incest-related PTSD and pathogenic schemas through imaginal exposure and rescripting. *Cognitive and Behavioral Practice, 2,* 63–92.

Smucker, M.R., Dancu, C., Foa, E.B., & Niederee, J.L. (1995). Imagery rescripting: A new treatment for survivors of childhood sexual abuse suffering from posttraumatic stress. *Journal of Cognitive Psychotherapy, 9,* 3–17.

Tarrier, N., Pilgrim, H., Sommerfield, C., Faragher, B., Reynolds, M., Graham, E., et al., (1999). A randomized trial of cognitive therapy and imaginal exposure in the treatment of posttraumatic stress disorder. *Journal of Consulting and Clinical Psychology, 67,* 13–18.

van der Kolk, B.A. (1989). The compulsion to repeat the trauma: Re-enactment, revictimization, and masochism. *Psychiatric Clinics of North America, 12,* 389–411.

CHAPTER 7

Issues in Conducting Exposure Therapy to Treat Combat Veterans' PTSD

Carlos G. Finlay

University of Buffalo

Judith A. Lyons

University of Mississippi Medical Center and G. V. ("Sonny") Montgomery VA Medical Center

Large-scale U.S. epidemiological studies show that combat is among the list of life experiences most commonly associated with symptoms of post-traumatic stress disorder among men (PTSD; Breslau & Kessler, 2001; Helzer, Robins, & McEvoy, 1987; Norris, 1992). For many veterans, war-related nightmares and dissociative flashbacks, near-paranoid ideation, and persistent hyperaroused states are common occurrences even decades after military service. These symptoms are further complicated by extreme and broad-based avoidance of war-related cues (e.g., discussions about war, war movies), social isolation, and a salient cognitive preoccupation with their past that impairs the traumatized veteran's ability to cope successfully with peacetime life.

Research on military samples shows the debilitating effects of combat-related PTSD are not restricted to any one sociodemographic group. For example, the absence of combat-related PTSD among women in general epidemiological studies can be attributed to the historical rarity of women in combat roles rather than to any gender difference in prevalence rates among those exposed to combat. To date, the largest epidemiological study of PTSD and other psychiatric conditions within a combat veteran population is the National Vietnam Veterans Readjustment Study (see Kulka, Schlenger, Fairbank, Hough, Jordan, Marmar, et al., 1990). Although the majority of returning veterans were observed to successfully readjust to civilian lifetime or peacetime military careers, estimates showed 31% of male and

Supported with resources and the use of facilities at the G.V. (Sonny) Montgomery VA Medical Center, Jackson, MS. The views expressed here represent those of the authors and do not necessarily represent the views of the Department of Veterans Affairs, MIRECC, or the University of Mississippi Medical Center.

Handbook of Exposure Therapies
169

29% of female veterans met criteria for PTSD at some time in their lives, and 15% of male and 9% of female veterans reported PTSD symptoms at the time of their assessment. Also, 11% of male and 9% of female veterans reported some symptoms associated with PTSD presentations but did not meet fully diagnostic criteria for the disorder. Similarly, a prospective study of reserve units serving in the Persian Gulf during Operation Desert Storm found no significant gender differences in either combat exposure or development of PTSD symptoms (Southwick, Morgan, Nagy, Bremner, Nicolaou, Johnson, et al., 1993). As the historical exclusion of women from frontline combat roles reduces—indeed, as the concept of war having a definable frontline may become obsolete—more women can be expected to present for treatment of combat-related PTSD.

A meta-analysis reports that a variety of treatments have demonstrated efficacy in reducing PTSD symptoms (Bradley, Greene, Russ, Dutra, & Westen, 2005). Compared to other populations, however, studies of combat trauma yield the lowest effect sizes across treatment modalities. Nevertheless, even within this difficult-to-treat population, data support the utility of exposure-based therapies (see Freuh, Turner, & Beidel, 1995). Across populations, exposure-based approaches yielded some of the largest effect sizes (Bradley, et al, 2005). Within studies of combat veterans, exposure therapy also yielded positive effect sizes when compared to other treatments or wait lists, although the effect sizes tended to be more modest.

Exposure therapy involves the direct and repeated presentation of learned trauma cues within a safe environment until subjective symptoms (e.g., distress ratings) or objective signs (e.g., psychophysiological measures, approach tasks) diminish over time (e.g., Freuh, et al., 1995; Levis & Hare, 1977). Exposure can range from very intense with abrupt onset (e.g., flooding) to procedures that are conducted more slowly across a hierarchy of cues with increasingly negative emotional valences, often combined with relaxation strategies (either interspersed with cue exposure as in systematic desensitization or before/after the exposure component of the session).

In vivo exposure protocols are nearly impossible to recreate for patients with combat-related post-traumatic stress. Some virtual reality programs that promote the illusion of immersion into a combat scenario are currently being tested, and some preliminary data support their use with combat veterans (e.g., Rothbaum, Hodges, Alarcon, Ready, Shahar, Graap, et al., 1999; Rothbaum, Hodges, Ready, Graap, & Alarcon, 2001), but such techniques can be expensive for many practitioners.

Thus, most treatment protocols for combat trauma have relied on imaginal exposure. Veteran clients are asked to recall traumatizing events in detail and explore possible motives and reasons for their and others' actions in combat. Situational cues (i.e., fear-related environmental stimuli and mental images of fear-related cues, including actual and potential negative consequences) are then selected based on their salience and ability to evoke intense emotional response. Veterans are then gradually exposed to these situational cues in either individual treatment (e.g., Lyons & Keane, 1989) or group therapy (e.g., Schnurr, Friedeman, Foy, Shea,

Hsieh, Lavori, et al., 2003) until the cue's affective valence reduces (Levis & Hare, 1977). Also, scenarios based on hypothetical motives are constructed and used in exposure trials along with cognitions about the actual event.

Despite the demonstrated success of the preceding techniques in the treatment of military veterans, there a number of special considerations in working with this population. This chapter reviews factors in the veteran's clinical profile and everyday life that may promote or impede progress in therapy and offers recommendations. These issues have been summarized into two domains of interest. First, factors that should be considered in treatment matching are discussed. In the second section, more pragmatic aspects of treatment implementation are presented. It is our hope that this review will increase mental health service providers' awareness of variables that often impact the treatment of veterans and thereby increase the likelihood of alleviating veterans' suffering.

SELECTION AND TIMING OF EXPOSURE AS THE TREATMENT OF CHOICE

The Complicating Role of Disability Status

Many veterans are eligible for disability benefits and free medical, mental health, and rehabilitation services from the Department of Veterans Affairs (VA). This process, known as *service-connection*, provides veterans financial assistance based on presenting medical/psychiatric conditions, the relation of each condition to active military duty, and the degree of impairment associated with each condition. Higher percentage ratings of disability can substantially augment personal incomes and increase access to a broader range of health, educational, and occupational opportunities for the veteran and veteran's family. Disability status can facilitate treatment by providing the veteran with a stable income base and broad access to care. The quest to obtain disability status or to increase percentage ratings, however, can lead to over-reporting of compensable symptoms (leading to misdiagnosis) and encourage under-reporting of other problems (e.g., substance abuse or preexisting conditions). Consequently, the resultant disability ratings are not always an accurate reflection of the veteran's true diagnosis and impairment. It is recommended that, before considering exposure therapy for trauma-related symptoms, each veteran's case be carefully reviewed to validate that PTSD is indeed an accurate and current diagnosis and that the level of impairment is such that exposure would be the appropriate treatment at that time. Unnecessary administration of exposure therapy has the potential to increase the salience of memories that had not previously been problematic and so carries the risk of harm to a patient who does not actually suffer from the intrusive reexperiencing symptoms that the exposure therapy would supposedly be prescribed to treat.

Developmental Factors

The timing of the traumatic event and when veterans enter treatment for post-traumatic stress symptoms can vary from a few months after their return from active duty to decades later. Veterans with prolonged post-traumatic stress symptoms (3 or more months after the event, American Psychiatric Association, 2000) or a delayed onset of clinically significant symptoms often report that the traumatic event happened decades before they initiate treatment. Indeed, it is not uncommon for changes in lifestyle or routine to transform subclinical post-trauma reactions into clinically significant impairment years after the traumatic event. Veterans often report delayed manifestation of PTSD symptoms after major life-span developmental milestones, such as retirement, death of a loved one, medical crisis, or onset of physical disability (e.g., Cassiday & Lyons, 1992; Macleod, 1994; Scaturo & Hayman, 1992). Because many veterans report a need to remain busy to suppress any stress reactions, the loss of daily activities resulting from employment termination or limited physical mobility undermines their ability to avoid anxiety or negative mood that was previously managed by these activities. Similarly, it is common for a successfully treated patient to need booster sessions in later life as new developmental milestones trigger new cognitive and emotional conflicts. For example, loss of a veteran's own child can precipitate renewed guilt and regret over civilian casualties during war. If the new or renewed distress is specific to a particular traumatic incident, it can often be addressed through exposure therapy.

Combat-related traumas can affect the veteran's everyday functioning differently at different points throughout the life span. Symptoms experienced by veterans in early adulthood are often overtly and functionally different from those experienced by veterans in their retirement years. Initial difficulties transitioning from military to civilian life are often couched in terms of the demands others place on them. A younger veteran with a new family may report difficulty managing home and work life, citing troubles applying strict military regimens and punishment contingencies to the more personal environment. Older veterans are more likely to report regret and sadness after personal reflection over life events and years of failed interpersonal relationships. Although consistent with normative phase-of-life issues, such concerns may augment or be augmented by the veteran's PTSD, and that connection can often be addressed within exposure-therapy sessions. In conjunction with reviewing a fit of vengeful rage that occurred on the battlefield, for example, it would be appropriate to eventually incorporate discussion of how this links to the veteran's fear of losing control while disciplining his or her child. Similarly, grief and guilt that stem from failure to save buddies in combat decades earlier can be processed in parallel with similar, normative feelings evoked by recent losses of loved ones as a result of natural causes.

Exposure therapy, however, is not automatically the treatment of choice for every case in which memories of past trauma are recounted among the presenting concerns. In many cases, the patient's distress stems from a broader life appraisal in which the veteran questions a variety of past actions and choices. If symptoms take the form of wide-ranging negative ruminations rather than specific trauma-related anxiety or dissociation, more general cognitive therapy may be most appropriate.

Sociopolitical Factors

Just as developmental events can influence symptom presentation and treatment needs, so, too, can wider cultural and political events. Veterans will often attribute mood deterioration, irritability, and impatience to world events that parallel their own combat experiences. Wars, insurgencies, rationales for combat, and local and worldwide reactions to these actions can spark tension in the veteran client. Veterans may find themselves drawn to day-by-day accounts of war and combat-related incidences, and recognize that these news items are exacerbating their anxiety, but have difficulty drawing their attention away from these reports. It is not uncommon for veterans of past wars to ruminate about current events and sociopolitical climates related to combat, actively comparing and contrasting their combat experiences with those of other warriors. As with developmental concerns, such thoughts are, to some degree, part of the normative process of appraising one's life within a larger context, and the clinician will need to make a judgment call as to whether and what type of intervention may be needed. The more global (as opposed to event-specific) and voluntary (versus intrusive and aversive) such ruminations, the less effective exposure therapy may be in improving any mood or anxiety symptoms they evoke.

Social Withdrawal and Role Pressure

Veterans diagnosed with PTSD commonly complain of an excessive need for social isolation and withdrawal, increased anxiety in social situations (e.g., eating at restaurants, large group gatherings), and an almost-immediate propensity to respond harshly (either verbally or physically) to increasing social pressure. Traumatized veterans' problems gaining and maintaining employment and marital/social difficulties are often attributed to this strong desire for social isolation (e.g., Prigerson, Maciejewski, & Rosenheck, 2001). Findings have suggested that social anxiety among veterans with PTSD is closely tied to negative mood states rather than a fear of negative evaluation by others (e.g., Hofmann, Litz, & Weathers, 2003).

Veterans may complain that their family and/or therapist "does not understand" them or appreciate their desire for solitude. Veterans will often assert that their wartime experiences distinguish them from others who have not gone through the same events. The strain of remaining vigilant for warlike threats in crowded public settings may be overwhelming and preclude family outings to malls or sporting events. Even tolerating the noise and activity levels at smaller family functions may be too demanding for a veteran who is chronically hyperaroused. Veterans often attribute their need for social isolation to combat events involving the deaths of military buddies with whom they developed strong attachments. To avoid experiencing such profound grief again in the future, veterans often deliberately forego developing strong relationships with family and friends. Survivor guilt has been linked with more debilitating presentations, including suicidal behavior (e.g., Hyer, McCranie, Woods, & Boudewyns, 1990).

Veterans' homecoming experiences also affect how they perceive social interaction and their need for social connections, including that of the therapy relationship. Some were denounced by war protesters on their return from their tour of duty. Others returned from months of life-threatening experiences to find most associates did not even notice they had been away. Veterans of unpopular wars or forgotten "peace-keeping" missions often cite negative receptions or neglect on return to civilian life as a further reason for social isolation and rejection of help from others.

Although likely to report decreased anxiety and a greater sense of calm when alone, veterans will state that others in their social network (e.g., spouses, children, family members, friends) are concerned or angered by the veteran's reluctance to engage in any social events. Also, such isolation does not afford the veteran client the necessary opportunities to learn or practice adaptive coping strategies for handling social situations effectively.

Treatment involves directly addressing not only the events of combat but also the interpersonal contexts surrounding those events and the current desire for social isolation. Each of these elements and their interrelationships can be effectively integrated within an exposure-therapy model through the selection of cues on which the veteran is encouraged to attend. Addressing the traumas that may underlie the veteran's avoidance can increase social engagement in the long term.

As with any intervention that is anticipated to impact a social system, an important caveat to consider is whether the social isolation is having deleterious effects on the veteran client's social and occupational functioning. Some veterans will report that their social withdrawal does not adversely affect them or their significant others. Therapists should keep in mind the possibility that friends and partners may have been selected based on compatibility with this lifestyle. In other cases, the family system may have adjusted to the veteran's presentation adaptively and not see social withdrawal as a problem. Alternatively, it is possible the network's adaptation to the veteran is short-lived and only served to delay onset of more severe symptomatology. Continued assessment of social and occupational impairment is important to identify when and how outside support systems continue to function over the course of treatment.

It is also important to consider the degree of resilience in the veteran's overall support network (including quality of relationship with employers) before initiating exposure therapy. In the short term, exposure therapy can increase the patient's distress. This can augment difficulties in social functioning until sufficient progress is made in therapy to attain reduced stress levels. It is preferable if initiation of exposure therapy can be timed so as not to begin during other periods of life upheaval or increased role demands.

Comorbidity

Veteran clients often present with multiple medical and psychiatric complaints beyond those inherent in the PTSD diagnosis. Many veterans return from active duty with significant physical and physiological damage (e.g., missing limbs) and sensory deficits (e.g., hearing loss). Exposure to wartime chemical agents is recognized as contributing to the development of various delayed medical conditions, including cancers and diabetes. Numerous studies show that combat-related PTSD has highly comorbid prevalence rates with various Axis I and Axis II disorders, including mood and anxiety disorders, antisocial personality disorder, borderline personality disorder, and alcohol and drug abuse and dependence (see Friedman, Schnurr, & McDonagh-Coyle, 1994). Kramer, Booth, Han, and Williams (2003) recently showed that veterans who report both PTSD and depressive symptoms report significantly greater psychological distress and impairment.

It has been our experience that cases of "pure" PTSD among combat veterans tend to be the exception rather than the rule, particularly if there is a time lag of several years between trauma and treatment. Determinations as to whether comorbid conditions contraindicate use of exposure therapy should be made on a case-by-case basis. Ability to be mindful of trauma cues and of cognitive, emotional, and interoceptive reactions while recognizing the safety of the current clinical environment appears critical to the treatment's effectiveness. Veterans with dementia, delirium, intoxication or acute substance withdrawal, paranoid delusions, or frightening hallucinations would thus not be expected to benefit from exposure therapy, even when combat-related outbursts and anxiety attacks are a presenting complaint.

Clinical management of PTSD symptoms and concomitant psychiatric presentations can require intensive oversight of therapeutic progress, and often such work is more daunting than one practitioner is capable of managing effectively. A close-working interdisciplinary treatment team is often the ideal for managing the many facets of each patient's symptom presentation. Embedded within such a team approach, exposure therapy is often the nucleus of care. Psychosocial skills training often plays a crucial supporting role. In many cases, monitoring and management of medical conditions determine the pace at which cue exposure can safely proceed.

TREATMENT IMPLEMENTATION

Maximizing Rapport and Treatment Engagement

Exposure therapy requires that the veteran be exposed to fear-related stimuli and be aware of the trial events and sensations elicited by the exposure. As can be expected, exposure therapy often involves a strengthening of PTSD symptoms before symptom abatement can be achieved. To be successful, an active involvement by the veteran is important, and motivation for treatment is key for adherence to any protocol. A cooperative atmosphere between the therapist and the veteran is important, as behavior change is dependent on the veteran's willingness to meticulously recount the thoughts, emotions, and events surrounding the trauma.

For many veterans, social interactions require caution and a vigilant eye on how others perceive their military experiences. Veterans are often hesitant to discuss wartime events with civilians for several reasons. First, even veterans who have PTSD have likely been successful in suppressing portions of their wartime memories. They are understandably reluctant to intentionally recall the events owing to the arousal and negative emotions this elicits. Second, veterans often feel that civilians cannot fully understand wartime events, and veterans often perceive in others a lack of appropriate appreciation for veterans' efforts. Third, across U.S. history, civilian reactions to declarations of war have varied widely. At the extremes of the distribution, most World War II veterans report feeling supported in many ways by civilians on their return, whereas many Vietnam veterans report years of verbal abuse, physical altercations, lack of employment options despite demonstrable skills, peer and family rejection, and a general devaluing of their efforts.

It is no surprise that many veterans extend their discomfort with others into the therapy session. Generally, veterans are reticent to disclose all of their wartime traumas during an initial assessment. Ethnicity and gender of the therapist can augment this discomfort. Veterans may be hesitant to talk to therapists of similar nationalities as prior enemy combatants. If they perceive a female therapist as needing to be protected from horror, they may be similarly reluctant to discuss extremely graphic events or to disclose the veteran's own role in perpetrating sexual assaults or other atrocities.

An important quality when establishing rapport with a veteran client is the concept of validation. Validation is often defined as the acknowledgment and appreciation of another's experiences and of the emotional and psychological impact of these experiences on that individual. As mentioned earlier, veterans' experiences subsequent to war have impacted their ability to interact socially with others as much as their wartime experiences. Negative homecoming experiences can foster a general distrust of others, including authority figures, civilians, and mental health professionals, who themselves report no combat experiences. To allay some of these barriers, it is important for the therapist to communicate genuineness and empathy. Even if a therapist has not seen combat, statements that relate an appreciation of the intensity of wartime events can be helpful. Many veteran clients report an appreciation for civilian mental health professionals who demonstrate interest in combat strategies, equipment, and lingo, so long as such interest remains in service of the veteran's treatment rather than an excessive level that would brand the clinician as a "wanna-be."

Honest directness is particularly valued by most veterans. As with any client and any treatment modality, the therapist is ethically bound to clearly outline the foreseeable risks and benefits of exposure therapy before embarking on this course of care. Combat veterans have experience with hardship and difficult missions. Most appreciate knowing that the "officer" in charge of this "operation" has a clear plan, with contingency plans already in place to deal with potential problems. It is particularly important to clearly convey the likelihood of an initial symptom increase during exposure therapy and the associated risk of not following through with treatment past that point to attain subsequent symptom reductions. Rather than scaring potential clients away, such honesty tends to affirm to the veteran that the therapist indeed appreciates the painfulness of the memories the veteran is being asked to divulge.

The most persuasive factor in winning a veteran's initial trust, however, is often an unsolicited testimonial on behalf of the therapist or treatment program from another veteran. Clinicians who work with many individual veterans or with veterans in a group setting may thus have an advantage in this regard.

Over time, rapport can be expected to develop into significant trust and even attachment as the client sees that the therapist can tolerate the details of the trauma, does not push the veteran beyond his coping limits, and remains accepting and respectful even when atrocities or shameful choices are confessed. Throughout the treatment process, patience and ongoing assessment are necessary, as the veteran may reveal additional traumas long after the initial assessment, thus requiring revision of the extant fear hierarchy being used in the exposure sessions.

Group Versus Individual Format

One important consideration is whether the veteran would receive added benefit from a group therapy format beyond that offered by individual treatment. Given the degree of social isolation among combat veterans who have PTSD, group therapy presents both unique benefits and challenges. Group formats are quite common across Vet Centers and Veterans Affairs medical centers (Resick & Calhoun, 2001), and many are now built on a model of exposure-based trauma-processing (e.g., Foy, Ruzek, Glynn, Riney, & Gusman, 1997, 2002). Koss and Harvey (1991) described the advantages of group treatments for PTSD among rape survivors, and many of these points appear to generalize to the veteran population. First, clients experience some ease and a sense of validation when they realize they share common posttraumatic symptoms with other veterans. Second, a group format provides a safe forum wherein veterans can express emotions and ideas about the traumatic event around others who share similar experiences. Third, a group format may be the only actual or perceived source of social support the veteran may feel he or she has. Finally, groups can afford the veteran the opportunity to learn more adaptive coping strategies from peers. In sum, a group format exposes clients to an analogue of outside social interactions whilst affording them the opportunities to identify with other group members and seek support.

Caution is warranted, however, when suggesting group therapy to the veteran client. It is not uncommon for veteran clients, who tend to be quite socially withdrawn, to be nervous and shy away from interacting with other group members when they start attending group sessions. Some veterans may need individual sessions first to get over the hurdle of acute symptom increases, learn to tolerate the social stress of the group format, prepare to hear peers recount their trauma histories, and learn how to express empathy to fellow group members. The degree to which a client can cope with individual differences within the group should be assessed judiciously. Concomitant psychiatric and medical conditions, symptom severity, and differences in global functioning can hinder group dynamics. Further, the therapist must be sensitive to details of the veteran's experience, as it may affect group dynamics during trauma processing. For example, a veteran who held a lower rank at the time of the traumatic incident or at discharge may feel subordinate to other group members who held higher military rank. Behaviors that are adaptive while on active duty (e.g., suppressing challenges to team members' maladaptive cognitions) could prove therapeutically detrimental in the context of group therapy. Additional variables to take into account include the following: war era, geographic theatre within a war era (e.g., Iraq versus Afghanistan), front line versus combat support role, branch of the armed services (Navy, Air Force, etc.), full-time military versus Guard or Reserve personnel, role in the traumatic event (victim, participant, observer), gender, and ethnicity. It is easy for such factors to promote multiple alliances within a group format. It can be particularly difficult for an individual to feel a part of the group if that person happens to be the sole outlier on one of the preceding variables. Decisions about homogeneity or heterogeneity of group membership should be made with care.

Inpatient Versus Outpatient Treatment

Veterans often report trauma processing is a profound and draining experience. Many report difficulty returning home or to work after a therapy session without intense residual effects. Most report feeling exhausted or keyed up for about 1 day after a treatment session but are able to proceed with treatment on an outpatient basis. For others who report dissociative episodes or poor impulse control, however, emotional reactions to trauma-related cues can elicit unsafe behaviors along with increased arousal. Such behaviors can include violent outbursts, intense reexperiencing/reenacting of events (i.e., flashbacks) with violent outbursts, feelings of despair and worthlessness with suicidal intent, and reactivation of maladaptive avoidance behaviors (e.g., substance abuse). These reactions can clearly endanger the veteran and others. Inpatient or residential treatment provides an environment for patients with severe PTSD to undergo exposure therapy, as it places the veteran client in a safe and highly controlled environment wherein unsafe behaviors can be monitored and managed effectively, and more stable moods can be reestablished.

Residential treatment can also be the treatment of choice for veterans whose chronic PTSD is not necessarily more severe or dangerous but who experience other barriers that hinder outpatient treatment progress. Residential programs typically include a variety of treatment modalities designed to attenuate arousal patterns and redirect veterans' efforts toward effectively and adaptively adjusting to civilian life. Before a veteran commits to an extended stay in a residential program that includes a major exposure therapy component, however, it may be advisable for the veteran to complete at least a few exposure sessions on an outpatient basis. Unless travel barriers or predicted risks in an individual case preclude such outpatient care, this sequencing allows a more gradual introduction to exposure therapy and helps the veteran make a truly informed decision before opting for the intensity that daily exposure therapy on an inpatient or residential basis may entail.

Clinicians should also be aware that veterans who have been rated as having a disability that is service-connected are often eligible for increased disability payments during months when they are hospitalized for treatment of that particular disability. Clinicians and veterans are advised to consult with the local VA Veterans Benefits Administration office for more specific details before program admission. Because the monthly payment differential can be quite significant (e.g., an increase by more than $2000 per month for a veteran who carries a 0–10% disability rating), the choice of inpatient versus outpatient care can have significant financial ramifications for the patient.

Addressing Guilt and Anger

Presentation of situational cues of what transpired during a trauma and how the client reacted at the time is conducted with combat veterans in much the same way as with any other client being treated for PTSD. Themes of guilt and anger, however, are common accompaniments of combat-related trauma and may take characteristic forms not always seen in response to other types of trauma. Such emotions are often attributed to the role the veteran was engaged in at the time of the traumatic events. Clinicians who have worked with civilian PTSD may be most accustomed to treating clients whose role in the trauma was that of victim. Many veterans' traumas fall into the victim category (e.g., suffering a direct attack by enemy combatants; victim of a "friendly fire" incident in which they were mistakenly fired on by allies or other Americans). Clinicians are often initially surprised, however, by the number of combat PTSD cases in which the veteran was in the role of trauma-initiator or indirect participant-observer. These include not only instances of inadvertently causing harm via a misjudgment or directly assaulting enemy combatants but also a wide range of other morally complex situations. A majority of treatment-seeking veterans in our clinic, for example, now struggle with their own action/complicity in the murder of a leader whose orders consistently placed troops at unnecessary risk or with their own commission of atrocities or failure to prevent commission of atrocities they witnessed.

Feelings of guilt or anger related to combat trauma can influence the effectiveness of exposure therapy by activating cognitive biases that suggest treatment progress is not or should not be possible. This is particularly seen in cases where veterans conceptualize their subsequent suffering as just punishment. For example, veterans who initiated an attack may report feelings of guilt about moving on with their lives with the knowledge that they killed or maimed other individuals, and they may therefore believe they do not deserve to put this event behind them. Veterans whose reported trauma suggests an indirect participant-observer role may focus on cues associated with their perceived inactivity at the time of the trauma (e.g., witnessing a fellow soldier impulsively commit suicide before the client could intervene). Those who committed acts that could be classified as war crimes may have difficulty emotionally reconnecting with the level of terror or vengeance experienced during the heat of combat that prompted them to act in a way that is now very discordant with their ideal self-image as a civilian. Clinicians should not underestimate the number of veterans who believe that symptom alleviation would represent a forgetting of deceased comrades or an endorsement of past actions they now deeply regret. Therapists can challenge such maladaptive cognitions and help the client fill in gaps in their retrospective conceptualization that rebuilds the context for actions taken at the time of the trauma. In a group format, such challenges are even more effective if put forth by peers rather than the therapist. Therapists can specifically invite peer feedback of this nature during group sessions.

Incorporation of Current Events

Inherent in the diagnosis of PTSD is the tendency to avoid trauma cues. Current governmental policies, politics, and national or world events are issues veterans very commonly raise during treatment. Sometimes these topics appear purely tangential distractions from trauma processing; however, there are frequently components of the topic that reflect core themes of the veteran's own trauma and that can be effectively used to more fully explore his/her own experiences. For example, a veteran may report elevated anxiety and panic after watching news of a terrorist incident involving American troops in another part of the world and may refer to elements of that event while processing his/her own experiences. Sometimes the commonalities between events are important, as when a veteran is able to identify with the troops shown on the news. Seeing others in similar situations can help normalize the veteran's own reactions and can make the client's own recall of aspects of his/her trauma more vivid. For example, seeing current events unfold in a contemporary news video clip may help the veteran accept how quickly decisions had to be made during combat and how little opportunity there was for careful deliberation. In other cases, it may be contrasts rather than commonalities that are important. A Vietnam veteran who was spat on and called "baby-killer" when he returned to the United States may ambivalently hope that current troops will receive a warmer welcome yet also be jealous or resentful when seeing new returnees receive more positive public attention. The therapist can easily incorporate discussion and imagery related to such ambivalence when addressing how the veteran's own combat experiences impacted self-concept. If media coverage of current war news is integrated into exposure therapy in this manner, it can actually provide opportunities for self-directed exposure to personally relevant war cues between therapy sessions. The appropriateness of such assignments would depend on the veteran's level of distress and mastery of anxiety-management techniques (diaphragmatic breathing exercises, progressive muscle relaxation, challenges to cognitive distortions, and availability of strong social support systems).

Acute Concomitant Psychiatric Episodes

It is not uncommon for brief elevations in symptom severity to occur during the early stages of treatment and to last more than one session after treatment onset (Lyons & Keane, 1989). Veterans may experience more frequent nightmares, trauma-related memories, visceral reactions to trauma cues, and increased desire to avoid trauma cues. This is largely because the veteran is being asked to fully and directly confront these images and cognitions for possibly the first time since active duty. Generally, these symptom elevations will produce notable, but transient, distress. During the informed consent process, the client should already have been prepared for such a symptom increase. Exposure therapy can usually continue with careful pacing of cue exposure and with support and encouragement being provided by the therapist.

Acute onset of secondary conditions (e.g., major depressive episodes, substance use relapse), however, may require the interruption of ongoing exposure trials, as the veteran may not be able to fully participate. Further, concomitant psychiatric conditions can introduce potentially life-threatening symptoms (e.g., strong suicidal and/or violent intent) that demand the therapist's attention. Decisions whether to postpone or abort exposure therapy, introduce additional cognitive-behavioral treatments to address the episodic condition, or merely monitor the episodes depend on the idiosyncratic nature of such presentation across clients. Continuous monitoring of emotions that typically rise and fall throughout treatment (e.g., overall anxiety, depressive or irritable moods, changes in appetite and/or sleep patterns, social withdrawal) may increase the likelihood of catching the onset of acute psychiatric episodes, thus allowing the therapist to tailor treatment to address clinically relevant changes in symptom presentation. In doing so, it is important to also consider the possibility that such symptom reports may be a learned evasion of trauma cue exposure and to address this with the client if such avoidance is suspected.

Managing Threat of Treatment Dropout

As with other anxiety disorders, it is not uncommon for patients to reappear and report reexperiencing symptoms after a premature dropout from earlier treatment. Although the literature reports no difference in dropout rates between exposure therapy and other treatments for PTSD (e.g., stress inoculation therapy, cognitive therapy; e.g., Hembree, Foa, Dorfan, Street, Kowalski, & Tu, 2003), premature dropout can hinder the veteran client's overall success in overcoming his or her PTSD symptoms. Dropout, although always the client's prerogative, prevents the veteran client from learning to tolerate anxiety and introduces yet another event in which he or she fails to learn or test more adaptive coping strategies (e.g., relaxation techniques).

If patients opt to withdraw prematurely from treatment, it is important to assess their reasons for leaving to the extent they wish to share their motives. Based on their responses, alternative treatment options can be considered, the clients can be invited to resume the therapy at some future point or can be provided with referral information to other mental health resources. Should their reasons involve a reported inability to directly confront their war memories, it is important to genuinely validate their concerns. Often, a frank review of the pros and cons of various treatment modalities and the veteran's concerns about the current treatment can reveal ways to shore up treatment readiness. For example, therapist and client might decide to revise the treatment plan to emphasize anxiety management skills training or other non-trauma–focused treatments while monitoring symptoms and social and occupational impairment. Some patients may choose not to resume exposure therapy, but many will soon recognize that they are not making the progress they desired and will be more resolute in approaching a second round of exposure therapy sessions.

CONCLUSION

Each war era brings with it unique nuances and social contexts that shape traumatic events, the way individuals perceive those events, and the availability of supportive social networks after such events. Individual dispositional factors add further variability. Most of the points stated throughout this text are based on clinical observations with veterans in the United States. It is reasonable to expect that the aforementioned factors may not influence PTSD symptom presentations similarly across different cultural and demographic groups. Further, as combat technologies continue to develop and new war theaters continue to emerge, it is expected that there will be new discoveries about the development, maintenance, and treatment of combat-related PTSD. In all, research into the etiology and treatment of PTSD represents a body of knowledge that can reasonably be expected to evolve as the role and structure of the military continues to be redefined.

REFERENCES

American Psychiatric Association. (2000). *Diagnostic and statistical manual of mental disorders* (4th ed., rev. text). Washington, D.C.: American Psychiatric Association.

Bradley, R., Greene, J., Russ, E., Dutra, L., & Westen, D. (2005). A multidimensional meta-analysis of psychotherapy for PTSD. *American Journal of Psychiatry, 162,* 214–227.

Breslau, N., & Kessler, R.C. (2001). The stressor criterion in DSM-IV posttraumatic stress disorder: An empirical investigation. *Biological Psychiatry, 50,* 699–704.

Cassiday, K.L., & Lyons, J.A. (1992). Recall of traumatic memories following cerebral vascular accident. *Journal of Traumatic Stress, 5,* 627–631.

Foy, D.W., Ruzek, J.I., Glynn, S.M., Riney, S.J., & Gusman, F.D. (1997). Trauma focus group therapy for combat-related PTSD. *Psychotherapy in Practice, 3,* 59–73.

Foy, D.W., Ruzek, J.I., Glynn, S.M., Riney, S.J., & Gusman, F.D. (2002). Trauma focus group therapy for combat-related PTSD: An update. *Psychotherapy in Practice, 58,* 907–918.

Friedman, M.J., Schnurr, P.P., & McDonagh-Coyle, A. (1994). Post-traumatic stress disorder in the military veteran. *Psychiatric Clinics of North America, 17,* 265–277.

Freuh, B.C., Turner, S.M., & Beidel, D.C. (1995). Exposure therapy for combat-related PTSD: A critical review. *Clinical Psychology Review, 15,* 799–817.

Helzer, J.E., Robins, L.N., & McEvoy, L. (1987). Post-traumatic stress disorder in the general population: Findings of the Epidemiological Catchment Area Survey. *New England Journal of Medicine, 317,* 1630–1634.

Hembree, E.A., Foa, E.B., Dorfan, N.M., Street, G.P., Kowalski, J., & Tu, X. (2003). Do patients drop out prematurely from exposure therapy for PTSD? *Journal of Traumatic Stress, 16,* 555–562.

Hofmann, S.G., Litz, B.T., & Weathers, F.W. (2003). Social anxiety, depression, and PTSD in Vietnam veterans. *Journal of Anxiety Disorders, 17,* 573–582.

Hyer, L., McCranie, E.W., Woods, M.G., & Boudewyns, P.A. (1990). Suicidal behavior among chronic Vietnam theatre veterans with PTSD. *Journal of Clinical Psychology, 46,* 713–721.

Koss, M.P., & Harvey, M. (1991). *The rape victim: Clinical and community approaches to treatment.* Lexington, MA: Stephen Green Press.

Kramer, T.L., Booth, B.M. Han, X., & Williams, D.K. (2003). Service utilization and outcomes in medically ill veterans with posttraumatic stress and depressive disorders. *Journal of Traumatic Stress, 16,* 211–219.

Kulka, R.A., Schlenger, W.E., Fairbank, J.A., Hough, R.L., Jordan, B.K., Marmar, C.R., & Weiss DS. (1990). *Trauma and the Vietnam War generation.* New York: Brunner/Mazel.

Levis, D.J., & Hare, N. (1977). A review of the theoretical rationale and empirical support for the extinction approach of implosive (flooding) therapy. In M. Hersen, A.M. Eisler, & P.M. Miller (Eds.), *Progress in behavior modification,* Vol. 2. New York: Academic Press.

Lyons, J.A., & Keane, T.M. (1989). Implosive therapy for the treatment of combat-related PTSD. *Journal of Traumatic Stress, 2,* 137–152.

Macleod, A.D. (1994). The reactivation of post-traumatic stress disorder in later life. *Australian and New Zealand Journal of Psychiatry, 28,* 625–634.

Norris, F.H. (1992). Epidemiology of trauma: Frequency and impact of different potentially traumatic events on different demographic groups. *Journal of Consulting and Clinical Psychology, 60,* 409–418.

Prigerson, H.G., Maciejewski, P.K., & Rosenheck, R.A. (2001). Combat trauma: Trauma with highest risk of delayed onset and unresolved posttraumatic stress disorder symptoms, unemployment, and abuse among men. *Journal of Nervous and Mental Disease, 189,* 99–108.

Resick, P.A., & Calhoun, K.S. (2001). Posttraumatic stress disorder. In D.H. Barlow (Ed.), *D.H. Barlow's clinical handbook of psychological disorders* (3rd ed.). New York: Guilford.

Rothbaum, B.O., Hodges, L., Alarcon, R., Ready, D., Shahar, F., Graap, K., et al. (1999). Virtual reality exposure therapy for PTSD Vietnam veterans: A case study. *Journal of Traumatic Stress, 12,* 263–271.

Rothbaum, B.O., Hodges, L.F., Ready, D., Graap, K., & Alarcon, R.D. (2001). Virtual reality exposure therapy for Vietnam veterans with posttraumatic stress disorder. *Journal of Clinical Psychiatry, 62,* 617–622.

Scaturo, D.J., & Hayman, P.M. (1992). The impact of combat trauma across the family cycle: Clinical considerations. *Journal of Traumatic Stress, 5,* 273–288.

Schnurr, P.P., Friedeman, M.J., Foy, D.W., Shea, M.T., Hsieh, F.Y., Lavori, P.W., Glynn S.M., Wattenberg, M., & Bernardy, N.C. (2003). Randomized trial of trauma-focused group therapy for posttraumatic stress disorder. *Archives of General Psychiatry, 60,* 481–489.

Southwick, S.M., Morgan, A., Nagy, L.M., Bremner, D., Nicolaou, A.L., Johnson, D.R., Rosenheck, R., & Chaney, D.S. (1993). Trauma-related symptoms in veterans of Operation Desert Storm: A preliminary report. *American Journal of Psychiatry, 150,* 1524–1528.

CHAPTER 8

Exposure Therapy for Obsessive-Compulsive Disorder

Jonathan S. Abramowitz and
Karin E. Larsen

Mayo Clinic

Exposure-based therapy is the most effective psychological treatment for obsessive-compulsive disorder (OCD). In this chapter, we review the theoretical basis for the use of exposure treatments for OCD, as well as the current parameters for delivering this therapy. We also review the outcome research establishing the efficacy of exposure and response prevention for OCD and the factors known to influence treatment response. The second half of this chapter presents an in-depth case history illustrating the use of exposure-based therapy for treating OCD.

Obsessive-compulsive disorder (OCD) is characterized by (1) recurrent, intrusive, and senseless thoughts, impulses, or doubts that evoke anxiety (obsessions) and (2) deliberate behavioral rituals or mental acts performed to neutralize obsessional anxiety (compulsions). The obsessional thoughts are often, but not always, evoked by environmental stimuli. For example, touching a doorknob might lead to anxiety-evoking thoughts of germs and illness, which in turn might lead to ritualistic hand washing to prevent or remove contamination. Common obsessions and compulsions include fears of contamination and washing rituals, fears of harming others and checking rituals, fears of discarding important information and saving rituals (hoarding), and blasphemous thoughts (fears of sinning) with praying rituals (e.g., McKay, Abramowitz, Calamari, Kyrios, Radomsky, Sookman, et al., 2004). Some patients also have excessive concerns about lucky/unlucky numbers or worries about orderliness and symmetry. In many instances, obsessional fear and ritualistic behavior produce significant distress and interfere with daily functioning in a variety of domains. In this chapter, we discuss the derivation of exposure-based treatment for OCD and the implementation of these treatment procedures and mechanisms proposed to account for their effectiveness, and we review the evidence for the effectiveness of this treatment approach. To illustrate these conceptual and practical points, we present a case history of a patient treated in our outpatient clinic.

The authors wish to thank Krista Aarnio for her assistance with preparing this chapter.

FROM THEORY TO THERAPY

Behavioral and cognitive-behavioral approaches to psychological treatment involve therapeutic procedures that have been derived from empirically based conceptualizations of the target problems. The case of exposure therapy for OCD is an excellent example. Mowrer's (1960) two-stage theory of the acquisition and maintenance of fear and avoidance behavior is often used to explain OCD from a learning perspective. The first stage of this process (acquisition) involves classical conditioning: a neutral stimulus or event (e.g., leaving the house) comes to evoke obsessional fear by being paired with another stimulus that, by its nature, provokes discomfort or anxiety (e.g., the idea that a house fire could occur while no one is home). In the second stage (maintenance), avoidance (e.g., unplugging the appliances) is used to reduce the anxiety or discomfort associated with the conditioned stimulus, in this case, leaving the house. The avoidance behavior is negatively reinforced because it provides an immediate reduction in anxiety (operant conditioning). Thus, the avoidance becomes habitual. Dollard and Miller (1950) adapted the two-stage theory to explain the development of compulsive rituals: Because of their ubiquitous nature, many obsessional stimuli cannot easily be avoided (e.g., leaving the house, thoughts about fires). Thus, compulsive rituals (e.g., returning home to check that the appliances are off) are developed as active avoidance strategies and subsequently maintained (negatively reinforced) by their success in reducing obsessional fear. Although rituals provide a temporary respite from obsessional fear, they prevent the natural extinction of obsessional anxiety, thereby perpetuating the fear.

Results of research conducted on the two-stage account of OCD have largely been mixed (for a review see Clark, 2004). There appears to be little empirical evidence that obsessive fear is acquired through classical conditioning. There is strong evidence, however, that compulsive rituals maintain obsessive fear via operant conditioning (negative reinforcement), and this leads nicely to the use of exposure therapy for weakening these maintenance processes. Meyer (1966) was the first to apply this approach in the treatment of OCD and eloquently articulated the rationale from a cognitive-behavioral perspective.

> Learning theories take into account the mediation of responses by goal expectancies, developed from previously reinforcing situations. When these expectations are not fulfilled, new expectancies may evolve, which, in turn, may mediate new behavior. Thus, if the obsessional is persuaded or forced to remain in feared situations and prevented from carrying out the rituals, he may discover that the feared consequences no longer take place. Such modification of expectations should result in the cessation of ritualistic behaviour (Meyer, 1966, p. 275).

Essentially, Meyer argued that when a patient with OCD confronts his or her obsessional fear without performing rituals, estimates of the probability and costs of feared outcomes are able to be corrected, leading to the reduction of obsessive fear and ritualistic behavior. These procedures, now commonly known as *exposure and response prevention* (ERP), form the backbone of effective psychological treatment of OCD.

In Meyer's (1966) initial report using ERP, his patients deliberately confronted for 2 hours each day obsessional situations and stimuli they usually avoided (e.g., floors, bathrooms), while also refraining from compulsive rituals (e.g., no washing or checking). Most of these individuals demonstrated at least partial improvement at post-treatment, and very few relapsed at follow-up evaluation (Meyer, Levy, & Schnurer, 1974). The interest generated by these initial findings led to additional studies in centers around the world using more advanced methodology in both inpatient and outpatient settings. Research conducted in the United Kingdom (Hodgson, Rachman, & Marks, 1972), Holland (Emmelkamp & Kraanen, 1977), Greece (Rabavilas, Boulougouris, & Stefanis, 1976), and the United States (Foa & Goldstein, 1978) with more than 300 patients and many therapists affirmed the beneficial effects and generalizability of exposure-based treatment for OCD. By the end of the 1980s, this form of therapy was widely considered the psychosocial treatment of choice for obsessions and compulsions.

A more contemporary advancement has been the proposal of cognitive theories to account for the development and maintenance of OCD presentations involving obsessions in the absence of overt compulsive rituals (e.g., Rachman, 1997, 1998). These theories are well supported by empirical evidence that intrusive thoughts (i.e., unwelcome ideas, images, and impulses that encroach into consciousness) are (1) normal and universal experiences and (2) indistinguishable (in terms of content) from clinical obsessions (Rachman & de Silva, 1978). Whereas most people correctly regard their unwanted thoughts as insignificant, those who misinterpret their unwanted intrusions as indicating a threat to themselves or others are at risk for developing obsessional problems. Catastrophic beliefs about normal intrusive thoughts lead to anxiety and the urge to control the thoughts to reduce anxiety (e.g., via compulsive rituals, avoidance, and other neutralizing strategies). Paradoxically, these "solutions" maintain obsessional fear by increasing preoccupation with the obsession and by blocking the acquisition of disconfirmatory evidence that would correct the dysfunctional beliefs.

To illustrate, consider a religious man who, while using the bathroom, experiences normal, yet unwelcome thoughts about God. Whereas most people might disregard such thoughts as nonsensical, the man described here believes that "having thoughts about God while in the bathroom is immoral and will lead to punishment." Thus, he becomes extremely fearful when such thoughts come to mind. To remove the anxiety-evoking thought, he takes precautions, such as compulsively repeating prayers, confessing, seeking reassurance, and thinking positive thoughts instead. Paradoxically, these responses become reminders of the unwanted thoughts and increase their frequency and intensity. Moreover, when this man fails to encounter "punishment," this avoidance of punishment is attributed to the precautionary responses. Thus, the man does not have the opportunity to learn that the intrusive thoughts are not dangerous. Therefore, the dysfunctional beliefs about the thought's importance are maintained.

IMPLEMENTATION OF EXPOSURE-BASED THERAPY FOR OCD

The specific procedures used in ERP have undergone modifications since Meyer's initial studies. In our clinic, we use cognitive-behavioral treatment procedures derived from learning and cognitive models of OCD. Specifically, our treatment involves methods to help the patient (1) gradually confront stimuli that evoke obsessive fear, (2) refrain from compulsive rituals that would terminate therapeutic exposure, and (3) correct dysfunctional beliefs that underlie obsessional thinking. Because pathological fear in OCD is evoked by both environmental stimuli and intrusive obsessional thoughts, the central elements of treatment include *situational* (in vivo) exposure to environmental cues and *imaginal* exposure to fear-evoking mental stimuli (e.g., intrusive thoughts). For example, an individual with the recurring obsession that she has hit a pedestrian while driving in a crowded parking lot would be instructed to practice driving through such parking lots for situational exposure. She would also practice imaginal exposure to thoughts and images of having hit someone. A patient with fears of becoming contaminated might be asked to touch objects of increasing "dirtiness"—a doorknob, the floor, a garbage can, a dumpster—for situational exposure. She would then confront images of germs and illnesses for imaginal exposure.

To illustrate further, consider the case of Mary, a young mother who was plagued with the unwanted idea that she could poison her baby by mistakenly putting lye-based household cleaning agents in his food. To ensure against any harm, Mary kept all poisonous substances locked in a basement closet. Although she frequently checked that the closet remained locked, Mary continued to have upsetting thoughts and doubts about whether her baby boy was truly safe from what she believed were her "mistake-prone ways." To reduce her fears, Mary ritualistically asked her husband, a doctor, to examine their child for intoxication. Mary's treatment included situational exposures in which she prepared food for her baby in the presence of open bottles of poisonous cleaning solution and while distracting herself (e.g., by listening to loud music or talking on the phone). For imaginal exposure, she purposely visualized a scene in which she had mistakenly poisoned the baby because she was not careful enough about toxic materials. Repetition of the scene continued, and Mary refrained from checking her son's health, or asking her husband to check her son's health until her anxiety habituated.

In contrast to situational fear cues, which are often concrete, obsessional thoughts, ideas, and images are intangible, and therefore, can be elusive targets when designing exposure. Although in vivo exposure often evokes obsessional thoughts, imaginal exposure provides a more systematic way of exposing the patient to the key fear-evoking elements of their obsessions. The recommended methods for conducting imaginal exposure include (1) using audiocassette tapes (continuous loop tapes work especially well) or (2) written scripts containing the anxiety-evoking material (Freeston & Ladouceur, 1999). Both media allow the therapist to prolong the patient's confrontation with an otherwise covert event and if necessary, manipulate the content of the stimulus. The use of an audiotape further ensures that unsupervised (homework) exposure will include confrontation with the correct stimuli.

TYPES OF IMAGINAL EXPOSURE

We have identified three kinds of imaginal exposure that can be used based on the specifics of the patient's symptoms. *Primary imaginal exposure* is essentially situational exposure to unwanted thoughts. It involves directly confronting spontaneously occurring repugnant thoughts, images, and urges (i.e., violent, sexual, or blasphemous obsessions) via methods such as loop tapes. *Secondary imaginal exposure* is used when situational exposure evokes fears of disastrous consequences (such as in Mary's case described previously). In such instances, imaginal exposure is begun during or after situational exposure and should involve visualizing the feared outcomes or focusing on uncertainty associated with the risk of feared outcomes. Finally, *preliminary imaginal exposure* entails imagining confronting a feared stimulus as a preliminary step in preparing for situational exposures. For example, a patient might vividly *imagine* touching the bathroom floor before actually engaging in situational exposure to the bathroom floor. This type of exposure might be used as an intermediate step in preparing the patient to confront a situation of which s/he is extremely fearful.

HABITUATION OF ANXIETY DURING EXPOSURE

At the start of exposure tasks (situational and imaginal), the patient typically experiences a rapid elevation in subjective anxiety and physiological arousal. In fact, patients are told that they must engage in the exposure task fully until such experiences are evoked. Over time, however, the subjective distress (and associated physiological responding) subsides, even if the individual remains exposed to the feared stimulus, a process known as *habituation*. Furthermore, habituation occurs more rapidly with repeated exposure to the same stimulus over time. Response prevention, which is a necessary accessory to exposure in the treatment of OCD, entails refraining from compulsive rituals and other safety-seeking or neutralizing behaviors that serve as an escape from obsessive fear (e.g., no hand washing after exposure to touching the floor). This allows for prolonged exposure and facilitates the extinction of obsessional anxiety. If the patient engages in compulsive rituals in an effort to reduce anxiety during exposure, habituation cannot occur, and the patient cannot learn that his or her anxiety would have eventually diminished without the ritual.

PROCEDURAL VARIATIONS

The delivery of ERP can vary along a number of parameters, including the frequency of treatment sessions and whether exposure is conducted in the session (i.e., supervised by the therapist) or for homework (self-controlled). Meta-analytic studies suggest that the greatest effectiveness is achieved when therapist-guided exposure sessions are held multiple times per week, as opposed to once a week (Abramowitz, 1996, 1997). This is probably because shorter intersession intervals prevent the return to maladaptive behaviors such as avoidance and rituals that maintain obsessional fear (the therapist is able to provide corrective feedback within a few days). Although therapist-directed exposure is important, treatment must also include homework exposure practice (Emmelkamp & Kraanen, 1977). Research also indicates that a limited number of sessions may be needed to produce substantial and durable symptom reduction. It is therefore recommended that an initial course of therapy be limited to about 15 to 20 sessions. One format that has been found to produce particularly potent effects includes a few hours of assessment and treatment planning followed by 15 daily treatment sessions, lasting about 90 minutes each, spaced over about 3 weeks (e.g., Franklin, Abramowitz, Kozak, Levitt, & Foa, 2000). When pragmatic concerns render this intensive regimen impractical, a schedule of twice-weekly sessions over 8 weeks affords greater flexibility without compromising clinical effectiveness (Abramowitz, Foa, & Franklin, 2003).

DELIVERING ERP

A course of ERP in our OCD treatment program begins with a functional assessment of obsessional stimuli (intrusive thoughts and environmental triggers), feared consequences of exposure to these stimuli, avoidance and rituals, or other strategies used to neutralize obsessive fear. This process might take from one to three treatment sessions. Before any exposure takes place, the therapist presents a conceptual model of OCD symptoms and how ERP weakens these symptoms. The patient is informed that exposure will evoke temporary distress that subsides over time if exposure is continued (habituation). We consider this treatment rationale a critical step in therapy because it helps motivate the patient to endure the distress that exposure evokes. Next, information gathered during the assessment process is used to plan the specific exposure exercises that will occur. Of importance, the term *response prevention* does not imply that the therapist forcefully prevents the patient from performing rituals. Instead, the therapist's conceptual model and explanation of ERP (i.e., the treatment rationale) serves to convince the patient to resist his or her own urges to carry out these behaviors. Self-monitoring—keeping a record of any response prevention violations—is used to identify stimuli that evoke ritualistic urges that could not be resisted.

The initial exposure exercises should involve confrontation with only moderately distressing situations, stimuli, and images. At each session, there is progression up a hierarchy of stimuli until the most distressing situations and obsessional thoughts, which *must* be confronted during treatment, are addressed. This hierarchical approach helps the patient learn to manage his or her distress and successfully complete early exposure tasks. It also increases confidence in the treatment and encourages the patient to persevere during later, more difficult, exposures. At the end of each treatment session, the therapist instructs the patient to continue with self-directed exposure to the same stimuli in different contexts. For example, after practicing exposure to contaminated clothes in the therapist's office, the patient would be instructed to touch these clothes to various objects in her house. Confrontation with the most anxiety-evoking situations is completed during the middle third of the treatment program. This allows the patient ample opportunity to repeat exposure to the most difficult situations in different contexts to allow generalization of treatment effects. The later treatment sessions involve exposure practice in varied contexts with the aim of generalizing the effects of treatment.

USING COGNITIVE TECHNIQUES DURING EXPOSURE THERAPY

One of the less well-described components of exposure therapy is the use of more or less informal cognitive therapy techniques during the exposure sessions. The therapist should take an active role in facilitating cognitive change during exposure by helping the patient challenge dysfunctional beliefs about feared stimuli and feared consequences relevant to the exposure exercise. Such discussions commonly turn to risk-taking. Rather than argue with patients about the exact probabilities of their most feared consequences, it is useful to emphasize the practicalities of taking low-level risks presented during exposure. That is, learning to take such risks is preferable to the consequences of trying to eliminate all risk (i.e., avoidance) or performing compulsive rituals to secure an absolute guarantee of safety, which is not feasible. It is counterproductive to try to convince the patient that exposure situations are "not dangerous." This is for the patient to discover for himself/herself through experience. Risk levels are best described as "acceptably low" rather than "zero."

MECHANISMS OF ACTION

How does exposure therapy reduce the symptoms of OCD? Foa and Kozak (1986) proposed that exposure helps patients correct their overestimates of the likelihood and severity of negative outcomes that underlie obsessional fear. For example, a patient who believes strongly that her unwanted violent thoughts will lead her to stab her infant would learn through exposure exercises that she is unlikely to perform this action. For such cognitive changes to occur, three criteria are necessary. First, the situations and stimuli chosen for exposure must match closely with the patient's obsessional fear to evoke subjective distress and physiological arousal. Second, exposure must be *prolonged* (perhaps 60 to 90 minutes) so that the patient experiences the habituation of fear while still exposed to the feared stimulus (within-session habituation). Third, exposure tasks must be repeated so that the intensity and duration of the initial fear response at the beginning of each exposure session declines with each successive session (between-sessions habituation). Figure 8.1 displays a plot of subjective anxiety across time during four daily sessions of exposure therapy for a patient with fears of knives and other sharp objects.

THE EFFICACY OF ERP

How effective is ERP in reducing OCD symptoms? A comprehensive meta-analysis of the ERP literature that included more than 800 patients in 24 studies conducted between 1975 and 1995 revealed large post-treatment effect sizes (1.16 for self-report measures, 1.41 on interview measures) (Abramowitz, 1996). Follow-up effect sizes were similarly large: 1.10 and 1.57 for self-report and interview scales, respectively. Using a different meta-analytic approach, Foa and Kozak (1996) found

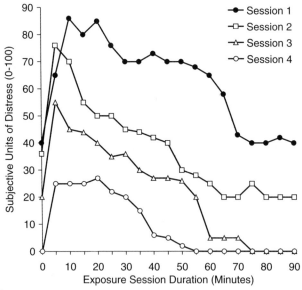

FIGURE 8.1   Graph depicting an OCD patient's subjective anxiety across four exposure sessions. In each session, this patient practiced holding knives, scissors, and other sharp objects while her infant was nearby. Note the reduction of anxiety within and between each trial of exposure.

that across 13 ERP studies, 83% of patients were responders (typically defined as achieving a pretreatment to post-treatment symptom improvement of at least 30%) at post-treatment, and across 16 studies, 76% were responders at follow-up evaluation (mean follow-up period was 29 months). These findings suggest that the majority of OCD patients who undergo treatment with ERP evidence substantial short- and long-term benefit.

Because meta-analysis combines controlled and uncontrolled studies, the effect sizes can be influenced by both specific factors (i.e., the ERP procedures themselves) and nonspecific features of therapy (e.g., time, expectancy) and therefore may be overstated. Thus, we review several randomized controlled trials (RCTs) that are designed to assess the specific efficacy of ERP procedures over and above nonspecific effects.

Most studies have used the 10-item Yale-Brown Obsessive Compulsive Scale (Y-BOCS; Goodman, Price, Rasmussen, Mazure, Fleischmann, Hill, et al., 1989a, 1989b) as the primary outcome measure; thus, comparing study results is relatively easy. Similarly, this allows for easy conversion of research findings into clinically meaningful information. The Y-BOCS yields a total score ranging from 0 (no symptoms) to 40 (extremely severe). Scores of 0 to 7 indicate subclinical symptoms, 8 to 15 indicate mild OCD, 16 to 25 represent moderate symptomatology, 26 to 30 represent severe symptoms, and 31 to 40 indicate profound or extreme symptoms. Because the Y-BOCS is so widely used and possesses adequate psychometric properties, we focus primarily on this measure in the following literature review.

Table 8.1 summarizes the results of four RCTs that have evaluated the efficacy of ERP. In the first such study, Fals-Stewart, Marks, and Schafer (1993) randomly

TABLE 8.1   Effects of Exposure and Response Prevention (ERP) in Randomized Controlled Trials

		Mean (SD) Y-BOCS total score					
		ERP group			Control group		
Study	Control condition	*n*	Pre	Post	*n*	Pre	Post
Fals-Stewart et al. (1993)*	Relaxation	31	20.2	12.1	32	19.9	18.1
Lindsay et al. (1997)	Anxiety management	9	28.7 (4.6)	11.0 (3.8)	9	24.4 (7.0)	25.9 (5.8)
Freeston et al. (1997)	Waiting list	15	25.1 (5.0)	12.2 (9.6)	14	21.2 (6.0)	22.0 (6.0)
Van Balkom et al. (1998)	Waiting list	19	25.0 (7.9)	17.1 (8.4)	18	26.8 (6.4)	26.4 (6.8)
Foa et al. (2005)	Pill placebo	29	24.6 (4.8)	11.0 (7.9)	26	25.0 (4.0)	22.2 (6.4)

Y-BOCS, Yale-Brown Obsessive Compulsive Scale.
*Standard deviation not reported in the study.

assigned patients to individual ERP, group ERP, or a progressive relaxation control treatment. All treatments included 24 sessions delivered on a twice-weekly basis over 12 weeks. Although both ERP regimens were superior to relaxation, there were no differences between group and individual ERP. Average improvement in the ERP groups was 41% on the Y-BOCS, and post-treatment scores fell within the mild range of severity. In the second study, Lindsay, Crino, and Andrews (1997) compared ERP to anxiety management training (AMT), a credible placebo treatment consisting of breathing retraining, relaxation, and problem-solving therapy. Both treatments were intensive: 15 daily sessions conducted over 3 weeks. On average, patients receiving ERP improved almost 62% from pretreatment to post-treatment on the Y-BOCS, with endpoint scores again in the mild range. In contrast, the AMT group showed no change in symptoms after treatment. The clear superiority of ERP over credible placebo therapies such as relaxation and AMT indicates that improvement in OCD symptoms can be attributed to the ERP procedures themselves, over and above any nonspecific factors such as time, attention, or expectancy of positive outcome.

Freeston, Ladouceur, Gagnon, Thibodeau, Rheaume, Letarte, et al. (1997) examined the efficacy of ERP with the addition of cognitive restructuring for OCD patients with severe obsessional thoughts without overt compulsive rituals. The treatment program was derived from cognitive models of obsessions and involved the use of primary imaginal exposure to intrusive anxiety-evoking thoughts and images. Situational exposure (e.g., holding a knife) was used when environmental stimuli (e.g., knives) evoked obsessive thoughts (e.g., images of stabbing one's child). Response prevention was also used. On average, patients attended between 25 and 30 twice-weekly and weekly treatment sessions. Compared to the wait-list comparison group, the treatment group evidenced encouraging results (see Table 8.1) for a group of patients that was previously considered by some (e.g., Baer, 1994) to be refractory to exposure-based therapy.

In the Netherlands, Van Balkom, De Haan, Van Oppen, Spinhoven, Hoogduin, Van Dyck (1998) examined the relative efficacy of four active treatments and a wait-list control. Treatment conditions included: (1) ERP, (2) cognitive therapy (CT), (3) ERP plus fluvoxamine, and (4) CT plus fluvoxamine; and all psychotherapy involved 16 weekly sessions. As Table 8.1 indicates, ERP fared somewhat less well in this study than in other RCTs. A likely explanation for the relatively disappointing improvement rate of 32% is that the ERP protocol was less than optimal: all exposure was conducted as homework assignments rather than in session and under the therapist's supervision. Moreover, therapists were not allowed to discuss expectations of disastrous consequences during the first 8 weeks of ERP because this would have overlapped substantially with CT procedures.

Most recently, Foa, Liebowitz, Kozak, Davies, Campeas, Franklin, et al. (2005) reported a multicenter double-blind RCT examining the relative efficacy of (1) intensive (15 daily sessions) ERP (including in-session exposure), (2) the antidepressant clomipramine (CMI), (3) combined treatment (ERP + CMI), and (4) pill placebo. ERP produced a 50% Y-BOCS reduction, which was far superior to the effects of pill placebo. Moreover, endpoint Y-BOCS scores fell within the mild range of OCD severity. ERP was also more effective than CMI but not CMI + ERP (which was equivalent to ERP alone). Overall, the findings from RCTs suggest that ERP produces substantial and clinically meaningful improvement in OCD symptoms and that symptom reduction is due to the specific effects of these treatment procedures and not to nonspecific or "common" factors of psychotherapy. The Foa, et al. (2005) study also demonstrates that ERP is more effective than medications that are often used in the treatment of OCD.

PREDICTORS OF TREATMENT OUTCOME

A number of factors have been identified as predictors of poorer response to ERP. These include the presence of extremely poor insight into the senselessness of OCD symptoms (Foa, 1979; Foa, Abramowitz, Franklin, & Kozak, 1999), severe depression (Abramowitz & Foa, 2000; Abramowitz, Franklin, Street, Kozak, & Foa, 2000; Steketee, Chambless, & Tran, 2001), generalized anxiety disorder (Steketee, et al., 2001), extreme emotional reactivity during exposure (Foa, Grayson, Steketee, Doppelt, Turner, & Latimer, 1983), and severe borderline personality traits (Steketee, et al., 2001). Whereas some studies found that more severe OCD symptoms predicted poorer outcome (e.g., Franklin, et al., 2000), other studies have not found such a relationship (e.g., Foa, et al., 1983). However, consistent evidence is emerging to suggest that patients who present with primarily hoarding symptoms respond less well to ERP (Abramowitz, et al., 2003; Mataix-Cols, Marks, Greist, Kobak, & Baer, 2002).

Several studies have also found a relationship between adherence with ERP instructions and treatment outcome (Abramowitz, Franklin, Zoellner, & DiBernardo, 2002; Lax, Basoglu, & Marks, 1992). For example, we found that better outcomes were associated with understanding the rationale for ERP and adhering to the therapist's instructions for conducting in-session and homework exposure tasks (Abramowitz, et al., 2002).

Results have been mixed regarding the relationship of marital satisfaction to the efficacy of CBT for OCD (e.g., Emmelkamp, de Haan, & Hoogduin, 1990; Riggs, Hiss, and Foa, 1992). What is clearer is that hostility from relatives toward the identified patient is associated with premature dropout from ERP and with poor response among patients who complete treatment (Chambless & Steketee, 1999). Chambless and Steketee (1999) found that when relatives express dissatisfaction with patients' symptoms, but do not express personal rejection, such constructive criticism may have motivational properties that enhance treatment response. This underscores the importance of educating family members about OCD and how to assist with ERP.

COMBINING MEDICATIONS WITH EXPOSURE THERAPY FOR OCD

Serotonin reuptake inhibitor (SRI) medications have demonstrated efficacy for OCD (e.g., Abramowitz, 1997). Because these medicines are easily obtained, most patients presenting for psychological treatment have already been tried on at least one of these agents. Thus, it is important to ask whether the concurrent use of SRI medication synergizes the effects of ERP (i.e., combination therapy is superior to ERP alone). A second possibility is that ERP is sufficiently powerful, leaving little room for SRIs to contribute. Finally, it is also conceivable that medications detract from the efficacy of ERP. This could happen, for example, if patients attributed their improvement to taking medication and subsequently failed to comply with exposure procedures.

The available research indicates that simultaneously using medication with ERP yields superior outcome compared to SRI monotherapy, but not compared to ERP alone (e.g., Foa, et al., 2005; Van Balkom, et al., 1998). That is, adding medication to ERP does not improve the effectiveness of ERP. In a study by Hohagen, Winkelmann, Rasche-Rauchle, Hand, Konig, Munchaeu, et al. (1998), however, combined ERP and fluvoxamine offered an advantage over ERP alone, but only for seriously depressed OCD patients. On the other hand, research consistently shows that ERP is an appropriate strategy to use for OCD patients who have residual symptoms despite having tried SRI medications. Clinical implications of this research are substantial because medication is the most widely available (and therefore the most widely used) form of treatment for OCD, yet it typically produces only modest improvement compared with ERP. This means that psychotherapists are likely to encounter patients who have already attempted treatment with medication but desire additional help. Thus, an important role for ERP is that it works well for patients who choose not to take medication, have serious side effects from medications, or do not respond to medications.

CASE DESCRIPTION

"Ilene" (not her actual name), a 29-year-old female, was referred to our clinic by her primary care doctor who recognized Ilene's complaints as symptoms of OCD. The patient had been married for 6 years and had a 4-month-old baby boy, "Robert." At her initial consultation, Ilene complained of upsetting thoughts and fears that she might violently harm her baby. In particular, she worried she might impulsively stab Robert, deliberately throw him down the stairs, drown him, roll his stroller into traffic, or put poisonous chemicals in his bottle during feedings. Because of these intrusive worries, Ilene was avoiding interacting with her son. She refrained from giving him baths, feeding him, and otherwise being alone with him. When her husband went to work, Ilene arranged for her mother to stay with her and Robert. Ilene said that her problems developed shortly after Robert was born and had worsened over the past few months. The fears and associated depressive symptoms were causing arguments between Ilene and her husband, and Ilene was unable to enjoy social functions that she had previously enjoyed. She felt hopeless and worried that she would never be a "normal" mother because of her bizarre fears.

Of importance, Ilene reported no psychiatric history, except for describing herself as "neurotic." She also denied any history of violent behavior and instead, considered herself very gentle. Robert was the result of a planned pregnancy, and Ilene had been looking forward to being a mother. Thus, she was perplexed as to how a "nice" person such as herself could have thoughts about doing such horrible things to a baby. Ilene had grown up in a rural area of the midwestern United States. She described her childhood as "normal" and denied any abuse or traumatic events. She described strong religious (Lutheran) beliefs and good relationships with her parents and two younger sisters. Ilene graduated from high school and earned a bachelor's degree in elementary education from her state university before getting married. She denied any previous psychological or psychiatric treatment, had no history of substance abuse issues, and no significant medical concerns.

Administration of the Yale-Brown Obsessive Compulsive Scale (Y-BOCS) Symptom Checklist revealed that Ilene's unacceptable obsessional thoughts of harming her baby were often cued by environmental stimuli. For example, seeing a car drive past would evoke images of Robert being hit by a car. Using a knife evoked unwanted images of stabbing Robert or carving letters into his body. Ilene reported avoiding knives for this reason. Ilene's Y-BOCS checklist results also indicated that she was compulsively checking Robert for signs that she *might* have injured him without realizing it. She checked his body for stab marks and bruises to reassure herself that she hadn't lost control and acted on her unwanted violent thoughts. Other compulsive rituals included repeating prayers to herself to "cancel out" her upsetting thoughts and mentally analyzing these thoughts to determine what their meaning could be.

Ilene's score of 24 on the Y-BOCS severity scale indicated that her symptoms were moderately severe. She reported spending several hours each day with frequent obsessional thoughts and compulsive rituals that were highly distressing and somewhat difficult to resist or control. Ilene also demonstrated good insight into the senselessness of her OCD symptoms, saying that she was probably not likely to act on her thoughts. Nevertheless, she remained quite fearful of these intrusive thoughts.

CLINICAL CASE CONCEPTUALIZATION

Ilene's complaints were conceptualized using the contemporary cognitive-behavioral model of OCD (e.g., Rachman, 1998; Salkovskis, 1999). According to this model,

Ilene's unwanted, intrusive thoughts, however unpleasant, were considered normal stimuli that occur from time to time in 90% of the population at large (Rachman & de Silva, 1978), and in the majority of parents with infants (Abramowitz, Schwartz, & Moore, 2003). Her excessive fear and anxiety associated with such thoughts were considered a result of her catastrophic misinterpretations of the presence and meaning of the thoughts. Indeed, Ilene worried that the thoughts meant that deep down she was really "an evil, cold-blooded, and dangerous person."

Ilene's avoidance of situations and stimuli that evoked the obsessional thoughts was conceptualized as a method of evading her unwanted thoughts, thereby reducing the chances of committing heinous acts. Similarly, her praying and checking rituals were seen as methods of escape from the anxiety associated with intrusive thoughts and doubts already in progress. For example, ritualistic prayers were used to reduce anxiety generated by unwanted thoughts of harm. Similarly, if plagued by intrusive thoughts that she had accidentally cut Robert with a knife, Ilene would check Robert's body to reduce her uncertainty and anxiety. According to the cognitive-behavioral model, these avoidant and compulsive checking responses become habitual because they are negatively reinforced by the short-term reduction in distress that they engender. In sum, Ilene experienced anxiety when she had an intrusive thought and then experienced a reduction in anxiety when she engaged in avoidance or checking behaviors; therefore, she continued to avoid and check in response to intrusive thoughts.

The cognitive-behavioral model of OCD also proposes that avoidance and compulsive (e.g. checking and praying) strategies are maladaptive because they maintain faulty interpretations of intrusive thoughts in the long run (Salkovskis, 1999). In Ilene's case, she interpreted the outcome of avoidance and rituals in ways that prevented her from learning that her catastrophic beliefs about her unwanted thoughts were false. That is, each time she had an intrusive thought of harm, performed a praying ritual, and did not harm her baby, she strengthened her belief that the praying ritual prevented her from harming her baby. In fact, Ilene reported believing that if she did not pray, she was "more likely to do something terrible." Thus, her belief that the presence of intrusive thought meant she was a cold-blooded and dangerous person was preserved. Given this belief system, Ilene was compelled to continue praying and checking to protect her baby and relieve her anxiety.

The conceptualization just described leads to exposure as a primary treatment procedure. Repeated and prolonged exposure to situations and thoughts that evoke Ilene's obsessional fears, and observation of the nonoccurrence of disastrous consequences, will help Ilene learn that these situations and thoughts pose a very low risk of harm—low enough that she need not worry about danger. Ilene must also have the opportunity to learn that her distress and compulsive urges dissipate over time even if she refrains from compulsive rituals and that rituals do not serve any protective purpose. Thus, response prevention is instituted to help weaken the associations between ritualizing and anxiety reduction. Exposure to her fear cues without performing rituals would thus provide Ilene with the unambiguous message that her thoughts were harmless, she is not a violent person, and she need not avoid, say, prayers, analyze the thoughts, or check her baby to reassure herself of this.

TREATMENT IMPLEMENTATION

Treatment consisted of three information-gathering and treatment planning sessions followed by 13 treatment sessions. Sessions occurred twice weekly over 8 weeks. During the first three sessions, the therapist collected detailed information about Ilene's obsessions, compulsions, and avoidance. In addition, the therapist provided a cognitive-behavioral conceptualization of OCD and an explanation for how OCD symptoms are weakened by the ERP procedures described above. Instructions to refrain from ritualistic or neutralizing behaviors (response prevention) were given during session 3. In vivo and imaginal exposures were conducted during sessions 4 through 16. One session was scheduled toward the beginning of each week, and the other toward the end of each week. Homework (described later) was assigned for days when there was no session. Telephone contacts were scheduled for 1 day between sessions. The purpose of phone contacts was for Ilene to check in with the therapist, and for the therapist to make any necessary corrections in the performance of exposure practices. The final session included an assessment of progress and discussion of methods Ilene could use to maintain her treatment gains.

During the first two sessions, the therapist conducted a functional assessment of the antecedents and consequences of obsessions, avoidance, and compulsive rituals. Ilene was then introduced to the cognitive-behavioral model of OCD as described previously. To normalize the presence of unwanted intrusive thoughts, the therapist showed Ilene a long list of examples of intrusive thoughts from OCD and non-OCD individuals. Several types of misinterpretations of these kinds of thoughts were also discussed (e.g., thought-action fusion; Shafran, Thordarson, & Rachman, 1996), and examples relevant to Ilene's symptoms were provided. Evidence that thoughts are not necessarily linked to actions was collected by having Ilene perform a brief experiment in which she was given a fragile glass thermometer and asked to think about smashing the easily breakable object to the ground. Using Socratic questioning, the therapist asked Ilene to explain how she was able to refrain from breaking the object, despite thinking about performing the action. Next, the therapist described how avoidance and compulsive rituals maintain erroneous interpretations of unwanted thoughts and prevent the realization that feared disastrous consequences are highly unlikely.

Once Ilene understood this conceptualization, the therapist introduced the concepts of exposure and response prevention as procedures to reduce obsessional thinking and the urges to perform rituals. Exposure was described as a way of weakening the association between unpleasant thoughts and distress by demonstrating that the thoughts are not harmful. Response prevention was explained as a strategy for weakening the urge to perform checking and praying rituals to reduce anxiety. It was also highlighted that ERP was intended not to eliminate unpleasant thoughts per se (indeed, everyone has the occasional unpleasant idea), but rather to change Ilene's faulty interpretation of these thoughts. A written summary of this treatment rationale was provided to the patient for her further review.[1]

In the third session, Ilene and the therapist developed a hierarchy of situations and thoughts to be confronted both in real life (in vivo) and in imagination. Items to be confronted first were those that evoked only moderate distress. The most distressing situations were confronted by the ninth treatment session. Ilene assessed the level of anxiety evoked by a given situation using the Subjective Units of Distress (SUDS) scale, with a rating from 0 (no anxiety) to 100 (intense anxiety). Ilene agreed to confront these situations without ritualizing or performing any neutralizing behaviors and continue the exposure until the obsessional distress had decreased significantly (a substantial decrease in SUDS). In this way, Ilene learned that her anxiety level would decrease even though she did not ritualize (e.g., pray or check her baby). These exposures served to weaken the link between ritualizing and anxiety reduction. Table 8.2 presents the exposure treatment plan and corresponding SUDS ratings.

In most cases, Ilene practiced each situation on the exposure hierarchy with the therapist before trying it on her own. For example, in one exposure session she held a knife in one hand and Robert in her other arm, initially with the therapist sitting nearby. Next, the therapist left the room. Then, Ilene was instructed to practice the exposure for at least 2 hours on her own for "homework." Ilene recorded her SUDS level on a homework chart every 10 minutes during practice exposures. In-session observations and inspection of completed homework forms indicated that her anxiety levels were decreasing both within and between exposure sessions. The patient was generally successful with abstaining from her ritualistic and/or neutralizing behaviors.

In addition to confronting actual situations that evoked unpleasant obsessional thoughts, Ilene practiced exposure to the thoughts themselves via primary imaginal exposures in which the intrusive thoughts were verbalized on a loop tape. The

TABLE 8.2   Ilene's Exposure Treatment Hierarchy

Exposure Number	Situation or thought	SUDS
1	Hold a large butcher knife	55
2	Take Robert for a walk in the stroller unaccompanied	65
3	Give Robert a bath unaccompanied	75
4	Cut meat with Robert nearby	75
5	Hold Robert while walking next to busy street	80
6	Hold Robert while standing on balcony of apartment	90
7	Think about stabbing Robert	90
8	Prepare a bottle for Robert with rat poison on the counter	95

SUDS, subjective units of distress scale.

*All patient handouts are available from the first author.

tape included a 3-minute recitation of the thought that was meant to evoke distress. After 3 minutes elapsed, the tape automatically repeated itself. Thus, Ilene could repeatedly listen to a description of her intrusive thoughts for an extended period of time. Just as with in vivo exposure, the intent of imaginal exposure was to help Ilene confront, rather than avoid, these intrusions and find that her distress attenuates over time even if no rituals are performed. An example of one imaginal exposure script was as follows:

> I am taking Robert for a walk on a beautiful spring day and we're coming to a street we have to cross. I start to get nervous because I usually try to avoid walking near the street with the baby. I grab the stroller very tightly as we wait for the traffic to slow down before crossing. Then I have the thought of sending the stroller off into the traffic. I feel so anxious, like I might lose control. Then I do it, I lose control and push the stroller with the innocent baby into the busy street. I scream with terror, but the baby has no idea what's happening to him, he's only 4 months old! I see the stroller get slammed by a car, then another. It's all mangled and I have killed my baby. I am standing there helpless as if in shock. Robert is dead. My husband will be horrified. How could I have let myself do this terrible thing?

By the tenth treatment session, Ilene was confronting nearly every situation and intrusive thought on the exposure hierarchy with very little distress. She had also given up her rituals. An excerpt from a Socratic style discussion about her success went as follows:

> THERAPIST: So, when we started this you were scared your thoughts of killing Robert meant you were a cold-blooded killer. What have you learned by doing the exposure and response prevention exercises?
>
> ILENE: Well, of course, I didn't hurt Robert.
>
> THERAPIST: Right; even though you were purposely thinking about it. Plus, your anxiety subsided. How do you explain that?
>
> ILENE: I didn't *want* to hurt him, so I didn't. I love my son.
>
> THERAPIST: But you still have intrusive thoughts sometimes, right?
>
> ILENE: Yes, from time to time.
>
> THERAPIST: So, what does this mean about your thoughts? What do they mean?
>
> ILENE: Not much. *I* decide what I do or don't do. If I don't want to hurt someone, I'm not going to do it. The thought of doing it is just a thought.
>
> THERAPIST: How strongly do you believe what you just told me?
>
> ILENE: Pretty strongly, like 80% to 90%.
>
> THERAPIST: Good. As long as you keep thinking that way, you'll find yourself less preoccupied with the thought since it's no longer threatening to you.

The final treatment session was devoted to maintaining therapeutic gains and preventing return of OCD symptoms. The importance of continuing exposure to obsessional thoughts or situations without ritualizing was discussed. Potential "high-risk" situations were identified, and Ilene was given suggestions for how to continue to develop and implement her own ERP exercises as needed. In addition, the difference between "lapse" and "relapse" was discussed, and Ilene was instructed to expect periodic lapses (particularly when under more stress) during which she would have to use the skills learned in CBT to maintain treatment her gains.

ASSESSMENT

Measures used to assess Ilene's progress in therapy at pretreatment and post-treatment were as follows:

- *Yale-Brown Obsessive Compulsive Scale* (Y-BOCS; Goodman, et al., 1989a, 1989b). Considered the gold-standard measure of OCD symptoms, the Y-BOCS is a semi-structured clinical interview that also includes a 10-item severity scale. Obsessions and compulsions are rated separately, yielding 2 subscores (range 0–20) that are added to produce a total score (range 0–40). Symptoms are rated on a 5-point Likert scale from 0 (no symptoms) to 4 (severe symptoms). Items include (1) time spent on symptoms, (2) interference, (3) distress, (4) resistance, and (5) control over symptoms. The Y-BOCS has satisfactory psychometric properties and has been found sensitive to treatment effects (e.g., Goodman, et al., 1989a, 1989b).
- *Beck Depression Inventory* (BDI; Beck, Ward, Mendelsohn, Mock, & Erbaugh, 1961). The BDI is a 21-item self-report scale that assesses the severity of affective, cognitive, motivational, vegetative, and psychomotor components of psychological distress. Because most individuals with OCD also report depressive symptoms, it is important to assess such symptoms over the course of therapy. Scores of 10 or less on the BDI are considered normal; scores of 20 or greater suggest the presence of clinical depression. The BDI has been shown to have excellent reliability and validity (Beck, Steer, & Garbin, 1988), and is widely used in treatment outcome research.
- *Revised Thought-Action Fusion Scale* (TAF; Shafran, et al., 1996). This is a 19-item self-report measure of the degree to which a person believes unwanted thoughts about disturbing events: (1) are the moral equivalent of the actions they describe, and/or (2) make the event more probable. Each item (e.g., "When I think unkindly about a friend, it is almost as disloyal as doing an unkind act") is rated on a scale from 0 (strongly disagree) to 4 (strongly agree). The TAF includes two subscales: Moral (12 items) and Likelihood (7 items), which possess high internal consistency (Cronbach's alphas = .95 and .96, respectively). Summed totals for each subscale are divided by the number of items so that scores on each subscale range from 0 to 4. The TAF was included to assess changes in cognitions believed to underlie OCD.

At the start of each session, Ilene and the therapist rated the following symptoms:

- *Fear of Intrusive Thoughts*. This was rated on a scale from 0 (none) to 8 (severe).
- *Avoidance*. The degree to which Ilene was avoiding situations associated with unpleasant intrusive thoughts was rated from 0 (never avoids) to 8 (invariably avoids).
- *Neutralizing (Rituals)*. Daily time spent performing compulsions (e.g., checking, praying) and neutralizing behaviors (e.g., rationalizing the meaning of unpleasant thoughts) was assessed on a scale from 0 (none) to 8 (30 times or over 2 hours per day).

RESULTS

Table 8.3 presents pretest and post-test scores on each assessment measure. Ilene's post-treatment BDI score was within the normal range, and her total Y-BOCS score indicated only subclinical OCD symptoms. TAF scores indicated that changes in cognition had also occurred as a result of ERP, and perhaps mediated the symptom improvement. As is indicated in Figure 8.2, Ilene had also substantially reduced her fears of intrusive thoughts, her avoidance patterns, and her rituals over the course of therapy. These scores were consistent with Ilene's verbal report. Moreover, her general functioning had improved as suggested by increased interest in socializing and reduced arguments with her husband. These final results were discussed with Ilene, and follow-up visits were scheduled for 3 and 6 months later.

TABLE 8.3   Scores on Measures of OCD, Depressive Symptoms, and OCD-Related Cognitions at Pre- and Post-Test

Symptom and Measure	Assessment	
	Pre-test	Post-test
Y-BOCS total score (0–40)	24	7
Obsessions (0–20)	12	5
Compulsions (0–20)	12	2
Beck Depression Inventory	18	4
Thought-action fusion scale		
Moral subscale	25	7
Likelihood subscale	14	4

Y-BOCS, Yale–Brown obsessive compulsive scale.

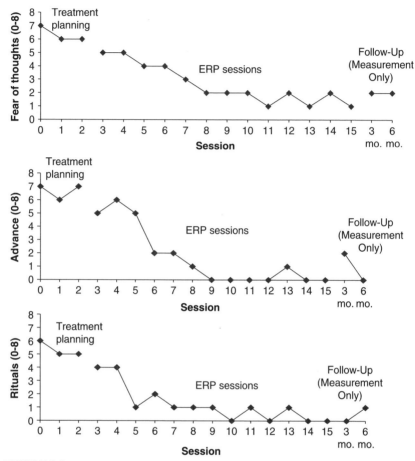

FIGURE 8.2   Ratings of fear of intrusive thoughts, avoidance, and rituals at each treatment session, and at follow-up evaluation.

DISCUSSION

Ilene's course of treatment was generally uncomplicated. She quickly understood the cognitive-behavioral model of OCD and rationale for using ERP procedures. She was also willing to take the "risks" of confronting feared situations and thoughts as part of her therapy. This speaks to the importance of providing a coherent rationale for the use of these techniques. It may be that Ilene would have refused to expose herself to these very unpleasant stimuli if she had not been educated about (1) the factors that maintain obsessional fear and compulsive urges as described in the cognitive-behavioral model, (2) the fact that intrusive thoughts are normal, and (3) the role that ERP procedures play in weakening processes maintaining OCD.

Ilene was seen 3 months after completing the ERP program. Between the end of therapy and follow-up visit, she had continued to practice self-exposure and response prevention with much success. At follow-up visit, Ilene reported occasional unwanted thoughts; however, they evoked only minor levels of distress. She was also able to remind herself that these cognitions, although strange, were meaningless and would not lead to horrific behavior. At the 6-month follow-up visit, OCD and depressive symptoms remained in check. Functionally, Ilene was enjoying motherhood, and she and her husband were planning another addition to their family.

Providing a clear and compelling model of OCD and rationale for treatment to patients is extremely important for successful ERP. After all, these treatment procedures are, by definition, anxiety-provoking. Patients who have a conceptual model for understanding their own difficulties, as well as knowledge of how and why exposure works to decrease these problems, will be much more likely to comply with the often difficult treatment instructions (Abramowitz, et al., 2002). In our treatment program, we often illustrate, for patients, idiosyncratic models of the relationships between their symptoms, anxiety, and factors maintaining their anxiety. Diagrams are also used to show how ERP procedures weaken associations between thoughts and anxiety.

SUMMARY AND CONCLUSIONS

This chapter has summarized the theoretical and empirical literature on exposure-based cognitive-behavioral therapy for OCD, and has illustrated the implementation and results of this treatment using descriptions of treatment procedures, verbatim dialogue from patient-therapist interactions, and data obtained throughout the course of therapy. In our clinical work with adults, we are guided by the empirical work described here, which indicates that the most effective outcome results when treatment involves therapist-supervised prolonged and repeated exposure (including exposure to the most feared stimuli) and full response prevention. Because obsessional fear in OCD is evoked by both tangible external stimuli and internal cognitive stimuli, treatment must often include both situational and imaginal exposure. Cognitive techniques are often helpful in engaging patients in exposure exercises and helping the patient process their experiences of confronting feared stimuli and experiencing the nonoccurrence of anticipated negative consequences. We find cognitive techniques especially useful for "tenderizing" the strongly held obsessional beliefs of patients who have difficulty recognizing the senselessness of their obsessions and rituals.

Exposure therapy for OCD, although often effective, is challenging for patients to undergo. Patients must commit to facing their fears and dropping the safety nets of avoidance and compulsive rituals. These procedures evoke temporary discomfort if undertaken correctly, and this highlights the importance of providing patients with a compelling rationale for engaging in therapy. Patients must be socialized to the conceptual model of OCD that forms the basis of treatment; they must be taught about the process of habituation; and they must develop a strong collaborative relationship with the therapist, who plays the role of a coach and a cheerleader. It is important to note that the role of the therapeutic relationship in exposure therapy departs from the role of this relationship in other forms of therapy (e.g., psychodynamic therapy). Particularly, whereas in some other forms of psychotherapy the relationship is considered an agent of change in itself, in exposure therapy, a good relationship is considered an essential foundation for implementing the specific treatment procedures (i.e., exposure and response prevention) hypothesized to produce change.

It is normal for novice therapists, or those new to the use of exposure-based therapy for anxiety, to feel trepidation in asking patients with OCD to purposely confront stimuli that evoke obsessional anxiety and then resist performing their rituals. Perhaps this seems unnecessarily painful. One might consider the following points if such discomfort sets in. First, as we have reviewed, exposure-based therapy is the treatment of choice for OCD. Second, exposure demands little of the patient that he or she is not already doing. For example, he or she is already thinking distressing thoughts repeatedly; this is the definition of an obsession. Instead, exposure asks that the patient to evoke the obsessional thoughts in a systematic and therapeutic fashion to practice more healthy ways of managing such situations. Third, there is no evidence that it is dangerous or harmful to interrupt a person who is engaged in compulsive rituals; at most, this evokes temporary discomfort. Fourth, it is clear that attempting to avoid, resist, and control obsessional stimuli are maladaptive responses that serve only to maintain the associated distress and impairment. Exposure therapy introduces the patient to a much healthier strategy for dealing with obsessions that leads to the development of adaptive responses. Fifth, the distress evoked during therapeutic exposure is temporary, and when it decreases, patients are left with important knowledge about situations and thoughts they once believed were dangerous, and about their own ability to manage their own subjective distress. Finally, there is no evidence that obsessional fears and rituals are caused by unconscious conflicts that persist until they are resolved. Thus, amelioration of certain fears by exposure will not cause "substitution" of additional symptoms.

REFERENCES

Abramowitz, J.S. (1996). Variants of exposure and response prevention in the treatment of obsessive-compulsive disorder: A meta-analysis. *Behavior Therapy, 27,* 583–600.

Abramowitz, J.S. (1997). Effectiveness of psychological and pharmacological treatments for obsessive-compulsive disorder: A quantitative review. *Journal of Consulting and Clinical Psychology, 65,* 44–52.

Abramowitz, J.S., & Foa, E. (2000). Does comorbid major depressive disorder influence outcome of exposure and response prevention for OCD? *Behavior Therapy, 31,* 795–800.

Abramowitz, J.S., Foa, E.B., & Franklin, M.E. (2003). Exposure and ritual prevention for obsessive-compulsive disorder: Effects of intensive versus twice-weekly sessions. *Journal of Consulting and Clinical Psychology, 71,* 394–398.

Abramowitz, J.S., Franklin, M.E., Street, G.P., Kozak, M.J., & Foa, E.B. (2000). Effects of comorbid depression on response to treatment for obsessive-compulsive disorder. *Behavior Therapy, 31,* 517–528.

Abramowitz, J.S., Franklin, M.E., Zoellner, L.A., & DiBernardo, C.L. (2002). Treatment compliance and outcome of cognitive-behavioral therapy for obsessive-compulsive disorder. *Behavior Modification, 26,* 447–463.

Abramowitz, J.S., Schwartz, S.A., & Moore, K.M. (2003). Obsessional thoughts in postpartum females and their partners: Content, severity and relationship with depression. *Journal of Clinical Psychology in Medical Settings, 10,* 157–164.

Baer, L. (1994). Factor analysis of symptom subtypes of obsessive compulsive disorder and their relation to personality and tic disorders. *Journal of Clinical Psychiatry, 55,* 18–23.

Beck, A.T., Ward, C.H., Mendelsohn, M., Mock, J., & Erbaugh, J. (1961). An inventory for measuring depression. *Archives of General Psychiatry, 4,* 561–571.

Beck, A.T., Steer, R.A., & Garbin, M.G. (1988). Psychometric properties of the Beck Depression Inventory: Twenty-five years of evaluation. *Clinical Psychology Review, 8,* 77–100.

Chambless, D.L., & Steketee, G. (1999). Expressed emotion and behavior therapy outcome: A prospective study with obsessive-compulsive and agoraphobic outpatients. *Journal of Consulting and Clinical Psychology, 67,* 658–665.

Dollard, J., & Miller, N.E. (1950). *Personality and psychotherapy: An analysis in terms of learning , thinking, and culture.* New York: McGraw-Hill.

Emmelkamp, P.M.G., & Kraanen, J. (1977). Therapist-controlled exposure *in vivo* versus self-controlled exposure *in vivo*: A comparison with obsessive-compulsive patients. *Behaviour Research and Therapy, 15,* 491–195.

Emmelkamp, P.M.G., de Haan, E., & Hoogduin, C.A.L. (1990). Marital adjustment and obsessive-compulsive disorder. *British Journal of Psychiatry, 156,* 55–60.

Fals-Stewart, W., Marks, A.P., & Schafer, J. (1993). A comparison of behavioral group therapy and individual behavior therapy in treating obsessive-compulsive disorder. *The Journal of Nervous and Mental Disease, 181,* 189–193.

Foa, E.B. (1979). Failure in treating obsessive-compulsives. *Behaviour Research and Therapy, 17,* 169–176.

Foa, E.B., & Goldstein, A. (1978). Continuous exposure and complete response prevention in the treatment of obsessive-compulsive neurosis. *Behavior Therapy, 9,* 821–829.

Foa, E.B. & Kozak, M.J. (1986). Emotional processing of fear: Exposure to corrective information. *Psychological Bulletin, 99,* 20–35.

Foa, E.B., & Kozak, M.J. (1996). Psychological treatment for obsessive-compulsive disorder. In M.R. Mavissakalian & R.F. Prien (Eds.), *Long-term treatments of anxiety disorders* (pp. 285–309). Washington, D.C.: American Psychiatric Press, Inc.

Foa, E.B., Abramowitz, J.S., Franklin, M.E., & Kozak, M.J. (1999). Feared consequences, fixity of belief, and treatment outcome in patients with obsessive-compulsive disorder. *Behavior Therapy, 30,* 717–724.

Foa, E.B., Grayson, J.B., Steketee, G.S., Doppelt, H.G., Turner, R.M., & Latimer, P.R. (1983). Success and failure in the behavioral treatment of obsessive-compulsives. *Journal of Consulting and Clinical Psychology, 51,,287–297.*

Foa, E.B., Liebowitz, M.R., Kozak, M.J., Davies, S., Campeas, R., Franklin, M.E., Huppert, J.D., Kjernisted, K., Rowan, V., Schmidt, A.B., Simpson, H.B., & Tu, X. (2005). Treatment of obsessive-compulsive disorder by exposure and ritual prevention, clomipramine, and their combination: A randomized, placebo controlled trial. *American Journal of Psychiatry, 162,* 151–161.

Franklin, M.E., Abramowitz, J.S., Kozak, M.J., Levitt, J.T., & Foa, E.B. (2000). Effectiveness of exposure and ritual prevention for obsessive-compulsive disorder: Randomized compared with nonrandomized samples. *Journal of Consulting and Clinical Psychology, 68,* 594–602.

Freeston, M.H., & Ladouceur, R. (1999). Exposure and response prevention for obsessive thoughts. *Cognitive & Behavioral Practice, 6,* 362–383.

Freeston, M.H., Ladouceur, R., Gagnon, F., Thibodeau, N., Rheaume, J., Letarte, H., & Bujold, A. (1997). Cognitive-behavioral treatment of obsessive thoughts: A controlled study. *Journal of Consulting and Clinical Psychology, 65,* 405–413.

Goodman, W.K., Price, L.H., Rasmussen, S.A., Mazure, C., Fleischmann, R.L., Hill, C.L., Heninger, G.R., & Charney, D.S. (1989a). The Yale-Brown Obsessive-Compulsive Scale I: Development, use, and reliability. *Archives of General Psychiatry, 46,* 1006–1011.

Goodman, W. K., Price, L. H., Rasmussen, S. A., Mazure, C., Fleischmann, R. L., Hill, C. L., Heninger, G.R., & Charney, D.S. (1989b). The Yale-Brown Obsessive-Compulsive Scale I: Development, use, and reliability. *Archives of General Psychiatry, 46,* 1006–1011.

Hodgson, R., Rachman, S., & Marks, I. (1972). The treatment of chronic obsessive-compulsive neurosis: Follow-up and further findings. *Behaviour Research and Therapy, 10,* 181–189.

Hohagen, F., Winkelmann, G., Rasche-Rauchle, H., Hand, I., Konig, A., Munchau, N., Hiss, H., Geiger-Kabisch, C., Kappler, C., Schramm, P., Rey, E., Aldenhoff, J., & Berger, M. (1998). Combination of behaviour therapy with fluvoxamine in comparison with behaviour therapy and placebo. *British Journal of Psychiatry, 173,* 71–78.

Lax, T., Basoglu, M., & Marks, I.M. (1992). Expectancy and compliance as predictors of outcome in obsessive-compulsive disorder. *Behavioural Psychotherapy, 20,* 257–266.

Lindsay, M., Crino, R., & Andrews, G. (1997). Controlled trial of exposure and response prevention in obsessive-compulsive disorder. *British Journal of Psychiatry, 170,* 135–139.

Mataix-Cols, D., Marks, I.M., Greist, J.H., Kobak, K.A., & Baer, L. (2002). Obsessive-compulsive symptom dimensions as predictors of compliance with and response to behaviour therapy: Results from a controlled trial. *Psychotherapy and Psychosomatics, 71,* 255–262.

McKay, D., Abramowitz, J.S., Calamari, J.E., Kyrios, M., Radomsky, A.S., Sookman, D., Taylor, S., & Wilhelm, S. (2004). A critical evaluation of obsessive-compulsive disorder subtypes: Symptoms versus mechanisms. *Clinical Psychology Review, 24,* 283–313.

Meyer, V. (1966). Modification of expectations in cases with obsessional rituals. *Behaviour Research and Therapy, 4,* 273–280.

Meyer, V., Levy, R., & Schnurer, A. (1974). The behavioral treatment of obsessive-compulsive disorders. In H.R. Beech (Ed.), *Obsessional states* (pp. 233–258). London: Methuen.

Mowrer, O. (1960). *Learning theory and behavior.* New York: Wiley.

Rabavilas, A., Boulougouris, J., & Stefanis, C. (1976). Duration of flooding sessions in the treatment of obsessive-compulsive patients. *Behaviour Research and Therapy, 14,* 349–355.

Rachman, S. (1997). A cognitive theory of obsessions. *Behaviour Research and Therapy, 35,* 793–802.

Rachman, S. (1998). A cognitive theory of obsessions: Elaborations. *Behaviour Research and Therapy, 36,* 385–401.

Rachman, S, & de Silva, P. (1978). Abnormal and normal obsessions. *Behaviour Research and Therapy, 16,* 233–238.

Riggs, D.S., Hiss, H., & Foa, E.B. (1992). Marital distress and the treatment of obsessive compulsive disorder. *Behavior Therapy, 23,* 585–597.

Salkovskis, P. (1999). Understanding and treating obsessive-compulsive disorder. *Behaviour Research and Therapy, 37,* S29–S52.

Shafran, R., Thordarson, D., & Rachman, S. (1996). Thought-action fusion in obsessive-compulsive disorder. *Journal of Anxiety Disorders, 37,* 231–237.

Steketee, G.S., Chambless, D.L., & Tran, G.Q. (2001). Effects of Axis I and II comorbidity on behavior therapy outcome for obsessive-compulsive disorder and agoraphobia. *Comprehensive Psychiatry, 42,* 76–86.

Van Balkom, A.J.L.M., De Haan, E., Van Oppen, P., Spinhoven, P., Hoogduin, K.A.L., & Van Dyck, R. (1998). Cognitive and behavioral therapies alone versus in combination with fluvoxamine in the treatment of obsessive compulsive disorder. *The Journal of Nervous and Mental Disorders, 186,* 492–49.

CHAPTER 9

Cognitive-Behavior Therapy and the Treatment of Childhood Obsessive-Compulsive Disorder

Sandra Mendlowitz

University of Toronto

Obsessive-compulsive disorder (OCD) affects between 1.9% and 3.6% of children and adolescents (Apter, Fallon, King, Ratzoni, Zohar, Binder, et al., 1996; Flament, Whitaker, Rapoport, Davies, Berg, Kalikow, et al., 1988; Thomsen, 1994; Valleni-Baile, Garrison, Jackson, Waller, McKeown, Addy, & Cuffe, 1994; Zohar, Ratzoni, Pauls, Apter, Bleich, Kron, et al., 1992). The most common symptom surrounds fears of germ contamination, although many children are plagued by horrific thoughts or images. Still others report symptoms such as excessive hand washing resulting in skin lesions, rereading of words, rewriting behaviors, retracing steps, and checking behaviors that result in hours of lost time. These behaviors can lead to needless anguish for the child, but, more importantly, they have a profound negative effect on academic functioning, peer relationships, and disruption in home life. Left untreated, many children with OCD suffer into adulthood and may develop comorbid anxiety, depression, and suicidality (Gravitz, 1998).

The efficacy of using cognitive-behavioral therapy (CBT) for OCD has been widely demonstrated in the adult literature (Baer, 1992; Marks, et al., 1988, Piacentini 1999; McLean, Whittal, Sochting, Koch, Paterson, Thordarson, et al., 2001). Also, March, Franklin, Nelson, & Foa (2001) noted that CBT is the only consistently successful treatment for OCD in pediatric populations with encouraging treatment efficacy in both individual (Bolton, Collins, & Steinberg, 1983; Franklin, Kozak, Cashman, Coles, Rheingold, & Foa, 1998; March, Mulle, & Herbel, 1994; March & Mulle, 1998) and group modalities (Mendlowitz & Saltzman, 1999; Thienemann, Martin, Cregger, Thompson, & Dyer-Friedman, 2001).

Although there is some clinical variation in CBT, the critical components when treating OCD in children include psychoeducation regarding OCD and the interrelationship among thoughts, feelings, and behaviors (cognitive restructuring, challenging thoughts, problem-solving strategies); training in anxiety management techniques (e.g., relaxation training and self-control strategies to prevent escape from the fearful

Handbook of Exposure Therapies

209

situation); exposure and response prevention (ERP); homework assignments; and parental involvement (i.e., transfer of control, co-therapist, and training in contingency management).

The ERP component involves gradually exposing the child to anxiety-eliciting cues until the anxiety or fear diminishes (Marks, 1997). ERP scenarios are relatively easy to design in an individual treatment session, and can be implemented in a group context (Mendlowitz & Saltzman, 1999; Thienemann, et al., 2001). Parental inclusion is a critical feature of ERP when working with pediatric populations because of the tendency for family members to make accommodations for the illness (Barrett, Dadds, & Rapee, 1996; Bouchard, Mendlowitz, Coles, & Franklin, 2004; Mendlowitz & Saltzman, 1999). For example, parents often unwittingly contribute to the expression of problem behaviors by becoming involved in, and enabling, the child's rituals. Reducing parental involvement in the child's rituals is important for treatment success (Walters, Barrett, & March, 2001). Parent training often involves educating parents in the use of cognitive and behavioral techniques (e.g., Silverman, Kurtines, Ginsburg, Weems, Lumpkin, & Carmichael, 1999; Silverman & Kurtines, 1996), and utilizing parents as co-therapists outside of therapy sessions (e.g., Mendlowitz, Manassis, Bradley, Scapillato, Miezitis, & Shaw, 1999). In the case reported here, a combination of these two approaches was used.

CASE STUDY: SUZIE

Background Information

Suzie is an average-size and well-groomed 10-year-old female and the youngest of two girls. Both of her parents work outside the home. Her mother has a high school education and her father a college education. She is described as a popular child with two best friends and participates in many peer-related activities. The family lives in a small town 3 hours from the hospital in which both the clinical assessment and treatment sessions were conducted.

The medical history was significant for numerous streptococcus infections before Grade 2; however, her tonsils were removed while she was in Grade 3, and there were no further episodes. Suzie's parents denied any temporal association between streptococcal or viral infections and the onset of OCD or other anxiety-like symptoms. Although no family history of psychiatric problems was initially acknowledged during the intake assessment, as Suzie's parents became knowledgeable of the disorder, they increasingly suspected that Suzie's paternal grandmother and a maternal cousin likely suffered from OCD.

Both Suzie and her parents were seen together for a diagnostic interview and assessment. Her parents noted behavioral problems since age three, but they had been unable to determine antecedents or causes. They first observed excessive hand washing, which, although still present, subsided in frequency by age five. A brief psychiatric assessment at that time resulted in no concrete treatment recommendations, although a diagnosis of OCD was suggested. Soon thereafter, other anxiety-related issues emerged; Suzie was described as becoming "clingy," expressing some mild concerns about being away from her parents, although more salient were issues of perfectionism regarding her school work. She also began to express physical complaints (e.g., stomachaches) about attending school, but her parents noted that they remained firm regarding school attendance, and her complaints of illness eventually discontinued, and she attended school without any complaints.

Unfortunately, the family was unable to locate a mental health professional who could provide functional assessment or behaviorally oriented treatment for their child. With some reluctance, and on the advice of their family physician, they agreed to pharmacotherapy, and Suzie was placed on 15 mg of paroxetine (Paxil) 10 months before assessment at our clinic. Pharmacotherapy had little, if any, benefit. Her parents observed both an exacerbation of existing symptoms and the emergence of new ones. Eventually, the parents concluded that pharmacotherapy was not the answer to their daughter's problems, and they investigated CBT treatment alternatives.

Assessment Results

Diagnosis of OCD was confirmed with a semi-structured diagnostic interview. Although no other anxiety disorder, or comorbid affective, attentional, or behavioral disorders, were noted, there was evidence of a tic disorder. Specifically, the parents reported a tendency in Suzie to "blink excessively" since age five. The blinking was exacerbated by stress, and Paxil had no therapeutic effect. Excessive blinking and throat clearing were observed during the intake assessment and were not temporally related to any specific thoughts or ritualized behavior.

Suzie was described as a good student, obtaining mostly As and Bs; however, she recently received a C in one of her subjects. No learning problems were reported, although Suzie acknowledged difficulty focusing in school because of her increasingly problematic obsessions. She reported that she was usually able to hide her rituals from her friends with no effect on peer relations to date. In contrast, familial conflict was increasing at an alarming rate. The quality of her relationship with her older sister was rapidly deteriorating because Suzie did not want to touch or go near anything her sister had come in contact with. For example, she refused to sit in any seat her sister recently occupied. She showered before but not after her sister. She moved the computer chair aside to avoid touching her sister when using the computer. She believed her sister's breath was contaminated with germs. She was distressed if her sister touched any of her belongings or entered her room. Although contamination fears were mostly specific to her sister, Suzie commented that she was periodically distressed when her mother yawned. No specific anxiety was associated with her father.

Further elaboration of symptoms revealed a myriad of obsessions and compulsions. Contamination obsessions vis-à-vis her sister were compounded by a fear that she might unwittingly contaminate her parents. To this end, she was concerned about the health effects of improper food handling and preparation. She also expressed self-doubt regarding the quality of her artwork and the accuracy of her schoolwork. She acknowledged vague fears of harming others, reported experiencing disturbing images containing sexual content, and indicated she had intrusive thoughts of songs with lyrics that included profanity.

Several compulsive behaviors appeared to be increasing in frequency and duration. For example, Suzie reported a ritualized order to the way she dressed in the morning. For a short period of time, she insisted on standing on her bed as she dressed to avoid having her clothes touch the ground. She also would touch both elbows when she passed through an open doorway.

Showering occupied significant amounts of time given both the frequency of her showering and the fact that she felt compelled to wash the curtain to cleanse it of germs before each showering occasion. So significant was her concern about contamination from the shower curtain that she would wash her hands if they brushed the shower curtain. She shampooed only occasionally for fear the subsequent rinsing would be inadequate to cleanse her of germs. She never used soap.

In addition to ritualized cleansing behaviors, she frequently confessed irrelevant information to her mother who was increasingly annoyed by this behavior. Her parents also reported a number of checking and counting behaviors that had escalated by the time treatment was initiated, with the appearance of hoarding behaviors as well.

The ever increasing stress associated with Suzie's OCD symptoms was also causing problems in her parents' marriage. Suzie's parents had different approaches to their daughter's problem, and they openly disagreed with how the other was managing Suzie's ritualized behaviors. Both parents had difficulty setting limits for fear of upsetting Suzie. Typically, Suzie reacted to limit-setting by becoming defiant, yelling, screaming, or threatening. Like many parents, they backed down in an effort to appease Suzie and decrease household tension. However, their backtracking only served to reinforce Suzie's inappropriate behavior and gave her too much control over family decision making.

After the initial intake assessment, Suzie's parents decreased her medication to 10 mg. They agreed to maintain the dosage for the duration of the treatment with the hope of discontinuing medication on termination.

Treatment Selection

Group-Based CBT Treatment

The treatment selected for Suzie was a 12-week group-based CBT intervention involving a treatment manual that detailed the therapy experiences of a similar-age child (Mendlowitz, 2001). The manual teaches children several treatment-related activities and therapeutic strategies: creation of a hierarchy, how to use an anxiety rating scale, relaxation techniques, two specific cognitive restructuring methods, use of a symbol or "superhero," and creation of a "cheat sheet" containing cognitive coping statements. The overall treatment plan emphasized psychoeducational concepts relevant to both OCD and CBT and the principles underlying anxiety management, cognitive restructuring, and exposure therapy with response prevention. Suzie's group included one other girl and three boys. Group treatment sessions were 90 minutes long.

Homework Assignments

Regular homework assignments supplemented group work and helped the treatment team obtain baseline ratings of symptoms. Homework included practice in targeting symptoms and rehearsing newly learned strategies. Homework and session worksheets were kept in a therapy binder that was used later as a reference for the child once treatment was terminated. Suzie's parents helped her implement therapist-generated and group-designed ERP plans that focused on reducing anxiety to specific stimuli (e.g., her sister, being touched, and so forth).

Parent Training Sessions

Suzie's parents also participated in a parent training group (Mendlowitz, Shulman, & Spenser, 2001) that followed the child group sessions and was led by the same therapists. Parents were given specific strategies each week to target problematic OCD behaviors using ERP techniques. Didactics in behavior management strategies, exploration of parenting issues, and instruction in contingency management programs formed a significant portion of the parent training sessions. Because of the aversive, and often coercive, interactions that characterize parental relationships with OCD children, parents are often reluctant to implement exposure therapy for fear of an escalation in inappropriate child behavior. It is therefore important for treatment facilitators to emphasize consistency and follow-through on all ERP plans. Parents are taught how to break the enabling cycle that negatively reinforces their child's symptoms. Because a parent's anxiety about treatment may interfere with treatment fidelity, parents are encouraged to address their own anxiety concerning exposure therapy. In addition to the training sessions, parents were provided weekly educational materials for future reference.

Assessment of Treatment Effects

Assessment was conducted at the diagnostic interview 3 months before treatment, immediately pretreatment, immediately post-treatment, at 6 months post-treatment, and at 12 months post-treatment. Measures were repeated for each assessment period by an independent assessor with postdoctoral training.

Intake Assessment Results

At the intake assessment, Suzie was diagnosed with Obsessive-Compulsive Disorder using the Anxiety Disorders Interview Schedule for DSM-IV, Parent Version (*ADIS*; Albano & Silverman, 1996), Children's Yale-Brown Obsessive-Compulsive Scale (*CY-BOCS*; Schahill, Riddle, McSwiggin-Hardin, Ort, King, et al., 1997), Multidimensional Anxiety Scale for Children (*MASC*; March 1997), and the Children's Depression Inventory (*CDI*; Kovacs, 1983).

Treatment Outcome

According to Suzie's CY-BOCS scores (Figure 9.1), a decline in both obsessions and compulsions was noted from pretreatment (Total Score = 26) to post-treatment (Total Score = 10) and 6 months post-treatment (Total Score = 2). Treatment gains were maintained at 12 months post-treatment (Total Score = 3).

A similar pattern was noted on the Harm-Avoidance scale (Table 9.1). The Harm-Avoidance scale is composed of two subscales: perfectionism and anxious coping. Like other children with OCD, Suzie's scores were mildly elevated on these scales. No other scales were elevated on the MASC profile. Declines were noted from pretreatment to post-treatment, and gains continued to be realized at 12 months post-treatment.

Changes in CDI T-scores were less dramatic. There were two elevated scores at pretreatment (Table 9.2): the Interpersonal Problems subscale was significantly

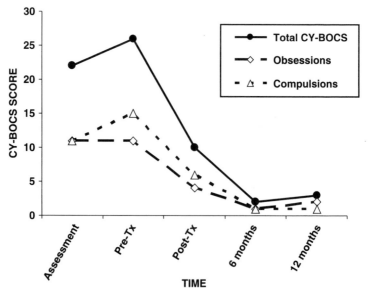

FIGURE 9.1   Suzie's CY-BOCS scores.

TABLE 9.1   MASC Harm-Avoidance T-Scores Across Time

MASC	Total Harm-Avoidance	Perfectionism	Anxious Coping
Initial Assessment	64	63	60
Pretreatment	64	63	60
Post-Treatment	56	50	60
6 Months Post-Treatment	40	50	35
12 Months Post-Treatment	38	45	35

elevated and the Negative Self-Esteem subscale was mildly elevated. Both subscales showed meaningful declines from pretreatment to post-treatment. Other subscales remained within the normal range across assessment periods.

The ADIS was administered twice after the initial intake: 6 months post-treatment and 12 months post-treatment. Suzie was symptom-free at both assessments and did not meet diagnostic criteria for OCD.

Discussion

The results clearly suggest that CBT was successful in treating Suzie's OCD symptoms and related anxiety. Treatment gains were maintained at 12 months post-treatment and appeared to have been maintained when the child was informally interviewed 2 years after treatment. In addition to a subsidence of OCD symptoms, the previously observed blinking behaviors that were thought to be a tic disorder had remitted entirely. Medication was tapered and eventually discontinued after treatment termination.

These results are consistent with other reports that support the use of combined CBT, exposure therapy, and parent training in the treatment of childhood OCD (e.g., Knox, Albano, & Barlow, 1996; Mendlowitz, et al., 1999; Piacentini, Bergman, Jacobs, McCracken, & Kretchman, 2002; Walters, et al., 2001). Suzie's treatment success was likely due to the many facets of the CBT treatment intervention, as well as the exposure therapy she practiced at home with her parents. Although it

TABLE 9.2   CDI T-Scores Across Time

CDI	Total Score	Negative Mood	Interpersonal Problems	Ineffectiveness	Anhedonia	Negative Self-Esteem
Initial Assessment	40	45	45	41	38	46
Pretreatment	46	45	67	41	38	57
Post-Treatment	37	40	45	41	38	40
6 Months	37	40	45	41	38	40
12 Months	39	40	45	41	38	40

may be preferable to conduct exposure therapy during treatment sessions, especially with adults, family members can be useful allies in conducting exposure therapy at home in the environment where OCD behaviors occur. In Suzie's case, the parents were able to facilitate exposure to her sister and other objects that appeared to be evoking anxiety in the child. A clear advantage of this approach is the apparent generalizability of treatment effects to an ecologically valid and relevant setting (Rapee, Wignall, Hudson, & Schniering, 2000).

Although ERP remains a key element in the treatment of OCD, training in coping strategies and cognitive restructuring techniques is crucial to the successful management of OCD, especially when addressing obsessions. The cognitive component of CBT focuses on the modification of distorted beliefs or thoughts. For example, the central theme in Suzie's belief system was perceived harm to others as well as herself and her perceived responsibility for preventing the harm. Distress arises because of the belief that one could be responsible to the lives of others (Van Noppen & Steketee, 2001). Although an ERP exercise could be developed to address the behavior, at the cognitive level, she would need to focus on the residual doubt. One caveat in working with children, however, is that once beliefs are tested, children will often say that the "bad thing" didn't occur because they performed the ritualistic behavior in their head, and not because they did not perform the ritual, per se. Thus, the child's underlying beliefs need to be challenged. Also, automatic thoughts often act as triggers for a particular behavior, and therefore by addressing the underlying obsession, the child can change her reaction (i.e., emotional response) to the thought and thus change her behavior (ritual or avoidance). In the process of challenging thoughts, children are taught that changes in thoughts produce changes in behavior and feelings. The reciprocal nature of this relationship between feelings, thoughts, and behaviors is addressed through the "triangle connection" (Figure 9.2).

An additional benefit of a group therapy program is that children have the opportunity to benefit from observation of their peers and peer feedback. As part of the group sessions, peers helped other group members challenge their obsessions and helped design ERP plans. This method not only educated the child in how to identify specific target behaviors but facilitated the development of more sophisticated exposure plans. It is noteworthy that the ERP plans developed by the children were often more challenging than those developed by the therapists. In addition, there was generally greater child compliance with peer-developed ERPs compared to therapist-developed ERPs. This group of children was also quick to use verbal praise for successfully addressing a problem and in doing so, reinforce appropriate behavior. Thus, peer recognition and support were strong motivators for the children to successfully complete their respective ERP plans. Anecdotally, Suzie said she was relieved that others struggled with concerns similar to hers and acknowledged a strong in-group identification with the other children. Of interest, her parents made similar comments about their parent training group.

Group ERPs are relatively easy to design given that many children suffer from topographically and functionally similar OCD behaviors and psychosocial issues

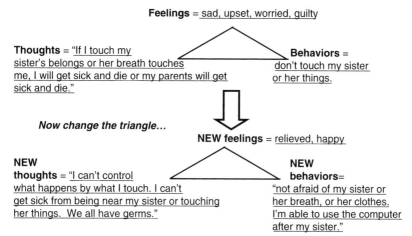

FIGURE 9.2 "The Triangle Connection."

related to the disorder. For example, one of Suzie's ERPs involved touching her sister's pajamas. To address her anxiety, some of her sister's clothing was brought to the group leader's office and used during treatment. While Suzie went through a graded process of touching the pajamas, holding them, placing them over her clothing, and then wearing them for the balance of the session, other children in the group were learning by observation to touch "contaminated" clothing items.

The combined effect of in-session and home-based exposure therapy was an important feature of the treatment program. Homework ERPs occurred every day through the week between sessions. For example, Suzie's parents created a hierarchy of fears related to her sister and implemented a graded exposure protocol. Suzie was required to sit in a chair previously occupied by her sister, touch objects her sister had touched, place her clothing together with her sister's clothing in the washing machine, allow her sister to touch objects in her room, wear clothing belonging to her sister for increasingly longer periods, sit beside her sister at home and in the family car, hold her sister's hand, and finally, hug her sister. Mastery of fears at lower levels of a hierarchy often result in more rapid resolution of more difficult steps (Bouchard, et al., 2004), and this was the result in Suzie's case. From a family systems perspective, both Suzie and her parents actively collaborated in the design and implementation of the ERP and practiced how to challenge Suzie's associated fears. These strategies allowed Suzie to benefit from ERP while strengthening her family relationships.

Not every ERP runs smoothly, especially in the initial stages. Most parents report that the child does not engage as willingly in the exposure tasks at home as compared to the hospital or clinic. Therefore it is important that much of the discussion in the parent training group address this issue before any home-based interventions. Equally important is that parents reinforce their child in the use of cognitive restructuring techniques before and after each ERP (Bouchard, et al., 2004). Children usually don't seek treatment on their own; they are generally brought to treatment by their parents. A frequent question that arises is their motivation for change; as long as parents are accommodating their behaviors, why would they want to do something that would, in the initial stages, increase their anxiety or distress? Another challenge in therapy is that ERP tasks are often too difficult for children to engage in because they do not want to risk that the feared outcome will occur. There may be some recognition by the child that they need to challenge their worries by demonstrating to themselves the fear is irrational, but this is generally not realistic or possible with children without providing some external motivator to initiate and maintain the process. Children can be motivated to attempt difficult tasks when their effort is rewarded. Suzie's parents regularly encouraged their daughter to complete cognitive restructuring worksheets from the workbook.

Immediately before treatment termination, Suzie's parents disclosed to other members of the parent training group a significant development in their marital relationship. Before treatment, their lives were chaotic and their approaches to Suzie so inconsistent that their marriage was in turmoil and on the verge of failing. The parent training sessions had taught them to work together as a cohesive unit, provided guidance on how to set appropriate limits, and helped them identify when they were enabling Suzie's OCD behaviors. They had come to understand their contribution to the problem and now viewed their relationship as a partnership. Success generated more success in both their child's life and other family interactions. They reported a dramatic decrease in the frequency of marital discord and their relationship continued to strengthen. The emotional tone of the entire family unit shifted to a more positive note as Suzie continued to make progress.

Although most studies demonstrate post-treatment success using CBT techniques, fewer have addressed the question of longer term follow-up evaluation. Treatment gains for Suzie were maintained at 12 months post-treatment, with some anecdotal evidence of treatment maintenance at 24 months. Her parents reported that they continued to "test" her fears by randomly exposing her to previously feared situations. For example, they periodically asked her to touch her sister's clothes and do the laundry. They also offered incentives for continuing to use the strategies she learned in the group and reminded her that her binder was available as a reference if she ever needed it.

Twenty-four months later, Suzie has maintained her treatment gains. She is symptom-free, doing exceptionally well in school, has earned a purple belt in martial arts, and has attended sleepover camp. Her parents now describe her relationship with her sister as "normal," and they borrow one another's clothes on a regular basis. There is no reason to believe these gains will not be maintained well into the future.

REFERENCES

Albano, A.M., & Silverman, W.K. (1996). *The anxiety disorders interview schedule for children for DSM-IV: Clinician manual (child & parent versions).* San Antonio, TX: Psychological Corporation.

American Psychiatric Association. (2000). Diagnostic and statistical manual of mental disorders. (4th ed.) Washington, D.C.: American Psychiatric Association.

Apter, A., Fallon, T.J., King, R.A., Ratzoni, G., Zohar, A.H., Binder, M., Weizman, A., Leckman, J.F., Pauls, D.L., Kron, S., & Cohen, D.J. (1996). Behaviour therapy for obsessive-compulsive disorder: a decade of progress. *Journal of the American Academy of Child and Adolescent Psychiatry, 35,* 907—912.

Astra, R.L., & Singg, S. (2000). The role of self-esteem in affiliation. *Journal of Psychology, 134*(1), 15–22.

Baer, L. (1992). Behavior therapy for obsessive-compulsive disorder and trichotillomania: Implications for Tourette syndrome. In T.N. Chase, A.J. Friedhoff, & D.J. Cohen (Eds.), *Tourette Syndrome: Genetics, Neurobiology, and Treatment* (pp. 333–340) New York: Raven Press.

Barrett, P.M., Dadds, M.R., & Rapee, R.M. (1996). Family treatment of childhood anxiety: A controlled trial. *Journal of Consulting and Clinical Psychology, 64*(2),333–342.

Bolton, D., Collins, S., & Steinberg, D. (1983). The treatment of obsessive-compulsive disorder in adolescence: a report of fifteen cases. *British Journal of Psychiatry, 142,*456–464

Brown, T.A., & Barlow, D.H. (1995), Long-term outcome in cognitive-behavioral treatment of panic disorder: Clinical predictors and alternative strategies for assessment. *Journal of Consulting and Clinical Psychology, 63,* 754–765

Bouchard, S., Mendlowitz, S.L., Coles, M.E., & Franklin, M. (2004). Considerations in the use of exposure with children. *Cognitive and Behavioral Practice, 11,* 56–65.

Flament, M.F., Whitaker, A., Rapoport, J.L., Davies, M., Berg, C.Z., Kalikow, K., et al. (1988), Obsessive-compulsive disorder in adolescence: An epidemiological study. *Journal of the American Academy of Child and Adolescent Psychiatry, 27,* 764–771.

Franklin, M.E., Kozak, J., Cashman, L.A., Coles, M.E., Rheingold, A..A., & Foa, E.B. (1998). Cognitive-behavioral treatment of pediatric obsessive-compulsive disorder: An open clinical trial. *Journal of the American Academy of Child and Adolescent Psychiatry, 37,* 412–419.

Gravitz, H.L. (1998). *Obsessive Compulsive Disorder: New Help for the Family.* Santa Barbara, California: Healing Visions Press.

Piacentini, J. (1999). Cognitive behavior therapy of childhood OCD. *Child and Adolescent Psychiatric Clinics of North America, 8*(3), 599–616.

Knox, L.S., Albano, A.M., & Barlow, D.H. (1996). Parental involvement in the treatment of childhood obsessive-compulsive disorder: A multiple baseline examination incorporating parents. *Behavior Therapy, 27,* 93–114.

Kovacs, M. (1983). *The Children's Depression Inventory: A self-rated depression scale for school-aged youngsters.* Toronto: Multi-Health Systems, Inc.

March, J.S. (1997). *Multidimensional anxiety scale for children.* Toronto: Multi-Health Systems, Inc.

March, J.S., Franklin, M., Nelson, A., & Foa, E. (2001). Cognitive-behavioral psychotherapy for pediatric obsessive-compulsive disorder. *Journal of Clinical and Child Psychology, 30*(1), 8–18.

March, J.S., & Mulle, K. (1998). *OCD in Children and Adolescents: A Cognitive-Behavioral Treatment Manual.* New York: Guilford Press.

March, J.S., Mulle, K., & Herbel, B. (1994). Behavioral psychotherapy for children and adolescents with obsessive-compulsive disorder: An open trial of a new protocol-driven treatment package. *Journal of the American Academy of Child and Adolescent Psychiatry, 33,*333–341.

Marks, I. (1997). Behaviour therapy for obsessive-compulsive disorder: A decade of progress. *Canadian Journal of Psychiatry, 42,* 1021–1027.

Marks, I., & O'Sullivan, G. (1988). Drugs and psychological treatments for agoraphobia/panic and obsessive-compulsive disorders: A review. *British Journal of Psychiatry, 153,* 650–658.

McLean, P.D., Whittal, M.L., Sochting, I., Koch, W.J., Paterson, R., Thordarson, D.S., et al. (2001). Cognitive versus behavior therapy in the group treatment of obsessive-compulsive disorder. *Journal of Consulting Clinical Psychology, 69,* 205–214.

Mendlowitz, S.L. (2001). Step on a crack. (Unpublished manuscript).

Mendlowitz, S, & Saltzman, J. (1999). Cognitive-behavioral group therapy for adolescents with OCD: An open clinical trial. 20th National Conference ADAA, March 23–26, 2000. (Poster presentation).

Mendlowitz, S.L., Manassis, K., Bradley, S., Scapillato, D., Miezitis, S., & Shaw, B.F. (1999). Cognitive-behavioral group treatments in childhood anxiety disorders: The role of parental involvement. *Journal of the American Academy of Child and Adolescent Psychiatry, 38,*1223–1229.

Mendlowitz, S.L., Shulman, I., & Spenser, H. (2001). Lucky charms, little habits,why can't I just snap out of it. (Unpublished manuscript).

Piacentini, J. (1999). Cognitive behavior therapy of childhood OCD. *Child and Adolescent Psychiatric Clinics of North America, 8*(3), 599–616.

Piacentini, J., Bergman, R.L., Jacobs, C., McCracken, J., & Kretchman, J. (2002). Open trial of cognitive behavior therapy for childhood obsessive compulsive disorder. *Journal of Anxiety Disorders, 16,* 207–219.

Rapee, R.M., Wignall, A., Hudson, J.L., & Schniering, C.A. (2000). *Treating anxious children and adolescents: An evidence-based approach.* Oakland, CA: New Harbinger Publications.

Silverman, W.K., & Kurtines, W.M. (1996). Transfer of control: A psychosocial intervention model for internalizing disorders in youth. In E.D. Hibbs & P.S. Jensen (Eds.), *Psychosocial treatments for child and adolescent disorders: Empirically based strategies for clinical practice* (pp. 63 – 81). Washington, D.C.: American Psychological Association.

Silverman, W.K., Kurtines, W.M., Ginsburg, G.S., Weems, C.F., Lumpkin, P.W., & Carmichael, D.H. (1999). Treating anxiety disorders in children with group cognitive-behavior therapy: A randomized clinical trial. *Journal of Consulting and Clinical Psychology, 76,* 995–1003

Thienemann, M., Martin, J., Cregger, B., Thompson, H.B., & Dyer-Friedman, J. (2001). Manual-driven group cognitive-behavioral therapy for adolescents with obsessive-compulsive disorder: A pilot study. *Journal of the American Academy of Child and Adolescent Psychiatry, 40,*1254–1260.

Thomsen, P.H. (1994). Children and adolescents with obsessive-compulsive disorder: An analysis of sociodemographic background. *Psychopathology, 27,* 303–311.

Valleni-Baile, L.A., Garrison, C.Z., Jackson, K.L., Waller J.L., McKeown, R.E., Addy, C.L., & Cuffe, S.P. (1994). Frequency of obsessive-compulsive disorder in a community sample of young adolescents. *Journal of the American Academy of Child and Adolescent Psychiatry, 33,* 782–791.

Van Noppen, B.L. & Steketee, G. (2001). Individual, group and multifamily cognitive-behavioral treatments. In M.T. Pato & J. Zohar (Eds.), *Current treatments of obsessive-compulsive disorder* (2nd ed.). Washington DC: American Psychiatric Publishing, p. 134–172.

Walters, T.L., Barrett, P.M., & March, J.S. (2001). The role of the family in childhood obsessive-compulsive disorder. *Clinical Child and Family Psychology Review, 3*(3), 173–84.

Zohar, A.H., Ratzoni, G., Pauls, D.L., Apter, A., Bleich, A., Kron, S., et al. (1992). An epidemiological study of obsessive-compulsive disorder and related disorders in Israeli adolescents. *Journal of the American Academy of Child and Adolescent Psychiatry, 31,*1057–1061.

CHAPTER 10

Exposure Treatments for Panic Disorder with and without Agoraphobia

Ellen I. Koch
Eastern Michigan University

Andrew T. Gloster
Technical University of Dresden, Germany

Stacey A. Waller
West Virginia University

Panic disorder is characterized by recurrent unexpected panic attacks that create intense fear or discomfort and involve at least four symptoms that develop quickly (peaking within 10 minutes). Panic attack symptoms include tachycardia (accelerated heart rate); sweating; trembling; dyspnea (shortness of breath); a feeling of choking; chest pain; nausea; dizziness or light-headedness; derealization or depersonalization; fear of losing control, going crazy, or dying; paresthesias (numbness or tingling sensations); and chills or hot flushes. Also, at least one panic attack must be followed by persistent concern of having another attack, worry about physical sensations or potential consequences, or significant changes in behavior. Agoraphobia is characterized by anxiety about being in places or situations where escape would be difficult or help would not be available in the event of a panic attack (e.g., being away from home alone, in a crowd or standing in line, on a bridge, or traveling by bus, train, or automobile). Problematic situations are avoided or endured with intense distress (American Psychiatric Association, 2000).

Modern behavioral researchers have developed a model for the etiology of panic disorder and agoraphobia (Barlow, 2002; Bouton, Mineka, & Barlow, 2001). Specifically, individuals who develop panic are hypothesized to have a generalized biological vulnerability to respond emotionally to events and a

The authors wish to thank Christie Hosek for her assistance with preparing this chapter.

Handbook of Exposure Therapies

generalized psychological propensity to become anxious. In addition, heightened anxiety sensitivity contributes to misinterpretations of normal somatic sensations as dangerous. Hypervigilance of somatic sensations and apprehension of future panic attacks subsequently increase anxiety and the likelihood of panic recurrence (see Barlow, 2002, for a more detailed explanation).

Individuals with panic disorder are fearful of both symptoms and the potential consequences of an attack. Catastrophic misinterpretations of physiological responses cause many individuals to present at the emergency room. Given that panic symptoms mimic other medical conditions, a full medical examination is often conducted before commencing psychological or psychopharmacological treatment.

In addition to physical symptoms, avoidance behavior is a hallmark of panic disorder. Typically, individuals with panic disorder will avoid any situations, settings, or behaviors that have been associated with panic in the past. Over time, avoidance behaviors generalize to broad classes of stimuli. For example, White and Barlow (2002) note that individuals with panic disorder may avoid "substances (e.g., caffeine, alcohol, taking medication) or physical activities (e.g., exercise, sexual activity) that produce somatic sensations resembling the symptoms associated with panic" (p. 330). Avoidance behaviors are often complemented by compensatory protective measures meant to increase subjective feelings of safety and provide a contingency plan in the event of a panic attack. For example, individuals may engage in preemptive safety behaviors or rituals (e.g., always carrying a water bottle, having immediate access to anxiolytic medication, chewing gum), confront feared situations only in the presence of a preferred "safety person," or distract themselves to stem burgeoning panic attacks. According to White and Barlow (2002), about half (46%) of individuals with panic disorder and agoraphobia report having at least one safety-seeking strategy and 24% have two. The three most common safety-seeking strategies include immediate access to anxiety medication (48%), food or drink (14%), and bags, bracelets, or other personally relevant objects (6%).

Whereas a full-blown panic attack involves marked somatic changes (i.e., increase in blood pressure, heart rate), individuals with agoraphobia also report significant anticipatory anxiety surrounding availability of help should a panic attack occur. Situations where escape is difficult or where a panic attack would be embarrassing frequently elicit the most anxiety (e.g., on an airplane or bridge, or in a crowd or traffic jam) and are avoided at all costs or endured with significant distress. In many ways, the situational specificity of these fears looks remarkably similar to a phobic reaction and differential diagnosis can be challenging. However, understanding the function of the avoidance behavior can help pinpoint the correct diagnosis. For example, an individual with a fear of flying may report very specific catastrophic imagery about a plane crashing. However, a person with panic disorder and agoraphobia may report that the fear of having a panic attack in the cabin of the airplane is of greater concern than the potential for a plane crash. For more details about specific assessment procedures utilized for panic disorder and agoraphobia, see White and Barlow (2002).

INTEROCEPTIVE EXPOSURE

The primary fear for individuals with panic disorder concerns their physical symptoms and the misinterpretation of somatic sensations as more dangerous than they actually are. Systematic exposure to the bodily sensations that occur during a panic attack, referred to as interoceptive exposure, was developed by Barlow and colleagues (Barlow & Cerny, 1988; Barlow, Cohen, Waddell, Vermilyea, Kloska, Blanchard, et al., 1984; Barlow & Craske, 2000; Barlow, Craske, Cerny, & Klosko, 1989). Examples of interoceptive exposure exercises that produce somatic sensations similar to those that occur during a panic attack include head shaking, head lifting, running in place, breath holding, body tensing, spinning, hyperventilating, straw breathing, and staring (Barlow & Craske, 2000). These exercises can be completed within-session or as homework assignments.

As with all exposure-based treatments, interoceptive exposure exercises are individually titrated or modified to achieve the desired physiological response. Exercises are also presented at a mild intensity level to provide exposure without creating undue anxiety (e.g., running in place for a few minutes at a time; Barlow & Craske, 2000). Interoceptive exposure exercises typically do not use graded hierarchies and appear to be most effective when strong sensations are evoked (White & Barlow, 2002). Although individuals can discontinue the exposure session at any time, patients are generally encouraged to continue as long as possible. From a therapeutic standpoint, ceasing an interoceptive exposure session prevents the person from acquiring new information regarding the harmlessness of normal somatic sensations. In addition, prematurely ceasing a session reinforces escape behavior and increases the chance that the patient will attribute failure to a personal defect. Not surprisingly, each instance of premature escape makes subsequent sessions more difficult to complete. Conversely, completion of an interoceptive exposure session often causes patients to realize that the feared outcome will not occur and that avoidance behaviors are not necessary.

Two studies have compared interoceptive exposure to alternative treatments (Ito, De Araujo, Tess, De Barros-Neto, Asbahr, & Marks, 2001; Arntz, 2002). Ito, et al. (2001) compared three groups: interoceptive exposure, in vivo exposure, and a combination of interoceptive exposure and in vivo exposure within a self-exposure format for panic disorder with agoraphobia. All three treatment groups significantly improved with gains maintained at a 1-year follow-up period. No differences were found among treatment conditions. Arntz (2002) compared interoceptive exposure plus in vivo exposure to a cognitive therapy intervention that included exposure without habituation to bodily sensations. Both treatment groups improved without any significant differences between treatments in terms of dropout, panic frequency, anxiety levels, mean responses to fear and anxiety questionnaires, and medication use.

IN VIVO EXPOSURE

If agoraphobia is present, in vivo exposure is often added to cognitive and behavioral interventions. The focus of in vivo exposure is systematic and repeated contact with avoided situations. The first step in the treatment process involves creating an exposure hierarchy where the patient identifies a variety of avoided situations that produce a range of distress when confronted. Exposure sessions can vary in intensity and whether they are therapist-directed or self-directed, massed or spaced (see White & Barlow, 2002 and later for more information).

Efficacy of Cognitive-Behavioral Treatments for Panic Disorder and Agoraphobia

A variety of cognitive and behavioral interventions have been used with and without medication for treatment of panic disorder and agoraphobia. In an attempt to classify the efficacy of various procedures, Chambless, Baker, Baucom, Beutler, Calhoun, Crits-Christoph, et al. (1998) developed specific criteria for empirically-supported treatments. A treatment is classified as "well-established" when at least two experiments (1) demonstrate superiority over a placebo or another treatment or is equivalent to an already established treatment, (2) use treatment manuals, (3) clearly specifies participant characteristics, and (4) when effects are demonstrated by two different investigators/investigatory teams. Procedures are rated as "probably efficacious" when two experiments are more effective than a wait-list control group or meet all but the last criterion for well-established treatments.

Two predominant psychosocial procedures for panic disorder have been recognized as well-established and empirically supported treatments: panic control treatment (Barlow & Craske, 2000) and cognitive therapy (Salkovskis & Clark, 1991). For agoraphobic avoidance, in vivo exposure is also considered a well-established and empirically supported treatment (Chambless, et al., 1998). No other psychosocial treatments for panic or agoraphobia have been accorded similar status (Chambless, et al., 1998). Also, the American Psychiatric Association practice guidelines recommend cognitive-behavioral treatments for panic disorder with "substantial clinical confidence" (1998).

PANIC CONTROL TREATMENT

The major elements of panic control treatment include psychoeducation, cognitive restructuring, breathing retraining, and interoceptive exposure exercises (Barlow & Craske, 2000). Psychoeducational exercises focus on helping the client to understand physiological reactions associated with anxiety, including the fight-or-flight response. The purpose of cognitive restructuring is to identify and challenge anxious thoughts and beliefs related to panic. Breathing retraining exercises are taught to counteract the exacerbating effects of hyperventilation. The main function of interoceptive exposure exercises, as noted earlier, is to provide experiential evidence that somatic sensations are not dangerous (White & Barlow, 2002).

COGNITIVE THERAPY

Cognitive therapy for panic disorder includes psychoeducation, cognitive restructuring, and behavioral experiments (Clark, Salkovskis, Hackmann, Middleton, Anastasiades, & Gelder, 1994). Psychoeducation helps clients understand the reciprocal effect catastrophic cognitions have on exacerbation of somatic sensations (Beck, Sokol, Clark, Berchick, & Wright, 1992). Cognitive restructuring includes identifying and challenging patients' interpretations of bodily sensations, substituting realistic interpretations of bodily sensations for catastrophic misinterpretations, and restructuring anxiety-related imagery. Behavioral techniques include inducing feared somatic sensations through hyperventilation, focusing attention on the body, or reading word pairs that describe feared sensations or catastrophes. A response prevention component is also commonly used (e.g., encouraging the patient not to cling to safety objects when feeling dizzy) to facilitate disconfirmation of negative predictions regarding the effects of symptoms (Clark, et al., 1994).

It should be apparent that both treatments include similar elements, although they differ in their respective emphases and the proposed mechanisms by which change is hypothesized to occur. For example, panic control treatment emphasizes extinction training through interoceptive exposure, whereas cognitive therapy has used cognitive restructuring techniques to modify catastrophic misinterpretations of somatic sensations. In truth, both approaches likely effect change through similar mechanisms of action. Both procedures address misinterpretations of body sensations and use evidence from interoceptive exposure or behavioral experiments to counteract these beliefs. Also, both treatment programs incorporate in vivo exposure to address agoraphobic avoidance.

TREATMENT EFFICACY

Meta-Analyses

Four meta-analyses of cognitive-behavioral and medication interventions for panic disorder have been published (Chambless & Gillis, 1993; Clum, Clum, & Surls, 1993; Gould, Otto, & Pollack, 1995; Westen & Morrison, 2001). Exposure constituted a significant portion of the treatment protocol in each meta-analysis, although cognitive restructuring and psychoeducation techniques were also included within the treatment packages.

Chambless and Gillis (1993) reviewed cognitive-behavioral treatment studies for generalized anxiety, panic disorder with and without agoraphobia, and social phobia. For panic disorder, they concluded that 72% of clients were panic free at post-test after a combination of exposure and cognitive strategies versus 25% of individuals in wait-list and pill placebo control groups (Chambless & Gillis, 1993). Large effect sizes (based on Glass's delta) were also found for cognitive-based interventions without significant exposure components (see Chambless & Gillis, 1993, for more details).

In Gould, et al.'s (1995) meta-analysis, 19 studies were reviewed that used cognitive-behavioral treatment components (including exposure, exposure plus cognitive restructuring, exposure plus relaxation, cognitive restructuring plus interoceptive exposure with and without relaxation, etc.) without pharmacotherapy. Despite the variety of procedures used, an overall mean Glass's delta effect size of 0.68 was found. The mean effect size for panic frequency reduction was 0.58, with 74.3% of participants panic-free, whereas only 27.1% of control subjects (conditions consisted of wait-list, psychological placebo, and supportive therapy) were panic-free. The overall attrition rate was 5.6% for treatment and 7.2% for controls, which is significantly better than the 19.8% dropout rate for any pharmacological intervention, and 32.5% for pill placebo control groups. In the seven studies that used interoceptive exposure and cognitive restructuring, Gould, et al. (1995) found a mean overall Glass's delta effect size of 0.88, with a mean effect size for reduction in panic frequency of 0.66 compared to wait-list or supportive therapy control conditions. The authors concluded that "CBT [cognitive-behavioral therapy] interventions that include a combination of cognitive restructuring and exposure elements appear to be the most effective" (Gould, et al., 1995, p. 836).

In a more recent meta-analysis, Westen and Morrison (2001) found that 82.4% of individuals with panic disorder improved because of various treatment procedures including cognitive therapy, interoceptive exposure, relaxation, and in vivo exposure. Preeffect to posteffect sizes were very large for panic control treatment (Cohen's $d = 2.2$) and large (Cohen's $d = 0.6$ to 1.9) for cognitive therapy. Portions of these treatments also produced large to very large effect sizes for prechanges to postchanges, including panic education (1.0), exposure (0.9), cognitive restructuring (3.2), and relaxation (0.5). Of the 17 studies reviewed, two provided information regarding the percentage of participants that maintained their gains from treatment for at least 12 to 18 months (85.5%), and 54% remained improved after 2 years (Westen & Morrison, 2001).

COMBINED COGNITIVE-BEHAVIORAL AND PSYCHOPHARMACOLOGICAL INTERVENTIONS

Finally, cognitive-behavioral interventions for panic have been combined with antidepressant and anxiolytic medications. An early review by Clum (1989) indicated that behavior therapies were generally more effective than pharmacological agents, especially at reducing rates of relapse; however, this review was completed before the development of the widely used selective serotonin reuptake inhibitors (SSRIs). Complicating matters is the fact that participants were more likely to drop out of medication and placebo trials (except for benzodiazepines) than exposure or behavior therapy. Also, individuals with agoraphobia were more likely to drop out than those with panic disorder only (Clum, 1989).

Clum, et al. (1993) conducted the first meta-analysis comparing psychological and pharmacological treatments for panic disorder. Specifically psychosocial interventions consisting of exposure, psychological coping (including instructions to confront the feared situations), and a combination of cognitive-behavioral techniques and medication were all more effective than benzodiazepines and other drugs alone. Additionally, panic disorder with agoraphobia interventions involving exposure were superior to cognitive restructuring alone. Finally, Clum, et al. (1993) found significant reductions in Glass's delta effect sizes when exposure alone or exposure plus placebo were used as comparison conditions indicating the power of the exposure procedures as an active portion of treatment and the lack of incremental improvement when comparing exposure to other treatment procedures.

Gould, et al. (1995) also included pharmacological interventions and combined cognitive-behavioral therapy (CBT) treatment with medication in their meta-analysis (see Gould, et al., 1995 for pharmacotherapy-only interventions that do not include cognitive or behavioral treatment components). Cognitive-behavioral procedures produced the highest mean effect size (Glass's Δ = 0.68), followed by combined CBT and pharmacotherapy (Glass's Δ = 0.56), and pharmacotherapy only (Glass's Δ = 0.47). The effect size for CBT was significantly higher than that for pharmacotherapy and produced higher panic-free rates (70%) compared to pharmacotherapy (57%). Gould, et al. (1995) also found higher attrition rates (22.0%) for combined cognitive-behavioral and medication interventions similar to other medication and pill placebo conditions. There was evidence that cognitive-behavioral completers maintained their treatment gains and were less likely to relapse than those in medication conditions. Finally, imipramine and group CBT were identified as the most cost-effective interventions (Gould, et al., 1995). In conclusion, Gould, et al. (1995) remarked, "there appears to be no convincing evidence to call into question the effectiveness of CBT for patients with panic disorder" (p. 835).

IN VIVO EXPOSURE FOR AGORAPHOBIA

An early review of behavioral treatments for agoraphobia found that approximately 60–70% of individuals treated with in vivo exposure showed clinically significant improvements in agoraphobia symptoms at post-test and 6-month follow-up period. Better experimental support was also found for treatments that used more direct exposure techniques (Jansson & Öst, 1982).

Two studies attempted to partial out the impact of in vivo exposure and cognitive restructuring for agoraphobia (van den Hout, Arntz, & Hoekstra, 1994; Burke, Drummond, & Johnston, 1997). Both studies found that the addition of cognitive restructuring did not improve the effectiveness of in vivo exposure. In the study by van den Hout, et al. (1994), cognitive therapy reduced the frequency of panic attacks initially, but not symptoms of agoraphobia, anxiety, or depression. These symptoms were significantly reduced after in vivo exposure; however, the small sample size (van den Hout, et al., 1994; Burke, et al., 1997) and attrition rate (Burke, et al., 1997) of these studies prevent drawing firm conclusions.

Several other treatment studies have compared exposure-based procedures with various interventions. One such comparison by Öst, Westling, and Hellström (1993) found no significant differences between applied relaxation, in vivo exposure, and cognitive therapy at 1-year follow-up evaluation, except that more individuals in the cognitive therapy group sought additional treatment before the follow-up period. Murphy, Michelson, Marchione, Marchione, and Testa (1998) compared cognitive therapy plus in vivo exposure, relaxation plus in vivo exposure, and in vivo exposure alone. All three treatments were administered in a group format, and all participants completed self-directed exposure assignments as homework. Unlike other studies, participants with chronic and severe agoraphobia were included in the sample. All groups significantly improved over time, with cognitive therapy plus in vivo exposure superior to relaxation plus in vivo exposure on anxiety measures (Murphy, et al., 1998).

Barlow, Gorman, Shear, and Woods (2000) recently completed a very large ($N = 312$) double-blind, placebo-controlled, clinical trial across four sites. The treatment groups included imipramine only, panic control treatment (PCT)-only, placebo-only, PCT plus imipramine, and PCT plus placebo. Participants received 3 months of active treatment and responders entered a 6-month maintenance phase involving monthly appointments. Treatment was discontinued for maintenance phase responders and these individuals were reassessed after 6 months (15 months post-treatment initiation).

After acute treatment, imipramine was significantly superior to placebo for both the acute phase completers (global response rate 78.4% and 64.3%, respectively) and intent-to-treat sample (48.7% and 37.5%) in reducing panic disorder symptom severity. However, the imipramine group experienced higher attrition rates for adverse effects than the placebo group. Also, the combination of PCT and imipramine was better at reducing panic severity than PCT alone for both the completer (global response rate 89.1% and 74.5%, respectively) and intent-to-treat (64.1% and 53.9%) samples. In the intent-to-treat sample only, PCT was significantly better than placebo in reducing symptom severity (global response rate 53.9% and 37.5%). No other comparisons were significantly different after acute treatment.

At the end of the maintenance phase, the combination of PCT and imipramine was significantly better at reducing panic symptoms than PCT plus placebo and PCT-only for both the completer and intent-to-treat samples. Also, PCT plus imipramine was superior to imipramine alone in the intent-to-treat sample only. In terms of single treatments, both PCT and imipramine alone were superior to placebo for the intent-to-treat sample. Responders for clinician rating of global severity (based on the intent-to-treat sample) were significantly different between PCT plus imipramine and imipramine-only (response rate 56.3% and 37.8%, respectively), PCT-only and placebo (42.1% and 13.0%), and imipramine-only and placebo (37.8% and 13.0%).

The outcome of the follow-up assessment produced different results. Specifically, the PCT plus placebo and PCT-only groups were significantly superior to PCT plus imipramine for panic symptom severity in the completer sample only. Also, PCT-only was superior to placebo for the intent-to-treat sample based on panic symptom severity response rate (32.4% compared to 9.1%). In terms of single interventions, both PCT and imipramine were superior to placebo after the treatment and maintenance phases for the intent-to-treat analyses, but (after discontinuing treatment) at follow-up evaluation, only PCT was superior to placebo. No significant differences were found between the PCT and imipramine-only groups at any point. For combined treatments, PCT plus imipramine was superior to PCT-only during treatment and maintenance for the completer and intent-to-treat samples. However, this difference was no longer significant at follow-up evaluation, and the combination of PCT and imipramine was significantly worse than PCT-only within the completer sample. Also, PCT plus imipramine was superior to PCT plus placebo during maintenance, and the opposite was true at follow-up evaluation. Finally, PCT plus imipramine was significantly better than imipramine-only at maintenance.

This study demonstrated that PCT and imipramine are equally superior over placebo for panic disorder with PCT resulting in less relapse (4% compared to 25% for imipramine) over time. Also, the combination of PCT and imipramine produced little benefit over either treatment alone. The authors concluded that PCT may be more durable and somewhat better tolerated when not combined with medication (Barlow, et al., 2000).

GROUP DISMANTLING STUDIES FOR PANIC CONTROL TREATMENT

A dismantling study conducted by Schmidt, Woolaway-Bickel, Trakowski, Santiago, Storey, Koselka, et al. (2000) assessed the added benefit of the breathing retraining component in PCT. Participants were assigned to PCT (including psychoeducation, cognitive therapy, interoceptive exposure, and in vivo exposure) with or without breathing retraining or a wait-list condition. The treatments were administered within a group format. Both active treatments resulted in significant improvements over wait-list at post-treatment and follow-up evaluation and no differences were found between the treatments.

Craske, Rowe, Lewin, and Noriega-Dimitri (1997) also compared cognitive restructuring and in vivo exposure with either interoceptive exposure or breathing retraining for agoraphobia within a group format. Inclusion of interoceptive exposure was associated with reduced panic frequency and decreased overall severity/impairment at post-test. At follow-up evaluation, the group that received interoceptive exposure also reported reduced panic frequency, fear of social situations, general anxiety, and overall severity/impairment (Craske, et al., 1997).

One study has looked at the ability of noncognitive-behavioral therapists to implement PCT in a managed care setting. Addis, Hatgis, Krasnow, Jacob, Bourne, and Mansfield, (2004) compared PCT to treatment-as-usual for individuals with panic disorder. Both treatment groups improved from pretest to post-test, with the PCT group showing greater change. Clinically significant improvement occurred for 42.9% of the PCT group participants and 18.8% of the treatment-as-usual group (Addis, et al., 2004). However, the results are less impressive when compared to the 73% response rate for PCT reported by Barlow, et al. (2000).

Innovations in Exposure Therapy for Panic and Agoraphobia

The documented success of exposure therapy in the treatment of panic and agoraphobia over the last 20 years has led some to proclaim that a first plateau in treatment development has been achieved (Barlow & Lehman, 1996) and that future research should address issues of treatment delivery and dissemination (Antony, 2002; Hofmann & Spiegel, 1999). Indeed, many innovations and adaptations of CBT for panic and agoraphobia have been studied. These include the administration of treatment via group therapy (Lidren, Watkins, Gould, Clum, Asterino, & Tulloch, 1994), the use of bibliotherapy as an adjunct to treatment (Côté, Gauthier, Laberge, Cormier, & Plamondon, 1994; Lidren, et al., 1994), intensive and massed exposure procedures (Hahlweg, Fiegenbaum, Frank, Schroeder, & von Witzleben, 2001), enlisting the help of family members (Byrne, Carr, & Clark, 2004; Gore & Carter, 2003), briefer forms of CBT (Clark, Salkovskis, Hackmann, Wells, Ludgate, & Gelder, 1999; Craske, Maidenberg, & Bystritsky, 1995), and technological innovations. With the exception of technology-enhanced interventions, these innovations have been reviewed elsewhere (see Barlow, 2002; Byrne, et al., 2004; Hofmann & Spiegel, 1999). Therefore we concentrate here on the progress and potential of technologically enhanced exposure treatments for panic and agoraphobia.

Technological Enhancements

Handheld Computers

Advances in computer technology have spurred innovative therapeutic applications. An example is the use of handheld computers as an adjunct to traditional therapy. For instance, handheld computers have been programmed to facilitate numerous aspects of CBT, including self-monitoring, breathing retraining, cognitive restructuring, and exposure (Newman, Kenardy, Herman, & Taylor, 1997). With respect to exposure, handheld computers have been programmed to provide encouraging statements aimed at helping individuals complete self-directed exposure exercises. A clear advantage of this approach is that clients can interact with a readily available "computer coach" that can manage therapeutic homework assignments. Furthermore, sophisticated computer algorithms can provide differential feedback that is contingent on the individual's input.

Investigations of the efficacy and effectiveness of computer-augmented treatment for panic and agoraphobia have just started to appear in the literature (Kenardy, Dow, Johnston, Newman, Thomson, & Taylor, 2003; Newman, et al., 1997). Comparing three treatment groups, Kenardy, et al. (2003) found that a brief 6-week computer-augmented treatment led to clinically meaningful post-treatment improvements at a level above the brief 6-week therapist-guided treatment and below the standard 12-week therapist-guided treatment. Although group differences disappeared at the 6-month follow-up assessment, the data suggest that using handheld computers may accelerate reduction in panic symptoms.

Biofeedback

Another technological innovation relevant to the treatment of panic disorder has been the use of respiratory biofeedback for client breathing retraining. In an illustrative case study, Meuret, Wilhelm, and Roth (2004) used a biofeedback computer to train a patient with panic disorder to regulate her aberrant breathing. The procedure necessitated the wearing of a nasal cannula that had the serendipitous effect of exposing the woman to unusual, and initially feared, bodily sensations. In addition to the breathing retraining, the client engaged in exposure in vivo during the monitoring. The treatment was successful in reducing symptoms, although it was unclear which elements accounted for the most change. The approach may not be applicable for all patients with panic disorder, and further controlled research is clearly needed; it represents an innovative use of technology with exposure for panic disorder.

Computerized Self-Help

Another innovative treatment used a computer program to teach clients principles of exposure therapy and guide them through its implementation (Gega, Marks, & Mataix-Cols, 2004; Marks, Kenwright, McDonough, Whittaker, & Mataix-Cols, 2004). Computer-guided self-exposure took place in a clinic and included a program that presented a comprehensive treatment rationale, identified panic triggers, assigned exposure homework, discussed barriers to implementing exposure, trained participants in coping strategies for use during exposure, provided feedback on exposure homework, modified treatment goals, and addressed future problems via a troubleshooting algorithm. With respect to symptom change, there were non-significant differences between the computer-guided and therapist-led treatment, although a small sample size and its consequential effects on interpreting nonsignificant results made the finding difficult to interpret. There was also evidence of a higher attrition rate in the computer-guided condition relative to treatment–as usual. Despite methodological problems with the study, the use of computerized self-help programs represents a promising development as an adjunct to current treatment practice.

Virtual Reality

Virtual reality (VR) is a relatively new technology with much promise for mental health. Creation of virtual worlds can facilitate exposure to stimuli otherwise difficult to access or control. Moore, Wiederhold, Wiederhold, and Riva (2002) report the creation of numerous panic- and agoraphobia-related environments, including elevators, grocery stores, town squares, and so forth. One advantage of the virtual reality approach to exposure therapy is the amount of control therapists can exert over the virtual environment. For example, a virtual shopping market can be populated with virtual people or left completely vacant. Which virtual market should be used in the exposure session depends on the specific fears that a client might have about going out in public.

Virtual reality exposure therapy has been extensively evaluated with regard to phobic conditions (e.g., fear of flying, fear of heights), but it has yet to be thoroughly evaluated with respect to panic populations and compared to in vivo exposure. Furthermore, it is an empirical question as to whether controlled VR environments somehow act as a subtle safety signal to clients who choose it over in vivo exposure. That is, anxious clients may prefer VR over in vivo exposure because they perceive even the best technology as qualitatively different, more controllable, and less inherently "dangerous" than actual feared situations. In turn, generalizability of fear reduction from the virtual context to real-world situations may be reduced.

To date, only one controlled study has examined VR exposure therapy for panic disorder (Vincelli, Anolli, Bouchard, Widerhold, Zurloni, & Riva, 2003). The virtual environments included an elevator, a supermarket, a subway ride, and a large square. Each environment was varied in terms of the number of people present, size of the area, access to exits, and length of exposure. Participants in both the CBT and CBT plus VR groups significantly improved from baseline to post-test with no significant differences between treatments. Like much of the VR research literature, however, this study suffered from low power given the extremely small sample size (i.e., each group contained only four participants). Nonetheless, all treatment participants showed clinically significant improvement at post-test, whereas none of the wait-list control participants improved.

Internet-Assisted Therapy

Clients have accessed psychoeducational materials on the Internet for years. As Internet accessibility grows, however, so do the possibilities to augment and improve current treatments. For example, Kenwright and Marks (2004) adapted the presentation of their computer-aided exposure self-help system (see previously) so that clients who could not travel to their clinic could access it via the Internet. Although the Internet version of this program awaits evaluation of a randomized controlled trial, preliminary results based on the Fear Questionnaire suggest the equivalency of Internet and clinic-based access. Two other studies have successfully combined CBT via the Internet with therapist contact by email (Carlbring, Westling, Ljungstrand, Ekselius, & Andersson, 2001; Carlbring, Ekselius, & Andersson, 2003). The results of these studies are promising, particularly for individuals who may not be able to participate in other forms of treatment because of their agoraphobic fears.

The innovative work of Alcañiz, Botella, Banos, Perpina, Rey, Lozano, et al. (2003) illustrates how the power of the Internet can allow clients to use VR technologies to engage in virtual exposures from their home computers. Alcañiz, et al. (2003) developed several modules allowing the titration of external and interoceptive virtual stimuli, as well as the intensity and predictability of these stimuli. Stimulus manipulations included auditory presentation of varied cardiac rhythms and visual symptoms (e.g., tunnel vision, double vision). Access to individual modules was controlled by the therapist based on client progress. To date, the system has not been empirically validated. However, it has potential to facilitate exposure and may prove especially beneficial to initiate treatment with home-bound clients.

Teleconferencing

Conducting therapy exclusively via the telephone may be indicated for individuals whose geographical location prohibits access to clinical services. In the case of panic disorder with agoraphobia, teleconferencing may allow clients who are homebound to receive care (Swinson, Fergus, Cox, & Wickwire, 1995). To date, two studies have reported clinically significant improvement in panic disordered individuals treated via teleconferencing (McNamee, O'Sullivan, Lelliott, & Marks, 1989; Swinson, et al., 1995). With respect to exposure, McNamee, et al. (1989) is especially interesting in that significant differences between clients treated with exposure and those treated with relaxation were observed even though telephone contact was limited to 2 hours total across 12 weeks. Although these initial findings were promising, more studies are required to explore the feasibility of teleconferencing for clients with panic disorder. It is interesting to note the paucity of publications investigating teleconference-based exposure treatments for this population. Explanations for the lack of research in this area are necessarily multifactorial. Further, it cannot be assumed that the quantity of publications directly correlates with clinicians' behavior and therefore may misrepresent the frequency with which tele-conference-based exposure treatments are implemented in practice. To the degree that teleconference-based exposure treatment is underused with a home-bound population (i.e., agoraphobia), however, one must wonder if clinicians' reluctance is related to the view of exposure as a relatively aversive process (Richard & Gloster, this volume) and thus, best implemented with closer oversight from the clinician.

Videoconferencing

Videoconferencing permits therapists and clients to see and hear each other via closed circuit connections. An advantage of videoconferencing is that clinicians have the opportunity to observe both verbal and nonverbal client communication. With respect to exposure, this affords therapists the opportunity to monitor exposure exercises and to observe any counter-therapeutic coping behaviors.

Bouchard, Paquin, Payeur, Allard, Rivard, Fournier, et al. (2004) and Bouchard, Payeur, Rivard, Allard, Paquin, Renaud, et al. (2000) studied the feasibility of delivering treatment via videoconferencing for clients diagnosed with panic disorder with agoraphobia. This study examined the effectiveness of a 12-week CBT in 21 individuals delivered either face-to-face or via videoconferencing. Their analyses point to large pretreatment to post-treatment effect sizes that were similar for the two groups. Patients who were too afraid to travel long distances before treatment were able to travel hundreds of kilometers to large cities after the videoconferencing treatment. Interestingly, Bouchard, et al. also reported higher therapeutic alliance ratings in the videoconference group compared to the face-to-face group.

Telemedicine also presents ethical quandaries unique to this treatment modality. For instance, an individual who decompensates during therapy may be hundreds of miles away from his or her therapist. This concern applies to all telemedicine populations, but may be especially salient for unstable clients who undergo exposure procedures that may initially exacerbate symptoms (see Richard & Gloster, this volume).

In summary, technological advances offer promising new dissemination possibilities, although not without complications, for one of psychology's most efficacious treatments. Far from simple technological fascination, these innovations may offer psychological services to those otherwise unable to access them (e.g., rural populations), jump-start therapy for clients whose agoraphobia is too severe to leave their home, facilitate homework and in vivo exercises, reduce health care costs, and promote treatment dissemination. These potential promises alone should justify future research.

As we move toward our second "plateau," however, researchers should take care to design carefully controlled and statistically powerful studies. Recent work demonstrates the promise of international, multisite collaborations as a method of pooling resources (Kenardy, et al., 2003). Such efforts are crucial if researchers are to increase sample sizes and design studies of sufficient power to determine whether new treatments are equivalent or superior to currently established treatments. The ultimate yardstick against which all treatment innovations must be measured is the prevailing gold standard. In such comparisons, we should avoid concluding equivalency of treatments based on nonsignificant differences between conditions, especially in studies with low statistical power.

BARRIERS TO EFFECTIVE EXPOSURE THERAPY

Most psychological treatments include components that are challenging to practice effectively. If the challenge is so significant that the therapist is unlikely to engage in the treatment, the challenge may be properly termed a barrier. With regard to the use of exposure therapy with panic disordered patients, several barriers may be present that therapists should anticipate and address. After identifying each potential barrier, we discuss strategies to help therapists resolve issues and increase the likelihood of high fidelity treatment delivery.

Client Perceptions that Interoceptive Exposure Is Not Effective

Individuals sometimes report that the sensations they experience during interoceptive exposure do not feel like real panic or that the session environment does not faithfully replicate the surprisingness of symptom onset. In these situations, therapists are urged to check that the individual is adequately engaged in the exposure exercise. One might consider increasing the duration of the exercise to produce a greater intensity of symptoms, reexamine whether the most salient discriminative stimuli for the client have been identified and used in the interoceptive exposure, or reassess the ability of the client to imagine feared situations. If none of these approaches work, it may be possible that the client can pinpoint other situations that produce similar sensations or times/situations when they are likely to experience heightened anxiety.

Session Length

As with any exposure procedure, interoceptive exposure and in vivo exposure sessions usually require additional time. Therapists must ensure that clients begin to habituate within-session and do not leave a session in a heightened state of anxiety. Premature termination of an exposure trial may inadvertently negatively reinforce escape and avoidance behavior and be counterproductive. Further, establishing the correct mix of interoceptive exposure exercises required to elicit symptoms and activate the client's fear structure (Foa & Kozak, 1986) can be a time-consuming trial-and-error process.

Resistance and Treatment Avoidance

Individuals sometimes experience difficulty completing their interoceptive exposure exercises or in vivo exposure assignments. When this occurs, therapists need to assess carefully the reason for failed assignments. Although failure to complete an assignment does not necessarily imply resistance, it may also be a first manifestation of clinically relevant avoidance behavior. Therapists should be watchful for signs that the client does not understand or believe the rationale for exposure, lacks confidence in his or her ability to overcome fears, or considers the graded hierarchy to be too daunting. Any discussion of noncompletion should help clients understand that failure to complete exercises can be a form of avoidance behavior. In this way, clients are not "put on the spot" to justify their behavior, but are encouraged to reflect upon it and understand its function.

Overly Eager Therapist or Patient

Therapists using exposure procedures should be careful not to move too quickly through the collaboratively established hierarchy. A reasonable criterion of anxiety/ subjective distress reduction, perhaps by 50%, should be reported before progressing to the next step in an exposure hierarchy. Correspondingly, clients should be warned against becoming too overzealous and jumping to the top of their hierarchy. Prematurely jumping to difficult situations on the hierarchy without solidifying easier items could precipitate subjectively dangerous symptoms that, in the most extreme case, may derail treatment. Steady systematic progression in the context of a hierarchy is preferred to sudden increases in exposure exercises.

Novice Therapists

Exposure therapy is not for the faint of heart, and clinicians must be able to tolerate the anxiety that clients experience, especially during the initial stages of treatment. A frequent clinician concern involves whether treatment has an iatrogenic effect. If the clinician's concerns are so significant that the treatment itself is modified or weakened, the therapeutic effects of exposure may be attenuated. For example, interoceptive exercises may not be undertaken with enough vigor to elicit physiological responses. Novice therapists may be helped by acknowledging their concerns while pointing out that clients are resilient, that there is strong empirical support for the use of exposure techniques, and that clients have already endured symptoms as severe as or worse than those produced via in vivo exposure before treatment. Also, we recommend a physical examination before treatment to allay any fears regarding the health of the client.

Pharmacotherapy

As indicated, combined pharmacotherapy and CBT is an empirically supported treatment approach. If the client attributes reduction of anxiety symptoms to his or her medication, rather than to the exposure techniques, the client's motivation to continue with potentially aversive exposure sessions will likely wane. If this is the case, therapists should discuss with clients why it is important to continue with both treatment components and the relapse risks associated with pharmacotherapy-only treatment. If resistance to exposure continues, the therapist should consider transitioning the client to a treatment model that emphasizes medication maintenance, coping skills, and other strategies designed to help the client identify maladaptive cognitions.

Acceptance of Psychological Factors

Many individuals do not comply with treatment because they don't believe they have a psychological problem. Individuals who present to emergency services with panic-related chest pain may undergo extensive medical procedures to rule out cardiac or other physiological etiologies. These experiences, along with the somatic and intensive nature of their symptoms, lead some to resist a psychological explanation. In turn, interoceptive exposure is viewed as suspect or even dangerous. Therapists should anticipate that some clients will resist psychological explanations and should take this into account when presenting assessment results and treatment rationale.

The Ultimate "What If"

Individuals with panic disorder sometimes dismiss the opinions of mental health professionals because they are convinced that their condition will ultimately lead to an untimely demise. Although these thoughts and beliefs are usually targeted as part of cognitive restructuring, therapists should be aware that some clients may not be convinced that they provided the best, or even a safe, treatment. As a result, the client may meet the prospect of purposefully evoking symptoms through interoceptive exposure with a less than enthusiastic response. In cases where clients may overestimate the harm that may befall them by participating in treatment, therapists should matter-of-factly note that any symptom exacerbation in the short term will be more than offset by long-term reductions in panic symptoms. In addition, therapists should reemphasize the theoretical rationale for exposure therapy to ensure that the client understands the mechanisms by which the treatment exerts its effect.

CASE STUDY

Case Description

"Jim" (not his real name) is a 40-year-old married Caucasian male. He was referred to the clinic for treatment of panic disorder with agoraphobia by his primary care physician. Secondary comorbid diagnoses included generalized anxiety disorder and dysthymic disorder.

Jim reported experiencing panic attacks at least once per day. Onset of symptoms was 10 years before the initial evaluation and was associated with a period of multiple psychosocial stressors, including a divorce and the deaths of two close family members. His symptoms at the time included increased heart rate, shortness of breath, feeling hot, sweating, shaking, weakness in his legs, light-headedness, dizziness, derealization, numbness in his left arm and hand, diarrhea, and fear of having a heart attack. In addition, he experienced frequent bouts of worry over having future panic attacks. As a consequence of his symptoms, he reported four to five emergency room visits when he feared he was having a heart attack. Extensive diagnostic testing did not find a medical explanation for his symptoms.

Jim also developed classic agoraphobic avoidance behaviors (e.g., reluctance to ride as a passenger in a car and avoidance of crowded public places). He was also avoidant of many situations that evoked the same physiological sensations that preceded panic. For example, he was unable to ride in a warm car, avoided music with melancholy lyrics, and limited his physical exertion during exercise. He attributed a significant weight gain to his avoidance of exercise. Jim was able to endure a variety of other situations, but only with intense anxiety and distress.

Jim became so fearful of nocturnal panic attacks that he had trouble falling asleep and reported receiving only 4 hours of sleep per night. He also avoided sleeping in his bed because it had been associated with nocturnal panic attacks.

Assessment and Case Conceptualization

Pretreatment assessment consisted of a diagnostic interview and administration of the following self-report questionnaires: Anxiety Sensitivity Index (ASI; Reiss, Peterson, Gursky, & McNally, 1986), Mobility Inventory (MI; Chambless, Caputo, Gracely, Jasin, & Williams, 1985), State-Trait Anxiety Inventory (STAI; Spielberger, Gorsuch, & Lushene, 1970), and the Beck Depression Inventory-II (BDI-II; Beck & Steer, 1987). Jim's scores on these measures are displayed in Table 10.1.

TABLE 10.1   Pretreatment and Post-Treatment Scores on Standardized Measures

Measure	Pretreatment	Post-Treatment
Anxiety Sensitivity Index	44	28
Mobility Inventory		
Accompanied	60	49
Alone	65	52
State-Trait Anxiety Inventory		
State	55	51
Trait	59	54
Beck Depression Inventory	29	12

Jim's treatment history included multiple trials of SSRI medications prescribed by his primary care physician; however, each trial terminated prematurely because the side effects of the medications tended to exacerbate his panic symptoms. At the initial visit, he was taking clonazepam, 1 mg three times per day, with minimal symptom relief. He also completed two- to three-therapy sessions with a psychologist 8 years earlier. As best we could tell, the prior treatment did not involve any exposure components.

Jim's case was conceptualized from a cognitive-behavioral perspective (Barlow, 2002). Like the majority of patients diagnosed with panic disorder with agoraphobia, Jim's initial panic attack occurred shortly after significant aversive life events. Jim initially developed gastroesophageal reflux disease, a common stress-related response. We hypothesized that Jim's heightened sensitivity to somatic sensations engendered catastrophic misinterpretations of sensations associated with reflux disease. For example, discomfort in his esophagus was misinterpreted as evidence of impending cardiac arrest. As additional somatic sensations came to be associated with panic attacks, there was a generalization of cues that could trigger panic. Jim's anxiety was maintained via active avoidance of all cues and behaviors that might trigger panic symptoms.

This conceptualization, which is consistent with both Mowrer's (1960) two-stage theory of fear acquisition and maintenance and Clark's (1986) cognitive theory of catastrophic misinterpretations, was explained in detail to Jim. He then began a trial of panic control treatment that was modeled after the procedures outlined by Barlow and Craske (2000).

Treatment

Overview

During treatment, Jim self-monitored his anxiety, depression, and panic attack frequency, intensity, and duration. Treatment consisted of 17 sessions of CBT. In addition, Jim attended two maintenance sessions during a 6-month period after active treatment. Four additional sessions that focused on bereavement were added during the maintenance period at his request owing to the death of a family member during treatment. Concurrently, Jim was treated by a psychiatrist who tapered and discontinued his clonazepam and prescribed venlafaxine at an initial dose of 37.5 mg per day with a gradual increase to 150 mg per day.

Treatment Sessions

Sessions 1 and 2 focused on education and treatment planning. Educational components focused on the nature of anxiety and panic and conveyed the rationale for cognitive and behavioral procedures. These strategies were included to correct misinformation about the symptoms associated with anxiety and panic, as well as the potential for adverse consequences of having these symptoms. Sessions 3 through 5 focused on relaxation procedures. These included both diaphragmatic breathing and progressive muscle relaxation. These skills helped Jim gain control over his physiological arousal, and he was able to decrease the frequency of panic attacks. To further decrease the frequency of panic attacks and to further correct the maladaptive beliefs contributing to panic, cognitive therapy was introduced. Sessions 6 through 9 focused on cognitive therapy and included an introduction to the role of cognition, identifying automatic thoughts, and realistically evaluating the probability of adverse life events. Throughout these sessions, Jim continued learning about medication side effects and learned how to correctly interpret somatic sensations associated with the medication.

Although Jim's panic attack frequency remained low, he continued to avoid stimuli he associated with panic attacks. To reduce avoidance behaviors and improve functioning, Sessions 10 through 17 focused on interoceptive and in vivo exposure. Hierarchies were developed based on Jim's avoidance behaviors and identification of those bodily sensations most likely to trigger a panic attack. For example, one somatic sensation Jim avoided was feeling warm, and he avoided situations that produced this sensation such as traveling in warm cars. One of his exposure exercises, therefore, involved sitting or driving in his car at progressively warmer temperatures.

Sessions 18 to 21 focused on grief and bereavement in response to a family member's short illness and death, which occurred unexpectedly during treatment. Interventions included normalization of grief reactions and encouragement of approach behaviors to facilitate grief (e.g., visiting the cemetery, viewing pictures, crying). Sessions 22 and 23 focused on developing strategies to maintain treatment gains.

Treatment Results

Table 10.1 shows Jim's scores on standardized measures at pretreatment and posttreatment (Week 17). He showed decreases in scores across all measures, with the greatest improvement demonstrated on the ASI, MI, and BDI-II.

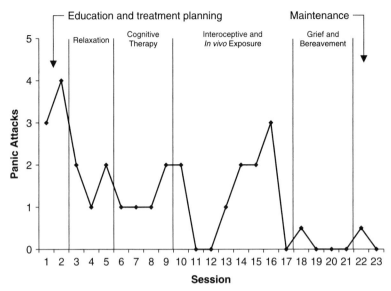

FIGURE 10.1   Jim's self-reported panic attacks per week across treatment sessions.

Weekly panic attack frequencies are presented in Figure 10.1. Jim showed a decreasing trend in panic attack frequency over time. There was an increase in reported panic attacks from the 13th through 17th sessions when he experienced several panic attacks during exposure practice. He remained relatively panic-free during the 6-month follow-up period, with two panic attacks in response to specific psychosocial stressors and one panic attack without an identifiable cue.

Jim also reported improved functioning and quality of life over the course of treatment. He was able to participate successfully in regular vigorous exercise, which contributed to a reduction in excess bodyweight. His sleep improved dramatically once he started sleeping in his bed rather than a living room chair. He also reported improvement in his relationship with his wife and indicated enjoying several of his children's activities, as opposed to enduring them with acute distress.

Identifying the most active treatment component is difficult in this case given that the frequency of Jim's panic attacks was highly variable during the exposure therapy phase. It appears that exposure was associated with an elimination of panic symptoms in the weeks after the first two sessions but increased shortly thereafter, a pattern that is unusual and not consistent with habituation. It is probably the case that the terminal illness experienced by one of Jim's family members interfered with treatment by making Jim more sensitive to issues of mortality and, correspondingly, his own somatic sensations. Therefore it may be noteworthy that after the family member's death, Jim's panic symptoms decreased rather than increased. This was not the case 10 years beforehand when the death of two family members led to the initial onset of symptoms.

SUMMARY AND CONCLUSIONS

Panic control treatment and cognitive therapy are both empirically validated and efficacious treatments for panic disorder. These treatments are used in conjunction with in vivo exposure for individuals that experience agoraphobia. Also, pharmacotherapy may be beneficial for panic disorder, although the combination of CBT with medications may not produce a significant benefit over either treatment alone. Given the efficacy of panic disorder and agoraphobia treatments, several recent innovations have been studied, including the use of handheld computers, virtual reality, Internet-based programs, teleconferencing, and videoconferencing. These applications may be particularly beneficial for individuals unable to engage in traditional treatment owing to geographic distance or being housebound because of anxiety. This chapter also identified some potential barriers to effective implementation of exposure-based procedures for panic disorder and agoraphobia and suggested possible solutions for the clinician. Finally, the case study demonstrated an effective implementation of panic control treatment.

REFERENCES

Addis, M.E., Hatgis, C., Krasnow, A.D., Jacob, K., Bourne, L., & Mansfield, A. (2004). Effectiveness of cognitive-behavioral treatment for panic disorder versus treatment as usual in a managed care setting. *Journal of Consulting and Clinical Psychology, 72,* 625–635.

Alcañiz, M., Botella, C., Banos, R., Perpina, C., Rey, B., Lozano, J. A., Guillen, V., Barrera, F., & Gil, J.A. (2003). Internet-based telehealth system for the treatment of agoraphobia. *CyberPsychology & Behavior, 6,* 355–358.

American Psychiatric Association. (2000). *Diagnostic and Statistical Manual of Mental Disorders* (4th ed., text revision, *DSM-IV-TR*). Washington, D.C.: Author.

American Psychiatric Association. (1998). Practice guideline for the treatment of patients with panic disorder. *American Journal of Psychiatry, 155,* 1–34.

Antony, M.M. (2002). Enhancing current treatments for anxiety disorders. *Clinical Psychology: Science and Practice, 9,* 91–94.

Arntz, A. (2002). Cognitive therapy versus interoceptive exposure as treatment of panic disorder without agoraphobia. *Behaviour Research and Therapy, 40,* 325–341.

Barlow, D.H. (2002). *Anxiety and its disorders: The nature and treatment of anxiety and panic* (2nd ed.). New York: Guilford.

Barlow, D.H., & Craske, M. (2000). *Mastery of your anxiety and panic (MAP-3): Client workbook for anxiety and panic* (3rd ed.). San Antonio, TX: Graywind/Psychological Corporation.

Barlow, D.H., & Cerny, J.A. (1988). *Psychological treatment of panic.* New York: Guilford Press.

Barlow, D.H., & Lehman, C.L. (1996). Advances in the psychosocial treatment of anxiety disorders. *Archives of General Psychiatry, 53,* 727–735.

Barlow, D.H., Cohen, A.S., Waddell, M., Vermilyea, J.A., Klosko, J.S., Blanchard, E.B., & Di Nardo, P.A. (1984). Panic and generalized anxiety disorders: Nature and treatment. *Behavior Therapy, 15,* 431–449.

Barlow, D.H., Craske, M., Cerny, J.A., & Klosko, J.S. (1989). Behavioral treatment of panic disorder. *Behavior Therapy, 20,* 261–282.

Barlow, D.H., Gorman, J.M., Shear, M.K., & Woods, S.W. (2000). Cognitive-behavioral therapy, imipramine, and their combination for panic disorder. *Journal of the American Medical Association, 283,* 2529–2536.

Beck, A.T., & Steer, G. (1987). *Manual for the revised Beck Depression Inventory*. San Antonio, TX: Psychological Corporation.

Beck, A.T., Sokol, L., Clark, D.A., Berchick, R., & Wright, F. (1992). A crossover study of focused cognitive therapy for panic disorder. *American Journal of Psychiatry, 149,* 778–783.

Bouchard, S., Paquin, B., Payeur, R., Allard, M., Rivard, V., Fournier, T., Renaud, P., & Lapierre, J. (2004). Delivering cognitive-behavior therapy for panic disorder with agoraphobia in videoconference. *Telemedicine Journal and e-health, 10,* 13–25.

Bouchard, S., Payeur, R., Rivard, V., Allard, M., Paquin, B., Renaud, P., & Goyer, L. (2000). Cognitive behavior therapy for panic disorder with agoraphobia in videoconference: Preliminary results. *CyberPsychology & Behavior, 3,* 999–1007.

Bouton, M.E., Mineka, S., & Barlow, D.H. (2001). A model learning theory perspective on the etiology of panic disorder. *Psychological Review, 108,* 4–32.

Burke, M., Drummond, L.M., & Johnston, D.W. (1997). Treatment choice for agoraphobic women: Exposure or cognitive-behaviour therapy? *British Journal of Clinical Psychology, 36,* 409–420.

Byrne, M., Carr, A., & Clark, M. (2004). The efficacy of couples-based interventions for panic disorder with agoraphobia. *Journal of Family Therapy, 26,* 105–125.

Carlbring, P., Ekselius, L., & Andersson G. (2003). Treatment of panic disorder via the internet: A randomized trial of CBT vs. Applied relaxation. *Journal of Behavior Therapy and Experimental Psychiatry, 34,* 129–140.

Carlbring, P., Westling, B.E., Ljungstrand, P., Ekselius, L., & Andersson, G. (2001). Treatment of panic disorder via the internet: A randomized trial of a self-help program. *Behavior Therapy, 32,* 751–764.

Chambless, D.L., & Gillis, M.M. (1993). Cognitive therapy of anxiety disorders. *Journal of Consulting and Clinical Psychology, 61,* 248–260.

Chambless, D.L., Baker, M.J., Baucom, D.H., Beutler, L.E., Calhoun, K.S., Crits-Christoph, P., et al. (1998). Update on empirically validated therapies. *The Clinical Psychologist, 51,* 3–16.

Chambless, D.L., Caputo, G., Gracely, S., Jasin, E., & Williams, C. (1985). The Mobility Inventory for agoraphobia. *Behaviour Research and Therapy, 23,* 35–44.

Clark, D.M. (1986). A cognitive approach to panic. *Behaviour Research and Therapy, 24,* 461–470.

Clark, D.M., Salkovskis, P.M., Hackmann, A., Middleton, H., Anastasiades, P., & Gelder, M. (1994). A comparison of cognitive therapy, applied relaxation and imipramine in the treatment of panic disorder. *British Journal of Psychiatry, 164,* 759–769.

Clark, D.M., Salkovskis, P.M., Hackmann, A., Wells, A., Ludgate, J., & Gelder, M. (1999). Brief cognitive therapy for panic disorder: A randomized controlled trial. *Journal of Consulting and Clinical Psychology, 67,* 583–589.

Clum, G.A. (1989). Psychological interventions vs. drugs in the treatment of panic. *Behavior Therapy, 20,* 429–457.

Clum, G.A., Clum, G.A., & Surls, R. (1993). A meta-analysis of treatment for panic disorder. *Journal of Consulting and Clinical Psychology, 61,* 317–326.

Côté, G., Gauthier, J.G., Laberge, B., Cormier, H.J., & Plamondon, J. (1994). Reduced therapist contact in the cognitive behavioral treatment of panic disorder. *Behavior Therapy, 25,* 123–145.

Craske, M.G., Maidenberg, E., & Bystritsky, A. (1995). Brief cognitive-behavioral versus nondirective therapy for panic disorder. *Journal of Behavior Therapy and Experimental Psychiatry, 26,* 113–120.

Craske, M.G., Rowe, M., Lewin, M., & Noriega-Dimitri, R. (1997). Interoceptive exposure versus breathing retraining within cognitive-behavioral therapy for panic disorder with agoraphobia. *British Journal of Clinical Psychology, 36,* 85–99.

Foa, E.B., & Kozak, M.J. (1986). Emotional processing of fear: Exposure to corrective information. *Psychological Bulletin, 99,* 20–35.

Gega, L., Marks, I., & Mataix-Cols, D. (2004). Computer-aided CBT self-help for anxiety and depressive disorders: Experience of a London clinic and future directions. *Journal of Clinical Psychology/In Session, 60,* 147–157.

Gore, K.L., & Carter, M.M. (2003). Incorporating the family in the cognitive-behavioral treatment of an African-American female suffering from panic disorder with agoraphobia. *Journal of Family Psychotherapy, 14,* 73–92.

Gould, R.A., Otto, M.W., & Pollack, M.H. (1995). A meta-analysis of treatment outcome for panic disorder. *Clinical Psychology Review, 15,* 819–844.

Hahlweg, K., Fiegenbaum, W., Frank, M., Schroeder, B., & von Witzleben, I. (2001). Short- and long-term effectiveness of an empirically supported treatment for agoraphobia. *Journal of Consulting and Clinical Psychology, 69,* 375–382.

Hofmann, S.G., & Spiegel, D.A. (1999). Panic control treatment and its applications. *Journal of Psychotherapy Practice and Research, 8,* 3–11.

Ito, L.M., De Araujo, L.A., Tess, V.L.C., De Barros-Neto, T.P., Asbahr, F.R., & Marks, I. (2001). Self-exposure therapy for panic disorder with agoraphobia. *British Journal of Psychiatry, 178,* 331–336.

Jansson, L., & Öst, L-G. (1982). Behavioral treatments for agoraphobia: An evaluative review. *Clinical Psychology Review, 2,* 311–336.

Kenardy, J., Dow, M.G.T., Johnston, D.W., Newman, M.G., Thomson, A., & Taylor, C.B. (2003). A comparison of delivery methods of cognitive-behavioral therapy for panic disorder: An international multicenter trial. *Journal of Consulting and Clinical Psychology, 71,* 1068–1075.

Kenwright, M., & Marks, I.M. (2004). Computer-aided self-help for phobia/panic via internet at home: A pilot study. *British Journal of Psychiatry, 184,* 448–449.

Lidren, D.M., Watkins, P.L., Gould, R.A., Clum, G.A., Asterino, M., & Tulloch, H.L. (1994). A comparison of bibliotherapy and group therapy in the treatment of panic disorder. *Journal of Consulting and Clinical Psychology, 62,* 865–869.

Marks, I., Kenwright, M., McDonough, M., Whittaker, M., & Mataix-Cols, D. (2004). Saving clinicians' time by delegating routine aspects of therapy to a computer: A randomized controlled trial in phobia/panic disorder. *Psychological Medicine, 34,* 9–17.

McNamee, G., O'Sullivan, G., Lelliott, P., & Marks, I. (1989). Telephone-guided treatment for housebound agoraphobics with panic disorder: Exposure vs. relaxation. *Behavior Therapy, 20,* 491–497.

Meuret, A.E., Wilhelm, F.H., & Roth, W.T. (2004). Respiratory feedback for treating panic disorder. *Journal of Clinical Psychology/In Session, 60,* 197–207.

Moore, K., Wiederhold, B.K., Wiederhold, M.D., & Riva, G. (2002). Panic and agoraphobia in a virtual world. *CyberPsychology & Behavior, 5,* 197–202.

Mowrer, O.H. (1960). *Learning theory and behavior.* Hoboken, NJ: John Wiley & Sons, Inc.

Murphy, M.T., Michelson, L.K., Marchione, K., Marchione, N., & Testa, S. (1998). The role of self-directed *in vivo* exposure in combination with cognitive therapy, relaxation training, or therapist-assisted exposure in the treatment of panic disorder with agoraphobia. *Journal of Anxiety Disorders, 12,* 117–138.

Newman, M.G., Kenardy, J., Herman, S., & Taylor, C.B. (1997). Comparison of palmtop-computer-assisted brief cognitive-behavioral treatment to cognitive-behavioral treatment for panic disorder. *Journal of Consulting and Clinical Psychology, 65,* 178–183.

Öst, L.-G., Westling, B.E., & Hellström, K. (1993). Applied relaxation, exposure *in vivo* and cognitive methods in the treatment of panic disorder with agoraphobia. *Behaviour Research and Therapy, 31,* 383–394.

Reiss, S., Peterson, R.A., Gursky, D.M., & McNally, R.J. (1986). Anxiety sensitivity, anxiety frequency, and the prediction of fearfulness. *Behaviour Research and Therapy, 24,* 1–8.

Richard, D.C.S., & Gloster, A.T. (this volume). Law, ethics, and professional issues in exposure therapy. In D.C.S. Richard & D. Lauterbach (Eds.), *Handbook of Exposure Therapies*: Burlington, MA: Academic Press.

Salkovskis, P.M. & Clark, D.M. (1991). Cognitive therapy for panic attacks. *Journal of Cognitive Psychotherapy, 5,* 215–226.

Schmidt, N.B., Woolaway-Bickel, K., Trakowski, J., Santiago, H., Storey, J., Koselka, M., et al. (2000). Dismantling cognitive-behavioral treatment for panic disorder: Questioning the utility of breathing retraining. *Journal of Consulting and Clinical Psychology, 68,* 417–424.

Spielberger, C.D., Gorsuch, R.L., & Lushene, R.E. (1970). *Manual for the State-Trait Anxiety Inventory (Form Y Self-Evaluation Questionnaire)*. Palo Alto, CA: Consulting Psychologists Press.

Swinson, R.P., Fergus, K.D., Cox, B.J., & Wickwire, K. (1995). Efficacy of telephone-administered behavioral therapy for panic disorder with agoraphobia. *Behavior Research and Therapy, 33,* 465–469.

van den Hout, M., Arntz, A., & Hoekstra, R. (1994). Exposure reduced agoraphobia but not panic, and cognitive therapy reduced panic but not agoraphobia. *Behaviour Research and Therapy, 32,* 447–451.

Vincelli, F., Anolli, L., Bouchard, S., Wiederhold, B.K., Zurloni, V., & Riva, G. (2003). Experiential cognitive therapy in the treatment of panic disorders with agoraphobia: A controlled study. *CyberPsychology & Behavior, 6,* 321–328.

Westen, D., & Morrison, K. (2001). A multidimensional meta-analysis of treatments for depression, panic, and generalized anxiety disorder: An empirical examination of the status of empirically supported therapies. *Journal of Consulting and Clinical Psychology, 69,* 875–899.

White, K.S., & Barlow, D.H. (2002). Panic disorder and agoraphobia. In D.H. Barlow (Ed.), *Anxiety and Its Disorders: The Nature and Treatment of Anxiety and Panic* (2nd ed.). New York: Guilford.

CHAPTER 11

Exposure Therapy for Phobias

Michiyo Hirai
Washington State University

Laura L. Vernon
Auburn University

Heather Cochran
University of Oklahoma

In the United States, approximately 11% of people will suffer from a specific phobia and 13.3% from a social phobia at some point in their lives (Kessler, McGonagle, Zhao, Nelson, Highes, Eshleman, et al., 1994). Various treatment approaches including exposure have been developed for specific phobia and social phobia. In this chapter, we review the empirical literature examining exposure-based interventions and their effectiveness, and discuss issues related to exposure therapy for phobias.

SPECIFIC PHOBIA AND EXPOSURE-BASED TREATMENT: OVERVIEW

Specific phobia is diagnosed when an individual experiences persistent and irrational fear of particular objects or situations, and displays avoidance of those objects or situations. Ample evidence exists that exposure-based approaches are some of the most effective treatment methods for phobic fear and avoidance behavior (e.g., Öst, 1989; Öst, Ferebee, & Furmark, 1997; Öst, Fellenius, & Sterner, 1991). Typically, exposure therapy uses a graded exposure hierarchy that is either standardized or idiosyncratically developed. Initial sessions involve exposing the person to the stimulus that is least feared, with subsequent sessions helping the client progress through the hierarchy and situations that elicit greater anxiety. A variety of exposure modalities (e.g., in vivo, imaginal, computer-assisted or virtual reality-based), and combinations of these approaches may be applied in individual or group format. Exposure interventions can be brief (e.g., single session; Öst, Hellström, & Kåver, 1992; Öst, Alm, Brandberg, & Breitholtz, 2001) or extended (e.g., 8 weeks or more; Rothbaum, Hodges, Smith, Lee, & Price, 2000). Progress within-session and therapeutic gain between-sessions is typically assessed through self-report ratings using a Subjective Units of Distress scale (SUDS), Behavioral Avoidance Test (BAT), self-report questionnaires, physiological measures (e.g., heart rate, blood pressure, galvanic skin response), and observer ratings.

Adjunctive techniques frequently supplement exposure sessions. For example, cognitive interventions are often incorporated to help a client identify automatic negative thoughts about the feared situation or object. Behavioral relaxation techniques, such as deep breathing and muscle relaxation, may also be used for individuals with high levels of arousal or tension. With patients who have developed a blood-injection-injury phobia, muscle tension and relaxation can be a useful strategy in restoring blood pressure and preventing vasovagal syncope (Hellström, Fellenius, & Öst, 1996).

In the following sections, we review the effectiveness of exposure approaches for a variety of specific phobias. Although phobias may develop to a number of objects and situations, we focus on phobic stimuli that have been investigated in controlled treatment outcome studies. These primarily include spider phobia, blood-injection-injury phobia, claustrophobia, and flying phobia.

SPIDER PHOBIA

Overview

Spider phobia is one of the most common specific phobias and is more common among women than men (e.g., Bourdon, Boyd, Rae, Burns, Thompson, & Locke, 1988; Öst, 1987). Historically, treatments with exposure elements, including imaginal flooding and implosion (Marshall, Gauthier, Christie, Currie, & Gordon, 1977), systematic desensitization (Marshall, Strawbridge, & Keltner, 1972; Rachman, 1966a, 1966b), and modeling (Denney, Sullivan, & Thiry, 1977) have proven effective for decreasing spider fear and avoidance in response to spiders. Surprisingly, however, no systematic large-scale evaluation of the efficacy of various exposure components has been undertaken.

This shortcoming in the research base has not prevented the development of successful variations on the exposure paradigm. For example, researchers have reported successful clinical outcomes using single-session in vivo exposure (e.g., Öst, 1989), group treatments (Öst, 1996; Öst, Ferebee, & Furmark, 1997), and self-help formats (Öst, Salkovskis, & Hellström, 1991; Hellström, & Öst, 1995). More recently, virtual reality exposure takes advantage of advanced computer technology (e.g., Garcia-Palacios, Hoffman, Carlin, Furness, & Botella, 2002). Next we review the empirical literature, as well as ancillary issues in the use of exposure therapy with phobic individuals.

Single-Session Exposure Therapy for Spider Phobia

There is compelling evidence that brief, one-session exposure therapy for spider phobia can reduce or completely eliminate spider phobia. The efficacy of single-session exposure treatment for phobias was first suggested by Öst (1989), who described its format and a series of 20 consecutive single-session specific phobia treatment cases in which 90% of individuals showed clinically significant reduction in fears at follow-up evaluation.

Since then, two studies have compared one-session therapist-directed individual treatment to self-help interventions for spider phobia (Hellström & Öst, 1996; Öst, Salkovskis et al., 1991). In both studies, spider-phobic individuals treated in one session for 2.5 to 3 hours improved significantly more than the self-help intervention group. Approximately 70–80% of participants in the single-session exposure groups showed clinically significant improvement on a variety of measures, including performance on a behavioral avoidance test, physiological measures, self-reported symptoms, and observer-rated symptoms.

Group Treatment

Decades ago, researchers found that systematic desensitization could be successfully administered in a group setting (Lazarus, 1961; Paul, 1966; Paul & Shannon, 1966; Robinson & Suinn, 1969). More recently, one-session group exposure treatment has been shown to be effective in reducing spider phobia (Götestam, 2002; Öst, 1996; Öst, Ferebee, et al., 1997), and research has begun to focus on identifying the active treatment components of group formats. For example, Öst (1996) examined the effect of group size on treatment outcome. Forty-two diagnosed treatment-seeking spider-phobic women were treated either in a small group with three to four individuals or in a large group of seven to eight individuals. Each group received a 3-hour therapy session that included a combination of gradual exposure and modeling. The therapist modeled approach behavior with one member of the group before instructing other group members to engage in the behavior. Fear reduction was observed in both groups, with no difference between groups in the magnitude of the reduction at post-treatment.

In a slightly different vein, Öst, Ferebee, et al. (1997) explored which forms of single-session group exposure were associated with greatest symptom reduction. They compared the effectiveness of gradual in vivo group exposure, in vivo observation (i.e., live modeling), and video observation for 46 clinically diagnosed spider-phobic women. In the live modeling condition, participants observed an individual engaging in exposure treatment. In the video observation condition, participants viewed a videotape of an individual undergoing exposure treatment. Although each group showed significant improvement on a variety of outcome measures at post-treatment, the in vivo exposure condition achieved the greatest treatment gains. Similarly, Götestam (2002) compared group versions of in vivo exposure, modeling, and video observation using 38 individuals with spider phobia. The results largely replicated Öst, et al.'s findings in that all groups demonstrated significantly improved spider-related fear with better progress in the in vivo group at post-treatment and 12-month follow-up evaluation.

There are obvious time- and cost-effectiveness advantages to group treatment. The advisability of using a treatment, however, is contingent on a number of factors, not just its efficiency. Group-based exposure could prove problematic for other reasons. For example, Öst (1996) observed that affectively strong reactions by a group member could have the potential to interfere with treatment of other group members. Further, detection of adverse responses is difficult because the therapist's attention is divided among the group, making it more likely that individuals who are not the current focus of treatment could successfully engage in avoidance behavior (Götestam, 2002; Öst, Ferebee, et al.,1997). At this point, there has been no systematic analysis of the relative advantages and disadvantages of group exposure.

Virtual Reality

Virtual reality (VR) exposure involves the use of advanced computer technology to create a virtual environment that simulates a feared stimulus or situation (see the chapter by Bouchard, Côté, and Richard in this volume for an in-depth treatment). Position tracking sensors monitor the individual's head and hand movements and synchronize the movements with orientation changes in the virtual environment. Visual displays are usually included in a helmet that includes miniature television screens to provide a continuous visual virtual environment.

Several studies suggest the efficacy of VR exposure treatment for spider phobia. Garcia-Palacios, et al. (2002) compared VR exposure sessions to a wait-list control condition with 23 clinically phobic participants. Individuals in the treatment condition spent four 1-hour sessions completing a standardized graded hierarchy (e.g., coming within arm's reach of a virtual spider, touching the virtual spider who would then flee on contact, and finally holding a virtual spider in hand). Relative to the wait-list condition, the virtual exposure group reported significant improvement in spider-related anxiety and symptom severity, behavior performance, and clinician-rated symptom severity. In addition, 83% of individuals in the VR group met the clinical improvement criterion relative to 0% in the wait list.

There is also preliminary evidence to suggest that the efficacy of VR exposure can be increased via tactile augmentation. Hoffman, Garcia-Palacios, Carlin, Furness, and Botella-Arbona (2003) examined the incremental effects of including tactile cues by exposing individuals to a virtual spider they could touch through physical texture and force feedback cues. VR exposure with and without tactile cues was compared to a no treatment condition with 28 spider-fearful and eight clinically phobic individuals. The two treatment groups underwent three 1-hour VR exposure sessions and displayed similarly significant improvement in self-reported fear and avoidance behavior. The tactile treatment group, however, was able to approach closer than the no-tactile group during the post-treatment BAT, suggesting some incremental efficacy for tactile augmentation.

Virtual reality exposure techniques possess several unique advantages. Most obviously, the degree of control available to the clinician by using a virtual environment has several implications. First, virtual environments eliminate unanticipated events during the exposure session (e.g., a sudden spider movement or an otherwise agitated spider). In addition, the properties of the spider itself can be modified. Therapists can control the virtual spider's size, color, orientation, position, speed, and movements. The novelty and technology of the treatment may also be more attractive to some individuals than conventional exposure, and pioneers of the treatment are hopeful that VR may be successful in increasing the number of individuals who seek treatment (e.g., Garcia-Palacios, Hoffman, See, Tsai, & Botella, 2001). Whether VR treatments are as effective for spider phobia as in vivo treatments has yet to be examined and might depend on the degree to which the technology accurately captures the reality of the exposure experience.

Disgust

There is a growing body of evidence suggesting that disgust plays an important role in specific phobias, particularly spider phobia. Recent research suggests that the majority of spider phobic individuals experience disgust in response to phobic stimuli (e.g., Sawchuk, Lohr, Tolin, Lee, & Kleinknecht, 2000; Vernon & Berenbaum, 2002, 2004). Woody and Teachman (2000) have suggested that synergistic influences between fear and disgust may be the mechanism underlying such findings.

Several studies have provided evidence that the exposure techniques applied to reduce fear of spiders also diminish disgust responses. Smits, Telch, and Randall (2002) found that 27 spider-fearful individuals reported declines in disgust and fear during 30 minutes of self-directed in vivo exposure to a tarantula. Teachman and Woody (2003) examined the effect of exposure treatment on cognitive processes related to disgust and fear of spiders. Diagnosed spider-phobic individuals underwent a weekly three-session group treatment based on a manualized exposure protocol (Antony, Barlow, & Craske, 1997). Spider-phobic individuals in the treatment group showed improvement and short-term maintenance of treatment gains on spider phobia symptoms measured by self-report questionnaires, behavioral tests, and cognitive associations linking spiders with disgust and fear. The no-treatment control group did not show similar changes. Of interest, however, global disgust sensitivity, such as one's response of disgust to contaminated food products, was not changed by exposure (de Jong, Andrea, & Muris, 1997; Smits, et, al., 2002).

Given emerging evidence regarding the importance of disgust in spider phobia, there has been recent examination of whether additional treatment techniques, designed specifically to target disgust responding, demonstrate incremental efficacy beyond that of unmodified exposure protocols. In a study addressing negative evaluations of spiders, de Jong, Vorage, and van den Hout (2000) compared a single-session, 3-hour exposure treatment to an identical treatment that also included counter-conditioning in 34 spider-phobic females. The purpose of the counter-conditioning techniques was to associate spiders with positively valenced experiences to change the negative affective evaluation of spiders to a neutral one. For example, individuals were encouraged to eat their favorite foods during regular exposure, listen to their favorite music, and so forth. Although de Jong, et al. hypothesized that the counter-conditioning exercises would be incrementally better at reducing disgust responses and a person's negative affective response to spiders, no group differences in symptom improvements emerged post-treatment or at 1-year follow-up period. In another attempt to supplement conventional exposure treatment for spider phobia with components targeting disgust, Hirai, Vernon, Cochran, Butcher, Stransky, and Meadows (2003) compared the efficacy of two single-session 2-hour individual exposure treatments for 37 spider-fearful individuals. Standardized conventional fear-focused exposure and educational information aimed to correct potentially fear-provoking misconceptions about spiders (e.g., not all spiders are dangerous or poisonous) were given to both groups. In addition, the disgust treatment group received information to correct misconceptions about potentially disgust-related aspects of spiders (e.g., not all spiders are dirty or contaminated) and completed three additional disgust-targeted exposure steps related to possible contamination (i.e., touching one's clothing, arm, and hair after touching the spider). Both groups demonstrated improved spider phobia symptoms, as well as disgust responses on various measures, including clinician-rated symptom severity, and behavior tasks at post-treatment and 1-week follow-up. No treatment group differences were found. Unfortunately, more than a third of the disgust treatment group did not complete the disgust exposure steps due either to treatment refusal or time constraints, which might explain the failure to find group differences.

The preceding findings suggest that single-session conventional exposure treatment is effective for decreasing both fear and disgust (Hirai, et al., 2003; Smits, et al., 2002; Teachman & Woody, 2003). It may be the case that exposure tasks that require a tactile response provide sufficient exposure to both the disgust-eliciting elements of spiders (e.g., contamination) and the fear-eliciting elements. Perceptions of spider contamination relevant to disgust likely take place under circumstances of direct physical contact, referred to as "physical contamination" by Rozin and Follin (1987, p. 29) and "biological contamination" by Klieger and Siejak (1997, p. 374). In this way, exposure treatments likely have the by-product of eliciting and treating disgust. The possible synergistic qualities of the two affective states suggest that any intervention that targets one may indirectly target the other (Woody & Teachman, 2000), but that the effect may not generalize to other nonfeared or disgusting stimuli (de Jong, et al., 1997; Smits, et al., 2002). Because exposure treatments are remarkably successful at decreasing both fearfulness and disgust, recent treatment components specifically designed to elicit and treat disgust may not have been sufficiently potent to add much therapeutically beyond the exposure component (de Jong, et al., 2000; Hirai, et al., 2003).

Cognitive Processes

Cognitive processes have been examined as a mediator of the effectiveness of exposure treatment. It has been theorized that coping styles under conditions of threat encourage stereotypic information processing (e.g., Steketee, Bransfield, Miller, & Foa, 1989), and there is some support for this assertion among spider-phobic individuals (e.g., Muris, Merckelbach, & de Jong, 1995). Individuals classified as *monitors* seek out threat information, whereas individuals classified as *blunters* attempt to distract and psychologically blunt threatening information (Miller, 1987). Rodriguez and Craske (1993) theorized that treatment approaches selected to match a person's coping style might produce better treatment outcomes. Specifically, they predicted that fear reduction would be greatest in a focused condition for individuals classified as monitors while individuals classified as blunters would show the greatest fear reduction in a distraction condition. In contrast, Foa and Kozak's emotional processing model (1986) suggests that distraction would interfere with emotional processing, affecting the activation of the fear network and the presentation of corrective information that is incompatible with pathological elements in the fear network. Distraction would disrupt the process of habituation thought to occur during exposure therapy.

Several studies have examined the effect of distraction versus focused attention on outcome in exposure therapy. Johnstone and Page (2004) compared cognitive distraction, in the form of a stimulus-irrelevant, personally relevant, conversation, during three 10-minute exposure sessions, to attentional focus via a stimulus-relevant conversation. Outcome was assessed at post-treatment and 4-week follow-up period with 27 diagnosed spider phobics. Somewhat surprisingly, they found that distraction, regardless of coping style, was associated with greater reported fear reduction, better BAT performance, higher levels of self-efficacy, and greater perceived internal control. Findings in this area have been inconsistent (c.f., Muris, de Jong, Merckelbach, & Van Zuuren, 1993a, 1993b; Muris, et al., 1995), however, and the importance of information preference coping styles in relation to spider exposure treatment outcome is unclear.

Return of Fear

Return of fear is an increase of self-reported fear from post-treatment to follow-up period (Rachman, 1979, 1989). Return of fear in spider phobics has been associated with several treatment variables, including shorter exposure duration (Rachman & Lopatka, 1988), massed exposure sessions completed consecutively in a single day (Rowe & Craske, 1998b), exposure to a single spider relative to multiple spiders (Rowe & Craske, 1998a), and depressed mood during exposure (Salkovskis & Mills, 1994). Findings suggest that exposure techniques that produce better habituation during treatment do not necessarily prevent return of fear. For example, Rowe and Craske (1998a) examined treatment involving either exposure to a single spider or exposure to four different spiders. Although exposure to a single stimulus was associated with more habituation across exposure trials, it was also associated with return of fear at 3-week follow-up period. Rowe and Craske (1998b) examined a massed exposure group relative to an expanding-spaced exposure group for which intertrial intervals doubled between sessions. The massed exposure group demonstrated more habituation across exposure trials, but also showed more return of fear at 1-month follow-up evaluation than the other group.

There is also evidence for a relationship between treatment context and relapse. Two recent studies reported that spider-fearful students displayed greater return of fear 1 week after exposure treatment when they were assessed in a room that was different from the treatment context (Mineka, Mystkowski, Hladek, & Rodriguez, 1999; Mystkowski, Craske, & Echiverri, 2002). Internal physiological state has also been conceptualized as a treatment context. Mystkowski, Mineka, Vernon, and Zinbarg (2003) examined the effects of internal state on return of fear by manipulating arousal via caffeine. Participants were assigned to conditions in which they either consumed caffeine or placebo during exposure or at 1-week follow-up evaluation. Individuals who experienced incongruent physiological states across the two sessions (i.e., caffeine/placebo or placebo/caffeine) exhibited greater return of fear than those in the congruent conditions (i.e., caffeine/caffeine, placebo/placebo), suggesting that state-dependent learning may mediate the likelihood of fear reemergence.

The preceding findings suggest the potential limitations of typical exposure techniques for providing generalizable treatment gains. An increased understanding of relapse-related variables should provide ways to maximize long-term exposure treatment retention.

Summary for Spider Phobia

There is a great deal of evidence documenting the efficacy of exposure treatments for spider phobia. Several modifications, including single-session and group treatments, may make exposure treatment more accessible by decreasing the amount of therapist involvement and treatment costs. In addition, there is preliminary evidence suggesting the efficacy of VR exposure. Exposure treatments have been shown to be effective for the reduction of both fear and disgust responses to spiders. The addition of exposure exercises specifically targeting disgust has not demonstrated incremental efficacy. Research on the return of fear has revealed several factors that potentially influence maintenance of treatment effects and generalization. As research in relapse continues, researchers should strive for a better understanding of how long-term gains can be maintained.

BLOOD-INJECTION-INJURY (BII) PHOBIA

The lifetime prevalence of BII phobia has been estimated at 3.1% of the population (Bienvenu, & Eaton, 1998). BII phobics typically avoid medical and health care situations, including doctors, dentists, and hospitals. Individuals with BII phobia report worrying about their ability to undergo necessary medical procedures, such as an operation, treatment, medical examination, and vaccination, as well as being able to take their children to doctors (e.g., Öst 1989; Öst, et al., 1992; Thyer, Himle, & Curtis 1985). Consequences of the avoidance associated with BII fear are potentially life-threatening, particularly for those who require acute or ongoing medical attention.

Exposure-based techniques combined with applied muscle tension, cognitive restructuring, and modeling are effective strategies for decreasing BII phobia–related fear and avoidance behavior (e.g., Marks, 1988; Page, 1994). In the available literature, three controlled treatment outcome studies investigated the effectiveness of pure exposure interventions (Öst, Fellenius, et al., 1991; Öst, et al., 1992; Öst, Lindahl, Sterner, & Jerremalm, 1984). These studies tested the efficacy of therapist-directed in vivo exposure and targeted one aspect of BII phobia alone, either blood (Öst, Fellenius, et al., 1991; Öst, et al., 1984) or injection phobia (Öst, et al., 1992). Exposure items were selected based on which feature of BII phobia was targeted. For example, exposure hierarchies for blood phobia typically included examining photos of blood, holding a blood sample vial, having blood drawn, and observing surgical operations. Studies of injection phobia have involved having the individual either observe or receive a finger prick or injection. Duration of treatment has varied from a single session to multiple sessions over 3 months. Therapeutic gains have been reported up to 1 year (Öst, Fellenius, et al., 1991).

Comparative Studies

It seems evident that exposure-based techniques can successfully alleviate BII pbobia–related symptoms; however, the relative effectiveness of exposure techniques compared to combined techniques or to treatment modalities that are not exposure-based is less clear. Öst, et al. (1984) compared individual, prolonged *in vivo* exposure to applied tension and relaxation techniques in 18 people with a phobic fear of blood. Individuals in the exposure group developed individually tailored hierarchies that gradually increased in intensity. The applied relaxation group practiced muscle tension-relaxation techniques while viewing slides of blood samples or visiting the blood bank. Treatment was for nine sessions over 3 months. Small-group differences at post-treatment were reported with a better outcome in the exposure-only group. At the 6-month follow-up evaluation, there were no significant group differences on self-report, physiological, or behavior measures. That individuals in the applied tension group also underwent some exposure makes it unclear whether changes in this group could be solely attributable to applied muscle tension practices. Another study (Öst, Fellenius, et al., 1991) attempted to answer this question by dismantling the exposure and applied tension components. Their study included an in vivo only condition, an applied tension condition, and a combined condition across five weekly individualized sessions with 30 diagnosed BII phobics primarily afraid of blood. All groups improved significantly at post-treatment and maintained therapeutic gains at 1-year follow-up. In contrast to Öst, et al. (1984), the group that received only in vivo exposure demonstrated the least improvement based on behavioral tests and observer ratings, and the combined group demonstrated the greatest improvement. Self-report and physiological measures revealed no group differences at post-treatment and follow-up evaluation.

For injection phobia, one study has demonstrated that a single-session exposure format may be effective. Öst, et al. (1992) compared single-session individual exposure with durations up to 3 hours to five 1-hour sessions. Forty individuals with a diagnosis of BII phobia and an injection fear gradually confronted common injection-related situations in a standardized order. Both groups demonstrated comparable and significant treatment gains that were maintained over the next year.

The preceding studies provide evidence that multiple session and single-session prolonged exposure delivered in an individual format alleviate fear of BII successfully. As discussed for spider phobia, single-session exposure provides some advantages, including time- and cost-effectiveness. Given the fact that individuals with BII phobia often report experiencing vasovagal syncope, applied tension techniques to prevent fainting would likely be beneficial for such individuals. Empirical research suggests some therapeutic augmentation by adding applied tension to simple exposure techniques (Öst, Fellenius, et al., 1991). The sparse number of controlled studies make conclusions about interactions among treatment parameters such as type of exposure (e.g., imaginal exposure), format of therapy (e.g., group vs. individual), venue of exposure (e.g., VR), and ways to construct hierarchies (e.g., idiosyncratic or therapist-determined) and treatment outcome tenuous at this time.

Disgust

As we have discussed previously, the role disgust plays in symptom exacerbation and treatment has been examined with regard to spider phobia. Likewise, disgust has received attention in the treatment of BII phobia (e.g., de Jong & Merckelbach, 1998). For example, researchers have reported that a majority of BII-phobic individuals report disgust in response to phobic stimuli, suggesting the importance of disgust in maintenance of BII phobia (e.g., Sawchuk, et al., 2000).

Investigation into how treatment for disgust can be incorporated into exposure-based techniques for BII phobia has just begun. Hirai, Cochran, Stransky, Butcher, and Meadows (2004) developed a single-session, individual exposure protocol targeting both disgust and fear for injection phobia and compared it to an exposure intervention without disgust-specific techniques and information. A total of 38 highly injection-fearful subclinical individuals were treated. Both treatments included psychoeducational and exposure components. The psychoeducational elements in the disgust-focused protocol were designed to identify and clarify misperceptions about disgust-related features of BII phobia stimuli (e.g., blood and injection always introduce contamination, diseases, and viruses), as well as fear-related properties (e.g., degree of pain during injections). Steps in the fear hierarchy were shared by both groups, including looking at photos and films of injection, finger-painting with rat blood, and finger-pricking. The disgust group also completed three additional exposure steps meant to provoke disgust-related contamination concerns, such as touching one's arm, hair, and face with the same hand used to hold the blood vial and the hypodermic needle. No group differences emerged on fear and disgust responses to BII phobia stimuli measured by various types of assessments at post-treatment and at 1-week follow-up evaluation. Both groups showed not only lowered disgust to BII phobia–related stimuli but also a reduction in global disgust sensitivity. The failure to find a main effect for treatment is consistent with results from the spider study (Hirai, et al., 2003). It is likely that common exposure tasks, such as holding a hypodermic needle and blood vial, elicited both fear and disgust reactions, thereby providing therapeutic effects for both reactions. Unlike previous spider studies that have not found changes in nonspider disgust sensitivity after exposure (de Jong, et al., 1997; Smits et al., 2002), participants showed a reduction in global disgust sensitivity and BII phobia–specific disgust responding.

Summary for BII Phobia

Exposure-based interventions, including single-session exposure treatment, appear to be effective for BII phobia with stable treatment gains maintained up to 1 year. It is probable that the addition of applied tension to exposure is beneficial for BII phobia sufferers with vasovagal syncope. A recent modification adding disgust elements to exposure did not provide incremental effects. However, the shortage of studies investigating the role of disgust in exposure treatment for BII phobia renders any conclusions regarding disgust tentative. It is expected that continued research investigating relationships among disgust, BII phobia, and exposure treatment will shed further light on this topic. Future studies need to identify the incremental effect of select treatment components and parameters in relation to maintenance of short-term and long-term therapeutic gains.

CLAUSTROPHOBIA

According to data from the national comorbidity survey, the lifetime prevalence rate of claustrophobia is 4.2% (Curtis, Magee, Eaton, Wittchen, & Kessler, 1998). This makes claustrophobia the third most prevalent phobia, following animal and height phobias. Several controlled treatment outcome studies have examined exposure techniques for claustrophobia (Booth & Rachman, 1992; Öst, et al, 2001; Öst, Johansson, & Jerremalm, 1982), all of which demonstrate that individual exposure approaches produce significant improvements in claustrophobia symptoms.

Comparative Studies

There is some evidence that exposure interventions are as effective as cognitive and relaxation interventions. One of the earliest studies conducted by Öst, et al. (1982), who randomly assigned 34 claustrophobic individuals to exposure, applied relaxation, or control conditions for 8 to 10 weeks over 3 months. Participants were classified as either behaviorally reactive or physiologically reactive based on pretreatment behavioral testing. In the exposure condition, participants progressed through idiosyncratically developed hierarchies. Relative to the control condition, individuals in the treatment conditions showed greater improvement at post-treatment and 14-month follow-up period. The exposure group yielded better outcomes than the relaxation group at post-treatment, but differences disappeared at follow-up evaluation. Behaviorally reactive individuals improved to a greater extent with exposure than relaxation, whereas the reverse pattern was seen with physiologically reactive participants.

In a later study, Booth and Rachman (1992) compared three independent treatments (i.e., gradual in vivo exposure, interoceptive exposure, and cognitive therapy) to a control condition. Individuals in the exposure condition developed hierarchies using situations available in the laboratory setting (e.g., staying in the laboratory closet with the door open and the light on, being in the closet with the door locked and the light off) and completed the hierarchy over the course of three sessions. Individuals in the interoceptive exposure condition completed a series of behavioral tasks (e.g., overbreathing, spinning, running in place) to simulate physical sensations they experienced when anxious. At post-treatment, the in vivo exposure condition showed the greatest gains on self-report, behavioral, and physiological measures of anxiety on exposure to claustrophobic situations. In contrast, the cognitive and interoceptive exposure groups demonstrated marginal improvement relative to the control condition. However, no differences among the treatment groups were found at post-treatment and 6- to 8-week follow-up evaluation.

Another study by Öst and colleagues (2001) compared 3-hour single-session individual in vivo exposure, five 1-hour weekly individual in vivo exposure, and five 1-hour weekly individual cognitive therapy to a wait-list control condition. A total of 46 claustrophobic individuals were treated. Individuals in the exposure groups selected personally relevant fear-eliciting situations (e.g., elevator, window-less room, subway). Individuals in the single-session group were exposed to two or three situations while accompanied by a therapist. Individuals in the five-session group confronted four to five situations with the therapist. All treatment groups showed improvement across a variety of assessment measures relative to the wait-list condition at post-treatment, with treatment gains maintained at 1-year follow-up evaluation.

The preceding studies demonstrate the effectiveness of in vivo individual exposure techniques, including short-term treatment strategies (i.e., single-session). At this point, the available controlled treatment outcome studies for claustrophobia support similar efficacies of several types of psychological interventions, including exposure, with long-term treatment gain up to 14 months.

Factors Affecting the Efficacy of Exposure for Claustrophobia

Several studies using individuals with subclinical levels of claustrophobia have examined factors that mediate the effectiveness of in vivo exposure (Kamphuis & Telch, 2000; Powers, Smits, & Telch, 2004; Sloan & Telch, 2002; Telch, Valentiner, Ilai, Petruzzi, & Hehmsoth, 2000; Telch, Valentiner, Ilai, Young, Powers, & Smits, 2004). In these studies, brief exposure trials of about 5 minutes, with several different behavioral and cognitive conditions, were repeated for up to 30 minutes in a small room. These studies yielded three primary conclusions. First, instructing individuals to focus on claustrophobia-related cognitions during exposure enhanced the effectiveness of exposure therapy, whereas distracting thoughts or mental processes appeared to impede treatment. Second, treatment was also impeded if participants were aware that they could engage in an escape behavior that could decrease their anxiety (e.g., opening a window). Finally, physiological feedback enhanced the effectiveness of exposure therapy. These findings appear to be consistent with Foa and Kozak's emotional processing theory (1986) in that they suggest activation of the fear network, and the presentation of corrective information that is incompatible with pathological elements in the fear network, are two important requisites for fear reduction. These studies, however, were conducted with nonclinical individuals, and the question remains whether the results will generalize to clinical populations.

Summary for Claustrophobia

Overall, brief in vivo exposure techniques are effective in the treatment of claustrophobia. The available research results suggest that exposure is at least as effective for treating claustrophobia as cognitive therapy and relaxation. It also seems to be the case that maximizing emotional processing during exposure is a key factor for modifying less severe symptoms. Little is known, however, regarding optimal treatment delivery and whether a combination of disparate treatment modalities (e.g., in vivo exposure plus cognitive restructuring) might enhance treatment outcome. In addition, other issues remain: the effects of varying the way exposure is delivered, how the hierarchies are constructed, and whether clinical samples respond to treatment in a way that is similar to nonclinical participants.

FLYING PHOBIA

The available literature suggests that exposure treatments and cognitive-behavioral approaches that include in vivo exposure components are equally effective and superior to no-treatment conditions for flying phobia (e.g., Howard, Murphy, & Clarke, 1983; Öst, Brandberg, & Alm, 1997; Van Gerwen, Spinhoven, Diekstra, & Van Dyck, 2002). Because many people have a fear of flying, and because the fear may interfere with an individual's professional obligations, a relatively large research base has developed in this area. More recently, fear of flying has received increased attention because of the ease with which flight cabins can be simulated in a virtual environment (in addition to the following section, see Bouchard, Côte, & Richard in this volume).

Virtual Reality

Compared to other in vivo exposure situations, taking a commercial airplane flight is a costly part of treatment. The creation of a virtual flight cabin with all the attendant sounds made on takeoff, landing, and so forth offers a cost-effective treatment option for clinicians that allows a degree of control not possible in real environments.

The most impressive series of studies on fear of flying was performed by Rothbaum and colleagues (Rothbaum, Hodges, Anderson, Price, & Smith, 2002; Rothbaum, et al., 2000). In these two studies they reported treatment and follow-up results for 49 individuals assigned to VR, in vivo exposure, or wait-list conditions. Participants were eligible for the study if they had a phobic fear of flying, panic with agoraphobia, or agoraphobia without panic. Participants completed eight sessions over 8 weeks or were placed on a treatment wait list. VR exposure included simulation of flight-related events (e.g., taking off, flying, a thunderstorm, turbulence, and landing). Prolonged in vivo exposure with standardized exposure hierarchy items took place at the airport terminal and on a stationary airplane where individuals engaged in imaginal exposure. Both the VR and in vivo exposure groups received anxiety management and cognitive restructuring training before exposure. Both exposure groups displayed significant reductions in self-reported fear of flying and were superior to the wait-list control at post-treatment, 6-month follow-up, and 12-month follow-up. More than 90% of individuals in both treatment groups took an actual flight during the 12-month follow-up period. There were no differences in treatment outcome between the exposure groups.

Other controlled treatment outcome studies support the efficacy of VR exposure for flying phobia. Mühlberger, Herrmann, Wiedemann, Ellgring, and Pauli (2001) compared a single-session VR program to a single-session relaxation program. The VR program consisted of 18 minutes of audiovisual information with motion simulations of all flight components, including leaving the terminal, taking off, turbulence, and landing. The VR group repeated the program four times. In addition, both groups underwent VR exposure (6 minutes, no audio or turbulence effects) as part of the assessment process. Results from a total of 30 individuals with flying phobia revealed that the exposure group yielded more significant improvement in some self-reported symptoms than the relaxation group at post-treatment. At 14–week follow-up evaluation, a trend in favor of the VR group was found.

Another study (Mühlberger, Wiedemann, & Pauli, 2003) compared two single-session, VR exposure programs (VR with motion simulation plus cognitive treatment, VR without motion simulation plus cognitive treatment) and a cognitive intervention to a nonrandomized wait-list control condition in a total of 47 diagnosed flying phobics. The VR programs provided audiovisual with or without motion simulation of all flight components similar to those used by Mühlberger, et al. (2001). Individuals in the VR groups briefly learned cognitive techniques and completed four successive 18-minute VR flights in the session. The cognitive therapy group received one session of cognitive restructuring psychoeducation. Results revealed that both VR exposure conditions were significantly superior to the wait-list condition in reducing symptoms at post-treatment and the 6-month follow-up period, whereas the cognitive and wait-list control groups were not significantly different. This latter finding is not especially surprising given that cognitive therapy is not intended to be delivered in only one session. Presence or absence of motion simulation also had no impact on the effectiveness of the virtual treatments. At 6-month follow-up evaluation, 62% of individuals in the VR groups had taken a commercial flight since treatment relative to 45% of those in the cognitive treatment condition. There was no follow-up evaluation for the control group.

The burgeoning VR treatment literature for fear of flying suggests that virtual treatments for flight phobia are superior to wait-list control conditions and may be superior to other treatments, although the evidence is limited. No study to date has shown VR exposure to be superior to in vivo exposure. It may be the case that VR and in vivo exposure treatments are equally effective. On the other hand, the relatively small sample sizes of these studies makes the power of the design an issue. The efficacy of single-session VR programs without sophisticated elements such as motion simulation effects further supports the notion that it has considerable potential to become a popular cost-effective treatment strategy for flight phobia. More studies are needed to further examine parameters that affect the treatment efficacy VR for fear of flying.

SOCIAL PHOBIA

Individuals with social phobia experience intense anxiety in situations in which negative social evaluation might occur, such as public performances or social interactions. Avoidance likely leads these individuals to experience impaired social or occupational functioning. Treatment packages often include in-session as well as between-session exposure, cognitive restructuring to target misinterpretations of social cues and distorted self-perceptions, and relaxation. In addition, inclusion of a social skills training component has been suggested (e.g., Turner, Beidel, Cooley, & Woody, 1994; Turner, Beidel, & Cooley-Quille, 1995). Regardless of the types of psychological intervention components incorporated, exposure typically includes confronting social situations, either in a standardized treatment context or by contrived exposure to feared social situations. The duration of exposure treatment is relatively long compared to that for specific phobias, ranging from 6 to 16 weeks (e.g., Feske & Chambless, 1995). Interventions are delivered in either a group or an individual format. Three meta-analytic studies for treatments of social phobia suggest that simple exposure techniques can alleviate social phobia symptoms significantly and therapeutic gains remain for at least 6 months to a year (Feske & Chambless, 1995; Taylor, 1996).

Comparative Studies

The three meta-analytic studies have shown that exposure interventions are comparable to other types of psychological treatments such as cognitive-behavioral treatment, cognitive therapy, and social skills training for treating social phobia. In addition, some pharmacological treatments, including benzodiazepines and selective serotonin reuptake inhibitors (SSRIs), may have some advantages over exposure (Feske & Chambless, 1995; Taylor, 1996; Fedroff & Taylor, 2000). No clear evidence has been provided with regard to the influence of treatment variables such as therapy format (e.g., individual or group) and exposure duration on treatment effects, based on these meta-analytic studies.

Several controlled exposure-only treatment outcome studies have been published since the meta-analyses described here (Blomhoff, Haug, Hellström,

Holme, Humble, Madsbu, et al., 2001; Clark, Ehlers, McManus, Hackmann, Fennell, Campbell, et al.; 2003; Haug, Blomhoff, Hellström, Holme, Humble, Madsbu, et al., 2003; Hofmann, 2004). Again, more recent studies have supported the effectiveness of exposure-based interventions. The question regarding the relative effectiveness of conventional exposure to combined or other psychological interventions or pharmacological treatments remains less clear. Hofmann (2004) examined 12-week group exposure and a group cognitive-behavioral intervention targeting speech anxiety, comparing these groups to a wait-list control. Among 90 individuals, 76% received a social phobia diagnosis at pretreatment. Both treatment groups followed standardized treatment protocols with common exposure steps in sessions and completed individual exposure homework. Both groups demonstrated significantly improved social anxiety symptoms and behavioral performance (i.e., increased public speaking time during behavioral tests) relative to the wait-list condition. The two treatments did not yield differences in outcome at post-treatment, but at 6-month follow-up evaluation, the cognitive behavioral group showed greater improvement than the exposure group.

Clark, et al. (2003) examined three 16-week individual treatments for 60 diagnosed social phobics, including fluoxetine (an antidepressant) plus self-exposure between sessions, placebo plus self-exposure between sessions, and cognitive-behavioral therapy, with a strong emphasis on cognitive elements. Exposure hierarchies were developed individually for self-exposure. At post-treatment, all groups demonstrated significantly reduced symptoms, with a better outcome found in the cognitive behavioral group on social anxiety measures. At 12-month follow-up evaluation, cognitive behavioral therapy remained superior to the other two groups. Because the exposure elements in the self-exposure groups were administered as homework without therapist-directed in-session exposure, whereas the cognitive behavioral group had some therapist-directed exposure practice in sessions, the superiority of the cognitive behavioral group should be interpreted with caution.

A series of studies (Blomhoff, et al., 2001; Haug, et al., 2003) compared exposure treatment with sertraline (a class of SSRIs) and placebo, sertraline only, and placebo only. Approximately 80 participants per treatment condition completed eight individual sessions over 12 weeks. The exposure elements consisted of in-session exposure for 15 to 20 minutes and between-session exposure practice based on idiosyncratically developed hierarchies. At post-treatment, all of the three active treatment groups demonstrated equally significant symptom reduction, though the exposure with placebo group did not differ from the placebo-only group in improvement. At the 1-year follow-up, symptom levels in all four groups were improved compared to pretreatment. However, the exposure with placebo and placebo-only groups demonstrated continued symptom improvement after treatment, while the sertraline groups, with and without exposure, displayed significant deterioration from post-treatment.

Overall, the three meta-analytic studies, as well as the recent literature, have provided evidence that exposure-based treatment in general is an effective treatment strategy for social phobia, and that pharmacological treatments, particularly SSRIs, may provide superior symptom relief in the short term. Results have been inconclusive regarding whether (1) adding cognitive restructuring and social skills training components augment exposure's therapeutic effects; and (2) treatment parameters, such as treatment format and duration, affect therapeutic gain.

Factors Affecting the Efficacy of Exposure for Social Phobia

Researchers have attempted to identify factors influencing the effectiveness of exposure therapy for social phobia. For example, the presence of comorbid psychological disorders has been investigated as a factor in the effectiveness of exposure treatment for social phobia. Van Velzen, Emmelkamp, and Scholing (1997) examined psychopathology factors including the presence of a personality disorder, or other Axis I comorbid psychopathology such as depression, in relation to exposure treatment outcome. In this study, individuals with a diagnosis of social phobia and an additional diagnosis received 10 to 14 sessions over 10 weeks with standardized in vivo exposure tasks during and between sessions. No relationship between the psychopathology variables and the effectiveness of exposure was found.

Several studies have also examined how safety behavior and levels of emotional engagement mediate the effectiveness of exposure treatment. Morgan and Raffle (1999) investigated whether safety behaviors during 10 exposure sessions over 3 weeks affected the efficacy of cognitive-behavioral group treatment for 30 individuals with social phobia. Examples of safety behaviors during a speech included wearing makeup to hide blushing and holding a cup tightly to avoid shaking. Individual safety behaviors were targeted for elimination during treatment in the "safety" condition, whereas those in the "usual" treatment group were not instructed to discontinue their safety behaviors. Self-reported social phobia decreased more in the safety condition than in the group that did not discontinue the use of safety behaviors.

Level of emotional engagement may also mediate the efficacy of exposure therapy. Coles and Heimberg (2000) investigated relationships between pretreatment patterns of emotional engagement in ideographically selected BAT situations and therapeutic outcome. Individuals with social phobia were treated in twelve 2.5-hour weekly cognitive-behavior sessions. It was reported that higher emotional engagement in the initial BAT predicted better treatment outcome.

Thus, recent research indicates that the presence of safety behaviors during exposure and a lack of emotional engagement may interfere with the effectiveness of exposure. Again, these findings are consistent with the theoretical mechanisms of exposure postulated by emotional processing theory (Foa & Kozak, 1986).

Summary for Social Phobia

Overall, it has been demonstrated that exposure-based interventions reduce social phobia symptoms over time. The evidence is less clear about the effectiveness of pure exposure interventions relative to combined psychological and pharmacological treatments. Because individuals with social phobia typically avoid performance and social interaction situations, incorporating practice of such activities into exposure treatment is likely a requisite for increased efficacy.

More controlled exposure treatment studies are warranted to examine the effects of various factors and treatment parameters on outcome. Although an increasing number of studies have investigated computerized or VR-based interventions for anxiety disorders including specific phobias, application of such techniques to social phobia have not yet been widely examined in controlled treatment outcome research. One small-scale controlled study compared a VR exposure program to a wait-list control condition in a student population and reported notable group differences on self-reported public speaking anxiety and physiological symptoms at post-treatment (Harris, Kemmerling, & North, 2002). This small but successful study provides an encouraging step in developing VR as an alternative exposure method for social phobia.

CONCLUSIONS

This chapter provided evidence that exposure-based interventions can be used to treat specific phobias, such as fear of spiders, BII phobia, closed places, and flying, and social phobia successfully. These improvements are usually maintained at short-term follow-up evaluation. A search of the literature, however, revealed that there is still a need for exposure outcome studies targeting a broader array of phobic objects and environments. Furthermore, the role of exposure components when combined with other psychological interventions and the relative effectiveness of conventional exposure to combined treatments or other psychological interventions are less clear.

The question of what treatment variables enhance the effectiveness of exposure treatments is an important one in understanding how to maximize treatment outcome. At this point, it is not conclusive what treatment parameters, such as duration, format, and venue of exposure, are related to treatment outcome. Regarding duration, single-session exposure appears comparably effective to prolonged exposure for many specific phobias (e.g., Mühlberger, et al., 2003; Öst, 1996; Öst, et al., 1992).

Theorists have generally predicted that distraction would weaken the effectiveness of exposure. Results are somewhat varied across phobic targets. For claustrophobia, maximizing emotional engagement and minimizing distraction appears to be important for successful exposure. Similarly, increasing emotional engagement and decreasing safety-seeking could improve the effectiveness of exposure for social phobia. Findings regarding the role of distraction in spider phobia treatment are less consistent.

There is mounting evidence that disgust plays an important role in the maintenance and treatment of spider and BII phobia. The findings of the studies reviewed here suggest that conventional fear-focused exposure treatment effectively decreases both fear and disgust for spider and BII phobia. Despite the apparent role of disgust in BII and spider phobia, supplemental exposure techniques targeting disgust did not demonstrate incremental efficacy.

The future of exposure programs in the treatment of phobias seems to be heading toward increased use of advanced technology, including VR. The potential of VR is noteworthy, particularly in its ability to tailor exposure experiences to the specific needs of the client and augment the treatment experience with audiovisual displays, tactile cues, and motion simulation. At this point, preliminary successful outcomes have been reported for VR exposure for a limited array of phobic targets.

The efficacy of exposure treatment for the anxiety disorders, particularly the specific phobias and social phobias, seems undisputed. Further, our understanding of factors contributing to the maintenance of exposure treatment gains is improving. Research continues to attempt to delineate its underlying mechanisms and the factors that contribute to short- and long-term gains.

REFERENCES

Antony, M.M., Barlow, D.H., & Craske, M.J. (1997). *Mastery of your specific phobia: Therapist guide.* San Antonio, TX: Therapy Works.

Bienvenu, O.J., & Eaton, W.W. (1998). The epidemiology of blood-injection-injury phobia. *Psychological Medicine, 28,* 1129–1136.

Blomhoff, S., Haug, T.T., Hellström, K., Holme, I., Humble, M., Madsbu, H.P., & Wold, J.E. (2001). Randomised controlled general practice trial of sertraline, exposure therapy and combined treatment in generalised social phobia. *British Journal of Psychiatry, 179,* 23–30.

Booth, R., & Rachman, S. (1992). The reduction of claustrophobia: I. *Behaviour Research and Therapy, 30,* 207–221.

Bourdon, K.H., Boyd, J.H., Rae, D.S., Burns, B.J., Thompson, J.W., & Locke, B.Z. (1988). Gender differences in phobias: Results of the ECA community survey. *Journal of Anxiety Disorders, 2,* 227–241.

Clark, D.M., Ehlers, A., McManus, F., Hackmann, A., Fennell, M., Campbell, H., Flower, F., Davenport, C., & Louis, B. (2003). Cognitive therapy versus fluoxetine in generalized social phobia: A randomized placebo-controlled trial. *Journal of Consulting and Clinical Psychology, 71,* 1058–1067.

Coles, M.E., & Heimberg, R.G. (2000). Patterns of anxious arousal during exposure to feared situations in individuals with social phobia. *Behaviour Research and Therapy, 38,* 405–424.

Curtis, G.C., Magee, W.J., Eaton, W.W., Wittchen, H.-U., & Kessler, R.C. (1998). Specific fears and phobias: Epidemiology and classification. *British Journal of Psychiatry, 173,* 212–217.

de Jong, P.J., Andrea, H., & Muris, P. (1997). Spider phobia in children: Disgust and fear before and after treatment. *Behaviour Research and Therapy, 35,* 559–562.

de Jong, P.J., & Merckelbach, H. (1998). Blood-injection-injury phobia and fear of spiders: Domain specific individual differences in disgust sensitivity. *Personality and Individual Differences, 24,* 153–158.

de Jong, P.J., Vorage, I., & van den Hout, M.A. (2000). Counterconditioning in the treatment of spider phobia: Effects of disgust, fear, and valence. *Behaviour Research and Therapy, 38,* 1055–1069.

Denney, D.R., Sullivan, B.J., & Thiry, M.R. (1977). Participant modeling and self-verbalization training in the reduction of spider fears. *Journal of Behavior Therapy and Experimental Psychiatry, 8,* 247–253.

Feske, U., & Chambless, D.L. (1995). Cognitive behavioral versus exposure only treatment for social phobia: A meta-analysis. *Behavior Therapy, 26,* 695–720.

Foa, E.B., & Kozak, M.J. (1986). Emotional processing of fear: Exposure to corrective information. *Psychological Bulletin, 99,* 20–35.

Garcia-Palacios, A., Hoffman, H.G., Carlin, A., Furness, T.A. III, & Botella, C. (2002). Virtual reality in the treatment of spider phobia: A controlled study. *Behaviour Research and Therapy, 40,* 983–993.

Garcia-Palacios, A., Hoffman, H.G., See, S.K., Tsai, A., & Botella, C. (2001). Redefining therapeutic success with virtual reality exposure therapy. *CyberPsychology and Behavior, 4,* 341–348.

Götestam, K.G. (2002). One session group treatment of spider phobia by direct or modelled exposure. *Cognitive Behaviour Therapy, 31,* 18–24.

Harris, S.R., Kemmerling, R.L., & North, M.M. (2002). Brief virtual reality therapy for public speaking anxiety. *CyberPsychology and Behavior, 5,* 543–550.

Haug, T.T., Blomhoff, S., Hellström, K., Holme, I., Humble, M., Madsbu, H.P., & Wold, J.E. (2003). Exposure therapy and sertraline in social phobia: 1-year follow-up of a randomised controlled trial. *British Journal of Psychiatry, 182,* 312–318.

Hellström, K., Fellenius, J., & Öst, L-G. (1996). One versus five sessions of applied tension in the treatment of blood phobia. *Behaviour Research and Therapy, 34*(2), 101–112.

Hellström, K., & Öst, L.-G. (1995). One-session therapist directed exposure vs. Two forms of manual directed self-exposure in the treatment of spider phobia. *Behaviour Research and Therapy, 33,* 959–965.

Hellström, K., & Öst, L.-G. (1996). Prediction of outcome in the treatment of specific phobia: A cross validation study. *Behavioural Research and Therapy, 34,* 403–411.

Hirai, M., Cochran, H., Stransky, J., Butcher, J., & Meadows, E. (2004). Assessing the efficacy of treatment techniques targeting disgust in BII phobia. Unpublished manuscript.

Hirai, M., Vernon, L, Cochran, H., Butcher, J., Stransky, J., & Meadows, E. (2003). The efficacy of exposure treatment with disgust components in spider phobia and its generalizability to blood-injection-injury phobia. (Unpublished manuscript.)

Hoffman, H.G., Garcia-Palacios, A., Carlin, A., Furness, T.A. III, & Botella-Arbona, C. (2003). Interfaces that heal: Coupling real and virtual objects to treat spider phobia. *International Journal of Human-Computer Interaction, 16,* 283–300.

Hofmann, S.G. (2004). Cognitive mediation of treatment change in social phobia. *Journal of Consulting and Clinical Psychology, 72,* 392–399.

Howard, W.A., Murphy, S.M., & Clarke, J.C. (1983). The nature and treatment of fear of flying: A controlled investigation. *Behavior Therapy, 14,* 557–567.

Johnstone, K.A., & Page, A.C. (2004). Attention to phobic stimuli during exposure: The effect of distraction on anxiety reduction, self-efficacy and perceived control. *Behaviour Research and Therapy, 42,* 249–275.

Kamphuis, J.H., & Telch, M.J. (2000). Effects of distraction and guided threat reappraisal on fear reduction during exposure-based treatments for specific fears. *Behaviour Research and Therapy, 38,* 1163–1181.

Kessler, R.C., McGonagle, K.A., Zhao, S., Nelson, C.B., Hughes, M., Eshleman, S., Wittchen, H.U., & Kendler, K.S. (1994). Lifetime and 12-month prevalence of DSM-III-R psychiatric disorders in the United States: Results from the National Comorbidity Survey. *Archives of General Psychiatry, 51,* 8–19

Klieger, D.M., & Siejak, K.K. (1997). Disgust as the source of false positive effects in the measurement of ophidiophobia. *Journal of Psychology: Interdisciplinary & Applied, 131,* 371–382.

Lazarus, A.A. (1961). Group therapy of phobic disorders by systematic desensitization. *Journal of Abnormal and Social Psychology, 63,* 504–510.

Marks, I.M. (1988). Blood-injury phobia: A review. *American Journal of Psychiatry, 145,* 1207–1213.

Marshall, W.L., Gauthier, J., Christie, M.M., Currie, S.W., & Gordon, A. (1977). Flooding therapy: Effectiveness, stimulus characteristics, and the value of brief in vivo exposure. *Behavior Research and Therapy, 15,* 79–87.

Marshall, W.L., Strawbridge, H., & Keltner, A. (1972). The role of mental relaxation in experimental desensitization. *Behaviour Research and Therapy, 10,* 355–366.

Merckelbach, H., de Jong, P., Arntz, A., & Schouten, E. (1993). The role of evaluative learning and disgust sensitivity in the etiology and treatment of spider phobia. *Advances in Behaviour Research and Therapy, 15,* 243–255.

Miller, S.M. (1987). Monitoring and blunting: validation of a questionnaire to assess styles of information seeking under threat. *Journal of Personality and Social Psychology, 52,* 345–353.

Mineka, S., Mystkowski, J., Hladek, D., & Rodriguez, B.I. (1999). The effects of changing contexts on return of fear following exposure therapy for spider fear. *Journal of Consulting and Clinical Psychology, 67,* 599–604.

Morgan, H., & Raffle, C. (1999). Does reducing safety behaviors improve treatment response in patients with social phobia? *Australian and New Zealand Journal of Psychiatry, 33,* 503–510.

Mühlberger, A., Herrmann, M.J., Wiedemann, G., Ellgring, H., & Pauli, P. (2001). Repeated exposure of flight phobics to flights in virtual reality. *Behaviour Research and Therapy, 39,* 1033–1050.

Mühlberger, A., Wiedemann, G., & Pauli, P. (2003). Efficacy of a one-session virtual reality exposure treatment for fear of flying. *Psychotherapy Research, 13,* 323–336.

Muris, P., de Jong, P.J., Merckelbach, H., & Van Zuuren, F. (1993a). Monitoring coping style and exposure outcome in spider phobics. *Behavioural and Cognitive Psychotherapy, 21,* 329–333.

Muris, P., de Jong, P.J., Merckelbach, H., & Van Zuuren, F. (1993b). Is exposure therapy outcome affected by a monitoring coping style? *Advances in Behaviour Research and Therapy, 15,* 291–300.

Muris, P., Merckelbach, H., & de Jong, P.J. (1995). Exposure therapy outcome in spider phobics: Effects of monitoring and blunting coping styles. *Behaviour Research and Therapy, 33,* 461–464.

Mystkowski, J., Craske, M.G., & Echiverri, A.M. (2002). Treatment context and return of fear in spider phobia. *Behavior Therapy, 33,* 399–416.

Mystkowski, J., Mineka, S., Vernon, L., & Zinbarg, R. (2003). Changes in caffeine state enhance return of fear in spider phobia. *Journal of Consulting and Clinical Psychology, 71,* 243–250.

Öst, L.-G. (1987). Age of onset in different phobias. *Journal of Abnormal Psychology, 96,* 223–229.

Öst, L.-G. (1989). One-session treatment for specific phobias. *Behaviour Research and Therapy, 27,* 1–7.

Öst, L.-G. (1996). One-session group treatment of spider phobia. *Behaviour Research and Therapy, 34,* 707–715.

Öst, L.-G., Alm, T., Brandberg, M., & Breitholtz, E. (2001). One vs. five sessions of exposure and five sessions of cognitive therapy in the treatment of claustrophobia. *Behaviour Research and Therapy, 39,* 167–183.

Öst, L.-G., Brandberg, M., & Alm, T. (1997). One versus five sessions of exposure in the treatment of flying phobia. *Behaviour Research and Therapy, 35,* 987–996.

Öst, L.-G., Fellenius, J., & Sterner, U. (1991). Applied tension, exposure in vivo, and tension-only in the treatment of blood phobia. *Behaviour Research and Therapy, 29,* 561–574.

Öst, L.-G., Ferebee, I., & Furmark, T. (1997). One-session group therapy of spider phobia: Direct versus indirect treatments. *Behaviour Research and Therapy, 35,* 721–732.

Öst, L.-G., Hellström, K., & Kåver, A. (1992). One versus five sessions of exposure in the treatment of injection phobia. *Behavior Therapy, 23,* 263–282.

Öst, L.-G., Johansson, J., & Jerremalm, A. (1982). Individual response patterns and the effects of different behavioral methods in the treatment of claustrophobia. *Behavioural Research and Therapy, 20,* 445–460.

Öst, L.-G., Lindahl, I., Sterner, U., & Jerremalm, A. (1984). Exposure in vivo vs. Applied relaxation in the treatment of blood phobia. *Behaviour Research and Therapy, 22,* 205–216.

Öst, L.-G., Salkovskis, P. M., Hellström, K. (1991). One-session therapist-directed exposure vs. self-exposure in the treatment of spider phobia. *Behavior Therapy, 22,* 407–422.

Page, A.C. (1994). Blood-injury phobia. *Clinical Psychology Review, 14*, 443–461.

Paul, G.L. (1966). *Insight vs. desensitization in psychotherapy.* Stanford, CA: Stanford University Press.

Paul, G.L., & Shannon, D.T. (1966). Treatment of anxiety through systematic desensitization in therapy groups. *Journal of Abnormal Psychology, 71*, 123–135.

Powers, M.B., Smits, J.A.J., & Telch, M.J. (2004). Disentangling the effects of safety-behavior utilization and safety-behavior availability during exposure-based treatment: A placebo-controlled trial. *Journal of Consulting and Clinical Psychology, 72*, 448–454.

Rachman, S.J. (1966a). Studies in desensitization: II. Flooding. *Behaviour Research and Therapy, 4*, 1–6.

Rachman, S.J. (1966b). Studies in desensitization: III. Speed of generalization. *Behaviour Research and Therapy, 4*, 7–15.

Rachman, S.J. (1979). The return of fear. *Behaviour Research and Therapy, 17*, 164–166.

Rachman, S.J. (1989). The return of fear: Review and prospect. *Clinical Psychology Review, 9*, 147–168.

Rachman, S.J., & Lopatka, C. (1988). Return of fear: Underlearning and overlearning. *Behaviour Research and Therapy, 26*, 99–104.

Robinson, C., & Suinn, R. (1969). Group desensitization of a phobia in massed sessions. *Behaviour Research and Therapy, 7*, 319–321.

Rodriguez, B.I., & Craske, M.G. (1993). The effects of distraction during exposure to phobic stimuli. *Behaviour Research and Therapy, 31*, 549–558.

Rothbaum, B.O., Hodges, L., Anderson, P.L., Price, L., & Smith, S. (2002). Twelve-month follow-up of virtual reality and standard exposure therapies for the fear of flying. *Journal of Consulting and Clinical Psychology, 70*, 428–432.

Rothbaum, B.O., Hodges, L., Smith, S., Lee, J.H., & Price, L. (2000). A controlled study of virtual reality exposure therapy for the fear of flying. *Journal of Consulting and Clinical Psychology, 68*, 1020–1026.

Rowe, M.K., & Craske, M.G. (1998a). Effects of varied-stimulus exposure training on fear reduction and return of fear. *Behaviour Research and Therapy, 36*, 719–734.

Rowe, M.K., & Craske, M.G. (1998b). Effects of an expanding-spaced vs. Massed exposure schedule on fear reduction and return of fear. *Behaviour Research and Therapy, 36*, 701–717.

Rozin, P., & Fallon, A. (1987). A perspective on disgust. *Psychological Review, 94*, 23–41.

Salkovskis, P., & Mills, I. (1994). Induced mood, phobic responding and the return of fear. *Behaviour Research and Therapy, 32*, 439–445.

Sawchuk, C.N., Lohr, J.M., Tolin, D.F., Lee, T.C., & Kleinknecht, R.A. (2000). Disgust sensitivity and contamination fears in spider and blood-injection-injury phobias. *Behaviour Research and Therapy, 38*, 753–762.

Sloan, T., & Telch, M.J. (2002). The effects of safety-seeking behavior and guided threat reappraisal on fear reduction during exposure: An experimental investigation. *Behaviour Research and Therapy, 40*, 235–251.

Smits, J.A.J., Telch, M.J., & Randall, P.K. (2002). An examination of the decline in fear and disgust during exposure-based treatment. *Behaviour Research and Therapy, 40*, 1243–1253.

Steketee, G., Bransfield, S., Miller, S.M., & Foa, E.B. (1989). The effect of information and coping style on the reduction of phobic anxiety during exposure. *Journal of Anxiety Disorders, 3*, 69–85.

Taylor, S. (1996). Meta-analysis of cognitive-behavioral treatments for social phobia. *Journal of Behavior Therapy and Experimental Psychiatry, 27*, 1–9.

Teachman, B.A., & Woody, S.R. (2003). Automatic processing in spider phobia: Implicit fear associations over the course of treatment. *Journal of Abnormal Psychology, 112*, 100–109.

Telch, M.J., Valentiner, D.P., Ilai, D., Petruzzi, D., & Hehmsoth, M. (2000). The facilitative effects of heart-rate feedback in the emotional processing of claustrophobic fear. *Therapy and Experimental Psychiatry, 38*, 373–387.

Telch, M.J., Valentiner, D.P., Ilai, D., Young, P.R., Powers, M.B., & Smits, J.A.J. (2004). Fear activation and distraction during the emotional processing of claustrophobic fear. *Journal of Behavior Therapy and Experimental Psychiatry, 35*, 219–232.

Thyer, B.A., Himle, J., & Curtis, G.C. (1985). Blood-injury-illness phobia: A review. *Journal of Clinical Psychology, 41*, 451–459.

Turner, S.M., Beidel, D.C., Cooley, M.R., & Woody, S.R. (1994). A multicomponent behavioral treatment for social phobia: Social effectiveness therapy. *Behaviour Research and Therapy, 32,* 381–390.

Turner, S.M., Beidel, D.C., & Cooley-Quille, M.R. (1995). Two-year follow-up of social phobics treated with social effectiveness therapy. *Behaviour Research & Therapy, 33,* 553–555.

Van Gerwen, L.J., Spinhoven, P., Diekstra, R.F.W., & Van Dyck, R. (2002). Multicomponent standardized treatment programs for fear of flying: Description and effectiveness. *Cognitive and Behavioral Practice, 9,* 138–149.

Van Velzen, C.J.M., Emmelkamp, P.M.G., & Scholing, A. (1997). The impact of personality disorders on behavioral treatment outcome for social phobia. *Behaviour Research and Therapy, 35,* 889–900.

Vernon, L.L., & Berenbaum, H. (2002). Disgust and fear in response to spiders. *Cognition and Emotion, 16,* 809–830.

Vernon, L.L., & Berenbaum, H. (2004). A naturalistic examination of positive expectations, time course, and disgust in the origins and remission of spider distress. *Journal of Anxiety Disorders, 18,* 707–718.

Woody, S.R., & Teachman, B.A. (2000). Intersection of disgust and fear: Normative and pathological views. *Clinical Psychology: Science and Practice, 7,* 291–311.

CHAPTER 12

Applications of Exposure Techniques in Behavioral Medicine

Flora Hoodin and Mary Gillis

Eastern Michigan University

Exposure interventions in behavioral medicine have been applied to a variety of presenting problems, some more extensively than others. Specifically, blood-injection-injury phobia (BII) has generated a substantial line of research because the biphasic vasovagal fainting response associated with BII phobia presents special safety and ethical issues, ultimately giving rise to modifications of the exposure protocol. Although dental phobia might once have been considered a BII type specific phobia, it has long been considered a specific phobia, situational type, and has generated an independent line of research. In contrast, pain anxiety, fear of reinjury, and pain catastrophizing more appropriately belong to the pain disorder diagnostic category, and have a more recently developed and still-evolving literature.

All three of these problems (BII phobia, dental phobia, and pain anxiety) include a significant avoidant component and pose similar treatment dilemmas for clinicians. Whereas the behavioral avoidance manifested by individuals with BII or dental phobia is situational, discrete, and specific to conditional stimuli, the health sequelae secondary to avoidance behaviors are potentially serious. For example, patients with diabetes who are unable to self-administer insulin injections are at significant short- and long-term health risks. Likewise, avoidance caused by fear of dental procedures can potentiate dental crises greater in magnitude than the patient's initial complaint. Similarly, avoidance behaviors secondary to pain anxiety may contribute to development and maintenance of chronic pain, and may engender excessive functional disability as a result. Although these examples represent typographically dissimilar health problems, the functional equivalence of avoidance behaviors in each case implies amenability to exposure techniques.

This chapter reviews diagnostic criteria for each condition, provides a historical overview of research, and offers observations about clinical issues. Finally, we review a nascent line of research with much potential for further empirical investigation involving a miscellaneous category of disease states and chronic conditions that span cancer, asthma, rheumatoid arthritis, pelvic pain, HIV, and others. These disparate medical diagnoses have all been investigated for responsiveness to treatment of emotional avoidance using written emotional disclosure procedures. We argue that written emotional disclosure is active *because* it is an exposure technique. We also argue that the efficacy of written emotional disclosure would be enhanced by modifying the disclosure protocol to conform more explicitly to exposure procedures. The chapter closes by summarizing the state of research in exposure applications in behavioral medicine, and highlighting directions for further investigation.

SPECIFIC PHOBIA, BLOOD-INJECTION-INJURY TYPE

Blood-injection-injury phobia is a subtype of specific phobia characterized by intense fear of seeing or imagining blood or injury in self or others and/or by receiving an injection or undergoing an invasive medical procedure (APA, 2000, p. 445). It is considered to be one of the most commonly occurring phobias, and possesses a strong hereditary component, with between 50% and 70% of group-study participants reporting incidence of the disorder in a first-degree relative (Öst, Sterner & Fellenius, 1989; Öst, Fellenius, & Sterner, 1991; Öst, Lindahl, Sterner, & Jerremalm, 1984). BII phobia is frequently marked by a loss of consciousness, which has been characterized as a vasovagal faint (Connolly, Hallam, & Marks, 1976; Marks, 1988; Thyer, Himle, & Curtis, 1985). Reports of phobic patients who suffer from one, two, or all three fears (i.e., blood, injection, and/or injury) appear in the BII literature, although some research indicates these should be treated as separate fears (e.g., Rainwater, Sweet, Elliott, Bowers, McNeill, & Stump, 1988; Willemsen, Chowdhury, & Briscall, 2002). Exposure (in the form of systematic desensitization, flooding, implosion, and some applications of modeling, in addition to imaginal and in vivo exposure) is a well-established treatment for BII, although the replacement of relaxation (in systematic desensitization) with a muscle tension or pumping instruction is suggested in cases of fainting. In contemporary applications, some form of exposure is often one facet of a treatment plan that may include information, positive reinforcement, prompting, or a variety of cognitive interventions.

HISTORICAL OVERVIEW

The history of the use of exposure therapies for BII phobia is dominated by case studies, starting with Stanley Rachman's 1959 account of a 24-year-old female school teacher who was desensitized to injection stimuli through imaginal and in vivo exposure over the course of 11 sessions, after the successful desensitization of an unrelated fear. No other reports of the use of exposure with BII patients appear for another 10 years, when clinicians began reporting case studies that highlighted the efficacy of exposure in unusual settings (e.g., Nash, 1971), with children (e.g., Ollendick & Gruen, 1972), and with clients presenting with multiple pathologies (e.g., Hsu, 1978; Tilley, 1985).

Other case studies conducted before 1985 demonstrate success with modified exposure protocols. For example, Fazio (1970) began treatment with sessions of implosion (imaginal exposure to exaggerated accounts of the client's greatest fear), followed by in vivo exposure to needle-like items and photographs of BII phobia stimuli. Nimmer and Kapp (1974) took a different approach, following daily sessions of imaginal exposure to BII stimuli with homework assignments consisting of in vivo exposure to sights and smells associated with medical procedures.

When explaining the treatment choice of exposure for BII phobias, these early researchers often cited Wolpe's success in treating a variety of anxiety disorders with systematic desensitization. The relative brevity of exposure treatments, however, was likely another decisive factor. Although no treatment outcome studies gave empirical imprimatur to the use of exposure for BII phobias, the publication of numerous case studies succeeded in establishing exposure-based therapies as "quicker, cheaper, and more effective" than other treatments (Taylor, Ferguson, & Wermuth, 1977, p. 28).

A quick, inexpensive, and effective intervention is nowhere more crucial than in a hospital setting, where patients with BII phobias may refuse or avoid medical treatment even for potentially fatal disorders. The urgency of medical treatment also inspires creative interventions, and the BII phobia literature through the mid-1980s abounds with case histories that highlight the "flexibility" of applied exposure treatments in medical settings (Elmore, Wildman, & Westefeld, 1980, p. 28). For example, Katz (1974) used information, deep relaxation training, a single session of imaginal exposure, and positive reinforcement to extinguish the intense anxiety experienced by a new hemodialysis patient. Similarly, Horne and McCormack (1984) recount a successful intervention composed of relaxation training, graded imaginal exposure, and videotaped modeling to help a mastectomy patient with a lifelong avoidance of needles accept postsurgical chemotherapy. In these cases and others like them, considerable ingenuity on the part of hospital clinicians made possible the rapid deployment of an idiographic psychotherapeutic intervention that necessarily preceded medical treatment for a life-threatening illness.

Beyond the establishment of exposure as an efficacious treatment for BII phobia in a wide variety of populations, the exposure literature before 1985 reveals attempts to come to terms with the effects of fainting in treatment. Unique to BII phobia is the phenomenon that a significant subgroup of sufferers lose consciousness when confronted with BII phobia–relevant visual or auditory stimuli. The BII faint has been characterized as a diphasic response composed of initial arousal of the sympathetic nervous system (marked by increased heart rate, blood pressure, respiration, etc.) followed by an exaggerated parasympathetic response characterized by a rapid drop in heart rate and blood pressure. This second phase is frequently accompanied by nausea, light-headedness, and sometimes loss of consciousness (Marks, 1988; Page, 1994; Willemsen, et al., 2002). In all, 80% or more of BII phobics report some fainting or near-fainting episodes (Öst, et al., 1984; Thyer et al., 1985), although fainting is not a characteristic response of BII phobics in other stressful situations (Öst, 1987), or of other phobics in response to BII phobia stimuli.

A number of case studies reported during this period document attempts to modify the exposure protocol to prevent patient fainting. Some suggested conducting exposure with the patient in a reclining position to prevent interruption of the exposure session (fainting as escape from phobic stimuli), as well as possible injury to the patient from falling while fainting (Wardle & Jarvis, 1981; Yule & Fernando, 1980). However, others came to realize that the relaxation training that was a standard feature of most exposure protocols did nothing to prevent the steep drop in blood pressure that precipitated fainting. Thus, Cohn, Kron, and Brady (1976) succeeded in eliminating fainting in a phobic patient by replacing relaxation with instructions to evoke imagery that stimulated feelings of anger in the patient. A similar success was reported by Babcock and Powell (1982) and Kozak and Montgomery (1981), who replaced relaxation with muscle tension exercises, eliminated fainting behavior and, in the latter case, replaced fearful cognitions with those more appropriate to the patient's role as a hospital rehabilitative therapist. This small literature inspired Swedish researcher Lars-Goren Öst to develop applied tension, an exposure variant created especially to counteract fainting.

In sum, early case study work established exposure (in the form of systematic desensitization, flooding, implosion, participant modeling, or imaginal and in vivo exposure) as a fast and flexible method of extinguishing BII phobias in a wide variety of populations and settings. Individual cases also established fainting as a potentially complicating factor in exposure treatment and lighted the path toward the development of a significant adaptation of the exposure protocol.

CONTEMPORARY TRENDS

The most important development in the BII phobia literature since 1985 is the emergence of applied tension as a more appropriate treatment than exposure alone for BII phobia patients who faint. Through a series of group treatment outcome studies, Öst and colleagues developed and validated a five-session protocol that eliminates fainting, with attendant reductions in anxiety and negative cognitions. Analysis of various dependent measures suggests that the treatment works as well for nonfainters as it does for fainters (Öst, et al. 1989), and results are maintained or improved at 1-year follow-up evaluation (Öst, et al. 1991). Although Öst ultimately suggested that exposure to phobic stimuli is not necessary to achieve the results obtainable by practicing the coping skill of tension only (Öst, et al. 1991), in practice, it appears that applied tension rather than tension only is preferred (cf. Roden, 2001; Fernandes, 2003).

The protocol developed by Öst and colleagues is a five-session treatment, and includes homework practice of the tension technique and self-monitoring of incidental exposures to BII phobia stimuli. Session 1 consists of teaching and practicing the tension technique. During Sessions 2 and 3, the patient undergoes repeated exposure to photographic slides of BII phobia stimuli to teach recognition of early signs of fainting and to practice the tension technique (both to avoid fainting and to accelerate recovery should fainting occur). Session 4 is a trip to a blood donation center that culminates in blood donation, and Session 5 consists of viewing a thoracic surgery. A 6-month follow-up procedure calls for behavioral contracting for continued exposure to BII phobia situations (often via blood donation), self-monitoring reports, and brief phone calls (Öst & Sterner, 1987).

Fainting presents a fascinating problem in the history of the application of exposure for BII phobias for the following reason. Exposure as a psychological technique reduces fear and avoidance through habituation, when an unlearned environment-behavior relation is disrupted through the repeated presentation of the environmental event in the absence of the feared/avoided consequence (Haynes & O'Brien, 2000). Thus, exposure for BII phobia patients consists of repeated, often graded, contacts (either imaginal, visual, or physical) with stimuli such as needles, blood, and injuries in the absence of negative consequences (such as unbearable pain or excessive blood loss) to reduce the patient's fear. In this model, fainting is assumed to be an extreme fear response (indeed, the vasovagal faint was sometimes called an "emotional faint"; Kleinknecht, 1987), and thus should submit to habituation via exposure just as other fear behaviors do.

Over time, however, it became clear that fainting may have a different etiology than other phobic responses to BII phobia stimuli, one less receptive to the habituation model of treatment. For example, Ellinwood and Hamilton (1991) successfully desensitized a physician to self-injection, but the patient continued to faint when a blood draw was attempted by someone else. Analysis of the patient's blood levels of stress hormones indicated that extensive exposure therapy had failed to habituate an "unconditioned physiological response" to the threat posed by needles (Ellinwood & Hamilton, 1991, p. 422). The case reported by Trijsberg, Jelicic, van den Broek, Plekker, Verheij, and Passchier (1996) presents perhaps the extreme example of a negative outcome produced by a lack of understanding of the nature of the BII faint. These researchers applied relaxation and graduated exposure via participant modeling in the case of a patient who typically responded to injections with violent resistance, and actually induced fainting behaviors in their previously nonfainting patient. The example of fainting blood donors may provide further evidence that fear and fainting are separate phenomena, for this presumably nonphobic population (4% of blood donors; Kaloupek, Scott, & Khatami, 1985) is unlikely to have volunteered for blood donation had they known it would precipitate a faint. Finally, examination of individual accounts of the etiology of the phobia underlines the fact that an unpredicted loss of consciousness when confronted with BII phobia stimuli is sufficient to condition the phobia (cf. Fazio, 1970; Jacobsen, 1991; Babcock & Powell, 1982; Cohn, et al., 1976; Roden, 2001). In sum, the vasovagal faint may emerge before, or even in the absence of, fear of BII phobia stimuli, and it may persist when fear has been deconditioned. In such cases it makes sense to treat fainting separately from other aspects of BII phobia, such as catastrophic cognitions or avoidant behavior.

The development of applied tension shifts the target of treatment from fear/avoidance to fainting, with a consequent shift away from exposure alone toward the use of exposure sessions as a means to practice the coping skill of applied tension. Results obtained by Öst and colleagues indicate that the anxiety and negative cognitions abate with the fainting behavior (Öst, et al. 1989, 1991), requiring no separate clinical attention. Thus, whereas in the past, exposure treatment targeted BII fear in the belief that the fainting would disappear with it, Öst's group work with both fainting and non-fainting BII phobics suggests that this model is inverted, and that a more effective approach is to treat the fainting that mediates the phobic response.

The subsequent use of exposure with BII phobia patients indicates that applied tension (in the form of imaginal and/or in vivo exposure with muscle tension as a counter-conditioner) has become standard procedure when treating patients with a history of fainting (Thompson, 1999; Roden, 2001; Fernandes, 2003). The rise of interest in cognitive psychology during the 1990s has also influenced the treatment of BII, as researchers reported the successful addition of elements such as cognitive coping skills training (Albano, Miller, Zarate, Cote, & Barlow, 1997), cognitive restructuring (Panzarella & Garlipp, 1999), and challenging negative automatic thoughts (Thompson, 1999) to their exposure treatments. Other recent case studies document the successful application of exposure as part of a multi-component program for BII phobia in special populations, specifically children (Albano, et al., 1997) and the developmentally disabled (Hagopian, Crockett, & Keeney, 2001).

CLINICAL ISSUES

Examining this literature raises several issues. First, BII phobia is a phenomenon that has the potential to affect the medical arena like few other mental health issues. Presence of these fears, even at subclinical levels, may determine whether an individual seeks treatment for a non-life-threatening disorder before it becomes life-threatening, or seeks treatment at all. Although the prevalence estimates for this phobia are fairly high (between 3% and 5%; Agras, Sylvester, & Oliveau, 1969;

Costello, 1982), it has been suggested that an accurate estimation of the proportion of the population with this disorder is impossible to obtain because "those with this disorder tend to remove themselves from the patient population" (Ellinwood & Hamilton, 1991, p. 423). It appears, however, that with treatment, former BII phobics can be influenced to become compliant patients, and even regular blood donors (e.g., Öst, et al., 1984; Tilley, 1985), a shift of tectonic proportions. In fact, becoming a regular blood donor may be a valuable treatment goal, as it offers continued opportunities to renew exposure to BII and medical stimuli, thus contributing to maintenance of treatment gains.

A second issue that arises in this literature is whether BII phobia should be considered one or several separate phobias. There is both case study (Daniels, 1976; Kleinknecht, 1993) and group study evidence to suggest that the "simple" phobia of BII may be composed of elements that are only semantically related, for treatment did not generalize between explicitly and implicitly treated fears (e.g., Rainwater, et al., 1988; Kleinknecht, 1987). However, a factor analysis of responses to the Multidimensional Blood/Injury phobia Inventory (Wenzel & Sawchuk, 2004) suggests that each of the phobic domains investigated (blood, injection, and injury) is part of the higher-order construct of BII phobia. So, although statistical analyses suggest that the three components of BII phobia may be considered unitary, clinical work suggests that they be treated as distinct fears or discrete behavioral constellations.

A third issue is the continuing debate over the mechanism of action in exposure. Before the introduction of applied tension, positive treatment outcome was commonly attributed to habituation (when no counter-conditioning is present) or extinction (when counter-conditioning is present). But with the introduction of applied tension, the model is significantly altered. Öst (1987) and Öst, et al. (1989) explained that the duration of exposure in the applied tension protocol is abbreviated compared to other exposure protocols because the goal of treatment is not to extinguish the subject's anxiety, but to evoke it in as many kinds of situations as are likely to occur in real life for the purpose of practicing the coping skill. It has been noted, however, that patients often spontaneously give up use of the coping skill after learning and practicing it over a period of time (cf. Cohn, et al., 1976; Öst, et al., 1989), without a return of fainting. Öst, et al. (1989) attribute this result to an increase in self-confidence, but it appears that it might be what Babcock and Powell called "deconditioning an autonomic syndrome" (1982, p. 969).

Finally, it is worth mentioning that the vasovagal faint continues to mystify the scientific community. Several theories have been advanced to explain the evolutionary advantage of an inherited tendency to lose consciousness at the sight or even the mention of blood, injury, or needles. It has been likened to tonic immobility, a protective maneuver available to some animals to fool predators ("playing dead"), although it differs from the latter in that animals in this state only give the appearance of disability and escape as soon as the threat recedes (Marks, 1988). The vasovagal faint, on the other hand, is a loss of consciousness in which the person is unaware of his/her surroundings, including disposition of the threat stimuli (Page, 1994). Thyer, Himle, and Curtis (1985) suggest the evolutionary advantage of a highly developed fear or revulsion to blood and wounds is two-fold, serving to check human aggression and to protect individuals from excessive blood loss (due to low blood pressure experienced during loss of consciousness). Barlow (1988) echoed this last argument, suggesting that those of our ancestors who lost consciousness when injured suffered less blood loss and were more likely to survive. However, Page (1994) marshaled evidence from contemporary emergency room observations to the effect that the phobic reaction to BII stimuli is similar to what normal patients experience only after a loss of about 30% of total blood volume, and is the opposite of what is normally experienced with minor blood loss. In fact, although the exact nature of the advantage BII fainting poses for those who possess it remains obscure, Page goes so far as to suggest that it may in fact represent an evolutionary *disadvantage* by increasing vulnerability to attackers (and, one might add, by decreasing the likelihood of the sufferer seeking out prompt medical attention). As such, it may be expected to slowly decline in the population.

SPECIFIC PHOBIA, DENTAL PHOBIA TYPE

Although not explicitly listed in the DSM, excessive dental fear or avoidance may be considered a specific phobia of the situational subtype. Dental phobia is some-times understood as one of the situations in which BII phobia expresses itself (an injection phobia may center on fear of dental injections; e.g., Camner, Andersson, & Eurenius,1983), although De Jongh, Bongaarts, Vermeule, Visser, De Vos, and Makkes (1998) concluded that the two phobias are not related. Early researchers found that pain anticipation, based on direct or indirect prior dental experience, is the primary antecedent for dental avoidance in individuals with access and finan-cial resources (Shoben & Borland, 1954; Lautch, 1971). Long-term avoidance may result in significant pain as a result of untreated dental problems. Once treated successfully, previously avoidant patients often report improvements in social and occupational functioning, as well as increased self-confidence.

Historical Overview

The first account of an exposure treatment for dental fear is from Gale and Ayer (1969), who successfully used systematic desensitization to injections, drilling, and extraction in nine therapeutic sessions. Subsequent research conducted before 1985 explored the addition of shock therapy (Klepac, 1975), biofeedback (Carlsson, Linde & Ohman,1980; Berggren & Carlsson, 1984; Berggren & Linde, 1984; Har-rison, Carlsson & Berggren, 1985), and coping skills training (Mathews and Rezin,

1977; Gauthier, Savard, Halle & Dufour, 1985) to exposure-based treatments for dental fears.

A review of early group studies on exposure-based treatments for dental fears reveals a lack of consensus among researchers about what constitutes treatment success. For example, Wroblewski, Jacob, and Rehn (1977) found that "symbolic modeling" (imaginal exposure using a videotaped hierarchy of images), with and without relaxation, was an effective treatment for dental anxiety, although only subjects in the relaxation condition were able to undergo subsequent dental treatment without the use of general anesthesia or nitrous oxide. Thus, a reduction in self-reported anxiety immediately post-treatment appears to be insufficient to substantiate successful treatment. Contrarily, Gatchel (1980) used post-treatment dental visits to measure treatment success and found that an education and discussion control condition worked as well as desensitization; however, desensitization was associated with a significantly greater reduction in patient self-reported anxiety. Eventually, both reductions in self-reported anxiety *and* increases in post-treatment dental visits were considered necessary to determine the success of treatment.

Some early group studies were successful in ameliorating symptoms of dental phobia with exposure-based protocols, but reported equivalent effects in control conditions. For example, in Wroblewski, et al. (1977), an attention-control condition was found to be as effective as either of two exposure conditions in improving dental anxiety and avoidance. Likewise, Bernstein and Kleinknecht (1982) reported no reliable difference in degree of improvement between patients randomly assigned to exposure, symbolic modeling, participant modeling, or either of two control conditions. Bernstein and Kleinknecht concluded that patients assigned to their control conditions may have benefited from a combination of expectancy effects and a mild form of exposure, but Getka and Glass (1992), who reported a similar finding, came to a different conclusion. They speculated that for a subset of dental avoiders, a positive dental experience is sufficient treatment. In sum, an evaluation of early successes with exposure treatments for dental anxiety should be considered relative to outcomes achieved in various placebo conditions.

Modeled exposure was a popular exposure variant in research on dental fear reduction conducted before 1985. Gordon, Terdal, and Sterling (1974) and Klesges, Malott, and Ugland (1984) reported successful case studies in which a family member modeled compliant, nonfearful behavior in a dental situation for increasing lengths of time for a fearful child. Chertock and Bornstein (1979) compared single and multiple models in coping or mastery mode to a no-model control group and achieved significant decrements in dental anxiety in every experimental condition. (This finding is noteworthy in that the "models" in all conditions were imaginal, not live.) In another group study, Shaw and Thoresen (1974) found modeling to be as effective as systematic desensitization, with less therapy time.

In sum, during the first 15 years of the use of exposure treatments for dental fears, researchers established that several varieties of exposure treatment, including variations on modeling (live, imaginal, or videotaped), sometimes accompanied by coping skills training or biofeedback, are equally efficacious in reducing patient fear and increasing post-treatment dental appointments. For some patients, however, these results may be obtained by attention-placebo or other nonexposure interventions, such as information and discussion.

Contemporary Research

When R.K. Klepac surveyed the first 15 years of research in psychological treatments for dental fear, he concluded, "anything behavioral works" (Klepac, 1986, p. 21). Research efforts since 1985 have sought ways to increase the efficacy of exposure-based treatments by adding cognitive elements, to increase the efficiency of treatment through standardization, and to obtain more consistent results by matching select exposure treatments to client characteristics.

The growing interest in cognitive therapy in recent years has led many researchers in the area of dental anxiety to explore how it may improve outcomes obtained by exposure therapy. Case studies reported by De Jongh, van der Burg, van Overmeir, Aartman, and Zuuren (2002) and Mansell and Morris (2003) attest to the successful incorporation of cognitive elements (eye movement desensitization and reprocessing [EMDR] and cognitive restructuring, respectively), and Getka and Glass (1992) found equivalent effects in a group study comparison of behavioral (exposure) and cognitive-behavioral (exposure plus a form of Meichenbaum's Stress Inoculation Treatment) conditions with regard to anxiety reduction. On the other hand, Harrison, Berggren, and Carlsson (1989) concluded that the addition of a cognitive-coping element to a systematic desensitization condition appeared to interfere with the spontaneous cognitive restructuring experienced by subjects in a desensitization-alone condition. Overall, then, no clear case can be made for or against the addition of elements of cognitive therapy to exposure treatments for dental phobia.

In contrast, the efficacy of various prepackaged or automated exposure-based treatments for dental fear has been widely supported by research conducted since 1985. Smith, Kroeger, Lyon, and Mullins (1990) reported the successful use of "the Kroeger method," a two-session standardized protocol for fearful dental subjects composed of modeling, systematic desensitization, and homework practice, in a large, multisite experiment. A 3-year follow-up study found that 96% of subjects who had completed one or two sessions of the Kroeger "fear control" method reported that they felt more trusting of their dentist and dental staff (Kroeger & Smith, 1989). Ning and Liddell (1991) created a group therapy approach to standardized treatments for dental fear that included imaginal exposure to dental situations in session and as homework. Horowitz (1992) detailed the successful use of "Overcoming Your Fear of the Dentist," a multimedia package that offers relaxation training and implosion therapy in the form of prompted recall of earlier dental-related traumas. Coldwell, Getz, Milgrom, Prall, Spadafora, and Ramsay (1998) reported on the successful use of an automated, exposure-based treatment for dental fear delivered via computer terminal, and the maintenance of treatment gains at 1-year follow-up evaluation. In sum, contemporary research supports the use of standardized treatment protocols, in a variety of formats, for both individuals and groups, in alleviating dental fear and avoidance.

Another significant line of research pursued since 1985 concerns efforts to match treatment variables to client characteristics to obtain more consistently positive outcomes. Jerremalm, Jansson, and Öst (1986) characterized participants in a study on dental fear as either physiological or cognitive reactors based on their response to a dental examination, and randomly assigned them to one of two exposure conditions. The first, applied relaxation, is somewhat similar to Öst's applied tension technique, in which a coping skill is taught and then rehearsed in a series of graded exposures to the phobic stimuli; it was hypothesized that this treatment would be most effective with participants categorized as physiological responders. The second treatment condition, self-instructional training, was hypothesized to be most effective for those participants considered cognitive responders, and entailed learning to confront negative thoughts elicited by dental contact and practice during graded exposure to in vivo stimuli. Although no outcome differential was obtained in this study, in a subsequent study a third category was added (i.e., participants were categorized as either physiological, behavioral, or cognitive responders), and it appeared that applied relaxation was the more effective treatment when the patient's response to phobic stimuli was predominantly physiological (Olsson-Jerremalm, 1988).

Litt, Kalinowski, and Shafer (1999) approached the topic of treatment matching from a different angle. In two large studies, participants classified as low-fear, high-fear, or cue-anxious were randomly assigned to one of five treatment conditions, including standard dental treatment, premedication, relaxation, distraction, or desensitization. In the first study, both low- and high-fear subjects responded best to relaxation-based treatments, and cue-anxious subjects improved most in the premedication and desensitization interventions. In the second study, all interventions worked equally well at decreasing distress in low-fear subjects, whereas music distraction worked best for high-fear subjects and desensitization was again shown to be the most efficacious treatment for cue-anxious subjects. As this brief review indicates, treatment matching is an issue that would benefit from greater research attention.

Long-term follow-up evaluation of patients treated with exposure for dental fears reveals that subjects who received a form of systematic desensitization are more likely than those who received pharmacological interventions to regularly attend to their dental health postintervention (Hakeberg, Berggren, Carlsson, & Grondahl, 1993; Thom, Sartory, & Johren, 2000; Johren, Jackowski, Gangler, Sartory, & Thom, 2000). Analysis of post-treatment variables indicates consistent differences between former study participants on this criterion (Liddell, Di Fazio, Blackwood, & Ackerman, 1994). Those who do not regularly visit the dentist report higher levels of post-treatment anxiety, a greater number of invasive relative to noninvasive procedures post-treatment, and less concordance between overt and covert anxiety. Thus, it appears that although patients who receive exposure for dental avoidance are more likely to attend to their dental health post-treatment than those who undergo other (or no) treatment, this result may be moderated by pretreatment symptom severity, both in terms of dental health and level of anxiety.

In sum, contemporary research in treatments for dental phobia has actively pursued refinements to the exposure protocol for the purpose of achieving more consistent results in less time at less expense to the patient. Although cognitive additions such as thought challenging have not been conclusively supported, automated and multimedia packages report success with both individuals and groups. A review of comparative studies supports the use of exposure over education and discussion (Gatchel, 1980), anesthesia (Berggren & Linde, 1984; Hakeberg, et al., 1993), or pharmacological treatment (Thom, et al., 2000; Johren, et al., 2000). Results obtained by exposure, however, are frequently matched by those obtained in conditions such as medicating patients before dental treatment (Hakeberg, et al., 1993; Litt, et al., 1999), coping skills training (Gauthier, et al., 1985), and in one study, a host of other treatments, including standard dental treatment, music distraction, and relaxation plus self-efficacy enhancement (Litt, et al. 1999). However, long-term follow-up of participants in dental fear reduction studies is beginning to shed light on the variables that may lead to differential treatment outcome, such as initial and post-treatment anxiety levels, and amount of invasive dental work required.

Clinical Issues

If, as Klepac said, "anything behavioral works," how is the clinician to choose the best treatment for the individual patient? The small research into treatment matching is inconclusive on this question, and comparative research serves to underline the initial point: some patients who find relief from dental anxiety through desensitization would be equally well served by a host of less expensive treatments, including music distraction, premedication, or a single dental appointment with an unusually gentle dentist. In other words, not only does anything *behavioral* work for some dental phobics, it appears that anything at all works. Because there are so many roads to reducing dental fear, researchers who hope to more conclusively champion one form of treatment over another need to first uncover the variables that will help clinicians determine the minimum treatment sufficient to reduce fear and increase dental visits for each individual.

How best to measure a successful treatment for dental fear is an issue that arose early in this research, for both self-reported levels of anxiety and post-treatment dental visits appeared to be inadequate on their own. Several researchers have attempted to use physiological measures of distress as a means of providing a less subjective report of treatment outcome than patient self-report. Several studies, however, found that physiological measures of distress such as heart rate and blood pressure are an unreliable measure of treatment success or failure for they may not reduce even when self-reported or dentist-observed improvements in anxiety are present (e.g., Gatchel, 1980; Bernstein & Kleinknecht, 1982; Harrison, et al., 1985; Carlsson, Linde, Berggren, & Harrison, 1986). Getka and Glass (1992) attempted to correlate overt patient behavior in the dental chair (e.g., presence or absence of signs of distress such as clenched hands, or excessive talking) with other treatment outcomes, but found no difference in overt patient behavior pretreatment to post-treatment, despite significant reductions in self-reported anxiety and increases in dental visits post-treatment. Thus, physiological and behavioral measures of treatment outcome have so far been unable to provide a more objective measure than self-report or a more easily obtained measure than long-term follow-up evaluation of dental visits.

Among other things, long-term follow-up monitoring of participants in dental-fear studies has provided insights into a number of positive side effects of exposure-based treatments for dental anxiety for both dentists and patients. Smith and associates (1990) found that dentists trained in the Kroeger method reported increased confidence and empathy with fearful patients, and a decreased tendency to take a patient's fearful behavior as a personal affront. As for patients, Hakeberg, et al. (1993) reported the use of relaxation in other stressful situations, improved self-esteem and confidence, reduced use of sedatives and alcohol, and reduced fear of medical care as positive side effects that emerged post-treatment. In sum, choice of treatment, measures of treatment success, and treatment generalization remain issues to be contended with by present and future researchers.

PAIN ANXIETY

Recent trends in the chronic pain literature focus on a set of related constructs and their association with chronic pain: pain-related fear, pain-related anxiety, kinesiophobia (irrational, debilitating fear of movement-related reinjury; Kori, Miller, & Todd, 1990), and pain catastrophizing (beliefs that characterize pain as awful, horrible, and unbearable). These constructs may be apparent in patients who meet criteria for the DSM-IV-TR diagnostic category Pain Disorder (with psychological factors and/or a general medical condition), for whom psychological factors are "judged to play a significant role in onset, severity, exacerbation or maintenance of the pain" (APA, 2000, p. 498).

According to Rhudy and Meagher (2000), the constructs of pain-related fear and pain-related anxiety differ in their physiological and behavioral correlates. Fear is accompanied by a surge of sympathetic arousal, impulses to escape, and reduced pain reactivity or analgesia. In contrast, pain-related anxiety, a state of anxious apprehension, is accompanied by hypervigilance and increased pain reactivity or hyperalgesia. Norton and Asmundson (2003) note that anxiety involves passive avoidance behavior, more cognitive processing, and less autonomic arousal. They point to accumulating evidence that disability in chronic pain patients is more strongly linked to pain-related fear than to pain severity.

Empirical investigations of kinesiophobia support the notion that this fear contributes to development and maintenance of chronic pain. Kinesiophobia is associated with muscle guarding during flexion in chronic low back pain patients (Watson, Booker, & Main, 1997). Through limiting flexion, pain-related fear of movement or reinjury indirectly influences maximum electromyography in flexion and extension (Geisser, Haig, Wallbom, & Wiggert, 2004), mediated by decreased range of motion. Thus, fear of movement-related reinjury potentially contributes to physical deconditioning, muscular atrophy, and degeneration that in turn promote pain. Although kinesiophobia shares the salient features of specific phobias, it differs in that most kinesiophobic pain patients do not recognize their fear and related avoidance behaviors as excessive or irrational (Vlaeyen, de Jong, Sieben, & Crombez, 2002), but as protective.

Catastrophizing chronic pain patients report more pain intensity, disability, and distress than noncatastrophizers (Severijns, Vlaeyen, van den Hout, & Weber, 2001). In contrast to early understandings of catastrophizing as symptomatic of depression (cf. Rosenstiel & Keefe, 1983; Sullivan & D'Eon, 1990), catastrophizing has been subsequently found to be independent of depression in its association with pain and disability (Geisser & Roth, 1998; Sullivan, Standish, Waite, Sullivan, & Tripp, 1998). Further, functional magnetic resonance imaging studies revealed that pain catastrophizing is significantly associated with increased activity in brain areas related to anticipation of and attention to pain, emotional aspects of pain, and motor control (Gracely, Geisser, Gieseke, Grant, Petzke, Williams, et al., 2004). Catastrophizing responses tend to be associated with pain-related avoidance behaviors (Cipher & Fernandez, 1997), thereby interfering with exposure to experiences that might disconfirm pain-related schemas. Avoidance behavior not only contributes to disability, loss of physical fitness, and increased muscle weakness, but may also be negatively reinforced by escape from or avoidance of the catastrophizing cognitions themselves.

Thus, common to this set of constructs is their association with escape and avoidance behavior. In light of empirically validated treatment for other disorders in which escape and avoidance are central, the use of exposure techniques has been investigated in some laboratory studies and in some clinical populations with pain anxiety.

Overview of Empirical Studies

The fear-avoidance model of pain by Lethem, Slade, Troup, and Bentley (1983) posits that pain avoidance is maintained by fear, which heightens pain sensitivity by desynchronizing pain experience, pain sensation, and behavior. Philips (1987) argued that avoidance behavior actively changes cognitions, reduces the patient's sense of control over the pain, increases the expectation that nonavoidance (i.e., exposure) would increase pain, and thus, fosters increased withdrawal and intolerance of stimulation. Because avoidance reduces fear, avoidance behavior (for example, a migraineur's preemptive analgesic-taking for a headache that is nonexistent but feared to be incipient) is negatively reinforced and more likely to recur. According to Lethem, et al. (1983), avoidance is more strongly associated with fear of the stimulus than the actual pain-inducing power of the stimulus.

Within the framework of this model, Philips and Jahanshahi (1985) exposed 100 chronic headache sufferers to 2-minute periods of noise, an auditory headache trigger, which was idiographically calibrated for each participant into three intensity levels. Avoidance of the noise stimulus was operationally defined as the participant terminating the noise during the 2-minute interval; noise tolerance was defined as the latency in seconds before doing so. Of interest, under optimal conditions of low arousal (relaxation), exposure to the noise stimulus was associated with increased tolerance at the graded intensity levels. Exposure without relaxation was not. On this basis, Philips and Jahanshahi (1985) created a case for repeated, graded, and controlled exposures in vivo to disconfirm negative expected painful consequences of physical activity and other headache triggers.

Behavioral operant conditioning approaches to the management of chronic back pain could also be viewed as increasing exposure, reducing avoidance, and thus facilitating habituation. These operant approaches use the systematic use of differential reinforcement of increasing duration, frequency, and variety of functional activities (Fordyce, 1976). The heart of interventions such as activity scheduling, physical exercise, and phased return to work, operant approaches in the form of graded activity functionally expose the patient to previously avoided situations. However, this form of "exposure" addresses pain anxiety indirectly and incidentally, and provides ample opportunity for avoidance of feared movements or activity.

An example of indirect and incidental exposure for pain anxiety was reported by McCracken and Gross (1998), who noted that of their patients undergoing rehabilitation, those who also decreased their pain anxiety significantly improved their functioning, even though pain anxiety was not directly targeted for intervention. A more direct approach would be to use fear modification processes (i.e., habituation and/or disconfirmation) to target respondently conditioned patterns of behavior. In doing so, either the association between the conditioned and unconditioned stimuli would be weakened by repeated presentation of the conditioned stimulus without the unconditioned stimulus, or the catastrophic expectancies would be challenged and disconfirmed. In subsequent research, Vlaeyen and colleagues explored the comparative efficacy in reducing pain anxiety of graded activity versus graded exposure to *fears* related to pain.

Chronic Low Back Pain

Exposure in vivo with the chronic low back pain population has been investigated in five single case design studies, each building on the first study by Vlaeyen, de Jong, Geilen, Heuts, and van Breukelen (2001). Vlaeyen and colleagues compared exposure in vivo for kinesiophobia with graded activity in a crossover design with four patients with chronic low back pain and high scores on the Tampa Scale of Kinesiophobia (TSK; Kori, et al., 1990). The exposure protocol involved first constructing a hierarchy of fear-eliciting movements using a visual analogue scale, then challenging expectations in idiographic behavioral tests of the movements in the hierarchical situations. All four participants exhibited clinically significant reductions in fear, catastrophizing, and disability.

In a replication study, time series analyses revealed exposure in vivo alone was associated with decreases in pain-related fear and catastrophizing, regardless of treatment order (Vlaeyen, de Jong, Geilen, Heuts, & van Breukelen, 2002), and the gains in decreased disability, decreased pain vigilance, and increased physical activity levels associated with pre-post treatment differences in pain-related fear were maintained for 1 year. Furthermore, the changes in fear were abrupt, and the authors speculated whether the abruptness was indicative, not of habituation, but of cognitive change inadvertently induced by the rationale given at the beginning of the exposure phase.

In another replication study, TSK scores did not decrease, even though mean ratings on the "fear thermometer" visual analogue scale did reduce (Linton, Overmeer, Janson, Vlaeyen, & de Jong, 2002). This discrepancy suggests a possible time lag in the development of cognitive change following disconfirmatory experiences. Substantial increases in function, however, were associated with reductions in both fear and avoidance beliefs in another replication study by Boersma, Linton, Overmeer, Jansson, Vlaeyen, & de Jong (2004). In contrast, in vivo exposure produced more rapid decreases in pain-related fear than in pain reports in yet another replication by Vlaeyen, de Jong, Onghena, Kersckhoffs-Hanssen, and Kole-Snijders (2002), suggesting that decreases in fear might actually precede decreases in pain. In sum, research with this population indicates that exposure to pain-related fear stimuli per se has been effective in reducing pain anxiety and increasing functionality. Implications are that rather than simply relying on its reduction as a secondary effect of operant treatment, the pain anxiety itself could be, and possibly should be, a bona fide target for exposure.

Headache

Whereas research with pain-anxious chronic back pain patients has explored in vivo exposure, research with pain-anxious headache patients has investigated imaginal exposure. In an exploratory systematic replication series using multiple baseline single case designs, Potter (1999) and later Bamford (2001) each investigated whether migraine-related pain anxiety would respond to direct behavioral intervention, either imaginal exposure (systematic desensitization) or cognitive restructuring (decatastrophizing). The original studies varied the timing of systematic desensitization in the context of a structured multi-component cognitive behavioral headache self-management program. The timing of the systematic desensitization protocol was counterbalanced with a decatastrophizing protocol. All four pain-anxious participants across the two studies reported significant reductions in Subjective Units of Distress scales ratings from pretreatment to post-treatment. Retrospective reanalysis, using critical difference score analysis for single-subject designs based on Yarnold's (1988) approach, revealed that for the three participants whose pain anxiety also decreased significantly, such reduction was achieved after hierarchy formation and written hierarchy embellishment homework, but *before* the in-session exposure protocol was implemented. This reanalysis suggests that the written hierarchy formation and embellishment (i.e., writing about the upsetting headache scenarios to flesh out details for later exposure sessions) functioned in a manner expected of exposure techniques (Hoodin, Potter, & Bamford, 2002). Resembling in many ways the written emotional disclosure procedures described in detail later, the exposure facilitated by written hierarchy embellishment appears to have contributed to and potentiated the systematic desensitization. The extent to which this is so is yet to be elucidated.

Clinical Issues

The pain anxiety and kinesiophobia literature raises several questions regarding the mechanisms of exposure, etiological processes by which the pain anxiety is acquired, the distinctions between graded exposure and graded activity interventions, the promotion of generalization and maintenance, and the optimal timing of intervention in the treatment of chronic pain. Attempts at answering these questions suggest fertile directions for future research, with clinical implications for improving the quality of life of people suffering from chronic pain.

The first question centers on the debate about the mechanism by which exposure in vivo is operating in these studies, and weighs extinction of conditioned associations (between, for example, movement and severe pain), against a cognitive process (in which, for example, catastrophic expectations associated with fear activation are disconfirmed when challenged). Basic research (Bouton, 1988, 2000) and clinical studies (e.g., Goubert, Francken, Crombez, Vansteenwegen, & Lysens, 2002) suggest that during exposure, *exceptions to the rule* are learned, consistent with the extinction model: the previously learned association will not recur in the particular situation in which exposure is taking place. In contrast, Vlaeyen, de Jong, Sieben, et al. (2002) take the cognitive view that what is learned during in vivo exposure is fundamental changes to the rule, for example, that movements are less harmful or painful than anticipated. Directly and cognitively challenging the rules that govern patients' activity appears to be ineffective, however, whereas the situational exposure approach leads to spontaneous cognitive restructuring that has potential through cognitive processes to generalize across situations.

The second question about potential respondent conditioning etiological mechanisms has been recently addressed by an innovative program of study investigating exposure interventions for headache triggers. In a group design including chronic headache sufferers and headache-free controls, Martin (2001) exposed participants to five durations of the visual disturbance: 0, 5, 15, 25, and 35 minutes. The visual disturbance induced headaches in both the headache group and the control group, but to a greater degree in the headache group. In this sense, the findings support a sensitization model: that increased sensitization to headache triggers precipitates headaches. Nevertheless, longer exposure to the visual disturbance produced *decreased* rather than increased headache. Martin hypothesized that these results support the use of prolonged exposure to headache triggers to facilitate a desensitization process to counter the sensitization process that he hypothesized to result from prior long-term avoidance of triggers. Using single-case design methodology with six participants for whom visual stimuli triggered headaches, Martin (2000) also demonstrated that nine sessions of repeated, prolonged exposure to visual disturbance (flicker, glare, eyestrain) reduced subsequent self-reports of visual disturbance, negative affect, and headache in response to that trigger. If sensitization to headache triggers suggests a respondent conditioning etiological mechanism, and avoidance of triggers over time contributes to increased sensitization, then the intervention of prolonged exposure to the triggers could be argued to have both theoretical and empirical support.

A third question focuses on the extent to which graded exposure in vivo and graded activity programs might be functionally distinct processes. As Vlaeyen, de Jong, Sieben, et al. (2002) point out, graded exposure is based on extinction of respondent conditioning and incorporates activities identified in idiographic fear hierarchies, whereas graded activity is embedded in instrumental learning principles, and uses shaping and positive reinforcement to increase functional capacity in order to achieve behavioral objectives often defined in terms of physical demands. Nevertheless, the goals of both graded exposure and graded activity are recovery of functional capacity, never elimination or reduction of pain. The question that remains to be answered more definitively concerns what incremental benefit graded activity programs may be afforded by addressing the anxiety about pain per se as a specific intervention target, as is done in graded exposure protocols.

A fourth question is how generalization and maintenance of reductions in pain anxiety and kinesiophobia may best be promoted. The current literature suggests generalization and maintenance can be enhanced by ensuring that exposure occurs to the full gamut of natural contexts in which pain has been experienced (Mineka, Mystkowski, Hladek, & Rodriguez, 1999), to the full range of stimuli during the exposure itself (e.g., cycling uphill as well as downhill; Rowe & Craske, 1998a), and to an expanded spaced (versus massed) exposure schedule (Rowe & Craske, 1998b). However, the empirical pain anxiety literature at present is far from definitive on this issue.

A final question concerns the optimal timing of intervention. Exposure studies to date have been conducted in tertiary care settings. As fear-avoidance beliefs have been shown to be a powerful predictor of disability (Sieben, Vlaeyen, Tuerlincks, &

Portegijs, 2002), however, Vlaeyen, de Jong, Sieben, et al. (2002) recommend early screening in the primary care setting for pain-related fear, and implementation of preventive intervention with at-risk acute pain patients. A program of research empirically testing this recommendation may lead to important developments in preempting pain-related disability with its attendant personal and societal costs.

WRITTEN EXPOSURE/EMOTIONAL DISCLOSURE

In the 1990s, an intervention technique emerged that has the potential to expand the reach of exposure interventions beyond the specific phobias and pain disorder categories featured in this chapter to a multitude of disorders: Pennebaker's written emotional disclosure protocol (Pennebaker & Beall, 1986; Pennebaker, 1997). This protocol requires repeated writing of one's deepest thoughts and feelings about a traumatic event not previously disclosed to others.

The written emotional disclosure protocol was first tested in non-health-care–seeking healthy younger adults, and yielded effect sizes in the moderate range or better for overall outcome, psychological well-being, and physiological functioning (Cohen's d = .47, .66, and .69 respectively; Smyth, 1998). Thereafter, the protocol was investigated for its impact on improving health of patients with medical conditions. Results from 19 studies of medical patients between 1997 and mid-2004 have been mixed. No significant effects were found for breast cancer patients (Walker, Nail, & Croyle, 1999), and emotional distress was found to reduce in only a subset of patients with prostate or gynecological cancer who were high in social constraint (Zakowski, Ramati, Morton, Johnson, & Flanigan, 2004).

Particularly intriguing, however, are results indicating positive changes in physiological indicators and concomitant decreased medical use for patients after treatment with the written disclosure protocol. For example, some disease-related physiological indicators improved for patients with asthma, arthritis (Smyth, Stone, Hurewitz, & Kaell, 1999), and HIV (Petrie, Fontanilla, Thomas, Booth, & Pennebaker, 2004). Sleep improved in patients with fibromyalgia (Gillis, 2002) and metastatic renal cell carcinoma (de Moor, Sterner, Hall, Warneke, Gilani, Amato, et al., 2002). Reported pain intensity decreased for dental, migraine, and pelvic pain patients (Sullivan & Neish, 1999; D'Souza, 2002; Norman, Lumley, Dooley, & Diamond, 2004, respectively), but not for arthritis or tension headache patients (Kelley, Lumley, & Leisen, 1997; D'Souza, 2002, respectively). Inpatient hospital stays decreased for patients with cystic fibrosis (Taylor, Wallander, Anderson, Beasley, & Brown, 2003) and outpatient health care use decreased for cancer patients and older primary care patients (Stanton, Danoff-Burg, Sworowski, Collins, Branstetter, Rodriguez-Hanley, et al., 2002; Klapow, Schmidt, Taylor, Roller, Li, Calhoun, et al., 2001, respectively).

Curiously, use of this written protocol does not appear to influence the majority of psychological variables assessed. However, short-term increases of negative mood were observed for patients with arthritis, pelvic pain, fibromyalgia, and headache, as well as for caregivers of children with chronic illness (Kelley, et al., 1997; Norman, et al., 2004; Gillis, 2002; D'Souza, 2002; Schwartz & Drotar, 2004, respectively). This short-term distress, which either resolves over time (e.g., Gillis, 2002) or is associated with better functioning (e.g., Kelley, et al., 1997), has been observed in emotional disclosure studies conducted with nonmedical populations and has often been interpreted as a sign that the writer is engaged in the written exposure task (e.g., Pennebaker & Beall, 1986).

Pennebaker holds that the efficacy of his protocol is due to mechanisms that are physiological (removal of stress caused by active inhibition or suppression of traumatic thoughts and feelings) and cognitive (insight, the cognitive integration of expressed emotions related to troublesome personal events into linguistic structures) (Francis & Pennebaker, 1992). Our review of Pennebaker's procedure and related research, however, suggests written emotional disclosure may well be legitimately viewed as an exposure technique, and has the potential to be as effective in producing habituation as imaginal contact with the aversive stimuli. A theoretical shift of this kind has significant clinical implications.

According to Sloan and Marx (2004), the written emotional disclosure paradigm shares important qualities with exposure techniques in directing individuals to confront personally distressing historical events. Behavioral theorists would concur and assert that the writing should be extended both within and across writing sessions until distress abates. In fact, using ecological momentary assessment technology, Lynch and Hoodin (2004) demonstrated that habituation of negative affect occurs within and across writing sessions when writers follow the instruction to continue writing until they are no longer upset. Although Kloss and Lisman (2002) explicitly set out to test the hypothesis that emotional disclosure is a form of exposure, they did not follow this particular instruction, and their results did not disconfirm the null hypothesis. Even following the typical written emotional disclosure protocol, which specifies only fixed duration (15–30 minutes) and frequency (on 3–5 days) of writing (Pennebaker, 1997), extinction could occur coincidentally for a subset of writers who are able to habituate within the protocol parameters. This may explain some of the variability in outcomes in written emotional disclosure research in medical samples. Whether following the pivotal exposure procedure dictum to continue exposure until subjective distress resolves will result in better or more consistent outcomes remains to be determined.

Conceptualizing the written emotional disclosure protocol as an exposure procedure may also cast some light on whether medical patients should be directed to write about their medical condition as the stressful event (e.g., Sullivan & Neish, 1999; Stanton, et al., 2002), or whether they should be allowed to self-select and even change topics (e.g., Rosenberg, Rosenberg, Ernstoff, Wolford, Amdur, Elshamy, et al., 2002). Although the DSM-IV (APA, 1994) first stipulated that "being diagnosed with a life-threatening illness" would qualify for Criterion A-1 of Posttraumatic Stress Disorder, researchers seeking to apply the written disclosure/exposure protocol should neither assume that the diagnosis is the most traumatic experience in the person's life, nor that the reaction to it was necessarily intense "fear, helplessness, or horror." Thus, future researchers would be well advised to evaluate how "traumatic" medical versus nonmedical writing topics are in the context of behavioral moderators already identified among medical written emotional disclosure patients, such as higher baseline avoidance, negative affect, alexithymia or nonexpressiveness, and social constraint (Stanton, et al., 2002; Norman, et al., 2004; Solano, Donati, Pecci, Persichetti, & Colaci, 2003; Lumley, 2004; Smyth, Anderson, Hockemeyer, & Stone, 2002; Zakowski, et al., 2004, respectively).

Explicitly adding the missing exposure characteristics to the written emotional disclosure protocol spotlights promising directions for improving its efficacy for medical populations. Systematic study of behavioral permutations of the Pennebaker protocol would be enlightening on both theoretical and clinical levels. Further, an attractive aspect of written emotional disclosure as an intervention is its potential for distance-delivery and self-guided administration for medical populations whose mobility may be constrained by illness or pain. Two such pioneering studies successfully delivered instructions for written emotional disclosure at home by telephone (Zakowski, et al., 2004), and video supplemented by written instructions (Broderick, Stone, Smyth, & Kaell, 2004). The feasibility for distance-delivery with medical populations is yet another important practical clinical question yet to be fully addressed by behavioral medicine researchers.

CONCLUSION

The four areas of exposure applications in behavioral medicine discussed in this chapter have widely divergent histories. There is a 40-year history of treating BII and dental phobias with a wide variety of exposure-based therapies. This extensive literature seems to indicate that BII phobia with fainting is best considered an inherited physiological response that yields to a treatment that teaches patients a compensatory maneuver (muscle tension) during exposure. Cognitive restructuring and fear abatement appear to occur as spontaneous sequelae to treatment with applied tension. Why the coping skill is often spontaneously discarded after treatment, *with no return of fainting,* is unclear. As for dental phobia, such a broad range of exposure-based treatments are successful in ameliorating symptoms of this disorder that a review of the literature demands a careful choice of treatment modality, with "exposure" in the form of a single dental appointment under the care of a dentist skilled in treating fearful patients a viable first choice.

The pain anxiety and emotional disclosure literatures are much more recent than those of BII and dental phobia, and concomitantly less developed. Nevertheless, a well-designed set of small-sample replication studies suggests that in chronic pain rehabilitation programs based on instrumental learning principles, targeting pain anxiety directly with in vivo exposure to pain-related fear stimuli not only extinguishes pain anxiety, but also appears to facilitate increasing functional capacity. In the migraine headache literature, a case has been made for prolonged exposure to headache triggers to facilitate desensitization of trigger-sensitization hypothesized to develop through long-term avoidance. Yet unresolved is whether the active agent in these exposure processes is habituation, cognitive restructuring, or the practicing of compensatory coping strategies in problematic contexts.

The burgeoning emotional disclosure literature has expanded into medical populations as diverse as cancer, HIV, pelvic pain, fibromyalgia, rheumatoid arthritis, and asthma, with inconsistent but intriguing salutary effects on physiological indicators and medical use. Viewing the emotional disclosure protocol as an exposure technique, rather than as a means to reduce the stress of inhibition and bring about insight, has implications for modifying the protocol in a way that may potentially enhance its efficacy. Theory would dictate that if writers continue writing until no longer upset (as called for by the exposure paradigm), extinction of distress related to previously avoided traumatic memories is more likely to result. Whether this proposed adjustment to the protocol indeed improves outcomes is a question for future empirical validation. Honing the protocol is important, as this methodology holds promise for distance delivery and self-guided administration well suited to patients whose illness status and pain may restrict their mobility.

The state of research presents a full slate of programmatic research for behavioral medicine applications of exposure. Despite the great deal yet to be learned, we know enough to be able to benefit many patients clinically with BII phobia, dental phobia, pain anxiety, and traumatic responses to a medical condition.

REFERENCES

Agras, S., Sylvester, D., & Oliveau, D. (1969). The epidemiology of common fears and phobias. *Comprehensive Psychiatry, 10,* 151–156.

Albano, A.M., Miller, P.P., Zarate, R., Cote, G., & Barlow, D.H. (1997). Behavioral assessment and treatment of PTSD in prepubertal children: Attention to developmental factors and innovative strategies in the case study of a family. *Cognitive & Behavioral Practice, 4,* 245–262.

American Psychiatric Association. (1994). *Diagnostic and statistical manual of mental disorders* (4th ed.). Washington, D.C.: Author.

American Psychiatric Association. (2000). *Diagnostic and statistical manual of mental disorders* (4th ed., rev. Text). Washington, D.C.: Author.

Babcock, H.H., & Powell, D.H. (1982). Vasovagal fainting: Deconditioning an autonomic syndrome. *Psychosomatics, 23,* 969–973.

Bamford, A. (2001). Comparative utility of systematic desensitization and decatastrophizing for pain anxiety related to migraine. Unpublished master's thesis, Eastern Michigan University, Ypsilanti, Michigan.

Barlow, D.H. (1998). *Anxiety and Its Disorders: The Nature and Treatment of Anxiety and Panic.* New York: Guilford Press.

Berggren, U., & Carlsson, S.G. (1984). A psychophysiological therapy for dental fear. *Behaviour Research and Therapy, 22,* 487–492.

Berggren, U., & Linde, A. (1984). Dental fear and avoidance: A comparison of two modes of treatment. *Journal of Dental Research, 63,* 1223–1227.

Bernstein, D.A., & Kleinknecht, R.A. (1982). Multiple approaches to the reduction of dental fear. *Journal of Behavior Therapy and Experimental Psychiatry, 13,* 287–292.

Boersma, K., Linton, S., Overmeer, T., Jansson, M. Vlaeyen, J., & de Jong, J. (2004). Lowering fear-avoidance and enhancing function through exposure in vivo. A multiple baseline study across six patients with back pain. *Pain, 108*(1–2), 8–16.

Bouton, M.E. (1988). Context and ambiguity in the extinction of emotional learning. Implications for exposure therapy. *Behaviour Research and Therapy, 26,* 137–149.

Bouton, M.E. (2000). A learning theory perspective on lapse, relapse, and the maintenance of behavior change. *Health Psychology, 19*(1 Suppl.), 57–63.

Broderick, J.E., Stone, A.A., Smyth, J.M., & Kaell, A.T. (2004). The feasibility and effectiveness of an expressive writing intervention for rheumatoid arthritis via home-based videotaped instructions. *Annals of Behavioral Medicine, 2*(1), 50–59.

Camner, L., Andersson, E., & Eurenius, M. (1983). Treatment of a dental patient with injection phobia. *Quintessence International, 14,* 759–760.

Carlsson, S.G., Linde, A., & Ohman, A. (1980). Reduction of tension in fearful dental patients. *Journal of the American Dental Association, 101,* 638–641.

Carlsson, S.G., Linde, A., Berggren, U., & Harrison, J.A. (1986). Reduction of dental fear: Psychophysiological correlates. *Community Dental Oral Epidemiology, 14,* 253–257.

Chertock, S.L., & Bornstein, P.H. (1979). Covert modeling treatment of children's dental fears. *Child Behavior Therapy, 1,* 249–255.

Cipher, D.J., & Fernandez, E. (1997). Expectancy variables predicting tolerance and avoidance of pain in chronic pain patients. *Behaviour Research and Therapy, 35,* 437–444.

Cohn, C.K., Kron, R.E., & Brady, J.P. (1976). A case of blood-illness-injury phobia treated behaviorally. *Journal of Nervous and Mental Disease, 162,* 65–68.

Coldwell, S.E., Getz, T., Milgrom, P., Prall, C.W., Spadafora, A., & Ramsay, D.S. (1998). CARL: A Lab-VIEW 3 computer program for conducting exposure therapy for the treatment of dental injection fear. *Behaviour Research and Therapy, 36,* 429–441.

Connolly, J., Hallam, R.S., & Marks, I.M. (1976). Selective association of fainting with blood-injury-illness fear. *Behavior Therapy, 7,* 8–13.

Costello, C.G. (1982). Fears and phobias in women: A community study. *Journal of Abnormal Psychology, 91,* 280–286.

D'Souza, P.J. (2002). The effects of relaxation training and written emotional disclosure for people with migraine or tension headaches. (Doctoral dissertation, Wayne State University, 2002). *Dissertation Abstracts International, 63*(11-B), 5509.

Daniels, L.K. (1976). Rapid in-office and in-vivo desensitization of an injection phobia utilizing hypnosis. *American Journal of Clinical Hypnosis, 18,* 200–203.

De Jongh, A., Bongaarts, G., Vermeule, I., Visser, K., De Vos, P., & Makkes, P. (1998). Blood-injury-injection phobia and dental phobia. *Behaviour Research and Therapy, 36,* 971–982.

De Jongh, A., van der Burg, J., van Overmeir, M., Aartman, I., & Zuuren, F.J. (2002). Trauma-related sequelae in individuals with a high level of dental anxiety. Does this interfere with treatment outcome? *Behavior Research and Therapy, 40,* 1017–1029.

de Moor, C., Sterner, J., Hall, M., Warneke, C., Gilani, Z., Amato, R., et al. (2002). A pilot study of the effects of expressive writing on psychological and behavioral adjustment in patients enrolled in a phase II trial of vaccine therapy for metastatic renal cell carcinoma. *Health Psychology, 21*(6), 615–619.

Ellinwood, E.H., & Hamilton, J.G. (1991). Case report of a needle phobia. *Journal of Family Practice, 32,* 420–422.

Elmore, R.T., Wildman, R.W., & Westefeld, J. (1980). The use of systematic desensitization in the treatment of blood phobia. *Journal of Behavior Therapy and Experimental Psychiatry, 11,* 277–279.

Fazio, A.F. (1970). Implosive therapy in the treatment of a phobic disorder. *Psychotherapy: Theory, Research and Practice, 7,* 228–232.

Fernandes, P.P. (2003). Rapid desensitization for needle phobia. *Psychosomatics: Journal of Consultation Liaison Psychiatry, 44,* 253–254.

Fordyce, W.E. (1976). *Behavioral methods in chronic pain and illness.* St. Louis: Mosby.

Francis, M.E., & Pennebaker, J.W. (1992). Putting stress into words: Writing about personal upheavals and health. *American Journal of Health Promotion, 6,* 280–287.

Gale, E.N. & Ayer, W.A. (1969). Treatment of dental phobias. *Journal of the American Dental Association, 78,* 1304–1307.

Gatchel, R.J. (1980). Effectiveness of two procedures for reducing dental fear: group-administered desensitization and group education and discussion. *Journal of the American Dental Association, 101,* 634–637.

Gauthier, J., Savard, F., Halle, J.-P., & Dufour, L. (1985). Flooding and coping skills training in the management of dental fear. *Scandinavian Journal of Behaviour Therapy, 14,* 3–15.

Geisser, M.E., Haig, A.J., Wallbom, A.S., & Wiggert, E.A. (2004). Pain-related fear, lumbar flexion, and dynamic EMG among persons with chronic musculoskeletal low back pain. *Clinical Journal of Pain, 20*(2), 61–69.

Geisser, M.E., & Roth, R.S. (1998). Knowledge of and agreement with pain diagnosis: Relation to pain beliefs, pain severity, disability, and psychological distress. *Journal of Occupational Rehabilitation, 8,* 73–88.

Getka, E.J., & Glass, C.R. (1992). Behavioral and cognitive-behavioral approaches to the reduction of dental anxiety. *Behavior Therapy, 23,* 433–448.

Gillis, M.E. (2002). The effects of written emotional disclosure on adjustment in fibromyalgia syndrome. (Doctoral dissertation, Wayne State University, 2002). *Dissertation Abstracts International, 63*(3-B).

Gordon, D.A., Terdal, L., & Sterling, E. (1974). The use of modeling and desensitization in the treatment of a phobic child patient. *ASDC Journal of Dentistry for Children, 41,* 102–105.

Goubert, L., Francken, G., Crombez, G., Vansteenwegen, D., & Lysens, R. (2002). Exposure to physical movement in chronic back pain patients: No evidence for generalization across different movements. *Behaviour Research and Therapy, 40,* 415–419.

Gracely, R.H., Geisser, M.E., Gieseke, T., Grant, M.A.B., Petzke, F., Williams, D.A., & Clauw, D.J. (2004). Pain catastrophizing and neural responses to pain among persons with fibromyalgia. *Brain, 127,* 835–843.

Hagopian, L.P., Crockett, J.L., & Keeney, K.M. (2001). Multicomponent treatment for blood-injury-injection phobia in a young man with mental retardation. *Research in Developmental Disabilities, 22,* 141–149.

Hakeberg, M., Berggren, U., Carlson, S.G., & Grondahl, H.G. (1993). Long-term effects on dental care behavior and dental heath after treatments for dental fear. *Anesthesia Progress, 40,* 72–77.

Harrison, J.A., Berggren, U., & Carlsson, S.G. (1989). Treatment of dental fear: Systematic desensitization or coping? *Behavioural Psychotherapy, 17,* 125–133.

Harrison, J.A., Carlsson, S.G., & Berggren, U. (1985). Research in clinical process and outcome methodology: Psychophysiology, systematic desensitization and dental fear. *Journal of Behavior Therapy and Experimental Psychiatry, 16,* 201–209.

Haynes, S.N., & O'Brien, W.H. (2000). *Principles and practice of behavioral assessment.* New York: Kluwer Academic.

Hoodin, F., Potter, R., & Bamford, A. (2002, May). What component of systematic desensitization decreases migraine-related pain anxiety? Paper presented at Association for Behavior Analysis Conference, Toronto, Canada.

Horne, D.J. De L., & McCormack, H. (1984). Behavioural psychotherapy for a blood and needle phobic mastectomy patient receiving adjuvant chemotherapy. *Behavioural Psychotherapy, 12,* 342–348.

Horowitz, L.G. (1992). Audiotaped relaxation, implosion, and rehearsal for the treatment of patients with dental phobia. *General Dentistry, 40,* 242–247.

Hsu, L.K.G. (1978). Novel symptom emergence after behavior therapy in a case of hypodermic injection phobia. *American Journal of Psychiatry, 135,* 238–239.

Jacobsen, P.B. (1991). Treating a man with needle phobia who requires daily injections of medication. *Hospital and Community Psychiatry, 42,* 877–878.

Jerremalm, A., Jansson, L., & Öst, L-G. (1986). Individual response patterns and the effects of different behavioral methods in the treatment of dental phobia. *Behaviour Research and Therapy, 24,* 587–596.

Johren, P., Jackowski, J., Gangler, P., Sartory, G., & Thom A. (2000). Fear reduction in patients with dental treatment phobia. *British Journal of Oral and Maxillofacial Surgery, 38,* 612–616.

Kaloupek, D.G., Scott, J.R., & Khatami, V. (1985). Assessment of coping strategies associated with syncope in blood donors. *Journal of Psychosomatic Research, 29,* 207–214.

Katz, R.C. (1974). Single session recovery from a hemodialysis phobia: A case study. *Journal of Behavior Therapy & Experimental Psychiatry, 5,* 205–206.

Kelley, J.E., Lumley, M.A., & Leisen, J.C. (1997). Health effects of emotional disclosure in rheumatoid arthritis patients. *Health Psychology, 16*(4), 331–340.

Klapow, J.C., Schmidt, S.M., Taylor, L.A., Roller, P., Li, Q., Calhoun, J.W., et al. (2001). Symptom management in older primary care patients: feasibility of an experimental, written self-disclosure protocol. *Annals of Internal Medicine, 134*(9), 905–911.

Kleinknecht, R.A. (1987). Vasovagal syncope and blood/injury fear. *Behaviour Research and Therapy, 25,* 175–178.

Kleinknecht, R.A. (1993). Rapid treatment of blood and injection phobias with eye movement desensitization. *Journal of Behavior Therapy and Experimental Psychiatry, 24,* 211–217.

Klepac, R.K. (1986). Fear and avoidance of dental treatment in adults. *Annals of Behavioral Medicine, 8,* 17–22.

Klepac, R.K. (1975). Successful treatment of avoidance of dentistry by desensitization or by increasing pain tolerance. *Journal of Behavior Therapy and Experimental Psychiatry, 6,* 307–310.

Klesges, R.C., Malott, J.M., & Ugland, M. (1984). The effects of graded exposure and parental modeling on the dental phobias of a four-year-old girl and her mother. *Journal of Behavior Therapy and Experimental Psychiatry, 15,* 161–164.

Kloss, J.D., & Lisman, S.A. (2002). An exposure-based examination of the effects of written emotional disclosure. *British Journal of Health Psychology, 7,* 31–46.

Kori, S.H., Miller, R.P., & Todd, D.D. (1990). Kinesiophobia: A new view of chronic pain behavior. *Pain Management, 1,* 35–43.

Kozak, M.J., & Montgomery, G.K. (1981). Multimodal behavioral treatment of recurrent injury-scene-elicited fainting (vasodepressor syncope). *Behavioural Psychotherapy, 9,* 316–321.

Kroeger, R.F., & Smith, T.A. (1989). Three-year results of a behavioral fear control program. *General Dentistry, 37,* 112–115.

Lautch, H. (1971). Dental phobia. *British Journal of Psychiatry, 119,* 151–158.

Lethem, J., Slade, P.D., Troup, J.D., & Bentley, G. (1983). Outline of a Fear-Avoidance model of exaggerated pain perception -I. *Behaviour Research and Therapy, 21,* 401–408.

Liddell, A., Di Fazio, L., Blackwood, J., & Ackerman, C. (1994). Long-term follow-up of treated dental phobics. *Behaviour Research and Therapy, 32,* 605–610.

Linton, S.J., Overmeer, T., Janson, M., Vlaeyen, J.W.S., & de Jong, J. (2002). Graded in vivo exposure treatment for fear-avoidant pain patients with functional disability: A case study. *Cognitive Behaviour Therapy, 31*(2), 49–58.

Litt, M.D., Kalinowski, L., & Shafer, D. (1999). A dental fears typology of oral surgery patients: Matching patients to anxiety interventions. *Health Psychology, 18,* 614–624.

Lumley, M. (2004). Alexithymia, emotional disclosure, and health: A program of research. *Journal of Personality, 72*(6), 1271–1300.

Lynch, T.J., & Hoodin, F. (2004). An examination of the mechanism of change of written disclosure using computerized EMA procedures with two bone marrow transplant participants. [Abstract]. *Annals of Behavioral Medicine, 27*(Suppl.), S10.

Mansell, W., & Morris, K. (2003). The dental cognitions questionnaire in CBT for dental phobia in an adolescent with multiple phobias. *Journal of Behavior Therapy and Experimental Psychiatry, 34,* 65–71.

Marks, I. (1988). Blood-injury phobia: A review. *American Journal of Psychiatry, 145,* 1207–1213.

Martin, P.R. (2000). Headache triggers: To avoid or not to avoid, that is the question. *Psychology and Health, 15,* 801–809.

Martin, P.R. (2001). How do trigger factors acquire the capacity to precipitate headaches? *Behaviour Research and Therapy, 39,* 545–554.

Mathews, A., & Rezin, V. (1977). Treatment of dental fears by imaginal flooding and rehearsal of coping behaviour. *Behaviour Research and Therapy, 15,* 321–328.

McCracken, L.M., & Gross, R.T. (1998). The role of pain-related anxiety reduction in the outcome of multidisciplinary treatment for chronic low back pain: Preliminary results. *Journal of Occupational Rehabilitation, 8*(3), 179–189.

Mineka, S., Mystkowski, J.L., Hladek, D., & Rodriguez, B.I. (1999). The effects of changing contexts on return of fear following exposure therapy for spider fear. *Journal of Consulting and Clinical Psychology, 67,* 599–604.

Nash, J.L. (1971). Behavior therapy in an army mental hygiene clinic: Deconditioning of a phobia: Case report. *Military Medicine, 136,* 639.

Nimmer, W.H., & Kapp, R.A. (1974). A multiple impact program for the treatment of injection phobias. *Journal of Behavior Therapy and Experimental Psychiatry, 5,* 257–258.

Ning, L., & Liddell, A. (1991). The effect of concordance in the treatment of clients with dental anxiety. *Behaviour Research and Therapy, 29,* 315–322.

Norman, S.A., Lumley, M.A., Dooley, J.A., & Diamond, M.P. (2004). For whom does it work? Moderators of the effects of written emotional disclosure in a randomized trial among women with chronic pelvic pain. *Psychosomatic Medicine, 66*(2), 174–183.

Norton, P.J., & Asmundson, G.J.G. (2003). Amending the fear-avoidance model of chronic pain: What is the role of physiological arousal. *Behavior Therapy, 34,* 17–30.

Ollendick, T.H., & Gruen, G.E. (1972). Treatment of a bodily injury phobia with implosive therapy. *Journal of Consulting and Clinical Psychology, 38,* 389–393.

Olsson-Jerremalm, A. (1988). Applied relaxation in the treatment of phobias. *Scandinavian Journal of Behaviour Therapy, 17,* 97–110.

Öst, L.-G. (1987). Applied relaxation: Description of a coping technique and review of controlled studies. *Behaviour Research and Therapy, 25,* 397–409.

Öst, L.-G., Fellenius, J, & Sterner, U. (1991). Applied tension, exposure in vivo, and tension-only in the treatment of blood phobia. *Behaviour Research and Therapy, 29,* 561–574.

Öst, L.-G., Lindahl, I-L, Sterner, U., & Jerremalm, A. (1984). Exposure in vivo vs applied relaxation in the treatment of blood phobia. *Behaviour Research and Therapy, 22,* 205–216.

Öst, L.-G., & Sterner, U. (1987). Applied tension: A specific behavioral method for treatment of blood phobia. *Behaviour Research and Therapy, 25,* 25–29.

Öst, L.-G., Sterner, U., & Fellenius, J. (1989). Applied tension, applied relaxation, and the combination in the treatment of blood phobia. *Behaviour Research and Therapy, 27,* 109–121.

Page, A.C. (1994). Blood-injury phobia. *Clinical Psychology Review, 14,* 443–461.

Panzarella, C., & Garlipp, J. (1999). Integration of cognitive techniques into an individualized application of behavioral treatment of blood-injection-injury phobia. *Cognitive and Behavioral Practice, 6,* 200–211.

Pennebaker, J.W. (1997). Writing about emotional experiences as a therapeutic process. *Psychological Science, 8*(3), 162–166.

Pennebaker, J.W, & Beall, S.K. (1986). Confronting a traumatic event: Towards an understanding of inhibition and disease. *Journal of Abnormal Psychology, 95,* 274–281.

Petrie, K.J., Fontanilla, I., Thomas, M.G., Booth, R.J., & Pennebaker, J.W. (2004). Effect of written emotional expression on immune function in patients with human immunodeficiency virus infection: A randomized trial. *Psychosomatic Medicine, 66,* 272–275.

Philips, H.C. (1987). Avoidance behavior and its role in sustaining chronic pain. *Behavior Research and Therapy, 24*(4), 273–279.

Philips, H.C., & Jahanshahi, M. (1985). Chronic pain: An experimental analysis of the effects of exposure. *Behavior Research and Therapy, 23*(3), 281–290.

Potter, R. (1999). Effects of Behavioral Treatment for Migraine and Systematic Desensitization for Pain Anxiety in Migraineurs referred by a University Health Center. Unpublished master's thesis, Eastern Michigan University, Ypsilanti, Michigan.

Rachman, S. (1959). The treatment of anxiety and phobic reactions by systematic desensitization psychotherapy. *Journal of Abnormal and Social Psychology, 58,* 259–263.

Rainwater, N., Sweet, A.A., Elliott, L., Bowers, M., McNeill, J., & Stump, N. (1988). Systematic desensitization in the treatment of needle phobias for children with diabetes. *Child and Family Behavior Therapy, 10,* 19–31.

Rhudy, J.L., & Meagher, M.W. (2000). Fear and anxiety: divergent effects on human pain thresholds. *Pain, 84,* 65–75.

Roden, S.K. (2001). Blood-injection-injury phobia in a commercial aviator: A case report. *Aviation Space and Environmental Medicine, 72,* 1138–1140.

Rosenberg, H.J., Rosenberg, S.D., Ernstoff, M.S., Wolford, G.L., Amdur, R.J., Elshamy, M.R., et al. (2002). Expressive disclosure and health outcomes in a prostate cancer population. *International Journal of Psychiatry in Medicine, 32*(1), 37–53.

Rosensteil, A.K., & Keefe, F.J. (1983). The use of coping strategies in chronic low back pain patients: Relationship to patient characteristics and current adjustment. *Pain, 17,* 33–44.

Rowe, M.K., & Craske, M.G. (1998a). Effects of varied-stimulus exposure training on fear reduction and return of fear. *Behavior Research and Therapy, 36,* 719–734.

Rowe, M.K., & Craske, M.G. (1998b). Effects of an expanding-space vs massed exposure schedule on fear reduction and return of fear. *Behavior Research and Therapy, 36,* 701–717.

Schwartz, L., & Drotar, D. (2004). Effects of written emotional disclosure on caregivers of children and adolescents with chronic illness. *Journal of Pediatric Psychology, 29*(2), 105–118.

Severijns, J.M., Vlaeyen, J.W., van den Hout, M.A., & Weber, W.E. (2001). Pain catastrophizing predicts pain intensity, disability and psychological distress independent of the level of physical impairment. *Clinical Journal of Pain, 17,* 165–172.

Shaw, D.W., & Thoresen, C.E. (1974). Effects of modeling and desensitization in reducing dentist phobia. *Journal of Counseling Psychology, 21,* 415–420.

Shoben, E.J., & Borland, L. (1954). An empirical study of the etiology of dental fears. *Journal of Clinical Psychology, 10,* 171–174.

Sieben, J.M., Vlaeyen, J.W., Tuerlincks, S., & Portegijs, P. (2002). Pain related fear in acute low back pain: The first two weeks of a new episode. *European Journal of Pain, 6*(3), 229–237.

Sloan, D.M., & Marx, B.P. (2004). A closer examination of the structured written disclosure procedure. *Journal of Consulting and Clinical Psychology, 72*(2), 165–175.

Smith, T.A., Kroeger, R.F., Lyon, H.E., & Mullins, M.R. (1990). Evaluating a behavioral method to manage dental fear: A 2-year study of dental practices. *Journal of the American Dental Association, 121,* 525–530.

Smyth, J.M. (1998). Written emotional expression: Effect sizes, outcome types and moderating variables. *Journal of Consulting and Clinical Psychology, 66*(1), 174–184.

Smyth, J.M., Anderson, C.F., Hockemeyer, J.R., & Stone, A.A. (2002). Does emotional non-expressiveness or avoidance interfere with writing about stressful life events? An analysis in patients with chronic illness. *Psychology and Health, 17*(5), 561–569.

Smyth, J.M., Stone, A.A., Hurewitz, A., & Kaell, A. (1999) Effects of writing about stressful experiences on symptom reduction in patients with asthma or rheumatoid arthritis: A randomized trial. *Journal of American Medical Association, 281*(14), 1304–1309.

Solano, L., Donati, V., Pecci, F., Persichetti, S., & Colaci, A. (2003). Postoperative course after papilloma resection: Effects of written disclosure of the experience in subjects with different alexithymia levels. *Psychosomatic Medicine, 65*(3), 477–484.

Stanton, A.L., Danoff-Burg, S., Sworowski, L.A., Collins, C.A., Branstetter, A.D., Rodriguez-Hanley, A., et al. (2002). Randomized, controlled trial of written emotional expression and benefit finding in breast cancer patients. *Journal of Clinical Oncology, 20*(20), 4160–4168.

Sullivan, M.J.L., & D'Eon, J.L. (1990). Relation between catastrophizing and depression in chronic pain patients. *Journal of Abnormal Psychology, 99,* 260–263.

Sullivan, M.J.L., & Neish, N. (1999). The effects of disclosure on pain during dental hygiene treatment: the moderating role of catastrophizing. *Pain, 79*(2–3), 155–163.

Sullivan, M.J.L., Standish, W., Waite, H., Sullivan, M., & Tripp, D.A. (1998). Catastrophizing, pain and disability in patients with soft tissue injuries. *Pain, 77,* 253–260.

Taylor, C.B., Ferguson, J.M., & Wermuth, B.M. (1977). Simple techniques to treat medical phobias. *Postgraduate Medical Journal, 53,* 28–32.

Taylor, L.A., Wallander, J.L., Anderson, D., Beasley, P., & Brown, R.T. (2003). Improving health care utilization, improving chronic disease utilization, health status, and adjustment in adolescents and young adults with cystic fibrosis: A preliminary report. *Journal of Clinical Psychology in Medical Settings, 10*(1), 9–16.

Thom, A., Sartory, G. & Johren, P. (2000). Comparison between one-session psychological treatment and benzodiazepine in dental phobia. *Journal of Consulting and Clinical Psychology, 68,* 378–387.

Thompson, A. (1999). Cognitive-behavioural treatment of blood-injury-injection phobia: A case study. *Behaviour Change, 16,* 182–190.

Thyer, B.A., Himle, J., & Curtis, G.C. (1985). Blood-injury-illness phobia: A review. *Journal of Clinical Psychology, 41,* 451–459.

Tilley, S. (1985). Multiple phobias and grief: a case study. *Behavioural Psychotherapy, 13,* 59–68.

Trijsburg, R.W., Jelicic, M., van den Brock, W.W., Plekker, A.E.M., Verheij, R., & Passchier, J. (1996). Exposure and participant modelling in a case of injection phobia. *Psychotherapy and Psychosomatics, 65,* 57–61.

Vlaeyen, J.W.S., de Jong, J., Geilen, M., Heuts, P.H.T.G., & van Breukelen, G. (2001). Graded exposure in vivo in the treatment of pain-related fear: a replicated single-case experimental design in four patients with chronic low back pain. *Behaviour Research and Therapy, 39,* 151–166.

Vlaeyen, J.W.S., de Jong, J., Geilen, M., Heuts, P.H.T.G., & van Breukelen, G. (2002). The treatment of fear of movement/(re)injury in chronic low back pain: Further evidence on the effectiveness of exposure in vivo. *The Clinical Journal of Pain, 18,* 251–261.

Vlaeyen, J.W.S., de Jong, J.R., Onghenga, P., Kerckhoffs-Hanssen, M., & Kole-Snijders, A.M.J. (2002). Can pain-related fear be reduced? The application of cognitive-behavioural exposure in vivo. *Pain Research and Management* 7(3), 144–153.

Vlaeyen, J.W.S., de Jong, J., Sieben, J., & Crombez, G. (2002). Graded exposure in vivo for pain-related fear. In D.C. Turk, & R.J. Gatchel. *Psychological approaches to pain management: A practitioner's handbook.* New York: Guilford Press.

Walker, B.L., Nail, L.M., & Croyle, R.T. (1999). Does emotional expression make a difference in reactions to breast cancer? *Oncology Nursing Forum, 26*(6), 1025–1032.

Wardle, J., & Jarvis, M. (1981). The paradoxical fear response to blood, injury, and illness: A treatment report. *Behavioural Psychotherapy, 9,* 13–24.

Watson, P.J., Booker, C.K., & Main, C.J. (1997). Evidence for the role of psychological factors in abnormal paraspinal acitivity in patients with chronic low back pain. *Journal of Musculoskeletal Pain, 5,* 41–56.

Wenzel, A., & Sawchuk, C.N. (2004). Psychometric properties of the multidimensional blood/injury phobia inventory. *Behavior Therapist, 27,* 10–15.

Willemsen, H., Chowdhury, U., & Briscall, L (2002). Needle phobia in children: A discussion of aetiology and treatment options. *Clinical Child Psychology and Psychiatry, 7,* 609–619.

Wroblewski, P.F., Jacob, T., & Rehn, L.P. (1977). The contribution of relaxation to symbolic modeling in the modification of dental fears. *Behaviour Research and Therapy, 15,* 113–115.

Yarnold, P.R. (1988). Classical test theory methods for repeated measures N = 1 research designs. *Educational and Psychological Measurement, 48,* 913–919.

Yule, W., & Fernando, P. (1980). Blood phobia-beware. *Behaviour Research and Therapy, 18,* 587–590.

Zakowski, S.G., Ramati, A., Morton, C., Johnson, P., & Flanigan, R. (2004). Written emotional disclosure buffers the effects of social constraints on distress among cancer patients. *Health Psychology, 23*(6), 555–563.

CHAPTER 13

Exposure Therapy
for Hypochondriasis

Joseph A. Himle and
Jody Hoffman
University of Michigan

Persons with hypochondriasis experience a persistent fear of having a serious illness or disease. Most people with hypochondriasis base these concerns about illness on a misinterpretation of bodily symptoms. The preoccupation with disease persists despite appropriate medical testing and reassurance. Although some health concerns are quite common in the general population, persons meeting diagnostic criteria for hypochondriasis experience clinically significant distress and/or substantial impairment in social, occupational, or other areas of functioning (DSM-IV-TR; American Psychiatric Association, 2000). Persons with hypochondriasis may have concerns focused on single or multiple diseases (Hiller, Leibbrand, Rief, & Ficter, 2005). Common health worries for persons with hypochondriasis include fears of cancer, heart disease, and other serious diseases (Hiller, et al., 2005).

Some individuals with hypochondriasis also have limited insight into the senselessness of their concerns, whereas others view their concerns as at least somewhat excessive or unreasonable but are unable to dismiss them. As a result, many people with hypochondriasis seek expensive medical evaluations, often repeatedly, and incur significant health care costs (Barsky, Ettner, Horsky, & Bates, 2001). In addition to seeking reassurance from medical professionals, persons with hypochondriasis often seek reassurance from family members, friends, medical books, and the Internet. Repetitive body checking for signs of illness (e.g., palpating lymph nodes, examining moles) is another commonly used method to temporarily reduce anxiety.

Handbook of Exposure Therapies

Hypchondriasis is a common disorder with general population prevalence estimates generally ranging from 4.5% to 7.7% of the general population and up to 10.7% among primary care samples (Creed & Barsky, 2004). Prevalence appears to be greater among women, but men are also clearly at risk as well (Creed & Barsky, 2004). Hypochondriasis is associated with significant impairment in many areas of functioning (Looper, & Kirmayer, 2001) and co-varies with many other conditions including anxiety disorders, somatization disorder, and depression (Noyes, Kathol, Fischer, Phillips, Suelzer, & Woodman, 1994). The disorder can closely resemble obsessive-compulsive disorder in that sufferers often complain of unwanted, intrusive thoughts that are frightening in nature and often engage in repetitive or ritualized avoidance behaviors in response to these thoughts. Differential diagnosis of hypochondriasis and obsessive-compulsive disorder (OCD) is made by determining whether a person's intrusive thoughts and accompanying behaviors are restricted to concerns about having an illness. If the thoughts and behaviors are restricted to illness concerns, the diagnosis of hypchondriasis is made (American Psychiatric Association, 2000).

Current treatments of choice for hypochondriasis include a variety of medications and cognitive-behavioral therapy (CBT). Serotonin reuptake inhibitors such as fluoxetine (Fallon, Qureshi, Schneier, Sanchez-Lecay, Vermes, Feinstein, et al., 2003), paroxetine (Oosterbaan, Van Balkom, Van Boeijen, De Meij, & Van Dyck, 2001), and nefazodone (Kjernisted, Enns, & Lander, 2002) have all been shown in open trials to be helpful for hypochondriasis. The most extensively tested psychosocial intervention for hypochondriasis is CBT. Cognitive-behavioral therapy for hypochondriasis focuses on correcting inaccurate, catastrophic misinterpretations of bodily sensations (e.g., my headache is a sure sign of a terminal brain tumor) coupled with response prevention strategies (i.e., preventing reassurance-seeking, body checking, consulting family or friends, using the Internet).

Four controlled studies in the literature examine the effect of CBT on hypochondriasis. Warwick and colleagues (Warwick, Clark, Cobb, & Salkovskis, 1996) were first to randomly assign persons with hypochondriasis to CBT versus a wait-list control condition. The 16-week treatment resulted in substantial improvement in hypchondriacal symptoms over the wait-list control condition, and these improvements were maintained at a 3-month follow-up evaluation. Clark and colleagues further advanced the literature in this area (Clark, Salkovskis, Hackmann, Wells, Fennel, Ludgate, et al., 1998) by comparing CBT, behavioral stress management (relaxation, problem solving, time-management training), and a wait-list control condition. CBT and behavioral stress management were equally effective and significantly more efficacious than the wait-list control. Avia and colleagues (Avia, Ruiz, Olivares, Crespo, Guisado, Sanchez, et al., 1996) also found CBT conducted in a group format to be superior to a wait-list control condition among patients meeting either full or subclinical criteria for hypochondriasis.

Finally, a recent randomized trial of CBT versus medical care as usual was completed on a large sample of individuals with hypochondriasis presenting to primary care facilities (Barsky & Ahern, 2005). Intent to treat analyses again found substantial benefits for CBT over medical care as usual. Improvements were observed in hypochondriacal beliefs and attitudes, health-related anxiety, social role functioning, and activities of daily living. It is interesting to note that somatic symptoms were not significantly improved by CBT, suggesting that CBT likely primarily benefits recipients by providing an appropriate way of responding to somatic symptoms rather than by eliminating them.

Although CBT is quite helpful for hypochondriasis, not all patients respond to this treatment. One promising alternative treatment involves exposure to illness-related stimuli coupled with prevention of reassurance seeking and bodily checking. This intervention is similar to exposure and response prevention used in the treatment of OCD (Marks, Lelliott, Basoglu, Noshirvani, Monteiro, Cohen, et al., 1988). Two studies have been completed comparing the relative efficacy of exposure therapy versus CBT in the treatment of hypochondriasis. Bouman and Visser (1998) compared cognitive therapy to exposure and response prevention. Exposure exercises focused on exposure to a hierarchy of illness-related concerns including: interoceptive exposure to activities that elicited feared body sensations (e.g., spinning around to create dizziness); conversations about feared diseases; visits to hospitals or cemeteries; and watching disease related videotapes. In addition to exposure exercises, participants were asked to refrain from both body checking and seeking reassurance from medical professionals or others. Results showed that the cognitive therapy and the exposure/response prevention treatments two treatments were equally effective in reducing hypochondriacal symptoms, although results were difficult to interpret because there was no control condition in the study. However, Visser and Bouman (2001) later examined the two treatments using a randomized controlled design in which hypochondriacal participants were randomly assigned to receive cognitive therapy, exposure and response prevention, or a wait-list control condition. Like the first study, the two active treatment modalities appeared to be equally effective. In addition, both treatments led to significantly better outcomes than a wait-list control.

The preceding findings with respect to CBT and exposure treatments of hypochondriasis present the practitioner with somewhat of a dilemma regarding which treatment to select for a given patient. One could make the argument that CBT is the logical, initial choice given that it has been more extensively tested in randomized controlled studies. Exposure-based treatments, however, may be indicated in cases where another disorder may be present (e.g., obsessive-compulsive symptoms including contamination washing obsessions, checking compulsions, and so forth) or when illness concerns are present with especially repetitive and/or exacting checking routines. The following case report discusses a patient who was not responsive to CBT with a cognitive restructuring focus, but responded well to a combination of in vivo and imaginal exposure.

CASE STUDY: MATT

Background Information

Matt is a 19-year-old college student with an undeclared major. He is the only child of a lawyer and a counselor. His personality could be described as somewhat shy. He is fortunate to have a strong social support network, and he attends a well-respected university approximately 1000 miles from his parents.

Matt's medical history included a minor nasal surgery and an unrelated brief course of pneumonia, both before the age of nine. His father has a history of major depressive disorder and obsessive compulsive disorder; his mother has a history of generalized anxiety disorder.

According to his parents and his own report, Matt generally had a well-adjusted childhood. Although he reported having periods of high stress, he denied the presence of anxiety until the summer after his senior year of high school. At that time, he had gone to his physician for a yearly physical, and the physician suggested that a small, superficial lump on his forearm should be surgically removed, primarily for aesthetic reasons. A dermatologist subsequently confirmed that the lump was of no medical concern; however, from the time of his initial referral to dermatology, Matt developed significant anxiety regarding his health. At first his anxiety focused on the possibility, already ruled out by medical personnel, that the lump could be cancerous. Once Matt relocated to the university at the beginning of his freshman year, his anxiety generalized to include other health worries (e.g., fear of indeterminate illnesses, fear of cancer, and fear of a brain tumor).

At the urging of his parents, Matt was seen for a diagnostic interview and a brief course of therapy at the college counseling service before the beginning of his freshman year. Therapy focused on helping him develop coping skills to manage his adjustment to college life. He was also prescribed escitalopram, 10 mg per day, and lorazepam, 0.5 mg up to three times a day. The counseling service then referred him for specialized anxiety disorder treatment at our clinic, noting they were unable to meet his needs in this regard.

At intake, Matt presented with concerns about his physical health. These included beliefs that body aches, nausea, dizziness, and small bumps signaled an undiagnosed, serious, noncancerous disease, and that headaches as well as retinal floaters were symptoms of a brain tumor. Common cognitions included (1) "I'm having a retinal floater (or headache)—what if I have a brain tumor?"; (2) "I must have cancer and my parents aren't telling me"; (3) "What if the doctors were wrong and I have a disease?"; (4) "I must be sick (i.e., with cancer, another disease)"; (5) "I feel dizzy (or nauseous), what if I have a disease that will put me in the hospital for the rest of my life?" Matt's concerns about his health were primarily triggered by physical symptoms, but could also be exacerbated by encountering someone with a disease or learning about a disease via the media.

Matt engaged in various reassurance-seeking behaviors, including (1) frequent doctor visits for medical concerns (once or twice monthly at the time of intake, and several weekly telephone calls to physicians); (2) reading literature on Internet health websites for more than an hour per day, particularly in response to new or indeterminate physical symptoms; (3) asking others, especially his parents, if he had a disease or other problematic health problem; and (4) frequent checking of his body for new bumps and lumps, and hypervigilance of internal physical sensations (particularly signs of headache or nausea). These behaviors functioned to reassure him for a short period of time, generally until he noted the recurrence of a physical symptom. Matt did not meet criteria for other anxiety or psychiatric disorders, although he noted mild levels of depressed mood secondary to periods of intense worry about his health. In addition, no medical illnesses were found despite repeated physical examinations. At intake, Matt's medication was increased to 20 mg of escitalopram, and he was referred to a CBT specialist for psychosocial treatment.

Treatment Selection

Two options appeared appropriate for Matt given his presentation. The first, cognitive therapy, was chosen because Matt did not meet criteria for OCD, and he expressed an interest in cognitive restructuring activities. The second treatment, exposure therapy, followed the cognitive therapy sessions and was selected only after cognitive therapy failed to effect clinically significant change in Matt. Each of the treatment modalities is described in more detail next.

Cognitive Therapy

Matt was initially provided an eight-session course of cognitive therapy that targeted thoughts and beliefs about his physical symptoms. Therapy included *psychoeducation* about the nature of his symptoms and disease etiology. For example, the therapist impressed on Matt the fact that medical illnesses present with symptoms that do not dissipate, as his did, with reassurance from others. Rules were developed regarding *reassurance-seeking*, including restricting medical appointments and related phone calls to once a year and clearly delineated emergency situations, as well as eliminating reassurance-seeking from valued others (including his therapist, psychiatrist, and parents). Matt's psychiatrist and parents were consulted by his therapist regarding effective strategies in this regard. Matt also monitored his anxious thoughts regarding illness and was taught how to restructure his thinking using cognitive techniques. Socratic strategies were used to help Matt develop alternative explanations for his physical symptoms and modify his belief that he had a serious disease. Matt quickly learned the principles of this therapy and was able to apply restructuring techniques to other situations (e.g., for stress management). Anxiety regarding his health, however, did not substantially improve and, after eight sessions, significant residual symptoms of health worry remained.

Exposure

A decision was then made to alter Matt's treatment from a cognitive approach to an exposure-based approach. Exposure included creation of a hierarchy of feared physical sensations and daily, sustained, repetitive exposure to them. In particular, therapy focused on exercises that created low-level nausea and head tension, the construction of bumps of various sizes on his body, and creation of visual disturbances by having him stare at lights and then closing his eyes (see Table 13.1 for Matt's exposure hierarchy).

Matt also reported substantial time spent worrying, almost obsessively, about his health. His worry was extremely distracting and significantly impeded his school performance, as it consumed large portions of his day. Given the inordinate amount of time he devoted to health worries, we decided to supplement in vivo exposure exercises with repetitive exposure to the 10 most anxiety-eliciting thoughts he had using three methods: listening to an audiotape of his thoughts, rewriting the thoughts, and reading the thoughts aloud. The thoughts were transcribed as brief phrases or statements that identified his worst-case health worries (e.g., "This bump is definitely a sign of a serious disease," "I am having headaches because I have a

TABLE 13.1   Matt's Symptom Exposure Hierarchy

Symptom	Anticipated SUDS Rating
Dizziness	40
Nausea	45
Head tension	65
Miniscule (< 1 mm) lump on body	74
Small (2 mm) lump on body	75
Large (4 mm) lump on body	79
Several lumps on body	80
Small lump + nausea and dizziness	85
Small lump + head tension	85
Miniscule (< 1 mm) lump on forehead	85
Small (2 mm) lump on forehead	90
Large (4 mm) lump on forehead	95
Several lumps on forehead	99
Multiple lumps + head tension + nausea + dizziness	99
Induce retinal disturbance via staring at lights	100

brain tumor and every doctor has missed it," "I have cancer and my parents aren't telling me," "I'm going to be in the hospital for the rest of my life"). The approach we took was similar to that used by Freestone and colleagues for treating primary obsessional OCD (see Freeston, Ladouceur, Gagnon, Thibodeau, Rhéaume, Letarte, & Bujold, 1997). Matt carried out these thought-based exposure exercises for 1 hour per day, all in one sitting. Interoceptive and in vivo exercises were conducted once per hour while he was awake, with an average of 8 to 10 exposures per day. While the program was intensive, Matt was extremely dedicated to his treatment and rarely missed a homework practice. Matt was instructed to continue with cognitive restructuring for other concerns (e.g., stress management), but ceased to use it for addressing hypochondriacal concerns. He continued with restrictions regarding reassurance-seeking, as well as checking of physical symptoms.

Assessment of Treatment Effects

Matt completed several measures of anxiety and depression. Each measure is briefly described next.

- *Illness Attitude Scales* (IAS; Kellner, 1987). The IAS assesses various components of hypochondriasis, including: (1) general worry about illness; (2) concern about pain, namely that physical pain is indicative of disease; (3) health habits, namely avoidance of harmful health behaviors; (4) belief in existence of an undiagnosed disease; (5) thanatophobia (fear of death); (6) disease phobia (worry about having specific diseases); (7) bodily preoccupations (sensitivity to bodily sensations that may be indicative of illness); and (8) treatment experiences, or the number of times the individual seeks medical treatments.
- *Anxiety Sensitivity Index* (ASI; Reiss, Peterson, Gursky, & McNally; 1986). The ASI is a 16-item measure of fear of anxiety-related symptoms.
- *Penn State Worry Questionnaire* (Meyer, Miller, Metzger, & Borkovec, 1990). The Penn State Worry Questionnaire is a 16-item questionnaire that measures symptoms of worry and appears to discriminate between worry and other symptoms of anxiety and depression (Brown, Antony, & Barlow, 1992).
- *Beck Depression Inventory* (BDI; Beck, Ward, Mendelson, & Erbaugh, 1961). The BDI is a 21-item, commonly used measure of depressive symptoms.
- *Beck Anxiety Inventory* (BAI; Beck, Epstein, Brown & Steer, 1988). The BAI is a 21-item measure that assesses severity of anxiety symptoms that overlap minimally with depression.

Table 13.2 details Matt's pretreatment scores on these measures. These indicated minimal levels of depressed mood and substantial health anxiety.

TABLE 13.2   Matt's Pretreatment and Post-Treatment and Follow-Up Scores on
Measures of Anxiety and Depression

Measure	Pretreatment	Post-Treatment	Follow-Up
Illness Attitudes Scale			
Worry About Illness	12	4	2
Physical Pain	12	2	2
Health Habits	8	4	3
Hypochondriacal Beliefs	9	3	4
Beliefs	2	1	1
Fear of Death	6	1	1
Disease Phobia	11	4	4
Bodily	6	1	2
Preoccupations			
Treatment			
Experiences			
Beck Anxiety Inventory	20	7	9
Penn State Worry Questionnaire	68	47	49
Anxiety Sensitivity Index	33	19	18
Average SUDS Rating of Most Feared			
Symptom (Retinal Floaters)	95	35	25
Beck Depression Inventory	9	7	7

Treatment Outcome

According to Matt's pretreatment versus post-treatment scores on the various
measures used to assess his progress, one can conclude that treatment was helpful
in reducing symptoms of health worry. At post-treatment, Matt's scores on most
assessment measures were in ranges comparable to nonanxious individuals. Six and
a half months post-treatment, he had maintained his therapy gains per assessment
scores, clinician observation, and his own report.

Matt's SUDS (Subjective Units of Distress) ratings during exposure therapy also
implied clinically significant progress. Matt completed logs of his exposure homework, including a rating from 0 (no anxiety whatsoever) to 100 (most anxiety possible) during each exposure practice. As indicated in Figure 13.1, over the course
of the 2-month active phase of exposure therapy, Matt's average daily SUDS ratings
(average of ratings across in vivo and thought exposure exercises) moved from the
high range at the beginning of treatment to the low anxiety range by the end of
treatment. Matt continued self-conducted exposure for 2 months after the cessation of formal therapist-guided exposure, and his SUDS scores remained in the low
anxiety range.

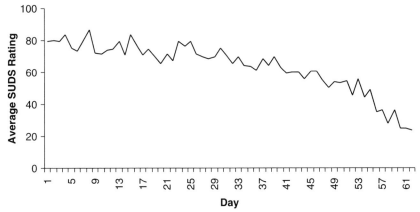

FIGURE 13.1 Average daily SUDS ratings over the course of active phase homework exposure practice.

Discussion

Matt's case supports the use of exposure and response prevention in the treatment of hypochondriasis. Although the initial cognitive therapy protocol did not yield satisfactory results, he was able to maintain commitment to therapy and adhere well to exposure and response prevention. He responded well to exposure and response prevention, although he did not have any formal symptoms of OCD, suggesting that exposure and response prevention had a direct effect on his hypochondriacal symptoms. At the end of treatment, his symptoms were markedly improved and these gains were maintained at follow-up monitoring.

Although Matt's outcomes are consistent with studies supporting the benefits of exposure and response prevention for hypochondriasis (Bouman & Visser, 1998, Visser & Bouman, 2001), broader conclusions about treatment efficacy must await larger controlled studies. The positive outcome for Matt was probably due in part to his high level of motivation and his gradual adaptation to university life. Matt's motivation to pursue treatment for his disorder was evidenced by his willingness to seek help at the student counseling center, take medication, undergo a failed course of cognitive therapy, and finally participate in a rigorous, anxiety-provoking course of exposure and response prevention therapy. This sort of persistence and determination is particularly valuable given the demands of exposure and response prevention protocols and may be unusual among hypochondriasis patients. Indeed, in our clinical experience Matt exhibited a level of treatment adherence and conscientiousness well above that of the average patient.

A central issue in this case report is why Matt did not improve with cognitive therapy. As noted earlier, Matt had little difficulty learning the techniques of cognitive restructuring, yet they did not substantially remediate his hypochondriacal cognitions. Although Matt had no other apparent history of formal obsessions or compulsions, in retrospect, his health worry had obsessional characteristics. Specifically, Matt's hypochondriasis was characterized by repetitive, intrusive hypochondriacal thoughts, coupled with numerous checking and reassurance-seeking behaviors. These characteristics, which were reminiscent of OCD, may help to explain why Matt responded better to exposure and response prevention versus cognitive therapy, as exposure and response prevention is the psychosocial treatment of choice for OCD (Abramowitz, 1997).

This case report illustrates the need to conduct further research into treatment matching for patients with hypochondriasis. Current research does not provide clear recommendations as to when cognitive- or exposure-based procedures are indicated. Clinical experience suggests several possible predictors, including the presence or absence of obsessive-compulsive symptoms; level of anxiety and ability of the patient to tolerate anxiety; personality characteristics suggesting an aggressive, confrontive, or affectively dysregulated style in treatment; and the presence or absence of distorted cognitions and maladaptive core beliefs. How these factors differentially predict treatment outcome or indicate the use of one approach over another is currently not known. Currently, a patient's acceptance of treatment and a practitioner's expertise and preference for a given technique are the factors that are most likely taken into consideration when selecting a therapeutic modality. Matt's case clearly illustrates a need to conduct research designed to identify predictors of treatment response, as many patients would not have persisted in treatment after a failed regimen of cognitive therapy.

REFERENCES

Abramowitz, J.S. (1997). Effectiveness of psychological and pharmacological treatments for obsessive-compulsive disorder: A quantitative review. *Journal of Counseling and Clinical Psychology, 65,* 44–52.

American Psychiatric Association. (2000). *The diagnostic and statistical manual of mental disorders* (4th ed., rev. Text). Washington, D.C.: American Psychiatric Association.

Avia, M.D., Ruiz, M.A., Olivares, M.E., Crespo, M., Guisado, A.B., Sanchez, A., & Valera, A. (1996). The meaning of psychological symptoms: effectiveness of a group intervention with hypochondriacal patients. *Behaviour Research and Therapy, 34,* 23–32.

Barsky, A.J., & Ahern, D.K. (2005). Cognitive behavioral therapy for hypochondriasis: A randomized controlled trial. *Journal of the American Medical Association, 291,* 1464–1470.

Barsky, A.J., Ettner, S.L., Horsky, J., & Bates, D.W. (2001). Resource utilization of patients with hypochondriacal health anxiety and somatization. *Medical Care, 39,* 705–715.

Beck, A.T., Epstein, N., Brown, G., & Steer, R.A. (1988). An inventory for measuring clinical anxiety: Psychometric properties. *Journal of Consulting and Clinical Psychology, 56,* 893–897.

Beck, A.T., Ward, C.H., Mendelson, M., & Erbaugh, J. (1961). An inventory for measuring depression. *Archives of General Psychiatry, 4,* 561–571.

Bouman, T.K., & Visser, S. (1998). Cognitive and behavioural treatment of hypochondriasis. *Psychotherapy and Psychosomatics, 463,* 214–221.

Brown, T.A., Antony, M.M., & Barlow, D.H. (1992). Psychometric properties of the Penn State Worry Questionnaire in a clinical anxiety disorders sample. *Behavioral Research and Therapy, 30* (1), 33–37.

Clark, D.M., Salkovskis, P.M., Hackmann, A., Wells, A., Fennell, M., Ludgate, J. Ahmad, S., Richards, H.C., & Gelder, M. (1998). Two psychological treatments for hypochondriasis, *British Journal of Psychiatry, 173,* 218–225.

Creed, F., & Barsky, A. (2004). A systematic review of the epidemiology of somatization disorder and hypochondriasis. *Journal of Psychosomatic Research, 56,* 391–408.

Fallon, B.A., Qureshi, A.I., Schneier, F.R., Sanchez-Lecay, A., Vermes, D., Feinstein, R., Connelly, J. & Liebowitz, M.R. (2003). An open trial of fluvoxamine for hypochondriasis. *Psychosomatics, 44,* 298–303.

Freeston, M.H., Ladouceur, R., Gagnon, F., Thibodeau, N., Rhéaume, J., Letarte, H., & Bujold, A. (1997). Cognitive-behavioral treatment of obsessive thoughts: A controlled study. *Journal of Consulting & Clinical Psychology, 65,* 405–413.

Hiller, W., Leibbrand, R., Rief, W., & Fichter, M.M. (2005). Differentiating hypochondriasis from panic disorder. *Journal of Anxiety Disorders, 19,* 29–49.

Kellner, R. (1987). *Abridged manual of the Illness Attitudes Scale.* Department of Psychiatry, School of Medicine, University of New Mexico, Albuquerque, NM.

Kjernisted, K.D., Enns, M.W., & Lander, M. (2002). An open-label clinical trial of nefazodone in hypochondriasis. *Psychosomatics, 43,* 290–294.

Looper, K.J., & Kirmayer, L.J. (2001). Hypochondriacal concerns in a community population. *Psychological Medicine, 31,* 577–584.

Marks, I.M., Lelliott, P., Basoglu, M., Noshirvani, H., Monteiro, W., Cohen, D., & Kasvikis, Y. (1988). Clomipramine, self-exposure and therapist-aided exposure for obsessive-compulsive rituals. *British Journal of Psychiatry, 152,* 522–534.

Meyer, T.J., Miller, M.L., Metzger, R.L., & Borkovec, T.D. (1990). Development and validation of the Penn State Worry Questionnaire. *Behaviour Research and Therapy, 28,* 487–495.

Noyes, R., Kathol, R.G., Fisher, M.M., Phillips, B.M., Suelzer, M.T., & Wooodman, C.L. (1994). Psychiatric comorbidity among patients with hypochondriasis. *General Hospital Psychiatry, 16,* 78–87.

Oosterbaan, D.B., Van Balkom, A.J.L.M., Van Boeijen, C.A., De Meij, T.G.J., & Van Dyck, R. (2001). An open study of paraxetine in hypochondriasis. *Progress in Neuro-Psychopharmacology and Biological Psychiatry, 25,* 1023–1033.

Reiss, S., Peterson, R.A., Gursky, D.M., & McNally, R.J. (1986). Anxiety sensitivity, anxiety frequency and the prediction of fearfulness. *Behaviour Research and Therapy, 24,* 1–8.

Visser, S., & Bouman, T.K. (2001). The treatment of hypochondriasis: Exposure plus response prevention vs cognitive therapy (2001). *Behaviour Research and Therapy, 39,* 423–442.

Warwick, H.M.C., Clark, D.M., Cobb, A.M., & Salkovskis, P.M. (1996). A controlled trial of cognitive-behavioural treatment of hypochondriasis. *British Journal of Psychiatry, 169,* 189–195.

CHAPTER 14

The Effect of Pharmacotherapy on the Effectiveness of Exposure Therapy

Brett Deacon

University of Wyoming

Exposure therapy is the psychological treatment of choice for the anxiety disorders. Exposure involves confronting feared stimuli while eliminating safety-seeking behaviors so that individuals learn the negative consequences they fear are unlikely to occur. Although cognitive interventions are typically combined with exposure in current treatment packages (e.g., Barlow & Craske, 2000), exposure alone elicits powerful reductions in fear (Deacon & Abramowitz, 2004) and produces cognitive changes similar to those observed in more cognitively focused treatment (Foa & Rauch, 2004; McLean, Whittal, Thordarson, Taylor, Söchting, Koch, et al., 2001; Whittal, Thordarson, & McLean, 2005). Whether delivered with a habituation or cognitive change rationale, exposure therapy provides patients with corrective information that may exert a powerful effect on pathological fear structures (Foa & Kozak, 1986).

Despite the well-established efficacy of exposure therapy, many individuals with anxiety disorders do not benefit from this treatment. For example, approximately 45% of patients with obsessive-compulsive disorder (OCD) drop out, fail to respond acutely, or relapse after treatment (Stanley & Turner, 1995). This observation has spurred the development of modifications to exposure therapy (e.g., McLean, et al., 2001), and it has also led to interest in the effects of augmenting exposure with pharmacotherapy. Medications such as serotonin reuptake inhibitors, tricyclic antidepressants, monoamine oxidase inhibitors, and benzodiazepines are effective monotherapies for anxiety disorders (Lydiard, Brawman-Mintzer, & Ballenger, 1996; Schmidt, Koselka, & Woolaway-Bickel, 2001), with short-term effects that are often comparable to those produced by cognitive-behavioral therapy (CBT) (Fedoroff & Taylor, 2001; Gould, Buckminster, Pollack, Otto, & Yap, 1997;

Gould, Otto, Pollack, & Yap, 1997). Although its precise mechanism of action is unclear, pharmacotherapy is generally thought to produce symptom relief by acting on various neurotransmitter systems to reduce somatic arousal and subjective anxiety in response to fear cues.

Given the existence of two distinct but effective therapies for the anxiety disorders, the question naturally arises as to whether their combination is more beneficial than either treatment alone. Optimism about combined treatment is often based on the assumption that because exposure therapy and pharmacotherapy affect anxiety in different ways, patients will receive the major advantages of both treatments. For example, Hegel, Ravaris, and Ahles (1994) argued that augmenting exposure-based CBT for panic disorder with alprazolam provides patients with both (1) fast-acting relief from panic produced by the medication, and (2) long-lasting suppression of panic following habituation to somatic cues produced by exposure. A related assumption is that medication will dampen patients' anxiety symptoms, thereby improving their ability to tolerate distress experienced during prolonged exposures. Indeed, panic disorder patients undergoing exposure therapy who exhibit intense somatic anxiety symptoms are often prescribed benzodiazepine medication for this reason (Starcevic, Linden, Uhlenhuth, Kolar, & Latas, 2004).

Alternatively, it is possible that pharmacotherapy might interfere with the effects of exposure therapy. The reduction of anxiety symptoms with pharmacotherapy may block fear activation during exposure, thus impeding a process believed necessary for cognitive change (Foa & Kozak, 1986). Medications may be used as safety aids and acquire the power to prevent catastrophe in the minds of their users. This phenomenon is observed in the panic disorder patient who uses a high-potency benzodiazepine on an as-needed basis to prevent the feared consequences of exposure to somatic cues. Although such pill-taking is negatively reinforced because of the immediate reduction of anxiety it engenders, it may also interfere with the disconfirmation of inaccurate beliefs about somatic sensations by (1) preventing opportunities for exposure to high somatic arousal, and (2) providing an excuse for the nonoccurrence of catastrophe (i.e., "I didn't have a heart attack because of the medication"). And last, research on context effects in fear extinction (Bouton, 2002) suggests that safety learning occurring in the context of pharmacotherapy may not generalize to the context of being medication-free. In other words, when the internal context of a drug state is withdrawn, so is the learned safety. Collectively, these reservations caution that pharmacotherapy might attenuate the effects of exposure therapy, particularly after medication is discontinued.

Theoretical matters notwithstanding, there is an important practical reason to consider the effects of combined treatment. The fact is that in most clinical settings, the majority of anxious patients are currently receiving pharmacotherapy. To illustrate, Stein, Sherbourne, Craske, Means-Christensen, Bystritsky, Katon, et al. (2004) reported that 58.7% of anxiety-disorder patients had received one or more psychotropic drugs during the previous 3 months. Thus, exposure therapy for most patients is likely to be initiated in the context of ongoing pharmacotherapy, making combined treatment the norm for patients who participate in exposure therapy. It is imperative that clinicians understand how, and under what circumstances, concurrent pharmacotherapy influences the effects of exposure therapy.

The purpose of this chapter is to consider the effects of pharmacotherapy on exposure therapy for anxiety disorders, as well as to highlight clinical issues that arise in the context of combined treatment. In the next section, clinical trials that compare combined treatment to exposure-based CBT alone for each anxiety disorder are reviewed in an attempt to disentangle the short-term and longer term effects of adding pharmacotherapy to exposure therapy. Where available, studies on the sequencing of these treatments and the effects of exposure therapy for patients already taking medications are also considered. Because a comprehensive examination of individual studies in these areas is beyond the scope of the present chapter, interested readers are encouraged to consult excellent reviews by Foa, Franklin, and Moser (2002), Otto, Smits, and Reese (2005), Schmidt, et al. (2001), and Westra and Stewart (1998) for more information. As will be seen, this body of research is complex and does not yield simple, unambiguous conclusions about the overall effects of combined treatment. Ultimately, however, it is apparent that the hope for consistently superior outcomes with combined treatment relative to exposure therapy alone has not yet been realized.

REVIEW OF STUDIES ON COMBINED TREATMENTS FOR ANXIETY DISORDERS

Panic Disorder

Far more research on combined treatments has been conducted for panic disorder and agoraphobia than for other anxiety disorders. This is perhaps not surprising given the long-standing recognition of these problems and the fact that effective pharmacotherapies for panic disorder have been available for decades. Most early studies of combined treatment for panic disorder examined the effects of situational exposure augmented with the tricyclic antidepressant imipramine. Short-term efficacy studies by Mavissakalian and Michelson (1986a, 1986b) and Telch, Agras, Taylor, Roth, and Gallen (1985) found that the combination of imipramine plus situational exposure was more effective than exposure therapy alone. In contrast, Marks, Gray, Cohen, Hill, Mawson, Ramm, and Stern (1983) reported that when agoraphobic patients participated in systematic self-exposure, imipramine was no more effective than pill placebo at up to 1-year follow-up. Although the effects of adding imipramine to exposure therapy are thus somewhat unclear, research has more reliably demonstrated that the effects of imipramine are augmented by situational exposure (Mavissakalian, Michelson, & Dealy, 1983; Telch, et al., 1985).

In their meta-analysis of treatments for panic disorder, Gould, Otto, and Pollack (1995) calculated mean effect sizes for exposure-based CBT, imipramine, and eight studies of combined treatment, six of which examined imipramine plus exposure therapy. Mean effect sizes for imipramine monotherapy (ES = 0.55) and combined treatment (ES = 0.56) were essentially identical. Moreover, an average of 22% of patients dropped out of both treatments, suggesting that addition of exposure therapy does not make the side effects of imipramine more tolerable. The mean effect size of CBT was 0.68, and with a mean dropout rate of 5.6% there appears to be little reason to augment exposure therapy with imipramine as a matter of course.

Before the mid-1980s, exposure therapy for panic disorder emphasized confronting feared agoraphobic situations. Situational exposure was generally effective in reducing avoidance, but it failed to eliminate panic attacks in most patients (Michelson, Mavissakalian, & Marchione, 1985). A shift toward understanding panic disorder as a product of the "fear of fear" (Goldstein & Chambless, 1978) led to treatment innovations that emphasized exposure to feared internal sensations (interoceptive exposure) and cognitive strategies designed to disconfirm inaccurate beliefs about the dangerousness of these stimuli. Compared to situational exposure, current CBT packages for panic disorder target more completely the cognitive and behavioral mechanisms involved in this problem and produce superior therapeutic effects (Gould, et al., 1995). Accordingly, research on the effects of combining imipramine with current CBT is particularly relevant to contemporary clinical practice.

In the largest study of combined treatment for panic disorder conducted to date, Barlow, Gorman, Shear, and Woods (2000) examined the separate and combined effects of imipramine and current CBT that included interoceptive exposure. A total of 312 patients at four study sites received one of five treatments: (1) CBT, (2) imipramine, (3) CBT + imipramine, (4) CBT + pill placebo, or (5) pill placebo. CBT included 11 therapy sessions over 12 weeks, and patients in the imipramine and placebo groups received 11 weekly 30-minute medical management sessions. Patients were assessed by independent evaluators at pretreatment and after acute treatment, after 6 months of maintenance treatment, and 6 months after treatment discontinuation.

After acute and maintenance treatment, patients receiving the combination of CBT and imipramine had significantly better outcomes than those receiving CBT alone. Among completers, response rates on the Panic Disorder Severity Scale (PDSS; Shear, Brown, Barlow, Money, Sholomskas, Woods, et al., 1997) at acute and maintenance assessments were 84.4% and 90.0%, respectively, for combined treatment and 67.3% and 73.2%, respectively, for CBT. However, the opposite pattern emerged 6 months after treatment was discontinued: combined treatment was associated with the worst outcome of any active intervention. PDSS response rates among completers at follow-up evaluation were 50.0% for combined treatment versus 85.2% for CBT alone. Taken together, these findings demonstrate that adding imipramine to CBT improves shorter term efficacy but impedes the durability of therapeutic gains after medication is discontinued.

In contrast to patients in the CBT + imipramine condition, patients receiving a combination of CBT and pill placebo maintained their gains after placebo medication was discontinued (PDSS response rate = 83.3%; Barlow, et al., 2000). This finding indicates that the negative effects of imipramine discontinuation are not simply due to the psychological effects of no longer taking a medication believed to be effective. Rather, it appears likely that the withdrawal of imipramine produced a shift in context (internal drug state) that compromised the safety learning that previously occurred in the context of imipramine. An important implication of the results of Barlow, et al. (2000) is that patients who remain adherent to ongoing imipramine pharmacotherapy over time may benefit from combined treatment. On the other hand, individuals who do not want to take imipramine indefinitely, or who are unlikely to adhere to dosing instructions, may be better off with CBT alone.

Two clinical trials have examined the effects of augmenting exposure therapy for panic disorder with a selective serotonin reuptake inhibitor (SSRI) medication. In the first study, de Beurs, van Balkom, Lange, Koele, and van Dyck (1995) randomly assigned 96 panic disorder patients to receive either situational exposure alone or the combination of situational exposure and fluvoxamine, hyperventilation provocations, or respiratory training. At post-treatment, combined exposure and fluvoxamine were superior to the other three active treatments (which did not differ from each other) and had twice as large an effect size on agoraphobic avoidance. The second trial by Sharp, Power, Simpson, Swanson, Moodie, Anstee, et al. (1996) compared the efficacy of fluvoxamine, placebo, CBT including situational exposure, CBT + fluvoxamine, and CBT + placebo among 190 panic disorder patients. All active treatments were effective and did not significantly differ from each other. Combined treatment with fluvoxamine was not more effective than CBT alone, nor was it more effective than the combination of CBT and pill placebo.

SSRI medications have rapidly emerged as first-line pharmacotherapies for panic disorder and have largely displaced tricyclic antidepressants in clinical practice. Because of the contradictory findings yielded by a small number of studies, however, the effects of adding SSRI medication to exposure therapy for panic disorder are unclear. Further, no published clinical trials have examined the effect of SSRI pharmacotherapy on current CBT for panic disorder. Given the ubiquity of SSRI pharmacotherapy among patients with panic disorder, additional studies are needed on how this treatment affects the outcome of CBT. In the meantime, research indicating that SSRIs are equivalent to tricyclic antidepressants such as imipramine in their clinical effects and dropout rates (Otto, Tuby, Gould, McLean, & Pollack, 2001) suggests a more cautionary approach to the use of these medications for the treatment of panic disorder until more conclusive data are available.

Despite the increasing popularity of antidepressant medications, benzodiazepines appear to be the most commonly used pharmacotherapy for individuals with panic disorder (Swinson, Cox, & Woszczyna, 1992). A well-designed and influential randomized controlled trial of situational exposure and the high-potency benzodiazepine alprazolam was conducted by Marks, Swinson, Basoglu, Noshirvani, O'Sullivan, Lelliott, et al. (1993). A total of 154 patients were randomly assigned to receive 8 weeks of treatment in one of four conditions: (1) exposure + alprazolam (combined treatment), (2) alprazolam + relaxation, (3) exposure + pill placebo, and (4) relaxation + pill placebo (double placebo). Alprazolam was slowly tapered from weeks 8 to 16, and follow-up assessments were conducted up to 43 weeks after treatment was initiated. At post-treatment, the exposure + alprazolam and exposure + pill placebo conditions evidenced larger reductions in phobic avoidance than did the nonexposure conditions. At follow-up evaluation, however, exposure + pill placebo was superior to combined treatment with alprazolam. In fact, after drug taper, patients in both alprazolam conditions lost their gains and fared significantly worse at follow-up evaluation than patients receiving double placebo. These results were replicated in a smaller-scale trial by Echeburua, De Corral, Bajos, and Borda (1993). Taken together, these findings suggest that the negligible short-term benefits of augmenting exposure therapy with alprazolam are negated by the iatrogenic effects that reliably occur when the drug is withdrawn.

In a randomized controlled trial of two combined treatments, Cottraux, Note, Cungi, Legeron, Heim, Chneiweiss, et al. (1995) examined whether augmenting 16 sessions of current CBT, including interoceptive exposure with the antianxiety agent buspirone produced outcomes superior to those of CBT combined with pill placebo. Buspirone was administered simultaneously with CBT and then tapered over 1 week after completion of CBT. No significant differences between treatment conditions were found at post-treatment or at 1-year follow-up monitoring. In all, 68% of patients receiving CBT plus placebo were considered responders compared to 44% of patients receiving CBT plus buspirone (a nonsignificant difference).

Given the clinical reality that most panic disorder patients are already taking medication, it is important to understand how preexisting pharmacotherapy regimens affect response to exposure therapy. Oei, Llamas, and Evans (1997) reported that concurrent pharmacotherapy with either antidepressants or benzodiazepines had no negative effect on the long-term benefits of exposure. Similarly, Schmidt, Woolaway-Bickel, Trakowski, Santiago, and Vasey (2002) reported that patients already taking SSRI medication responded equally well to exposure-based CBT at post-treatment and 6-month follow-up evaluation, regardless of whether they discontinued their medication during CBT.

In contrast, other studies have reported poor long-term outcomes among patients who took benzodiazepines during exposure-based CBT (Biondi, & Picardi, 2003; Otto, Pollack, & Sabatino, 1996). The manner in which these medications are used is also important. Westra, Stewart, and Conrad (2002) found that the use of benzodiazepines on an as-needed basis to cope with anxiety was associated with markedly worse outcomes after CBT, whereas regular benzodiazepine users fared just as well as unmedicated patients. Fortunately, patients who are able to discontinue their benzodiazepine medication during the course of exposure therapy may still receive the full benefits of this treatment (Bruce, Spiegel, & Hegel, 1999; Hegel, et al., 1994; Otto, Pollack, Sachs, Reiter, Meltzer-Brody, & Rosenbaum, 1993). To illustrate, Spiegel, Bruce, Gregg, and Nuzzarello (1999) randomly assigned 20 panic disorder patients to taper alprazolam with or without concurrent exposure-based CBT. At 6-month follow-up evaluation, half of the patients who discontinued alprazolam without CBT had relapsed compared to none whose taper occurred during CBT.

What can be concluded from studies of the effects of pharmacotherapy on exposure therapy for panic disorder? With respect to short-term efficacy, a number of studies suggest that both tricyclic antidepressants and SSRIs may enhance the effects of exposure-based CBT. However, an approximately equal number of clinical trials provide no support for this conclusion, and a meta-analysis of this literature indicates that combined treatment is no more effective than CBT alone (Gould, et al., 1995). On the other hand, clinical trials have consistently failed to support an advantage of combined treatment when long-term outcomes are considered. In fact, the two largest and most well-designed trials of combined treatments provide unambiguous evidence that pharmacotherapy (imipramine or alprazolam) interferes with the durability of exposure-based CBT (Barlow, et al., 2000; Marks, et al., 1993). Concurrent use of benzodiazepines, particularly on an as-needed basis, may impede the short- and long-term effects of exposure therapy. By avoiding as-needed usage and initiating a slow taper that occurs during the administration of exposure, however, the problematic effects of benzodiazepines may be circumvented. When short- and long-term outcomes are considered together, it appears that exposure-based CBT alone is preferable to combined treatment for panic disorder.

Obsessive-Compulsive Disorder

A number of randomized controlled trials have examined the effects of integrating antidepressant pharmacotherapy with exposure therapy for OCD (exposure and response prevention [ERP]). An initial clinical trial of combined treatment with fluvoxamine (an SSRI) and ERP was conducted by Cottraux, Mollard, Bouvard, Marks, Sluys, Nury, et al. (1990). A total of 60 OCD patients were randomly assigned to receive either 24 weekly sessions of ERP plus pill placebo, ERP plus 24 weeks of fluvoxamine followed by a 4-week taper, or the combination of ERP and fluvoxamine. Patients in all three treatment conditions improved from pretreatment to post-treatment on rituals and depressive symptoms, and there was a nonsignificant trend for combined treatment with fluvoxamine to be superior to ERP plus pill placebo on assessor's ratings of the daily duration of rituals. Between-group differences decreased by 6-month follow-up evaluation, and no significant differences between treatments were evident on any outcome measure at this point.

In a second trial by van Balkom, de Haan, van Oppen, Spinhoven, Hoogduin, & van Dyck (1998), 117 OCD patients were randomly assigned to one of five treatment conditions: (1) cognitive therapy (CT), (2) ERP, (3) CT + fluvoxamine, (4) ERP + fluvoxamine, and (5) wait-list control. CT and ERP were delivered in 16 weekly 45-minute sessions. Fluvoxamine was administered alone for 8 weeks, followed by 10 sessions of either ERP or CT for an additional 8 weeks in the combined treatment conditions. At post-treatment, all four active treatments were effective in reducing OCD symptoms, and there was no advantage of combined treatment relative to either cognitive therapy or ERP alone.

A third randomized controlled trial of combined treatment with fluvoxamine was conducted by Hohagen, Winkelmann, Rasche-Rauchle, Hand, Konig, Munchaeu, et al. (1998). In all, 58 OCD patients were randomly assigned to either the combination of ERP and fluvoxamine or ERP and pill placebo. After the authors excluded nine patients who had outlying baseline scores on the Yale-Brown Obsessive Compulsive Scale (Y-BOCS) symptom severity scale (Goodman, Price, Rasmussen, Mazure, Fleischmann, Hill, et al., 1989a; 1989b), 49 patients were available for statistical analyses. A statistically significant difference in clinical response between treatments was found on only 1 of 11 outcome measures: combined treatment with fluvoxamine produced greater reductions in the severity of obsessions than did ERP plus pill placebo. Post-treatment Y-BOCS total scores did not significantly differ between groups. When dichotomizing patients as responders on the Y-BOCS based on the criterion of > 35% reduction from pretreatment to post-treatment, combined treatment with fluvoxamine (87.5%) was significantly more effective than ERP plus placebo (60.0%). This study suggests a slight augmentation effect of ERP with fluvoxamine. However, the unusually high post-treatment Y-BOCS scores for the ERP plus placebo group ($M = 15.9$) raises the possibility that the mild synergistic effect of fluvoxamine would not have been evident if ERP had produced more typical levels of symptom reduction.

A recent multisite, randomized controlled trial examined the acute efficacy of ERP, the tricyclic antidepressant clomipramine, their combination, and pill placebo in 112 patients with OCD (Foa, Liebowitz, Kozak, Davies, Campeas, Franklin, et al., 2005). ERP was administered in an intensive format consisting of daily, 2-hour exposure sessions for 3 weeks. Patients receiving combined treatment initiated ERP and clomipramine simultaneously. At week 12, all active treatments were superior to pill placebo, and both ERP monotherapy and combined treatment were superior to clomipramine alone. The combination of clomipramine and ERP was no more effective than ERP alone.

A glaring weakness in the anxiety treatment literature is the paucity of studies on combined treatments for children and adolescents. The Pediatric OCD Treatment Study (2004) represents an important exception to this trend. In this study, 112 children and adolescents with OCD ages 7 through 17 years were randomly assigned to receive ERP, the SSRI sertraline, their combination, or pill placebo for 12 weeks. ERP consisted of 14 one-hour sessions over 12 weeks, and ERP and medication were initiated simultaneously for patients receiving combined treatment. At 12 weeks, all three active treatments were superior to pill placebo. Combined treatment was more effective than either ERP alone or sertraline alone, which did not differ from each other. Rates of clinical remission at post-treatment were 53.6% for combined treatment, 39.3% for ERP, 21.4% for sertraline, and 3.6% for placebo. Significant site differences were found in outcomes across different treatment conditions. At one site, ERP alone ($ES = 1.6$) was as effective as combined treatment ($ES = 1.5$), whereas at a second site combined treatment ($ES = 1.3$) was more effective than ERP alone ($ES = 0.5$).

In summary, randomized controlled trials demonstrate little or no short-term advantage to augmenting exposure therapy with pharmacotherapy in the treatment of OCD. The longer term effects of combined treatment are largely unknown, although 6-month follow-up analyses conducted by Cottraux, et al. (1990) further suggest that combined treatment is equivalent to ERP alone. Of importance, there is no evidence to suggest that pharmacotherapy interferes with the effects of exposure; rather, medication appears largely superfluous for OCD patients engaged in ERP. Longer term studies are necessary to examine whether ongoing pharmacotherapy or its discontinuation interferes with the durability of ERP. Initial evidence suggests that preexisting antidepressant pharmacotherapy does not impede the short-term effects of ERP (Franklin, Abramowitz, Bux, Zoellner, & Feeny, 2002). Accordingly, at present there is little cause for concern that patients already taking serotonergic medications will have an incomplete response to exposure therapy.

Social Phobia

Several recent randomized controlled trials have evaluated the efficacy of combined treatments for individuals with social phobia, generalized type. In a large multicenter trial, Davidson, Foa, Huppert, Keefe, Franklin, Compton, et al. (2004) examined the short-term efficacy of group CBT including situational exposure, the SSRI fluoxetine, and their combination. Social phobic patients ($N = 295$) were randomly assigned to receive one of five treatments: (1) CBT alone, (2) fluoxetine alone, (3) CBT + fluoxetine, (4) CBT + pill placebo, and (5) pill placebo. CBT was administered over 14 weekly sessions in group format and emphasized social skills training and exposure via role plays. Based on independent evaluators' assessments, the percentage of responders in each condition were as follows: 54.2% (combined treatment), 51.7% (CBT alone), 50.9% (fluoxetine alone), 50.8% (CBT + pill placebo), and 31.7% (pill placebo alone). No differences were found between the active conditions at post-treatment, and each was superior to pill placebo on most outcome measures. Fluoxetine alone produced more rapid changes early in treatment, whereas patients receiving CBT evidenced more significant changes later in treatment.

A large randomized controlled trial by Blomhoff, Haug, Hellstrom, Holme, Humble, and Wold (2001) examined the efficacy of combined treatment for generalized social phobia in a primary care setting. Patients ($N = 387$) were randomly assigned to receive sertraline alone, pill placebo, the combination of sertraline and CBT involving situational exposure, or the combination of CBT and pill placebo. CBT was administered in eight 15- to 20-minute sessions by primary care physicians who had received 30 hours of didactic training. The authors categorized patients as responders, partial responders, or nonresponders and did not report descriptive statistics on outcome measures. The percentage of responders in each group was 45.5% (sertraline + CBT), 40.2% (sertraline alone), 33.0% (CBT + placebo), and 23.9% (placebo alone). Chi-square analyses indicated that sertraline-treated patients had better outcomes than nonsertraline-treated patients. Conversely, no significant difference emerged between CBT-treated patients and those who did not receive CBT. The authors concluded that sertraline enhances the effects of CBT in the short-term treatment of social phobia. The obvious caveat to this conclusion is that CBT may not have been delivered in a sufficiently high dose to achieve its typical therapeutic effects.

Haug, Blomhoff, Hellstrom, Holme, Humble, Madsbu, et al. (2003) reported 1-year follow-up analyses of the patients treated in the Blomhoff, et al. (2001) study. Patients in all four conditions improved significantly from baseline to 1-year follow-up period; however, different symptom trajectories were evident among patients who received acute treatment with sertraline and exposure-based CBT. From weeks 24 to 52, patients in the CBT + placebo and placebo groups continued to experience reductions in social phobic symptoms. In contrast, patients treated with sertraline, either alone or in combination with CBT, did not improve after week 24 and evidenced a slight deterioration in their symptoms. These findings are consistent with those reported in a large randomized controlled trial of phenelzine and CBT for social phobia (Heimberg, Liebowitz, Hoe, Schneier, Holt, Welkowitz, et al., 1998; Liebowitz, Heimberg, Schneier, Hope, Davies, Holt, et al., 1999). In this trial, phenelzine produced somewhat more rapid and robust effects on social phobic symptoms during acute and maintenance treatment. However, after a 6-month treatment-free period, patients receiving phenelzine were more likely to relapse than those receiving CBT.

Overall, insufficient data exist for making reliable conclusions about the effects of combining pharmacotherapy with exposure therapy in the treatment of social phobia. A large and well-designed randomized controlled trial (Davidson, et al., 2004), however, found no advantage of combined treatment relative to exposure-based CBT alone at post-treatment. Several studies have highlighted a trend for pharmacotherapy to produce more rapid reductions in social phobic symptoms, although exposure therapy appears to "catch up" with pharmacotherapy by the end of acute treatment and may produce more long-lasting effects.

Generalized Anxiety Disorder

Only one published clinical trial has examined the effects of combined treatment for generalized anxiety disorder (GAD). Power, Simpson, Swanson, and Wallace (1990) randomly assigned 101 patients with GAD to one of five treatments: (1) CBT alone, (2) the benzodiazepine diazepam, (3) CBT + diazepam, (4) CBT + pill placebo, and (5) pill placebo alone. CBT was administered in a maximum of seven sessions over 9 weeks and included cognitive therapy, progressive muscle relaxation, and homework assignments involving exposure to anxiety-provoking thoughts and situations. Diazepam and placebo were administered for 6 weeks followed by a 3-week taper. At post-treatment and 6-month follow-up, CBT (either alone or in combination with diazepam) was associated with significantly better outcomes than diazepam and pill placebo, which did not differ from each other. The percentage of responders in each group at follow-up evaluation was 71% for CBT alone, 71% for CBT + diazepam, 67% for CBT + placebo, and 41% for diazepam alone. Thus diazepam did not augment CBT for GAD, whereas adding CBT to diazepam was superior to diazepam monotherapy.

Post-Traumatic Stress Disorder

Despite the existence of effective psychological and pharmacological treatments for post-traumatic stress disorder (Otto, Penava, Pollack, & Smoller, 1996), no published studies at the time of this writing have investigated whether concurrent pharmacotherapy augments exposure therapy for this disorder. Some evidence that exposure-based CBT may augment pharmacotherapy was provided by Otto, Hinton, Korbly, Chea, Phalnarith, Gershuny, et al. (2003), who reported that Cambodian refugees who failed to respond to sertraline benefited from the addition of CBT that included interoceptive and imaginal exposure to ongoing sertraline pharmacotherapy.

Specific Phobia

Little research is available on the effects of combined treatments, or pharmacotherapy more generally, in the treatment of specific phobias. A small number of studies have examined the effects of combined treatment with diazepam (Whitehead, Blackwell, & Robinson, 1978) and imipramine (Zitrin, Klein, & Woerner, 1978; Zitrin, Klein, Woerner, & Ross, 1983). In each case, the authors concluded that concurrent pharmacotherapy did improve treatment response beyond that obtained with exposure alone.

Each clinical trial described thus far investigated the effects of augmenting exposure therapy with medications thought to have a specific, antianxiety pharmacological effect. An entirely different approach to combined treatment involves augmenting exposure with medication that has no antianxiety effect per se but that may enhance learning and facilitate fear extinction. Following the latter method, an important study by Ressler, Rothbaum, Tannenbaum, Anderson, Graap, Zimand, et al. (2004) examined the effects of augmenting exposure therapy for acrophobia (fear of heights) with D-cycloserine (DCS), a putative "cognitive enhancer." A total of 27 adults with acrophobia were randomly assigned to receive virtual reality exposure combined with either pill placebo, 50 mg of DCS, or 500 mg of DCS. Patients underwent two 35 to 45 minute exposures separated by 1 to 2 weeks. A single pill of DCS or placebo was ingested 2 to 4 hours before each exposure. Assessments were conducted 1 week after the first exposure, 2 weeks after the second exposure, and 3 months later.

All three groups evidenced equivalent levels of fear during the first exposure session, indicating that DCS did not affect within-session habituation. During the second exposure session, 1 week later, and at 3-month follow-up evaluation, however, patients who had received DCS demonstrated less fear during virtual acrophobic exposures than did placebo patients. The beneficial effects of DCS extended beyond the virtual world, as patients receiving DCS reported fewer real-world acrophobic symptoms than patients receiving placebo at each assessment. Results of this study clearly demonstrate that combining DCS (but not placebo) with exposure facilitates extinction. The substantial and durable therapeutic effects of simply taking DCS on two occasions during exposure are nothing short of remarkable. If current efforts to replicate these findings with other anxiety disorders are successful, the result could be a dramatic change in the theory and practice of psychology and psychiatry (Ressler, et al., 2004).

Summary of Research on Combined Treatments

Randomized controlled trials provide little evidence for the superiority of combined treatment over exposure therapy alone for the anxiety disorders. There are no consistently replicable circumstances under which concurrent pharmacotherapy appears to facilitate exposure. A number of studies have reported evidence for a short-term advantage of combined treatment in panic disorder; however, some of these same studies indicate that the beneficial acute effects of pharmacotherapy disappear after medication discontinuation, leaving many patients worse off than if they had not taken medication to begin with. It appears that combined treatment is especially likely to interfere with the effects of exposure-based CBT for panic disorder, particularly with benzodiazepine pharmacotherapy used in an as-needed fashion. In contrast, there is no evidence that medication actively interferes with the therapeutic benefits of exposure therapy for patients with other anxiety disorders. Rather, in most cases concurrent pharmacotherapy appears superfluous. Taking into account research on the short- and long-term effects of combined treatment, as well as its greater expense and increased risk of side effects and attrition, there is little empirical justification for recommending this treatment over exposure therapy alone as a first-line treatment for any anxiety disorder.

It is noteworthy that the effects of augmenting exposure therapy with pharmacotherapy appear to be duplicated by augmenting exposure with placebo. Of the 13 clinical trials that directly compared exposure with the addition of an active drug or a pill placebo, only one found a clear advantage of the active drug (Ressler, et al., 2004), whereas three found a long-term disadvantage (Barlow, et al., 2000; Haug, et al., 2003; Marks, et al., 1993). Thus, the therapeutic benefits produced by the specific pharmacological effects of antianxiety medications seem to disappear in the context of exposure therapy. This observation contradicts the commonly held assumption that the nonoverlapping therapeutic effects of pharmacotherapy and exposure will synergistically combine to produce a superior treatment. Rather, it appears that exposure therapy and medications for anxiety disorders work through different mechanisms that are not complementary, and may be contradictory in some instances.

In summary, the addition of pharmacotherapy does not appear to adequately address the important issue of how to improve the effectiveness of exposure therapy. However, an important exception is found in the study by Ressler, et al. (2004) in which acrophobic patients given a cognitive enhancer showed a markedly improved response to exposure therapy. Replication of this finding could fundamentally change the manner in which physicians and therapists work together to treat anxious patients. In the meantime, additional research is needed on the effects of combined treatment for social phobia, GAD, post-traumatic stress disorder, and specific phobias. At present, we have little idea whether concurrent pharmacotherapy for patients with these disorders is helpful, unnecessary, or harmful. Given that most anxious patients presenting for exposure therapy are already taking medications, more research is needed on treatment outcomes for such individuals and how to optimally sequence multiple therapeutic modalities. Fortunately, the available evidence suggests that in most cases ongoing pharmacotherapy regimens do not interfere with a patient's ability to benefit from exposure.

ISSUES THAT ARISE IN COMBINED TREATMENT

Pharmacotherapy is by far the most common treatment modality for patients with anxiety disorders (Stein, et al., 2004). Given the widespread use and acceptance of psychotropic medications, most patients who elect to participate in exposure therapy will do so in the context of ongoing pharmacotherapy. Concurrent medication use presents clinicians with a number of unique challenges, three of which are reviewed in this section: (1) conveying an integrated treatment rationale, (2) managing context effects, and (3) working with prescribing physicians.

Conveying an Integrated Treatment Rationale

A crucial task in the beginning stages of therapy is to communicate a compelling treatment rationale. This process includes discussion of factors that contribute to the development and maintenance of the disorder, as well as the advantages and disadvantages of available treatment options. Under ideal circumstances, the treatment rationale logically integrates the conceptualization and treatment of the problem and engenders positive expectancies about the likelihood of success. Indeed, research demonstrates that patients who agree with the treatment rationale are more engaged in treatment and have better outcomes (Addis & Jacobson, 1996, 2000).

Cognitive-behavioral theories (e.g., Beck, Emery, & Greenberg, 1985) emphasize the role of inaccurate threat-related cognitions and avoidance behaviors in the development and persistence of anxiety disorders. Anxiety itself is seen as a by-product of the maladaptive cognitions and behaviors that are the real targets of exposure therapy. The direct reduction of anxiety for its own sake is antithetical to exposure therapy; indeed, the experience of high anxiety during exposure is viewed as essential to successful outcome in this treatment (Foa & Kozak, 1986). Accordingly, the treatment rationale in exposure therapy emphasizes (1) the role of modifiable psychological processes in the development and maintenance of anxiety, and (2) the importance of acquiring corrective information through exposure and related interventions that promote fear extinction and "unconditional safety learning" (see later).

Biological models typically emphasize the role of neurotransmitter dysregulation in the development of anxiety disorders (e.g., Krystal, Deutsch, & Charney, 1996; Pigott, 1996). Pharmacotherapy is believed to reduce anxiety symptoms by regulating neurotransmitter activity. Clinical experience suggests that the rationale for pharmacotherapy is often presented from a reductionist perspective in which patients are informed that their symptoms are caused by a "chemical imbalance in the brain" that may be "corrected" with medication. Although the intended target of pharmacotherapy is neurotransmitter activity, the direct reduction of anxiety is often considered its most central therapeutic effect.

Confusion is likely to result when patients in combined treatment receive a one-sided, biologically based treatment rationale from their prescribing physician and a narrow cognitive-behavioral rationale from their therapist. A deterministic chemical imbalance rationale appears incompatible with the notion that anxiety symptoms are caused by fully modifiable psychological factors. The exposure therapist's emphasis on confronting feared situations may contradict the physician's suggestion that medication be taken at the first sign of panic. Acceptance of a one-sided cognitive-behavioral rationale may produce poor compliance with medication, whereas belief in a deterministic chemical imbalance rationale may create the perception that nonpharmacological treatment will be of little or no benefit.

To avoid these potential pitfalls, clinicians should convey an integrated rationale that acknowledges the role of biology but emphasizes the need to develop durable anxiety management strategies. Biological factors (e.g., genetics, neurotransmitter dysregulation) may be described as one of many variables that contribute to anxiety. These factors may increase an individual's vulnerability to anxiety in general, and as such they are legitimate targets for intervention; however, biological factors alone are insufficient for the development of an anxiety disorder. The specific content of an individual's fear structure and the persistence of inaccurate threat-related beliefs over time are best viewed as the product of psychological processes that may be modified by cognitive-behavioral procedures. According to this integrated model, pharmacotherapy may facilitate recovery by producing symptom relief, but the central task of directly modifying problematic cognitive and behavioral responses is accomplished by exposure.

This integrated model is well accepted by most patients. Occasionally, an individual will express skepticism that exposure will benefit them based on the belief that their symptoms are caused by a chemical imbalance. In such instances it may be helpful to educate the patient about research demonstrating that (1) exposure is an effective treatment that often enhances the effects of pharmacotherapy (Schmidt, et al., 2001), and (2) successful exposure therapy actually produces changes in brain function (Schwartz, Stoessel, Baxter, Martin, & Phelps, 1996). Moreover, patients may be reminded that even biologically induced anxiety symptoms can be effectively managed by cognitive and behavioral strategies.

The integrated model presented previously is most applicable when combined treatment includes pharmacotherapy with antidepressant medications or other substances that do not produce an immediate anxiety-reducing effect. Circumstances are markedly different when patients present for exposure therapy in the context of ongoing benzodiazepine pharmacotherapy on an as-needed schedule. In such cases, it may be difficult to integrate the competing rationales for exposure and benzodiazepine treatment (Westra & Stewart, 1998). In fact, it may be unwise to do so in light of research findings that combined treatment with benzodiazepine pharmacotherapy interferes with the effects of exposure (e.g., Marks, et al., 1993). The recommended course of action with such patients is to frankly discuss these matters and review the possibility of discontinuing the benzodiazepine during exposure therapy. If the patient is amenable to this approach, he or she may still derive substantial benefit from exposure provided that the benzodiazepine taper occurs slowly and is completed before the termination of exposure therapy (Spiegel & Bruce, 1997). If the patient is unwilling to consider altering their pattern of benzodiazepine use, it may be best not to initiate exposure therapy.

Managing Context Effects

The central task of exposure therapy for anxiety disorders is to unambiguously disconfirm patients' inaccurate threat-related beliefs through the provision of corrective information. This process involves the active learning of alternative meanings of fear cues, not simply the unlearning of old meanings (Bouton, 2002). After fear extinction, memories of the original fear learning and extinction learning are in competition, with the dominant memory determined by the current context. Exposure therapy facilitates unconditional safety learning by demonstrating to patients that the consequences they fear are unlikely to occur *in any context*.

Consider the case of Susan, a 70-year-old woman with significant agoraphobic avoidance motivated by the inaccurate belief that she is likely to lose bowel control in public. Susan participated in several situational exposures that triggered her fear of losing bowel control (briskly walking, riding a bus). Despite clear evidence of within-session habituation, Susan's belief in the probability of losing bowel control remained strong and unchanged for 3 weeks. In discussing this paradox with the author, Susan revealed that she had taken diphenoxylate/atropine (Lomotil) (an antidiarrheal medication) before each exposure to prevent herself from having an accident. Susan reluctantly agreed to abstain from Lomotil before the next session. One week later, Susan accompanied the author to a fast food restaurant and ate a greasy cheeseburger before participating in another situational exposure (shopping in a crowded mall). Although she experienced intense anxiety during the exposure, Susan habituated after 45 minutes and reported a significant decrease in her fear of losing bowel control 1 week later.

Susan's response to exposure therapy illustrates the importance of context in fear reduction. Her failure to benefit from initial exposures was most likely a product of the context in which these exposures occurred. Susan had acquired conditional safety (i.e., "I am unlikely to lose bowel control *provided that I take antidiarrheal medication*") that failed to generalize to contexts in which this condition did not apply. It was not until exposure incorporated multiple contexts (not taking antidiarrheal medication, eating greasy food) that Susan experienced significant cognitive change.

How is Susan's case relevant to combined treatment? The use of pharmacotherapy during exposure introduces a number of potential contexts and conditions that may, like Susan's use of antidiarrheal medication, interfere with safety learning when a change in context occurs. One such context is the internal state created by the pharmacological effects of the medication. For example, interoceptive cues associated with the context of imipramine include dry mouth, sweating, and increased heart rate (Mavissakalian, Perel, & Guo, 2002). Research suggests that safety learning acquired in the context of a given drug state is diminished when a shift in drug state occurs (Mystkowski, Mineka, Vernon, & Zinbarg, 2003). A large randomized controlled trial of combined treatment for panic disorder with imipramine (Barlow, et al., 2000) provides powerful evidence of an internal context effect; following imipramine discontinuation, patients in combined treatment (who had previously responded quite well) experienced a marked increase in panic symptoms. Practically speaking, the context effect of internal drug state increases the risk of relapse after patients withdraw from their medication. The negative effects of this context shift may be managed by discontinuing medication during ongoing exposure therapy, which provides patients with the opportunity to actively acquire safety learning in this new internal context.

An additional pharmacotherapy-induced context effect occurs when the physiological symptoms of anxious arousal are blocked or diminished. In this context, the safety learning produced by exposure may be conditional on the experience of no more than moderate arousal (e.g., "I am unlikely to have a heart attack *provided that my heart doesn't beat too rapidly*"). For patients who fear high somatic arousal itself, the context of diminished anxiety may interfere with safety learning by preventing exposure to sufficiently intense interoceptive cues. In addition, the pharmacologically induced dampening of anxiety symptoms may deprive patients of the opportunity to practice cognitive-behavioral skills under conditions of high arousal.

Pharmacotherapy is especially likely to interfere with unconditional safety learning when it is used as a safety aid. This phenomenon is observed when patients take high-potency benzodiazepines on an as-needed basis to avert or cope with perceived threat. When used in this manner, these medications may acquire in the minds of their users the power to prevent the very catastrophes that exposure seeks to disconfirm. To illustrate, the author assessed a 35-year-old woman with panic disorder who described an intense fear of suffocation during her panic attacks. When asked why she continued to fear this consequence despite its failure to occur in more than 100 previous attacks, she responded that only by taking alprazolam during each attack had she managed to prevent suffocation. This case exemplifies two problematic cognitive effects of using medications as safety aids. First, patients are effectively prevented from acquiring information that might disconfirm their inaccurate threat-related beliefs. Second, these beliefs may actually be strengthened based on the notion that the nonoccurrence of catastrophe constitutes a "near-miss" that was achieved only through the power of the medication (Salkovskis, 1991).

When treating patients receiving concurrent benzodiazepine pharmacotherapy, exposure therapists should be vigilant for the possibility that medication is serving as a safety aid. Patients should be instructed to refrain from this form of medication use, particularly before and during exposures. Of importance, research suggests that safety aids merely need to be available, not used, for them to interfere with safety learning during exposure (Powers, Smits, & Telch, 2004). In other words, a tablet of alprazolam may weaken the effects of exposure to the same extent regardless of whether it is ingested or kept in one's pocket. Unconditional safety learning is facilitated when patients do not have access to medications or any other safety aids (e.g., cell phone, water bottle, paper bag) during exposure. The unambiguous disconfirmation of inaccurate threat-related beliefs is most likely to occur when there is only one plausible explanation for the nonoccurrence of catastrophe during exposure.

Working with Prescribing Physicians

It is often helpful for therapists to work directly with prescribing physicians to minimize the potential contradictions between exposure therapy and pharmacotherapy. When patients are engaged in exposure therapy and do not over attribute their improvement to pharmacotherapy, consultation with the prescribing physician may be unnecessary. In other cases, however, the failure of both treatment providers to work together may result in the rigid delivery of two seemingly incompatible treatment modalities, leaving it up to the unfortunate patient to determine which competing approach to follow.

Ideally, the prescribing physician and exposure therapist both present an integrated treatment rationale that accommodates psychological and biological interventions. This ideal, however, may not reflect the clinical reality in which therapists and physicians often present a one-sided psychological or neurochemical rationale. A related problem occurs when well-meaning physicians advise patients to avoid exposure to fear cues, or recommend the as-needed use of medication to dampen anxious arousal. These practices may undermine the apparent value of exposure and interfere with safety learning during exposure. In such circumstances, the therapist should consult the prescribing physician to better coordinate the treatment rationale and plan.

The informed consent process in combined treatment should include discussion of the possibility of relapse on medication discontinuation. Patients who plan on taking medication for the foreseeable future are usually willing to accept this risk. Individuals who wish to discontinue their medication in the near future, however, may express concern about their prognosis. For these patients, the best time to initiate medication taper may be during ongoing exposure therapy (Spiegel & Bruce, 1997). Exposure therapists must involve the prescribing physician in the process of deciding whether or not, and how, to taper the patient's medication. Because withdrawal symptoms and other adverse effects may occur during drug discontinuation, this process should always occur under the supervision of a physician.

In the author's experience, most physicians are eager to learn about exposure therapy and are quite willing to consider prescribing medication in a judicious manner, or not at all, when effective nonpharmacological treatment options exist. In support of this observation, Hunt, Gibbons, Paraison, and Rabik (2004) found that residency training program directors in various medical specialties were very interested in receiving training in cognitive-behavioral models and interventions for panic disorder. Proactive therapists may have the opportunity to educate prescribers about how to optimally integrate exposure therapy and pharmacotherapy. More to the point, clinicians who foster collaborative relationships with prescribing physicians may avoid the aforementioned problems associated with combined treatment and facilitate consistently better outcomes for their patients.

CONCLUDING COMMENTS

Most patients who participate in exposure therapy also take medication for their anxiety symptoms. Unfortunately, relatively little is known about how concurrent pharmacotherapy affects the outcome of exposure for most anxiety disorders. The randomized controlled trials literature suggests that combined treatment is no more effective in the short term than exposure therapy alone. When longer term outcomes are considered, exposure may actually be more effective than combined treatment in some circumstances (e.g., for panic disorder, after medication discontinuation). Existing research does not support the assumption that exposure therapy and pharmacotherapy will synergistically combine to produce uniquely robust therapeutic effects. Instead, it appears that these treatment modalities exert their effects through different, noncomplementary mechanisms.

Additional research is needed to replicate and extend the exciting finding that the short-term use of cognitive enhancing medication facilitates exposure therapy (Ressler, et al., 2004). This line of research has the potential to revolutionize combined treatment by fundamentally changing the purpose of pharmacotherapy from that of complementing exposure to directly facilitating exposure. In the meantime, existing data are insufficient for recommending combined treatment over exposure therapy alone for patients with any anxiety disorder.

REFERENCES

Addis, M.E., & Jacobson, N.S. (1996). Reasons for depression and the process and outcome of cognitive-behavioral psychotherapies. *Journal of Consulting and Clinical Psychology, 64,* 1417–1424.

Addis, M.E., & Jacobson, N.S. (2000). A closer look at the treatment rationale and homework compliance in cognitive therapy for depression. *Cognitive Therapy and Research, 24,* 313–326.

Barlow, D.H., & Craske, M.G. (2000). *Mastery of Your Anxiety and Panic* (3rd ed.). San Antonio, TX: Graywind Publications Inc./The Psychological Corporation.

Barlow, D.H., Gorman, J.M., Shear, M.K., & Woods, S.W. (2000). Cognitive-behavioral therapy, imipramine, or their combination for panic disorder: A randomized controlled trial. *Journal of the American Medical Association, 283,* 2529–2536.

Beck, A.T., Emery, G., & Greenberg, R. (1985). *Anxiety disorders and phobias: A cognitive perspective.* New York: Basic Books.

Biondi, M., & Picardi, A. (2003). Increased probability of remaining in remission from panic disorder with agoraphobia after drug treatment in patients who received concurrent cognitive-behavioural therapy: A follow-up study. *Psychotherapy and Psychosomatics, 72,* 34–42.

Blomhoff, S., Haug, T.T., Hellstrom, K., Holme, I., Humble, M., & Wold, J.E. (2001). Randomised controlled general practice trial of sertraline, exposure therapy and combined treatment in generalized social phobia. *British Journal of Psychiatry, 179,* 23–30.

Bouton, M.E. (2002). Context, ambiguity, and unlearning: Sources of relapse after behavioral extinction, *Biological Psychiatry, 52,* 976–986.

Bruce, T.J., Spiegel, D.A., & Hegel, M.T. (1999). Cognitive-behavioral therapy helps prevent relapse and recurrence of panic disorder following alprazolam discontinuation: a long-term follow-up of the Peoria and Dartmouth studies. *Journal of Consulting and Clinical Psychology, 67,* 151–156.

Cottraux ,J., Mollard, E., Bouvard, M., Marks, I., Sluys, M., Nury,A.M., Douge, R., & Ciadella, P. (1990). Controlled study of fluvoxamine and exposure in obsessive-compulsive disorder. *International Clinical Psychopharmacology, 5,* 17–30.

Cottraux, J., Note, I.D., Cungi, C., Legeron, P., Heim, F., Chneiweiss, L., Bernard, G., & Bouvard, M. (1995). A controlled study of cognitive behaviour therapy with buspirone or placebo in panic disorder with agoraphobia. *British Journal of Psychiatry, 167,* 635–641.

Davidson, J.R., Foa, E.B., Huppert, J.D., Keefe, F.J., Franklin, M.E., Compton, J.S., Zhao, N., Connor, K.M., Lynch, T.R., & Gadde, K.M. (2004). Fluoxetine, comprehensive cognitive behavioral therapy, and placebo in generalized social phobia. *Archives of General Psychiatry, 61,* 1005–13.

de Beurs, E., van Balkom, A.J.L.M., Lange, A., Koele, P., & van Dyck, R. (1995). Treatment of panic disorder with agoraphobia: Comparison of fluvoxamine, placebo, and psychological panic management combined with exposure and of exposure in vivo alone. *American Journal of Psychiatry, 152,* 683–691.

Deacon, B.J., & Abramowitz, J.S. (2004). Cognitive and behavioral treatments for anxiety disorders: A review of meta-analytic findings. *Journal of Clinical Psychology, 60,* 429–441.

Echeburua, E., De Corral, P., Bajos, E.G., & Borda, M. (1993). Interactions between self-exposure and alprazolam in the treatment of agoraphobia without current panic: An exploratory study. *Behavioural and Cognitive Psychotherapy, 21,* 219–238.

Fedoroff, I.C., & Taylor, S. (2001). Psychological and pharmacological treatments of social phobia: A meta analysis. *Journal of Clinical Psychopharmacology, 21,* 311–324.

Foa, E.B., Franklin, M.E., & Moser, J. (2002). Context in the clinic: How well do cognitive-behavioral therapies and medications work in combination? *Biological Psychiatry, 10,* 987–997.

Foa, E.B., & Kozak, M.J. (1986). Emotional processing of fear: Exposure to corrective information. *Psychological Bulletin, 99,* 20–35.

Foa, E.B., Liebowitz, M.R., Kozak, M.J., Davies, S., Campeas, R., Franklin, M.E., Huppert, J.D., Kjernisted, K., Rowan, V., Schmidt, A.B., Simpson, H.B., & Tu, X. (2005). Randomized, placebo-controlled trial of exposure and ritual prevention, clomipramine, and their combination in the treatment of obsessive-compulsive disorder. *American Journal of Psychiatry, 162,* 151–161.

Foa, E.B., & Rauch, S.A. (2004). Cognitive changes during prolonged exposure versus prolonged exposure plus cognitive restructuring in female assault survivors with posttraumatic stress disorder. *Journal of Consulting and Clinical Psychology, 72,* 879–884.

Franklin, M.E., Abramowitz, J.S., Bux, D.A., Zoellner, L.A., & Feeny, N.C. (2002). Cognitive-behavior therapy with and without medication in the treatment of obsessive-compulsive disorder. *Professional Psychology: Research and Practice, 33,* 162–168.

Goldstein, A.J., & Chambless, D.L. (1978). A reanalysis of agoraphobia. *Behavior Therapy, 9,* 47–59.

Goodman, W.K., Price, L.H. Rasmussen, S.A., Mazure, C., Fleischmann, R.L., Hill, C.L., Heninger, G.R., & Charney, D.S. (1989a). The Yale-Brown Obsessive Compulsive Scale: I. Development, Use, and Reliability. *Archives of General Psychiatry, 46,* 1006–1011.

Goodman, W.K., Price, L.H., Rasmussen, S.A., Mazure, C., Delgado, P., Heninger, G.R., & Charney, D.S. (1989b). The Yale-Brown Obsessive Compulsive Scale: II. Validity. *Archives of General Psychiatry, 46,* 1012–1016.

Gould, R.A., Buckminster, S., Pollack, M.H., Otto, M.W., & Yap, L. (1997). Cognitive-behavioral and pharmacological treatment of social phobia: A meta-analysis. *Clinical Psychology: Science and Practice, 4,* 291–306.

Gould, R.A., Otto, M.W., & Pollack, M.H. (1995). A meta-analysis of treatment outcome for panic disorder. *Clinical Psychology Review, 8,* 819–844.

Gould, R.A., Otto, M.W., Pollack, M.H., & Yap, L. (1997). Cognitive behavioral and pharmacological treatment of generalized anxiety disorder: A preliminary meta-analysis. *Behavior Therapy, 28,* 285–305.

Haug, T.T., Blomhoff, S., Hellstrom, K., Holme, I., Humble, M., Madsbu, H.P., & Wold, J.E. (2003). Exposure therapy and sertraline in social phobia: 1-year follow-up of a randomised controlled trial. *British Journal of Psychiatry, 182,* 12–18.

Hegel, M.T., Ravaris, C.L., & Ahles, T.A. (1994). Combined cognitive-behavioral and time-limited alprazolam treatment of panic disorder. *Behavior Therapy, 25,* 183–195.

Heimberg, R.G., Liebowitz, M.R., Hope, D.A., Schneier, F.R., Holt, C.S., Welkowitz, L.A., Juster, H.R., Campeas, R., Bruch, M.A., Cloitre, M., Fallon, B., & Klein, D.F. (1998). Cognitive behavioral group therapy vs phenelzine therapy for social phobia: 12-week outcome. *Archives of General Psychiatry, 55,* 1133–1141.

Hohagen, F., Winkelmann, G., Rasche-Rauchle, H., Hand, I., Konig, A., Munchau, N., Hiss, H., Geiger-Kabisch, C., Kappler, C., Schramm, P., Rey, E., Aldenhoff, J., & Berger, M. (1998). Combination of behaviour therapy with fluvoxamine in comparison with behaviour therapy and placebo: Results of a multicentre study. *British Journal of Psychiatry, 173 (suppl. 35),* 71–78.

Hunt, M., Gibbons, L., Paraison, H., & Rabik, C. (2004). Report of the committee on academic training: Medical specialty training on panic disorder. *Behavior Therapist, 27,* 18–20.

Krystal, J.H., Deutsch, D.N., & Charney, D.S. (1996). The biological basis of panic disorder. *Journal of Clinical Psychiatry, 57* (suppl. 6), 23–31.

Liebowitz, M.R., Heimberg, R.G., Schneier, F.R., Hope, D.A., Davies, S., Holt, C.S., Goetz, D., Juster, H.R., Lin, S.H., Bruch, M.A., Marshall, R.D., & Klein, D.F. (1999). Cognitive-behavioral group therapy versus phenelzine in social phobia: long-term outcome. *Depression and Anxiety, 10,* 89–98.

Lydiard, R.B., Brawman-Mintzer, O., & Ballenger, J.C. (1996). Recent developments in the psychopharmacology of anxiety disorders. *Journal of Consulting and Clinical Psychology, 64,* 660–668.

Marks, I.M., Gray, S., Cohen, D., Hill, R., Mawson, D., Ramm, E., & Stern, R.S. (1983). Imipramine and brief therapist-aided exposure in agoraphobics having self-exposure homework. *Archives of General Psychiatry, 40,* 153–162.

Marks, I.M., Swinson, R.P., Basoglu, M., Noshirvani, H., O'Sullivan, G., Lelliott, P.T., Kirby, M., McNamee, G., Sengun, S. & Wickwire, K. (1993). Alprazolam and exposure alone and combined in panic disorder with agoraphobia: A controlled study. *British Journal of Psychiatry, 162,* 776–787.

Mavissakalian, M., & Michelson, L. (1986a). Relative and combined effectiveness of therapist-assisted in vivo exposure and imipramine. *Journal of Clinical Psychiatry, 47,* 117–122.

Mavissakalian, M., & Michelson, L. (1986b). Two-year follow-up of exposure and imipramine treatment of agoraphobia. *American Journal of Psychiatry, 143,* 1106–1112.

Mavissakalian, M., Michelson, L., & Dealy, R.S. (1983). Pharmacological treatment of agoraphobia: Imipramine versus imipramine with programmed practice. *British Journal of Psychiatry, 143,* 348–355.

Mavissakalian, M., Perel, J., & Guo, S. (2002). Specific side effects of long-term imipramine management of panic disorder. *Journal of Clinical Psychopharmacology, 22,* 155–161.

McLean, P.D., Whittal, M.L., Thordarson, D.S., Taylor, S., Söchting, I., Koch, W.J., Paterson, R., & Anderson, K.W. (2001). Cognitive versus behavior therapy in the group treatment of obsessive-compulsive disorder. *Journal of Consulting and Clinical Psychology, 69,* 205–214.

Michelson, L., Mavissakalian, M., & Marchione, K. (1985). Cognitive-behavioral treatments of agoraphobia: Clinical, behavioral, and psychophysiological outcome. *Journal of Consulting and Clinical Psychology, 53,* 913–925.

Mystkowski, J.L., Mineka, S., Vernon, L.L., & Zinbarg, R.E. (2003). Changes in caffeine states enhance return of fear in spider phobia. *Journal of Consulting and Clinical Psychology, 71,* 243–250.

Oei, T.P.S., Llamas, M., & Evans, L. (1997). Does concurrent drug intake affect the long-term outcome of group cognitive behaviour therapy in panic disorder with or without agoraphobia? *Behaviour Research and Therapy, 35,* 851–857.

Otto, M.W., Hinton, D., Korbly, N.B., Chea, A., Phalnarith, B., Gershuny, B.S., & Pollack, M.H. (2003). Treatment of pharmacotherapy-refractory posttraumatic stress disorder among Cambodian refugees: A pilot study of combination treatment with cognitive-behavior therapy vs. sertraline alone. *Behaviour Research and Therapy, 41,* 1271–1276.

Otto, M.W., Penava, S.J., Pollock, R.A., & Smoller, J.W. (1996). Cognitive-behavioral and pharmacological perspectives on the treatment of post-traumatic stress disorder. In M.H. Pollack, M. W. Otto, &

J.F. Rosenbaum (Eds.), *Challenges in clinical practice: Pharmacologic and strategies* (pp. 219–260). New York: Guilford Press.

Otto, M.W., Pollack, M.H., & Sabatino, S.A. (1996). Maintenance of remission following cognitive-behavior therapy for panic disorder: Possible deleterious effects of concurrent medication treatment. *Behavior Therapy, 27,* 473–482.

Otto, M.W., Pollack, M.H., Sachs, G.S., Reiter, S.R., Meltzer-Brody, S., & Rosenbaum, J.F. (1993). Discontinuation of benzodiazepine treatment: Efficacy of cognitive-behavioral therapy for patients with panic disorder. *American Journal of Psychiatry, 150,* 1485–1490.

Otto, M.W., Smits, J.A.J., & Reese, H.E. (2005). Combined psychotherapy and pharmacotherapy for mood and anxiety disorders in adults: Review and analysis. *Clinical Psychology: Science and Practice, 12,* 72–86.

Otto, M.,W., Tuby, K.S., Gould, R.A., McLean, R.Y.S., & Pollack, M.H. (2001). An effect-size analysis of the relative efficacy and tolerability of serotonin selective reuptake inhibitors for panic disorder. *American Journal of Psychiatry, 158,* 1989–1992.

Pediatric OCD Treatment Study (POTS) Team. (2004). Cognitive-behavior therapy, sertraline, and their combination for children and adolescents with obsessive-compulsive disorder: The Pediatric OCD Treatment Study (POTS) randomized controlled trial. *Journal of the American Medical Association, 292,* 1969–1976.

Pigot, T.A. (1996). OCD: Where the serotonin selectivity story begins. *Journal of Clinical Psychiatry, 57* (suppl. 6), 11–20.

Power, K.G., Simpson, R.J., Swanson, V., & Wallace, L.A. (1990). Controlled comparison of pharmacological and psychological treatment of generalized anxiety disorder in primary care. *British Journal of General Practice, 40,* 2889–294.

Powers, M.B., Smits, J.A.J., & Telch, M.J. (2004). Disentangling the effects of safety-behavior utilization and safety-behavior availability during exposure-based treatment: A placebo-controlled trial. *Journal of Consulting and Clinical Psychology, 72,* 448–454.

Ressler, K.J., Rothbaum, B.O., Tannenbaum, L. Anderson, P., Graap, K., Zimand, E., Hodges, L., & Davis, M. (2004). Cognitive enhancers as adjuncts to psychotherapy: Use of D-cycloserine in phobic individuals to facilitate extinction of fear. *Archives of General Psychiatry, 61,* 1136–1144.

Salkovskis, P.M. (1991). The importance of behaviour in the maintenance of anxiety and panic: A cognitive account. *Behavioural Psychotherapy, 19,* 6–19.

Schmidt, N.B., Koselka, M., & Woolaway-Bickel, K. (2001). Combined treatments for phobic anxiety disorders. In M. Sammons & N.B. Schmidt (Eds.), *Combined treatment for mental disorders: A guide to psychological and pharmacological interventions* (pp. 81–110). Washington, D.C., US: American Psychological Association.

Schmidt, N.B., Woolaway-Bickel, K., Trakowski, J.H., Santiago, H.T., & Vasey, M. (2002). Antidepressant discontinuation in the context of cognitive behavioral treatment for panic disorder, *Behaviour Research and Therapy, 40,* 67–73.

Schwartz, J.M., Stoessel, P.W., Baxter, L.R., Martin, K.M., & Phelps, M.E. (1996). Systematic changes in cerebral glucose metabolic rate after successful behavior modification treatment of obsessive-compulsive disorder. *Archives of General Psychiatry, 53,* 109–113.

Sharp, D.M., Power, K.G., Simpson, R.J., Swanson, V., Moodie, E., Anstee, J.A., & Ashford, J.J. (1996). Fluvoxamine, placebo, and cognitive behaviour therapy used alone and in combination in the treatment of panic disorder and agoraphobia. *Journal of Anxiety Disorders, 10,* 219–242.

Shear, M.K., Brown, T.A., Barlow, D.H., Money, R., Sholomskas, D.E., Woods, S.W., Gorman, J.M., & Papp, L.A. (1997). Multicenter collaborative panic disorder severity scale. *American Journal of Psychiatry, 154,* 1571–1575.

Spiegel, D.A., & Bruce, T.J. (1997). Benzodiazepines and exposure-based cognitive behavior therapies for panic disorder: Conclusions from combined treatment trials. *American Journal of Psychiatry, 154,* 773–781.

Spiegel, D.A., Bruce, T.J., Gregg, S.F., & Nuzzarello, A. (1991). Does cognitive behavior therapy assist in slow-taper alprazolam discontinuation in panic disorder? *American Journal of Psychiatry, 151,* 876–881.

Stanley, M.A., & Turner, S.M. (1995). Current status of pharmacological and behavioral treatment of obsessive-compulsive disorder. *Behavior Therapy, 26,* 163–186.

Starcevic, V., Linden, M., Uhlenhuth, E.H., Kolar, D., & Latas, M. (2004). Treatment of panic disorder with agoraphobia in an anxiety disorders clinic: Factors influencing psychiatrists' treatment choices. *Psychiatry Research, 125,* 41–52.

Stein, M.B., Sherbourne, C.D., Craske, M.G., Means-Christensen, A., Bystritsky, A., Katon, W., Sullivan, G., & Roy-Byrne, P.P. (2004). Quality of care for primary care patients with anxiety disorders. *American Journal of Psychiatry, 161,* 2230–2237.

Swinson, R.P., Cox, B.J., & Woszczyna, C.B. (1992). Use of medical services and treatment for panic disorder with agoraphobia and for social phobia. *Canadian Medical Association Journal, 147,* 878–883.

Telch, M.J., Agras, W.S., Taylor, C.B., Roth, W.T., & Gallen, C. (1985). Combined pharmacological and behavioral treatment for agoraphobia. *Behaviour Research and Therapy, 23,* 325–335.

van Balkom, A.J., de Haan, E., van Oppen, P., Spinhoven, P., Hoogduin, K.A., & van Dyck, R. (1998). Cognitive and behavioral therapies alone and in combination with fluvoxamine in the treatment of obsessive-compulsive disorder. *Journal of Nervous and Mental Disease, 186,* 492–499.

Westra, H.A., & Stewart, S.H. (1998). Cognitive behavioural therapy and pharmacotherapy: Complimentary or contradictory approaches to the treatment of anxiety? *Clinical Psychology Review, 18,* 307–340.

Westra, H.A., Stewart, S.H., & Conrad, B.E. (2002). Naturalistic manner of benzodiazepine use and cognitive behavioral therapy outcome in panic disorder with agoraphobia. *Journal of Anxiety Disorders, 16,* 233–246.

Whitehead, W.E., Blackwell, B., & Robinson, A. (1978). Effects of diazepam on phobic avoidance behavior and phobic anxiety. *Biological Psychiatry, 13,* 59–64.

Whittal, M.L., Thordarson, D.S., & McLean, P.D. (2005). Treatment of obsessive-compulsive disorder: Cognitive behavior therapy vs. exposure and response prevention. *Behaviour Research and Therapy, 43,* 1559–1576.

Zitrin, C.M., Klein, D., & Woerner, M.G. (1978). Behavior therapy, supportive psychotherapy, imipramine, and phobias. *Archives of General Psychiatry, 35,* 303–321.

Zitrin, C.M., Klein, D., Woerner, M.G., & Ross, D.C. (1983). Treatment of phobias: Comparison of imipramine hydrochloride and placebo. *Archives of General Psychiatry, 40,* 125–138.

CHAPTER 15

Pharmacological Enhancement of Learning in Exposure Therapy

**Kerry J. Ressler, Michael Davis,
and Barbara O. Rothbaum**

Emory University

Historically, medication and psychotherapy approaches have been used as independent, and presumably mechanistically different, methods for treating anxiety disorders
(Birk, 2004; Davidson, 1997; Foa, Franklin, & Moser, 2002; Otto, 2002; Schatzberg &
Nemeroff, 1998). In fact, pharmacotherapy has been thought to be contraindicated
in combination with behavior therapy for the treatment of many anxiety disorders,
particularly phobias and performance anxiety, because it was thought to interfere
with the effectiveness of exposure therapy. Recent progress has been made in understanding the learning processes that underlie a potential mechanism of exposure
therapy—namely extinction. This work has brought new promise to the potential
use of pharmacological agents that are used specifically in combination with exposure therapy to enhance this form of emotional learning. This chapter reviews the
preclinical evidence, clinical rationale, and one recent clinical study that together
provide empirical support for this novel and exciting approach to treatment.

EXTINCTION IS A NEURAL MECHANISM
THAT MAY UNDERLIE EXPOSURE THERAPY

Extinction refers to the decrement in a conditioned response (CR) over time following the repeated exposure to a conditioned stimulus (CS) in the absence of the
expected unconditioned stimulus (UCS). Pavlov provided the first report of extinction in his studies of digestive physiology in dogs (Pavlov, 1927). He observed that

the conditioned salivation of dogs in response to an external food-signaling cue slowly decreased and eventually disappeared when the cue was presented repeatedly in the absence of food.

More recent work has focused on extinction of fear behaviors in addition to the extinction of appetitive behaviors. Experimentally conditioned fear has been studied in both animals and humans as a useful model of anxiety disorders. With fear conditioning, a *learned* fear response is established following the pairing of an aversive UCS to a neutral CS. During extinction, repeated presentation of the CS in the absence of the UCS results in the loss of the conditioned fear to the CS. From an operational perspective, extinction may thus be defined as "a reduction in the strength or probability of a conditioned fear response as a consequence of repeated presentation of the CS in the absence of the UCS" (Rothbaum & Davis, 2003).

Although the precise clinical meanings and relative roles of the processes of habituation, desensitization, and counter-conditioning are somewhat debatable (Tryon, 2005), the process of extinction as simply defined previously likely plays a critical role in the mechanism of exposure therapy. Some of the initial explanations of a mechanism of exposure therapy date back to Mowrer's two-factor theory (Mowrer, 1960). Mowrer suggested that fears are acquired according to classical conditioning and are maintained by fear reduction that comes from escape and avoidance of the phobic object. In terms of extinction, it is known that avoidance of experience with the CS will interfere with the process of extinction of fear. Thus maintenance of fear through avoidance is directly opposed to extinction of fear that is allowed to occur with controlled exposure.

In a similar manner, advances in information-processing theories were also consistent with an extinction-based understanding of reduction of fear and anxiety (Lang, 1977). More recently, Foa and Kozak developed *emotional processing theory*, in which fear is viewed as a cognitive structure in memory that serves as a blueprint for escaping or avoiding danger (Foa & Kozak, 1986). This structure contains information about the feared stimuli and fear responses. According to emotional processing theory, two conditions are necessary for therapeutic fear reduction: (1) the fear structure must be activated, and (2) the information that is inconsistent with the fear structure must be available and incorporated into the existing structure. These are the same conditions that are met with the process of extinction in animal conditioning paradigms.

Although the specifics of the theories are different, these various approaches to a mechanistic understanding of exposure therapy all incorporate some component of the basic concept of extinction (Foa, et al., 2002; Mowrer, 1960; Otto, 2002; Tryon, 2005; Zinbarg, 1993). That is, diminished expression of a conditioned response (e.g., fear) will occur with repeated nonreinforced *exposures* to the conditioned stimulus (e.g., feared object, place). The remainder of this chapter focuses on how this process of extinction during exposure can be enhanced in animals and humans.

EXTINCTION INVOLVES NEW EMOTIONAL LEARNING

A variety of behavioral observations support the hypothesis that extinction is a form of new learning as opposed to "unlearning" or forgetting of the original conditioned association (reviewed in Bouton, 2004; Myers & Davis, 2002). The most nonspecific of these observations is the phenomenon of *spontaneous recovery*. This refers to the reappearance over time of a conditioned fear that had been previously extinguished through extinction training. An additional characteristic of extinction is context specificity. Through a process known as *renewal*, previously extinguished conditioned fear will return if tested in a new context. Finally, the phenomenon of *reinstatement* occurs when uncued presentations of the UCS or other stressor interrupt extinction and lead to reemergence of the previously diminished conditioned fear response. Collectively, these data suggest that extinction is a labile form of learning that is specific with respect to environmental and temporal context and is vulnerable to degradation by stress, as well as the passage of time. More simply put, extinction appears to involve learning a new inhibitory response that competes with, but does not replace, the original excitatory fear memory.

Data obtained with rodents indicate that extinction appears to be dependent on events occurring within, and interactions between, the prefrontal cortex and the amygdala (Milad & Quirk, 2002; Quirk, Russo, Barron, & Lebron, 2000). The amygdala is the primary brain region involved in fear-conditioned learning and the extinction of fear. Activation of the central nucleus of the amygdala serves to initiate the full fear response. This "fear response" occurs through the hardwired neural connections that exist between the central nucleus and a number of other neural pathways. For example, activation of various midbrain nuclei by the central amygdala results in freezing, potentiation of reflexes such as the acoustic startle reflex, and increased respiration during elicitation of the fear response. Parallel projections to the lateral hypothalamus activate the sympathetic nervous system leading to cardiovascular effects, pupil dilation, and increased sweating. Lesions of these individual brain regions that are downstream of the central nucleus serve to block specific aspects of the fear response, whereas ablation of the central nucleus itself blocks the entire fear response. Functional brain imaging studies in humans are consistent with this hypothesis and demonstrate engagement of the amygdala and prefrontal cortex during acquisition training and early extinction of fear (Phelps, Delgado, Nearing, & LeDoux, 2004).

Several lines of data suggest that glutamate has a central role in this process. Like associative fear conditioning, extinction is dependent on activation of N-methyl-D-aspartate (NMDA) receptors. In a variety of neural systems throughout the brain, the glutamatergic NMDA receptors are thought to perform the function of mediating associative learning at the level of the synapse. Blockade of these receptors has been shown to block learning of new fear associations and extinction of fear associations, but not to block expression of learned fear responses. As with other memories, fear memories and extinction memories appear to have short- and long-term phases of consolidation. The short-term memory formation appears to be dependent on a number of receptors including the NMDA receptor, the voltage gated calcium channel, and the norepinephrine receptor. In contrast, the consolidation of the memory from a short- to a long-term representation appears to require the addition of new mRNA and protein synthesis.

Administration of NMDA receptor antagonists either systemically (Baker & Azorlosa, 1996; Cox & Westbrook, 1994) or by direct infusion into the amygdala before extinction training (Falls, Miserendino, & Davis, 1992; Lee & Kim, 1998) blocks the extinction of fear memories. In addition, other investigators have found that blockade of NMDA receptors after extinction training also impairs extinction suggesting that NMDA receptors participate in the consolidation of extinction memories (Santini, Muller, & Quirk, 2001). Together these data have demonstrated clearly that extinction of fear memories in animals requires functioning of NMDA receptors within the amygdala.

PHARMACOLOGICAL ENHANCEMENT OF EXTINCTION IN ANIMAL MODELS

In contrast to previous experiments showing extinction to be dependent on the functional integrity of NMDA receptors, we were interested in testing the reciprocal hypothesis that enhancing neurotransmission at NMDA receptors would facilitate extinction (Walker, Ressler, Lu, & Davis, 2002). Because administration of full agonists at the NMDA receptor is associated with excitotoxic effects on neurons (Olney, 1994), the partial NMDA agonist D-cycloserine (DCS) was used. Curiously, for entirely separate pharmacological characteristics, DCS was initially and primarily used in humans for the treatment of tuberculosis. However, DCS also acts at the strychnine-insensitive glycine recognition site of the NMDA receptor complex to enhance NMDA receptor activity (Monahan, Handelmann, Hood, & Cordi, 1989). As a putative cognitive enhancer, DCS was initially found to act as an enhancer of contextual learning in spatial memory tasks (Baxter, Lanthorn, Frick, Golski, Wan, & Olton, 1994; Quartermain, Mower, Rafferty, Herting, & Lanthorn, 1994; Schuster & Schmidt, 1992; Thompson, Moskal, & Disterhoft, 1992).

Based on these data, we tested the effects of DCS on enhancing extinction of conditioned fear (Walker, et al., 2002). We found that systemic administration of DCS dose dependently enhanced extinction of previously conditioned fear-potentiated startle but did not influence fear-potentiated startle in rats that had not received extinction training. Similar effects on extinction were found when DCS was given by infusion directly into the amygdala. The general findings of this study have been replicated by Richardson and colleagues (Ledgerwood, Richardson, & Cranney, 2003, 2004, 2005) using a cue-conditioned freezing paradigm and shown to occur in a time-dependent manner, suggesting an effect on consolidation. In addition, this same group has demonstrated that postextinction training admin-istration of DCS interferes with reinstatement of conditioned fear (Ledgerwood, et al., 2004). They also recently reported that extinction training enhanced by DCS appears to result in generalized extinction such that fear behavior after exposure to a nonextinguished CS is reduced (Ledgerwood, et al., 2005). Collectively, data from these rodent studies suggest that DCS, a drug shown to be safe for use in humans, may have significant potential use in the facilitation of extinction-based therapies for human anxiety disorders.

PHARMACOLOGICAL ENHANCEMENT OF BEHAVIORAL EXPOSURE THERAPY FOR ACROPHOBIA

We directly tested this hypothesis to demonstrate that DCS facilitates exposure therapy for the treatment of specific phobia in humans (Ressler, Rothbaum, Tannenbaum, Anderson, Graap, Zimand, et al., 2004). We wished to examine the ability of DCS to enhance emotional learning in humans using the most optimally controlled form of psychotherapeutic learning available. Virtual reality exposure (VRE) therapy is ideal for clinical research assessment because exposure and testing are identical between patients, is well controlled by the therapist and occurs within the spatial and temporal confines of the limited therapy environment (Rothbaum, Hodges, Kooper, Opdyke, Williford, & North, 1995). This method has proven to be successful for the treatment of specific phobias, as well as post-traumatic stress disorder (Rothbaum, Hodges, Smith, Lee, & Price, 2000; Rothbaum, et al., 1995; Rothbaum, Hodges, Ready, Graap, & Alarcon, 2001). With VRE for fear of heights, we used a virtual glass elevator, in which participants stood while wearing a VRE helmet and were able to peer over a virtual railing. Previous work has shown improvements on all acrophobia outcome measures for treated as compared to untreated groups after seven weekly therapy sessions (Rothbaum, et al., 1995).

To examine whether DCS would enhance the learning that occurs during expo-sure therapy for humans with specific phobia, we enrolled 28 volunteer participants who were diagnosed with acrophobia by DSM-IV (Ressler, et al., 2004). Partici-pants were randomly assigned to three treatment groups, placebo + VRE therapy, or DCS + VRE therapy at two different doses of DCS (50 mg or 500 mg). Treatment condition was double-blinded, such that the subjects, therapists, and assessors were not aware of assigned study medication condition. Although we used two differ-ent doses of DCS, preliminary analysis of our data indicated that there were no significant differences between the 50 mg and 500 mg drug groups for the primary outcome measures of acrophobia. Therefore we combined the two drug groups for analysis.

Participants underwent two therapy sessions, which is a suboptimal amount of exposure therapy for acrophobia (Rothbaum, et al., 1995) . They were instructed to take a single pill of study medication 2 to 4 hours before each therapy session, such that only two pills were taken for the entire study. A post-treatment assessment was performed within a week after the two therapy sessions, and an additional follow-up assessment was performed 3 months after the therapy.

At both 1 and 2 weeks and 3 months after treatment, subjects who received DCS in conjunction with VRE therapy had significantly enhanced decreases in fear within the virtual environment (Figure 15.1, $p < .05$). Furthermore, within the virtual environment, skin conductance fluctuations, a psychophysiological measure of anxiety, was significantly decreased in the group that received DCS in conjunction with therapy (data not shown).

One of the cardinal features of extinction in animal models is the context specificity of the extinction environment. However, Richardson and colleagues have demonstrated that DCS enhancement of extinction in animal models appears to lead to generalization across contexts (Ledgerwood, et al., 2005). Therefore we wondered if the decreased fear of heights found within the virtual environment would generalize to other settings. This question was assessed in two ways, first, by asking questions related to the subject's fear of heights in the real world, and second, by assessing how much the subjects had decreased their avoidance of heights since the treatment. We found that all measures of fear were decreased at the early assessment (not shown) and the 3-month assessment (Figure 15.2, A, B). We also found that subjects' self-exposure to heights in the "real world" had increased, suggesting

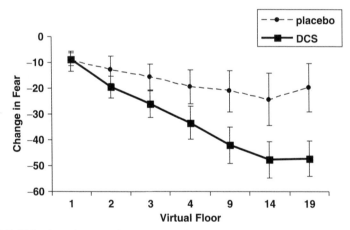

FIGURE 15.1   D-Cycloserine administration with exposure therapy results in a greater reduction in fear within the virtual environment. Change in subjective units of discomfort (SUDS) from pretest to post-test after two therapy sessions that occurred ~1 week before this short-term follow-up assessment. Decrease in SUDS level (y axis) is shown for each floor (1–19) of the virtual glass elevator. Overall ANOVA was performed using pre-post difference and floor as within subjects variables and drug group as between subjects variable. Significant overall pre-post changes were seen: $F(1,25) = 38, p < .001$. Significant effect of floor was found: $F(6, 150) = 89, p < .001$. Most important, significant effect of pre-post X floor X drug interaction was found: $F(6,150) = 3.8, p < .001$. Similar improvements in subjects treated with DCS as compared to placebo were maintained at 3 months (data not shown). Figure adapted from Ressler, et al. (2004).

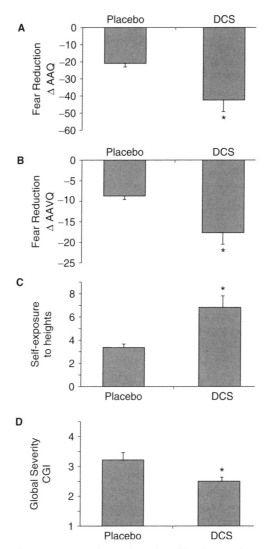

FIGURE 15.2   Reduction in acrophobia in the real world with D-cycloserine augmentation of virtual reality therapy. Assessment scores of acrophobia measures are shown at 3-month follow-up evaluation. *A*, Acrophobia Anxiety Questionnaire (AAQ) pre-post difference score, t(19) = 2.4; p < .05. *B*, Acrophobia Avoidance Questionnaire (AAVQ) pre-post difference score, t(19) = 2.4; p <. 05. *C*, Self-report of number of in vivo exposures to heights since the treatment. T(17) = 3.0; p < .01. *D*, Self-report of Clinical Global Improvement (scale: "1" = very much improved," 4" = no change) t(19) = 2.3; p <. 05. ★ = p <. 05. Figure adapted from Ressler, et al. (2004).

decreased avoidance (Figure 15.2,*C*). Finally, subjects that received DCS in conjunction with therapy felt that they had improved significantly compared to the placebo group in their overall acrophobia symptoms (Figure 15.2, *D*).

Our data indicate that participants receiving DCS experienced no increase in anxiety or fear during the exposure paradigm so that the enhancement of extinction is not due simply to enhanced intensity of exposure. Participants in the DCS group showed some evidence of enhanced extinction after only a single dose of medication and therapy. After two doses of medication and therapy, they showed significant reductions in levels of fear to the specific exposure environment. Finally, we found that 3 months after the two treatment sessions, the DCS participants showed significant improvements on all acrophobia outcome measures, their own self-exposures in the real world, and their impression of clinical self-improvement (Ressler, et al., 2004).

Although it is possible that DCS somehow specifically enhances extinction, the current literature would suggest that it enhances learning in general, and thus enhances extinction as a form of learning. The specific evidence that DCS is enhancing extinction in a learning-specific way again comes from preclinical evidence in rodents. When combined with the conditioned stimulus, the DCS-treated animals showed accelerated extinction. However, this reduction was not seen when the animals were simply placed back in the fear-conditioning context in the absence of the conditioned stimulus. Thus DCS did not reduce fear by itself, but only facilitated the specific process of extinction of fear in combination with the exposure (Ledgerwood, et al., 2003; Walker, et al., 2002).

It is important to note that the timing of dosing of DCS may be critical in the use of this agent in the augmentation of exposure therapy. Despite animal studies suggesting enhancement of spatial learning (Baxter, et al., 1994; Quartermain, et al., 1994; Schuster & Schmidt, 1992; Thompson, et al., 1992), the studies of human trials in patients with dementia have found only minor improvements (Schwartz, Hashtroudi, Herting, Schwartz, & Deutsch, 1996; Tsai, Falk, & Gunther, 1998) or no significant effect on memory enhancement (Fakouhi, Jhee, Sramek, Benes, Schwartz, Hantsburger, et al., 1995; Jones, Laake, & Oeksengaard, 2002; Randolph, Roberts, Tierney, Bravi, Mourandian, & Chase, 1994). We believe that a principal difference between those studies, our human acrophobia study, and the animal literature is the frequency and chronicity of drug dosing. The human memory enhancement studies used daily dosing for weeks to months compared to single dosing before the learning event in animal experiments and in our exposure study. In fact, Quartermain and colleagues (Quartermain, et al., 1994) explicitly examined single versus chronic dosing of DCS in animals for improvement of learning. They found that a single dose of drug before training enhanced the learning of the task, whereas 15 days of drug before the task had essentially no effect on the learning (Quartermain, et al., 1994). This has been explicitly tested with extinction by Richardson and colleagues who found that rats receiving five doses of DCS on an every-other-day schedule received no benefit when given in combination with exposures during the extinction training session compared with significant facilitation of extinction with acute dosing (Parnas, Weber, & Richardson, 2005).

Of interest, it is now accepted that most psychiatric medications have their intended psychotropic effect, not through their acute mechanisms but through chronic mechanisms that often involve receptor, cellular, and systemic regulatory mechanisms that are quite distinct from the acute pharmacological drug effect. Tachyphylaxis,* among other regulatory phenomena, is also likely to occur with prolonged activation of the NMDA receptor. In the case of DCS augmentation of exposure therapy, chronic treatment may actually result in a loss of efficacy. In contrast to other psychotropic medication, to achieve the intended effect of enhancing NMDA receptor activity, DCS may need to be taken on an acute schedule specifically in combination with the exposure-based treatment.

FUTURE DIRECTIONS

Following on the work outlined here, several other groups have pursued the use of DCS in augmentation of exposure treatment for other disorders. Michael Otto and colleagues have now replicated the effect in patients with social phobia. In a double-blind trial, they found that those receiving DCS instead of placebo in combination with exposure treatment had significantly better improvement at followup evaluation (Hoffman, Meuret, Smits, Simon, Pollack, Eisenmenger, et al., 2006). Furthermore, the use of DCS to enhance extinction of addictive disorders has now been demonstrated in rats. Stewart and colleagues recently reported that DCS facilitates the extinction of cocaine-induced conditioned place preference without affecting initial acquisition of place preference (Botreau & Stewart, 2005). From these sorts of studies, there is significant excitement in the field that DCS may facilitate extinction in treatment of substance abuse disorders in humans, as well as anxiety- and fear-based disorders (Li & Volkow, 2005).

CONCLUSIONS

Exposure therapy is likely to involve emotional learning processes, such as extinction, that have been well defined in animal models of the acquisition and inhibition of conditioned fear. As the neurobiological mechanisms of such emotional learning is increasingly well understood, novel and powerful pharmacological tools will be developed that may enhance the learning process of extinction. Sophisticated combinations of precise exposure paradigms with such cognitive enhancers may offer the promise of significantly increasing the effectiveness of behavioral exposure therapy for the treatment of refractory psychiatric disorders.

---

* Tachyphylaxis is a rapid decrease in drug responsivity after administration of initial doses.

REFERENCES

Baker, J.D., & Azorlosa, J.L. (1996). The NMDA antagonist MK-801 blocks the extinction of Pavlovian fear conditioning. *Behavioral Neuroscience, 110*(3), 618–620.

Baxter, M., Lanthorn, T., Frick, K., Golski, S., Wan, R., & Olton, D. (1994). D-cycloserine, a novel cognitive enhancer, improves spatial memory in aged rats. *Neurobiology and Aging, 15*(2), 207–213.

Birk, L. (2004). Pharmacotherapy for performance anxiety disorders: Occasionally useful but typically contraindicated. *Journal of Clinical Psychology, 60,* 867–879.

Botreau, F., & Stewart, J. (2005). D-cycloserine, an NMDA agonist, facilitates extinction of a cocaine-induced conditioned place preference but does not alter the initial training Abstract 112.9. Washington, D.C.: Society for Neuroscience.

Bouton, M.E. (2004). Context and behavioral processes in extinction. *Learning and Memory, 11*(5), 485–494.

Cox, J., & Westbrook, R. (1994). The NMDA receptor antagonist MK-801 blocks acquisition and extinction of conditioned hypoalgesia responses in the rat. *Quarterly Journal of Experimental Psychology, 47B,* 187–210.

Davidson, J.R. (1997). Biological therapies for posttraumatic stress disorder: An overview. *Journal of Clinical Psychiatry, 58*(Suppl 9), 29–32.

Fakouhi, T., Jhee, S., Sramek, J., Benes, C., Schwartz, P., Hantsburger, G., et al. (1995). Evaluation of cycloserine in the treatment of Alzheimer's disease. *Journal of Geriatric Psychiatry and Neurology, 8*(4), 226–230.

Falls, W.A., Miserendino, M.J., & Davis, M. (1992). Extinction of fear-potentiated startle: Blockade by infusion of an NMDA antagonist into the amygdala. *Journal of Neuroscience, 12*(3), 854–863.

Foa, E., Franklin, M.E., & Moser, J. (2002). Context in the clinic: How well do cognitive-behavioral therapies and medications work in combination? *Biological Psychiatry, 52,* 987–997.

Foa, E.B., & Kozak, M.J. (1986). Emotional processing of fear: exposure to corrective information. *Psychological Bulletin, 99*(1), 20–35.

Hofmann S.G., Meuret, A.E., Smits, J.A., Simon, N.M., Pollack, M.H., Eisenmenger, K., Shiekh, M., & Otto, M.W. (2006). Augmentation of exposure therapy with D-cycloserine for social anxiety disorder. *Archives of General Psychiatry, 63,* 298–304.

Jones, R., Laake, K., & Oeksengaard, A.R. (2002). D-cycloserine for Alzheimer's disease. *Cochrane Database of Systemic Reviews,* Issue 2.

Lang, P.J. (1977). Imagery in therapy: An information processing analysis of fear. *Behavior Therapy, 9,* 862–886.

Ledgerwood, L., Richardson, R., & Cranney, J. (2003). Effects of D-cycloserine on extinction of conditioned freezing. *Behavioral Neuroscience, 117*(2), 341–349.

Ledgerwood, L., Richardson, R., & Cranney, J. (2004). D-cycloserine and the facilitation of extinction of conditioned fear: consequences for reinstatement. *Behavioral Neuroscience, 118*(3), 505–513.

Ledgerwood, L., Richardson, R., & Cranney, J. (2005). D-cycloserine facilitates extinction of learned fear: Effects on reacquisition and generalized extinction. *Biological Psychiatry, 57*(8), 841–847.

Lee, H., & Kim, J. (1998). Amygdalar NMDA receptors are critical for new fear learning in previously fear-conditioned rats. *Journal of Neuroscience, 18,* 8444–8454.

Li, T.K., & Volkow, N. (2005). The neuroscience of addiction. *Nature Neuroscience, 8*(11), 1429–1430.

Milad, M.R., & Quirk, G.J. (2002). Neurons in medial prefrontal cortex signal memory for fear extinction. *Nature, 420*(6911), 70–74.

Monahan, J.B., Handelmann, G.E., Hood, W.F., & Cordi, A.A. (1989). D-cycloserine, a positive modulator of the N-methyl-D-aspartate receptor, enhances performance of learning tasks in rats. *Pharmacology Biochemical Behavior, 34*(3), 649–653.

Mowrer, O.H. (1960). *Learning theory and the symbolic processes.* New York: Wiley.

Myers, K.M., & Davis, M. (2002). Behavioral and neural analysis of extinction. *Neuron, 36*(4), 567–584.

Olney, J. (1994). New mechanisms of excitatory transmitter neurotoxicity. *Journal of Neural Transmission Supplement, 43,* 47–51.

Otto, M. (2002). Learning and "unlearning" fears: preparedness, neural pathways, and patients. *Biological Psychology, 52,* 917–920.

Parnas, A.S., Weber, M., & Richardson, R. (2005). Effects of multiple exposures to D-cycloserine on extinction of conditioned fear in rats. *Neurobiology, Learning, and Memory, 83*(3), 224–231.

Pavlov, I. (1927). *Conditioned reflexes.* Oxford: Oxford University Press.

Phelps, E.A., Delgado, M.R., Nearing, K.I., & LeDoux, J.E. (2004). Extinction learning in humans: Role of the amygdala and vmPFC. *Neuron, 43*(6), 897–905.

Quartermain, D., Mower, J., Rafferty, M., Herting, R., & Lanthorn, T. (1994). Acute but not chronic activation of the NMDA-coupled glycine receptor with D-cycloserine facilitates learning and retention. *European Journal of Pharmacology, 257*(1–2), 7–12.

Quirk, G.J., Russo, G.K., Barron, J.L., & Lebron, K. (2000). The role of ventromedial prefrontal cortex in the recovery of extinguished fear. *Journal of Neuroscience, 20*(16), 6225–6231.

Randolph, C., Roberts, J., Tierney, M., Bravi, D., Mourandian, M., & Chase, T. (1994). D-cycloserine treatment of Alzheimer's disease. *Alzheimers Disease and Associated Disorders, 8*(3), 198–205.

Ressler, K.J., Rothbaum, B.O., Tannenbaum, L., Anderson, P., Graap, K., Zimand, E., et al. (2004). Cognitive enhancers as adjuncts to psychotherapy: Use of D-cycloserine in phobic individuals to facilitate extinction of fear. *Archives of General Psychiatry, 61*(11), 1136–1144.

Rothbaum, B.O., & Davis, M. (2003). Applying learning principles to the treatment of post-trauma reactions. *Annals of the New York Academy of Science, 1008,* 112–121.

Rothbaum, B.O., Hodges, L., Smith, S., Lee, J.H., & Price, L. (2000). A controlled study of virtual reality exposure therapy for the fear of flying. *Journal of Consulting and Clinical Psychology, 68*(6), 1020–1026.

Rothbaum, B.O., Hodges, L.F., Kooper, R., Opdyke, D., Williford, J.S., & North, M. (1995). Effectiveness of computer-generated (virtual reality) graded exposure in the treatment of acrophobia. *American Journal of Psychiatry, 152*(4), 626–628.

Rothbaum, B.O., Hodges, L.F., Ready, D., Graap, K., & Alarcon, R.D. (2001). Virtual reality exposure therapy for Vietnam veterans with posttraumatic stress disorder. *Journal of Clinical Psychiatry, 62*(8), 617–622.

Santini, E., Muller, R.U., & Quirk, G.J. (2001). Consolidation of extinction learning involves transfer from NMDA-independent to NMDA-dependent memory. *Journal of Neuroscience, 21*(22), 9009–9017.

Schatzberg, A., & Nemeroff, C.B. (Eds.). (1998). *Textbook of psychopharmacology.* Washington, D.C.: American Psychiatric Press.

Schuster, G.M., & Schmidt, W.J. (1992). D-cycloserine reverses the working memory impairment of hippocampal-lesioned rats in a spatial learning task. *European Journal of Pharmacology, 224*(1), 97–98.

Schwartz, B.L., Hashtroudi, S., Herting, R.L., Schwartz, P., & Deutsch, S.I. (1996). D-Cycloserine enhances implicit memory in Alzheimer patients. *Neurology, 46*(2), 420–424.

Thompson, L.T., Moskal, J.R., & Disterhoft, J.F. (1992). Hippocampus-dependent learning facilitated by a monoclonal antibody or D-cycloserine. *Nature, 359*(6396), 638–641.

Tryon, W.W. (2005). Possible mechanisms for why desensitization and exposure therapy work. *Clinical Psychology Review, 25,* 67–95.

Tsai, G., Falk, W., & Gunther, J. (1998). A preliminary study of D-cycloserine treatment in Alzheimer's disease. *Journal of Neuropsychiatry and Clinical Neuroscience, 10*(2), 224–226.

Walker, D.L., Ressler, K.J., Lu, K.T., & Davis, M. (2002). Facilitation of conditioned fear extinction by systemic administration or intra-amygdala infusions of D-cycloserine as assessed with fear-potentiated startle in rats. *Journal of Neuroscience, 22*(6), 2343–2351.

Zinbarg, R.E. (1993). Information processing and classical conditioning: Implications for exposure therapy and the integration of cognitive therapy and behavior therapy. *Journal of Behavior Therapy and Experimental Psychiatry, 24*(2), 129–139.

CHAPTER 16

Virtual Reality Applications for Exposure

Stéphane Bouchard
*Université du Québec
en Outaouais*
Sophie Côté
University of Ottawa
David C. S. Richard
Rollins College

WHAT IS IN VIRTUO EXPOSURE?

By definition, virtual reality (VR) is "an application that lets users navigate and interact with a three-dimensional, computer-generated (and computer-maintained) environment in real time" (Pratt, Zyda, & Kelleher, 1995, p. 17). The key concept that differentiates VR from the use of other audiovisual media to deliver exposure is interactivity. Even if anxiety-provoking stimuli are presented on slides, videotape, computer screen, or even IMAX theater, those exposure methods should not be considered as VR. The mediated experience becomes an alternate reality when participants can explore the surroundings (e.g., look under a closet, open a door, or walk out of a room), and the displayed images change accordingly. The selected technology can immerse the patient to different degrees in the virtual environments, from a simple presentation on a computer screen to the use of head-mounted displays and motion trackers, and even to a full-size 10 × 10 × 10-foot room with stereoscopic images projected on walls, floor, and ceiling. Although it could be considered as VR by Pratt, et al.'s (1995) definition, the simple use of a computer screen is probably not immersive enough to provide an optimal exposure tool. The room-size system, often referred to by the trade name of CAVE

Supported in part by a research grant from the Canada Research Chairs program. Corresponding address: Stéphane Bouchard, Département de psychoéducation et de psychologie, Université du Québec en Outaouais, PO Box 1250, Station Hull, Gatineau, Qc, J8X 3X7. E-mail: *stephane.bouchard@uqo.ca*.

347

(Automated Virtual Environment™,* Fakespace Technology), is an attractive medium to deliver virtual stimuli. But it costs more than $250,000 and the space requirements are significant deterrents for most clinical researchers and psychologists. The solution that has attracted most researchers is the use of smaller head-mounted displays (HMD, see Figure 16.1) and motion trackers. From a therapeutic perspective, performing in virtuo exposure (Tisseau & Harrouet, 2003) could be attractive for a number of reasons. Before addressing the advantages of VR, however, we should be clear that VR researchers do not propose in virtuo exposure is more effective than in vivo exposure. Instead, it is an alternative exposure therapy medium that may be more practical and effective than imaginal exposure and other presentation modalities.

In virtuo exposure offers a standardized, controlled, replicable environment that can be used to induce emotions for therapeutic purposes. Whenever such a situation is required, VR should be considered (see Wiederhold & Wiederhold, 2005, for examples). However, the advantages of in virtuo exposure may not apply to all exposure situations.

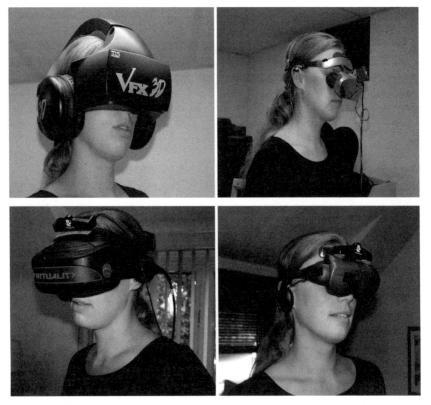

FIGURE 16.1   Head-mounted display. (Images courtesy of the Cyberpsychology Lab.)

*The letter C was added at the beginning of this acronym to reference Plato's Cave.

Because of the rapid development of the field, and for a variety of practical reasons (e.g., sample availability, protocol development, computer programming restrictions, use of reliable behavioral avoidance/approach measures), most published studies have focused on specific phobias. However, applications directed at more complex anxiety disorders are currently in development. Nevertheless, it is possible to create a list of the advantages (Table 16.1) of current

TABLE 16.1   Advantages of in virtuo exposure relative to in vivo exposure in the treatment of selected disorders

	Specific phobia: spiders	Specific phobia: heights	Specific phobia: enclosed space	Specific phobia: public speaking	Specific phobia: flying	Specific phobia: driving	Specific phobia: snakes	Specific phobia: thunder	Post-traumatic stress disorder	Social anxiety disorder	Panic disorder with agoraphobia	Substance abuse (for cue exposure)	Eating disorders (for body image)	Stuttering (for social performance)	Anger management
Increased treatment standardization	✓	✓	✓	✓	✓	✓	✓	✓	✓	✓	✓	✓	✓	✓	✓
Treatment is more attractive to patients	✓	✓	✓	✓	✓	✓	✓	✓	✓	✓	✓	✓	✓	✓	✓
Increased control over the pace of exposure	✓	✓	✓	✓	✓	✓	✓	✓	✓	✓	✓	✓	✓	✓	✓
More stimuli readily available than in vivo	✓	✓		✓	✓	✓	✓	✓	✓	✓			✓	✓	✓
No more need to conduct imaginal exposure		✓			✓		✓	✓	✓		✓	✓			
Better protection of confidentiality		✓		✓	✓	✓		✓		✓		✓			✓
Increased patient's safety during exposure		✓			✓	✓									
No more need to care for animals (stimuli)	✓						✓								
More attention devoted to avoidance behaviors		✓					✓								
Reduced costs					✓	✓									

The absence of a check mark indicates that either the situation does not apply (e.g., there is usually no need to conduct imaginal exposure for claustrophobia) or that VR does not offer any significant advantage over in vivo (e.g., it is rarely a problem to create a simple hierarchy of enclosed situations to treat claustrophobia).

VR programs that are used to provide exposure. A reasonable question involves whether computerized and virtual reality approaches for the treatment of phobias and related anxiety disorders are acceptable to clients. Little research has been conducted on treatment acceptance specifically (i.e., Davis, 1993), but in the published literature, results appear to suggest openness, especially among younger generations, to using VR technology. In one clinical study, Botella, et al. (unpublished manuscript) treated 24 adults suffering from panic disorder with agoraphobia either with exposure in vivo or in virtuo and assessed treatment satisfaction. In both conditions, all ratings were above 9 out of 10 for how logical the treatment appeared, how satisfied the patients were, to what extent the patients would recommend the treatment, how useful the treatment was for their problem, and how the exposure strategy used seemed useful. Other studies have confirmed that in virtuo exposure seems more attractive to patients. For example, Garcia-Pallacios, Hoffman, Kwong See, Tsai, and Botella (2001) surveyed undergraduate students with high levels of spider fear. When students were asked whether they would prefer a multisession in vivo or a multisession in virtuo intervention, 81% chose virtual therapy. When asked whether they would prefer one session in vivo treatment or a multisession in virtuo intervention, 89% still chose VR. When this research team conducted the same survey with 102 diagnosed phobic patients, 70% of them chose in virtuo exposure (Garcia-Palacios, Botella, Hoffman, Villa, & Fabregat, 2004). When asked whether they would refuse to go into therapy if one form of exposure or the other was used, 23.5% refused in vivo exposure, compared to 3% in the case of in virtuo exposure. One obvious limitation to these studies was the speculative nature of what the virtual intervention entailed. Asking individuals which treatment modality they would prefer, in the absence of actually experiencing both treatments, provides no evidence about treatment satisfaction and about which treatment they actually preferred. Nevertheless, it tells a lot about which treatment would be chosen if a choice was made available. These results clearly show that VR is more attractive, or enticing, than traditional in vivo exposure. This issue is especially important in the case of children and adolescents, for whom getting psychological treatments is not always based on a strong intrinsic motivation. In the case of adults, it could represent a substantial advantage when seeking in vivo treatment is considered too frightening.

The clinician's control over the virtual environment often allows for smoother and better hierarchical exposure sessions, such as flight conditions and turbulences in a virtual flight or intensity of commuting traffic in a virtual driving exposure session. It also allows for standardized and behaviorally relevant analogue observation techniques. Whereas analogue observation methods have historically involved exposing individuals to functionally relevant challenging situations in a controlled environment such as a clinic, virtual analogue observation refers to assessment of the individual in a virtual environment that closely approximates the feared naturalistic setting. Assessing behavioral responses in virtual environments (Renaud, Bouchard, & Proulx, 2002) is a new and rapidly evolving form of analogue observation.

In cases such as social anxiety, where performance in front of other people is necessary, or acrophobia, where therapists have to accompany the patient to exposure situations outside the office, VR provides better protection against breached confidentiality. Patient safety can also be increased when the exposure session involves engaging in behaviors that subject the patient to some degree of risk (e.g., the risk of falling when treating acrophobia or the risk of having an accident when treating a driving phobia). And in other instances, the controlled situation allows the therapist to pay more attention to the actual behavior of the patient than to personal safety concerns (i.e., the therapist paying attention to upcoming cars and patient's driving skills at the expense of patient's avoidance and safety-seeking behaviors).

Because of the standardized nature of the stimuli presented to the participants, virtual environments also provide the opportunity to measure treatment processes more reliably in terms of both subjective and physiological responses. For example, some researchers have examined changes in event-related potentials as a function of exposure to a virtual environment (see Mager, Bullinger, Mueller-Spahn, Kuntze, & Stoermer, 2001). Others have studied the relative contribution of changes in self-efficacy, beliefs, and information processing to treatment outcome (Côté & Bouchard, unpublished), and some have looked at the benefits of including NMDA partial agonist (D-cycloserine) medication to facilitate exposure (Ressler, Rothbaum, Tannenbaum, Anderson, Graap, Zimand, et al., 2004). Methodologically, all these experimental studies benefited from treatments in which exposure stimuli were highly standardized.

CAN VR INDUCE ANXIETY?

VR's potential to elicit a genuine fear reaction when people are exposed to virtual phobogenic stimuli is a prerequisite for using VR in exposure-based therapies. VR's capacity to produce anxiety reactions reliably has been repeatedly documented. For example, Robillard, Bouchard, Fournier, and Renaud (2003) immersed 13 paired phobic and control participants in the same VR environments. Results confirmed that immersions in phobogenic virtual environments elicit subjective fear reactions in nonphobic participants, and that reactions are significantly more intense among phobic participants. Using motion tracking devices, Renaud, et al. (2002) have shown that exposure to phobogenic virtual stimuli leads to objective behavioral avoidance patterns that are significantly more pronounced in phobics than in nonphobics. Using physiological measures, Moore, Wiederhold, Wiederhold, and Riva (2002) found that immersing nonphobics into potentially phobogenic virtual situations such as elevators and grocery stores with virtual people could lead to significant changes in heart rate and skin conductance. Meehan (2001) and Zimmons (2004) assessed nonphobic participants' reactions under a variety of conditions while immersed in a virtual height environment and confirmed that VR can produce strong and significant changes in heart rate, skin conductance, and skin temperature when participants are exposed to phobogenic situations.

People's reactions to virtual stimuli also apply to virtual humans. For example, James, Lin, Steed, Swapp, and Slater (2003) immersed nonphobics in various virtual social environments and observed an increase in anxiety when participants had to interact with virtual humans who appeared disinterested to their presence. Later on, the same research team (Slater, Pertaub, Barker, & Clark, 2004) compared the effect of giving a speech in an empty seminar room or to a virtual audience on the anxiety of individuals with and without public speaking phobia. The level of anxiety, measured subjectively and physiologically, was low among nonphobics in both conditions, but it was significantly higher among phobics in the empty room condition and even higher when the phobics delivered their speeches to the virtual humans. Pursuing their research on virtual people, Pertaub, Slater, and Barker (2002) compared the reaction of 43 people suffering from fear of public speaking when they delivered two speeches to an audience of virtual humans that were programmed to respond neutrally (no reaction), positively (leaning forward, eyes wide open, etc.), or negatively (leaning back, discussing among themselves, etc.) to the speeches. Delivering a speech to the negative audience was significantly more anxiety inducing and rated as less satisfying than delivering a speech to a neutral audience. Of interest, all these studies used virtual environments and virtual people that were not perfectly realistic. Taken together, these results illustrate that VR can be used to expose people to virtual stimuli. All these studies have also found significant correlations between the anxiety reaction and the feeling of presence (the illusion of being *in* the virtual environment), which might give us clues to explain why VR can elicit emotions.

It is not clear, however, whether physiological responses to virtual environments show a consistent pattern across individuals. Wiederhold and Wiederhold (2000) found that participants do not show consistent changes in peripheral skin temperature or heart rate when being exposed to virtual environments. Similarly, Jang, Kim, Nam, Wiederhold, Wiederhold, and Kim (2002) exposed 11 nonphobic individuals for 15 minutes to virtual environments depicting a flying or driving scenario. Heart rate variability analyses showed no significant differences between the interactive driving condition and the passively explored flying environment. Within environments, however, baseline and exposure heart rates were significantly different in the driving, but not the flying, virtual environment. Consistent with habituation, participants initially showed an increased skin conductance in the driving environment that dissipated after 7 minutes.

Although this chapter focuses on anxiety disorders, it is important to mention studies that were made on exposure for substance abuse (smoking and crack/cocaine). Bordnick, Graap, Copp, Brook, and Ferrer (2005) and Lee, Lim, Graham, Kim, Wiederhold, Wiederhold, & Kim (2004) found that a virtual environment depicting venues and objects known to be associated with cigarette craving elicited higher self-reported craving than did pictures of the same objects, and Graap (2004) reported the same finding with crack and cocaine cues. VR is also used for other disorders, such as eating disorders and body image dysphoria (Riva, Bacchetta, Baruffi, & Molinari, 2002), and anger management (Rizzo, Neumann, Pintaric, & Norden, 2001).

EFFICACY OF IN VIRTUO EXPOSURE

In preparing this chapter, we counted about 21 individual case studies, three studies using a multiple baseline across subjects design, three uncontrolled group studies or open clinical trials, six controlled group design studies that included a passive control condition (wait list, placebo, or no treatment), and nine studies that compared virtual treatment to an alternative active treatment control condition (usually in vivo, relaxation, or cognitive). The longest follow-up assessments were 12 months (e.g., Bullinger, 2005; Rothbaum, Hodges, Anderson, Price, & Smith, 2002) and 3 years (Widerhold & Wiederhold, 2003). The two largest sample sizes in a controlled design were 73 (Rothbaum, et al., in press) and 213 (Bullinger, 2005). Given the rate of publications in this area—the majority of the VR treatment outcome literature has been published in the last 6 or 7 years—the rapid evolution of relevant technology, and the number of outcome studies under way and presented in scientific conferences, we fully expect this review to be outdated by the time it is published. Based on that, and given the fact that many comprehensive reviews are being published (e.g., Côté & Bouchard, unpublished; Miyahira, 2005; Wiederhold & Wiederhold, 2005), the following pages describe and comment on selected studies rather than pretending to be comprehensive and detailed for each study.

FEAR OF FLYING

The most common therapeutic application of virtual technology has been in the treatment of flight phobia. There are several reasons for this development. First, virtual environments simulating flight cabins and virtual flights are less difficult to develop and achieve an interesting degree of realism. Second, virtual exposure is attractive because of the cost-efficiency and logistical ease relative to in vivo exposure. Third, fear of flying is a pervasive problem associated with significant economic impact. Estimates are that up to a quarter of the flight population experiences anxiety when flying, and 20% of those with flight phobia use sedatives or alcohol to cope with flying (Greist & Greist, 1981).

Indices of treatment efficacy came initially from individual case studies, with controlled group designs published in the last 4 or 5 years. The case studies vary widely in terms of their quality and reliance on quantitative measures to infer clinical change. For example, Klein (1998, 1999) reported five case studies in separate publications. In each case, clinical change was measured either in Subjective Units of Distress scales (SUDs) scores or other forms of self-report. Similarly, other researchers (e.g., North, North, & Coble, 1997; Kahan, 2000) relied almost exclusively on anecdotal report to infer clinical change. Although some researchers report whether a client completed a post-treatment flight (e.g., Kahan, 2000; Rothbaum, Hodges, Watson, Kessler, & Opdyke, 1996), some criticisms have been raised about using post-treatment flight as an outcome measure. For example, Öst, Brandber, and Alm (1997) noted that it could be a questionable measure of clinical change given that most clients are not afforded the opportunity to complete a pretreatment flight. Also, many flight phobic individuals can fly despite their anxiety. Therefore a pretreatment flight must be offered at pretreatment (to exclude participants who can actually fly) and the post-treatment flight should be carefully designed to avoid methodological problems (such as patients' sense of security gained by flying accompanied by a therapist). Fortunately, some of the randomized control design studies described here did offer flight tickets for free and excluded participants who agreed to fly at pretreatment.

Relative to other anxiety disorders, the published literature on the application of virtual reality in the treatment of fear of flying is the most developed from a research design standpoint. Controlled group designs have been published by a number of independent research groups. In every case, the virtual reality intervention has yielded treatment effects comparable to in vivo exposure or other appropriate comparison interventions.

The most often cited controlled group design was reported by Rothbaum, Hodges, Smith, Lee, and Price (2000) in which 49 participants were randomly assigned to in virtuo exposure, in vivo exposure to an airplane at the airport, or a wait-list control group. Participants in the exposure conditions first completed four sessions of anxiety management training before in virtuo or in vivo exposure. Results showed that the exposure groups were largely equivalent in treatment effects and superior to the wait-list control group. Treatment effect sizes ranged from .21 to .70 on subjective questionnaires and the in virtuo and in vivo groups were 3.5 times more likely than the wait-list control group to take a post-treatment flight. There were no group differences in treatment satisfaction ratings between the exposure groups and treatment gains were maintained at the 6-month follow-up period.

Later, Rothbaum, et al. (2002) reported results from a 12-month follow-up evaluation of the aforementioned study. In all, 80% of participants from the initial study responded. No significant differences were found between the two treatment groups at follow-up evaluation on any of the outcome measures. Treatment effects relative to the wait-list group, however, were maintained at 12 months. There were no differences between treatment groups in the number of group members flying since the end of treatment, but there were some signs of greater alcohol and drug use in the in virtuo group to quell in-flight anxiety.

In a replication and extension of their previous study, Rothbaum, et al. (in press) reported on the results from an independent sample of 75 participants (25 completers per condition out of 83 initially enrolled). Analyses included an intent-to-treat approach, as well as traditional completer analyses. With a new and larger sample than in their previous studies, they demonstrated once more that (1) both traditional exposure and in virtuo exposure were superior to the waiting list and (2) the differences between the two active treatments were not significant. Once participants in the waiting list were reassigned to the experimental conditions and treated, the comparisons between the treatment involving in virtuo and in vivo exposure were conducted with 42 and 40 patients in each condition, respectively. Effect sizes for the difference in treatment efficacy at 12-month follow-up evaluation ranged from $\eta^2 = .016$ to $\eta^2 = .001$. This suggests small to trivial effect sizes according to Cohen's (1988) criteria. More important, the gains did not deteriorate at follow-up evaluation. For example, 71% and 76% of the participants in the in virtuo and in vivo conditions, respectively, did not meet the diagnostic criteria for specific aviophobia at the 6-month follow-up period. And in this study, there was no evidence of differences in anxiety during the post-treatment flight, as self-rated anxiety was rather low and similar in both treatment conditions.

Results by Rothbaum, et al. (2000; 2002; in press) appear to echo those from other researchers. For example, Maltby, Kirsch, Mayers, and Allen (2002) published a study in which 45 participants were assigned to either a five-session in virtuo intervention or an attention-group placebo condition. Results showed large pre-post differences in measures of subjective flight anxiety, with 77% of the treatment group reporting a meaningful decline in flight anxiety compared to only 22% for the control group; however, group differences disappeared or were attenuated at the 6-month follow-up period. Although 65% of the in virtuo exposure group had been able to complete a post-treatment flight, 57% of the control group completed it as well. Mean SUDs ratings of in-flight anxiety did not differ between groups. These follow-up results are difficult to interpret, although the methodological issues raised by Öst, et al. (1997) might provide some tentative answers. Because the post-treatment flight was conducted using a small aircraft and accompanied by a therapist (albeit not the one treating the patient), some participants in the control condition might have felt confident enough to try the graduation flight. This successful behavioral experiment at post-treatment could also have a positive impact on their fear, explaining why statistical differences on questionnaires completed at post-treatment disappear at follow-up evaluation.

Another controlled study was reported by Mühlberger, Wiedemann, and Pauli (2003). In their dismantling study, they examined the treatment effects of motion simulation by randomly assigning 45 flight phobics to one of four treatment conditions: cognitive treatment and in virtuo exposure with motion simulation, cognitive treatment and in virtuo exposure without motion simulation, cognitive treatment alone, or wait-list control. The 3-hour therapy session consisted of identifying and analyzing catastrophic cognitions and discussing concepts related to anxiety and exposure, and then performing four consecutive flights in VR (each flight included take off, quiet flight, turbulences, and landing). Results showed that the VR groups differed significantly from the cognitive-only and wait-list control groups on most self-report measures of anxiety after treatment and at the 6-month follow-up evaluation; however, there were no significant group differences in rates of flying between the three groups receiving treatment at post-treatment and at the 6-month follow-up period. Although somewhat surprising, the efficacy of the cognitive therapy control condition might be explained by results from Hunt, Fenton, Goldbert, and Tran (unpublished) who showed that cognitive restructuring alone could be effective in the treatment of specific phobias. The results of the VR immersion were consistent with an earlier study by Mühlberger, Hermann, Wiedemann, Ellgring, and Pauli (2001), who found greater reduction in subjective and physiological measures of anxiety for a group of flight phobics completing a virtual intervention than for participants completing a relaxation training session. In the latter study, however, the difference between the two conditions remained significant at the 3-month follow-up period.

In an interesting study, Wiederhold, Jang, Gevirtz, Kim, Kim, and Wiederhold (2002) compared imaginal exposure to in virtuo exposure and in virtuo exposure plus physiological feedback. Physiological feedback was presented verbally by the therapist about participants' skin resistance levels while they were immersed in the virtual environment. Feedback was also displayed on a computer monitor at pre- and post-VR immersion for heart rate, skin conductance, and respiration rate. All 30 participants received two sessions of anxiety management skills training, plus six sessions of exposure. At post-treatment, only 10% of control participants agreed to fly (alone, without medication) as compared to 80% of participants in the in virtuo exposure-only condition and 100% of participants in the in virtuo exposure plus physiological feedback condition. Statistical differences from pretreatment to post-treatment and between conditions on questionnaires mirrored these results. At the 3-year follow-up evaluation (Wiederhold & Wiederhold, 2003), the 10% in the imaginal exposure condition were still flying on their own, 60% in the exposure in virtuo condition, and 100% in the exposure in virtuo plus physiological feedback condition. The fact that the physiological feedback improved treatment efficacy is interesting and may contribute to our understanding of the treatment mechanism of in virtuo exposure. First, taking physiological measures allows the therapist to see if patients' physiology is in concordance with their subjective report of anxiety. According to Wiederhold and Wiederhold (2000), obtaining such information can help the therapist, notably when participants are reporting high levels of anxiety that are not accompanied with physiological arousal. These cases may represent patients who are more difficult to treat or have issues related to secondary gains. Second, it is possible that by observing improvements objectively in their ability to face their fear, participants could increase their perceived self-efficacy (Bandura, 1986) to cope with their phobia, a variable that was found to be a significant predictor of treatment outcome, at least for arachnophobia (Côté & Bouchard, 2005).

In sum, VR interventions for flight phobia have been studied empirically more than any other anxiety disorder. Results from individual case studies and uncontrolled group designs are uniformly favorable. With regard to random-ized controlled trials, there is strong evidence for treatment efficacy from the Rothbaum group (with a replication study, large sample sizes and comparisons with the in vivo gold-standard form of exposure, and waiting list conditions, as well as 12-month follow-up evaluations) and from the Wiederhold's group (with a comparison with imaginal exposure and a 3-year follow-up evaluation). The results from Mühlberger, et al. (2003) and Maltby, et al. (2002) are encouraging at post-treatment, but follow-up data are less impressive. These results, and the methodological differences between the studies, have to be weighed against the very favorable ones from of the 3-year follow-up period by Wiederhold and Wiederhold (2003) and both 12-month follow-up eval-uations of Rothbaum, et al. (2002; in press). There is no evidence to sug-gest that virtual treatments are more efficacious than in vivo exposure. As mentioned earlier in this chapter, however, researchers in the field of VR never claimed that in virtuo exposure was meant to be more efficacious.

SPIDER PHOBIA

Although a significant proportion of the literature surrounding virtual treatments has focused on flight phobia, researchers have creatively applied the technology to other anxiety disorders as well. Despite the smaller literature bases, results have been emphasizing that virtual environments may be useful. Evidence for the efficacy of virtual treatments for spider phobia comes from two case studies, two uncontrolled studies, and one controlled group design. Carlin, Hoffman, and Weghorst (1997) provided a 37-year-old female 12 weekly 1-hour sessions of VR exposure therapy. By the end of treatment, SUD ratings had decreased dramatically. In addition, the authors reported the elimination of compulsive, avoidance-related rituals. At the end of treatment, the patient was able to hold a live tarantula in her hands and control her anxiety.

In a study with children using a multiple baseline across subjects design, St.-Jacques, Bouchard, and Renaud (2004) treated nine children (8 to 16 years old) with eight sessions of in virtuo exposure. Questionnaire data were collected at pretreatment and post-treatment, as well as at a 6-month follow-up period. Weekly self-monitoring was completed during baseline (lasting from 3 to 5 weeks) and during the treatment phase. Self-monitored fear of spiders was reduced after the introduction of treatment in all subjects, and the statistical analyses conducted on each questionnaire revealed a significant reduction from pretreatment to post-treat-ment and no relapse at follow-up evaluation.

In a pilot study, Bouchard, Côté, St.-Jacques, Robillard, and Renaud (2006) assessed the efficacy of five sessions of in virtuo exposure using a virtual environment created by extensively modifying three-dimensional game software. This prelimi-nary study was conducted with a small sample ($N = 8$) and had no control group.

Statistical analyses revealed significant improvement on the behavioral avoidance test, the Spider Beliefs Questionnaire, the Fear of Spider Questionnaire, and a measure of perceived self-efficacy. Results were maintained after 6 months. To document the impact of virtual reality exposure on cardiac response and automatic processing of threatening stimuli, and later on study treatment processes, Côté and Bouchard (in press) treated 28 adults suffering from arachnophobia with in virtuo exposure. The treatment was manualized and lasted five sessions. This study used classical paper and pencil tests, but also a behavioral avoidance test, a pictorial emotional Stroop task with spider and control color-filtered images, and a physiological measure of anxiety (interbeat intervals) while participants were performing the behavioral avoidance test. As expected from other studies' results, repeated measures ANOVAs revealed that in virtuo exposure had a significant impact on questionnaire data, as well as on the behavioral avoidance test. What is more original is that the authors also found significant improvement on the pictorial Stroop task, showing that information processing of spider-related stimuli changed after treatment. Analyses of heart rate data also confirmed that improvement could be observed on psychophysiological parameters while patients were facing a live tarantula. In a subsequent article (Côté & Bouchard, 2005), researchers used these data to compare the predictive power of three possible explanations for treatment efficacy: changes in beliefs toward spiders, changes in information processing, and changes in self-efficacy. All three variables changed significantly and were significantly correlated with patients' improvement in symptomatology and performance on the behavior avoidance test. However, the hierarchical regression analyses revealed that increased perceived self-efficacy was the best predictor of treatment outcome, over and above the variance explained by the other process variables.

In the only controlled study, Garcia-Palacios, Hoffman, Carlin, Furness III, and Botella (2002) assigned 23 participants to a VR or wait-list control condition. Treatment duration was flexible and averaged four 1-hour sessions. Of interest, this is the only study in which tactile sensations were used in therapy. During the last therapy session, participants in the in virtuo exposure condition were invited to virtually "touch" a spider while simultaneously physically contacting a furry toy spider. By the end of treatment, 83% of the patients in the VR group, but none of the wait-list group members, showed clinically significant improvement. All subjective measures (completed by the patients, the therapists, and an independent assessor), as well as the behavioral avoidance test, showed significant reductions in anxiety and avoidance favoring the VR group.

Studies in the application of VR to arachnophobia do not have the methodological strength of those in aviophobia. There is clearly a need for a study comparing in virtuo to two control conditions, the gold-standard (in vivo), as well as an inactive control one (wait list, placebo, etc.) and a long-term follow-up period. Some studies, however, are providing new information on in virtuo exposure, such as documenting the impact of treatment on information processing using tactile stimulation to enhance the virtual experience, or shedding some light on the treatment mechanism of phobias.

FEAR OF PUBLIC SPEAKING AND SOCIAL ANXIETY

The first series of outcome studies on fear of public speaking were conducted by North, North, and Coble (1998). They assigned 16 participants diagnosed with specific phobia of public speaking to an in virtuo exposure treatment or a no-treatment control condition (they were immersed in a trivial VR scene and were advised by the experimenters to manage their fear and expose themselves on their own, without any systematic treatment program). The treatment was delivered over five brief 10- to 20-minute therapy sessions. Six of the eight participants who completed the in virtuo exposure treatment showed significant improvement at post-treatment, and no significant changes were noticed in the control condition.

Harris, Kemmerling, and North (2002) assigned 14 students to either an in virtuo exposure treatment or a wait-list control group. The VR treatment involved four 12- to 15-minute sessions of speaking in public in a virtual environment. There were no between-group differences in state-trait anxiety or SUDs ratings, but the VR group reported significant increases in public speaking confidence over time relative to the control group. In addition, the VR group showed significant decreases in heart rate (and resting heart rate) over time while giving a speech to the simulated audience.

Three studies have been conducted with people suffering from social phobia. Anderson, Rothbaum, and Hodges (2003) reported two cases (a 46-year-old female and a 50-year-old female) of social phobics in which the patients were provided an anxiety management program, cognitive restructuring, and in virtuo exposure to an audience while giving a speech. In both cases, pre-post reductions in SUDs ratings across all virtual stimuli conditions were observed and decreases in trait anxiety were noted. In addition, both women were able to give a speech to a small audience at the end of treatment and rated their own performance as acceptable. Only a 46-year-old client completed the follow-up measures, and results suggested that treatment gains were maintained. In an uncontrolled case study, Riquier, Herbelin, and Chevalley (2005; Herbelin, Ponder, & Thalmann, 2005) exposed three social phobics (between the ages of 14 and 23) to highly realistic and complex virtual people. Participants, who were invited to give speeches in front of a small and a large audience for five therapy sessions, reported significant clinical improvements at post-treatment.

Klinger, Bouchard, Légeron, Roy, Lauer, Chemin, and Nugues (2005) completed a group trial comparing 12 sessions of traditional group cognitive-behavioral therapy (CBT) and in vivo exposure to individual CBT and in virtuo exposure. Participants in the in virtuo exposure condition received minimal cognitive therapy training as therapy sessions were mostly devoted to exposure in the virtual environments. Four virtual situations were created to tackle different aspects of social phobia: assertiveness anxiety (being assertive to virtual people who are criticizing the patient), performance anxiety (giving a talk to a group of virtual people in a meeting room), intimacy anxiety (discussing with a virtual friend and unknown virtual people in an apartment), and observation anxiety (engaging in conversations with a virtual friend and a virtual waiter while being looked at by virtual people in the surroundings). Results on a clinician's rating scales as well as clients' ($N =$ 36) self-report questionnaires (quality of life, social anxiety felt in different contexts, etc.) showed a significant improvement in both conditions, with no condition being superior to the other. On the Liebowitz scale, a well-known measure of social anxiety disorder symptomatology, the effect size of the difference between CBT with in vivo and in virtuo was so small that a sample of more that 300 participants would have been required to detect a statistically significant difference (and would then have suggested that VR therapy was more effective than group-CBT). On some other measures, such as performance anxiety or fear of scrutiny and intimacy, the differences were so trivial that a sample of more than 3000 participants would have been required to reach statistical significance. Despite its innovative features, some limitations of this study warrant further replication, notably the lack of a no-treatment control condition and long-term follow-up evaluation.

Although preliminary results are suggestive, research surrounding the virtual treatment of public speaking and social anxiety is still in its infancy. More studies with larger sample sizes and relevant comparison treatments are needed, but current results are promising. The application of VR to more complex anxiety disorders such as social anxiety, compared to specific phobias, is especially valuable. Although treatments protocols become more complex and are not limited to in virtuo exposure only, the applications of VR are also becoming more attractive to therapists who are dealing with difficult patients and social exposure sessions.

FEAR OF HEIGHTS

Virtual reality technology has also been applied to assist the treatment of fear of heights. With regard to case studies (Choi, Jang, Ku, Shin, & Kim, 2001; Bouchard, St.-Jacques, Robillard, Côté, & Renaud, 2003), results suggest that in virtuo exposure to heights situations was effective in reducing symptoms of acrophobia over five or six sessions. Both studies found reductions in subjectively reported anxiety, and one person in Choi, et al.'s study (2001) also showed physiological evidence consistent with habituation over time to the virtual stimulus. In a pioneering work, Lamson (1997) reported the treatment of 32 cases of acrophobia. After a single therapy session of in virtuo exposure and 60 additional minutes of discussions with their therapists, post-treatment results showed that 90% of the participants were considered much improved. At a 3-month follow-up evaluation, 90% of the participants were able to use a glass elevator and ride to the 15th floor. The first published controlled study of any virtual treatment was Rothbaum, Hodges, Kooper, Opdyke, Williford, and North's (1995) study with 20 students suffering from a fear of heights. Participants were assigned to either a 7-week in virtuo treatment protocol or a wait-list condition. Results showed that measures of anxiety, distress, and avoidance all declined for the VR group but not the wait-list control group. Mean ratings of discomfort significantly decreased across sessions for the VR group as well, suggesting habituation to the virtual stimulus. Although 7 of the 10 VR participants were able to complete an in vivo exposure to a heights situation, three were not. No data were presented regarding wait-list controls on the behavior avoidance test.

After a presentation of their preliminary results (Emmelkamp, Bruynzeel, Drost, & van der Mast, 2001), Emmelkamp, Krijn, Hulsbosch, de Vries, Schuemie, and van der Mast (2002) reported results of an outcome study in which 33 adults suffering from chronic acrophobia (mean duration of 31.5 years) were randomly assigned to either three 1-hour sessions of in vivo exposure (exposure in a mall, a fire escape, and a rooftop) or to three 1-hour exposure sessions to the same locations reproduced in VR. In addition to a 6-month follow-up evaluation, an interesting asset of this study is the use of a gold-standard control condition (in vivo exposure) where the virtual environments were replicas of the physical environments that were used in therapy. They found significant within-group differences in both conditions on all subjective and objective measures of anxiety from pretreatment to post-treatment, and stability of the results from post-treatment to follow-up periods. They did not find any significant differences in treatment efficacy between both conditions. The effect sizes of the differences suggest that any potential one would be marginal, if not trivial.

In the study with the largest sample so far, Bullinger (2005) recruited 213 adults who were randomly assigned to in virtuo exposure (74 using HMD technology and 40 using a highly immersive system similar to a CAVE), in vivo exposure (n = 52), and a wait-list control (n = 47). Participants received three sessions of exposure and completed questionnaires and physiological measures (heart rate, salivary cortisol, etc.). At 6 months, participants performed a behavioral avoidance test in which they were invited to climb to the top of the bell tower of the Münster of Basel and look down. As was the case in the Emmelkamp, et al. (2002) study, the virtual environment was a replica of the physical environment used for in vivo exposure. Results showed that in virtuo exposure was as effective as in vivo exposure, which were all superior to the waiting list. As discussed later in this chapter, there was no significant difference between the two different technologies that were used to immerse the patients (HMD vs. CAVE).

The three controlled studies in this area again suggest that virtual interventions are efficacious in the treatment of fear of heights, with no differences between virtual and in vivo exposure. The studies published so far documented comparisons of in virtuo with either in vivo or passive wait-list control conditions. The exceptionally large sample in Bullinger's (2005) study, as well as the comparison with two control conditions, should reassure those who worry about the power of VR outcome studies. With the evidence collected to date on different phobias, including acrophobia, it is doubtful that VR will be shown to be more or less effective than in vivo exposure.

POST-TRAUMATIC STRESS SYMPTOMS AND POST-TRAUMATIC STRESS DISORDER

Another innovative use of virtual technology applied to complex anxiety disorders has been the creation of virtual environments that are relevant to individuals suffering from post-traumatic stress symptoms or post-traumatic stress disorder (PTSD). Three studies, two case studies (Difede & Hoffman, 2002; Hodges, Rothbaum, Alarcon, Ready, Shahar, Graap, et al., 1999) and one uncontrolled group study (Rothbaum, et al., 2001), have been published detailing such efforts.

In the Difede and Hoffman study, a 26-year-old female who survived the World Trade Center attacks was treated with in virtuo exposure after imaginal exposure had been ineffective. Six graded 1-hour VR sessions were completed with scenes detailing virtual planes crashing into the World Trade Center, people jumping to their deaths, and the towers collapsing. SUDs ratings decreased over the six sessions with a corresponding 83% reduction in depression symptoms and a 90% reduction in PTSD symptoms. By the end of treatment, the patient no longer met diagnostic criteria for PTSD or major depression. A larger outcome study from the same group is currently under way (Difedee, Hoffman, Cukor, Patt, & Giosan, 2005) and preliminary results showed a marked improvement in the seven patients treated with in virtuo exposure (change in Clinician-Administered PTSD Scale [CAPS] scores of an average of 28 points) and few changes in the 14 participants assigned to the waiting list (average change of five points on the CAPS). Results are therefore preliminary but encouraging.

Rothbaum and her colleagues, on the other hand, have focused on the treatment of PTSD in the chronic and difficult population of Vietnam veterans. Rothbaum, Hodges, Alarcon, Ready, Shahar, et al. (1999) reported the case of a Vietnam helicopter pilot who they exposed to a virtual helicopter and jungle combat scenes over fourteen 90-minute sessions. In addition to in virtuo exposure, imaginal exposure was also used. The authors reported a 22-point reduction in the CAPS by the end of treatment. However, arousal scores changed by only two points at 6-month follow-up evaluation. Also, trait anxiety scores did not show much change at follow-up evaluation. In a more recent open clinical trial, Rothbaum, et al. (2001) reported the results of eight Vietnam veterans who completed the same virtual scenes over ten 90-minute sessions. Similar to the individual case reported earlier, CAPS ratings were out of the clinical range at 6 months with a reduction in intrusion symptoms on the Impact of Events Scale at 6-month follow-up evaluation.

To sum up, the validation of VR applications for PTSD is still in development. A few interesting case studies have been reported. More control studies are needed to further document the efficacy of in virtuo exposure. In the addition of the current clinical trial by Difede, et al. (2005) for the World Trade Center attacks, other trials are in preparation for war-related traumas such as the Middle-East (see Kaplan, 2005) and other war zones (Gamito, Pacheo, Ribeiro, Pablo, & Saraiva, 2005), or for stress inoculation training for noncombatants (see Kaplan, 2005).

DRIVING PHOBIA

Researchers are only beginning to document the efficacy of VR for the fear of driving. Although in vivo stimuli are easily accessible to conduct exposure, in virtuo exposure provides a safer context to conduct treatment for patients who are suffering from driving phobia, some of whom have been in a motor vehicle accident and may be suffering from PTSD. Only a few case studies have been conducted so far. Wiederhold, Wiederhold, Jang, and Kim (2000) mention three females in their forties who were successfully treated with an exposure-based protocol in which in virtuo was used early in the hierarchy. The treatment also involved in vivo exposure between sessions and during some therapy sessions.

Walshe, Lewis, Kim, O'Sullivan, and Wiederhold (2003) presented the results from seven patients treated with in virtuo exposure and a mix of VR environments designed for the fear of driving or adapted from three-dimensional racing games. Improvement was statistically significant on all questionnaire data.

In two related articles, Wald and Taylor (2000; 2003) reported a client treated with three sessions of driving simulations in VR. Wald (2004) also describes a multiple baseline design in which five women received eight sessions of in virtuo exposure. Questionnaire data were collected at pretreatment and post-treatment and at 1-, 3- and 12-month follow-up evaluations. Statistical analyses applied to the daily self-monitoring data revealed a modest but significant improvement in fear for four of five patients. However, these improvements did not lead to a significant increase in driving frequency. Three of the five patients did not meet the diagnostic criteria for specific phobia, the other two having benefited from the treatment only moderately.

Overall, these results suggest that in virtuo exposure shows some promise for the treatment of driving phobia. The field is now ready for larger studies using classical group designs. Worthy of note is the use of off-the-shelf three-dimensional games, compared to more expensive VR 'systems.

PANIC DISORDER WITH AGORAPHOBIA

The treatment of more complex anxiety disorders like panic disorder with agoraphobia involves many therapeutic strategies such as cognitive restructuring and interoceptive exposure. Only one study reports on the sole use of VR to treat agoraphobia and it was conducted with a non-clinical sample (North, et al., 1997). Other investigations used VR to conduct exposure to agoraphobic cues (e.g., subway, mall, elevators), and in some cases interoceptive cues (e.g., hyperventilating, hearing others hyperventilate, tunnel vision), in combination with other CBT techniques.

For example, Vincelli, Anolli, Bouchard, Widerhold, Zurloni, and Riva (2003) reported preliminary results from 12 adults enrolled in an ongoing clinical trial. The treatment lasted eight sessions and participants were randomly assigned to either traditional CBT with in vivo exposure, CBT with in virtuo exposure, or a waiting list. Nonparametric statistical analyses revealed that both treatments were superior to the waiting list on every measure, including the Fear Questionnaire. Naturally, results from the completed trial must be awaited before reaching any firm conclusion.

In a larger study by Botella, et al. (unpublished), 36 people diagnosed with panic disorder with agoraphobia were assigned to traditional CBT with in vivo exposure, CBT with in virtuo exposure, or a waiting list. Although follow-up data are still being analyzed, post-treatment data showed significant improvements in fear, catastrophic beliefs, and anxiety sensitivity in both treatment conditions, and not in the wait-list control condition. These findings were also observed on measures of agoraphobic avoidance, which should be particularly sensitive to the difference between the two active treatments. The effect sizes for the difference among both treatments were small, suggesting that both forms of treatment were equally efficacious.

Based on the currently available data, it is still too early to state that using VR is an effective alternative for the treatment of panic disorder with agoraphobia. The sample size of the study by Vincelli, et al. (2003) is too small and follow-up data from Botella, et al. (unpublished) have yet to be analyzed; however, these two studies will be completed in the next year or so. If the promising results hold, there should soon be strong evidence to support the use of in virtuo exposure for panic disorder with agoraphobia. In addition, a larger study with 90 participants using a design similar to the other two is in progress in France (Cottraux, Berthoz, Jouvent, Pull, Zaoui, Pelissolo, et al., 2005). A total of 46 patients have been enrolled so far and results are to be analyzed in 2006.

CLAUSTROPHOBIA

Six studies have reported the use of virtual technology in the treatment of claustrophobia. All but one of the reports are case studies (Bouchard, St.-Jacques,

Côté, Robillard, & Renaud, 2003; Botella, Baños, Perpiñá, Villa, Alcañiz, & Rey, 1998; Botella, Villa, Baños, Perpiñá, & García-Palacios, 1999; Bullinger, Roessler, & Mueller-Spahn, 1998; Wiederhold & Wiederhold, 2000). In each case, individuals completing VR treatment sessions that exposed them to scenes designed to evoke sensations associated with claustrophobia (e.g., tunnels, locked rooms, elevators, sliding walls allowing small rooms to "shrink") were able to complete relevant behavioral avoidance tests. In the only multiple baselines study, Botella, Baños, Villa, Perpiñá and García-Palacios (2000) had four participants complete eight 35-minute virtual reality exposure sessions. Each participant reported decreased fear of enclosed spaces at termination and follow-up evaluation. Also, all participants were able to complete a behavioral avoidance test.

As with other fears, initial results across these studies suggest that VR interventions may be efficacious in the treatment of claustrophobia. However, there has been no randomized group controlled study to date.

SUMMARY OF OUTCOME STUDIES

Based on the available literature, what can we conclude about the efficacy of VR when used for exposure purposes? Obviously, there exists a research community that is highly stimulated by the applications of in virtuo exposure. Researchers followed a natural progression in the design of their studies, with single case and uncontrolled studies being conducted first, followed by more rigorous randomized control trials, and ultimately leading to studies assessing treatment processes and dismantling therapeutic ingredients. No study has reported that in virtuo exposure was ineffective, and only three studies reported weak effects compared to the control condition (Maltby, et al., 2002; Mühlberger, et al., 2003; Wald & Taylor, 2003). No study has shown that VR is more effective than in vivo exposure, but none was conducted with that aim in mind. It is in fact other assets of VR that may make the treatment more effective, rather than more efficacious.

One might argue that each of the studies published so far can be criticized on at least one ground (small sample size, lack of long-term follow-up data, poor treatment standardization, reliance on subjective measures only, etc.), but such a conclusion would not be fair. For each study's weakness, there are two or more studies that do not suffer from such weakness yet reach the same conclusion. For example, some studies have long follow-up periods (e.g., Wiederhold & Wiederhold, 2003); others use a combination of self-report, behavioral, and physiological measures (e.g., Côté & Bouchard, in press); others have very large sample size (Bullinger, 2005); some compare VR with a gold-standard in vivo control condition (e.g., Emmelkamp, et al., 2002) or to basic waiting-list control (e.g., Rothbaum et al., 2000); and some target more complex anxiety disorders (e.g., Klinger, et al.,

2005). There is even a replication study with very strong methodology (Roth-baum, et al., in press) and a comparison with imaginal exposure (Wiederhold, et al., 2002). Overall, the converging evidence and replications using different method-ologies and populations indicate that VR offers an attractive alternative to in vivo exposure.

ISSUES IN VR TREATMENT

Presence and Pictorial Realism of the VR Environments

It is intriguing that VR may work given the fact that virtual reality does not perfectly replicate physical reality. Advocates of VR interventions contend that virtual environments create a superior sense of presence relative to imaginal exposure and, as a result, are more likely to activate the underlying neural net-work associated with fear processing (see Rothbaum, et al., 1996; Foa & Kozak, 1986). The sense of presence is often defined as the subjective impression of being *there* in the virtual environment (Sadowski & Staney, 2002). Presence is also thought to be related to the suspension of disbeliefs (Wiederhold & Wie-derhold, 2005), or when the user fails to perceive the existence of a medium in his interactions with the environment (the illusion of nonmediation; Lombard & Ditton, 1997). Presence may occur when a person interacting with a virtual environment reports a greater degree of interactivity with the virtual environ-ment than with their physical environment (Wiederhold & Wiederhold, 2000). Several variables have been found to influence presence (Sadowski & Stanney, 2002), such as: ease of interaction, user-initiated control, maximal pictorial real-ism, length of immersion in the virtual environment, social interactions in the virtual environment, subjective factors from the user, and hardware/software factors.

According to Wiederhold and Wiederhold (1999; 2005), the quality of presence that is felt in the virtual environment may be related to treatment outcome. This hypothesis is appealing, especially as some people do not seem to react emotionally to virtual environments (e.g., Walshe, et al., 2003). To relate presence and patient's emo-tional involvement in VR therapies, Wiederhold and Wiederhold (1999) affirmed that individuals receiving VR treatment should be classified into four functional groups. The first subgroup exhibits high subjective and objective arousal to the vir-tual environment. Such individuals are described as "highly phobic" and "capable of becoming highly immersed in the VR environment" (Wiederhold & Wiederhold, 1999, p. 163). The second subgroup of individuals evidence a high level of physi-ological arousal, but a low level of subjective arousal. These individuals may show significant decreases, for example, in autonomic arousal, but not report any change in subjective discomfort (or may deny becoming anxious when exposed to vir-tual stimuli despite measurable increase in physiological arousal). A third subgroup evidences high levels of subjective arousal, but objective indices of physiological arousal are normal. Wiederhold and Wiederhold suggest this may occur in situations where the individual may have something to gain by inaccurately reporting his or her level of anxiety (e.g., secondary gain issues, if litigation is pending, and so forth). A fourth group, and one not often seen in treatment, includes individuals who are not able to immerse themselves in the virtual world and do not derive any benefit from in virtuo exposure.

A common misconception about VR relates to the level of pictorial realism. Many virtual environments that are used in the studies described earlier look cartoonish, and none of the virtual environments represent an excellent replica of the physical reality. However, judgments about the perceived realism of the VR environments differ significantly between phobics and nonphobics. The Robillard, et al. (2003) study is a nice example where the comparison between phobics and nonphobics revealed significant differences, and large effect sizes on measures of anxiety, presence, and sense of realism. Taking the realism to a minimum, Herbelin, Riquier, Vexo, and Thalmann (2002) asked 10 nonphobics to deliver a speech in a virtual room filled with images of just and only eyes starring at them. Even in this unrealistic condition, participants reported significant increases in anxiety and heart rate. Zimmons (2004) immersed 42 nonphobics in a virtual height simulation (throwing balls down a pit) and, in an attempt to assess whether the texture or the lighting quality of the image played a role in the experience felt in VR, used a simple black and white grid representation of the virtual pit as a control condition. Of interest, there was a statistically significant increase in anxiety (heart rate) even in the black and white environment. These are only a few examples reminding us that emotions are not logical and that anxiety can be triggered by the simple perception of a threat, even if the stimuli are virtual, cartoonish, and not really dangerous.

The relationship between presence and the level of anxiety felt in the VR environment may be more complex than it appears at first glance. As mentioned earlier, there is a strong relationship between anxiety and presence. For example, Robillard, et al. (2003) reported a significant correlation ($r = .74$, $p < .001$) between anxiety and presence. To document the direction of the causal relationship between anxiety and presence, two studies were conducted by Bouchard and his colleagues. In a first study conducted with snake phobics, participants were told that the virtual environments were either infested or not infested with snakes (Bouchard, St.-Jacques, Robillard, & Renaud, 2004). Because the VR environments were exactly the same, changing the instructions allowed the researchers to manipulate experimentally the level of anxiety and assess its impact on presence. Using a counter-balanced design, they found that inducing anxiety lead to a significant increase in presence. To test the inverse relationship, Michaud, Bouchard, Dumoulin, and Zhong (2004) asked acrophobics to do a feared task (i.e., riding a glass elevator up to a selected floor, crawling outside the building while looking down to the streets, walking on wooden scaffolds toward a building across the street, etc.) while immersed in VR with conditions that were favorable or unfavorable to presence (lights turned on in the laboratory, surrounding physical environment visible in the participant's field of view, etc.). The level of anxiety was higher in the immersions conducted when presence was higher, and vice versa. Taken together, these two studies suggest that there is a reciprocal determinism between anxiety and presence; increasing anxiety leads to more presence, and more presence leads to increase in anxiety. What remains to be tested is whether this relationship is linear or if it holds only if a minimal level of presence is reached.

What is the relationship between presence and treatment outcome? Many researchers in the VR research community assume that degree of presence in the virtual environment is related to treatment outcome. Garcia-Palacios, Quero, Botella, and Baños (2005) treated 45 phobics with in virtuo exposure and conducted a regression analysis examining the relationship between change in fear/avoidance and presence. The results were not significant: measures of presence, dissociation, and emotional involvement did not correlate significantly with treatment outcome. In their study on treatment mechanism with arachnophobics, Côté and Bouchard (2005) also failed to find any predictive power of presence on treatment outcome. These results echoed findings from Krinj, Emmelkamp, Biemond, de Wilde de Ligny, Schuemie, and van der Mast (2004), and Bullinger (2005), who compared the efficacy of a highly immersive CAVE-like system and the less immersive but more affordable HMD technology. Both research teams reported more presence and more anxiety in the CAVE system, but no difference in treatment outcome. Another known attempt to assess realism and treatment outcome is from Mühlberger, Wiedemann, and Pauli (2005), who reanalyzed their previous data in comparing participants who went in the virtual flight while airplane motion was either simulated (n = 12) or not simulated (n = 13). The motion mirrored the VR flight, with speed acceleration and deceleration as well as turbulence. They also found that motion induced statistically stronger anxiety, but had no effect on treatment outcome.

These data do not mean that Wiederhold and Wiederhold's (2005) hypothesis, that "the efficacy of VR is related to the *quality* of presence" (p. 77, italics added) is erroneous. Patients in the fourth subgroup of the Wiederhold's classification did not become present and did not feel any anxiety in VR. It is quite possible that future research will show that a minimal level of presence is necessary to trigger the anxiety reaction. Once this threshold is passed, becoming more present may be interesting but may have limited impact on treatment outcome. Thus it may be more a matter of quality than quantity.

Cybersickness: Virtual Reality-Induced Symptoms

It has been reported in the literature that immersions in virtual reality can induce unpleasant side effects, such as nausea, dizziness, and headache (Lawson, Graeber, Mead, & Muth, 2002). The term *cybersickness* is also often used to describe symptoms similar to motion sickness (McCauley & Sharkey, 1992), although some side effects are irrelevant to motion sickness and are easier to control. In a review chapter on the topic, Lawson, et al. (2002) concluded that about 5% of people immersed in a virtual environment might experience significant side effects. The scientific studies on the side effects of VR immersions are often difficult to generalize to clinical populations, because most studies were conducted on nonclinical samples (e.g., fighter pilots, astronauts, soldiers) performing tasks that significantly differ from treatment protocols (e.g., flight simulations for fighter pilots) and using old and heavy equipment compared to what is currently used during therapy. In a study with 23 children and 35 adults selected from the community and immersed in VR environments used in therapy, St.-Jacques and Bouchard (2005) found that the VR immersions could induce minor side effects in some people, but no side effects lasted according to participants when they were interviewed 24 hours after the immersion.

Some VR-induced symptoms and effects could be directly related to the equipment used. For example, heavy HMD may cause neck strain or headache if the strapping band is too tight around the forehead. Also, as staring at TV monitors for a long time can induce eye strain, looking into an HMD for a long time can cause the same phenomenon. Adapting stereoscopic displays in the HMD to inter-pupillary distance is also necessary, although very few VR environments used for in virtuo exposure involved a stereoscopic HMD. Nevertheless, problems caused by the equipment become less and less frequent given the fast pace of technological advances. For example, most affordable commercial HMDs can now offer a 800 × 600 resolution and weigh less than 7 ounces, which is not problematic for adults and most children. The problem of eye accommodation occurring over long immersions is also easily solved by taking small pauses once every 20 or 30 minutes of immersion, which is also useful to allow time for therapist and patient discussion.

Another potential source of side effects is caused by conflict between sensory information. For example, think of an acrophobic who is immersed in VR with an HMD. When he turns his head around, he can contemplate the scenery. If he looks down, he can see the depth of the cliff, and by pressing a mouse button with a finger, he can walk forward towards the edge of the cliff. When that user "walks" in the virtual environment, his visual perceptual system signals movement, while part of the vestibular and the proprioceptive systems do not detect forward motion. When the user turns his head around, the vestibular system also detects this motion immediately, but there may be a small lag in time while the computer processes the information and displays the corresponding visual stimuli in the HMD. These incongruities between the sensory systems (vision, proprioception, and inner ear otolith/semicircular canal systems) could cause symptoms of nausea, vertigo, dizziness, etc. These symptoms of cybersickness are related to motion sickness; however, they are usually transient, neither severe nor dangerous, and often disappear during the immersion in VR. Because some people are more sensitive to motion sickness than others, it is recommended to pay attention to VR side effects during the exposure session (Stanney, 2002). It is important, however, not to confound VR side effects with anxiety symptoms, or other naturally occurring side effects, such as vertigo induced by looking down a cliff during exposure.

One last set of VR-induced side effects relates to the task the user has to perform in the virtual environment. In regrouping factors related to VR side effects, Stanney, Mourant, and Kennedy (1998) found that many side effects could be explained by task characteristics, such as the speed of movements, the degree of control the user can have on the immersion, images shown in peripheral visual field, etc. These task characteristics may explain why very few patients mention symptoms of cybersickness during therapy, compared to immersions for leisure or training purposes.

Wiederhold and Wiederhold (1999) have also reported unexpected reactions from patients in response to the virtual environment, just as it would happen during in vivo exposure. They discuss the case of a flight phobic who had a panic attack during VR therapy. What makes this case especially interesting is that the panic attack occurred in the third VR session and after unsuccessful imaginal exposure therapy. Also, the case illustrates the importance of using both subjective and objective indices of anxiety. The authors report that the only indication a panic attack was occurring was the sudden and unexpected change in heart rate. In the same report, Wiederhold and Wiederhold (1999) also report the case of a motor vehicle accident survivor who experienced a flashback during VR treatment. As with the prior case, imaginal exposure had not been successful. Executing a left turn in the VR environment elicited the flashback and necessitated cessation of the session. Subsequently, the individual reported cessation of nightmares and treatment was ultimately successful.

To sum up, in some cases, immersion in VR can induce a few side effects. Some of these side effects could be related to the equipment or the tasks the client has to perform during the in virtuo exposure. These symptoms are usually easy to prevent. Other symptoms are related to motion sickness and may occur in people who are sensitive to motion sickness, intoxicated, or suffering from inner-ear problems. Questionnaires can be used to assess these symptoms, and clinical studies report few, if any, side effects. Finally, these symptoms have to be different from sensations induced by the exposure itself.

Cost Issues

A frequent objection to the use of virtual reality exposure programs is the cost involved and whether the technology warrants such an investment. VR headsets and peripheral devices can easily run into thousands of dollars. Whether such an expense is cost-effective will ultimately depend on the incremental treatment utility of VR interventions. In other words, given the nontrivial costs associated with the technology, the results of

VR interventions cannot simply be as effective as in vivo exposure. Given the impressive success rates of this traditional and less expensive form of exposure, the incremental gains that VR interventions can possibly post will, mathematically, be minimal at best. As such, a demonstration of equivalence, although useful from a research perspective, does not necessarily imply widespread clinician acceptance.

In a similar vein, claims of cost-effectiveness are almost always made relative to in vivo exposure techniques. Although in vivo exposure for some behavioral disorders can be logistically untenable and cost prohibitive (e.g., fear of flying), this does not necessarily mean that VR therapy is cost-effective, as other forms of exposure (e.g., imaginal exposure) have been shown empirically to successfully treat a variety of anxiety disorders and phobias. Thus, the term *cost-effective* must always be considered relative to an alternative therapeutic criterion. If the criterion is itself cost prohibitive, VR interventions will, of course, gain the appearance of being a cost-effective alternative.

On a more positive note, costs are likely to decrease significantly. For example, a decent HMD could have cost almost $6,000 seven years ago and $1,000 by January 2005. Today, units are probably substantially less as new and very powerful products are now being sold for half that amount. In addition, once the initial hardware is purchased, it becomes easier and less costly to invest in new software and applications. Nevertheless, despite these improvements, VR still involves costs. As listed in Table 16.1, the incremental gains of VR therapy include its attractiveness for patients and the increased control over the stimuli for therapists. In some cases, the increase in safety, confidentiality, stimuli, variety, and treatment standardization are worth the investment.

CASE HISTORY

Josée, a 38-year-old administrative assistant and mother of three, cannot always travel where she wants. She suffers from spider phobia. Because of her fear, she limits her trips to locations that are as close as possible to the sea or water spots, in the hope she will not be taken by surprise by spiders. But what she fears can be found anywhere, as she realized during a vacation in Florida. While standing on a large veranda in a museum looking at some animals, her boyfriend told her suddenly to look to her left. Approximately 15 meters from where she stood, she saw a large web with two big spiders (approximately 15 cm in diameter). She immediately felt panicky, disgusted, and had the urge to go back inside the museum. She subsequently refused to return to the veranda for the remainder of the visit.

Spider phobia, also called arachnophobia, is a relatively common disorder, although most people typically do not seek professional help to get rid of their fear. Accordingly, Josée has never sought treatment until she read about a research program in a local newspaper, called the clinic, and scheduled an intake evaluation.

At the time of the intake, Josée reported having always been scared of spiders, and she could not identify any particular event that would have caused her phobia. She reported that, whenever she saw a spider, she felt a sudden rush of anxiety and had to run away. She would then ask someone else to kill the spider for her. She reported avoiding certain places because of her fear and usually remained vigilant, checking for spiders around her. She even avoided pictures of spiders and conceded that she had to fold the research project ad in the newspaper to hide the spider picture so that she could call for an appointment. She acknowledged that her fear of spiders was unjustified.

Clinical Case Conceptualization

The etiology of her anxiety cannot be detailed precisely, as she could not remember any traumatic event that might have initiated her fear of spiders; however, she could remember many past events that illustrated the level of her fear. For example, she remembered being on a swing at the age of 7 when she observed two spiders crawling across clothes. She reported being so frightened that she jumped immediately off the swing. She hypothesized that this event remained salient in her memory because she did not see the spiders after jumping off the swing, and was therefore not afforded the opportunity of knowing she was safe. She also mentioned being the victim of many practical jokes by her brothers with plastic spiders and reported feeling uncomfortable around her siblings at family reunions as a result.

Consistent with a functional analysis of any anxiety disorder, it is fruitful to focus on those mechanisms that maintain a phobia (Antony & Swinson, 2000; Barlow, 2002). The information gathered at the intake suggested that through a series of episodes involving unfortunate experiences with spiders or practical jokes, Josée started avoiding spiders. Avoidance behavior exacerbated her fear in two ways: (1) by preventing her from confronting her fears and correcting the associations she had developed between spiders and threat or disgust (Thorpe & Salkovskis, 1997), and (2) by accumulating evidence that she cannot cope with spiders because of her fearfulness (Bandura, 1986). As Josée put it, when she saw a spider, she felt a strong rush of anxiety that quickly rose to maximal distress levels. As a result, she was constantly vigilant, and if she saw a spider she would immediately ask someone to kill it. Thus, flight behavior was reinforced and she accumulated evidence that she was ineffectual at dealing with spiders. With time, she also developed many dysfunctional beliefs about spiders and about herself when confronted with spiders, such as "if I saw a spider now, it would try to jump on me," or "if I saw a spider now, I would panic."

Treatment Selection

VR was selected because it offers many opportunities for clinical psychologists who want to use standardized or specific stimuli to conduct exposure to feared stimuli.

In virtuo exposure gives the therapist total control over the situation. For example, in the treatment of the fear of spiders, the therapist can control the number, speed, and aggressiveness of spiders, providing a multilevel hierarchy. For example, in some virtual environments, clients can begin their hierarchy while immersed in VR and look at pictures, then move to rooms with very small spiders that stay perfectly still or move very slowly, and then go to other locations filled with spiders that have different sizes and behaviors. Such a degree of control over the stimuli would be difficult to achieve with traditional in vivo exposure. In virtuo exposure also allows clients to be exposed to the exact same situation over and over again, or even to go far beyond what they could try during in vivo sessions (e.g., standing next to a giant tarantula or being surrounded and followed by dozens of spiders). In the case of in virtuo treatment for arachnophobia, protecting the spiders' safety can be useful, especially if it is difficult to find spiders and keep them alive (e.g., during winter). Panicking clients could drop the spider, which could be fatal for a tarantula. Finally, in virtuo exposure is more enticing for patients than in vivo, as Garcia-Palacios, et al. (2001) have demonstrated.

Assessment

It is to be noted that Josée was participating in a study on the cognitive treatment mechanisms underlying in virtuo exposure (Côté & Bouchard, 2005), which explains why so many questionnaires were used. Although this number of measures is not necessary outside a research context, objective measures can greatly help a client following his progress over time. Also note that results from the emotional Stroop task are not presented for the sake of simplicity.

The diagnosis was based on the Structured Clinical Interview for DSM-IV (SCID; First, Spitzer, Gibbon, & Williams, 1996). At pretreatment, the *Immersive Tendencies Questionnaire* (Witmer & Singer, 1998) was also administered. It measured individual's susceptibility to feel present in VR.

Two weeks before treatment and every week during treatment (immediately after the session), Josée was asked to rate, on a scale of 0–100, the intensity of her fear, her avoidance behavior, and her perceived self-efficacy toward spiders. At pretreatment, midtreatment, and post-treatment, Josée's spider phobia was assessed with the *Spider Beliefs Questionnaire* (Arntz, Lavy, van der Berg, & van Rijsoort, 1993), the *Fear of Spiders Questionnaire* (Szymanski & O'Donoghue, 1995) and the *Perceived Self-Efficacy Towards Spiders*. The latter was constructed and validated specifically for Côté and Bouchard's (2005) study to measure patients' perception about their ability to perform efficiently in certain tasks involving spiders and/or to remain calm while doing so.

In a *Behavioral Avoidance Test* (*BAT*), a live tarantula was placed in a transparent Plexiglas cage, with the lid closed, on a sliding motorized platform that the client controlled by holding a switch button (see McGlynn, Rose, & Lazarte, 1994). She sat on a chair, at the end of the motorized platform, and had to let the therapist lift the cardboard box (Step 1) and let her remove the box's lid (Step 2). After looking at the spider for 1 minute, she had to move the platform closer (each 25 cm forward constituted Steps 3 to 9). Once the platform was the closest possible to her (23 cm to the chest), she had to bend forward and place her face above the opening of the box and look at the spider for 1 minute (Step 10). She was instructed to go through the steps until her anxiety was too uncomfortable and then she could stop.

After each in virtuo exposure session, she completed the *Presence Questionnaire* (Witmer & Singer, 1998) and the *Simulator Sickness Questionnaire* (Kennedy, Lane, Berbaum, & Lilienthal, 1993).

Treatment

Josée's treatment consisted of 11 weekly 60-minute sessions. There was a 5 minute pause in the middle of each in virtuo exposure session to reduce the risk of cybersickness. No homework was given, as this treatment was part of an experimental study and in vivo homework would have contaminated the results. After each in virtuo session, Josée remained in the waiting room for 15 minutes before she left to ensure that she did not feel any cybersickness symptoms. Treatment was administered by a Ph.D. candidate (S.C.) using a computer working with Windows 2000 (Pentium III, 4.2 GHz, 1 Go of RAM, equipped with a nVidia™ Geforce4 Ti 4200 128 MB graphics card), an Intertrax² motion tracker from Intersense™ (USB model, 3dof, update rate 256 Hz), an I-Glass SVGA head mounted display by IO-Display™ (resolution 800 × 600, 26 degrees FoV diagonal) and a wireless mouse by Gyration™. The VR environments were created by adapting a 3D game (Max Payne™; see Figure 16.2). The evolution of Josée's progress during treatment is detailed next.

Session 2

After the intake session, Josée was provided the clinical case conceptualization regarding the factors that likely caused and maintained her phobia and the justification for an in virtuo treatment approach. Josée listened carefully to this information and demonstrated her understanding by illustrating with examples from her own experience. She was instructed in ways to reduce cybersickness symptoms (turn her body completely when in motion in virtuo, not moving too fast, etc.), and how to use the equipment. She then practiced these skills in virtuo in a spider-free environment. Within a few minutes of entering the virtual world, she was able to move reasonably well through the virtual space (an apartment) and use objects found there.

Session 3

To maintain a meaningful level of presence during her exposure sessions, instructions were always given as if the exposure was taking place in physical reality. For

FIGURE 16.2   Illustration of a person immersed in virtuo and images of the VR environment used to treat arachnophobia.

example, the therapist would instruct Josée to "walk forward" instead of asking her to "press the left button." In this way, Josée quickly incorporated the equipment in her natural movements and its manipulations became automatic within the first exposure session. The intensity of the exposure was monitored with Josée's subjective evaluation of her anxiety level on a scale of 0-100.

Josée chose to begin the exposure with only framed pictures of spiders that were hung on the walls of the virtual apartment, which was the lowest intensity level of the in virtuo hierarchy. She gradually approached 3 virtual cm from the pictures, and afterward, she exposed herself to a "live" virtual spider staying still on a stove. She mentioned that she was very surprised to be able to come close to this spider and said she was happy to see progress so soon in therapy. Indeed, she reported that her anxiety lowered more quickly at the end of the session.

Sessions 4–6

Josée rapidly understood and integrated the exposure principles, so only minimal instructions were given throughout the session. Indeed, without any suggestion from the therapist, she would take initiative and approach spiders once her anxiety had decreased to manageable levels (i.e., to approximately 40%). We also encouraged her to turn her back on the spiders because losing track of their physical location triggered anxiety. The last phobogenic stimuli used in a previous session were systematically revisited to assess whether they still triggered anxiety. If they did, exposure was continued until her anxiety diminished. Generally, Josée still felt anxious with those previously seen stimuli, but she could approach them much faster and closer (e.g., in 3 minutes instead of 25) before her anxiety reached high levels.

During exposure, Josée mentioned that she had the same reactions she usually felt in the presence of a spider (itchiness, worrying hands, feeling hot, etc.). This suggested a strong feeling of presence. She generally reported few cybersickness symptoms, but was sometimes uncomfortable with the weight of the HMD or the time lag between her physical moves and the corresponding motions in VR. She usually ignored these elements after a few minutes, however, especially when her anxiety was high.

Although reporting between 9 and 11 anxiety exacerbations per session, Josée's evolution through the hierarchy was surprisingly slow. After session five, she was still confronting the same relatively easy situations (small spiders, staying still), as opposed to the worse scenarios available in the virtual environment (being surrounded by spiders of different sizes and behaviors). At session six, she reported a dream about a colleague opening an envelope and many plastic spiders falling on her pillow, which woke her up. She then had to turn the lights on and reassure herself that she was safe. During this session, she could move to the next level, but spent all the session exposing herself to the same two spiders: tarantulas that moved toward her or unexpectedly on the side and then stayed still. She reported feeling more anxious that particular week, for work-related reasons, and cried during the session when the spiders moved and surprised her, which made her anxiety peak at 100%. She mentioned that she often felt sad and vulnerable when she exposed herself, because she had remembrances of her brothers' practical jokes. Nevertheless, she could go through with the exposure and ended the session standing between the two spiders, each at less than a virtual foot from her, and let her anxiety decrease at 40%. She mentioned that she saw progress at home, as she could watch a TV program with many tarantulas, a thing she could not have done before.

Sessions 7–10

Josée's progress, although still moderately slow, was accelerated during those sessions. Indeed, Josée began to see the positive effects of therapy at home. She reported being able to watch a movie scene involving a lot of giant spiders and remain calm. She also reported that, seeing a spider walking on her husband's foot, she kept talking normally and did not react. She said that before treatment, she would have felt a rush of anxiety and would have shaken her clothes and hair to make sure there was no spider on her. What seemed to particularly help Josée going through the hierarchy was an awareness of her tendency to anticipate negative reactions from either herself or the spiders during exposure. For example, she would often say: "I am ok now, but if that one moves, I will jump out the window!" She acknowledged the steps she had successfully negotiated, but never her capacity to go further, as if she doubted future success. The therapist noted when she was anticipating failure and moderated these cognitions by encouraging her to think in the present tense (as if she was doing an observation experiment) or by walking in the virtual world toward the object of her fear. Both strategies were successful and did not intensify Josée's self-reported anxiety. At the conclusion of therapy, Josée acknowledged that the tendency to anticipate failure mediated her anxiety.

Final Session

During the last session, Josée completed the final VR exposure scenario: crossing a room filled with spiders and going into a bedroom with a particularly huge and aggressive spider. She was able to remain calm as she successfully approached the spider to a distance of 1 virtual foot. Information was then provided concerning relapse prevention. With the therapist, Josée developed a graded hierarchy so that she could conduct exposure sessions at home. The graded in vivo hierarchy involved approaching a medium-size domestic spider in a plastic bowl, then touching the bowl with her hand, touching the spider with a pencil, placing her hand in the bottom of the bowl, and touching the spider with a finger. The last step involved killing spiders with a tissue. To ensure that Josée continued to expose herself to spiders, practice her skills, and reduce the opportunity for resurgence of avoidance behavior, we encouraged Josée to think of herself as "the designated person to kill spiders."

Results

As previously mentioned, measures were taken before the intake and after each session, as detailed in Figure 16.3.

Josée's rating of her fear and avoidance were high at the beginning of the therapy before plateauing and then slowing as she progressed and was able to control her anticipation during the exposure exercises. Her perceived self-efficacy rating also followed the same pattern: a rapid increase that corresponded with progress in therapy and at home.

Standardized questionnaires were administered after sessions 1 (pretreatment), 7 (midtreatment), and 11 (post-treatment). Scores on the *BAT* and the *Perceived*

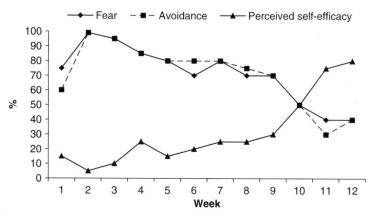

FIGURE 16.3 Weekly measures of fear, avoidance, and perceived self-efficacy during VR treatment.

Self-Efficacy Towards Spiders Questionnaire are reported in Figure 16.2, and scores of the *Fear of Spiders Questionnaire* (FSQ) and the *Spiders Beliefs Questionnaire* (SBQ) (both the beliefs toward the spiders and the beliefs toward self-scales) are reported in Figure 16.4.

As therapy progressed, Josée was able to interact further with the live spider in the *BAT*. Indeed, even if her BAT score was only 1 at midtreatment, she could let the therapist remove the cardboard box over the Plexiglas cage and look at the spider for 1 minute, something she had refused to do at the pretreatment. After therapy, Josée was able to let the therapist remove the lid over the Plexiglas cage and move it 70 cm closer to her chin. Although not part of the BAT procedures,

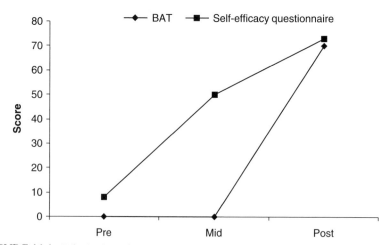

FIGURE 16.4   Behavioral avoidance test (in steps) and self-efficacy (in %).

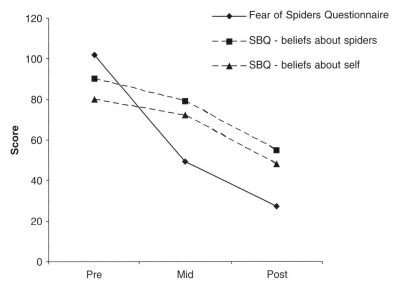

FIGURE 16.5   Fear of Spiders and Spider Beliefs Questionnaire.

she could also stand 2 feet from the cage with the lid closed. For Josée, this was a clinically significant change, even though it was not scored in the standard BAT protocol. In the same fashion, her perceived self-efficacy score gradually increased as treatment progressed. Josée's beliefs toward spiders and fear of spiders as measured by the SBQ and the FSQ also gradually decreased throughout treatment to reach nonclinical levels after treatment (Figure 16.5).

Case Discussion

At the end of treatment, Josée wrote a note about her experience with VR therapy. She wrote that, although feeling a lot of skepticism, apprehension, and anxiety before treatment, she considered herself to have been more successful than she originally anticipated. She mentioned that in virtuo exposure allowed her to interact with spiders and gain mastery. She also learned that she frequently anticipated negative outcomes and that she could impede negative self-statements. She concluded by saying that the treatment had significantly increased the quality of her life.

CONCLUSION

Over the last 2 decades, the exponential growth and use of computer technology have precipitated dramatic changes in business practices in both the public and private sector. A survey conducted in the 1990s suggested that at that time, clinical psychologists had readily accepted computer technology for purposes of office management and assistance in completing mundane tasks (e.g., generating assessment reports), but that computer applications to deliver therapeutic protocols were slow to catch on. McMinn, Buchanan, Ellens, and Ryan (1999) surveyed 420 psychologists and found modest rates of computer use for treatment intervention purposes. In fact, when comparing their results to survey results reported by Farrell (1989), they concluded that clinical psychologists have not accepted the computer as an adjunctive therapy tool despite large advances in technology and development of computer software for that purpose. Although respondents to the questionnaire generally viewed computerized test reporting and test scoring assistance as ethical, respondents were critical of computer-delivered adjunctive therapies. A total of 60% considered using a computer in lieu of traditional, face-to-face therapy to be unethical. Although only 12.8% considered virtual treatments for anxiety disorders to be unethical, 45.5% were not sure. At best, results suggested that computer applications resulting from the latest wave of technology (i.e., applications designed to deliver treatments rather than helping the clinicians perform clerical tasks) were considered by clinicians to be ethically questionable. Although McMinn and colleagues ultimately concluded that computer technology was having a "minimal impact" (p. 172) on clinical practice, they remained optimistic for the future. In a more recent Delphi poll on the future of psychotherapy, 62 experts in the field of psychotherapy listed the changes they considered the most likely to occur in the next 10 years (Norcross, Hedges, & Prochaska, 2002). The panel concluded that VR therapy will flourish, ranking the use of VR as the therapeutic intervention third most likely to increase the greatest in the next 10 years (after homework assignments and relapse prevention). In line with the prediction in the Norcross, et al. (2002) survey, there has been an important increase of studies using virtual reality in the treatment of mental disorders.

Despite the advantages mentioned earlier in this chapter, and the fact that more than 40 empirical articles have been published on the efficacy of in virtuo exposure, results from the survey reported by McMinn and colleagues (1999) raise the question of different trajectories between clinicians and researchers. Specifically, juxtaposing McMinn's results against those presented by Richard and Lauterbach (2004) leads to some interesting conclusions. In a review of computer applications in behavioral assessment, Richard and Lauterbach entered key word terms into the PsycInfo database and counted publications and dissertations related to computerized behavioral assessment applications over the last 40 years. Not surprisingly, the number of publications has increased exponentially over time at a rate much greater than other assessment instruments (e.g., MMPI, Rorschach, WAIS). The interest in virtual treatments has also spawned a number of relevant organizations, journals, and businesses. Scientific journals such as *Cyberpsychology and Behavior* and *Presence* publish frequent studies about VR applications, and VR publications have popped up in established American Psychological Association journals (e.g., *Journal of Consulting and Clinical Psychology*). Taken in conjunction with McMinn's study, these results suggest that increased interest in computer applications by researchers has not yet been met with a corresponding enthusiasm by clinicians. Informal discussions with mental health professionals also support this impression. We suspect several reasons to explain this slow transfer from the research labs to the clinics: (1) the vast majority of clinicians have little to no experience with computerized or virtual treatment procedures, (2) graduate training does not emphasize adjunctive computerized interventions, (3) some clinicians remain concerned about the effect computer programs will have on therapist-client rapport and treatment outcome, (4) the costs associated with a devoted computer or virtual reality system remain high, and (5) the incremental usefulness of treatment using computer and VR programs has not yet been demonstrated convincingly.

Important information must be provided to counter the last three issues. The consideration that there is no significant advantage of using VR to conduct exposure is partly based on the impression that in vivo stimuli can always be used instead of in virtuo ones, or that imaginal exposure is as effective as in vivo. The population used in the early outcome studies certainly contributed to this impression, with studies on acrophobia, arachnophobia, or claustrophobia using stimuli that are easily available in vivo. The interest to use VR may seem low for therapists who receive few people consulting for specific phobias and where the available VR environments depict situations where in vivo stimuli are easily accessible. In early studies, sample selection was often based on methodological and practical considerations. Researchers initially began to validate in virtuo exposure for disorders for which behavioral avoidance tests could be devised (rather than relying solely on subjective measures), for which in vivo exposure could be used as a gold-standard control condition, and for which treatment was more simple and straightforward to adapt (compared to more complex anxiety disorders). As illustrated in Table 16.1 and previous sections of this chapter, VR environments are currently available for more complex disorders and for situations where in vivo stimuli are more difficult to find. Applications where in vivo stimuli are less available are now being tested (e.g., fear of thunderstorms), as well as for more complex anxiety disorders (e.g., post-traumatic stress disorder, panic disorder with agoraphobia, social anxiety disorder). New and original applications are also being tested for in virtuo exposure in the treatment of mental disorders other than anxiety, such as substance abuse, eating disorders, stuttering, or anger management. In addition, the availability of in vivo exposure stimuli is certainly not the only issue to consider. In some cases, therapists may be interested in VR for treatment attractiveness, increased standardization, and control over the stimuli or confidentiality.

As for the cost issue, there has been a significant reduction in the price of the required hardware and software. With the increase in demands from mental health professionals and developments in computer science, the price of VR was prohibitive years ago, is still currently high, and will soon be affordable.

Finally, although no study has measured the direct impact of using VR on therapist-client rapport, it must be pointed out that using VR should not hinder the therapeutic alliance, as the computer does not replace the therapist; it is merely a tool to deliver potent and emotionally relevant stimuli, just as television does when therapists use videotaped stimuli. A potentially more threatening technology for the therapeutic alliance and bond is the use of videoconference to deliver the treatment, and even in the case where the patient and the therapist never meet face to face, the therapeutic bond remains very strong (Allard & Bouchard, 2005; Bouchard, Paquin, Payeur, Allard, Rivard, Fournier, et al., 2004).

To conclude, although more studies are warranted, the bulk of evidence from converging results from outcome studies point to the fact that in virtuo exposure is effective. Results were replicated over and over with different methodologies: (1) sample sizes varied from single case studies to more than 200 patients; (2) follow-up time sometimes extended as far as 3 years posttreatment; (3) a wide variety of measures have been used, from questionnaire to behavioral, physiological, and information processing ones; (4) a number of control groups have been used, from waiting-list to imaginal and in vivo exposure; and (5) a variety of populations have been tested, including complex cases. The difference in treatment efficacy between in vivo and in virtuo exposure seems minimal. VR presents some assets that justify, in some circumstances, considering in virtuo exposure. It generally offers the advantage of treatment standardization, increasingly realistic environments, and control of aversive stimuli. From an exposure therapy standpoint, VR treatments are convenient for both therapists and clients, as the therapy protocols can be completed in an office rather than outdoors or in public settings. VR software also allows clinicians considerable control over environmental parameters, thereby maximizing salient environmental features that trigger fears in the client. What remains to be seen is whether the advantages of VR will be sufficient to offset the burden imposed by costs.

REFERENCES

Allard, M., & Bouchard, S. (2005). Effectiveness of CBT delivered through videoconferencing and face-to-face for panic disorder with agoraphobia. Paper presented at the Cybertherapy Conference 2005, June, Basel. In Wiederhold, B., Riva, G., and Bullinger, M.D. (Eds.), *Cybertherapy 2005*. San Diego: Interactive Media Institute.

Anderson, P., Rothbaum, B.O., & Hodges, L.F. (2003). Virtual reality in the treatment of social anxiety: Two case reports. *Cognitive and Behavioral Practice, 10,* 240–247.

Antony, M., Swinson, R. (2000). *Phobic disorders and panic in adults.* Washington, D.C.: American Psychological Association.

Arntz, A., Lavy, E., van der Berg, G., & van Rijsoort, S. (1993). Negative beliefs of spider phobics: A psychometric evaluation of the spider phobia beliefs questionnaire. *Advances in Behaviour Research and Therapy, 15*(4), 257–277.

Bandura, A. (1986). *Social foundations of thoughts and action. A social cognitive theory.* Englewoods Cliffs: Prentice Hall.

Barlow, D.H. (2002). *Anxiety and its disorders* (2nd ed.). New York: Guilford Press.

Bordnick, P., Graap, K., Copp, H. Brooks, J. & Ferrer, M. (2005). Virtual reality cue reactivity assessment in cigarette smokers. *Cyberpsychology and Behavior, 8*(5), 487–492.

Botella, C., Baños, R. M., Perpiñá, C., Villa, H., Alcañiz, M., & Rey, A. (1998). Virtual reality treatment of claustrophobia: A case report. *Behaviour Research and Therapy, 36,* 239–246.

Botella, C., Baños, R.M., Villa, H., Perpiñá, C., & García-Palacios, A. (2000). Virtual reality in the treatment of claustrophobic fear: A controlled, multiple-baseline design. *Behavior Therapy, 31,* 583–595.

Botella, C., Villa, H., Baños, R.M., Perpiñá, C., & García-Palacios, A. (1999). The treatment of claustrophobia in virtual reality: Changes in other phobic behaviors not specifically treated. *Cyberpsychology and Behavior, 2* (2), 135–141.

Botella, C., García-Palacios, A., Quero, S., Baños, R.M., Alcañiz, M., & Riva, G. (Unpublished manuscript). Virtual reality exposure in the treatment of panic disorder with agoraphobia. Submitted to the journal *Behavior Therapy.* (In review.)

Bouchard, S., Côté, S., St-Jacques, J., Robillard, G., & Renaud, P. (2006). Efficacy of virtual reality exposure in the treatment of arachnophobia using 3D games. *Technology and Health Care, 14,* 19–27.

Bouchard, S., Paquin, B., Payeur, R., Allard, M., Rivard, V., Fournier, T., Renaud, P., & Lapierre, J. (2004). Delivering cognitive-behavior therapy for panic disorder with agoraphobia in videoconference. *Telemedicine Journal and e-Health, 10*(1), 13–25.

Bouchard, S., St-Jacques, J., Côté, S., Robillard, G., & Renaud, P. (2003). Exemples de l'utilisation de la réalité virtuelle dans le traitement des phobies/Using virtual reality in the treatment of phobias. *Revue Francophone de Clinique Comportementale et Cognitive, 8*(4), 5–12.

Bouchard, S., St-Jacques, J., & Renaud, P. (unpublished). Efficacy of a virtual reality treatment for children suffering from arachnophobia.

Bouchard, S., St-Jacques, J., Robillard, G., Côté, S., & Renaud, P. (2003). Efficacité de l'exposition en réalité virtuelle pour l'acrophobie : Une étude préliminaire. *Journal de Thérapie Comportementale et Cognitive, 13*(3), 107–112.

Bouchard, S., St-Jacques, J., Robillard, G., & Renaud, P. (Submitted/2004). Anxiety increases the sense of presence in virtual reality. *Presence: Teleoperators and Virtual Environments.* Already available online at Presence-connect.com, 4(1), Avril 2004.

Bullinger, A. (2005). Treating acrophobia in a virtual environment. Paper presented at the Cybertherapy Conference 2005, June, Basel. In Wiederhold, B., Riva, G. & Bullinger, M.D. (Eds.), *Cybertherapy 2005.* San Diego: Interactive Media Institute.

Bullinger, A.H., Roesler, A., & Mueller-Psahn, F. (1998). 3D VR as a tool in cognitive-behavioral therapy of claustrophobic patients. *Cyberpsychology and Behavior, 1*(2), 139–146.

Carlin, A.S., Hoffman, H.G., & Weghorst, S. (1997). Virtual reality and tactile augmentation on the treatment of spider phobia: a case report. *Behaviour Research and Therapy, 35,* 153–158.

Choi, Y.H., Jang, D.P., Ku, J.H., Shin, M.B., & Kim, S.I. (2001). Short-term treatment of acrophobia with virtual reality therapy (VRT): A case report. *CyberPsychology and Behavior, 4* (3), 349–354.

Cohen, J. (1988). *Statistical power analyses for the behavioral sciences.* Hillsdale, NJ: Lawrence Erlbaum Associates.

Côté, S. & Bouchard, S. (2005). Documenting the efficacy of virtual reality exposure with psychophysiological and information processing measures. *Applied Psychophysiology and Biofeedback, 30*(3), 217–232.

Côté, S. & Bouchard, S. (unpublished). Virtual reality exposure's efficacy in the treatment of specific phobias: A critical review.

Côté, S. & Bouchard, S. (submitted/2005). Cognitive mechanisms underlying virtual reality exposure's efficacy. Paper presented at the Cybertherapy Conference 2005, June, Basel. In Wiederhold, B., Riva, G., & Bullinger, M.D. (Eds.), *Cybertherapy 2005*. San Diego: Interactive Media Institute.

Cottraux, J., Berthoz, A., Jouvent, R., Pull, C., Zaoui, M., Pelissolo, A., Puccl C., Genouilhac, V., Giraud, N., Duinat, A., Znaidi, F., De Mey Guillard, C., Panagiotaki, P., Fanget, F., Viaud-Delmon, I., Mollard, E., & Gueyffier, F. (2005). A comparative controlled study of virtual reality therapy and cognitive behaviour therapy in panic disorder with agoraphobia: Design and methodological issues. *VRIC —Laval Virtual 2005 Proceedings*, pp. 125–130.

Davis, F. (1993). User acceptance of information technology: Systems characteristics, user perceptions and behavioural impacts. *International Journal of Man-Machine Studies, 38*, 475–487.

Difede, J., & Hoffman, H.G. (2002). Virtual reality exposure therapy for World Trade Center post-traumatic stress disorder: A case report. *CyberPsychology and Behavior, 5* (6), 529–535.

Difede, J., Hoffman, H., Cukor, J., Patt, Y., & Giosan, C. (2005). Virtual reality therapy for posttraumatic stress disorder following September 11, 2001. Paper presented at the Cybertherapy Conference 2005, June, Basel. In Wiederhold, B., Riva, G., & Bullinger, M.D. (Eds.), *Cybertherapy 2005*. San Diego: Interactive Media Institute.

Difede, J., Hoffman, H., & Jaysinghe, N. (2002). Innovative use of virtual reality technology in the treatment of PTSD in the aftermath of September 11. *Psychiatric Services, 53* (9), 1083–1085.

Emmelkamp, P.M.G., Bruynzeel, M., Drost, L., & van der Mast, C. (2001). Virtual reality treatment in acrophobia: A comparison with exposure in vivo. *CyberPsychology and Behavior, 4* (3), 335–339.

Emmelkamp, P.M.G., Krijn, M., Hulsbosch, A.M., de Vries, S., Schuemie, M.J., & van der Mast, C.A.P.G. (2002). Virtual reality treatment versus exposure in vivo: A comparative evaluation in acrophobia. *Behaviour Research and Therapy, 40*, 509–516.

Farrell, A.D. (1989). Impact of standards for computer-based tests on practice: Consequences of the information gap. *Computers in Human Behavior, 5*, 1–11.

First, M.B., Spitzer, R., Gibbon, M., & Williams, J.B.W. (1996). *Structured clinical interview for DSM-IV axis-I disorders—patient version*. New York: Biometrics Research Department, New York State Psychiatric Institute.

Foa, E.B., & Kozak, M.J. (1986). Emotional processing of fear: Exposure to corrective information. *Psychological Bulletin, 99*, 20–35.

Gamito, P., Pacheco, J., Ribeiro, C., Pablo, C., & Saraiva, T. (2005). Virtual war PTSD: A methodological thread. Paper presented at the Cybertherapy Conference 2005, June, Basel. In Wiederhold, B., Riva, G., & Bullinger, M.D. (Eds.), *Cybertherapy 2005*. San Diego: Interactive Media Institute.

Garcia-Palacios, A., Botella, C., Hoffman, H.G., Villa, H., & Fabregat, S. (2004). Comparing the acceptance of VR exposure vs in vivo exposure in a clinical sample. Paper presented at the Cybertherapy Conference 2004, San Diego, January 2004. In Wiederhold, B., Riva, G., & Wiederhold, M.D. (Eds.), *Cybertherapy 2004*. San Diego: Interactive Media Institute.

Garcia-Palacios, A., Hoffman, H., Carlin, A., Furness III, T.A., & Botella, C. (2002). Virtual reality in the treatment of spider phobia: A controlled study. *Behaviour Research and Therapy, 40*, 983–993.

Garcia-Palacios, A., Hoffman, H.G., Kwong See, S., Tsai, A., & Botella, C. (2001). Redefining therapeutic success of virtual reality exposure therapy. *Cyberpsychology and Behavior, 4* (3), 341–348.

Garcia-Palacios, A., Quero, S., Botella, C., & Baños, R. (2005). Outcome predictors in virtual reality exposure for the treatment of phobias. Paper presented at the Cybertherapy Conference 2005 , June, Basel.

Graap, K.M. (2004). Cue reactivity in a virtual crack house. Paper presented at the AABT convention. November 2004, New Orleans.

Greist, J.H., & Greist, G.L. (1981). *Fearless flying: A passenger guide to modern airplane travel*. Chicago: Nelson Hall.

Harris, S.R., Kemmerling, R.L., & North, M.M. (2002). Brief virtual reality therapy for public speaking anxiety. *CyberPsychology and Behavior, 5* (6), 543–550.

Herbelin, B., Ponder, M., & Thalmann, D. (2005). Building exposure: Synergy of interaction and narration through the social channel. *Presence, 14*(2), 234–246.

Herbelin, B., Riquier, F., Vexo, F., & Thalmann, D. (2002). Virtual reality in cognitive behavioral therapy: A preliminary study on social anxiety disorder. In *8th International Conference on Virtual Systems and Multimedia, VSMM2002.*

Hodges, L.F., Rothbaum, B.O., Alarcon, R., Ready, D., Shahar, F., Graap, K., Pair, J., et al. (1999). A virtual environment for the treatment of chronic combat-related post-traumatic stress disorder. *Cyberpsychology and Behavior, 2* (1), 7–14.

Hunt, M., Fenton, M., Goldberg, A., Tran, T. (Unpublished). Cognitive therapy versus in vivo exposure in the treatment of specific phobia. *Journal of Behavior Therapy and Experimental Psychiatry.*

James, L.K., Lin, C.Y., Steed, A., Swapp, D., & Slater, M. (2003). Social anxiety in virtual environments: Results of a pilot study. *Cyberpsychology & Behavior, 6* (3), 237–243.

Jang, D.P., Kim, I.Y., Nam, S.W., Wiederhold, B.K., Wiederhold, M.D., & Kim, S.I., (2002). Analysis of physiological response to two virtual environments: Driving and flying simulation. *Cyberpsychology and Behavior, 5*(1), 11–18.

Kahan, M. (2000). Integration of psychodynamic and cognitive-behavioral therapy in a virtual environment. *CyberPsychology and Behavior, 3* (2), 179–183.

Kaplan, A. (2005). Virtually possible: Treating and preventing psychiatric wounds of war. *Psychiatric Times, XXII*(4): www.vrphobia.com/library/print/VRPOS.pdf.

Kennedy, R.S., Lane, N.E., Berbaum, K.S., & Lilienthal, M.G. (1993). Simulator Sickness Questionnaire: An enhanced method for quantifying simulator sickness. *International Journal of Aviation Psychology, 3* (3), 203–220.

Klein, R.A. (1998). Virtual reality exposure therapy (fear of flying): From a private practice perspective. *Cyberpsychology and Behavior, 1* (3), 311–316.

Klein, R.A. (1999). Treating fear of flying with virtual reality exposure therapy. In VandeCreek, L., & Jackson, T. (Eds.), *Innovations in clinical practice: A source book* (pp. 449–464). Sarasota, FL: Professional Resource Press / Professional Resource Exchange, Inc.

Klinger, E., Bouchard, S., Légeron, P., Roy, S., Lauer, F., Chemin, I., & Nugues, P. (2005). Virtual reality therapy for social phobia: A preliminary controlled study. *Cyberpsychoplogy and Behavior, 8*(1), 76–88.

Krijn, M., Emmelkamp, P.M.G., Biemond, R., de Wilde de Ligny, C, Schuemie, M.J., & van der Mast, C.A.P.G. (2004). Treatment of acrophobia in virtual reality: The role of immersion and presence. *Behaviour Research and Therapy, 42,* 229–239.

Lamson, R.J. (1997). *Virtual Therapy.* Montreal: Polytechnic International Press.

Lawson, B.D., Graeber, D.A., Mead, A.M., & Muth, E.R. (2002). Signs and symptoms of human syndromes associated with synthetic experiences. In Stanney, K.M. (Ed.), *Handbook of Virtual Environments: Design, Implementation, and Applications* (pp. 589–618). Mahwah, NJ: Lawrence Erlbaum Associates, Publishers.

Lee, J., Lim, Y., Graham, S.J., Kim, G., Wiederhold, B., Wiederhold, M., & Kim, S.I. (2004). Nicotine craving and cue exposure therapy by using virtual environments. *Cyberpsychology and Behavior, 7*(6), 705–713.

Lombard, M., & Ditton, T. (1997). At the heart of it all: The concept of presence. *Journal of Computer-Mediated Communication, 3*(2). Available at http://www.ascusc.org/jcmc/vol3/issue2/

Mager, R., Bullinger, A.H., Mueller-Spahn, F., Kuntze, M.F., & Stoermer, R. (2001). Real-time monitoring of brain activity in patients with specific phobia during exposure therapy, employing a stereoscopic virtual environment. *Cyberpsychology and Behavior, 4*(4), 465–469.

Maltby, N., Kirsch, I., Mayers, M., & Allen, G.J. (2002). Virtual reality exposure therapy for the treatment of fear of flying: A controlled investigation. *Journal of Consulting and Clinical Psychology, 70*(5), 1112–1118.

McCauley, M.E., & Sharkey, T.J. (1992). Cybersickness: Perception of self-motion in virtual environments. *Presence, 1*(3), 311–318.

McGlynn, F.D., Rose, M., & Lazarte, A. (1994). Control and attention during exposure influence arousal and fear among insect phobics. *Behavior Modification, 18,* 371–388.

McMinn, M.R., Buchanan, T., Ellens, B.M., & Ryan, M.K. (1999). Technology, professional psychology, and ethics: Survey findings and implications. *Professional Psychology: Research and Practice, 30*(2), 165–172.

Meehan, M. (2001). *Physiological reaction as an objective measure of presence in virtual environments.* Ph.D. Dissertation. Chapel Hill, University of North Carolina.

Michaud, M., Bouchard, S., Dumoulin, S., & Zhong, X.-W. (2004). Manipulating presence and its impact on anxiety. Paper presented at the Cybertherapy Conference 2004, San Diego, January 2004. In Wiederhold, B., Riva, G., & Wiederhold, M.D. (Eds.), *Cybertherapy 2004.* San Diego: Interactive Media Institute.

Miyahira, S.D. (2005). The maturing of virtual reality research in behavioural health: A meta-analysis and review. Paper presented at the Cybertherapy Conference 2005, June, Basel. In Wiederhold, B., Riva, G., & Bullinger, M.D. (Eds.), *Cybertherapy 2005.* San Diego: Interactive Media Institute.

Moore, K., Wiederhold, B.K., Wiederhold, M.D., & Riva, G. (2002). Panic and agoraphobia in a virtual world. *Cyberpsychology and Behavior, 5,* 197–202.

Mühlberger, A., Herrmann, M.J., Wiedemann, G., Ellgring, H., & Pauli, P. (2001). Repeated exposure of flight phobics to flights in virtual reality. *Behaviour Research and Therapy, 39,* 1033–1050.

Mühlberger, A., Wiedemann, G., & Pauli, P. (2003). Efficacy of a one-session virtual reality exposure treatment for fear of flying. *Psychotherapy Research, 13*(3), 323–336.

Mühlberger, A., Wiedemann, G., & Pauli, P. (2005). Subjective and physiologic reactions of flight phobics during VR exposure and treatment outcome: What adds motion simulation? Paper presented at the Cybertherapy Conference 2005, June, Basel. In Wiederhold, B., Riva, G., & Bullinger, M.D. (Eds.), *Cybertherapy 2005.* San Diego: Interactive Media Institute.

Norcross, J.C., Hedges, M., & Prochaska, J.O. (2002). The face of 2010: A delphi poll on the future of psychotherapy. *Professional Psychology: Research and Practice, 33*(3), 316–322.

North, M., North, S., & Coble, J.R. (1997). *Virtual reality therapy: An innovative paradigm.* Colorado Springs: IPI Press.

North, M., North, S., & Coble, J.R. (1998). Virtual reality therapy : An effective treatment for the fear of public speaking. *International Journal of Virtual Reality, 3*(2), 2–6.

Öst, L.G., Brandberg, M., & Alm, T. (1997). One versus five sessions of exposure in the treatment of flying phobia. *Behaviour Research & Therapy, 35,* 987–996.

Pertaub, D.P., Slater, M., & Barker, C. (2002). An experiment on public speaking anxiety in response to three different types of virtual audience. *Presence: Teleoperators and Virtual Environments.* 11 (1):68–78.

Pratt, D.R., Zyda, M., & Kelleher, K. (1995). Virtual reality: In the mind of the beholder. *IEEE Computer, 28*(7), 17–19.

Renaud, P., Bouchard, S., & Proulx., R. (2002). Behavioral dynamics in the presence of a virtual spider. *IEEE Transactions on Information Technology in Biomedicine, 6*(3), 235–243.

Ressler, K.J., Rothbaum, B.O., Tannenbaum, L., Anderson, P., Graap, K., Zimand, E., Hodges, L., & Davis, M. (2004). Cognitive enhancers as adjuncts to psychotherapy. *Archives of General Psychiatry, 61,* 1136–1144.

Richard, D.C.S. & Lauterbach, D. (2004). Computers in the training and practice of behavioral assessment. In S.N. Haynes and E.M. Heiby (Eds.), Comprehensive Hanbook of Psychological Assessment (pp. 222–245). Hoboken, NJ, John Wiley and Sons.

Riquier, F., Herbelin, B., & Chevalley, F. (2005). Thérapies par réalité virtuelle dans le traitement et l'évaluation clinique de la phobie sociale. Paper presented at the 11th *Congrès de l'Association Francophone de Formation et de Recherche en Thérapie Comportementale et Cognitive.* June 2005, Aix-les-Bains.

Riva, G., Bacchetta, M., Baruffi, M., & Molinari, E. (2002). Virtual-reality-based multidimensional therapy for the treatment of body image disturbance in binge eating disorders: A preliminary controlled study. *IEEE Transactions on Information Technology in Biomedicine, 6*(1), 224–234.

Rizzo, A.A., Neumann, U., Pintaric, T., & Norden, M. (2001). Issues for application development using immersive HMD 360 degree panoramic video environments. In Smith, M.J., Salvendy, G., Harriss,

G., & Koubek R.J. (Eds.), *Usability evaluation and interface design* (Vol. 1, pp. 792–796). New York: L.A. Erlbaum.

Robillard, G., Bouchard, S., Fournier, T., & Renaud, P. (2003). Anxiety and presence during VR immersion: A comparative study of the reactions of phobic and non-phobic participants in therapeutic virtual environments derived from computer games. *CyberPsychology and Behavior, 6*(5), 467–476.

Rothbaum, B.O., Anderson, P., Zimand, E., Hodges, L., Lang, D., & Wilson, J. (In press). Virtual reality exposure therapy and standard (in vivo) exposure therapy in the treatment for the fear of flying. *Behavior Therapy*.

Rothbaum, B.A., Hodges, L.F., Alarcon, R., Ready, D., Shahar, F., Graap, K., et al. (1999). Virtual reality exposure therapy for PTSD Vietnam veterans: A case study. *Journal of Traumatic Stress, 12*(2), 263–271.

Rothbaum, B.A., Hodges, L.F., Anderson, P.L., Price, L., & Smith, S. (2002). Twelve-month follow-up of virtual reality and standard exposure therapies for the fear of flying. *Journal of Consulting and Clinical Psychology, 70* (2), 428–432.

Rothbaum, B.A., Hodges, L.F., & Kooper, R. (1997). Virtual reality exposure therapy. *Journal of Psychotherapy Practice, 6,* 219–226.

Rothbaum, B.A., Hodges, L.F., Kooper, R., Opdyke D., Williford, J.S., & North, M. (1995). Effectiveness of computer-generated (Virtual Reality) graded exposure in the treatment of acrophobia. *American Journal of Psychiatry, 152,* 626–628.

Rothbaum, B.O., Hodges, L., Ready, D., Graap, K., & Alarcon, R. (2001). Virtual reality exposure therapy for Vietnam veterans with posttraumatic stress disorder. *Journal of Clinical Psychiatry, 62,* 617–622.

Rothbaum, B.A., Hodges, L.F., Smith, S., Lee, J.H., & Price, L. (2000). A controlled study of virtual reality exposure therapy for the fear of flying. *Journal of Consulting and Clinical Psychology, 68* (6), 1020–1026.

Rothbaum, B.A., Hodges, L.F., Watson, B.A., Kessler, G.D., & Opdyke, D. (1996). Virtual reality exposure therapy in the treatment of fear of flying: A case report. *Behavior Research and Therapy, 34,* 477–481.

Sadowski, W., & Stanney, K. (2002). Presence in virtual environments. In Stanney, K.M. (Ed.), *Handbook of virtual environments: Design, implementation, and applications* (pp. 791–806). Mahwah, NJ: Lawrence Elbaum Associates, Publishers.

Slater, M., Pertaub, D.P., Barker, C., & Clark, D. (2004). An experimental study on fear of public speaking using a virtual environment. In *3rd International Workshop on Virtual Rehabilitation*. Lausanne, Switzerland.

Stanney, K.M. (2002), *Handbook of virtual environments. Design, implementation, and applications.* Mahwah, NJ: Lawrence Erlbaum Associates, Publishers.

Stanney, K.M., Mourant, R.R., & Kennedy, R.S. (1998). Human factors issues in virtual environments: A review of the literature. *Presence, 7*(4), 327–351.

St.-Jacques, J., & Bouchard, S. (2005). Clinical applications of virtual reality and cybersickness. Paper presented at the Cybertherapy Conference 2005, June, Basel. In Wiederhold, B., Riva, G., & Bullinger, M.D. (Eds.), *Cybertherapy 2005.* San Diego: Interactive Media Institute.

St.-Jacques, J., Bouchard, S., & Renaud, P. (2004). Long-term effectiveness of in VR exposure for phobic children. Paper presented at Cybertherapy Conference 2004, San Diego, January 2004. In Wiederhold, B., Riva, G., & Wiederhold, M.D. (Eds.), *Cybertherapy 2004.* San Diego: Interactive Media Institute.

Szymanski, J., & O'Donoghue, W. (1995). Fear of spiders questionnaire. *Journal of Behaviour Therapy and Experimental Psychiatry, 26* (1), 31–34.

Thorpe, S.J., & Salkovskis, P.M. (1997). The effect of one-session treatment for spider phobia on attentional bias and beliefs. *British Journal of Clinical Psychology, 36,* 225–241.

Tisseau, J., & Harrouet, F. (2003). Autonomie des entités virtuelles. In Fuchs P. (Ed.), *Le traité de la réalité virtuelle* (2nd ed.). Paris: École des Mines de Paris.

Vincelli, F., Anolli, L., Bouchard, S., Wiederhold, B.K., Zurloni, V., & Riva, G. (2003). Experiential cognitive therapy in the treatment of panic disorder with agoraphobia: A controlled study. *CyberPsychology and Behavior, 6*(3), 321–328.

Wald, J. (2004). Efficacy of virtual reality exposure therapy for driving phobia: A multiple baseline across-subjects design. *Behavior Therapy, 35*(3), 621–635.

Wald, J., & Taylor, S. (2003). Preliminary research on the efficacy of virtual reality exposure therapy to treat driving phobia. *CyberPsychology & Behavior, 6*(5), 459–465.

Wald, J., & Taylor, S. (2000). Efficacy of virtual reality exposure therapy to treat driving phobia: A case report. *Journal of Behavior Therapy and Experimental Psychiatry, 31*(3–4), 249–257.

Walshe, D.G., Lewis, E.J., Kim, S.I., O'Sullivan, K., & Wiederhold, B.K. (2003). Exploring the use of computer games and virtual reality in exposure therapy for fear of driving following a motor vehicle accident. *CyberPsychology & Behavior, 6*(3), 329–334.

Wiederhold, B.K., Jang, D.P., Gevirtz, R.G., Kim, S.I., Kim, I.Y., & Wiederhold, M.D. (2002). The treatment of fear of flying: A controlled study of imaginal and virtual reality graded exposure therapy. *IEEE Transactions on Information Technology in Biomedicine, 6,* 218–223.

Wiederhold, B.K., & Wiederhold, M.D. (1999). Clinical observations during virtual reality therapy for specific phobias. *CyberPsychology and Behavior, 2* (2), 161–168.

Wiederhold, B.K., & Wiederhold, M.D. (2000). Lessons learned from 600 virtual reality sessions. *CyberPsychology & Behavior, 3* (3), 393–401.

Wiederhold, B.K., & Wiederhold, M.D. (2003). Three-year follow-up for virtual reality exposure for fear of flying. *Cyberpsycholy and Behavior, 6*(4), 441–44.

Wiederhold, B.K., & Wiederhold, M.D. (2005). *Virtual reality therapy for anxiety disorders.* Washington, D.C.: American Psychological Association.

Wiederhold, B.K., Wiederhold, M.D., Jang, D.P., & Kim, S.I. (2000). Use of cellular telephone therapy for fear of driving. *CyberPsychology & Behavior, 3,* 1031–1039.

Witmer, B.G., & Singer, M.J. (1998). Measuring presence in virtual environments: A presence questionnaire. *Presence, 7* (3), 225–240.

Zimmons, S. (2004). Anxiety and image characteristics in virtual environments. The Virtual-Pit experiment. Ph. D. Dissertation. Preliminary results. Chapel Hill, University of North Carolina.

CHAPTER 17

Obstacles to Successful Implementation of Exposure Therapy

Elizabeth A. Hembree and
Shawn P. Cahill
University of Pennsylvania

In considering obstacles to clinicians' use of exposure therapy, two different types of barriers come to mind. First, the majority of therapists simply do not use evidence-based treatments such as exposure therapy, even when they are aware of their existence. Second, implementing exposure therapy in an effective or optimal manner is often easier said than done. Even when the exposure therapist has the benefit of good training and detailed treatment manuals, many clients with anxiety disorders present significant challenges in therapy. In this chapter, we address both of these issues. We begin by considering the problem of dissemination: why do so many therapists not use exposure therapy, an intervention that now has several decades of strong empirical support? We will then discuss some commonly encountered clinical challenges in implemewnting effective exposure treatment, and make recommendations for how to surmount these.

THE DISSEMINATION BARRIER

Despite the clear evidence for the efficacy of exposure therapy as a primary intervention in the treatment of specific phobias, obsessive-compulsive disorder (OCD), post-traumatic stress disorder, and acute stress disorder, as well evidence for the efficacy of cognitive behavior programs in which exposure is a major component for the treatment of panic disorder (PD), social anxiety disorder (SAD), and generalized

Handbook of Exposure Therapies
389

anxiety disorder, surprisingly few therapists use exposure therapy in treating their clients with anxiety disorders. For example, in one survey of licensed doctoral level psychologists who regularly treated anxiety disorders, Freihei, Vye, Swan, and Cady (2004) asked respondents to specify which of several specific exposure therapy procedures they used in the treatment of OCD, PD, and social phobia (e.g., exposure and response prevention in the treatment of OCD; interoceptive exposure in the treatment of PD; in vivo exposure and the use of group cognitive-behavioral therapy (CBT) in the treatment of SAD). They also inquired about respondents' use of nonexposure therapy interventions (e.g., cognitive restructuring, breathing retraining, relaxation training, bibliotherapy).

A strong majority of the respondents (71%) identified their theoretical orientation as "cognitive-behavioral," and an even greater number reported they had received training in CBT for anxiety (91%) and used CBT (88%) in the treatment of anxiety disorders. The most common reason given for using CBT, endorsed by 74% of the respondents, was that CBT was supported by research evidence. Yet, among therapists who had treated the three target disorders (OCD, SAD, PD), results of the survey revealed a considerable discrepancy between the specific treatments these therapists reported using, and recommendations derived from the APA Division 12 Task Force review of empirically supported treatments (American Psychological Association, 1995; Chambless, Sanderson, Shohma, Johnson, Pope, Crits-Christoph, et al., 1996; Chambless, Baker, Baucom, Beutler, Calhoun, Crits-Christoph, et al., 1998).

In the treatment of OCD, 67% of respondents frequently used cognitive restructuring and 41% frequently used relaxation training, whereas only 38% frequently used exposure and response prevention. In the treatment of PD, 71% of respondents frequently used cognitive restructuring and relaxation, but only 12% frequently used interoceptive exposure. In fact, 76% of respondents indicated they *rarely or never* used interoceptive exposure in the treatment of PD. In the treatment of SAD, 69% of respondents frequently used cognitive restructuring and 59% frequently used relaxation training, yet only 31% frequently used self-directed in vivo exposure and even fewer frequently used therapist-directed in vivo exposure (7%) or group CBT specifically targeting social anxiety (1%).

In another survey of licensed doctoral level psychologists, Becker, Zayfert, and Anderson (2003) inquired about the use of imaginal exposure therapy in the treatment of post-traumatic stress disorder (PTSD). Their sample of respondents included two groups: the main sample of participants was recruited through random selection of psychologists from listings provided by state licensing boards for two northeastern states, and in two major cities in the state of Texas. The second sample of participants was recruited from the Disaster and Trauma Special Interest Group (D&T SIG) of the Association for Advancement of Behavior Therapy. Most respondents in both samples reported having treated 11 or more clients with PTSD and, not surprisingly, somewhat more of the D&T SIG respondents (79%) had treated at least 11 PTSD clients in comparison to the main sample respondents (63%).

Given that exposure therapy has been designated as a first-choice intervention for treatment of PTSD on the weight of empirical evidence (Rothbaum, Meadows, Resick, & Foy, 2000) and by expert consensus (Foa, Davidson, & Frances, 1999), the results obtained by Becker, et al. Were disquieting: 83% of therapists from the main sample said they *never* used imaginal exposure in the treatment of their clients with PTSD; only 9% reported that they used it with at least 50% of their PTSD cases. D&T SIG members were more likely to use imaginal exposure in their treatment of clients with PTSD, but 34% indicated they had *never* used it, and only 55% said they used it with at least 50% of their cases.

Of importance, Becker, et al. (2003) also investigated the reasons that therapists did not use imaginal exposure in the treatment of PTSD. By far, the most common reason endorsed for not using imaginal exposure was limited training (60%), followed by therapist preference for "individualized treatment" over manualized treatment (25%) and concern that exposure treatment may cause clients to decompensate (22%). Formal training and degree of experience treating PTSD were both associated with higher use of imaginal exposure. A total of 28% of the main sample, and 93% of the D&T SIG sample reported receiving some training in imaginal exposure for PTSD. Among those who reported receiving such training, 54% had used it at least once, and those therapists with more experience in treating PTSD were more likely to use it with at least half of their clients (41%) than therapists with less experience (12%). A smaller percentage of therapists in both samples reported receiving training in exposure therapy for other anxiety disorders (12% and 45% for the main and D&T SIG samples, respectively).

The data described previously clearly demonstrate that most therapists do not provide exposure therapy to clients suffering from anxiety disorders. They further suggest that a significant barrier to clients receiving the benefits of exposure therapy is lack of training: most therapists have not been trained in the specific techniques of exposure therapy. Moreover, it appears that to be effective, training in exposure therapy must also address therapists' concerns about the safety of exposure therapy, as well as their hesitations about using treatment manuals.

MYTHS AND MANUALIZED TREATMENTS

The preceding findings, although recent, are not new. Barlow (1996) and Barlow, Levitt, and Bufka (1999) discussed barriers to successful dissemination of efficacious psychosocial interventions for a variety of disorders. Two important barriers identified by Barlow, et al. (1999) concerned myths and misconceptions about randomized clinical trials that seem to dissuade clinicians from learning to use these treatments, and the logistical challenges of training clinicians in the use of these treatments.

Myths

Common myths that are sometimes discussed in the clinical literature and are often further propagated in presentations and discussions during professional conferences include the ideas that (1) participants in randomized trials are easy, straightforward treatment cases with a single diagnosis and no significant comorbidity; (2) the results of treatment outcome studies, based on these simple, rarified samples of patients, will not generalize to real-world settings; and (3) exposure can be harmful, and will make people worse, or cause them to dropout from treatment.

Good research methodology includes the specification of inclusion and exclusion criteria. In an attempt to generate results that *are* generalizable, however, most recent studies of cognitive behavioral treatments have minimal exclusions, and those that are applied are typically dictated by good clinical judgment. In addition, many recent studies have specifically focused on outcomes obtained with samples characterized by comorbidity of other Axis I and II disorders. Overall, the research suggests that many patients with comorbid conditions benefit from treatment, although in some studies, the presence of severe comorbid pathology may reduce the efficacy of treatment for the target disorder relative to those without significant comorbidity. This has been shown for treatment of PTSD (Feeny, Zoellner, & Foa, 2002; Hembree, Cahill, & Foa, 2004), panic disorder (Brown, Anthony, & Barlow, 1995), generalized anxiety disorder (Borkovec, Abel, & Newman, 1995), and OCD (Abramowitz, Franklin, Street, Kozak, & Foa, 2000). Moreover, there is recent evidence that treatment of the target disorder can result in concomitant improvement on comorbid conditions (e.g., Blanchard, Hickling, Devineni, Veazey, Galovski, Mundy, et al., 2003; Tsao, Mystkowki, Zucker, & Craske, 2005). Other studies have shown that the outcome obtained with nonresearch or "clinic" patients is comparable to that obtained with patients in randomized clinical trials for OCD (Franklin, Abramowitz, Kozak, Levitt, & Foa, 2000) and social phobia (Juster, Heimberg, & Engelberg, 1995).

Safety and Tolerability of Exposure

The myth that exposure is harmful and is associated with poorer outcome and high rates of premature dropout from treatment warrants close examination. This concern has understandably led to reluctance on the part of many clinicians to learn and use this treatment. Nowhere in recent years has concern about the safety of exposure therapy been expressed more frequently than in its use in the treatment of PTSD.

Until recently, the basis of these concerns was primarily case reports and published cautionary statements, without any systematic research into the frequency of such incidents and whether such cases of symptom worsening really are associated with relatively poor outcome. For example, Kilpatrick and Best (1984) warned readers that imaginal exposure may exacerbate fear and anxiety, thus retraumatizing the clients. Their concerns were subsequently reinforced by the interpretation of results from several case reports and studies. Pitman, Altman, Greenwald, Longpre, Macklin, Poire, et al. (1991) described six cases of Vietnam veterans who were treated unsuccessfully with imaginal exposure that emphasized maximal arousal (flooding) and suggested that flooding may increase PTSD and related symptoms. In discussing results of a later dismantling study of eye movement desensitization and reprocessing (EMDR), Pitman, Orr, Altman, Longpre, Poire, and Macklin (1996) speculated that EMDR was better tolerated than flooding by patients *and* therapists because it was less anxiety provoking and less likely to produce negative consequences in comparison to exposure therapy. Notably, Pitman, et al. (1996) did not make a direct comparison of these two procedures, and thus their statements were not based on direct empirical evidence (cf. Cahill & Frueh, 1997). Such statements are nonetheless influential in maintaining clinicians' fears and concerns about the harmfulness of exposure therapy.

Some investigators have addressed the issues of exposure-related symptom worsening and its impact on outcome and attrition more directly. Tarrier, Pilgrim, Sommerfield, Faragher, Reynolds, Graham, et al. (1999) compared imaginal exposure therapy and cognitive therapy in the treatment of PTSD. Participants were randomly assigned to a treatment condition and provided up to 16 one-hour weekly therapy sessions. Results revealed that the imaginal exposure and cognitive therapy conditions did not differ on percentage of subjects dropping out of active treatment, incidence of PTSD at post-treatment, or post-treatment severity on measures of PTSD, depression, and anxiety. However, a significantly greater percentage of treatment completers receiving imaginal exposure obtained a post-treatment PTSD severity score, as measured by the Clinician Administered PTSD Scale (CAPS; Blake, Weathers, Nagy, Kaloupek, Gusman, Charney, & Keane, 1995), that was one or more points higher than their pretreatment score (31%) than those receiving cognitive therapy (10%). This difference disappeared at 6-month follow-up evaluation. On the basis of this result, Tarrier, et al. (1999) reported that imaginal exposure was more likely to lead to symptom worsening in a small percentage of patients.

Several cautions are warranted in interpreting the Tarrier, et al. (1999) results. First, as noted by Devilly and Foa (2001), an increase of one point on the CAPS is within the measurement error of the instrument. Thus, without additional information about the magnitude of the change, it is not clear whether these participants actually displayed symptom worsening or rather, failed to show symptom improvement. Second, because of the absence of a wait-list control group during the treatment period, it is not clear whether the difference between the two treatments reflects an increase in the percentage of participants that either show symptom worsening or failure to improve in the exposure therapy group, or a greater decrease in the cognitive therapy condition. And third, their relatively high rate of participants showing an increase in post-treatment scores has not been replicated in three recent CBT studies for the treatment of PTSD that have reported relevant data.

Gillespie, Duffy, Hackmann, and Clark (2002) administered a multi-component cognitive therapy program that included the use of cognitive restructuring, brief imaginal exposures, and behavioral experiments based on Ehlers and Clark's (2000) cognitive theory of PTSD to survivors of a 1998 terrorist car bombing in the Northern Ireland city of Omagh. *All* participants showed a minimum 20% *reduction* in PTSD severity. Cloitre, Koenen, Cohen, and Han (2002) randomly assigned female survivors of childhood assault with chronic PTSD to treatment with 8 weekly sessions of skills training in affect and interpersonal regulation followed by 8 weekly sessions of imaginal exposure to the trauma memory or to wait list. Among completers only one person (4.5%) showed symptom worsening in the treatment condition, compared with six (25%) in the wait-list condition, although the group difference was not statistically significant. Taylor, Thordarson, Maxfield, Federoff, Lovell, and Ogrodniczuk, (2003) randomly assigned men and women trauma survivors with chronic PTSD following a range of traumas to 8 weekly sessions of imaginal plus in vivo exposure therapy, EMDR, or relaxation training. At the end of treatment, there were no cases of symptom worsening in the exposure therapy condition and one case in each of EMDR (7%) and relaxation (7%).

In addition to these published studies, Cahill, Riggs, Rauch, and Foa (2003) presented results of additional analyses of data from a study in which female survivors of physical and sexual assault occurring in adulthood were randomly assigned to exposure therapy alone, stress inoculation training alone (a form of anxiety management training that does not involve intentional exposure to trauma memories or reminders), the combination of exposure plus stress inoculation training, or wait list (Foa, Dancu, Hembree, Jaycox, Meadows, & Street, 1999). Of 79 treatment completers, only two showed an increase on PTSD severity, one in the wait-list condition (6.7%) and one in the combined exposure therapy plus stress inoculation training condition (4.5).

Using data from a study comparing the outcome of women with chronic PTSD treated with either prolonged exposure (PE) alone or exposure combined with cognitive restructuring (PE/CR; Foa, Hembree, Cahill, Rauch, Riggs, Feeny, et al., 2005), Foa, Zoellner, Feeny, Hembree, and Alvarez-Conrad (2002) took advantage of a unique design feature to investigate reliable symptom worsening during treatment, its relationship with the initiation of imaginal exposure, and its association with treatment outcome and dropout. All participants completed self-report measures of PTSD, anxiety, and depression at pretreatment and the beginning of Sessions 2, 4, and 6. In vivo exposure was initiated in Session 2, and imaginal exposure to trauma memories was initiated in Session 3 or 4. Thus Foa, et al. (2002) were able to investigate the incidence of reliable worsening of PTSD, anxiety, and depression occurring between Sessions 2 and 4. Moreover, because participants had been randomly assigned to begin imaginal exposure in either Session 3 or Session 4, we were able to determine if there was an association between initiating imaginal exposure and the percentage of participants showing reliable symptom worsening. Results indicated that the majority of participants did not show any symptom worsening across measures of PTSD (85% and 97% for PE and PE/CR conditions respectively), anxiety (72% and 91%), and depression (87% and 97%). Results also indicated that reliable worsening did occur in a minority of participants, and such worsening was associated with the initiation of imaginal exposure therapy.

Of importance, however, participants who showed symptom worsening early in therapy were not more likely to dropout out from treatment (15%) than participants who did not experience symptom worsening (17%). Moreover, treatment outcome was not different for participants who showed symptom worsening compared to those who did not. Such findings have led us to tell clients early in treatment that while exposure has been shown to be effective at reducing symptoms for many people, "you may be one of those who feels worse before you feel better, but this doesn't mean that you won't *get* better."

In addition to concerns about exposure-induced symptom exacerbations, many have voiced concern that exposure therapy is associated with greater dropout from treatment. To investigate whether PTSD patients have particular difficulty tolerating exposure therapy, Hembree, Foa, Dorfan, Street, Kowalski, and Tu (2003) examined dropout rates across different conditions in 25 controlled trials of cognitive behavioral treatments for PTSD. The average rate of dropout was 20.6% from exposure only treatments, 22.1% from cognitive therapy and anxiety management conditions, 26.0% from combinations of exposure and cognitive therapy or anxiety management, and 18.9% from EMDR. No difference in dropout rate among these active treatments was detected. These findings suggest that using the criterion of premature termination, all cognitive behavioral treatments for PTSD are equally tolerable. Control treatments, including wait list, supportive counseling, and relaxation, seem more tolerable to patients, as the average dropout was only 11.4%.

An important remaining question, however, is how the 20.6% average dropout rate from exposure therapy for PTSD compares with dropout rates in other diagnostic groups. Heimberg, Liebowitz, Hope, Schneier, Holt, and Welkowitz (1998) reported a 19.5% dropout rate from CBT among clients diagnosed with social phobia; and Barlow, Gorman, Shear, and Woods (2000) reported a 28% dropout rate among panic-disordered clients. Overall, these dropout rates are most likely comparable to or lower than dropout rates found in regular outpatient, nonstudy treatments. Indeed, Persons, Burns, and Perloff (1998) reported a dropout rate of 50% among depressed clients who received cognitive therapy in a private practice setting.

With regard to medication treatment, a meta-analysis of 19 medication trials for PTSD by Van Etten and Taylor (1998) found an average dropout rate of 32% for active treatment and, in four trials, 23% for placebo. Six large-scale, placebo-controlled studies of medication for PTSD published, as the Van Etten and Taylor meta-analysis found dropout rates from active medications (fluoxetine, sertraline, and paroxetine) ranged between 22% and 38% and dropout from placebo ranged between 27% and 41% (Brady, Pearlstein, Asnis, Baker, Rothbaum, Sikes, et al., 2000; Connor, Sutherland, Tupler, Malik, & Davidson, et al., 1999; Davidson, Rothbaum, van der Kolk, Sikes, & Farfel, 2001; Marshall, Beebe, Oldham, & Zaninelli, 2001; Martenyi, Brown, Zhang, Prakash, & Koke, 2002; Tucker, Zaninelli, Yehuda, Ruggiero, Dillingham, & Pitts, 2001). Thus similar dropout rates seem to occur across a range of disorders and treatment conditions, although dropout may be higher from active psychotherapy than control conditions. Medication and active psychotherapy yield dropout rates similar to one another and to placebo medication.

Not only is exposure therapy as well tolerated as other treatments, female college students with PTSD given descriptions of exposure therapy and medication (sertraline) as treatments for PTSD expressed a nearly 4:1 preference for exposure therapy (Zoellner, Feeny, Cochran, & Pruitt, 2003). Although this study did not include other psychotherapy options and therefore may reflect a generic preference for psychotherapy over medication, the description of exposure apparently did not scare off large numbers of subjects.

The second important barrier to dissemination of evidence-based treatments discussed by Barlow, et al. (1999) concerned the logistical challenges of training clinicians in the use of these treatments. Two immediate questions arise when considering this issue: First, do clinicians want to be trained in these methods? And second, how is training in empirically supported treatments like exposure therapy most effectively provided?

Treatment Manuals

As described previously, Becker, et al. (2003) found that the two primary reasons clinicians reported not using exposure therapy were lack of training and reluctance to use manualized treatments. The latter concern appears to be generally common. Addis and Krasnow (2000) surveyed more than 800 members of the American Psychological Association about their experiences with, and attitudes toward, use of treatment manuals. Results showed that many psychologists had negative opinions about the use of manualized treatments, especially with regard to their effect on the process of psychotherapy. Many endorsed the view that use of treatment manuals would dehumanize the therapy process, or make the therapist more like a technician than a caring clinician.

This concern is important and valid. It can be difficult to learn to use therapy manuals, especially for clinicians who have not had the benefit of such training in their graduate school program or internship experiences. In the Center for the Treatment & Study of Anxiety (CTSA) at the University of Pennsylvania, we have trained many clinicians in the use of manualized exposure therapy for treatment of OCD, PTSD, and other anxiety disorders. It has been our experience that even experienced, skilled clinicians often go through a period of awkwardness in learning to use treatment manuals. The complexities are many. First, one must understand and operate from a clear conceptual model, one that may be new to the clinician. Next, one must know the treatment manual thoroughly, which often requires considerable investment of time in reading and practicing. The therapist must then apply the manualized treatment to clients while tailoring the interventions to each individual presentation. Finally, the therapist must remember throughout that first and foremost, he or she is a therapist and must bring into the session all of the basic therapy and relationship skills that form the foundation of any effective treatment process.

We have observed that for many therapists, this is just plain difficult. It often takes much practice to implement a manualized treatment while simultaneously providing the empathy and warmth and consistent attention to the therapeutic alliance that is so important in psychotherapy. Although it is a misconception that following treatment manuals dehumanizes the therapy process, tailoring the interventions of a treatment manual to the individual client while simultaneously "being a therapist" requires practice and skill. It is the "art" of effective use of treatment manuals and is built on knowledge and experience. How does one acquire this skill?

Training

Instruction in evidence-based treatment interventions takes place at many levels: graduate programs, internships, postdoctoral fellowships, continuing education trainings and seminars, and on-the-job experience. There is huge variability in the depth, focus, and quality of training at all levels. For clinicians who have completed their basic education and are already out working in the field, it can be particularly difficult to acquire the training necessary to instill confidence in using treatments such as exposure therapy. Most continuing education (CE) courses for licensing requirements are brief; 3 hours to 1 or 2 days is common. Unfortunately but perhaps not surprisingly, research has shown that brief CE courses generally do not lead to changes in practice behavior of participants (e.g., Davis, Thomson, Oxman, & Haynes, 1992). The training in delivery of empirically supported treatments that is provided in academic treatment clinics is much more involved.

For example, in the CTSA, our currently recommended method of training in PE therapy for treatment of PTSD begins with a 3- or 4-day intensive workshop that includes extensive didactics, discussion of underlying theory and empirical support, readings and a detailed treatment manual, demonstrations of therapy components by expert trainers via role-plays and videotaped therapy sessions, and role-play practice among participants with trainer observation and feedback. We then recommend that the trainee use PE with one or two PTSD clients while receiving session-by-session supervision from a PE expert, often via videotaped or audiotaped sessions.

Our experience has been that even after an intensive course such as described here, on-going consultation or supervision of the first case or two is often quite important in bolstering therapists' confidence in implementing exposure therapy. This level of training is not unusual in clinical research centers such as the CTSA, but is certainly not common in community settings. Yet to effectively disseminate exposure therapy and other evidence-based treatments to community clinicians and others working outside of academic research clinics, it is imperative that we develop cost-effective and broadly obtainable methods of training that really do change the practice behaviors of clinicians.

THE IMPLEMENTATION BARRIER

Successful exposure therapy is rooted in a strong foundation. As in most forms of CBT, a good foundation for exposure therapy has several cornerstones: a firm grounding in the conceptual model of treatment; a strong, collaborative, therapeutic alliance; a clear and compelling rationale for treatment; and effective implementation of the exposure techniques. After discussing these cornerstones, we present some commonly encountered challenges in implementing in vivo and imaginal exposure, and offer some guidance about how to navigate these to promote effective engagement with and habituation of excessive fear.

Strong Foundation

It is hard for people to confront and overcome their fears. If it were easy, most individuals probably would not be in your office seeking professional help. Usually, they have tried to face their fears and failed, or succeeded only a minority of the time, and at great emotional cost. These cornerstones—conceptualization, alliance, rationale, and effective implementation—are all integral to the process of good exposure therapy and helping people do things that will reduce their excessive fear.

Conceptual model of treatment

Detailed treatment manuals are valuable tools for an exposure therapist. But even more important is a clear understanding of the principles and aims underlying the procedures and techniques specified in those manuals. It is often this conceptual grounding that will guide the therapist's decision-making when choices are presented. For example, when building an effective in vivo exposure hierarchy for a person with phobia of heights, the therapist must be guided by the aim of matching the exposure situations with the individual's specific fear structure. Foa and Kozak (1986), in their seminal paper on emotional processing of fear, built on Peter Lang's work. They proposed that fear and anxiety signal the activation of a cognitive structure that serves as a program for escaping danger. This fear structure includes information about the feared stimulus; the verbal, physiological, and behavioral responses to the feared stimulus; and the meaning of the stimulus and response elements of the structure. Fear structures can be quite useful and enhance survival by leading to appropriate responses to threat.

When fear becomes pathological, according to Foa and Kozak, the fear structure includes (1) excessive response elements, so that the fear is very intense (e.g., extensive avoidance and hyperarousal); (2) associations among stimuli and responses that do not accurately represent reality (e.g., "all heights can be fallen from," "avoid being higher than I could survive if I fall"); and (3) incorrect interpretations such as "so, driving across tall bridges and riding in elevators is never safe." They suggested that treatment of such pathological fear requires (1) accessing the fear structure (i.e., bringing the person into contact with the feared and avoided situation in some way so that this fear network is triggered) and (2) providing corrective information or a "safe experience" that serves to modify the excessive or unrealistic aspects of the fear structure. In the example of the height phobic, this treatment would likely entail (1) gradual exposure to increasingly high places and (2) remaining unharmed (i.e., not falling from these heights), thus modifying the belief that all heights are dangerous.

Understanding the conceptual model underlying exposure treatment will guide the therapist's construction of an in vivo hierarchy, will help the therapist provide a rationale that makes sense to the client and will bolster the client's courage in choosing to approach heights rather than avoid them, and will help the therapist know how to respond to the client's struggles with avoidance behavior.

Therapeutic alliance

A critical component of any therapy is a strong therapeutic alliance. When working with clients with anxiety disorders, alliance can be promoted in several ways. First, it is important to acknowledge the client's courage in entering a therapy designed to help him or her face and overcome strong fears. The therapist should clearly align himself or herself with the client in supporting this endeavor and sometimes against the disorder. Second, using specific examples from the client's fears and symptoms when presenting education and treatment rationale in the early sessions of therapy conveys that the therapist has been listening, and is tailoring this treatment to the client's unique situation. Third, in constructing an in vivo hierarchy or planning targets for imaginal exposure to trauma memories, be collaborative. During joint decision-making, the therapist guides and makes recommendations while incorporating the client's judgment regarding the aims and pace of therapy. Finally, provide plenty of support, encouragement, and positive feedback. We often do the exposures right along side the client, thus both modeling exposure and supporting and encouraging the client. For example, working with a client with OCD-related fears of contamination, we often eat our lunches right off the office floor alongside the client, after touching the toilet flush handles and faucets with our hands along with the client.

Clear and compelling rationale for treatment

For anxiety-disordered clients, a good deal of exposure takes place outside of the therapist's office and out of the therapist's eyesight. Helping the client to understand and appreciate the rationale for treatment is critical to the success of exposure therapy, as the client must accept the rationale in order to follow the therapy plan both in and out of session. As discussed previously, being thoroughly grounded in the conceptual model underlying exposure therapy helps the therapist present a convincing rationale. It is also helpful to inform the client that research has shown exposure to be highly effective at reducing excessive fear (or the symptoms of the specific disorder that is the focus of treatment), and that the therapist is knowledgeable about the use of this treatment.

Some clients are uncertain about whether this approach will work for *them*. Some will say they have tried and failed to face their fears, or that they did face them, but their anxiety did not diminish. For clients who are uncertain about the efficacy of this treatment, the therapist should describe the treatment with the goal of helping the client see that the approach at least makes sense intellectually. With skeptics, acknowledge the difficulty of accepting the rationale while at the same time emphasizing that (1) facing, rather than avoiding, feared but low risk or safe situations repeatedly or for a long time will result in an eventual decrease in anxiety and will improve ability to discriminate safe or low risk from harmful situations; (2) avoidance prevents opportunities to learn this, and strengthens the urges to avoid; and (3) successfully confronting feared situations (or memories) and experiencing habituation is powerfully reinforcing, reduces symptoms, and makes people feel competent. Often, full acceptance—emotional acceptance—of these ideas requires *doing* the first few exposures and experiencing the results. Using analogies or metaphors is also often helpful in presenting a convincing rationale.

After hearing the rationale for confronting rather than avoiding feared situations, occasionally a client will say: "but I have tried that and it didn't work." "I *have* ridden in elevators but my fear has never decreased." In these cases it is often useful for the therapist to clarify the distinction between occasional, brief exposures and deliberate, repeated, prolonged exposures to feared situations. The therapist should explain that only the latter is effective in ameliorating phobia or excessive fear, and that together they will take a look at how the client has been trying to face his or her fears, with the aim of figuring out what is interfering with habituation or learning.

Implementing Exposure Effectively

Tailoring treatment interventions to the individual client's fear structure is key to successful exposure therapy. Throughout all phases of treatment—the initial evaluation, psychoeducation, and exposure sessions—the therapist should listen for the client's specific fears and avoidance behaviors, both passive and active. Many clients are not aware of their avoidance behavior, particularly when it has been long-standing and habitual, so the therapist may need to teach the client to recognize avoidance patterns.

In vivo exposure

Effective in vivo exposure begins with generating a list of situations or items that the person fears and avoids (or endures if necessary, but as briefly as possible) in an effort not to trigger the pathological fear. These situations are typically ranked according to their ability to elicit increasing levels of fear or distress. It is useful to maximize the potential for a successful learning experience early in treatment by carefully selecting the first few in vivo exposure assignments. For example, the first session in which we assign in vivo exposure homework to PTSD clients, we try to select a situation that the client has a high likelihood of successfully completing, with some resulting habituation. This may be a situation that the client has difficulty confronting, but can already manage if unavoidable. Early success increases confidence and motivation to continue by helping the client to learn that she or he *can* benefit from exposure.

As treatment progresses, some clients don't show expected fear reduction despite systematic exposures. In these cases, it is helpful to look closely at what the client is actually *doing* during exposure exercises. Inquire about subtle ritualistic or compulsive behavior, or look for subtle "safety behaviors" and avoidance (e.g., being with "safe" people, using one's elbow or foot to open doors, shopping only when the stores are less crowded, walking up several flights of stairs rather than taking the elevator, etc.) that may interfere with fear reduction by preventing the client from realizing that the situations are not dangerous. Discussion of the client's previous and successful experiences with natural exposure situations can help instill confidence (e.g., learning to ride a bike, becoming comfortable in the dark, speaking up in groups). By pointing to these, the therapist can help the client see that he or she has already successfully completed exposures.

Imaginal exposure

In imaginal exposure, most commonly used in the treatment of PTSD and OCD, the client vividly imagines himself or herself coming into contact with a feared situation. The imaginal scene typically includes a detailed description of events, as well as the thoughts, emotions, and physical sensations the person imagines would result from that contact. In PTSD treatment, imaginal exposure to traumatic experiences is used to help the client emotionally process and organize traumatic memory(s). In OCD treatment, imaginal exposure is used primarily as a means of exposure to the feared consequences of obsessions or to not performing compulsive behavior. Habituation to the feared image (or trauma memory) occurs over successive repetitions of the imaginal scene, and the anxiety and distress associated with the imagery diminish.

Imaginal exposure to feared memories or situations should be conducted in a manner that promotes emotional engagement. Through repeated imaginal confrontation with trauma memories, the images, thoughts, and feelings represented in the fear structure are organized, processed, and integrated. Emotional processing is facilitated when the client is emotionally connected with the memory and the feelings aroused by this process, but at the same time is not overwhelmed with anxiety. The experience should be conducive to learning that memories are not dangerous, and that anxiety does not last indefinitely.

The aim of encouraging emotional engagement during imaginal exposure has empirical support, as well as theoretical importance. Using self-reported distress level during imaginal exposure to the memory of a traumatic event as an index of emotional engagement, Jaycox, Foa, and Morral (1998) examined the relationship between changes in the women's distress levels during six successive sessions of exposure therapy, and treatment outcome. Results indicated that patients who showed high initial distress levels and gradual habituation across sessions improved more in treatment than those who showed either high or moderate initial distress and no habituation. Thus Jaycox, et al. (1998) concluded that high engagement and habituation over the course of treatment combined are associated with successful outcome.

It is common for PTSD sufferers to avoid feelings when thinking or talking about a trauma. Accordingly, the standard procedures in PE (Foa & Rothbaum, 1998) are designed to promote emotional engagement by asking the client to keep her eyes closed, vividly imagine the scene as if it is happening now, use the present tense, and to include the thoughts, feelings, physical sensations, and behaviors that she experienced during the traumatic event. The therapist prompts for details that are missing (i.e., "what are you feeling?" or "what are you thinking as he says that?"), and monitors the client's distress level throughout. When a client is not experiencing an effective level of emotional engagement during exposure, we recommend that procedures be modified so as to increase or decrease the client's level of arousal or distress accordingly (see later).

Obstacles to Successful Exposure

Avoidance

Avoidance behavior is a key feature of all anxiety disorders. Confrontation with feared situations or stimuli will reliably trigger urges to escape or avoid, so avoidance is the most commonly encountered impediment to effective exposure both in and out of the therapist's office. When struggles with avoidance are evident, the therapist should acknowledge the client's fear and urges to avoid, and normalize it in the context of his or her anxiety disorder. At the same time, remind the client that while avoidance reduces anxiety in the short term, in the long run it maintains fear and prevents the client from learning that the avoided situations (or thoughts, memories, impulses, images) are not harmful or dangerous. It is not unusual for a client's struggle with avoidance to intensify after the introduction of in vivo and/or imaginal exposure, several sessions into treatment. This middle phase of treatment is difficult for some clients. This is sometimes the "feeling worse before you feel better" stage of therapy, and their symptoms may directly reflect this. With extremely avoidant clients in particular, it can be helpful to predict early on that this may happen, and let them know that it is not associated with lesser outcome.

In some cases of repeated avoidance behavior, reiterating the exposure rationale, although important, may not be enough. The therapist and client may need to take a close look at progress with the in vivo exposure exercises and may need to break them down into a more gradual progression. In addition, metaphors or analogies can also be a useful tool in helping the client to overcome avoidance. For example, we sometimes describe this struggle as sitting on a fence between exposure and avoidance. We acknowledge the difficulty of getting off the fence, but stress that sitting on it prolongs the fear and slows progress. We sometimes encourage the client to "*choose* to feel" anxiety in the service of mastery and recovery, rather than only having it triggered against one's will. A core aim is to help the client learn that although anxiety is not comfortable, it is also not dangerous, and that treatment involves learning to tolerate the anxiety induced by exposures or by not avoiding.

Finally, it may be helpful to review the reasons that the client sought treatment in the first place (i.e., the ways in which his or her PTSD or panic or OCD symptoms interfere with life satisfaction) and to review the progress that has already been made. Simply revisiting these important issues, while also validating the client's fear and concerns that exposure can be difficult, may help the client to renew his or her struggle against avoidance.

Underengagement

The term *underengagement* refers to difficulty in accessing the emotional components of the fear structure. It is most commonly encountered in imaginal exposure, but may also occur with in-vivo exposure. In the case of imaginal exposure for treatment of PTSD, the client may describe the trauma, even in great detail, yet feel disconnected from it emotionally or not be able to visualize what happened. Distress or anxiety levels during the exposure are typically low when the client is underengaged. Alternatively, the underengaged client may report high distress levels yet the nonverbal behavior does not reflect high distress.

The therapist can encourage emotional engagement first by following procedures such as asking the client to keep his or her eyes closed and to use present tense. Occasionally probe for details, sensory information, feelings, and thoughts (e.g., "describe what you see ... describe the room ... how does it smell? ... what are you wearing? ... what are you feeling? ... what are you thinking?" etc.) with brief questions. This type of prompting sometimes promotes engagement in the imagery by activating elements of the fear structure. On the other hand, it is sometimes important with underengaged clients to not become *too* active in questioning or prompting, as this may risk getting into conversations with the client during imaginal exposure that reduces his or her connection to the image or emotional engagement with the memory.

If underengagement is persistent across sessions, the therapist should revisit the rationale for exposure and discuss with the client why it is important to experience the emotional impact of confronting fears. It may be helpful to inquire about what the client fears will happen if she or he connects emotionally. In other words, identify the feared consequences (e.g., "I'll lose control ... I'll cry ... I'll never stop feeling anxious"). Validate the client's feelings, and yet help the client realize that being distressed is not dangerous.

Overengagement

The term *overengagement* refers to excessive emotional distress elicited by imaginal or in vivo confrontation with feared stimuli. Imaginal confrontation with frightening memories or images is often distressing and so can elicit tears and emotional upset; it can be difficult to tell when a client has passed from emotional upset. One way that we identify excessive engagement or distress is by asking ourselves whether the client's experience in this moment is conducive to learning. Is the client able to observe and incorporate what is happening around him or her? Or, if this occurs during imaginal exposure to trauma memories, is the client's experience one of feeling as though she or he is actually reexperiencing the traumatic event? Is the client able to learn from this experience that memories are not dangerous, even if painful, and that anxiety does not last indefinitely? If not, the client is likely overengaged. During overengagement, distress levels are typically extremely high and habituation does not occur over successive repetitions of exposure. Sometimes the client may feel or appear detached or dissociated from present experience. Certain procedural modifications may help to decrease engagement in exposure.

For in vivo exposure, it is often useful to modify the hierarchy by breaking the target situation(s) into more manageable increments or steps. The therapist may need to be present in the actual situation with the client, or have some other person (family member, friend) be present during the exposure to provide emotional support. If a client seems overengaged during imaginal exposure, ask the client to keep his or her eyes open while describing the exposure scene, and to use the past rather than present tense in describing a traumatic event. Another standard therapist response to the overengaged client is greater use of voice to connect with and focus the client and to communicate empathy. These comments should be brief supportive statements that acknowledge the client's effort and encourage the client to remain with the memory (e.g., "I know this is really difficult; you are doing a great job"; "I know this is distressing, but you are safe here; the memory can't hurt you").

When an overengaged client is extremely distressed or overwhelmed by recounting and imagining a traumatic memory, it's sometimes best to begin by just having a conversation about the trauma. The aim is to increase client's sense of control and competence by disclosing the details of a trauma while maintaining contact with and feeling supported by the therapist. Another alternative procedure for overengaged clients is writing instead of talking about the trauma. The written narrative should include the client's thoughts, feelings, actions, and sensations, as well as events of what occurred.

Anger

The experience and expression of intense anger during imaginal exposure have been thought to interfere with emotional processing by dominating the client's affect and preventing access of the core fear. Some empirical findings have supported this concern (Foa, Riggs, Massie, & Yarczower, 1995). Accordingly, in the treatment of PTSD, when a client primarily expresses anger, we first validate that feeling as an appropriate response to the trauma and as a symptom of PTSD. We then present the idea that focusing on the anger during exposure may prevent the client from engaging with the fear and anxiety associated with the trauma memory. If needed, we may encourage the client to direct the energy of his or her anger toward getting better and/or to "move it aside" to focus on other equally important elements of his or her experience. Repeated conversations during the course of treatment may be needed when engagement with the memory and other trauma reminders trigger anger.

Notably, using a subset of the participants in the Foa, et al. (1999) PTSD treatment outcome study, Cahill, Rauch, Hembree, and Foa (2003) examined changes in self-reported anger over the course of treatment and found that the PE, stress inoculation training (SIT), and PE/SIT treatments resulted in significant decreases in anger even though treatment was focused on reduction of fear.

CONCLUSION

Despite literally decades of research demonstrating the efficacy of exposure therapy across the spectrum of anxiety disorders, only a minority of therapists are trained in this modality, and even fewer regularly use it to treat their patients suffering from anxiety. Three main reasons for this unfortunate state of affairs have been identified: lack of training (or inadequate training), therapist dislike of using manualized treatments, and therapist fears that exposure therapy will have harmful effects. From our perspective, the primary problem is lack of training. Research evaluating the safety and tolerability (to patients) of exposure therapy has not supported the excessive concerns that have been expressed about the use of this treatment, and yet such concerns continue to dissuade clinicians from learning or using this efficacious treatment.

In the second half of this chapter, we have attempted to debunk the myth that "manualized" treatment is dehumanizing to the client and restricts the therapist's creativity and individuality. Quite to the contrary, effective use of exposure therapy with anxious clients requires a thorough understanding of the clients' fears and behaviors, tailoring the treatment to the clients' responses, and heavy reliance on a strong therapist-client relationship to help clients overcome their debilitating anxiety.

REFERENCES

Abramowitz, J.S., Franklin, M.E., Street, G.P., Kozak, M.J., & Foa, E.B. (2000). Effects of comorbid depression on response to treatment for obsessive-compulsive disorder. *Behavior Therapy, 31,* 517–528.

Addis, M.E., & Krasnow, A.D. (2000). A national survey of practicing psychologists' attitudes toward psychotherapy treatment manuals. *Journal of Consulting and Clinical Psychology, 68,* 331–339.

American Psychological Association Division of Clinical Psychology (1995). Training in and dissemination of empirically-validated psychological treatments: Report and recommendations. *The Clinical Psychologist, 48,* 3–23.

Barlow, D.H. (1996). Health care policy, psychotherapy research, and the future of psychotherapy. *American Psychologist, 51,* 1050–1058.

Barlow, D.H., Gorman, J., Shear, M.K., & Woods, S.W. (2000). Cognitive-behavioral therapy, imipramine, or their combination for panic disorder: A randomized controlled trial. *JAMA, 283,* 2529–2536.

Barlow, D.H., Levitt, J.T., & Bufka, L.F. (1999). The dissemination of empirically supported treatments: A view to the future. *Behaviour Research and Therapy, 37*(Suppl 1), S147–S162.

Becker, C.B., Zayfert, C., & Anderson, E. (2003). A survey of psychologists' attitudes towards and utilization of exposure therapy for PTSD. *Behaviour Research and Therapy, 42,* 277–292.

Blake, D.D., Weathers, F.W., Nagy, L.M., Kaloupek, D.G., Gusman, F.D., Charney, D.S., & Keane, T.M. (1995). The development of the clinician-administered PTSD scale. *Journal of Traumatic Stress, 8,* 75–90.

Blanchard, E.B., Hickling, E.J., Devineni, T., Veazey, C.H., Galovski, T.E., Mundy, E., Malta, L.S., & Buckly, T.C. (2003). A controlled evaluation of cognitive behavioral therapy for posttraumatic stress in motor vehicle accident survivors. *Behaviour Research and Therapy, 41,* 79–96.

Borkovec, T.D., Abel, J.L., & Newman, H. (1995). Effects of psychotherapy on comorbid conditions in generalized anxiety disorder. *Journal of Consulting and Clinical Psychology, 63,* 479–483.

Brady, K., Pearlstein, T., Asnis, G.M., Baker, D., Rothbaum, B., Sikes, C.R., & Farfel, G.M. (2000). Efficacy and safety of sertraline treatment of posttraumatic stress disorder. *JAMA, 283,* 1837–1844.

Brown, T.A., Antony, M.M., & Barlow, D.H. (1995). Diagnostic comorbidity in panic disorder: Effect on treatment outcome and course of comorbid diagnoses following treatment. *Journal of Consulting and Clinical Psychology, 63,* 408–418.

Cahill, S.P., & Frueh, B.C. (1997). Flooding vs. EMDR: Relative efficacy has yet to be investigated: Comment on Pitman et al. (1996). *Comprehensive Psychiatry, 38,* 300–303.

Cahill, S.P., Rauch, S.A., Hemberee, E.A., & Foa, E.B. (2003). Effect of cognitive-behavioral treatments for PTSD on anger. *Journal of Cognitive Psychotherapy, 17,* 113–131.

Cahill, S.P., Riggs, D.S., Rauch, S.A.M., & Foa, E.B. (2003, March). Does prolonged exposure therapy for PTSD make people worse? Poster presented at the annual convention of the Anxiety Disorders Association of America, Toronto, Ontario, Canada.

Chambless, D.L., Baker, M.J., Baucom, D.H., Beutler, L.E., Calhoun, K.S., Crits-Christoph, P., Daiuto, A., DeRubeis, R., Detweiler, J., Haaga, D.A., Bennett Johnson, S., McCurry, S., Mueser, K.T., Pope, K.S., Sanderson, W.C., Shoham, V., Stickle, T., Williams, D.A., & Woody, S.R. (1998). Update on empirically validated therapies, II. *The Clinical Psychologist, 51,* 3–16.

Chambless, D.L., Sanderson, W.C., Shohma, V., Johnson, S.B., Pope, K.S., Crits-Christoph, P., Baker, M., Johnson, B., Woody, S.R., Sue, S., Beutler, L., Williams, D.A., & McCurry, S. (1996). An update on empirically validated therapies. *The Clinical Psychologist, 49,* 5–18.

Cloitre, M., Koenen, K., Cohen, L.R., & Han, H. (2002). Skills training in affective and interpersonal regulation followed by exposure: A phase-based treatment for PTSD related to childhood abuse. *Journal of Consulting and Clinical Psychology, 70,* 1067–1074.

Connor, K.M., Sutherland, S.M., Tupler, L.A., Malik, M.L., & Davidson, J.R.T. (1999). Fluoxetine in post-traumatic stress disorder: Randomised, double-blind study. *British Journal of Psychiatry, 175,* 17–22.

Davidson, J.R.T., Rothbaum, B.O., van der Kolk, B.A., Sikes, C.R., & Farfel, G.M. (2001). Multi-center, double-blind comparison of sertraline and placebo in the treatment of posttraumatic stress disorder. *Archives of General Psychiatry, 58,* 485–492.

Davis, D.A., Thomson, M.A., Oxman, A.D., & Haynes, R.B. (1992). Evidence for effectiveness of CME: A review of randomized controlled trials. *Journal of the American Medical Association, 268,* 1111–1117.

Devilly, G.J., & Foa, E.B. (2001). Comments on Tarrier et al.'s study and the investigation of exposure and cognitive therapy. *Journal of Consulting and Clinical Psychology, 69,* 114–116

Ehlers, A., & Clark, D.M. (2000). A cognitive model of posttraumatic stress disorder. *Behaviour Research and Therapy, 38,* 319–345.

Foa, E.B., Dancu, C.V., Hembree, E.A., Jaycox, L.H., Meadows, E.A., & Street, G.P. (1999). A comparison of exposure therapy, stress inoculation training, and their combination for reducing posttraumatic stress disorder in female assault victims. *Journal of Consulting and Clinical Psychology, 67,* 194–200.

Foa, E.B., Dancu, C.V., Hembree, E., Jaycox, L.H., Meadows, E.A., & Street, G.P. (1999). The efficacy of exposure therapy, stress inoculation training and their combination in ameliorating PTSD for female victims of assault. *Journal of Consulting and Clinical Psychology, 67,* 194–200.

Foa, E.B., Davidson, J.R.T., & Frances, A. (1999). The Expert Consensus Guidelines Series: Treatment of posttraumatic stress disorder. *Journal of Clinical Psychiatry, 60,* 4–76.

Foa, E.B., Hembree, E.A., Cahill, A.M., Rauch, S.A.M., Riggs, D.S., Feeny, N.C., & Yadin, E. (2005). Randomized trial of prolonged exposure for PTSD with and without cognitive restructuring: outcome at academic and community clinics, *Journal of Consulting and Clinical Psychology, 73,* 953–964.

Foa, E.B., & Kozak, M.J. (1986). Emotional processing of fear: Exposure to corrective information. *Psychological Bulletin, 99,* 20–35.

Foa, E.B., Riggs, D.S., Massie, E.D., & Yarczower, M. (1995). The impact of fear activation and anger on the efficacy of exposure treatment for posttraumatic stress disorder. *Behavior Therapy, 26,* 487–499.

Foa, E.B., & Rothbaum, B.O. (1998). *Treating the trauma of rape.* New York: Guilford Publications.

Foa, E.B., Zoellner, L.A., Feeny, N.C., Hembree, E.A., & Alvarez-Conrad, J. (2002). Does imaginal exposure exacerbate PTSD symptoms? *Journal of Consulting and Clinical Psychology, 70,* 1022–1028.

Feeny, N.C., Zoellner, L.A., & Foa, E.B. (2002). Treatment outcome for chronic PTSD among female assault victims with borderline personality characteristics: A preliminary examination. *Journal of Personality Disorders, 16*(1), 30–40.

Franklin, M.E., Abramowitz, J.S., Kozak, M.J., Levitt, J.T., & Foa, E.B. (2000). Effectiveness of exposure and ritual prevention for obsessive-compulsive disorder: Randomized compared with nonrandomized samples. *Journal of Consulting and Clinical Psychology, 68,* 594–602.

Freihei, S.R., Vye, C., Swan, R., & Cady, M. (2004). Cognitive-behavioral therapy for anxiety: Is dissemination working? *The Behavior Therapist, 27,* 25–32.

Gillespie, K., Duffy, M., Hackmann, A., & Clark, D.M. (2002). Community based cognitive therapy in the treatment of posttraumatic stress disorder following the Omagh bomb. *Behaviour Research and Therapy, 40,* 345–357.

Heimberg, R.G., Liebowitz, M.R., Hope, D.A., Schneier, F.R., Holt, C.S., Welkowitz, L.A., et al. (1998). Cognitive behavior group therapy vs. phenelzine therapy for social phobia. *Archives of General Psychiatry, 55,* 1133–1141.

Hembree, E.A., Cahill, S.P., & Foa, E.B. (2004). Impact of personality disorders on treatment outcome for female assault survivors with chronic posttraumatic stress disorder. *Journal of Personality Disorders, 18,* 117–127.

Hembree, E.A., Foa, E.B., Dorfan, N.M., Street, G.P., Kowalski, J., & Tu, X.(2003). Do patients drop out prematurely from exposure therapy for PTSD? *Journal of Traumatic Stress, 16,* 555–562.

Jaycox, L.H., Foa, E.B., & Morral, A.R. (1998). Influence of emotional engagement and habituation on exposure therapy for PTSD. *Journal of Consulting and Clinical Psychology, 66,* 185–192.

Juster, H., Heimberg, R.G., & Engelberg, B. (1995). Self selection and sample selection in a treatment study of social phobia. *Behaviour Research and Therapy, 33,* 321–324.

Kilpatrick, D.G., & Best, C.L. (1984). Some cautionary remarks on treating sexual assault victims with implosion. *Behavior Therapy, 15,* 421–423.

Marshall, R.D., Beebe, K.L., Oldham, M., & Zaninelli, R. (2001). Efficacy and safety of paroxetine treatment of chronic PTSD: A fixed-dose, placebo-controlled study. *American Journal of Psychiatry, 158,* 1982–1988.

Martenyi, F., Brown, E.B., Zhang, H., Prakash, A., & Koke, S.C. (2002). Fluoxetine versus placebo in posttraumatic stress disorder. *Journal of Clinical Psychiatry, 63,* 199–206.

Persons, J.B., Burns, D.D., & Perloff, J.M. (1998). Predictors of dropout and outcome in cognitive therapy for depression in a private practice setting. *Cognitive Therapy and Research, 12,* 557–575.

Pitman, R.K., Altman, B., Greenwald, E., Longpre, R.E., Macklin, M.L., Poire, R.E., & Steketee, G. (1991). Psychiatric complication during flooding therapy for posttraumatic stress disorder. *Journal of Clinical Psychiatry, 52,* 17–20.

Pitman, R.K., Orr, S.P., Altman, B., Longpre, R.E., Poire, R.E., & Macklin, M.L. (1996). Emotional processing during eye movement desensitization and reprocessing therapy of Vietnam veterans with chronic posttraumatic stress disorder. *Comprehensive Psychiatry, 37,* 419–29.

Rothbaum, B.O., Meadows, E.A., Resick, P., & Foy, D. (2000). Cognitive-behavioral therapy. In E.B. Foa, T.M. Keane, & M.J. Friedman (Eds.), *Effective treatments for PTSD* (pp. 60–83). New York: Guilford Press.

Tarrier, N., Pilgrim, H., Sommerfield, C., Faragher, B., Reynolds, M., Graham, E., & Barrowclough, C. (1999). A randomized trial of cognitive therapy and imaginal exposure in the treatment of chronic posttraumatic stress disorder. *Journal of Consulting and Clinical Psychology, 67,* 13–18.

Taylor, S., Thordarson, D.S., Maxfield, L., Federoff, I.C., Lovell, K., & Ogrodniczuk, J. (2003). Efficacy, speed, and adverse effects of three PTSD treatments: Exposure therapy, relaxation training, and EMDR. *Journal of Consulting and Clinical Psychology, 71,* 330–338.

Tsao, J.C.I., Mystkowski, J.L., Zucker, B.G., & Craske, M.G. (2005). Impact of cognitive-behavioral therapy for panic disorder on comorbidity: A controlled investigation. *Behaviour Research and Therapy, 43,* 959–970.

Tucker, P., Zaninelli, R., Yehuda, R., Ruggiero, L., Dillingham, K., & Pitts, C.D. (2001). Paroxetine in the treatment of chronic posttraumatic stress disorder: Results of a placebo-controlled, flexible-dosage trial. *Journal of Clinical Psychiatry, 62,* 860–868.

Van Etten, M.L., & Taylor, S. (1998). Comparative efficacy of treatments for post-traumatic stress disorder: A meta-analysis. *Clinical Psychology and Psychotherapy, 5,* 126–144.

Zoellner, L.A., Feeny, N.C., Cochran, B., & Pruitt, L. (2003). Treatment choice for PTSD. *Behaviour Research and Therapy, 41,* 879–886.

CHAPTER 18

Exposure Therapy Has a Public Relations Problem: A Dearth of Litigation Amid a Wealth of Concern

David C. S. Richard
Rollins College
Andrew T. Gloster
Technical University of Dresden, Germany

LAW, ETHICS, AND PROFESSIONAL ISSUES IN EXPOSURE THERAPY

"What? You're going to use exposure? I didn't know you were a sadist?!" (private communication with colleague who shall remain anonymous, 2005). For practitioners of exposure therapy, such statements in isolation can be humorous, irritating, or both. But what if the sentiment is widespread? Negative attitudes toward treatment may mediate the willingness of mental health practitioners to conduct exposure therapy and a client's willingness to engage in the treatment. For instance, a recent graduate textbook on psychotherapy stated, "Although patients typically accept the procedure because they experience its benefits firsthand, many mental health professionals are reluctant to use the anxiety-inducing techniques associated with exposure. Directly activating intense emotional expressions is too disconcerting for staid practitioners of 'talk' therapy" (Prochaska & Norcross, 1999, p. 270).

In summarizing the claims of others while also playing devil's advocate, Prochaska and Norcross (1999) levy charges against exposure therapy that seem to harken the

---

The authors thank Deborah Williams, Karen Saules, Lauren Connolly, Sarah Shafbuch, and Stuart Dotson for their assistance with data collection.

409

specter of *A Clockwork Orange* by claiming that exposure therapy (1) imposes crass exercises on clients for which the ends do not justify the means, (2) encourages the use of impersonal techniques that are done "to" a client, rather than "with" a client, and (3) is a cure worse than the original disorder. Although behavior therapists may object to these sentiments, they are not isolated. Recent articles in the popular press confirm the existence of negative stereotypes surrounding exposure therapy. One journalist likened the procedure to "torture, plain and simple" stating that the treatment is not for the "faint of heart" (Slater, 2003). This report also quoted a health care professional as saying, "very few patients can tolerate that adrenaline-based approach" (Slater, 2003).

Needless to say, behaviorally oriented practitioners do not endorse the view that exposure therapy is a sadistic enterprise. Feeny, Hembree, and Zoellner (2003) recently summarized prevailing myths of exposure therapy into four categories: (1) exposure therapy is rigid and insensitive to the ideographic needs of patients, (2) exposure therapy alone will not successfully treat complex cases: additional treatment components are necessary, (3) studies showing the efficacy of exposure therapy do not generalize to real world clinical settings, and (4) exposure therapy exacerbates symptoms and causes high rates of attrition. Although the authors provide compelling evidence to dispel each of these myths, the typology points to sentiments that exist in the therapeutic community (see also the chapter discussing obstacles to exposure treatment by Hembree and Cahill in this volume).

Given the prevailing myths about exposure therapy, its widely acknowledged aversive elements, and the litigious nature of modern society, we wondered to what extent exposure therapy had been litigated. To answer this question, we searched the Lexus-Nexus database for legal cases tried in the U.S. Supreme Court, the Federal Court of Appeals, District Court of Appeals, and Court of Veteran Appeals. The term *exposure therapy* resulted in a single hit. The case surrounded treatment of exposure to a chemical agent rather than exposure therapy. Other search terms conceptually related to exposure therapy were also used.[1] The 12 other search terms resulted in 2,561 hits. After reviewing the briefs, however, none explicitly discussed exposure therapy. A review of case abstracts found no evidence to substantiate concerns that exposure therapy has been litigated in any jurisdiction. Case abstracts concerned issues ranging from the psychological (disability cases, false memory syndrome, dual relationships) to the irrelevant (asbestos exposure).

The only relevant discussion of exposure therapy came in the case *Heller v. Doe* tried in the U.S. Supreme Court. This case centered on the definitions and burden of proof used to involuntarily commit persons with "mental retardation" and "mental illness." Discussing the treatment of the mentally retarded, Justice Souter indicated that they are often subject to "invasive" and "intrusive" procedures, includ-

---

1   Search terms included (1) exposure therapy, (2) PTSD, (3) psychiatric desensitization, (4) desensitization therapy, (5) phobia, (6) empirically validated treatments, (7) empirically validated therapy, (8) empirically and psychotherapy, (9) empirically supported treatment, (10) empirically validated intervention, (11) cognitive behavioral therapy, (12) psychotherapy, and (13) psychotherapy and malpractice.

ing "aversive conditioning as well as forced exposure to objects that trigger severe anxiety reactions." Although exposure therapy was not directly under review, Justice Souter's reference to the treatment of anxiety in the mentally retarded clearly implies exposure therapy is an aversive procedure.

Although encouraged by the paucity of evidence implicating exposure therapy in legal proceedings, we acknowledge the possibility that issues surrounding exposure therapy have been litigated, but did not reach the appellate system or were settled out of court. Many settlements include confidentiality clauses that might account for the absence of exposure therapy in the legal databases. This quagmire prompted us to contact insurance carriers for information about claims involving exposure therapy. Unfortunately, we were told that that information surrounding lawsuits is confidential. We know from previous research, however, that practicing psychotherapists have less than a 1% chance of being sued for malpractice (Montgomery, Cupit, & Wimberley, 1999). Further, many ethical complaints are withdrawn or winnowed out during the investigatory process.

If a behavior therapist were to encounter treatment dilemmas when using exposure techniques, it is likely that the issue would surround when to discontinue treatment. Of relevance is a taxonomy proposed by Williams (2000) delineating the various kinds of legal and ethical issues encountered by therapists. The taxonomic category "escape from unwanted treatment" is most germane for exposure therapists. For example, Williams presented the case of a minor who filed a false ethical complaint to escape unwanted treatment for drug abuse. It is conceivable that under the right circumstances, a patient might view exposure therapy as aversive enough to precipitate such a complaint if escape from the treatment venue was not possible (e.g., an inpatient treatment setting or a court-ordered observational period).

Purpose

Of course, a dearth of extant case law does not equate to an absence of concern regarding the ethicality of exposure therapy. Many of the concerns expressed by clinicians in the past about the use of exposure therapy have little or nothing to do with potential litigation. In a survey of 207 practicing clinicians of various orientations and 29 members of the Association for the Advancement of Behavior Therapy (AABT)'s* disaster and trauma special interest group, Becker, Zayfert, & Anderson (2002) found that clinicians consistently cited limited training, a preference for individualized treatment over manualized therapy, and concern that the patient would decompensate as factors that influenced the decision to use imaginal exposure with post-traumatic stress disorder (PTSD) patients. With regard to potential clinical complications, Becker and colleagues found that clinicians most commonly feared that imaginal exposure would lead to an increase in client arousal, reexperiencing symptoms, dissociation, substance abuse, and suicidality. In addition,

*AABT recently changed its name to the Association for Cognitive and Behavior Therapies.

concerns about self-injury and potential dropout were noted, with 68% of their main sample anticipating that self-injury was likely to be exacerbated by using imaginal exposure and 59% believing that imaginal exposure would increase the likelihood that patients would drop out of therapy. Overall, Becker and colleagues concluded that exposure treatments were underused, in part because of pervasive clinician concerns regarding the iatrogenic effects of exposure therapy.

In an attempt to address how exposure therapy in its various manifestations is viewed by treatment professionals who are likely to use the approach, we surveyed members of the Anxiety Disorders Association of America (ADAA) regarding their professional experiences with exposure therapy. As the only national organization dedicated exclusively to the study and treatment of anxiety disorders, members of the ADAA seemed most likely to possess knowledge of legal and/or ethical problems resulting from exposure therapy. Because exposure therapy may also be perceived by the public as a possibly harmful process (Feeny, et al., 2003; Slater, 2003; Zayfert, Becker, & Gillock, 2002), we then surveyed undergraduate students and clients at a university clinic to better understand their reactions to the use of exposure therapy and contrasted their reactions against other therapeutic modalities.

METHOD

Survey Measures

Two surveys were used to assess attitudes toward exposure therapy. One was given to members of the ADAA, and the other was given to both undergraduate students and clients. The version for ADAA members assessed demographics and issues surrounding training and implementation of exposure therapy. Specifically, items addressed topics such as percent of client case load diagnosed with an anxiety disorder, percent of clients treated with exposure therapy, judgments about the aversiveness of various clinical procedures, training in exposure therapy, special insurance, and ethical or legal difficulties resulting from implementation of exposure therapy. In addition, ADAA members rated the aversiveness of different therapy modalities.

The survey administered to students and outpatients presented 11 therapy vignettes designed to represent variations of exposure therapy (e.g., in vivo, imaginal, virtual reality) and other treatments (e.g., dynamic therapy, cognitive restructuring). Consistent with suggestions from prior treatment preference research (Ertl & McNamara, 2000), each vignette included a statement stating the efficacy of the procedure. For each vignette, participants answered four questions that assessed their judgment of (1) the perceived helpfulness of the procedure, (2) the acceptability of the procedure, (3) their reaction if asked to undergo the procedure, and (4) the ethicality of the procedure. The term *ethical* was defined for students and outpatients as behavior that is "professionally appropriate, justified, and in the best interest of the client." The survey used with students and outpatients can be found in the Appendix.

Participants

We sampled members of the ADAA (n = 84), undergraduate students (n = 119), and waiting room outpatients at the university's psychology clinic (n = 21). Data from students and outpatients were collected concurrently with another project, and the data collection procedure has been reported elsewhere (see Richard & Gloster, 2006). Both students and outpatients completed a questionnaire that presented vignettes of different therapies and their application to hypothetical client problems (see the Appendix).

ADAA members

ADAA members were recruited from the ADAA's online referral network. All association members listed with an email address were contacted and asked to participate in the study. A total of 708 emails were sent to association members. Of the 708 emails, 54 were returned due to delivery failure (i.e., the email address was not valid, mailbox full, etc.). Of the remainder, a total of 101 members responded. Seventeen cases were removed due to missing data, truncated emails, or duplicate submissions. Thus, our final sample consisted of 84 ADAA members, or 12.84% of all valid email contacts. ADAA members who agreed to participate completed a copy of the survey and returned it by email. The survey was embedded in the email rather than attached, as previous research has found significantly higher response rates for embedded surveys (Dommeyer & Moriarty, 1999).

Of those who participated, 48.8% were male (n = 41) and 51.2% were female (n = 43). The mean number of years, as obtainment of the terminal degree was 16.77 (SD = 10.86), with a range of 1 to 54 years. Although the majority of respondents held a Ph.D. (59.5%), other terminal degrees were reported: M.S.W (15.5%), M.D. (8.3%), M.A./M.S. (9.5%), B.S. (1.2%), and other (6.0%). Respondents indicated a range of clinical orientations: cognitive-behavioral (73.8%), eclectic (14.3%), behavioral (4.8%), humanistic (2.4%), medical/biological (1.2%), and other (3.6%). Professional affiliations were reported as follows: private practice (65.5%), university clinic (8.3%), educational institution (7.1%), hospital (6.0%), community mental health (4.8%), Veterans Administration hospital (2.4%), and other (6.0%). Slightly more than half of respondents (57.1%) reported receiving graduate training in exposure therapy, but nearly three-fourths (73.8%) reported receiving formal instruction or supervision in exposure therapy elsewhere. Qualitative responses suggested that supervised clinical work (i.e., practica and internship) was the most common venue for graduate training in exposure therapy. Other training modalities included formal classroom work, reading, and discussions with mentors. Professionals reported receiving other instruction/supervision from various sources, including postdoctoral training programs, treatment seminars, workshops, classes, continuing education credits, conferences, and consultation. The sample reported that over half of their clients have been provided anxiety diagnoses (M = 65.82%, SD = 25.77%) and that of those clients, nearly three-fourths (M = 70.48%, SD = 32.49%) were currently being treated with some form of exposure therapy.

Undergraduate students

The second group consisted of 119 undergraduate students enrolled in psychology classes at a large midwestern state university. Of the respondents, 30.3% were male (*n* = 36) and 69.7% were female (*n* = 83). The sample was mostly Caucasian (77.3%), with African American (12.6%), Asian (2.5%), and other (5.8%) students represented. The mean age of the sample was 21.1 years (SD = 5.3 years; range = 18 to 46). Class extra credit was provided at the instructor's discretion. Questionnaires were administered in a paper-and-pencil format.

In addition to completing the exposure therapy survey, undergraduates also completed the Beck Depression Inventory II (BDI-II) and several questions about their own psychotherapy experiences.[2] These measures were administered to determine if students had previous experience with psychotherapy and to assess general negative affect. We were curious if either factor moderated attitudes toward exposure therapy.

The student sample was relatively free of depression. The mean BDI-II score for the sample was 9.8 (SD = 7.8; range = 0 to 43). This score is similar to the nondepressed normative sample reported for the BDI-II (M = 7.65, SD = 5.9; Beck, 1996). Fifteen students (12.6%) reported attending one or more psychotherapy sessions in the last year, and three students (2.5%) reported attending more than 10 psychotherapy sessions in the same timeframe.

Outpatients

The third group of participants consisted of 21 outpatients seeking treatment at a university psychology clinic that served an urban midwestern community. Of the respondents, 33.3% were male (*n* = 7) and 66.6% were female (*n* = 14). The sample was mostly Caucasian (76.2%), with African American (4.8%), biracial (14.3%), and other (4.8%) represented. The mean age of the sample was 37.2 years (SD = 11.4 years; range = 20 to 55). Outpatients were provided a free therapy session in exchange for completing the survey. Questionnaires were administered in a paper-and-pencil format.

The mean BDI-II score for the outpatient sample was 18.1 (SD = 11.0; range = 1 to 38). This score is similar to the mild depression normative sample reported for the BDI-II (Beck, 1996). Outpatients reported attending between one and 50

---

2 When used as a screening measure for depression, the following BDI-II cutoff scores can be used: 0 to 13 minimal depression, 14 to 19 mild depression, 20 to 28 moderate depression, and 29 to 63 severe depression.

psychotherapy sessions in the past year (M = 22.5, SD = 17.8) As expected, BDI-II scores for outpatients were significantly higher than those of the students, $t(138)$ = 4.10, $p < .001$.

Procedures

The procedures were approved by the institutional Human Subjects Review Committee at Eastern Michigan University. For the ADAA sample, participants were contacted by email. Each email contained a brief introduction to the study, the survey, a demographic questionnaire, and the informed consent form. Participants were instructed to reply to the email and place asterisks next to their desired responses. The student sample was recruited from undergraduate psychology courses in exchange for extra credit provided by their instructors. Student participants completed the questionnaires in groups of two to 10 individuals. The outpatient sample was recruited from the university psychology clinic in exchange for a free session. Questionnaires were completed in the waiting room before therapy, or were completed at home and returned at the next therapy session. Questionnaires for both students and outpatients were administered in counterbalanced order.

RESULTS

Professionals

Aversiveness of therapeutic procedures

Professionals were asked to rate the aversiveness of various therapeutic modalities. As can be seen in Table 18.1, ADAA professionals clearly considered flooding to be the most aversive procedure. In fact, on a scale from 0 (not at all aversive) to 6 (very aversive), the mean aversiveness rating difference between flooding and the next most aversive procedure represented the largest difference across the 11 rated procedures. Of the six therapies rated as most aversive, four involved an exposure component. If eye movement desensitization retraining is included as a variant of exposure therapy, then five of the six most aversive therapies included an exposure component. The exception to this appears to be psychodynamic therapy, which was rated the third most aversive therapeutic modality. It is not clear what accounts for this rating, but it may be a function of the largely cognitive-behavioral orientation of the professionals who were sampled. Finally, a large proportion of participants appeared unfamiliar with acceptance and commitment therapy (ACT) and virtual reality (VR) therapies. Somewhat surprisingly, 36.9% of the sample indicated they did not know enough about ACT to provide a rating. For VR therapy the corresponding percentage was 23.8%. As a result, inferences regarding their perceived aversiveness should be interpreted with caution.

TABLE 18.1   Professionals' ratings of various therapeutic procedures' aversiveness (most aversive to least aversive)

Procedure	M (SD)	Don't Know Enough About It	N/A
Flooding	4.68 (1.87)	2.4 %	2.4 %
EMDR	3.34 (2.00)	4.8 %	17.9 %
Psychodynamic therapy	3.04 (2.06)	2.4 %	7.1 %
In vivo exposure	2.81 (2.14)	3.6 %	1.2 %
Virtual reality exposure	2.62 (1.92)	23.8 %	10.7 %
Imaginal exposure	2.53 (1.80)	2.4 %	–
Systematic desensitization	2.35 (1.75)	1.2 %	2.4 %
ACT	2.23 (1.75)	36.9 %	10.7 %
Cognitive therapy	1.66 (1.39)	1.2%	–
Group therapy	1.51 (1.54)	1.2 %	6 %
Client-centered therapy	1.46 (1.71)	2.4 %	8.3 %

Note: Ratings scale from 0 (not at all) to 6 (very much so).
EMDR, eye movement desensitization and reprocessing; ACT, acceptance and commitment therapy.

Knowledge of ethical/legal problems, complaints, and dilemmas

We also asked ADAA professionals about their knowledge of legal problems, ethical complaints, and ethical dilemmas resulting from the implementation of exposure therapy. Consistent with our review of legal databases, none of the professionals reported legal action or ethical complaints being filed as a result of using exposure therapy. However, 13.9% of valid responses ($n = 11$) reported knowledge of ethical dilemmas within their clinic that resulted from using exposure therapy. Overall, ADAA professionals estimated the mean percentage of ethical dilemmas experienced in their clinic as a result of exposure therapy to be 1.18% of all treated cases ($SD = 5.88\%$, range 0.0% to 50.0%). The exposure techniques associated with the most frequent ethical dilemmas were in vivo exposure, flooding, and imaginal exposure (e.g., loop tapes used in obsessive-compulsive disorder [OCD] treatment). Qualitative descriptions of the reported ethical dilemmas revealed five common themes: (1) maintaining proper boundaries, (2) proper implementation of in vivo exposure resulting from situational or logistic constraints (i.e., length of session limited by insurance company, flying phobia flight never got off the ground), (3) using exposure with minors (i.e., a boy initiating flooding without his parents, using pornographic images for a minor with scrupulosity OCD), (4) clients misunderstanding instructions, and (5) distinguishing between a legitimate reason to terminate an exposure treatment session versus the clinical manifestation of anxious avoidance.

Assuming that some problems may not be severe enough to be considered ethical dilemmas, we asked if any problems were commonly encountered using exposure-based procedures. Of the 14 participants (18.7% of valid responses) who reported experiencing treatment-related problems, the most common problems included (1) compliance with and understanding of instructions, (2) resistance to the procedures, (3) desire on the part of the therapist and/or client to move through the hierarchy too quickly, (4) difficulty motivating a client, (5) clients' anxiety about implementing the procedure, and (6) dropout.[3]

Student and Outpatient Samples

Both undergraduate students and outpatients at the clinic were asked to rate 11 anxiety-related treatment vignettes with respect to perceived efficacy of treatment, acceptability of the treatment, and how the participant would react if a therapist suggested the treatment for him or her. For example, a vignette designed to represent in vivo exposure for specific phobia stated:

> A client is afraid of spiders to the point that the client needs therapy. The client is told that handling a spider will eventually reduce fear of spiders. As part of therapy, the client must hold a tarantula and let the spider crawl over the client's arm.

Flooding results from these two groups are presented in Table 18.2. For each vignette, correlations were calculated between each of the three rated variables. All three variables were significantly correlated with each other across all 11 vignettes (Ranges: Vignette 1: $r = .61-.79$; Vignette 2: $r = .75-.89$; Vignette 3: $r = .32-.58$; Vignette 4: $r = .83-.84$; Vignette 5: $r = .75-.83$; Vignette 6: $r = .61-.69$; Vignette 7: $r = .72-.75$; Vignette 8: $r = .74-.79$; Vignette 9: $r = .65-.69$; Vignette 10: $r = .75-.82$; Vignette 11: $r = .87-.88$; all p's $< .001$). Thus we calculated an *Overall Rating* that collapsed across the two samples and represented the mean response to all three questions. A higher *Overall Rating* reflects a better appraisal of the treatment. Table 18.2 is organized by *Overall Rating* means. The vignette of graduated in vivo exposure treatment for social phobia (Vignette # 3) was rated most positively; the vignette of interoceptive exposure for panic disorder (Vignette # 11) was rated the least positively.

To assess whether individuals with greater levels of negative affect provided higher or lower *Overall Ratings* to the therapy vignettes, we conducted a series of 11 independent t-tests by splitting the student sample in half into a "high" negative affect group (i.e., BDI-II scores > 13) and "low" negative affect group (i.e., BDI-II scores $=13$). Using a Bonferroni correction for multiple comparisons, no comparisons yielded significant t values (Range: $t (117) = 0.11, p < .91$ to $t (117) = 2.13$,

---

3   One professional took care to indicate that attrition from exposure therapy occurred in less than 10% of cases.

TABLE 18.2   Outpatients' and students' mean appraisals of treatment vignettes

Vignette	Mean Overall Rating	Outpatients ($n = 21$)	Students ($n = 119$)
Graduated in vivo exposure: social phobia	4.62 (0.40)		
Helpful?		4.90 (0.30)	4.80 (0.42)
Acceptable?		4.81 (0.40)	4.71 (0.46)
Your reaction?		4.19 (1.08)	4.35 (0.59)
Imaginal exposure: social phobia	4.56 (0.57)		
Helpful?		4.67 (0.58)	4.57 (0.72)
Acceptable?		4.71 (0.56)	4.64 (0.62)
Your reaction?		4.57 (0.51)	4.44 (0.68)
Cognitive restructuring: GAD	4.31 (0.71)		
Helpful?		4.57 (0.81)	4.33 (0.80)
Acceptable?		4.67 (0.80)	4.40 (0.70)
Your reaction?		4.33 (0.91)	4.09 (0.79)
Virtual reality: fear of flying	4.00 (0.77)		
Helpful?		3.90 (1.14)	4.02 (0.94)
Acceptable?		4.05 (0.80)	4.16 (0.71)
Your reaction?		3.79 (0.93)	3.86 (0.91)
Hypnosis: PTSD	3.59 (0.91)		
Helpful?		3.95 (1.02)	3.50 (0.99)
Acceptable?		4.00 (0.95)	3.64 (0.95)
Your reaction?		3.86 (0.96)	3.43 (0.98)
Free association: specific phobia (fear of heights)	3.47 (0.95)		
Helpful?		3.71 (0.96)	3.13 (1.19) *
Acceptable?		4.05 (0.74)	3.75 (0.96)
Your reaction?		3.60 (1.02)	3.37 (1.02)
In vivo exposure: specific phobia (fear of spiders)	3.02 (1.06)		
Helpful?		3.00 (1.58)	3.37 (1.28)
Acceptable?		3.00 (1.18)	3.30 (1.04)
Your reaction?		2.12 (1.07)	2.55 (1.18)
Imaginal exposure: childhood sexual abuse	2.77 (1.16)		
Helpful?		2.67 (1.32)	2.91 (1.29)
Acceptable?		2.67 (1.32)	2.94 (1.18)
Your reaction?		2.48 (1.33)	2.56 (1.21)
Exposure and response prevention: OCD	2.72 (1.12)		
Helpful?		2.71 (1.42)	2.80 (1.27)
Acceptable?		2.71 (1.27)	2.86 (1.14)
Your reaction?		2.48 (1.21)	2.54 (1.14)

(Continued)

TABLE 18.2   Outpatients' and students' mean appraisals of treatment vignettes—*Cont'd*

Vignette	Mean Overall Rating	Outpatients ($n = 21$)	Students ($n = 119$)
Cue exposure: alcohol problem	2.69 (1.15)		
Helpful?		2.14 (1.24)	2.63 (1.31)
Acceptable?		2.48 (1.12)	3.03 (1.13) *
Your reaction?		2.03 (1.11)	2.67 (1.22) *
Interoceptive exposure: panic disorder	2.13 (1.07)		
Helpful?		2.33 (1.28)	1.97 (1.11)
Acceptable?		2.48 (1.25)	2.25 (1.11)
Your reaction?		2.33 (1.15)	2.04 (1.06)

Note: Higher numbers reflect more positive appraisals.

Overall Rating = Mean rating of the following three domain questions collapsed across outpatients and students; *Helpful?* = How helpful do you think this treatment would be?; *Acceptable?* = How acceptable is this kind of treatment?; *Your reaction?* = How would you react if a therapist suggested this treatment for you; * = mean difference between students and outpatients on domain question was significant at $p < .05$.

$p < .04$), suggesting that level of negative affect did not influence students' ratings of the therapy vignettes.

Several interesting trends can be observed in Table 18.2. First, there is an inverse relationship between variability of responses and overall ratings (i.e., the standard deviations increase as mean ratings of acceptability, helpfulness, and so forth decrease). This implies a greater consensus exists for positively appraised therapeutic procedures than for those less positively appraised. Second, subtracting ratings of how participants would react if their therapist suggested the procedure from ratings of how helpful they consider a procedure yields a discrepancy score that represents the difference between perceived treatment efficacy and treatment acceptability for self. For the outpatient sample, all comparisons yielded positive results. That is, on average, participants appraised procedures as acceptable even when admitting to lukewarm reactions if asked to engage in the treatment modality. For undergraduates, this general trend held, with the exception of three vignettes: (1) a free association task for a specific phobia (fear of heights), (2) cue exposure for an alcohol problem, and (3) interoceptive exposure for panic disorder.

Outpatients and students were also asked whether the treatments described in the vignettes were ethical. Table 18.3 shows that for the outpatient sample, two vignettes (graduated in vivo exposure for social phobia and imaginal exposure for social phobia) were unanimously rated as ethical. In addition, no participants rated virtual reality treatment of flight phobia as unethical. The treatment modality outpatients considered least ethical was exposure and response prevention for OCD. Similar to their outpatient counterparts, students unanimously judged graduated in

TABLE 18.3   Outpatients' and students' appraisals of treatment ethicality

	Ethical?				
Vignette	Yes	No	Undecided	Proportion *Yes* Of All Responses	Proportion *Yes* Excluding Undecided Responses
In vivo exposure: specific phobia (spider)					
Outpatients	10	6	5	.48	.63
Students	61	30	28	.51	.67
Imaginal exposure: childhood sexual abuse					
Outpatients	8	6	7	.38	.57
Students	50	43	26	.42	.54
Graduated in vivo exposure: social phobia					
Outpatients	21	0	0	1.0	1.0
Students	119	0	0	1.0	1.0
Cue exposure: alcohol problem					
Outpatients	5	8	8	.24	.38
Students	47	39	32	.40	.55
Exposure and response prevention: OCD					
Outpatients	7	10	4	.33	.42
Students	44	46	29	.37	.49
Imaginal exposure: social phobia					
Outpatients	21	0	0	1.0	1.0
Students	117	2	0	.98	.98
Cognitive restructuring: GAD					
Outpatients	20	1	0	.95	.95
Students	104	1	14	.87	.99
Free association: specific phobia (fear of heights)					
Outpatients	19	1	1	.90	.95
Students	86	15	18	.72	.85
Virtual reality: fear of flying					
Outpatients	18	0	3	.86	1.0
Students	103	6	10	.87	.94
Hypnosis: PTSD					
Outpatients	14	2	5	.67	.88
Students	82	13	24	.69	.86
Interoceptive exposure: panic disorder					
Outpatients	6	8	7	.29	.43
Students	23	72	24	.19	.24

Note: The term *ethical* was defined as "professionally appropriate, justified, and in the best interest of the client."

OCD, obsessive–compulsive disease; GAD, generalized anxiety disorder; PTSD, post-traumatic stress disorder.

vivo exposure of social phobia to be ethical. However, students perceived intero-ceptive exposure for panic disorder as the least ethical procedure.

We also calculated two indexes that standardized ethicality ratings across treat-ment modality. The first index was the proportion of *all* responses that were "Yes" responses (i.e., endorsement of the treatment as ethical). The second index excluded "Undecided" responses and represented the proportion of all "Yes" responses when only "Yes" and "No" responses were taken into account. We then rank ordered each treatment modality in Table 18.4 in terms of scores on the first calculated index.

Table 18.4 is striking in terms of the similarities of the rankings between out-patients and students. Of the top eight perceived most ethical treatments, there is only one transposition (virtual reality and the free association task switch places in the rankings across outpatients and students). In addition, the three treatments considered the least ethical are the same across the two groups, although their order varied (i.e., exposure and response prevention for OCD, interoceptive exposure for panic disorder, and cue exposure for an alcohol problem). These results suggest largely convergent attitudes across the outpatient and student samples. Of interest, these were also the three least well-received treatments by professionals.

It is striking that graduated in vivo exposure for social phobia was consistently the most positively appraised vignette and considered the most ethical. It is possible that the word "gradual" in the vignette favorably influenced participants' views of the ethicality of the treatment.

DISCUSSION

This study examined the ethical, legal, and professional experiences and opinions of specialized anxiety treatment providers, as well as issues of perceived efficacy and ethicality of treatment modalities with outpatient and student samples. We found no evidence of any legal or ethical complaints lodged against therapists as a result of using exposure therapy. This result is especially important given misperceptions of exposure therapy within the popular press and even among other mental health professionals not familiar with the principles of exposure therapy and relevant treat-ment outcome studies. A minority of professionals (13.9%) reported experiencing any ethical dilemmas while using exposure procedures. Professionals estimated that approximately 1.18% of *all* treated cases resulted in ethical dilemmas. Likewise, 18.7% of professionals reported the incidence of *any* problems resulting from the use of exposure therapy. It is unknown how these percentages compare to other treatment modalities.

Examination of qualitative responses to the questionnaire did not provide any evidence that exposure therapy is harmful for clients. Most dilemmas concerned complications with treatment implementation and probably occur across thera-peutic modalities (i.e., boundary issues, failure to follow directions). Although it is possible that we did not reach professionals who have had legal or ethical com-plaints resulting from the use of exposure therapy or that our sample is biased toward individuals who are sympathetic toward the procedures, the survey results in

TABLE 18.4 Rank order of outpatients' and students' ethicality appraisals

Rank	Outpatients	Proportion Yes of All Responses	Students	Proportion Yes of All Response
1.	Graduated in vivo exposure: social phobia	1.0	Graduated in vivo exposure: social phobia	1.0
2.	Imaginal exposure: social phobia	1.0	Imaginal exposure: social phobia	.98
3.	Cognitive restructuring: GAD	.95	Cognitive restructuring: GAD	.87
4.	Free association: specific phobia (fear of heights)	.90	Virtual reality: fear of flying	.87
5.	Virtual reality: fear of flying	.86	Free association: specific phobia (fear of heights)	.72
6.	Hypnosis: PTSD	.67	Hypnosis: PTSD	.69
7.	In vivo exposure: specific phobia (spider)	.48	In vivo exposure: specific phobia (spider)	.51
8.	Imaginal exposure: childhood sexual abuse	.38	Imaginal exposure: childhood sexual abuse	.42
9.	Exposure and response prevention: OCD	.33	Cue exposure: alcohol problem	.40
10.	Interoceptive exposure: panic disorder	.29	Exposure and response prevention: OCD	.37
11.	Cue Exposure: alcohol problem	.24	Interoceptive exposure: panic disorder	.19
	Mean for exposure treatments	.57	Mean of exposure treatments	.59
	Mean for non-exposure treatments	.84	Mean of non-exposure treatments	.76

GAD, generalized anxiety disorder; PTSD, post-traumatic stress disorder; OCD, obsessive-compulsive disorder.

conjunction with the legal case study review suggest that exposure therapy has not resulted in a litany of lawsuits or ethical complaints. One might also conclude from this finding that the temporary exacerbation of symptoms that frequently occurs with exposure therapy is not perceived by clients as being harmful, or unnecessary, given that a key criterion for a civil suit is that the plaintiff suffered undue harm as a result of treatment.

Given that exposure therapy possesses treatment components that can be especially aversive and anxiety-provoking, these results were somewhat surprising and suggest that a client's affective reactivity in treatment does not translate into treatment dissatisfaction, ethical complaints, lawsuits, and so on. In our view, when properly practiced, exposure therapy may insulate against dissatisfaction because of two factors: (1) the strong theoretical and empirical base from which the techniques are derived, and (2) the powerful therapeutic effects many clients experience. It is important to point out that individuals who undertake exposure therapy do not enter treatment "pain-free." Their emotional turmoil is often severe; otherwise they would not be in treatment to begin with, and, in many cases, turmoil has occupied a central place in their lives for a long time. Any discomfort that occurs as a result of treatment is framed by clients against a backdrop of long-standing emotion management and regulation problems. Thus, although an individual may experience emotional discomfort in exposure therapy, it is perceived by clients as an exacerbation of emotional responses that were occurring before treatment, not as sequelae uniquely attributable to the treatment. Because this is the case, how individuals view their exposure therapy experience is often different from the critical appraisals of dispassionate observers who are relatively free of the emotional problems that have significant disruptive effects in clients' lives.

That being said, an area that deserves more investigation concerns the meaning of informed consent in the context of exposure therapy. Specifically, although a client may consent to exposure therapy, he or she may not fully appreciate the potential aversiveness inherent in many exposure procedures. As a result, exposure therapists may confront a situation in which a client stresses his or her desire to terminate an exposure treatment in mid-session, thereby negatively reinforcing problematic escape behavior. It therefore becomes critical to decide a priori with the client the conditions under which an exposure session should be terminated. Although therapists may have the best interests of the client in mind when encouraging clients to continue with an aversive procedure, the consent of the client to treatment should always be viewed as conditional upon what the client thinks is in his or her own best interest.

Our results extended the findings of Becker, Zayfert, and Anderson (2002) by showing some degree of consensus among our three samples in terms of which exposure applications are perceived to be the most aversive. The fact that exposure therapies constituted four of the top six aversive procedures as rated by professionals confirms the common impression that strong emotional responses are often evoked by the techniques. Likewise, exposure therapies were among five of the six lowest

Overall Rating means found for clients and students. In addition, students, clients, and professionals rated procedures without an exposure component as the least aversive techniques. Thus, it appears that professionals' ratings of aversiveness generally converged with those provided by clients and students, especially with regard to those techniques considered the most aversive or least helpful. Although the current data do not allow us to conclude the underlying mechanism propelling these judgments, the perceived level of discomfort the client would experience probably was an important source of variance. Further, it is possible that the client and student judgments may have been confounded by the type of problem included in the treatment vignette (e.g., graduated exposure may have garnered a more negative rating if it had been paired with childhood sexual assault or an alcohol problem).

It is also interesting to note that although treatment procedures were generally viewed as potentially efficacious, that did not necessarily mean individuals wished to engage in them. It could be that people do not want to engage in treatments that require them to actively address their problems. Alternatively, it may simply be an issue of relevance. That is, because the clients and students in our sample were not primarily seeking treatment for an anxiety disorder, they may have considered a question concerning their reaction to engaging in an anxiety-focused treatment irrelevant.

In summary, exposure therapy appears to be relatively free of ethical and legal complaints even though it may be viewed as aversive by professionals and may not be the treatment of choice by outpatients and students. As such, a central issue in the acceptance of exposure therapy likely surrounds whether therapists receive appropriate training in the techniques and how they communicate treatment rationale to their clients and the public at large. To some degree, the criticism that clients will become overly aroused as a result of exposure therapy is ironic given that nonbehavioral practitioners have frequently argued that emotional arousal, by itself, may be a necessary component of effective treatment (e.g., cathartic reactions, primal scream therapy). Complicating matters is the fact that many faddish treatments gain popularity because of their "no pain, all gain" appeal, whereas other treatment orientations eschew treatment outcome research as insensitive to meaningful clinical change.

We must stress, however, the danger in equating perceived aversiveness with treatment efficacy and/or ethicality. There are many biomedical treatments, for example, that are inherently aversive (e.g., chemotherapy, bone marrow transplants) and yet remain the best chance a patient has for survival. Rarely does one hear that chemotherapy is an unnecessary or sadistic enterprise that is not useful for cancer patients, or that the cure is worse than the problem in conditions other than end-state functioning. Likewise, exposure therapy may represent the best chance a client has for resolving highly charged emotional responses in response to problematic cues, memories, rituals, and so forth. The perceived aversiveness of treatment is neither a de facto indicator of its ethicality nor its effectiveness. In fact, a more germane question may be whether it is ethical for therapists to engage in treatments for disorders that are known to be both less aversive *and* less efficacious. One wonders how ethical it is to have a client spend countless hours in therapy attempting to understand obscure personality dynamics when a more potent and empirically supported treatment is available. As evidenced in the preceding chapters of this book, the exposure therapies constitute a family of highly efficacious treatment procedures that are applicable to a wide variety of behavioral and mental health problems. Although their use may evoke strong responses from clients, it is probably the case that sustained change in anxiety symptoms can occur only in the context of a strong affective reaction and subsequent habituation to previously feared stimuli.

REFERENCES

Beck, A.T. (1996). *Beck Depression Inventory*. II. San Antonio: The Psychological Corporation.

Becker, C.B., Zayfert, C., & Anderson, E. (2004). A survey of psychologists' attitudes towards and utilization of exposure therapy for PTSD. *Behaviour Research and Therapy, 42*, 277–292.

Dommeyer, C.J., & Moriarty, E. (1999). Comparing two forms of an e-mail survey: Embedded vs. Attached. *International Journal of Market Research, 42*(1), 1999–2000.

Ertl, M.A. & McNamara, J.R. (2000). Predicting potential client treatment preferences. *Psychotherapy: Theory, Research, Practice, Training, 37*(3), 219–227.

Feeny, N.C., Hembree, E.A., & Zoellner, L.A. (2003). Myths regarding exposure therapy for PTSD. *Cognitive and Behavioral Practice, 10*, 85–90.

Leonard Heller, Secretary, Kentucky Cabinet for Human Resources, Petitioner v. Samuel Doe, by His Mother and Next Friend, Mary Doe, et al. (Supreme Court of the United States, 1993).

Montgomery, L.M., Cupit, B.E., & Wimberley, T.K. (1999). Complaints, malpractice, and risk management: Professional issues and personal experiences. *Professional Psychology: Research and Practice, 30*, 402–410.

Prochaska, J.O. & Norcross, J.C. (1999). *Systems of psychotherapy: A transtheoretical analysis* (4th ed.). Pacific Grove: Brooks/Cole Publishing.

Richard, D.C.S. & Gloster, A.T. (2006). Technology integration and behavioral assessment. In M. Hersen (Ed.), *Clinician's Handbook of Adult Behavioral Assessment*. San Diego, Academic Press, pp 461–495.

Slater, L. (November 2, 2003). Cruelest cure. *New York Times*.

Williams, M.H. (2000). Victimized by "victims": A taxonomy of antecedents of false complaints against psychotherapists. *Professional Psychology: Research and Practice, 31*, 75–81.

Zayfert, C., Becker, C.B., & Gillock, K.L. (2002). Managing obstacles to the utilization of exposure therapy with PTSD patients. In L. Vandecreek, & T.L. Jackson (Eds.), *Innovations in clinical practice: A source book* (Vol. 20). Sarasota, FL: Professional Resource Press.

Exposure Survey for Outpatients and Students

We are interested in your reaction to the use of certain kinds of treatment. Please read each of the following stories. After you have read each story, please answer the questions that follow. This survey asks you to judge how ethical certain treatments are. The term *ethical* means *professionally appropriate, justified*, and in the *best interest of the client*.

1. A client is afraid of spiders to the point that the client needs therapy. The client is told that handling a spider will eventually reduce fear of spiders. As part of therapy, the client must hold a tarantula and let the spider crawl over the client's arm. [In vivo exposure: specific phobia (fear of spiders)]

   1a. How helpful do you think this treatment would be?
   - A. Very helpful
   - B. Somewhat helpful
   - C. Neutral, undecided
   - D. Somewhat unhelpful
   - E. Very unhelpful

   1b. How acceptable is this kind of treatment?
   - A. Very acceptable
   - B. Acceptable
   - C. Neutral, undecided
   - D. Not acceptable
   - E. Very unacceptable

   1c. How would you react if a therapist suggested this treatment for you?
   - A. Very positively
   - B. Positively
   - C. Neutral, undecided
   - D. Negatively
   - E. Very negatively

1d. Would you consider this type of therapy ethical?
A. Yes
B. No
C. Undecided

[*The same response scales were then repeated for each of the following vignettes. Italicized subheadings were not included with the vignette*]:

2. *Imaginal exposure: childhood sexual abuse.* An adult client was sexually abused as a child. The client is told that reimagining the sexual abuse will help the client manage the memories better. The client is asked to recall as many aspects of the abuse in as much detail as possible. Then, as part of the therapy, the client must imagine that the situation is occurring again.

3. *Graduated in vivo exposure: social phobia.* A client has severe anxiety when speaking in front of other people. The client is told that gradually learning how to speak in front of others will help reduce anxiety. As part of therapy, the client must first raise a hand in meetings and ask for something to be repeated. Then, the client must make a short comment during a meeting. Gradually, the client works up to giving a speech during an important meeting.

4. *Cue exposure: alcohol problem.* A client is in therapy for a drinking problem. The client is told that being exposed to things that are associated with drinking may be helpful. As part of the therapy, the client must smell alcohol, sit in the presence of alcohol, and other things associated with alcohol use. However, the client is not allowed to taste alcohol.

5. *Exposure and response prevention: obsessive-compulsive disorder.* A client is extremely afraid of contaminating his/her hands and cleans the bathroom several times per day to keep it sanitary. The client is told that being exposed to unclean situations while not being allowed to escape will eventually help reduce anxiety. As part of therapy, the client must touch a toilet without washing afterward.

6. *Imaginal exposure: social phobia.* A client is a talented musician but is afraid to go on stage and perform. The client is told that relaxation exercises in combination with imagining a performance will be helpful. As part of therapy, the client must enter a state of relaxation and then imagine going on stage to perform.

7. *Cognitive restructuring: generalized anxiety disorder.* A client is constantly afraid that something dreadful is going to happen to loved ones. The client is always on guard and anxious. The client is told that challenging irrational thoughts will eventually lead to lower fear and anxiety. As part of therapy, the client must learn that most fears are irrational and learn other ways of thinking about problems.

8. *Free association: specific phobia (fear of heights).* A client has a serious fear of heights and can not ride an elevator. The client is told that saying whatever comes to mind will eventually help uncover the reason for the client's fear. As part of therapy, the client relaxes on a couch and says whatever comes to mind while a therapist listens and is quiet.

9. *Virtual reality: fear of flying.* A client has a fear of flying. The client is told that a treatment using a virtual reality headset could be helpful. The client wears the headset (which looks like a helmet) and views a video screen that shows the interior of an airplane cabin. The client sits in a special chair that simulates rough weather. As the plane flies through the computer-generated world it is in, engine sounds come through the headset.

10. *Hypnosis: PTSD.* A client experienced a car accident in which friends and family were hurt. As a result, the client has developed a fear of driving. The client is told that being placed in a hypnotic state will help the client be less anxious in the future. A hypnotic state is one in which a person is relaxed, can vividly imagine previous events, and can still respond to therapist questions.

11. *Interoceptive exposure: panic disorder.* A client experiences feelings of high anxiety and panic that come out of the blue. The client is told that producing these bodily sensations voluntarily will help the client be less fearful. As part of therapy, the client is encouraged to breathe rapidly and hyperventilate so the client can feel light-headed. The client is also turned around and around in a chair until the client is very dizzy.

Index